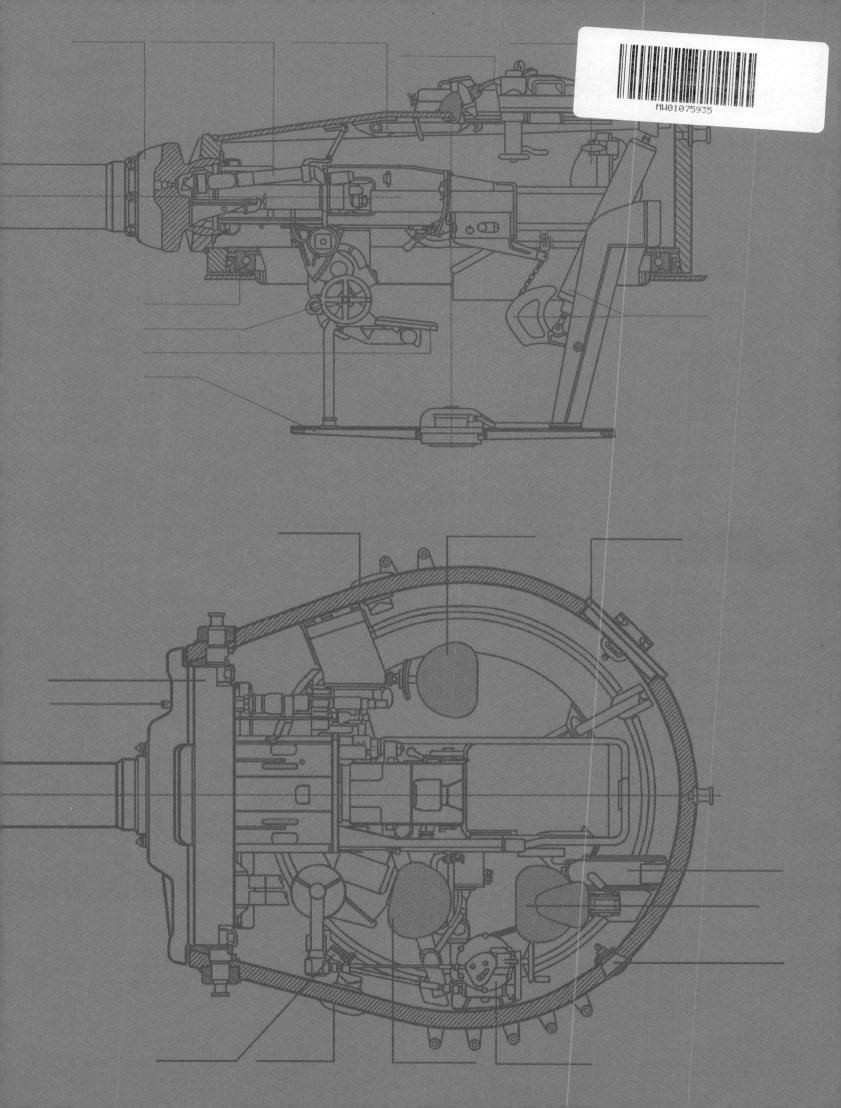

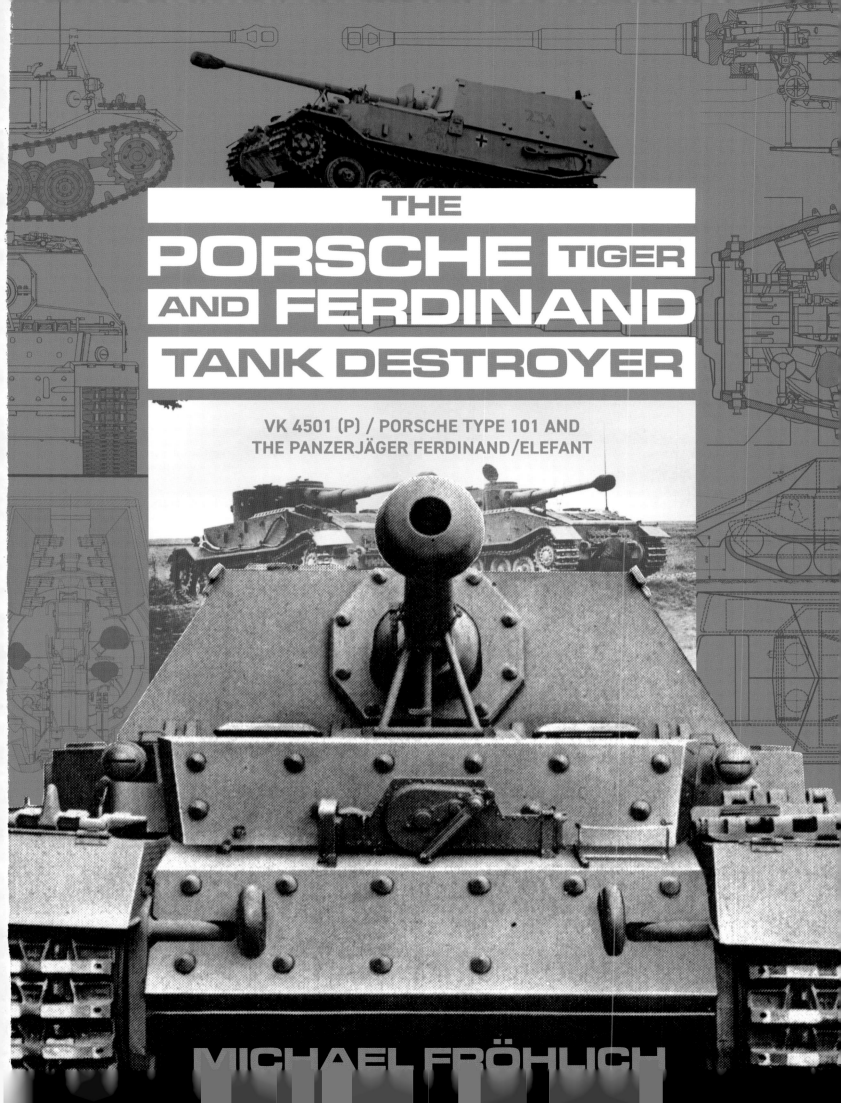

THE
PORSCHE TIGER
AND FERDINAND
TANK DESTROYER

VK 4501 (P) / PORSCHE TYPE 101 AND THE PANZERJÄGER FERDINAND/ELEFANT

MICHAEL FRÖHLICH

Originally published in two volumes as *Der Andere Tiger: Der Panzerkampfwagen Porsche Typ 101* by Motorbuch Verlag, Stuttgart © 2019 Motorbuch Verlag, translated from the German by David Johnston; *Der Panzerjäger "Ferdinand": Panzerjäger Tiger (P), Porsche Typ 131* by Motorbuch Verlag, Stuttgart © 2020 Motorbuch Verlag, translated from the German by David Johnston.

Library of Congress Control Number: 2021942588

Cover design by Justin Watkinson
Type set in Helvetica Neue LT Pro/Minion Pro

ISBN: 978-0-7643-6351-1
Printed in Serbia

Published by Schiffer Publishing, Ltd.
4880 Lower Valley Road
Atglen, PA 19310
Phone: (610) 593-1777; Fax: (610) 593-2002
Email: Info@schifferbooks.com
Web: www.schifferbooks.com

For our complete selection of fine books on this and related subjects, please visit our website at www.schifferbooks.com. You may also write for a free catalog.

Schiffer Publishing's titles are available at special discounts for bulk purchases for sales promotions or premiums. Special editions, including personalized covers, corporate imprints, and excerpts, can be created in large quantities for special needs. For more information, contact the publisher.

We are always looking for people to write books on new and related subjects. If you have an idea for a book, please contact us at proposals@schifferbooks.com.

Contents

The current generation always discovers
what the old one has already forgotten.

—Johann Wolfgang von Goethe

Foreword

While researching my books on the Maus battle tank (*Kampfpanzer Maus*, Schiffer, 2017) and the superheavy-tank projects (*German Superheavy Panzer Projects of World War II*, Schiffer, 2019), I kept coming across documents concerning the development of the so-called Porsche Tiger. When I then looked at the relevant literature, I found, for example, the following assessment of the Porsche development by W. Oswald: "The derisive nickname 'Ferdinand' remained more common for this blatantly faulty design by professor and honorary doctor Porsche."[1] Because Oswald's book is regarded as the standard work on the subject, despite numerous errors, other authors have incorporated his views into their own works. Even Ferdinand Porsche's biographers (from those written in 1951 to the latest biography from 2017) have not bothered to question these statements more closely.

However, I had doubts about these statements, because I already knew of Professor Porsche's brilliance and that of his hand-picked engineers. Karl E. Pawlas[2] was the only author to delve deeper into the reasons behind the tank project's failure and, in addition to technical problems that could not be remedied in a short time, concluded that the main reasons for its failure were the intrigues in the Heereswaffenamt (HWA, or Army Ordnance Office) and Albert Speer's dislike of the older professor. The so-called Henschel Tiger design was in reality a project of the Army Ordnance Office, specifically the "Amtsgruppe [office group] for Development and Testing, Motor Transport and Motorization Department, Vehicles, Tanks, and Motorization Branch," or Wa Prüf 6 for short. Particularly involved was Oberbaurat Kniepkamp, who strove to advance his own interests and those of Dr. Maybach. Amtsleiter Karl Otto Saur, head of the Technical Office and Speer's deputy, characterized the Henschel design as "the office's Tiger."[3]

These efforts by the Army Ordnance Office initially got nowhere because of Armaments Minister Todt, who was well known for pushing through his own ideas regardless of what the "big shots" thought. As well, Todt and Porsche had a good personal rapport thanks to their common points of view. With Todt's death in an aircraft accident on February 8, 1942, and the naming of the young architect Albert Speer as armaments minister, the tide turned for Porsche. Albert Speer was uncomfortable with the professor's good relations with Hitler. Concerning the relationship between Professor Porsche and the armaments minister, Porsche's secretary Ghislaine E. J. Kaes wrote: "Cooperation with Todt had always been ideal, but Porsche did not get along at all with the much-younger Speer."

I found the statements by the previously quoted Karl Otto Saur during his interrogation by the Americans on June 11, 1945, to be even more striking: "No three people agree about Porsche's person. He is a genius; in other words, one of those who are appreciated only by posterity. The majority reject him out of ignorance. He made life difficult for us, as he is stubborn and willful, but he is capable. He was the prototype or, more accurately, the extreme representative of the free engineer in this first committee [the Tank Committee]. Porsche was a pure developer. That was in part a mistake. Later the chairmen of the committees had to be developers, while their deputies were the leaders of the main committee and thus responsible for production."[4]

This recognition weighed all the more heavily, because unlike the architect Speer, Saur was himself an engineer and technician and knew what he was talking about.

Was the Porsche Tiger a bad design or did it simply fail because of the scheming HWA? Perhaps the truth lies somewhere in between. Both Tiger designs were plagued by errors. Which could be remedied more quickly? Due to the changing war situation, the time factor was the decisive point in fielding a tank that was at least the equal of the superior Soviet armored fighting vehicles. The German leadership, including the Army Ordnance Office, had previously wasted too much time on the development of heavy tanks.

In order to get the most-accurate answers possible, I went back to the archives to look for contemporaneous information about this tank project. Its prehistory was just as important as its final development: the Porsche Tiger heavy tank destroyer, also known as the "Ferdinand" or "Elefant."

During my research, the main focus was again on the technical details and development path of these vehicles. A detailed account of the tank destroyer's operational history was not to be the content of this work, since there are already several good books on this subject on the market.

I would like to thank all those who have actively contributed to the creation of this book. First and foremost, my family, who were once again a great help to me; Hendrik Müller for proofreading; the Porsche company archives, especially Mr. Gross; Rolf Hilmes and Joachim Deppmeyer for their contributions; Karlheinz Münch, Wolfgang Schneider, Dirk Hensel, and the archives of Dresden Technical University; the BAMA Freiburg; and the Institute for Contemporary History in Munich for providing material.

Michael Fröhlich
Dresden, March 2021

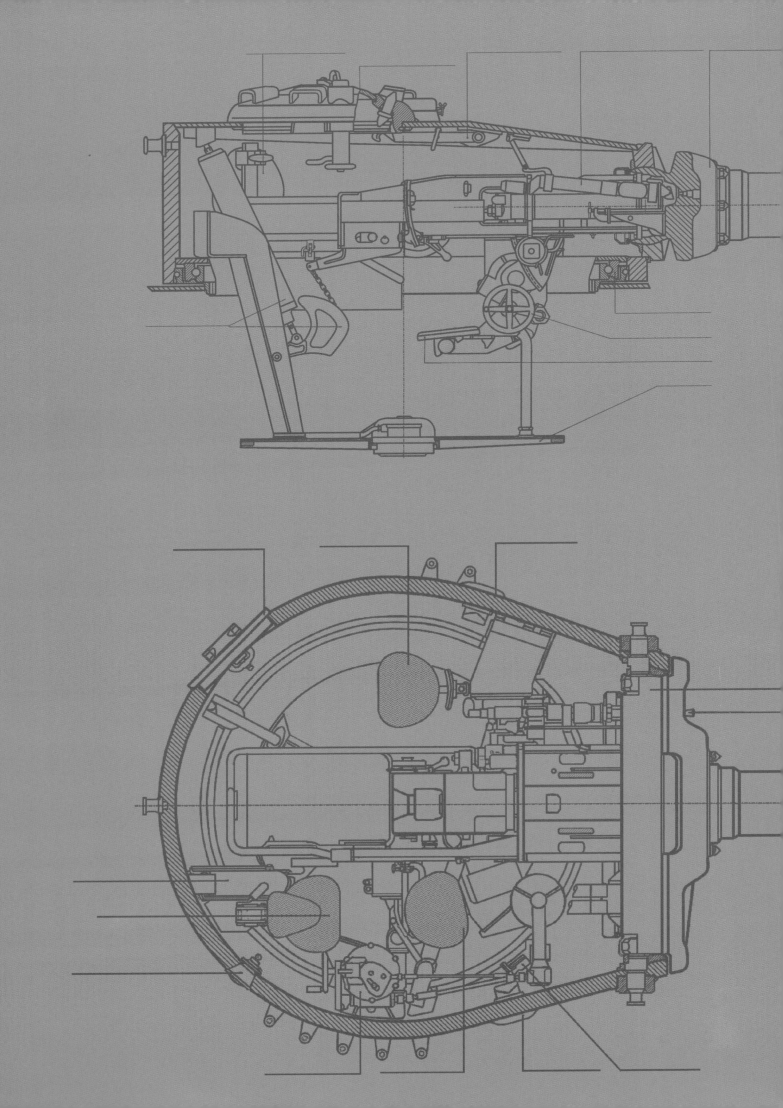

PART I

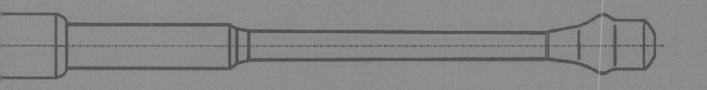

Introduction

Development of the heavy German vehicle designated the "breakthrough tank" (not counting the Grosskampfwagen K of the First World War) began in 1925 with the *Grosstraktor* (large tractor), so called for reasons of secrecy, which was in the 20-metric-ton (22 ton) class. The Treaty of Versailles of 1919 had forbidden tank development in Germany. For competitive reasons, three companies were tasked with the secret development program: Daimler-Benz, Rheinmetall-Borsig,

and Krupp. Each company designed and built two prototypes out of "soft steel." In addition to the same basic specification—such as the superstructure with a main and a secondary turret, armament consisting of a 75 mm L/24 gun and three MGs, maximum armor of 14 mm (armor-piercing, bulletproof), and engine performance of about 250 hp—different types of running gear were specified so that the best-performing variants could be selected:

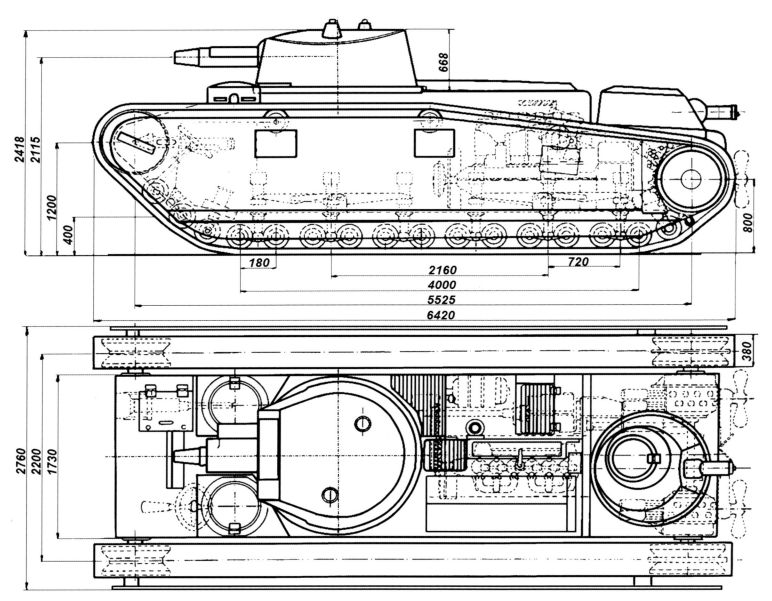

The Krupp tractor (large tractor) in cross section

The Daimler-Benz large tractor. *SB*

Daimler-Benz: Planetary gearbox with six forward and two reverse gears with hydraulic gearshift and band brakes, clutch coupling with planetary gearbox and worm gear brake, running gear consisting of four groups, each of four road wheels with hydraulic compensation, tracks of pressed sheet steel

Krupp: Multistep transmission with six forward and one reverse gears with pneumatic gearshift and coil clutch, clutch linkage with planetary transmission and band brake, one running gear with three groups with lever compensation and one running gear with two times six and three times four pairs of road wheels, rubber band tracks with wire cable, and one-bar guide

Rheinmetall: Multistep gearbox with eight forward and one reverse gears with electrically operated preselection shifting, one vehicle with clutch coupling and worm-gear

transmission, one vehicle with differential steering and continuously variable control by means of track drive (PIV transmission), one running gear with six pairs of road wheels without pressure compensation and one with two groups each with two times four pairs of road wheels with hydraulic pressure compensation, rubber band tracks with inlaid link track, and double-bar guide

For reasons of secrecy, Krupp assembled its vehicles at the Meppen artillery range, while Rheinmetall assembled its and Daimler-Benz's vehicles at the company's own artillery range at Unterlüß. In mid-June 1929, these six vehicles, which had yet to be tested, were packed in crates, disguised as tractors, and shipped to Kama in the Soviet Union. The basis for this was a secret agreement between the German Reich and the Soviet Union. During one of the first functionality checks,

Krupp's *Neubaufahrzeug* (new-build vehicle). *SB*

it was discovered that both Daimler-Benz vehicles had irreparable damage to their planetary gearboxes; as a result, it was impossible to change gears. Consequently, both vehicles had to be decommissioned.

The two remaining competitors also had serious problems with their rubber tracks, pneumatic controls, and differential steering. The planned swimming capability also had to be abandoned because of a fatal accident. The only thing that was incomprehensible was that Daimler-Benz did not attempt a redesign. Whether Ferdinand Porsche's unharmonious departure from Daimler-Benz, where he was technical director in 1930, played a role was unfortunately impossible to determine. Krupp and Rheinmetall, on the other hand, worked step by step to correct the shortcomings displayed by their vehicles.

The political relationship with the Soviet Union deteriorated after Hitler took power in 1933, and in July of that year a directive was issued to shut down the tank-testing facility at Kama. All six large tractors were shipped back to Germany,

where they were overhauled by Daimler-Benz. The company's two vehicles were given to the armored forces as monuments. The other four vehicles were used for further training, allowing valuable experience and important ideas for later tank development to be gained.

On the basis of experience gained with the British Vickers Mk. III multiturret tank—and the trend that it started—and its Soviet copies (T 28, T 29, and T 35), based on reworked designs, in 1934–35 three prototypes were produced by Krupp (Design A) and two by Rheinmetall (Design B), which later received the designation *Neubaufahrzeug* (new-build vehicle). By that time, Daimler-Benz was no longer active in tank development.

In addition to its 75 mm main gun, the three-turret tank had a coaxial 37 mm gun and single machine gun turrets fore and aft. The Krupp tanks were made of armor steel, while the Rheinmetall vehicles were built using mild steel. The 250 hp aeroengine chosen to power the vehicle did not prove suitable for use in a tank, however. The type of running gear used was also obsolete by that time. The armored forces used the vehicles mainly for training purposes.

The three Krupp vehicles did, however, see action in Norway in 1940. One tank was damaged by a mine and had to be blown up on the spot. The other two vehicles returned to Germany.

The development of heavy tanks had a low priority in Germany at that time, since the focus was on fast tanks, which better suited Guderian's Blitzkrieg strategy.

In January 1937, then Baurat Kniepkamp of Wa Prüf 6 was tasked by his superior, Oberstleutnant Philipps, with development of a superheavy tank. And so, at the beginning of 1937, Kniepkamp gave to Henschel & Sohn AG the general task of becoming involved in the development of superheavy armored vehicles. Krupp also became involved in the plan,

after it contacted the Army Ordnance Office and made inquiries about development contracts for a heavy tank.

The company received an answer from the Army Ordnance Office's advisor to the Motor Transport and Motorization Department on October 6, 1937: "Herr Kniepkamp states that while he is involved in the matter, his superior [Oberstleutnant Philipps] does not as yet have an official order for it, and that it is his superior and not he who will decide which company will be selected for the development of this vehicle."[6] And so, Henschel initially undertook the development of 33-metric-ton (36.37 ton) study vehicles on its own, with no official contract. It was inspired to do so by Wa Prüf 6 under Baurat Kniepkamp, since he actively supported the torsion bar's interleaved running gear and the Maybach engine, in part due to Kniepkamp's economic interests. He held patents for the interleaved suspension, which had been adopted for

One of the three VK 3001 (H) hulls to be built. *SB*

use on some half-track prime movers and was not always in line with the interests of the development companies. The interleaved suspension had the advantage that a maximum number of road wheels were used, having a positive effect on operating characteristics and ground pressure.

But it was again the Krupp company that criticized Kniepkamp. Krupp found, among other things, that assemblies that were suitable for tractors could not be used for tanks without modification. As well, the interleaved running gear was significantly heavier and wider and accumulated dirt more easily than conventional running gears. Its greater weight and complicated design also required more raw materials and workforces. Kniepkamp was criticized for having new transmissions and steering gear in production vehicles without first undergoing sufficient testing.[7]

Despite criticism, Henschel received from Kniepkamp, by way of his new superior, Oberstleutnant Fichtner, contracts for the design of a DW I (*Durchbruchswagen*, or breakthrough tank). The hull was of two-part construction, since at that time the rolling mills were not yet capable of producing 50 mm (1.96 in.) armor plates that were the complete length of the vehicle. The tank was equipped with a 280 hp Maybach HL 120 engine and a Maybach-Variorex type 328 145 gearbox. The steering system had a three-stage Cletrac gearbox, which in retrospect turned out to be a poor design. The medium-size road wheels were sprung by torsion bars following the Röchling principle of hollow and solid bars. The follow-up type, requested by Wa Prüf 6 in 1938, was the DW II, also called Panzerkampfwagen VI. It had a simple torsion bar suspension (Porsche patent) and modified components, including steering gear, reduction gearing, tracks, and brakes, One vehicle was built and tested. Maximum speed was 35 kph (21.75 mph).

The next design was designated VK 3001 (H). The now single-piece hull had 50 mm (1.96 in.) of armor on the sides and 60 mm (2.36 in.) in front. It was planned that the vehicle should be powered by the twelve-cylinder Maybach HL 190 P engine, producing 400 hp at 2,500 rpm. For space reasons, however, Maybach developed the six-cylinder HL 150 engine, producing 320 hp for the VK 3001 (H). Two engines were built and tested. The vehicle was ultimately powered by the more compact six-cylinder HL 116 gasoline engine, producing 300 hp, and the Maybach-Variorex gearbox. The L320C steering unit consisted of five oil-controlled couplings, which enabled three steering radii. The suspension had simple torsion bars with heads of different thicknesses, as per Porsche's patent. The seven interleaved road wheels on each side and the three return rollers had solid-rubber tires. Maximum speed was again 35 kph (21.75 mph). Three prototypes and a preproduction series of

Cross section through the 128 mm self-propelled K 40

eight VK 3001(H) vehicles were supposed to be built; however, the latter series was canceled.

Krupp had received a contract to prepare the corresponding turret with the short-barreled 7.5 cm KwK L/24 gun. A Maybach-Olvar type 401216 gearbox was fitted experimentally with a new SMG 90 steering gearbox. The Olvar gearbox was similar to the later Tiger H I gearbox, although it had actually been designed for a 400 hp engine. Its structure was reminiscent of Variorex gearboxes, but shifting of the Olvar gearbox was achieved by oil pressure produced in the gearbox rather than negative pressure of the gasoline engine. Of the three experimental vehicles built, numbers 1 and 3 were converted into 12.8 cm Selbstfahrlafetten L/61 (Panzerselbstfahrlafette für 12.8 cm K 40) self-propelled guns, also known by the name "Sturer Emil" ("stubborn Emil").

In 1937, Daimler-Benz and MAN (which originally stood for Maschinenfabrik Augsburg-Nürnberg AG) also received development contracts for tanks in the planned 30-metric-ton (33 ton) class. Under the impression made by the superior Soviet T-34 tank, at the end of 1941 the Daimler-Benz and MAN designs led via the VK 3001 (DB) and VK 3001 (MAN), to the VK 3002 (DB) and VK 3002 (MAN), which later became the Panzer V Panther, which is outside the scope of this book.

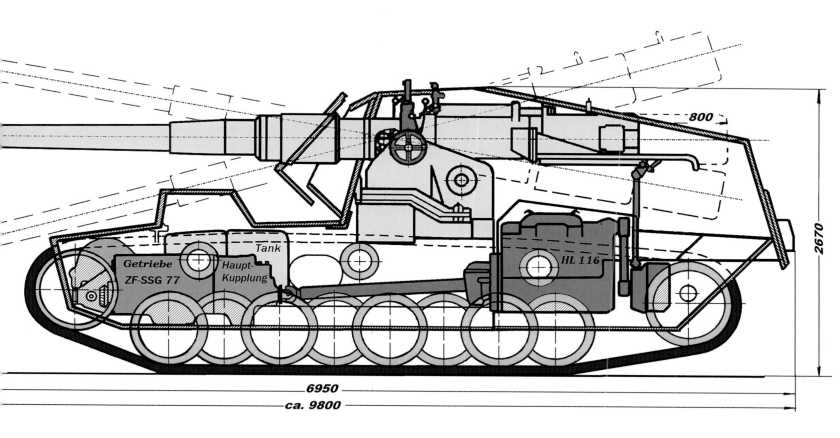

On September 1, 1939, Henschel had received a development contract from the Army Ordnance Office for an even-heavier tank in the 65-metric-ton (71.6 ton) class, the Panzerkampfwagen VII. Henschel was to build the chassis and superstructure of the VK 6501, and once again Krupp would produce the turret. Henschel designed the hull in three parts, to avoid exceeding the railroad loading gauge. An armor thickness of 80 to 100 mm (3.15–3.9 in.) (up-armored version) was planned. Special mobile 10-metric-ton (11 ton) cranes were designed, so that two could assemble and disassemble the vehicle. The sections were to be joined using clamping bolts.

The first two vehicles would be powered by a twelve-cylinder Maybach HL 320 P gasoline engine, while the other two chassis were to receive the larger HL 360 P.8 This did not happen, however, due to changes to the hull, so that ultimately three Maybach HL 224 P engines, each producing 600 hp at 3,000 rpm, and a newly developed Maybach preselector gearbox were used. The three-radius steering gear that was used was a Henschel development. The interleaved suspension with nine steel road wheels and torsion bars was adapted to the increased vehicle weight and in principle was similar to the design of the VK 3001 (H).

Maximum speed was supposed to be 25 kph (15.5 mph). Two prototypes made of mild steel were planned. The rotating turret was again supposed to accommodate (just) one 75 mm Kampfwagenkanone L/24 and one MG 34. The radio operator operated an MG 34 in a separate revolving turret. The contract issued to Krupp on March 14, 1940, for production of eight VK 6501 tank hulls and eight turrets was canceled by the Wa Prüf 6 on August 15. The two *Beschuss-Wannen*, literally hulls made of armor steel for the purpose of being fired at, were completed and underwent firing tests. A riveted tank hull had previously been fired at successfully at the Kummersdorf artillery range.

CHAPTER 1

The VK 3001 (P) Leopard Project

On December 6, 1939, Professor Porsche's independent design bureau, the "Dr. Ing. h. c. F. Porsche KG"—Designs and Consultation for Engine and Vehicle Design—received a development contract from the Army Ordnance Office for a 35-to-40-metric-ton (38.5–44 ton) tank, which was to have an air-cooled engine if at all possible. The tank's official designation was VK 3001 (P), while internally Porsche called it "Special Vehicle I" or Type 100. The later Leopard designation was an unofficial company name, at the time when a heavy-tank project with the name Tiger was begun.

This development had its origins in November 1939, when Hitler directed the Army Ordnance Office to make strategic preparations for a war with France. The army faced the task of reducing its technical inferiority to French tanks in regard to armor protection and armament. The office saw in Porsche a creative developer with much experience in air-cooled engines. Amtsleiter Saur characterized "Porsche as the first outsider, the Army Ordnance Office having believed until then that, with respect to tank developments, it had to determine the conditions in the details to the greatest possible extent—and even though it did not design itself—it still forced the companies so strongly to design according to its ideas that until then there could be no talk of a free development."[9]

Porsche's reputation as a genius at that time and Hitler's great respect for the designer of the "Strength through Joy" car may have played an important role. Since Henschel had already received a similar contract in 1937–38, the Army Ordnance Office was following the then-customary procedure of issuing identical development contracts to several competing companies independently of one another. The office would subsequently select the best technical solution. As the war went on, however, German industry could no longer afford this wastage of development capacities, whereupon by order of Armaments Minister Speer these double developments were forbidden. At this time, Professor Porsche faced the difficult task of catching up to the Henschel company's more than two-year lead in the VK 3001 tank project, especially since Porsche had no experience whatsoever in the field of tank design.

Porsche could achieve this only with a completely new approach. Instead of the Henschel path with Maybach gasoline engines and mechanical gearboxes, in Stuttgart they took the path of the air-cooled gasoline engine (not a diesel engine, as is often claimed in the literature) combined with an electric drive. Porsche had gained good experience with the air-cooled engine in his "Strength through Joy" car, and when it came to the electric drive he could fall back on his earlier success with vehicles with the so-called Mixte drive, the development of which lay decades in the past. That was in the year 1900, when Ferdinand Porsche broke new ground with the Semper Vivus, the world's first fully functional hybrid automobile. "In this vehicle two generators coupled with gasoline engines formed a charging unit, which simultaneously provided wheel hub motors and batteries with electricity."[10]

In return, the generators were used as electric starters in gasoline engines. Of course, this concept could be only partially adapted for the tank project. The principle of wheel hub motors and battery drive could not be housed in a 30-metric-ton (33 ton) tank. The solution to this challenging task took place in the Porsche-KG design bureau following the proven practice of division of work. Ferdinand Porsche had the creative ideas, after which his chief designer Karl Rabe drew up an original draft. On the basis of this preliminary design, the respective experts in a subarea worked on detailing, with Professor Porsche assisting in their completion. For example, the gearbox specialist Karl Fröhlich, the engine specialist Josef Kales, the suspension specialist Josef Zahradnik, the chassis specialist Erwin Kales, and the machining specialist

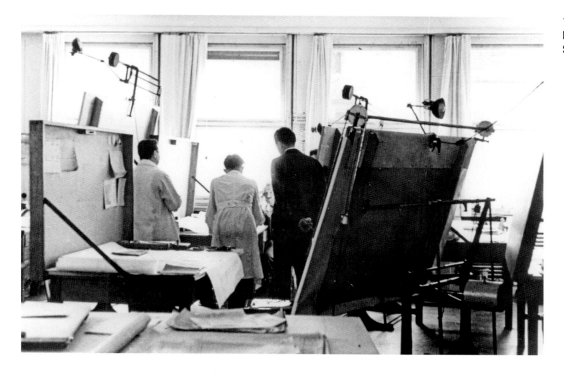

1937 in the old Porsche KG design bureau at Kronenstraße 24, Stuttgart. *PA*

The new bureau at Spitalwaldstraße 2 in Zuffenhausen. *PA*

Engineer Xaver Reimspieß examining a fan with Professor Porsche. *PA*

Oswald Kux worked on the detail designs, in order to create a complete design, which was ultimately checked once again and optimized by Josef Micki.

Then Porsche's engineers, in particular engine specialist Xaver Reimspieß, went to work. Just three days later, on December 9, 1939, Oberingenieur Reimspieß had the first designs in sketch form. The Porsche Type 100 had been created on paper.

The drawing showed a conventional tank, low at 2,250 mm (88.58 in.), in the style of that time, with a small turret for a short-barreled gun with a caliber of 75 mm and a length of L/24 plus a coaxial machine gun. The upper part of the hull protruded slightly over the tracked suspension, to keep open the option of accommodating larger guns (i.e., larger turret diameter). A lower ground pressure of 9.66 kilograms (kg) / cm^2 (137.4 psi) and 500 mm wide (19.68 in.) track links with arrow-shaped profile were the chief characteristics of the 8-meter-long vehicle. It is interesting that the drawing already included sloped armor. The upper front plate, because of the greater distance shells had to penetrate, was just 25 mm (0.98 in.) thick, while the almost vertical front plate and the turret were to have 50 mm (1.97 in.) of armor. This then-standard arrangement was probably due to the driver's visor and the radio operator's machine gun ball mount, which the Army Ordnance Office envisaged for most tanks. This almost vertical plate was explicitly a shot trap and therefore had to be sufficiently heavily armored.

The Porsche engineers also had to take into account a multitude of military requirements, such as the 75 mm gun, the ball mount to accommodate the MG 34, the previously mentioned driver's visor, and the driver's optics with vision slit and glass block, as well as the entry hatches, the machine gun ammunition belt feeds, and the radio equipment with transformer and their wiring diagram with antenna feed-throughs and fold-down mechanisms.

Also new to the Porsche engineers were parts such as armored hinges, spherical-head screws, guide wheel and drive sprockets for the drive wheels, and a track with central tooth.

These standard parts specified by Wa Prüf 6 were a new experience for the Porsche engineers, whose creativity was severely restricted as a result.

The design's breakdown was conventional, with driver's and fighting compartments in front and the engine compartment in the rear. In the initial design, for unknown reasons the driver sat on the right side and the machine gunner on the left front.

So as to get a good overview of the armored force's wishes and ideas, on December 20 the participating Porsche engineers (Rabe, Komenda, Reimspieß, and Klauser) visited the armored-forces school at Wünsdorf to inspect current tank technology for themselves. On January 6, 1940, the initial design of the VK 3001 (P) was discussed with Professor Porsche and Karl Rabe, the bureau's chief engineer. Porsche had doubts whether such a heavy tank could even be operated with a mechanical gearbox. He probably still remembered the gearbox problems encountered by the Großtraktor designed by Daimler-Benz, whose technical director he had been at that time. He held the view that only an electric or hydraulic drive was worth considering. He therefore wanted to solve the problem of power transmission his own way and take advantage of uninterrupted tractive power, since he had designed trains for especially heavy loads during the First

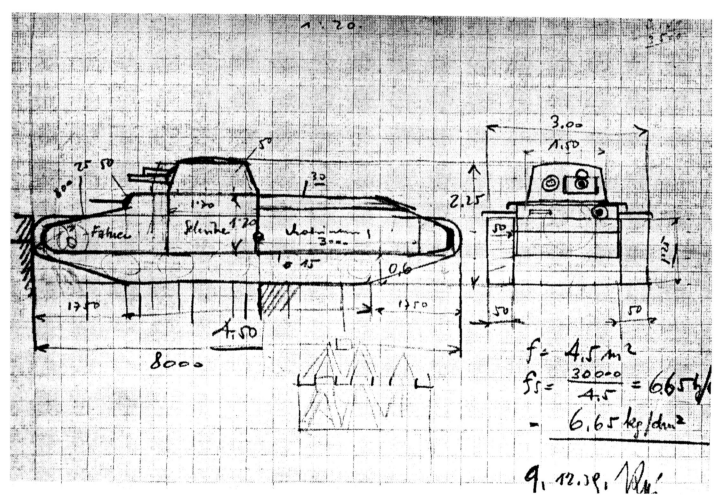

Xaver Reimspieß put his first ideas for a tank on paper on December 9, 1939. *PA*

World War. The professor recalled the B and C trains with their mixed propulsion, in which a combustion engine powered a generator, which in turn produced the necessary current for an electric motor. He therefore decided to add an expert in gasoline-electric mixed drive to his development team.

Dipl.Ing. Otto Zadnik visited the Porsche bureau in Stuttgart on January 19, 1940. Otto Zadnik had played a major part in the design of the gasoline-electric C trains during the First World War. At that time, Ferdinand Porsche had been technical director of Austro-Daimler, where Zadnik was

Professor Porsche and Otto Zadnik, his new electrical specialist. *PA*

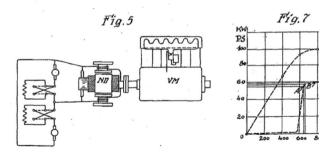

Otto Zadnik's patent for the efficient regulation of electric vehicle drives of March 24, 1927. *PA*

The C-Zug from the year 1918. Each trailer wheel had wheel hub motors, which were powered by the tractor's generator. *PA*

working on the development or aeroengines on the test benches. These so-called C trains consisted of a generator wagon with a 150 hp, six-cylinder gasoline engine and a flange-mounted, 300-volt, direct-current generator of 90 kW to produce electricity. As well as supplying the towing vehicle, this output also powered a large four-axle trailer, which was 5.8 meters (m) (19 ft.) long. It had electric motors in each of its eight wheels, each producing 15 horsepower. This trailer could be converted into an 8.2 m (26.9 ft.) flatbed by separating into two two-axle coupled chassis. Performance was sufficient for 15 kph (9.3 mph) on roads and 27 kph (16.77 mph) on tracks, since it could be operated both on roads and railroad tracks. The trailer weighed 15.3 metric tons (16.9 tons), and its payload was 22 metric tons (24.25 tons). The rear-wheel-driven generator wagon weighed 8.4 metric tons (9.25 tons).

The C train was used in the First World War to transport Skoda heavy howitzers for the Austrian army. Five C trains were required for one 81.3-metric-ton (89.61 ton) howitzer with base. One other special feature was that the all-wheel-drive trailer, which was normally connected to the generator car by a 100 m (328 ft.) power cable, was able to cross weak bridges alone after it had been separated from it.

On the basis of these experiences, another meeting on the Type 100 tank was held at Zuffenhausen on January 21, 1941, which, in addition to Professor Porsche, Otto Rabe, Xaver Reimspieß, and Josef Kales, was attended by Otto Zadnik. The same day, Porsche took these ideas to the Army Ordnance Office in Berlin. On February 5, 1940, Zadnik began the concrete electrical work for the new tank project. An important chapter in German armaments policy began on March 17, 1940, with the creation of a ministry for armaments and munitions under Reichsminister Todt. This ministry and later its special committees significantly strengthened industry's position relative to the army.

This was a reaction to industry criticisms; delivery delays were caused by excessive interference in the design process by the Army Ordnance Office. Associated with this was a restriction of the office to the function of a contracting entity, and while it could subject the delivered product to military scrutiny, it was forced out of the field of production and development. This also played into Porsche's hands, especially since the professor got along very well with the technicians and Minister Fritz Todt.

New organs were created for the two central areas of tank production and design. The object of these was a resource-sparing increase in the output of those tank types already in production, and the design of new, more-powerful tanks.

The first point had priority, and so on June 15 that year Special Committee VI "Tank" was created under Dr. Walter Rohland of the German Stainless Steel Mills. On July 17, the Tank Production Subgroup decided in the presence of General der Artillerie Leeb; Oberste Fichtner, Schroetter, and Phillipps; and Undersecretary Pollert to prioritize the Panzer III and

IV tank types and the 30- and 60-metric-ton-class (33 and 66 ton) tanks. The focus was on increasing production of the Panzerkampfwagen IV (BW), as well as on the goal of producing 20% as spare parts. Acting in an advisory role was the "Experience Community X Tanks," which was under Todt's influence. This committee's primary objective was to achieve a significant increase in tank production and, in the process, work in ways that reduced consumption of materials and personnel.[11] At that time, new designs were regarded as secondary. The first sitting of the special committee under Dr. Roland, which took place on August 15, put the emphasis on machine procurement and decided on a guideline for manufacture, according to which 300 heavy tanks were supposed to be delivered per month as of January 1, 1941.

A major meeting with Oberst Fichtner, the head of Wa Prüf 6, Oberst Holbrich, and Oberregierungsrat Kniepkamp about the Porsche Type 100 took place on June 5, 1940, and went on into the evening.[12] Another step followed on June 30, during a meeting at Steyr-Daimler-Puch AG. Professor

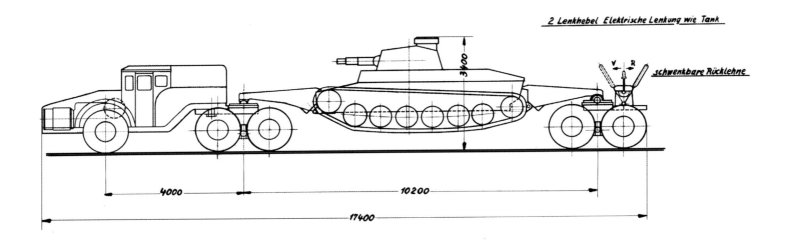

M. 1:50 Schwerlastzug Zusammenstellung

K 2972 Ⓖ

Typ	102
Entwurf Nr.	781
Tag	22. 11. 40
Entworfen	W.
Mappe	

The transport vehicle, still called the Type 102, that later became the Type 142. *PA*

Porsche, Ferry Porsche, Karl Rabe, and Baron von Malberg from the Porsche-KG met with Director-General Meindl, chief designer of the Steyr-Daimler-Puch AG, Director Oskar Hacker, and Dr. Junghold. The subject matter included the C train and the Porsche Type 100. A review of the Type 100 tank drawings and minutes of the previous meeting with Director Hacker and an inspection of the new Nibelungenwerk in St. Valentin, the only pure tank factory in Germany and Austria, took place from June 11 to 13.

This meeting led to important conclusions concerning cooperation with the Steyr company. On July 30, 1940, Oberst Fichtner of the Army Ordnance Office met with Steyr Director-General Meindl and Director Hacker at the Porsche office in Stuttgart to discuss fundamental problems concerning production of the Porsche Type 100.

In preparation for construction of the prototype, on September 10, 1940, following a demonstration of and test drives in captured French tanks at the Kummersdorf artillery range, there was a discussion concerning the necessary standard parts for the Porsche Type 100, such as the driver's visor, radio equipment, gunsights, etc. Engineers Rabe and Zadnik subsequently traveled to Berlin to secure the necessary electrical equipment. A further meeting with Directors Meindl and Hacker at Steyr was held on October 10 and 11, followed by an inspection of the Nibelungenwerk at St. Valentin. Several more meetings at this level followed by the end of the year. As well, design of a transport vehicle for the Type 100 tank was completed by November 22, 1940. The vehicle was also supposed to be able to transport other tanks, which was not a problem since the distance from the drawbar was variable. At that time, this design was dubbed the Porsche Type 102. The armored vehicle was suspended between an articulated lorry and a steerable chassis. The transport vehicle, through to the rear chassis, was also electrically powered. The Porsche designers selected a Daimler-Benz MB 819 twelve-cylinder diesel engine with a continuous output of 400 hp at 2,400 rpm as the generator, analogous to the design of the C train. The 17.7-liter (1,080 cubic inch) engine weighed 865 kg (1,907 lbs.), and the basic engine was similar to the MB 809B; however, the project was abandoned. It was later given the designation Porsche Type 142 (because of the danger of confusion with the later hydraulic variant, the Porsche Type 142) in the general Porsche classification.

In the first weeks of January 1941, there were several large conferences involving the entire circle with Porsche, Rabe, and Reimspieß at the Steyr company, where, in addition to the tank project, the possibility of whether the engines for the Type 100 could also be produced by the company was also sounded out. Porsche had also decided to test a gasoline-hydraulic drive by the Voith company in addition to its gasoline-electric drive. The first meeting on this subject had taken place at St. Pölten on December 17, 1940. Participants, in addition to Professor Porsche, were Director Hacker and, from the Voith company, chief engineer Kugel, Director Gsching, and engineer Mazanek. Among the topics of discussion were the possible methods of steering tracked vehicles. The Voith specialists anticipated the necessary performances and torques to design a suitable twin-turbo transmission. The possibility was also checked of solving the steering system by mechanical means in combination with fluid couplings. On February 5, 1941, Voith chief engineer Kugel presented the computed graph and patent application of January 13 of that year for a "Drive and Steering Arrangement for Tracked Vehicles," which was forwarded by Director Hacker.

On February 18, 1941, the Berger & Mössner company of Feuerbach completed a wooden model of the Porsche Type 100, which Professor Porsche and his driver Goldinger took to Hitler at Berchtesgaden the same day. Accordingly, it was at this point in time at the latest that Hitler was told about the VK 3001 (P) and VK 3001 (H) tank projects, since Henschel had also had a model produced. The first major tank conference therefore took place that day on the Obersalzberg.[13] This meeting began at 15:00, and soldiers were initially excluded. Hitler and Todt first spoke solely with engineers and designers from the tank industry, since these felt inhibited toward the military authorities. These internal discussions saw the participating designers give their opinions as to whether it would be possible to fit existing German tanks with a larger gun.

The Army Ordnance Office feared that the increased weight would cause the tanks to lose much of their speed. All the designers present thought it possible to fit the tanks with heavier armament without simultaneously having to accept reduced speed. After this pronunciation the military was brought in. In the discussion that followed, Hitler stressed that speed was the most important factor to the panzer arm, followed by armament and then, in third place, armor protection. He concluded with the sentence "The tank is not life assurance."[14]

The topic under discussion at that time was not new designs, but the redesign of existing weapons, especially better guns for the Panzer III and IV; for example, the Panzer III was to be equipped with the 50 mm KwK L/60. Hitler could not yet become excited about new designs. The hope of a quick end to the war caused new designs to take a back seat.

The upgrading of existing tanks moved to the foreground. Wa Prüf 6 subsequently illustrated the problems that went hand in hand with reaming the existing tanks, which included the following:

- disadvantages of longer barrels

- loading difficulties inside the turret

- impeding the commander

- jamming of the traverse mechanism

- reduction in ammunition supply

Hitler found that the engineers were of the opinion that these difficulties could be solved, and ordered the immediate mounting of the long 50 mm gun in one Panzer III and IV and their demonstration. He subsequently stressed that the Army Ordnance Office had to be limited to technological requirements and determining troop usability. It was to refrain

from design work on its own and reduce its staff.[15] How much the Waffenamt took this to heart could still be observed at a later time.

But on to the ongoing development work on the Porsche Type 100. To achieve the most compact engine possible, consultations were also held with the aeroengine manufacturer Hirth, since two air-cooled, ten-cylinder gasoline engines were supposed to power the vehicle. Porsche chose the configuration with two combustion engines, each driving a generator, to be able to effectively use the space in the restricted engine compartment. A single engine with double generator would have caused the vehicle to be too tall, like the later Maus battle tank: in the Maus, the double generator was below the turret-rotating platform, and as a result it was unnecessarily tall.

Two generators were necessary at that time so that each side would have a controllable drive, since the output of single generators could easily be controlled. The engineers were apparently not capable at that time of dividing such high currents from a generator and regulating them separately. The installation of the two electric motors in the front of the

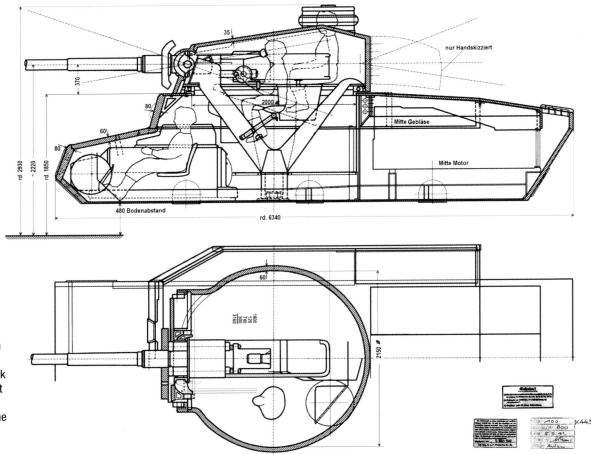

The dimensions taken from drawing K 4432 are marked with "rd."; the other dimensions are original. The gun in the drawing is, contrary to other accounts, a 75 mm tank gun, which is recognizable at the gun breech and barrel diameter in comparison to the 80 mm armor thickness. *PA*

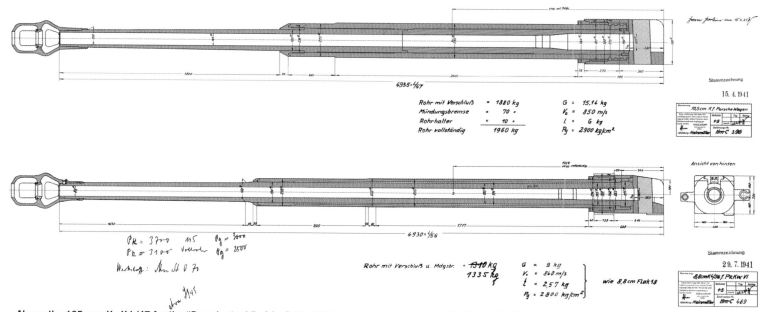

Above: the 105 mm KwK L/47 for the "Porsche tank" of April 15, 1941; *below*, for comparison, the 88 mm KwK 36 L/56 for the Pz.Kw. VI of July 29, 1941

tank corresponded to the Army Ordnance Office's desire for front-wheel drive and better weight distribution. The small gun turret with a short-barreled gun still had a minor influence on the vehicle's center of gravity.

Production planning for the Type 100 took place in Stuttgart on March 1, 1941, together with Director-General Meindl and chief designer Hacker of Steyr-Daimler-Puch. It envisaged six prototypes with a contract value of 4,500,000 reichsmarks (RM). Construction was to begin at the end of July. The specification revealed the following picture of the Porsche Type 100:

The drawing created by Xaver Reimspieß on March 5, 1941, depicted a design of the Porsche Type 100 with a large turret ring diameter of 2,000 mm (78.74 in.). Because of this turret ring diameter, the upper part of the hull extended over the tracks. The tank was thus capable of being equipped with the tank gun derived from the 88 mm Flak 18/36 instead of the smaller 75 mm KwK L/48 envisaged by the Henschel design. The short-listed 105 mm KwK L/47 was also usable on the Porsche chassis.

The large turret ring, of course, caused the turret to be positioned far forward, and therefore driver's and radio operator's hatches in the roof area had to be dispensed with. In their place the Porsche engineers envisaged side emergency exits, although the Wa Prüf 6 later had these sealed for reasons of safety under fire. The already-mentioned front-wheel drive was preferred by the Army Ordnance Office on account of its superior self-cleaning of the tracks and better accessibility to the brakes. The engine compartment was very compact. Two ten-cylinder gasoline engines in V configuration were envisaged, each producing 210 hp at 2,500 rpm. This engine, also designated the Porsche Type 100, achieved 49.4 ft.-lbs. of torque at 2,000 rpm.

Fuel consumption at maximum power was 270 gr/hp/l. Dry, ready for installation, and without cooling fan, a single engine weighed 420 kg (925.9 lbs.). The necessary cooling fan with drive added another 130 kg (286.6 lbs.). In this design the exhaust was in the rear of the armored hull, as on the later Type 101, with the muffler housed beneath the armor protection. The planned turret support on the floor of the hull was later abandoned because of the reduced armor thickness of the floor. The planned emergency exit in the floor further weakened the floor plate's strength. The roof components were subsequently reinforced so that the turret ring could be supported on the hull roof.

Instead of the gearbox, there were two electric motors installed longitudinally between the driver and radio operator. Power transmission from the electric motors was accomplished by bevel gears via hollow shafts. These transmitted the power by way of Cardan shafts to the reduction gear, designed as planetary gearing, and on to the drive wheels. Slip clutches protected the units from damage and impacts. The advantage was that the electric motors had a high starting torque, important for a tank off-road. The uninterruptible tractive power also gave the tank a big advantage off-road. Because tracked vehicles have a high frictional resistance, an armored vehicle

using a standard gearbox could decelerate so sharply during shifting through the gears that off-road a driver often drove in a lower gear than would actually have been technically possible.

Porsche also broke new ground when it came to the running gear. While the Army Ordnance Office preferred transverse torsion bars for its VK 3001 (H) project (as per Porsche's patent of August 10, 1931), on the Porsche Type 100 the professor used his longitudinal torsion bar suspension (also patented) externally, which helped give the vehicle a particularly low overall height, since the torsion bars did not

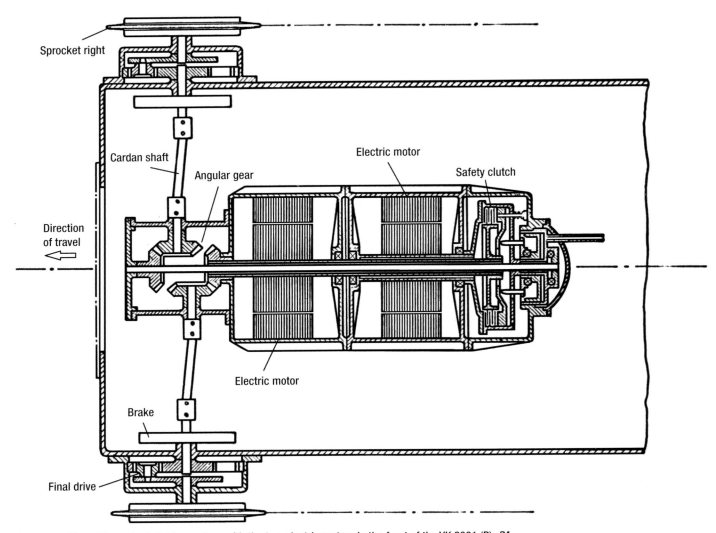

The composition of the patented drive system with the two electric motors in the front of the VK 3001 (P). *PA*

protrude into the interior space. Each side had six rubber-encapsulated, double road wheels with a diameter of 600 mm (23.62 in.). The upper half of the track ran over two return rollers on each side. Track width was 500 mm (19.68 in.), with a track pitch of 160 mm (6.3 in.).

The track ground contact length of 3,225 mm (126.97 in.) and a track of 2,600 mm (102.36 in.) gave the 35-metric-ton (38.58 ton) vehicle the relatively high ground pressure of 0.9 kg/cm² (12.8 psi). The longitudinal torsion bars and their exterior installation had very many advantages over the transverse installation: They enabled overall height to be

reduced; the lower vehicle height also resulted in a lower vehicle weight. Also, the manufacture of the armored hull was less expensive and took about half the time, since the large amount of high-quality drilling, necessary for the Henschel project, was not required.

These running-gear elements were very simple to install, which was an enormous advantage during repairs in the field. The time required to replace the middle inner road wheel, for example, of the later Tiger VK 4501 (H) was twelve to twenty-four hours, since no fewer than thirteen road wheels had to be removed, which was equivalent to five pairs of road

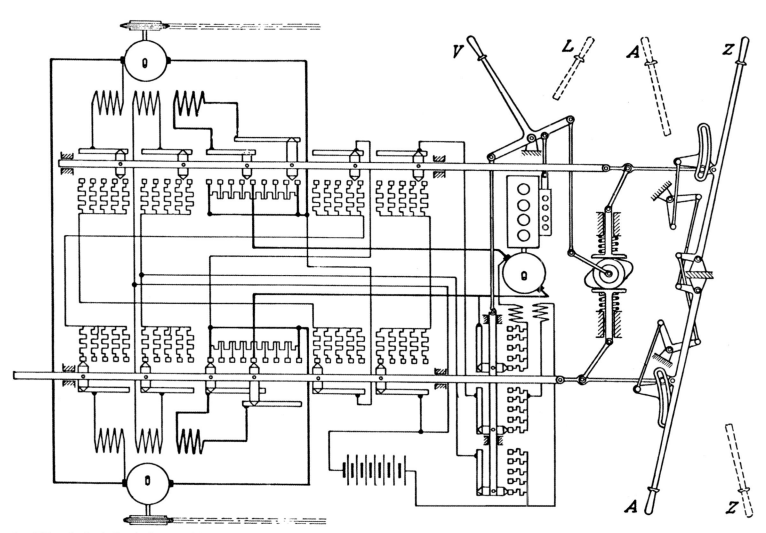

In addition, the basic circuit diagram of the tank's drive system. *PA*

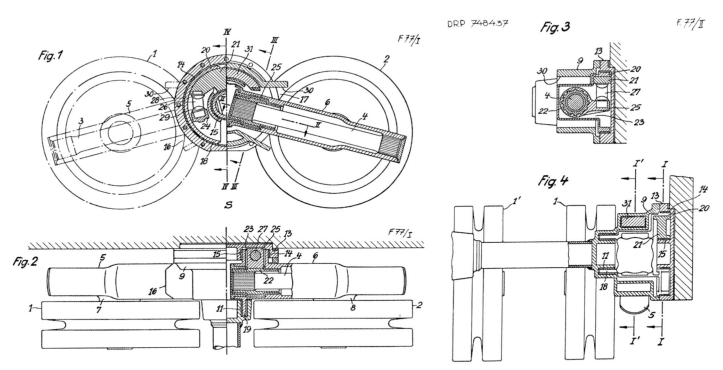

The first version of the Porsche company's knee lever torsion bar suspension. A

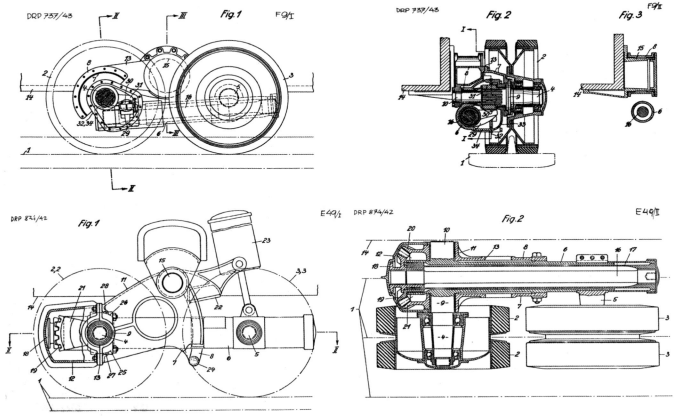

Professor Porsche's torsion bar suspension, which was also patented: the version here still has a shock absorber, which later became unnecessary because of the suspension's high spring rate. PA

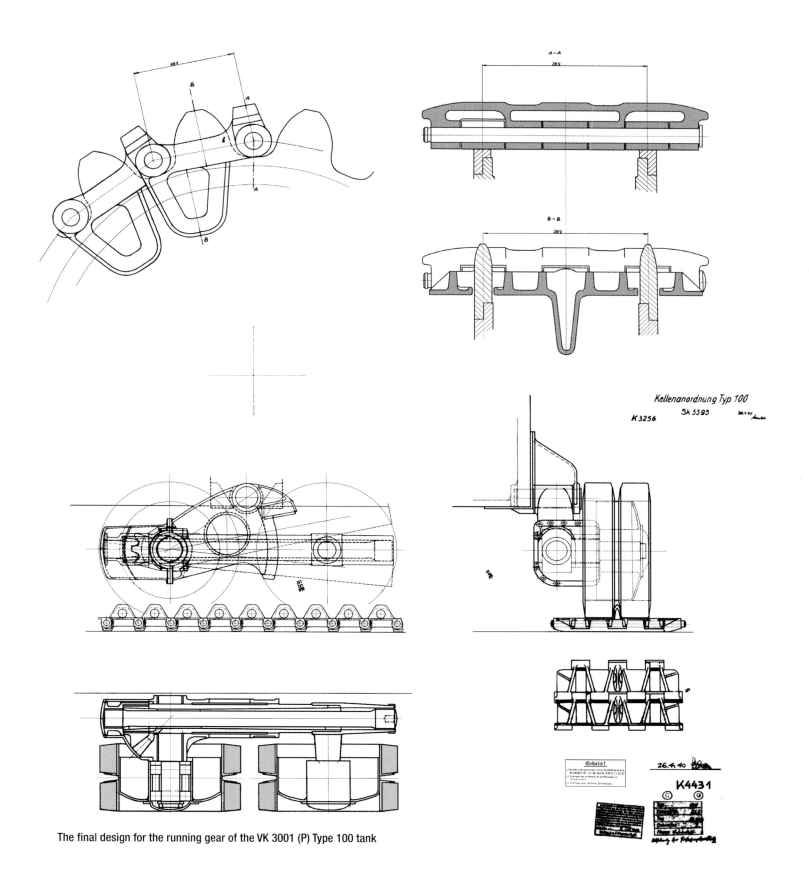

Kettenanordnung Typ 100

The final design for the running gear of the VK 3001 (P) Type 100 tank

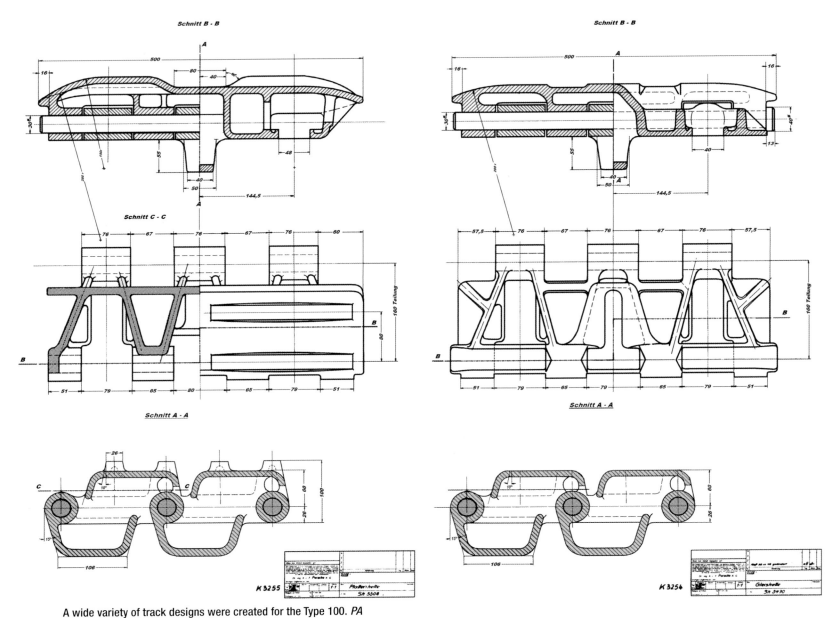

Schnitt B - B

Schnitt C - C

Schnitt A - A

Schnitt B - B

Schnitt A - A

K 3255   Plattenhälfte   K 3254   Gleishälfte

A wide variety of track designs were created for the Type 100. *PA*

wheels and three single road wheels. The time-consuming track change from the 520 mm (20.47 in.) travel track to the 725 mm (28.54 in.) operational track with installation of the outer road wheels took three hours on the Henschel vehicle.[16]

Changing the road wheels of the Porsche running gear was much simpler and was therefore much more popular with the troops. Shortcomings revealed themselves, however, in the relatively short spring deflections and the associated spring stiffness, which did not allow high speeds. On March 13, 1941, there was a meeting with Krupp about the penetrative ability of the guns under consideration. One day later there was another consultation about the hydraulic drive with Voith in Stuttgart, this time, however, with representatives of the parent plant from Heidenheim. The principal design work on the Porsche Type 100 was completed in April 1941.

This is no Tatzelwurm (from Alpine folklore, a lizard-like creature; translator) and also no millipede; rather, your Tiger from below.

5 3 1
4 2

Hier ist eine Übersicht über die Arbeiten, Schlüssel und Sonderwerkzeuge, die nötig sind, um eine Laufrolle, ein Triebrad, Leitrad oder einen Flansch zu wechseln.

Laufrolle Reihe	1	2	3	4	5
Wie bocke ich die Schwing-arme hoch?	Auflaufbock vor innerstes Laufrad des zu hebenden Armes legen, Pz auffahren **1**		Kette aufmachen. Mit Winden eine Pz-Seite über Kettenzahnhöhe hochheben		
	Am besten mit 2 soliden Stützplatten, 2 Ölhebern zu 30 t eine Längsseite hochbocken **2**				
Wieviele Rollen müssen ab?	1	3	4	8	13
Welche Steck-schlüssel, Sonderwerkzeuge brauche ich?	27	27	27	10 (2799/5) 70 50 C 2798 U5 **4** Gew. Zapfen M 39 × 1,5 Schraube 18 × 35	15 (2799/5) 70 50 C 2798 U5 **5** Gew. Zapfen M 39 × 1,5 Schraube 18 × 110

	1	3	3	5	
	Außen-flansch	Innen-flansch	Leitrad	Triebrad	
Welche Steck-schlüssel, Sonderwerkzeuge brauche ich?	27	27 2798 U10 Schrauben-zieher **3**	22 50 C 2798 U5 Schrauben M 14 × 90 Gew.Zapfen M 39 × 1,5 Rohr mit 15 mm Innen-⌀, 75 mm lang **6**	Schlüsselweite 50, 46 Triebrad mittels Abdrückschraube abdrücken, Kolben mit Feder entfernen. Vorrichtung C 2798 U3 mit Spindel und Mutter, Steckschlüssel 27, 46, Kopfschraube 50, Mitnehmer abnehmen, geteilten Ring abnehmen, Filzring erneuern **7**	

Wenn's finster wie in einer Kuh,
kalt, naß und dreckig noch dazu,
im Matsch versunken Bock und Winden,
Hammer und Schlüssel nicht zu finden,

wenn Stäbe brechen, Arme hängen,
drei Rollen fehlen, fünfe zwängen —
dann denkt man sich bei dem Malör:
„was tät hier wohl der Konstruktör?"

Extract from the so-called Tiger Primer (D 656/27), describing "the activities, wrenches, and special tools necessary to replace a road wheel, a drive wheel, idler wheel, or flange."

On April 2, 1941, the Krupp engineers again held internal discussions as to which guns the company could offer for the Porsche vehicle. As previously described, the 88 mm L/56 gun and the 105 mm L/47 were on the short list. Two days later, Krupp made a written offer to the Porsche bureau to produce six turrets with 80 mm (3.15 in.) of frontal and 60 mm (2.36 in.) of side armor for the six prototype chassis. The planned turret ring diameter was about 1,900 mm (74.8 in). Cost per turret, including an 88 mm L/56 gun (without the parts to be provided by the ordnance office), was 110,000 RM.

The previously required wooden model of the turret with weapons mockups cost another 5,000 RM. This full-scale model was sent to the Nibelungenwerk on May 25, 1941, raising the price to 7,724 RM. Furthermore, Krupp planned to initially complete three hulls for the project, now designated Panzerkampfwagen VI (P), for 75,000 RM each. Krupp envisaged delivery of the first hull in November 1941, likewise the first turret. The second hull was supposed to be delivered in December 1941, and the third in January 1942. The remaining turrets were to be produced after that date. Krupp intended to submit a proposal for a 105 mm gun with a length of L/47 by April 10, 1941, and one for an 88 mm L/56 gun by April 18, each with a larger loading chamber and higher muzzle velocity (940/920 m/sec. instead of 840/860 m/sec.—3,084/3,018 ft./sec. instead of 2,756/2,822 ft./sec.).

On April 24, 1941, Krupp and Porsche agreed on the 88 mm L/56 gun as the main weapon. Torsion bars for the bogie suspensions were to be manufactured by the Hoesch company. Herr Heerlein and Herr Lettmann of Krupp made their way to a meeting in the Porsche bureau in Stuttgart on May 2, 1941. Representing Porsche were junior manager Ferry Porsche, chief designer Rabe, and leading engineers Reimspieß and Zadnik.

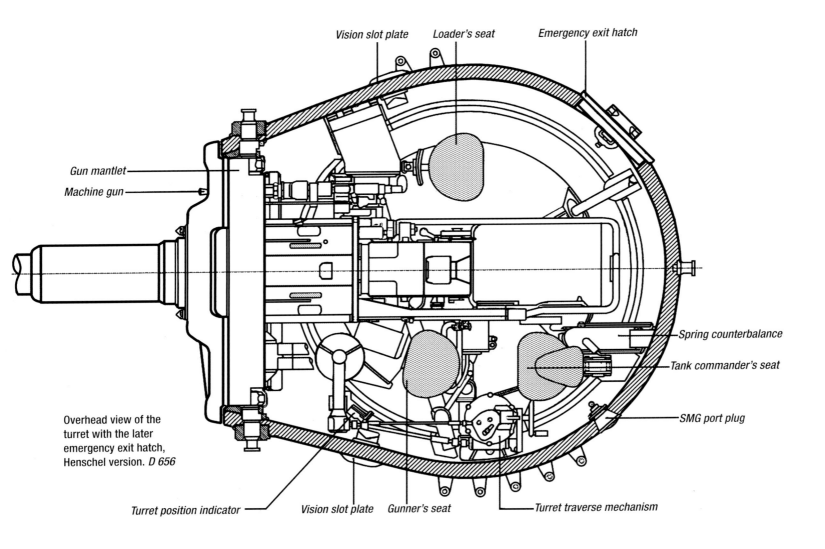

Vision slot plate   Loader's seat   Emergency exit hatch

Gun mantlet

Machine gun

Spring counterbalance

Tank commander's seat

Overhead view of the
turret with the later
emergency exit hatch,
Henschel version. *D 656*

SMG port plug

Turret position indicator   Vision slot plate   Gunner's seat   Turret traverse mechanism

Up for debate were the following details of the planned turret:

1. Modification of the turret ring, since because of the shell-casing chute, the turret could not be supported on the hull floor as planned. The hull roof had to be reinforced so that the turret was self-supporting. In addition, the deck under the turret had to be taken back by about 50 mm (1.97 in.), at the cost of the engine deck.

2. Design of the turret's electrical slip ring transformer

3. Ventilation of the turret could be achieved either via blowing or by sucking in the air with the help of the engine fan. The volume of air was to be controlled by flaps in the engine firewall.

4. Since the driver and radio operator were supposed to climb in through the turret hatches, unhindered access forward past the gunner's and loader's seats had to be ensured, and it was envisaged that the driver and radio operator would exit through side hatches in an emergency.

5. The Krupp representatives stated that the latest date for completion of the one-to-one-scale wooden model was May 20, 1941.

6. The basic electrical equipment was supposed to be the same as that of the *Panzer IV*. This also included the intercom system and the 12-volt lighting.

On May 13, 1941, there was another major meeting with all those responsible at the Nibelungenwerk in St. Valentin, during which chief designer Karl Rabe carried out an off-road drive in a Panzer IV chassis built at the factory.

On May 24, 1941, Krupp delivered the full-size wooden turret model by rail to the Nibelungenwerk in St. Valentin. The same day, there was another meeting in Stuttgart with engineer Esser of Krupp. That same month, there were discussions about an air-cooled, ten-cylinder diesel engine for the Type 100 with an unidentified Swiss company, probably Brown, Boveri & Cie, since a Dr. Bayer from that company had made contact with chief engineer Rabe in Stuttgart on March 20, 1941.

Among other things, the company was known for the production of exhaust gas turbochargers, a product that could not be made in Germany at that time because of patent and material problems. Exhaust gas turbochargers could be used only with diesel or gas Otto engines at that time due to high exhaust gas temperatures. Porsche gave the diesel project the internal company designation Porsche Type 200. It was initially not pursued, however, because the use of diesel engines in German tanks did not become of interest until later, with the ability to manufacture large quantities of synthetic diesel fuel.[17]

Strangely enough, the opinion prevails in the literature that the Porsche Type 100 was generally powered by two diesel engines. This is clearly contradicted by Xaver Reimspieß's notes, which describe the diesel engine only as a project that was not pursued.[18]

The second major tank conference, which set the trend for further development, was held at Hitler's Berghof on May 26, 1941. Participants at this important event included Professor Porsche; Reichsminister Dr. Fritz Todt; from the Army Ordnance Office, Oberste Philipps, Fichtner, and Crohn plus Oberstleutnant von Wilke and Oberbaurat Kniepkamp; Hauptamtsleiter Saur; and Dr. Hacker of Steyr. Oberst Fichtner of Wa Prüf 6 caused a stir when, in his opening remarks, he claimed that Germany had the best tanks in the world and also the most. Hitler regarded this as exaggerated and contradicted him energetically. (According to Saur, Oberst Fichtner's actions ensured that he would be replaced. Fichtner was to bring the Tiger project to a conclusion before this.)[19]

Further fundamental armament questions were then discussed. According to Hitler, it had now become necessary to equip the army with a new generation of heavy tanks, which were to have heavy firepower with relatively good mobility, since according to Hitler there was information that the English were planning to bring heavy tanks to the front. He therefore demanded a 50-to-60-metric-ton (55–66 ton) armored vehicle that was to have the following characteristics:

- a gun with greater penetrative ability compared to enemy tanks

- heavier armor than before (100 mm / 3.94 in. in front, 60 mm / 2.36 in. on the sides)

- a maximum speed of at least 40 kph (24.85 mph)

Hitler's most important decision thus affected the projects by Henschel and Porsche, which would become for Henschel the VK 3601 (H) and for Porsche the VK 4501 (P). Hitler demanded thicker frontal armor of 100 mm (3.94 in.), while 60 mm (2.36 in.) would suffice for the sides. The tank gun's penetrative ability was also supposed to be increased so that it would be capable of penetrating 100 mm (3.94 in.) of armor at a range of 1,500 m (4,921.26 ft.). This meant that a performance increase was required for the envisaged gun, the 88 mm Flak 18. This gun required a servicing diameter of about 1,850 mm (72.83 in.) and was envisaged for the VK 4501 (P), which met this requirement. The second weapon being considered by Hitler was the type 0725, envisaged by the Army Ordnance Office for the VK 3601 (H). This weapon had a conical section of barrel at the muzzle. Using so-called flanged ammunition, it easily achieved the penetrative abilities demanded by Hitler (the required high muzzle velocity was achieved by compressing the so-called cuff of the armor-piercing shot to a smaller final caliber).

Hitler saw another advantage in the smaller turret-servicing diameter of 1,650 mm (64.96 in.), which would have led to a lower turret weight of about 2.2 metric tons (2.42 tons), with 80 mm (3.15 in.) of frontal and 60 mm (2.36 in.) of side armor. The chassis could also be made smaller and lighter, or more ammunition could be stowed in the vehicle. He regarded the high demand for the strategic material tungsten as a disadvantage, since 1 kg would be required per projectile. Minister Todt drew his attention to the stockpile in Germany of just 700 metric tons (771 tons), of which just 260 metric tons (286 tons) was available for ammunition. The greater part was required for additives, tools, and machinery. The expected high barrel wear could also not be dismissed out of hand.

The VK 3601 prototype during a test drive. It has two rows of interleaved road wheels and narrow armored superstructure, which was, however, able to accommodate only a turret with a 75 mm gun. *SB*

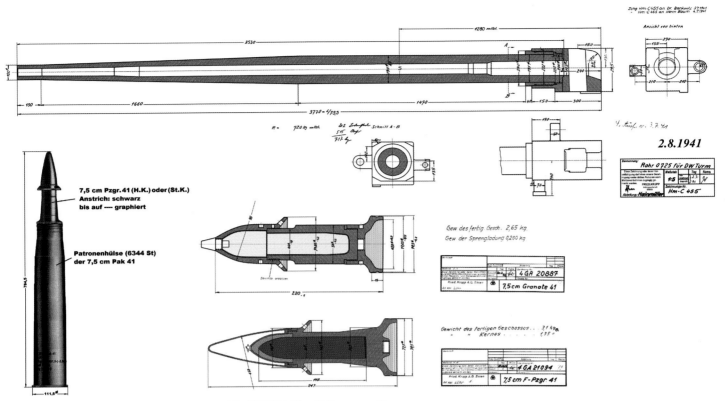

The conical 75 mm KwK 0725 for the turret of the VK 3001 (H) with its ammunition

In response to the first-named problem, Krupp later turned to steel as a replacement material; however, it fell far short of the penetrative ability of tungsten. Krupp tried to address the second problem by compensating with a cylindrical main barrel and a replaceable conical muzzle attachment, as implemented on the later Pak 41. For the abovementioned reasons, the Krupp turret with its 88 mm gun ultimately became the preferred weapon, since the 88 mm gun also had a greater moral and destructive effect on the target. For the Army Ordnance Office and Henschel, this resulted in the need to redesign the VK 3601 (H) so that it could accept the turret with larger servicing diameter and increased armor thickness. The goal was to have six Porsche and six Henschel vehicles delivered for testing by the summer of 1942.

Despite this, Henschel had received a contract to design a new turret with the 75 mm KwK 0725 for the Henschel vehicle. On this occasion, Hitler was again shown the small wooden models of the VK 3001 (P) and VK 3001 (H). The Army Ordnance Office—namely, Wa Prüf 6—advised Hitler that the two models would be breaking new ground. While the Porsche vehicle's gasoline-electric drive had not yet been tested, Henschel had gained a great deal of experience with

the drive and running gear of its 30-metric-ton vehicle over the past two years, which was necessary to deal with greater vehicle weights. Despite this, Hitler insisted that work should continue on both solutions.[20] Hacker subsequently gave a short presentation on the possibilities of rational tank production. Wa Prüf 6's first attack on the Porsche project had thus been repelled.

Following this, Hitler held an internal meeting with Minister Todt, Amtsleiter Saur, Dr. Porsche, and Director Hacker. About this meeting, Karl Otto Saur wrote: "The Tiger was first discussed with the führer on May 26, 1941. There were two designs: by Henschel of Kassel and by Porsche. . . . Porsche suggested a revolutionary innovation: an electric drive. Unfortunately, it lost out to the Henschel vehicle and never entered quantity production, since its timely start-up could not be guaranteed, in particular because of engine troubles."[21] One day later, Oskar Hacker of Steyr and the Porsche engineers met in Stuttgart to discuss this new task.

Another important chapter in German tank development began on June 21, 1941. In agreement with Generaloberst Fritz, head of army equipment, Minister Todt formed a tank committee. This date contradicts the claim made in the literature that Porsche received the development contract only because he was head of the tank committee. This committee had the task of bringing together all military, technical, and manufacturing forces of official and civilian agencies to achieve standardized planning, testing, and production.[22] According to Saur, however, the suggestion came from Hitler himself, "who determined that our tank development was too military, too bureaucratic. Design requirements were dictated to industry, and the latter, following these constraints, had to design the thing. There were no tanks, but compromises from the dictatorship and the desire to get out of this dictatorship. The object was to build the tanks from the maximum realization of military requirements and maximum performance by the engineers. The tank committee succeeded in this."[23]

The committee comprised officers of the chief of army equipment, of the Army Ordnance Office such as Oberst Fichtner (and later, Oberst Holzhäuer), industry representatives such as designer Michael of Alkett, Director Wiebecke of MAN, Director Wunderlich of Daimler-Benz, Dr. Maybach for engines, Director Dr. von Soden of ZF for gearboxes, engineer Aders of Henschel, and Director Bleichert of Miag, and, from the Ministry of Armaments and Munitions, the person of Karl-Otto Saur. They were later joined by Professor von Eberan of the Institute for Automotive Engineering, Dresden University of Technology, as scientific representative, and the tank expert and representative of the Ministry of Armaments, Generalleutnant Ritter von Radlmeier. Professor Porsche was named chairman (and later, Dr. Stiehler von Heydekampf, director of Henschel), and Director Oskar Hacker of Steyr was managing deputy.

The proposal to make Professor Porsche chairman came from Minister Todt. Daimler-Benz had previously had a contract with the Porsche company in the civilian field, but this ceased to exist with the outbreak of war in 1939. However, Daimler-Benz proposed to Dr. Todt that Porsche be employed as an advisor. Todt agreed. Todt and Porsche got on very well from the outset. With this step, Todt was able to limit the Army Ordnance Office's influence on new designs, since the Tank Committee had to check its demands at the outset. Industry's influence grew as a result, which also benefited Professor Porsche. Under these conditions he was able to fully develop his creativity.

The appearance of modern Russian tanks after June 22 resulted in a demand for product innovation from the German tank arm. Simultaneous with the commencement of work by the Tank Committee, there was a meeting with Henschel at the Army Ordnance Office on July 1, 1941, during which the company received a contract for development of a 45-to-50-metric-ton (49.6–55 ton) vehicle with a rotating turret and armored skirts that could be raised and lowered on the basis of previously developed study models. This was equivalent to the later VK 4501. The contract was initially limited to sixty vehicles, but because of the minimum-raw-materials requirement this was increased to 100 vehicles. Henschel took the most-important assemblies, such as the steering gear, final drives, and running gear with drive sprockets, from the VK 3601 (H). On the same day, in Stuttgart, representatives of the Simmering-Graz-Pauker and BBC companies met with Karl Rabe to discuss an engine for the new Porsche Type 101 project. The first discussions about the VK 4501 (P), which Hitler wanted and later became the Tiger P, took place with Heerlein of Krupp, representative of the hull maker, on July 10, 1941.

But work also continued on the Porsche Type 100 project. Steyr finally delivered the first engine for the Type 100 to Stuttgart by truck on July 7, 1941, and it was immediately mounted on the engine test bench there and was run for the first time on July 14. The second Type 100 engine followed on July 30 and was likewise run on the test bench. On July 22, Rabe, Reimspieß, and Fender traveled to Pilsen to negotiate the building of gearboxes for the Type 101. The next day there was a test drive in a Skoda tank on the factory grounds. Back in Stuttgart, there were talks with representatives of the Bosch, Voith, and Behr companies.

On July 31, 1941, following a presentation by Oberst Fichtner during the Tank Committee meeting, Professor Porsche had his first chance to examine captured Soviet tanks, which had been made serviceable again, at the Kummersdorf artillery range. He used the opportunity to examine the rubber-saving road wheels of the KV-I and K-II (so-called "Russian" road wheels) so that he could adopt this principle for his Type 101 project. The rubber tires were no longer subjected to pressure, and durability rose. As well, less rubber, of which there was a shortage at that time, was required. The quantity of rubber required for a Henschel VK 4501 vehicle was 370 kg (815.71 lbs.), while the later rubber-saving road wheels required just 110 kg (242.5 lbs.).

The Army Ordnance Office later designated the design as road wheels based on the "Porsche principle," and, after some hesitation, adopted them for the later Tiger H 1 and H 3 and in part also for the Panzerkampfwagen Panther. The Wa Prüf 6, exactly like the Soviet designers before them, were forced to accept the high level of track noise and greater track wear.

On August 25, 1941, the second Type 100 engine suffered connecting-rod damage, as a result of which the crankshaft was badly damaged and had to be replaced. Engine number 2 was running on the test bench again on September 2. The work overlapped with development of the Type 101, which now had special priority. The plan, which as of August was dubbed the "Tiger program," envisaged an unconditional focus on these new heavy tanks. As a result, the Type 100 had the character of only an experimental vehicle.

In a document dated September 23, 1941, however, an excited Minister Todt wrote to General von Leeb, head of the Army Ordnance Office, that the Army Ordnance Office was hindering the Porsche project to the advantage of the Henschel vehicle: "(1) The Army Ordnance Office has ordered that the Porsche tank will not be getting the turret envisaged by Prof. Porsche, with a diameter of 2,000 mm [78.74 in.], but instead the Henschel turret of 1,900 mm [74.8 in.]. Since the führer has commissioned Prof. Porsche, I cannot lose the impression that the Army Ordnance Office is putting prestige first, and

that an Army Ordnance Office tank will ultimately be produced. The Flak 41 can hardly be housed in the 1,900 mm turret. I must inform you that every time I am with the führer, he asks me whether the high-performance Flak 41 will really fit in the Porsche tank. Prof. Porsche has assured me that he is pursuing the possible installation of the Flak 41. I cannot relieve him of this task and accept the excuse that the Flak 41 can no longer be fitted because the Army Ordnance Office has ordered a smaller turret. The führer also has no real confidence that another 88 mm barrel is now being designed in place of the Flak 41. The führer wants to use the Flak 41 in the new heavy tank with no restrictive conditions. I would like to draw your attention to the fact that we can all expect the greatest complaints from the führer, if one day when the vehicle is first demonstrated it has a gun other than the Flak 41. For myself as Reich minister for armaments and munitions, out of conviction and because I represent the will of the führer, I see it as my duty to use all my energy to ensure that no other gun is considered for the heavy tank than the barrel of the Flak 41."[24]

To be on the safe side, Minister Todt sent a copy of the letter to Oberst Schmundt in the Reich Chancellery, who in turn sent a copy to the head of the OKW. The Army Ordnance Office could not accept this, and on September 27, 1941, Oberst Fichtner, the head of Wa Prüf 6, gave his opinion to General Leeb. In addition to stating that the reduction of turret size from 2,000 to 1,820 mm (76.74 to 71.65 in.) originated solely and exclusively from Krupp, his explanation of

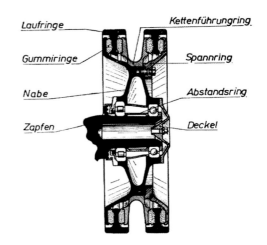

The rubber-saving road wheel of the Soviet KV-I tank, which served as an example for later German tanks. *Right:* the road wheel of the later Porsche Type 101.

the development of the VK 4501 was very interesting, and therefore extracts from it will be repeated here: "(2) . . . The Pz.Kfw. 4501 currently under development by Henschel is a further development of the 30[-metric]-ton [33 ton] tank that has been in design and testing there since early 1937. As per orders issued by the officers of the Army High Command, it was anticipated that the Henschel heavy tank would carry the 75 mm KwK L/24 and later a 105 mm KwK L/28, which required a turret servicing circle [diameter] of 1,650 mm [64.96 in.]. At the end of 1939, Professor Dr. Porsche was tasked with development of a 25-to-30[-metric]-ton [27.55–33 ton] heavy tank, for which at least a 75 mm L/24, and, if possible, a 105 mm gun, was demanded. In the course of the upgrading of tank armament, it was envisaged that an 88 mm L/36 gun would be installed in the Porsche tank. The Dr. Porsche KG issued a direct order to Krupp for the associated turret, and it was developed in direct cooperation between the two companies. Contrary to normal practice, the office did not issue a development order to Krupp. In evaluating war experiences and because of the führer's increased demands for improved penetrative ability, there crystallized for production—start of production May–June 1942—a Type 4501 Porsche vehicle with the 88 mm gun and a Type 3601 Henschel with the 0725 weapon. Due to further directives from the führer that conical barrels were not to be used, the turret developed by Prof. Porsche at Krupp had to be used for the Henschel tank, with minor modifications, since because of lack of time, no other solution was possible. This measure forced the development office to adopt a modification to its running gear, and the Henschel type also became a 45[-metric]-ton [49.6 ton] vehicle. There had thus never been a Henschel turret with an 88 mm gun and 1,900 mm [74.8 in.] servicing circle; on the contrary, the Porsche turret was placed on the Henschel vehicle."[25]

The remaining content consisted of a torrent of verbose assurances that the Wa Prüf 6 had always supported Porsche and had taken every opportunity to study captured and German equipment. Wa Prüf 6 assured that it would always be available to provide advice and assistance to the Porsche company, if Professor Porsche only wanted it. With this,

Porsche was indirectly accused of not listening to Wa Prüf 6, which, on the basis of Professor Porsche's character, was surely not entirely unfounded. As to the problem of the 88 mm Flak 41 installation, Oberst Fichtner advised that concerning this question, he had received information from Porsche KG to the effect that for the time being, only the L/56 was possible for the VK 4501.

Fichtner also pointed out that Hitler had originally insisted on the ability to penetrate 140 mm (5.5 in.) at 1,000 m (3,280 ft.), without expressly demanding the 88 mm caliber. The Rheinmetall company therefore tried to achieve this performance with a 75 mm tank gun with a cylindrical barrel, based on the Pak 44. This measure would also have led to a more favorably shaped turret. In point 6, the head of Wa Prüf 6 advised that they had now issued a contract to the Krupp and Rheinmetall companies for development of a turret mounting the 88 mm Flak 41 for the VK 4501 (Porsche and Henschel versions). The office meant the turret of the later VK 4502, of which fifty examples were later built. Eleven copies of this self-justifying letter were distributed to the various departments, as if to warn the other departments in the office.

On November 3, 1941, Rabe and Reimspieß inspected the first Type 100 hull, then being worked on, at the Nibelungenwerk in St. Valentin, which was followed by further discussions with Steyr in the days that followed. Meanwhile, on November 18, 1941, Krupp was able to report that the first Type 101 hull of the VK 4501 (P) was completely welded and that no problems had arisen. There was a setback, however, when a defect appeared in one of the Type 100 test bed engines and it once again had to be disassembled.

Professor Porsche was summoned to Berlin on November 16 to take part in a flight to Smolensk on the Eastern Front. There he would have the opportunity to examine the first captured examples of the new Russian T-34 tank. The Tank Special Committee, under the command of Oberst Fichtner, arrived at army headquarters in Orel on November 18, 1941. In addition to representatives of the Army Ordnance Office, such as Oberbaurat Kniepkamp, with Professor Porsche, Director Dr. Hacker (Steyr), Director Dr. Rohland (Verein. Stahlwerke), Director Wunderlich (Daimler-Benz), Director

A captured first-generation T-34 with rubber-tired road wheels at Kummersdorf. *SB*

4452.41

Here the improved driver's visor of the T-34, as was later used in the Porsche Type 180, can be seen clearly. The measured armor thicknesses were painted on the tank. The different track generations are interesting. The idler wheels also seem to have different diameters. *B*

Dorn (Krupp AK), Ober-Ing. Aders (Henschel), Ing. Oswald (MAN), and Ober-Ing. Zimmer (Rheinmetall), all the important tank development companies were represented.

The attendees were greeted by Generaloberst Guderian, who gave a speech on the desperate tank situation. He also laid out his demands for improvements to existing armored vehicles and new designs. The committee then set off on its drive to the front to visit the 35th Panzer Regiment. It also inspected the tank battlefield in the area of Orel and German frontline workshops. The latter complained about a lack of spare parts and the sensitivity of German tanks to cold. Moreover, the Wehrmacht's situation regarding spare-parts and equipment supply was catastrophic.

After the Tank Special Committee returned from its inspection trip, Guderian held a final meeting, and on November 22 it flew home. Professor Porsche returned to Stuttgart the same day and described his impressions and experiences to chief engineer Karl Rabe. In particular, he described the novel Soviet tank type, the T-34, which the Wehrmacht was having great problems dealing with at that time and which later would greatly influence German tank development.

The third major tank conference took place at the Reich Chancellery in Berlin on November 29, 1941, and was attended by Professor Porsche. The main topic was the accelerated development of the Panther, following the example of the Soviet T-34, and the establishment of an initial production

A captured T-34 tank from the second production series. The later version was equipped with simple steel road wheels on account of the rubber shortage. *SB*

capacity of 600 per month. In his address, Hitler declared that German tanks were no longer fully equal to some of the Russian tanks and British infantry tanks with respect to armor and the penetrative ability of their guns. Contrary to the opinion he had expressed at the second tank conference on February 18 of the year, he now regarded improved armor protection as the first priority, even at the expense of speed. As an initial measure, the existing tank types were to be improved through the addition of armor plates in front and the use of special ammunition (Panzergranate 40). For the future new designs, Hitler regarded a limitation in the number of types as being of primary importance. In the future, production was to be limited to three types:

- the light type, corresponding to the previous Panzer III

- the medium type, corresponding to the Panzer IV

- the heavy type: the Henschel and Porsche designs

In addition to the heavy-tank type, Porsche was also given the task of designing a superheavy-tank type (the later Maus).

Furthermore, Hitler demanded that the Sturmgeschütze (assault guns) must again be attached to the infantry and also be fitted with a gun enabling them to effectively combat enemy tanks. Hitler further directed that much more attention be paid to the production process when designing tanks, and, in the interest of fluid mass production, an effort be made to simplify design elements. Oberst Fichtner restated the opinion heard at the front, that the troops would prefer a gun with a greater firing range over heavier armor.

These final statements by Hitler were anything but advantageous for the Porsche Tiger project, since, to date, Professor Porsche had emphasized innovative technologies. With the Porsche Type 100, Professor Porsche could still work out his ideal design and then look for a manufacturer who could implement his project, but for the Porsche Type 101 he lacked time for development and production.

On December 21, a new problem arose. On the test bench, the first Type 100 engine tended to develop oil foaming.

Extensive experimentation with a modified lubrication system was carried out between Christmas and New Year's. An oil slinger was also installed. Shortly before the turn of the year from 1941 to 1942, the Porsche team carried out many tests with the engine to resolve existing lubrication problems. The lubrication system modifications finally produced good results, but the joy was short lived.

On January 1, 1942, another engine broke down on the test bench in Stuttgart. There followed a discussion with Dr. Wichelt and Professor Mader of the Junkers company about the engine mounting. On January 13, 1942, engineers Rabe and Zadnik made their way to the Nibelungenwerk to see for themselves the state of progress on the Type 100. It was planned

The VK 3001 (P)'s first drive at St. Valentin on February 24, 1942. *PA*

Professor Porsche and his electrical specialist Otto Zadnik in front of the Type 100. *PA*

that the vehicle, now called the Leopard, would finally be driven in the week following. They were also interested in the beginning assembly work on the running-gear parts for the Type 101.

The **fourth major tank conference**, which took place on **January 23, 1942,** at Rastenburg in East Prussia, was dominated by an answer to the Soviet T-34 tank. The T-34, which was clearly superior to the German designs, impressed the

The first test drive by the Porsche Type 100 tank took place in ice and snow on February 24, 1942. Here the engineers are examining the right drive wheel. Otto Zadnik and Professor Porsche are standing in the turret replacement weight. *PA*

attendees with the simplicity of its design and its robustness. The Russian W-2 diesel engine was also a milestone in engine development, since it had been developed solely for use in tanks and was not based on any existing power plant. As well, the T-34 was very well suited to mass production, and it is therefore not surprising that Professor Porsche's response to this design was "Copy it!," an idea that was rejected by the military and industry. Moreover, Hitler wanted to create a superiority in armor and armament for the future, which the enemy would not be able to match quickly. The VK 3001 project, already begun by Daimler-Benz and MAN, was to become the VK 3002, the German answer to the Soviet tank.

Hitler demanded the accelerated development of the Panzer V Panther, based on the example of the Soviet T-34

tank and the creation of a tank production capacity of 600 per month at first. However, at that time he saw that in all likelihood, the value of the tank arm would be diminished significantly by the imminent large-scale introduction of new and effective armor-piercing ammunition based on the principle of the hollow charge. He therefore endorsed a switch in production to large numbers of self-propelled guns, which could be produced faster and cheaper.[26]

Because of the new drive, construction of the VK 3001 (P) proved considerably more expensive for the Nibelungenwerk than the Panzer IV, which was also being built in the factory. Two of six prototypes were ultimately completed.[27] The long-awaited demonstration of the first prototype of the Porsche Type 100 took place on February 24, 1942, in the factory's

The tank drives out of the village into the surrounding countryside. *PA*

testing grounds in the presence of Professor Porsche and Ferry Porsche. The second vehicle was also ready to be test-driven on March 27, 1942. Several pictures of the Porsche Type 100 taken during these test drives, which internally was known only as the Leopard, have survived,

The later testing took place without a gun turret, since Krupp was unable to deliver the turrets on time and had meanwhile canceled the order in favor of the VK 4501 (P). To achieve a comparable driving weight, a turret replacement weight was mounted. Extensive testing was carried out on- and off-road, in order to obtain sufficient knowledge of the gasoline-electric drive's behavior in the armored vehicle and its cooling problems. This information was all the more important because, as described above, work had begun on the contract for the more heavily armored VK 4501 (P).

Since this project was given the code name "Tiger" by Hitler, to better distinguish the smaller VK 3001 (P) as the factory's smaller predator, it was given the name Leopard. The first mention of both code names appears in chief engineer Karl-Otto Saur's diary under January 13, 1942, or just before completion of the first Type 100 vehicle. Senior offices were also unaware of this name, as Karl-Otto Saur's postwar interrogation revealed. This shows that the Leopard mentioned in the literature had nothing to do with the Porsche vehicle, but rather that this designation was intended for the heavily armored VK 1602 battlefield reconnaissance vehicle, which was on the army's development list until January 1943.

Here the tank is seen passing through the village of St. Valentin. *PA*

Here the tank is seen passing through the village of St. Valentin. *PA*

On March 27, 1942, there was another demonstration in St. Valentin, which according to Xaver Reimspieß went well. The Nibelungenwerk's Leopard caused no further problems. The next day, another Type 100 engine arrived with a full-scale mockup of the new Porsche "Special Vehicle 2" (Porsche Type 101) under military guard from Stuttgart to St. Valentin.

According to Professor Porsche, the testing of "Special Vehicle 1" (Porsche Type 100) provided valuable information and experience about its electric controls and steering, and important knowledge about the behavior of air-cooled engines in tanks.

The test drives by the Leopard were carried out with no major problems. *PA*

The fresh air feed (*behind the turret*) and the two exhausts in front of the two mufflers can be seen in the photo above. The vehicle is carrying a turret replacement weight, from which Otto Zadnik is looking. *A*

Professor Porsche, wearing his familiar hat, during one of the later test drives (there is no more snow) in the factory's own testing area. *PA*

CHAPTER 2

The VK 4501 (P) Tiger Tank

As determined in the previous chapter, development of the Porsche Type 101 began at a time when the Porsche Type 100 existed only as a one-tenth-scale model. The contract for the new Type 101 resulted from experience in the Western Campaign, where heavily armored French tanks demonstrated the limits of the German panzers. Hitler's demand on May 26, 1941, for a more heavily armored vehicle caused a major problem for the Porsche and the Army Ordnance Office project. In addition to total weight, additional armor increased axle weight, and the running gear had to be made stronger. Mobility also had to be adapted to the new requirements. The necessary high engine performance required a larger engine compartment, which in turn resulted in increased chassis length.

Professor Porsche in the Porsche KG's drawing room. *PA*

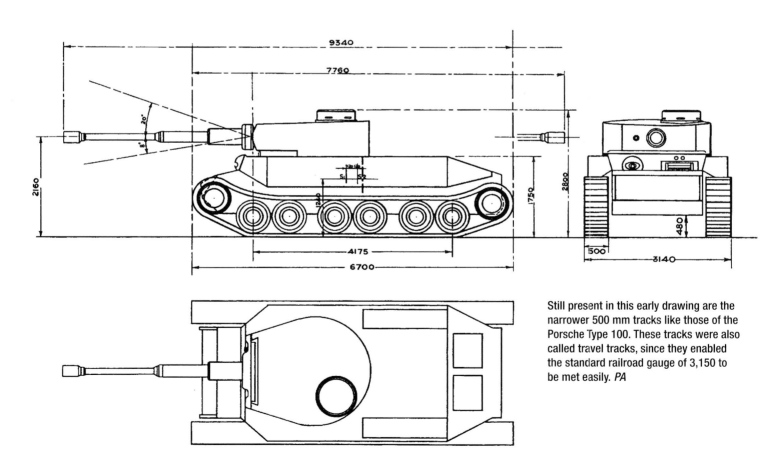

Still present in this early drawing are the narrower 500 mm tracks like those of the Porsche Type 100. These tracks were also called travel tracks, since they enabled the standard railroad gauge of 3,150 to be met easily. *PA*

The turret design resembled that of the Type 100. It was horseshoe shaped in outline, with the right side bending farther inward. The first eight turrets had lower 80 mm sidewalls and a profiled 25 mm thick turret roof. Because of the more heavily armored turret, which because of the large turret ring already sat far forward, the vehicle's center of gravity shifted, so that as a consequence Porsche was forced to move the two electric motors, previously in front of the vehicle, to the rear, where they were mounted transversely. Since the military preferred front drive because of its better self-cleaning characteristics, Porsche also used sprockets on the forward idler wheels, which was unusual and became a salient feature of the VK 4501 (P), or Porsche Type 101. Road wheels and bogie suspension were strengthened, and the tracks were widened from 500 mm (19.68 in.) to 600 mm (23.6 in.) and later 640 mm (25.2 in.). The return rollers could be deleted, since the diameter of the road wheels was increased to 794 mm (31.25 in.). Because of the vehicle's increased weight, the rubber tires were subject to very heavy loads. Since the raw material caoutchouc was a strategic material, Porsche decided to adopt rubber-saving road wheels similar to the road wheels used on the Soviet KV tanks.

On July 3, 1941, the Nibelungenwerk received information from the chief of the OKW, Wi Rü Office, that Hitler had directed that production of the heavy tank 4501 (P) was to be accelerated by all means and that there was no need to wait for the testing usually required for the issuing of an order. According to the documents in the office's possession, the completion of ten vehicles in May, ten in June, twelve in July, and fifteen in August 1942 was possible. The entire series was to comprise 100 vehicles.

The Porsche Type 101 was first mentioned in Karl Rabe's diary on July 10, 1941. The entry was made in connection to a meeting between Porsche and engineer Heerlein of Krupp. The first preliminary discussions with the Voith company concerning a hydraulic drive for the Type 101 were held two days later. The Porsche KG later designated this new hydraulic version the Porsche Type 102. At the end of July, the Skoda company received the order to build final drives for the Type 101. The spring rods for the toggle suspension were to be delivered by the Hoesch company.

On July 22, Krupp received the official armaments order for 100 hull shells and the manufacture and installation of 100 complete tank turrets. The Army Ordnance Office had chosen the Nibelungenwerk in St. Valentin as the recipient and assembly firm. The same day, Karl Rabe, with Reimspieß and Fender, visited the Skoda factory in Pilsen. It was primarily about the final drives for the Type 101. The next day a test drive took place in a Skoda tank. After they returned to Stuttgart, the planetary gearbox was redesigned.

As of July 24, 1941, there were further discussions at brief intervals with the Voight company, the Nibelungenwerk, and Krupp. On August 1, Porsche for the first time inspected captured Russian tanks at Kummersdorf, which was very interesting for the professor. The following discussions with Dr. Fritz Todt at the Armaments Ministry lasted until August 8. On August 9, Skoda submitted the first design for a track for the Type 101.

The handover of drawings for the new Type 101 engine to the Simmering-Graz-Pauker company took place on September 5, 1941. Discussions were also held with other firms, such as MAN, Junkers, and Krupp, seeking the best solutions for the project. At the end of the month, representatives of the Teves company came to Stuttgart to discuss details of the brake system. Starting in October 9, 1941, Porsche's engineers also concerned themselves with various diesel engines for the Type 101. For test purposes, two single-cylinder diesel engines, each with a displacement of 1.5 liters (91.5 in.^{3}), were built, one with direct fuel injection, the type 158, and one as a Simmering System prechamber engine, the type 159.

On October 10, there was a major discussion with representatives of Simmering-Pauker of Vienna and Steyr. Oskar Hacker, General von Radlmeier, Dr. Voith, and engineer Kugel completed the group. The next day, Professor Kamm and Dr. Huber of the Stuttgart Technical University took part in the discussions at Porsche. On October 17, 1941, the Porsche engineers attended a demonstration of a captured Russian tank in Stuttgart-Vaihingen. In the days that followed, there were discussions with Drs. Dorn and Heerlein of Krupp and with representatives of the Rheinmetall, Skoda, Knecht, and Teves companies.

On November 2, 1941, there was a long and intensive meeting in Vienna with Fritz Xaver Reimspieß, Professor Porsche, and Karl Rabe from the Porsche KG; Director-General Schuster; Dr. Hacker of Simmering-Pauker-Graz AG; and

Director Walter from Steyr concerning the Type 101. It dealt mainly with the planned engine program. The decision was made to also develop an engine with liquid cooling under the designation Porsche Type 130.

Individual departments were created in halls V and VI of the Nibelungenwerk under a so-called "Tiger" office. All experimental and assembly work on the Porsche Tiger took place in hall V, while the necessary running-gear parts were mechanically produced in hall VI.[28]

Porsche was at Führer Headquarters on November 13 and 14. The next day there were daylong deadline meetings with Steyr, Simmering, and Voith in Stuttgart. At the beginning of December, after Porsche's trip to see Hitler on November 29, there were stormy debates in the Stuttgart office between the professor and Karl Rabe. Numerous problems were encountered during construction, and therefore Porsche often drove to the Nibelungenwerk. Otto Zadnik usually remained on scene for several days, often accompanied by Xaver Reimspieß. The Porsche engineers repeatedly commuted between St. Valentin, Pilsen Fallersleben, and Stuttgart.

The first Type 101 engine ran on the test bench in Stuttgart on December 21, and once again heavy engine foam buildup was discovered. This required modification of the lubrication system, in which baffle plates were installed in the crankshaft housing. The necessary drawings were immediately sent to the Simmering firm, so that these modifications could be carried out on the next engine.

The first two hulls, which by then had been completely welded (with the numbers 150 001 and 150 002), plus accessories, which included the six drain-opening covers, the machine gun ball mount, the parts for the driver's visor, and the two engine doors in the bulkhead, had been delivered to the assembly plant in St. Valentin on December 27, 1941. Hulls 150 003 and 150 004 were also sent to the Nibelungenwerk on December 31. Meanwhile, in-depth running-gear tests for the Type 101 were carried out at the VF factory's laboratory in Fallersleben.

The year 1942 began with a visit by Professor Maier of the Waffenamt's armaments inspectorate. Rabe and Ferry Porsche visited Daimler-Benz on January 8, in search of a suitable diesel engine for the Porsche Type 101. Furthermore, Karl Rabe went to Junkers to seek advice on mounting the Type 100 and 101 engines. What he was told was evaluated

The hull shell of a Type 101 clearly shows the engine compartment for the two ten-cylinder engines and the side ventilation openings. *SB*

in Stuttgart the following day. While the Type 100 engine ran well on the test bench, as previously described, on January 17, 1942, the Type 101 engine suffered a piston seizure and had to be disassembled. In-depth discussions followed.

On January 18, 1942, at Krupp's own firing range at Meppen, the 88 mm KwK 36 L/56, designated device 5-38, was fired for the first time. The first twenty rounds served to break in the barrel, adjust the recoil brake, and test the breech and shell-casing ejection system. There were problems with several jams and more or less intense afterflaming. The latter problem was caused by the muzzle brake. The gun was fired

Hull shell number 150 002 in the Krupp factory. *PA*

with the normal powder of the 88 mm Flak 18, which as we know had no muzzle brake. To overcome this problem, it was directed that the gun henceforth be fired with a flash-reducing wad. In addition, the Army Ordnance Office had planned a mass firing of about 300 rounds, using a gun that had already been accepted.

Details of the rotating turrets of the VK 3601 and VK 4501 were also discussed by Krupp, Henschel, and Wa Prüf 6 on January 21. In addition to elimination of the center column, hatches were planned for the spare ammunition in the floor of the turret platform.

One week later, on January 20, there was a large round of meetings at St. Valentin with Director-General Meindl and all the participants in the Tiger production theme. At Krupp in Essen as well, the department heads discussed details of hull construction with Dr. Rohland of the Tank Committee. The main topic was simplification of the Porsche hulls. In advance, Krupp had fired at two 30 mm armor plates with a 37 mm gun. One of the plates was mechanically processed and welded at an angle of 90°, while the other plate was autogenous-cut and welded at an angle of 30°. The effect of the fire was the same, so that no particular advantage was detectable. Autogenous cutting as a production method could

represent a great savings potential. Rohland was supposed to present this testing protocol to Hitler at the next conference.

Another point of the Special Committee VI "Tank" revolved around the theme of the rational production of heavy turrets. The focus lay on the technique of pressing turrets, which offered a great potential saving. It was found that the horseshoe-shaped turret of the VK 4501, with its shape and wall thicknesses of 100/80 mm (3.94/3.15 in.), was unsuitable for pressing for reasons of time and weight.

Considerable follow-up work was required. In any case, the roof had to be cut out again and, for weight-saving reasons, replaced by a lighter metal sheet. If they wanted to achieve a nominal thickness of 80 mm (3.15 in.), a thickness of 90 to 95 mm (3.54–3.74 in.) would have to be accepted in the lower area. With this, however, a 100 mm (3.94 in.) turret front would not be possible, if the entire turret was not to be reduced from a thickness of 110 to 115 mm (4.33–4.53 in.) to 100 mm. Even the newly developed reinforced 4501 turret (the first mention of a new Tiger on January 23, 1942) was not suitable for pressing in its current form. Turrets with dimensions of those in the Tiger program, if suitably designed, required a press with 10,000 to 15,000 metric tons (11,023–16,535 tons)

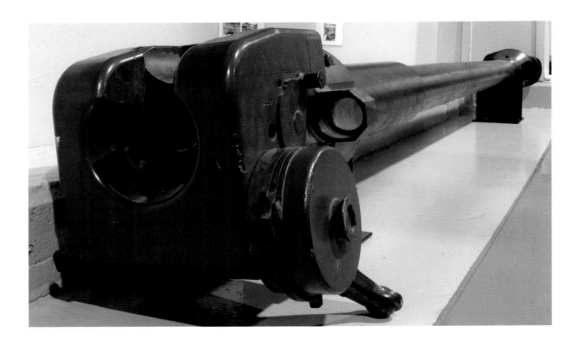

The 88 mm KwK 36 L/56 in the Bovington Tank Museum

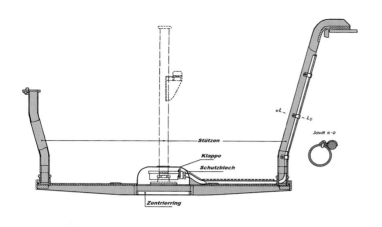

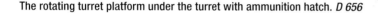

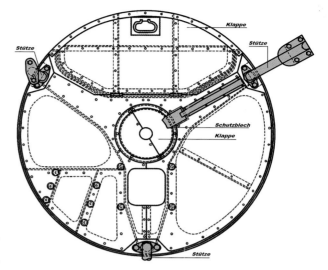

The rotating turret platform under the turret with ammunition hatch. *D 656*

of compression force. While such existed in the form of forging presses, they were already working at full capacity.[29]

Before January was over, Krupp ordered radio equipment for the one hundred Type 101 turrets from army department WuG 6. It was anticipated that six Fu 5 sets would be delivered in February 1942, nine in March, twelve in April, and, as of May, fifteen sets per month. Beginning in February, one set of radio equipment was required per month for the three VK 4501 Henschel turrets that had been ordered. Astonishingly, Krupp also ordered two sets of Fu 5 radio equipment per month for the six turrets for the VK 3601 (Henschel), which had been canceled.

Three more hulls—150 005, 150 007, and 150 008—were delivered to St. Valentin in January. A request was sent to Krupp that the next six hulls delivered be the electric version, in order to avoid the costly conversion process during fitting-out of the turrets. (Hull 150 004, delivered in December, was still the hydraulic version.)

On January 23, Porsche was summoned to Führer Headquarters. The same day, the Porsche company sent Krupp the information that the type designation was being changed from 101 to 102, to better differentiate between all the drawings and parts lists valid only for the hydraulic drive,. From that point in time, the designation of the hydraulic version of the Tiger P was Porsche Type 102. Another detail change affected the pneumatic system. The pneumatic system's two large pressure vessels were replaced by four smaller ones.

At the beginning of February, Krupp was sent the second 88 mm gun (device 5-38) as well as two type 0725 guns for the VK 3601 by the sole gunmaker, Wolf-Buckau. On January

27–28, the Dr. Porsche KG held meetings with representatives of the Krupp and Daimler-Benz companies. Reimspieß advised those in attendance that the front plate on future vehicles would not be sloped at 45°, as before, but instead were to be sloped at 30° to the horizontal. Further, the driver's visor was to be designed so that it could also be used as an exit, meaning that it could pivot outward (similar to that of the T-34).

Reimspieß anticipated that its dimensions would be about 450×350 mm (17.72×13.78 in.). Since this meeting ultimately concerned the hulls from number 150 101 onward, it will be examined more closely in a later chapter (Type 180). Two days later the Tank Committee met at Krupp to discuss the "Tiger program," with a subsequent tour of the production area led by Dr. Rohland. In the beginning the meeting focused on three proposals. First, Krupp proposed that the individual parts for the Type 101 hull be cut to finished size, largely eliminating the mechanical autogenous processing. Because Wa Prüf 6 feared a reduction in resistance to shellfire, Krupp was prepared to carry out comparative trials to refute the objection. From Professor Porsche came the wish that beginning with hull 150 101, the hull design be changed so that the front plate was sloped at just 30° to the horizontal. Dr. Rohland also made the suggestion that in the future, the armor of the VK 4501 should be welded only with chromium-nickel-containing austenitic electrodes. After a lengthy debate, the following decisions were agreed to:

The Krupp firm was to construct a ballistic model with the former hull shape, but in keeping with the proposal to cut without autogenous processing.

As of hull number 101, the Krupp firm should anticipate the delivery of hulls with the front plate sloped 30° and autogenously cut.

The Porsche firm was to provide the Krupp firm with about four designers for the extensive design work required to accomplish points 1 and 2.

During ballistic trials in April, in addition to the autogenously cut hull, a hull with panel joints exactly the same as those of the first 100 hulls should also be fired at.

Concerning the welding of the two ballistic bodies, both variants were to be welded, one in the previous fashion and the other only autogenously, in keeping with the proposal from Dr. Rohland (without hard cover layers).

Should firing at the autogenously cut hull suggested by Krupp produce an unfavorable result, in August 1942, after delivery of the first 100 hulls, subsequent hulls were to be manufactured in the previous mechanically processed form. The same should be done if the design work required for the new form with the autogenously cut and 30°-sloped front plate was not completed in time.

It was decided that the VK 4501 production hulls should in the future be welded only autogenously, with chrome-nickel-containing electrodes without hard cover layers. Wa Prüf 6 reserved the right to conduct a review.

According to the explanation given by the Krupp representatives, the technology of "pressing turrets" was not used because the period from design start to the start of production was always very short. To gain the time necessary for the construction and testing of the forming presses, the dimensions of the pressed parts had to have been set at the start of design work, with no significant press shape changes being possible. These requirements could not be met by the design. In addition, only a small number of suitable presses were available to carry out this work. Despite all difficulties, it was intended to pursue this possible production method in the future.

The question was asked about why the turret developed for the heavy tank was so wide at the front compared to the Russian vehicles. Krupp subsequently pointed out that it was entirely possible to design a narrow gun mantlet. It would, however, have to be correspondingly higher, so that the area exposed to fire was approximately the same in height times width. In conclusion, Oberst Fichtner advised that because of the large departure of labor forces, completion of the VK 3001 and VK 3601 vehicles by the Henschel company had been set back temporarily. Despite this, the armor for the four still-pending VK 3601 vehicles, which was being worked on, was to be completed. The previous deadlines could be exceeded. Krupp and Wa Prüf 6 still had to agree where these four hulls were to be stored. Of the eight VK 3001 vehicles, only four were to be completed as test vehicles. The remaining four hulls were likewise deferred indefinitely.[30]

On February 2, 1942, Professor Thoma from Munich presented his design for a tank drive with the aid of a hydrostatic gearbox (see chapter 5), which in later years he would be able to realize in a Panzer IV. However, the next day, Professor Porsche decided, on the occasion of another visit by representatives of the Voith firm, in favor of that company's hydrodynamic drive.

In February 1942, Krupp worked on further turret designs for the VK 4501 series. It was to be determined whether, because of its small servicing circle of 1,850 mm, the VK 4501—strengthened—turret with the 88 mm L/71 gun could also be mounted on the Henschel vehicle. This meant for the later Tiger H 3. The Porsche vehicle was instead to be checked to determine if a 105 mm L/70 gun (from the Löwe tank) could be accommodated in the strengthened turret, since the diameter of the hull roof cutout on the Porsche vehicle was 2,000 mm (78.74 in.).

Internally, Krupp once again summarized the heavy-tank turrets under development:

Design of an 88 mm L/56 turret with a servicing-circle diameter of 1,650 to 1,700 mm (64.96–66.93 in.), following the design of the VK 4501, was strengthened with a wall thickness of 80/50 mm (3.15/1.97 in.), or 80/40 mm (3.15/1.57 in.) if the weight should be too great. The turret was designated for the VK 3002 vehicle to be developed by Krupp, and for the MAN company's VK 3002 as a replacement for the 75 mm L/70 turret.

Design of an 88 mm L/71 turret for the VK 4501 was strengthened with a servicing-circle diameter of 1,850 mm (72.83 in.). According to Oberst Fichtner, this turret would

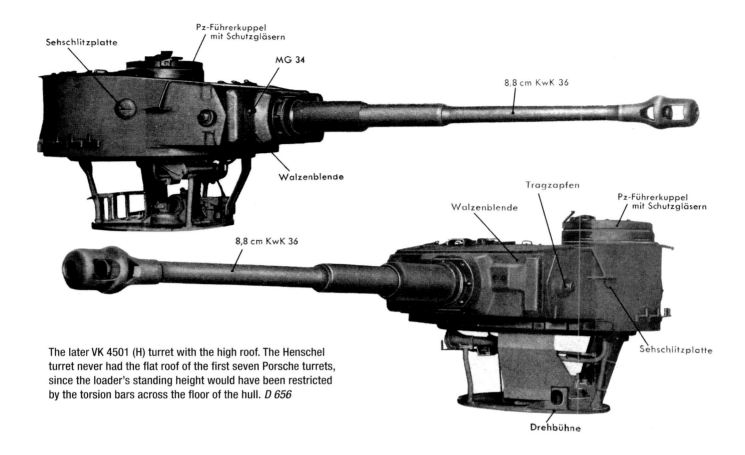

Sehschlitzplatte

Pz-Führerkuppel
mit Schutzgläsern

MG 34

8,8 cm KwK 36

Walzenblende

8,8 cm KwK 36

Tragzapfen

Walzenblende

Pz-Führerkuppel
mit Schutzgläsern

Sehschlitzplatte

Drehbühne

The later VK 4501 (H) turret with the high roof. The Henschel turret never had the flat roof of the first seven Porsche turrets, since the loader's standing height would have been restricted by the torsion bars across the floor of the hull. *D 656*

be suitable for the Henschel vehicle. As soon as *Wa Prüf 6* had received the design drawings, they were to be passed on to Henschel for review.

Design of a 105 mm L/70 turret (VK 7001) for the Porsche vehicle with a servicing-circle diameter of 2,000 mm (78.74 in.). Design: strengthened VK 4501 turret.

In addition to the design of a 105 mm L/70 turret for the VK 7001, the size of the smallest servicing-circle diameter for a 128 mm L/50 turret and a 150 mm L/40 turret was to be determined. For large and small elevations, it was also to be determined whether an additional smaller gun with a caliber of approximately 50 or 75 mm could be accommodated.

Meanwhile on February 5, Steyr-Daimler-Puch reminded Krupp of its obligation to also provide descriptions and a list of spare parts for the new vehicles. According to the OKH, the books were to include

- equipment description and operating instructions:
  for the turret
  for the superstructure without turret (chassis)

- care manual

- deadline booklet

- maintenance manual (removal and installation, disassembly)

- list of spares

Since the first four books were to be printed by Wa Prüf 6, the initial design was requested in March to ensure timely completion. The "Provisional Equipment List for VK 4501, Superstructure and Turret, Status January 1942" also appeared the same month. In addition to the turret with 88 mm KwK

36 (device 5-38), it also contained a 75 mm KwK 40 (device 5-37) turret by the Rheinmetall company.

February 8, 1942, was a black day for Professor Porsche personally but also for the tank project. On that day, Minister Dr. Fritz Todt was killed in an air crash under unexplained circumstances. As described in the introduction, the two technicians got along well; their interactions were filled with a high degree of mutual respect. Todt had been a technician and expert, but he also accepted advice from other experts if he didn't understand something. On February 10, Hitler named the younger Albert Speer as Todt's successor. Speer was no technician; rather, he was Hitler's star architect, who knew how to influence Hitler. He was the kind of man who would tolerate no contradiction from others, unless it was Hitler. Professor Porsche was therefore not the right contact person for him, since Porsche had to be convinced of the (divergent) opinion of his opposite number instead of blindly following him.

The shooting-in of five 88 mm KwK 36 guns began at the artillery range at Meppen, in the 3,500 m (11,483 ft.) position, at the beginning of February 1942, according to plan. The Dortmund-Hoerder Hüttenverein AG (DHHV), which appeared as the assembly firm, presented the weapons to the representatives of the Army Ordnance Office and Krupp. Each weapon was approved after firing fifteen rounds. Except for two failures, everything went smoothly. Once again, complaints were made about the afterflame after the guns were fired. *Wa Prüf 6* undertook another mass firing of a total of 250 rounds of ammunition, during which there was no afterflaming because of the hot barrels. The examining officer measured

a maximum barrel recoil of 555 mm (21.85 in.), which was acceptable since the upper limit was 560 mm (22.05 in.).

On February 3, hulls 150 006, 150 009, and 150 010 were on their way from Krupp to St. Valentin. The Krupp firm received an inquiry from the Nibelungenwerk as to which hull version would be in the next shipment, since the last two hulls had been the hydraulic version. Deliveries of assemblies for the electric hull version dominated at St. Valentin; therefore the successive delivery of six electric hulls was desirable.

Meanwhile. there were turret-manufacturing problems involving the delivery of turret ball bearings by the Kugelfischer company. An inquiry revealed that Kugelfischer had temporarily halted production due to shortages of coal and electrical power. Not until the Armaments Ministry had contacted the supplier of electricity in Schweinfurt could the delivery of two complete sets of ball bearings and the express production of nine more be secured. This delay also had consequences for subsequent production. In this case, without ball bearings, Krupp's second mechanical workshop was unable to complete the slip ring bodies required for the turret on time.

On February 24, Krupp and Porsche specified the installation steps for the assembly of turrets:

- Install the transformer.

- Center and attach the bend in the casing-chute bend by means of auxiliary units.

- Insert the slip ring transmitters by means of precise centering.

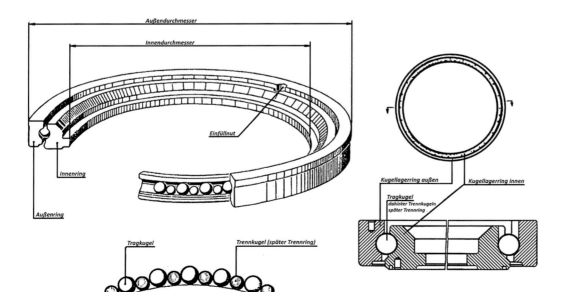

The rolling bearing of the turret traverse system, as used in the turret of the VK 4501. *D 656*

- Insert casing chute into sleeve-lock bend.

- Turret casings with ball bearings were to be mounted using 200 mm long (7.87 in.) mounting bolts. This was intended to avoid damaging the air inlet and the water downpipe.

- Install the lock stop bar.

- Screw in other loose parts, such as seat, protective shield, and turret-locking clamp.

Another hull reached St. Valentin on February 24. Since three of the hulls that had been delivered were the hydraulic variant, the Nibelungenwerk once again asked Krupp if it could not give priority to hulls for the electric drive. Krupp, however, was not in a position to reorganize existing production of 50% hydraulic and 50% electric hulls, since there was no storage space in Essen for the hydraulic hulls that had already been started. All tank parts had to be dispatched immediately after production.

On March 3, Krupp and the Army Ordnance Office agreed on the guns to be delivered for the VK 4501. The

Comparison of the Porsche VK 4501 (P) and AK-VK 7001 of February 27

Running Number	Name		VK 4501 (P)	VK 7001
I. Dimensions				
1	Hull length	mm	6,200	6,850 in part because of greater servicing diameter
2	Armor, forward	mm	100	100
3	Armor, side	mm	80	80
4	Floor thickness	mm	25	30
5	Roof thickness	mm	25	40
6	Turret		88 mm L.71v	105 mm L/70
7	Servicing diameter	mm	1,850	2,420
8	Track length	mm	14,300	15,000
9	Track width	mm	600	750
10	Track weight	kg/m	~ 150 (too low)	~ 250
11	Contact length	mm	4,200	4,340
12	Number of rounds (in turret)		50 (0)	76 (46)
13	Shell weight	kg	15	40/41
II. Weights				
1	Hull with installed parts	kg	20,960	27,000
2	Running gear without tracks, with final drives	kg	10,077	9,900
3	Tracks	kg	4,300	7,500
4	Power plants	kg	6,588	3,710
5	Turret with gun, complete	kg	9,600 (reinf. 12,500)	19,200
6	Gun ammunition with racks	kg	900	3,300
7	MG ammunition (2,000 rounds)	kg	80	80
8	Various	kg	1,084	1,300
9	Fuel	kg	510 640 l of fuel	1,000 l of fuel and water
10	Spare parts	kg	565	810
11	Crew with equipment	kg	500	500
12	Contingencies	kg	436	750
	Total Weight	**kg**	**55,000**	**75,000**

A comparison of the dimensions and weights of the VK 4501 (P) and the VK 7001.[31]

Maschinenfabrik-Buchau was to build 100 examples of the 88 mm KwK L/56, designated device 5/38, and the DHHV 150. Delivery of the first device 5/38 (Henschel) to the turret maker Wegmann was planned for the beginning of March. The same allocation of 100–150 examples also affected the 88 mm KwK L/71, designated device 5/808. The first batch of fifteen guns was to be delivered by Wolf-Buckau by September 1, 1942. It was envisaged that the manufacturer that was to produce the production guns would also provide the three 5/808 prototypes.

On March 12, Director Müller of Krupp wrote to engineer Krömer, the commissioner for the Tiger program in the Armaments Ministry, that the April deadline for the delivery of ten completed turrets to the Nibelungenwerk could not be met. The reason was the delayed or absent delivery of machinery. As well, the missing workers had arrived too late and occupied only 80% of the positions. The remaining requirement could be filled only with untrained Russian civilian workers.

Design work was also completed too late, especially since a number of changes were still required. Moreover, the first ten turret rolling bearings could not be delivered on February 1 as requested. Due to posttreatment, delivery did not take place until March 14–17. The first installment of guns and optics was also supposed to be available and ready for installation by the first-named date. As a result, the first Porsche turrets could not be delivered until the beginning of May 1942, and the Henschel turret several days later.

The answer came one day later. It was found that, though delayed, all the conditions had been created for delivery of the turrets in April. "The delays incurred so far due to the late delivery of various parts must therefore be made up for through suitable measures during assembly."[32] The content of the subsequent exchange of letters corresponded to the previous communications and does not need to explained further.

The armaments meeting held on March 5 and 6, 1942, concerned the Tiger program, because Hitler stressed that he thought it of great importance that the first Tigers should go

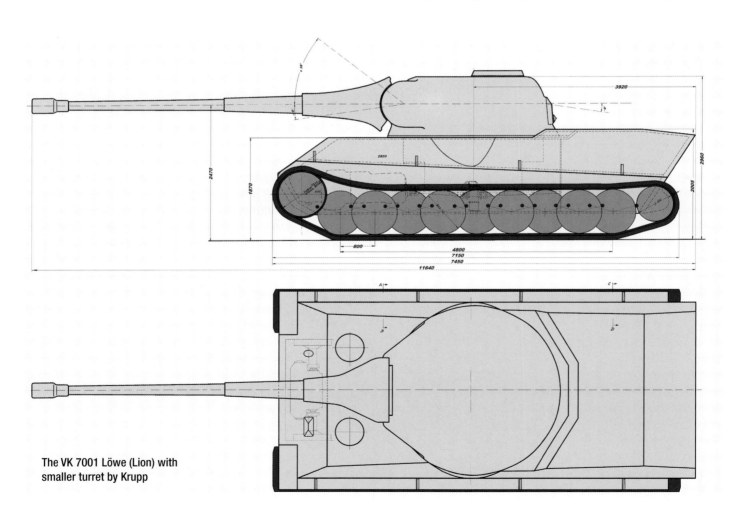

The VK 7001 Löwe (Lion) with smaller turret by Krupp

to the front immediately after completion. The necessary testing would take place at the front. This demand was absurd, because pointless losses of these valuable vehicles were inevitable. Furthermore, Hitler demanded that the planned 72-metric-ton (79.37 ton) Löwe tank must be a 100-metric-ton (110 ton) vehicle, and he wanted the first prototype to be running prior to the spring of 1943.

After negotiations with the state railway, the question of widening the tank was to be looked into again. To provide more leeway for rail transport, the state railway's central office was to consider increasing the rail loading gauge from 3,350 to 3,550 mm (131.89 to 139.76 in.) for the Tiger, since track spacing was still 3,500 mm (137.80 in.) in many places in the European rail network. On the basis of this distance and the deduction of 75 mm (2.95 in.) for the vehicle's permissible lateral displacement and 100 mm (3.94 in.) for operational irregularities, there was a need for the international passage profile for vehicles to be 3,150 mm (124 in.). The reduction of the figure for operating irregularities from 100 to 25 mm (3.94 to 0.98 in.) was a concession, so that this width could in exceptional cases be increased to 3,300 mm (129.92 in.) for the transport of tanks. This increase was applicable, however, only to a height of 2,600 mm (102.36 in.) above the tracks (status 1942).

Hitler was apparently not satisfied with the later answer, since on April 4 he asked Generalleutnant Gercke, head of the field transport organization, to again check the loading gauge on the spot with the aid of templates with widths of 3,350, 3,400, 3,500, and 3,550 mm (131.89, 133.86, 137.80, and 139.76 in.). The designers were given the task of determining whether this widening could yet be used for ongoing Panther and Tiger production.[33]

On March 9, 1942, the Simmering-Graz-Pauker factory delivered the first improved Type 101 engine to Stuttgart for testing. These tests were conducted successfully on March 15 and 21. Measured performance was 320 brake horsepower at 2,400 rpm. On March 22, however, the pistons of the reworked Type 101 engine burned out as the engine overheated. There was further trouble with the engine on the night of March 28, when the tenth cylinder's piston again seized.

On March 16, 1942, Hitler informed Amtsleiter Saur that a possible copy of the T-34 tank was no longer to be pursued, since the Panzerkampfwagen V and VI had better armor and armament at almost the same speed. Hitler requested to be shown photos of the Porsche Tiger. On March 19, Saur also showed him the planned Tiger production numbers: in October 1942 (up to and including September), sixty Porsche and

The later Simmering 101/2 engine on the test bench with the new air conveyance. *PA*

twenty-five Henschel Tigers, and in March 1943 (up to and including February), a further 135 vehicles of both types, making available a total of 220 Tigers. Hitler emphasized that the decision as to whether the Porsche or Henschel Tiger was to be built should be made as quickly as possible, so that just one would be produced in quantity. A preliminary decision was possible under certain circumstances, should the Porsche Tiger prove extremely satisfactory.[34]

The next day, Karl Rabe received a visit from an OKH committee to discuss the equipment planned for the Type 101, and this was followed by a discussion with Krupp on questions concerning the turret. On March 28, a wooden mockup of the Type 101 tank, together with a Type 100 engine, was sent under military guard to the Nibelungenwerk in St. Valentin. In addition, Rabe had issued an order to the firm of Berger & Mössner from Feuerbach for a one-tenth-scale model of the Tiger P.

On the occasion of another armaments conference, which took place on March 21, Hitler asked Professor Porsche if it was possible to install additional cooling—for example, for the desert—and also heating. Porsche replied that these were possible and that he had already found a solution for the Tiger. Furthermore, he received a development contract for the independent design of a 100-metric-ton (110 ton) tank, which later became the Maus. Porsche had thus received a new tank project before the previous project had even been driven. With his motto of accepting all contracts, the professor was running the risk of getting bogged down in a multitude of projects.

This later model of the Tiger already has the taller turret and emergency exit and roof ventilator. *SB*

Firing trials against the cylindrical gun mantlet made of tempered special cast steel took place at the Kummersdorf range on March 17. A large number of 50 mm and 75 mm armor-piercing rounds were fired at the mantlet from a distance of 100 m (328 ft.). The smaller-caliber ammunition succeeded only in penetrating weak spots, such as the openings for the telescopic sight and machine gun. From 100 m (328 ft.) the 75 mm was unable to penetrate with certainty, however. The proposed improved tempering could not be developed in time for the first series, since these first 100 cylindrical gun mantlets were already in production.

This came with the criticism that Porsche and Krupp had developed the mantlet without involving Wa Prüf 6 with respect to the design's resistance to shellfire, and its finished execution. On March 23, a vote was held in Stuttgart involving Porsche, Krupp, and the armaments ministry as to the numbers of individual tank hulls. The participants decided that fifty examples of the Porsche Type 101 electric and air-cooled hull and fifty examples of the Type 101 hydraulic and air-cooled version should be produced.

Furthermore, engine covers for twenty-five Type 130 electric and liquid-cooled hulls and for twenty-five Type 131

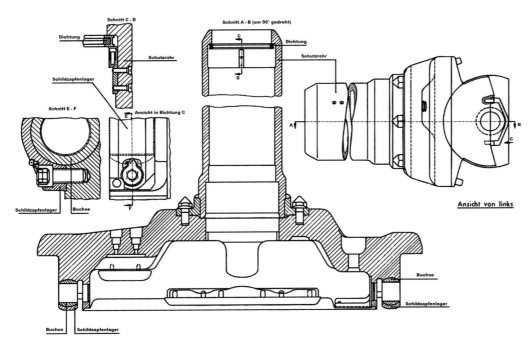

Cross section through the armored mantlet of the 88 mm KwK 36. *D* 656

hydraulic and liquid-cooled hulls should be prepared, the latter probably not being carried out. The participants decided that the driver's visor should receive a cutout 500 mm in diameter for hull numbers 150 101 to 150 165, or for the later Porsche Type 180 or VK 4502 (P). The position in the front plate was 570 mm (22.44 in.) from the center and 400 mm (15.75 in.) from the upper edge. The entire visor was to be produced by Krupp. The planned ball mount was also to be manufactured by Krupp if at all possible.

Porsche was to provide the final drawings for the visor by March 30. As well, an effort was to be made to extend the side panels above the hull roof far enough to create a protective edge for the turret traverse bearings. Soft rails were to be welded onto the roof plates. The holes for attachment of the running gear, steering gear, and drivetrain were supposed to precisely match those of the Type 4501 (P) hull. The exhaust openings were not supposed to be made through the hull walls.

All the openings in the hull bottom were also the same as those of the VK 4501 (P). The exception was the deleted spent-casing port. Porsche was to complete the necessary individual and assembly drawings by April 8. A further forty-five hulls were to be laid down immediately after completion of the first fifteen. According to the representative of the ministry, all the dates mentioned had to be kept, since otherwise for Krupp the connection to the delivery of the Type 101 hulls would have been lost. The slope of the VK 4502 (P)'s front plate was set at 35°, with a protruding top edge. For the time being, at least for the first fifteen hulls, the exit hatch with the driver's visor and ball mount were to be fashioned in the front plate. For this purpose, a front plate with the bow section of the Porsche Type 180 was to be used for firing trials. The front section of the hull bottom also received a 20 mm (0.79 in.) doubling for better protection against mines.

Two further meetings took place in Essen on the same day, March 23, 1942. The topic was the Tiger program and its deadlines. New there was Diplom-Ingenieur Krömer, whom Speer had installed as special representative for the Tiger program. Krömer again stressed the special high priority of this program. According to him, Hitler insisted that all deadlines must be met under all circumstances. Dr. Müller of Krupp responded that the Krupp firm had other tasks, given personally by the führer.

Some of the necessary labor forces and machinery promised for completion of the program were not in place. First-class workers had also been pulled from the Tiger production program, which negatively affected the deadlines that had been set. For example, the deadline set on July 4, 1941, for ten Porsche Tiger turrets and one Henschel turret by April 1942 could not be met. Further causes were the previously described delivery problems affecting ball bearings from the Kugelfischer firm, which had also delivered faulty bearings.

The provision of optical devices by the OKH was also delayed by one and a half months. The situation was similar when it came to weaponry, especially since the nine guns delivered late were seriously flawed. The Boehringer-Sturm L3S1 hydraulic drive for the Henschel turret had still not been delivered. Krömer criticized Krupp for failing to advise the ministry about the delivery difficulties on a timely basis, which Dr. Müller rejected. He declared that they had always kept the ministry up to date. He argued that if firm commitments were not kept, Krupp could not be made responsible for deadlines not being met. Krömer then demanded that two Porsche turrets be sent from Essen to the Nibelungenwerk on April 15, 1942, and eight Porsche turrets on April 30. He then conceded that the first 100 turrets did not have to be waterproof.

Under these conditions, engineer Talmon of Krupp committed to April 25 as the deadline for the first turret, May 1 for the second, and for the third to tenth turrets consecutively by May 15. Krömer found these dates intolerable, however. Dr. Müller pointed out that the delivery of one Henschel and ten Porsche turrets had been guaranteed by the end of April, and that the delay was thus just a few days. It was ultimately agreed that two turrets would be sent by April 15, 1942, even if their assembly was not complete. Final completion would then be carried out by Krupp fitters at the Nibelungenwerk. Krömer also informed Krupp on which precise dates the other turrets would be required. Krupp was given the task of determining the production state of the individual turrets.

The deadline of the end of May 1942 was not to be exceeded under any circumstances. The Nibelungenwerk requested the delivery in advance of those parts that had to be installed in the hull beforehand, such as, for example, the slip ring transformer and the turret traverse mechanism generators. Completion of the Henschel turret was also particularly urgent and was to be achieved in the first days of May 1942. On the subject of production of the Porsche Type 101 hull, Krömer advised that in the future, the hydraulic version was no longer to account for half of production, and instead emphasis was to be placed on production of the electric drive.

As of March 23, the following hulls had been sent to the Nibelungenwerk:

- fourteen hulls with hydraulic drive

- fourteen hulls with electric drive

Two more hulls of each type were delivered by the end of March. Krömer's further demands were

- by the end of April 1942:
  sixteen hulls with hydraulic drive and thirty hulls with electric drive

- in May 1942:
  two hulls with hydraulic drive and fourteen hulls with electric drive

- in June 1942:
  five hulls with hydraulic drive and twelve hulls with electric drive

- in July 1942:
  ten hulls with hydraulic drive and six hulls with electric drive

Because the demands exceeded the delivery commitments made by Krupp, an agreement on subsequent numbers was to be reached with the Krupp firm in the coming months.[35]

On April 4, the Nibelungenwerk wrote to Krupp that the hulls to be delivered in April must correspond to the latest state of development, since because of the existing delivery delay, extra work was no longer possible. Concerning the ten hydraulic hulls, the Nibelungenwerk declared that it was unable to carry out the subsequently requested changes, since all the boring mills were engaged in production of the electric hulls. Krupp was confronted with the choice of having Krupp fitters change the rear two covers at the Nibelungenwerk or

having the hulls sent back. Krupp was also asked if it could send the approximate timetable for the April delivery of hulls. The telegram with the desired list arrived the same day:

- Delivered to date were fourteen hydraulic hulls and fourteen electric hulls, plus the remaining two of each type of hull for the month of March.

- For the month of April, two hydraulic hulls and ten electric hulls

- For the month of May, two hydraulic hulls and fourteen electric hulls

- For the month of June, five hydraulic hulls and fourteen electric hulls

- For the month of July, fifteen hydraulic hulls

- For the month of August, ten hydraulic hulls

All in all, the plan was to deliver fifty examples of each hull type.

Krupp sent an inquiry to Porsche KG, asking when it could expect Type 101 liquid-cooled engines, so that the corresponding gratings could be produced in time. From Porsche came the answer that the use of liquid-cooled drives could not yet be clarified in principle.

There were further setbacks in engine production. On April 2, another Type 101 engine suffered a seized piston on the test bench. After the Mahle piston was replaced, the engine was running again in the laboratory the next day. The engine was further tested the following day, including a half hour at full power. Afterward, the engine was disassembled in the presence of both Porsches and an engineer from the piston maker Mahle. Work on the engines went on feverishly. Extensive air volume measurements were made. Representatives of Voith and Hirth were present because of the changes to the blower, since the engines were receiving insufficient air. A new oil pump was also sent by courier from Vienna and installed. The renewed air measurements were continued through the night on April 11, and even Professor Porsche was present until five in the morning. Throughput values had improved

In the photo above, the full-scale wooden model of the Type 101, including a turret mockup. Standing in front of it, the Nibelungenwerk factory management. *SB*

from a third to a half, but the desired success on the test bench was not achieved until April 13 and 14, after a two-stage Voith blower was installed.

On April 7, 1942, Krupp advised the Nibelungenwerk that the desired engine covers and the early Porsche turret would be dispatched by truck on April 10. The previously installed turret parts, such as the slip ring body, 24-volt contactors for 200 amperes, and generator (i.e., the Leonard transformer), had been en route by express rail since April 1. To counteract unwanted delays, Porsche suggested that the army acceptance office should be bypassed in delivery of the complete engine cover. These six engine gratings were, however, only sample castings, which after the planned demonstration were to be sent back to Krupp. As announced, turret 150 001, with barrel number 4 installed, arrived at the Nibelungenwerk on April 10.

The delivery also included TZF 9b (telescopic sight) no. 4, three seat cushions, machine gun plugs, and other individual parts. The turret still had a number of shortcomings, however. The hatch cover could not be closed from the outside, changing the machine gun barrel was impossible because of the mechanical firing mechanism's spring, the lock could not be fixed, and elevation was possible only to 16°, because the sealing frame hit the telescopic sight. For everyone, however, it was important that the turret could be placed on the hull in time.

After the problematic air experiments described above, the first Type 101 engine was sent to Steyr by truck at about 15:00 on April 13, 1942. Two days later the engine covers also arrived at the factory. This haste was not unfounded, since beforehand Hauptamtsleiter Karl Otto Saur had the "excellent" idea to have the first Porsche and Henschel Tigers demonstrated at Führer Headquarters in Rastenburg on April 20, 1942, Hitler's birthday, which naturally increased the pressure on everyone enormously. The Henschel fitters and those at the Nibelungenwerk worked day and night, and the assembly work resembled an anthill and no longer had anything to do with a rational mode of operation. Workers were more likely to get in each other's way.

The feat was completed on April 17, 1942, and at 18:30 the first Porsche Type 101 drove out of hall V under its own power, and a crane was able to load it onto a Krupp firm SSt low loader.

The transport arrived at a secondary station near the "Wolf's Lair" headquarters at Rastenburg, East Prussia, on April 19, 1942.

Karl Rabe made the following entry in his diary on April 20: "Today is the führer's birthday. I am in the office all day. At noon Prof. P. called; the demonstration of the Type 101 had gone well. Prof. P. received the War Merit Cross 1st Class with Swords."[36] The rest of the process is not documented; all that exists is a very subjective recollection by Dr. Erwin Aders, the chief engineer of the Henschel-Ordnance Office design, who many years later wrote: "The tracks protruded 50 mm [1.97 in.] beyond the railroad profile on both sides. The railway directorates therefore closed the Kassel-Rastenburg [East Prussia] line for all other trains to avoid encounters. The train steamed into a secondary station near the headquarters on April 19. A 70[-metric]-ton [77 ton] crane of the Reichsbahn was ready under steam at 9 a.m. We weren't allowed to drive straight to the headquarters on a public road but had to wait to use the blocked road with our 'rival' [Porsche]. We had to wait an hour and used it for test drives and adjustment work. . . . The train from St. Valentin [Nibelungenwerk] arrived at about ten. A platform car with an emergency generator was there; they had obviously carried out welding work on the way [the welding equipment was probably used to attach the spare track links lying on the rear of the tank]. The tracks were there. They were laid out, and the vehicle was placed on top of them [Why had they removed the tracks on the way? And how had they done it while the train was moving?]. Coincidentally and unfortunately, they were now across the track. Its first drive therefore had to start with a turn at right angles. That didn't work. The persistently repeated attempts caused the tracks [which were only 500 mm (19.69 in.) wide] to burrow deeper and deeper, and after half an hour they were on the hard core of the paving. Designer Reimspieß asked us for help, but his colleague from electrical planning [Zadnik]

The demonstration vehicle loaded on a railcar on April 17, 1942, in the transfer area of the factory's branch line. Unlike its competition, the Porsche vehicle was able to stay within the railroad loading gauge. *PA*

forbade it. Porsche stood by and let everything happen. We then received instructions to depart for the entrance to the headquarters and parked our vehicle in the forest. It was not until later that we learned that after our departure, the steam crane had once again been warmed up, and that the Porsche vehicle was turned in the direction of departure on the crane hook. On a solid road, it lived up to expectations and also

reached the parking area in the forest [which was no tour de force, since the Henschel vehicle, with its 725 mm wide (28.54 in.) tracks, had a ground pressure of about 1.05 kg/cm^2 (14.9 psi), while in contrast the Porsche vehicle, with its narrower 500 mm (19.69 in.) track, had a ground pressure of 1.41 kg/cm^2 (20 psi) on paved roads].

The 500 mm spare track links are
still lying on the floor of the railcar.
The vehicle is fitted with the
still-incomplete turret with the
number 150 001. *PA*

"The next morning—April 20, 1942—the two armored vehicles drove into the headquarters. The 'bigwigs' of the Third Reich and the Wehrmacht gathered at about 10:30. Goebbels and Göring were absent. When Hitler appeared at about eleven, the industry representatives were presented in the sequence Krupp–Nibelungenwerk–Henschel. Porsche then received the War Merit Cross First Class. Hitler subsequently spent an hour listening to an explanation of the design of the Porsche vehicle and its rotating turret [Ob. Ing. Heerlein, Krupp]. It was obvious that he was already biased in favor of Porsche.

"Hitler had just two or three minutes left for Henschel. He nevertheless climbed onto the Henschel tank, asked a question about the cooling system (because he saw the screen over the cooling air intake in the roof), and then climbed down again. I already had the feeling on this occasion that Hitler sensed my dislike and my cold attitude and was probably inhibited by it. The actual demonstration that morning consisted of the vehicles driving straight ahead on the good, solid country road that led past the 'Wolf's Lair'; both tanks quickly disappeared in the distance, but neither came back. The Henschel's still untested brakes had to be properly adjusted; about the Porsche we heard nothing. While we were still at the headquarters waiting for further instructions, it was announced that a second demonstration was going to take place in the afternoon for the benefit of Göring.

"The Reichsmarschall arrived at about 15:00 in an almost operetta-like presentation, in great splendor and magnificence. He passed his marshal's baton and dress sword to a folk comrade from St. Valentin to hold and, following Hitler, climbed onto the Porsche tank. Again it was explained, but this time the Henschel vehicle was ignored. When, during the driving exercises, the Porsche vehicle had exited, to my dismay Hauptamtsleiter Otto Saur urged that the Henschel tank drive onto the fallow field next to the road. I was prepared for a catastrophic failure but was disappointed in a 'triumphal' way. As if the demonstration had been rehearsed, our tank drove off, without hesitation crossed a dirt road with an easy stony stretch as if it were nothing, and in the distance gained the country road again."[37]

Because no photos exist, it is not proven whether the Henschel tank had a full-fledged turret at that time. The meeting notes of March 23, 1942, revealed that the Krupp firm was not able to deliver the first Henschel turret until the beginning of May at the earliest.

In addition to the first discussions about the successor to the Type 101, the new Type 180, on April 18, Krupp received from Porsche the new design drawings of the engine compartment for the Type 102, for which Voith had to develop the main gearbox as well as the steering system. However, a new problem had arisen in the meantime. The Nibelungenwerk found that it was no longer able to accommodate the delivered hull shells in the factory. Due to delivery problems and requests for changes, it could no longer follow up with the assembly. In particular, there was uncertainty as to how it was to proceed with the hydraulic Type 102; therefore these hulls in particular had to be sent back. On April 23, 1942, the Nibelungenwerk wrote to Krupp that the hydraulic hull with the number 150 009 was to be sent back to Krupp. They also asked Krupp not to send any more hydraulic hulls, since the storage and loading capabilities in the factory were much more limited than at Krupp. As well, a total of ten hydraulic hulls had to be so extensively modified by Krupp, on account of changes to the hydraulic assemblies, that it seemed simpler to convert them into electric hulls. It was surely also simpler for Krupp to carry out the installation of exit hatches, which had again been called for at the demonstration.

St. Valentin simultaneously informed the Porsche firm and the Armaments Ministry on this matter. But despite this, Krupp sent the fifth hydraulic hull with accompanying personnel to St. Valentin, where it arrived on April 27. The Nibelungenwerk immediately demanded that it and the five hydraulic hulls, including an escort party, who were on the way, be sent back at once. But there was no reaction from Krupp. Even after reminders by Director Dr. Judtmann on April 28 and 29, nothing happened. After the twenty-ninth, Krupp replied that it intended to modify the nine hulls that had since been returned; however, the tenth hull, with the number 150 009, was to remain at St. Valentin and be modified there. The Nibelungenwerk responded one week later, stating that hull number 150 009, which was just in the process of being sent back, could still be kept. However, it saw itself unable to change or modify the hull on the spot. Since it was known that Krupp was unwilling to accept the factory's proposal that the hydraulic hulls be converted into electric hulls, they did not see themselves in a position for a redesign. After a discussion with Krömer, it was suggested that the hull, with the first and second turrets, be sent back to Essen for the necessary modifications. The return was to take place after the arrival of the third turret; therefore on about May 10. This third turret, 150 003, was envisaged for the first fully equipped vehicle, with the hull number 150 002. This vehicle was supposed to be sent to Kummersdorf for ballistics trials by mid-May, since vehicle 150 001 was not suitable because of its provisional features.

For the purpose of initial instruction on the technically correct installation of the 88 mm gun in the Tiger turret, two Feldwebel armorers and twelve armorer assistants from the 501st and 502nd Heavy-Tank Companies received an initial briefing at the Krupp factory from April 27 to May 5. Meanwhile,

on April 22, 1942, there followed a shipping notice for an autogenously cut ballistics-trials hull for the Type 101 to the station at the Kummersdorf artillery range. These ballistics trials took place on April 30 and, as decided earlier, involved one autogenously cut and one machined hull. The machined ballistics trials hull cost 74,052 RM, and the autogenously cut hull was 61,983 RM. On each of the two Krupp hulls, one side had been soft-welded and the other hard-welded. Also present for comparison was a hull from the Dortmund-Hoerder Hüttenverein AG. Both companies used armor plates of similar composition and strength. The mean strength for the 80 mm (3.15 in.) plate was 110 kg/mm^2 (156,413 psi), and for the 100 mm (3.94 in.) plate it was 100 kg/mm^2 (142,194 psi). Because of its higher content of carbon and molybdenum, the DHHV material proved more brittle overall.

The Kummersdorf artillery range, April 30, 1942. The slope angles of the armor plates have been marked on the vehicle. *SB*

Side view of Krupp hull I. *SB*

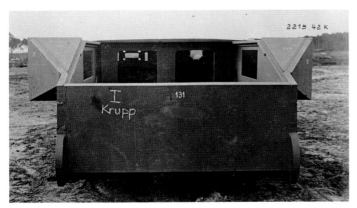

The ballistics test hull I at the Kummersdorf artillery range, seen from behind. *SB*

The second Krupp hull, Ia, ready to be fired on. *SB*

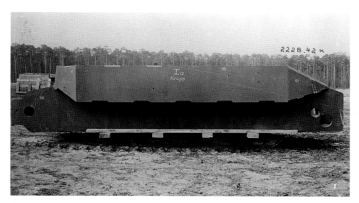

Side view of the second Krupp hull, Ia, prior to being fired on. *SB*

The track shields did not live up to expectations, failing to provide the desired track protection. *B*

The hull processed with flame cut produced a substantial saving in machining, which resulted from a reduction in machines and machine time. In contrast, the number of cutting devices as well as the gas and oxygen demand increased. In addition, suitable workers had to be trained. But even the flame-cut edges required a certain amount of finishing work, as a rule by grinding, so that the later weld seams could withstand stresses. The stresses the weld seams were exposed to were associated with

- shellfire

- the tensile and compressive forces that occurred while driving and steering

- the alternating pressure stress caused by the tracked running gear

- the torsional forces that occurred when armored vehicles were off-road

- the internal stress of the weld seams that was present before and after the relaxation of the finished hulls

The following methods of connecting armor plates were tested on the ballistics-trials hulls:

1. simply superimposed edges

2. interlocking

3. pins

4. shoulder plates

Firing at the hulls had shown that it was a mistake to use only one type of connection for armor plates. The above-described method no. 1 was the simplest, but also the weakest connection type, and was used where it could be assumed that drive and running-gear parts provided added protection. The no. 2 option was sufficient for the majority of welded edges if the subsequent sheets were secured by other means against being pushed inward or outward. Only on the main panels, which were directly exposed to fire, was an interlocking joint alone not sufficient, and additional pins were required. It was clearly shown that an interlocking joint between the front roof panel and the driver's front panel, as used on the Krupp hull, was poorer than the shoulder plate connection of the DHHV hull. Even a dovetail-shaped interlocking joint failed to suffice, apart from the fact that a dovetail executed roughly simultaneously in two planes was an expensive and complicated tooth shape. What was interesting was the statement that in the future, the joint between the front roof panel and driver's front panel would no longer be of significance, since the two panels were to be replaced by a single panel (VK 4501 P 2). The no. 3 option had proven itself perfectly. Pin length was to correspond to the thickness of the receiving sheet. The tenons had to be fitted neatly, since a subsequent repair in the field was difficult. Method no. 4 still had to be machined and was used when thinner panels were placed on thicker ones, such as, for example, the hull roof on the driver's front panel.

Also tested was the usefulness of a movable screen forward of the hull front, to protect the running gear and especially the tracks. The screen mounted on the VK 4501 (H) ballistics trials hull from DHHV showed that this purpose was only partly achieved and was not worth the effort. The screen and

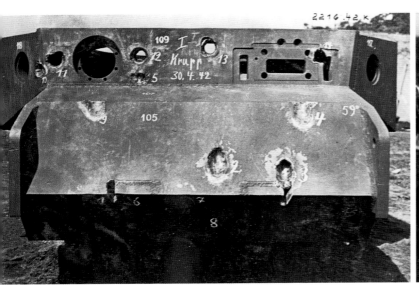

Krupp hull I after the firing trials. A high-explosive shell caused the weld seam at the top of the bow plate to break open. *SB*

the associated lever assembly were so damaged or completely torn off that the harm was greater than the benefit.

The welding on all the armored hulls was austenitic. The electrodes, V 4 A and Thermanit M, represented one of the most alloyed austenitic electrode forms. Following a test, no clear difference was found in the comparison of hard and soft roofs. These alloy-rich electrodes were later replaced by alloy-poor V 12C extra electrodes.

On the other hand, the sometimes gross welding defects, which led to cracks when the hulls were fired on, were harshly criticized. It had to be stated that when struck by 50- and 75 mm armor-piercing shells, the formation of cracks in the vicinity of the hit could not be avoided. A 150 mm high-explosive shell striking the upper roof panel of Krupp hull 1 caused serious damage, since the weld seam was torn open along its entire length, and because of the resulting large gap, the hull was no longer bulletproof. This DHHV hull's shoulder plate arrangement was able to prevent this damage. The effects of hits by 150 mm high-explosive shells were minimal to meaningless.

It was shown that when struck by a 75 mm armor-piercing shell (muzzle velocity of 630 m/sec. or 2,067 ft./sec.) at an angle of 90° and a range of 100 m (328 ft.), a 100 mm thick armor plate did not guarantee safety. Safety from penetration first occurred with armor thicknesses of 105 to 110 mm (4.13–4.33 in.). Oberst Fichtner was deeply disappointed by the result, when the bow plate (according to Parts List No. 109) was cleanly penetrated by a 7.5 cm Panzergranate-Rot

armor-piercing round. Baurat Rau of Wa Prüf 6 found numerous flakes and eruptions, which suggested that there was a problem with the armor steel. In a later evaluation, on May 13, Baurat Rau admitted that on the basis of trials with comparison areas, no guarantee could be given for the invulnerability of the bow plates to shellfire.

An increase in strength was scarcely possible even if the analysis was changed. Further strengthening of the bow plates could not be undertaken on the first 100 hulls. In the meantime, however, surface-hardened bow plates were fitted; therefore a certain increase in resistance to fire was to be expected. The flakes that were found were ultimately determined to be contamination, which produced no noteworthy reduction in resistance to fire.

Because of the problems with penetration of the armor, on June 19, Krupp carried out another ballistics test on the VK 4501 (P) armored hull. In this case, a 100 mm bow plate (109), which had since received a production-standard surface hardening, was fired at. This tempering had an effect, since both shots, fired under the same conditions, at 90° with 7.5 cm Panzergranate-Rot armor-piercing rounds, failed to penetrate. The first shot caused a 7 to 8 mm deep flaking off of the chromium layer, the second shot a 4 cm pockmark, with a 20 × 40 mm (0.79 × 1.57 in.) piece flying away. That was clearly better than before, but it also showed that complete safety against penetration was not ensured.

Because of the raw material and alloy situation, Wa Prüf 6 decided to change the analysis regulations, lowering the chromium content to 1.7% to 2.3% and introducing a nickel content of 0.4% to 1.0%. The sum of both contents was to be at least 2.7%. The nickel content was to be obtained exclusively from scrap. Plates with these new qualities—60, 80, and 100 mm (2.36, 3.15, and 3.94 in.) thick—were to undergo firing tests at Kummersdorf. The strength regulations, however, remained unchanged, meaning that plates from 55 to 80 mm (2.17 to 3.15 in.) had a strength of 100 to 115 kg/mm^2 (142,194–163,523 psi) and plates from 85 to 120 mm (3.35 to 4.72 in.) were to be delivered with a strength of 95 to 105 kg/cm^2 (135,084–149,303 psi). During the manufacture of armor plates, mistakes caused by incorrect melting or rolling

Krupp hulls I and Ia from the inside after being fired on. The different types of stiffener are readily apparent. *B*

defects kept cropping up, often manifesting themselves as more or less large cracks. After approval of the tolerance application by the Army Ordnance Office's inspection authority, these cracks had to be sanded down and welded at great expense. Under such time pressure, manufacturer's defects were also no rarity, resulting, for example, from incorrect drilling. These holes subsequently had to be welded shut again.

Krupp received the following instructions for further production: of the Porsche Type 101, ninety hulls were to be built for electric drive and ten hulls for hydraulic drive. Final delivery date was planned for October 1942. The Army Ordnance Office asked Krupp to change the designation of the new Porsche Type 180 uniformly to VK 4502 (P) instead of VK 4501/2 P. Furthermore, Krupp was to produce a Type 101 hull for ballistics trials in accordance with the new

flame-cutting procedure. To avoid later finishing work, Krupp was to initially produce just thirty examples of the new Type 180. The remaining hulls should only be prepared.

Regarding the Type 101, a directive was issued stating that the envisaged spent-casing chute would not be used and instead should be sealed. A semicircular or polygonal bar was to be provided to protect the turret ring. Since the gun mantlet brushed the engine fan's side air inlets when the gun barrel was pointing downward, the gun mantlet had to be changed accordingly (*see illustration opposite*).

On May 1 and 2, the Porsche firm received two Type 101 engines. Two days later, the Nibelungenwerk again contacted Krupp to inquire about precisely when turret 150 003 could be in St. Valentin at the earliest, since, as is known, turret 150 001 was unsuitable for testing at Kummersdorf. They also

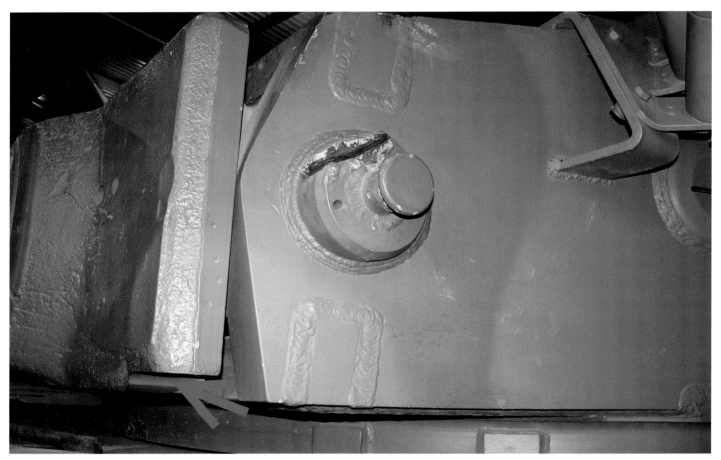

This notch (*see arrow*) was an identifying feature of the former Porsche turrets converted for use on Henschel Tigers, as here on Tiger 131 in the Bovington Tank Museum.

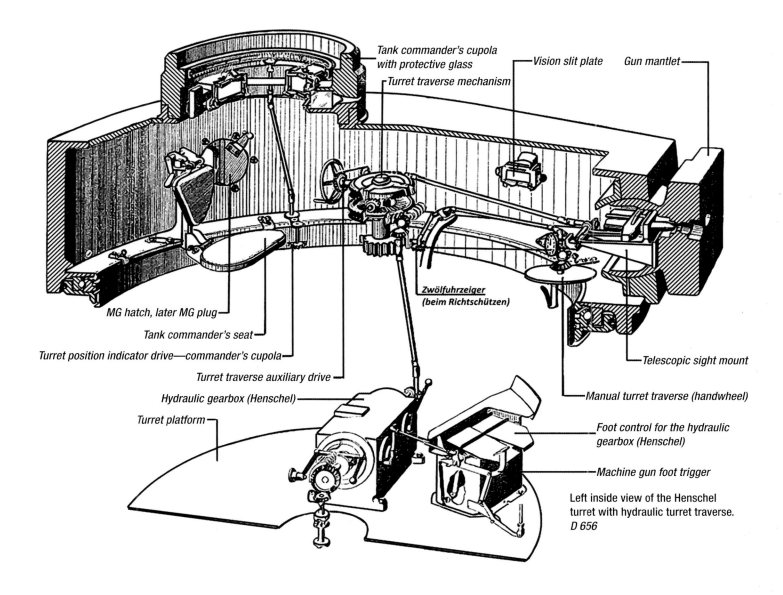

Tank commander's cupola with protective glass

Turret traverse mechanism

Vision slit plate

Gun mantlet

MG hatch, later MG plug

Tank commander's seat

Turret position indicator drive—commander's cupola

Turret traverse auxiliary drive

Hydraulic gearbox (Henschel)

Turret platform

Zwölfuhrzeiger (beim Richtschützen)

Telescopic sight mount

Manual turret traverse (handwheel)

Foot control for the hydraulic gearbox (Henschel)

Machine gun foot trigger

Left inside view of the Henschel turret with hydraulic turret traverse. D 656

required the equipment list that had already been agreed on with Henschel. The answer came the next day. Turret 150 003 with barrel 103 was to be dispatched on May 10, so that it would be available to the Nibelungenwerk on May 12. To avoid further delays in delivery of turrets, on May 5 a meeting was held with representatives of Krupp, the Nibelungenwerk, and Wa Prüf 6. The following questions were up for debate:

1. Which changes should be made immediately and retrospectively to the first vehicle?

2. Which changes from which specific vehicle would be effective?

3. Which changes in the running series could no longer be carried out?

As immediate changes from the first turret, the participants identified that the accessory storage would be done as specified, and that the direction numbers on the commander's cupola should first be improved by highlighting with different colors. Krupp would later deepen this scale arrangement. It had already been decided that a stowage bin like that of the Panzerkampfwagen IV (BW) was to be fitted on the rear of the turret. Spare track links, probably fifteen, were to be placed between the stowage bin and the turret. The firing-control lamp was to be moved forward. Moving the elevating arc and the direction clock forward was also to be checked by Krupp.

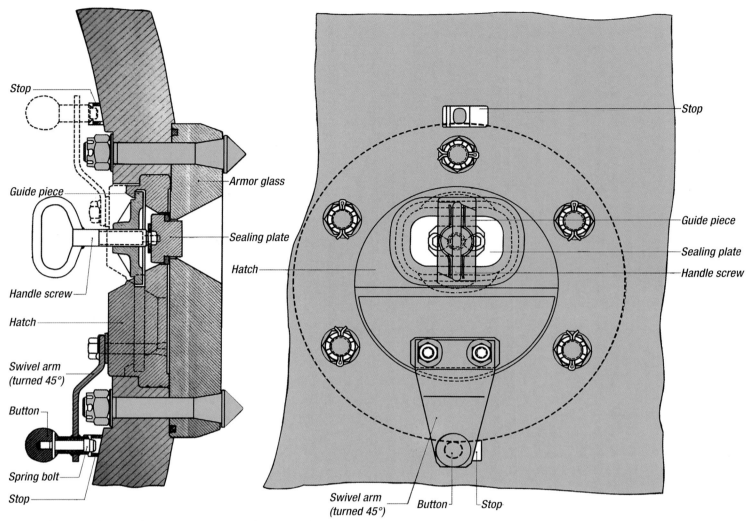

Stop

Guide piece

Handle screw

Hatch

Swivel arm
(turned 45°)

Button

Spring bolt

Stop

Armor glass

Sealing plate

Hatch

Stop

Guide piece

Sealing plate

Handle screw

Swivel arm
(turned 45°)

Button

Stop

The MG hatches for close-in defense were located in the rear right and left of the turret.

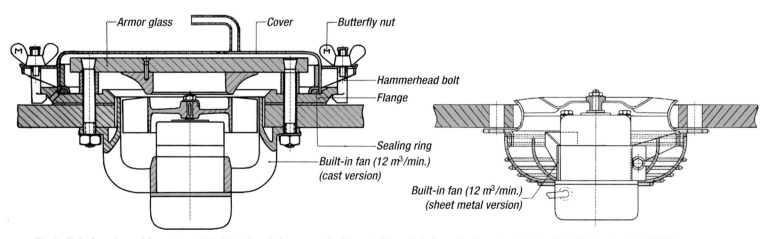

Armor glass

Cover

Butterfly nut

Hammerhead bolt

Flange

Sealing ring

Built-in fan (12 m³/min.)
(cast version)

Built-in fan (12 m³/min.)
(sheet metal version)

The built-in fan planned from turret 150 011, already in use on the Henschel turret. *Left*: made of cast material; *right*: of sheet metal. *D 656*

Difficult operation of the elevating mechanism was criticized. Easier operation was to be achieved with the previous compensator, at least in the central range of +10° to −3°.

Furthermore, Krupp was looking into the possibility of fitting an emergency escape hatch in the rear right of the turret, in place of the previous machine gun flap. This investigation was regarded as especially urgent, since the entire crew of the Porsche vehicle was forced to rely on the two hatches in the turret roof, and the danger existed that while under fire, the second man might not get out. Another point of discussion concerned the determination that the planned spent-casing chute had been abandoned and, in the interim, it

should serve as a spent-casing catcher. Krupp was given the task of finding a more convenient and space-saving arrangement for a spent-casing catcher. Regarding a change in shape of the commander's cupola, Wa Prüf 6 was to conduct ballistics tests to determine its resistance to fire. The last point established that from turret 150 011 onward, a raised fan was to be fitted like the one on the turret of the Henschel vehicle.

Further technical details, like the abovenamed points, were set between Porsche and Wa Prüf 6:

- installation of deflector bars from turret number 150 001

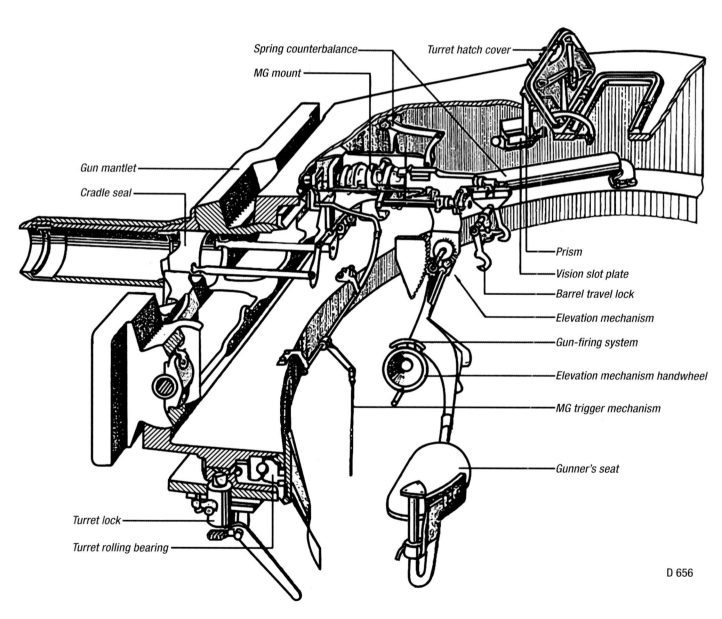

Spring counterbalance

Turret hatch cover

MG mount

Gun mantlet

Cradle seal

Prism

Vision slot plate

Barrel travel lock

Elevation mechanism

Gun-firing system

Elevation mechanism handwheel

MG trigger mechanism

Gunner's seat

Turret lock

Turret rolling bearing

D 656

- fitting of snap rings and track bolts from outside, as well as a ramp bar

- revision of the internal equipment in the turret: elimination of the impractical group hanging of gas masks, mess kits, and earphone boxes

- Porsche regarded the complete sealing of the brakes demanded by the office as inexpedient, since it prevented the removal of condensation and leakage oil.

- Special tools, such as track tensioners, jacks, two jack stands, and the tow bars, were to be supplied from the first vehicle. From vehicle 150 101 onward, Porsche planned to install a hydraulic jack, which could jack up the vehicle at four points. The telescopic jack's jack stand was also to be designed to serve as a floor valve.

- Installation of mine projectors could allow the turret hatch for hand grenades to be eliminated.

- A deflector for the antenna was no longer needed, since the antenna was insulated.

- installation of wire screens over all gratings, beginning with the first vehicle

- Turret 150 002 had to be reworked, since the gun with barrel number 3 tilted and its traverse mechanism was too sluggish.

- installation of an emergency escape hatch with a diameter of 50 cm, either on the right reverse side of the turret or under the radio operator's seat in the hull floor

- An inertia starter or a second starter independent of the battery was to be provided in the vehicle.

- Armor protection for the brakes was present on the sides. This was not possible from the front and below until the twenty-first vehicle. Up to the twentieth vehicle, this could not be fitted until a repair was necessary.

- From the first vehicle, scrapers had to be installed for the drive and idler wheels.

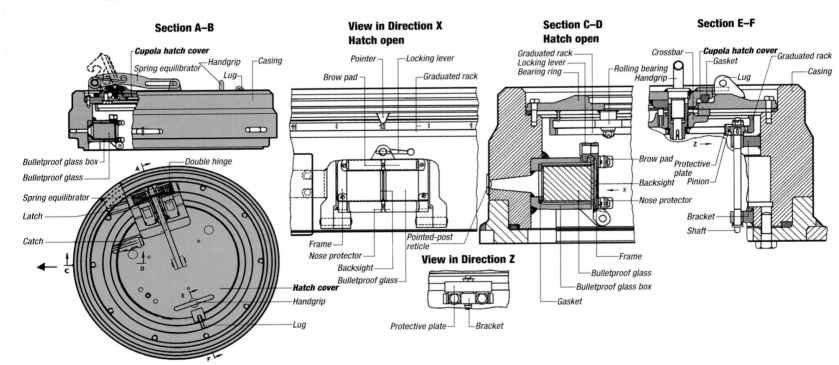

The early version of commander's cupola was very exposed and, as a result, vulnerable to fire. In addition, the commander had his head at the level of the vision blocks. A hit on the cupola usually meant that the commander was put out of action. The later new cupola was not only more favorably shaped, but its angled mirrors also better protected him against injury caused by hits from enemy fire. *D 656*

- The Porsche firm was to look into a turret crane for changing road wheels.

- Thickening of the front third of the hull floor to 40 mm was regarded as necessary for adequate mine protection. Weight compensation could take place by thinning the lower parts of the sidewalls behind the road wheels.

- Concerning the problem of the exposed commander's cupola, Wa Prüf 6 suggested additional tapered armor up to the height of the vision ports.

- The muzzle brake in its current form entailed the risk of early detonations caused by casting in dirt and the like; therefore it was necessary to check whether the shortcoming could be eliminated by a wire screen or by turning the muzzle brake.

- Two limiting spheres were to be fitted on the front outer edges of the vehicles to serve as a guide to the driver.

The first test drives at the factory had to be carried out purely electrically, since the gasoline engines were still not ready. Type 100 generators provided the power. It was transferred to the turretless Type 101 by a cable. Thus, a use was still found for the Type 100 in May 1942. Porsche had also planned this energy transfer system for possible underwater travel.

Professor Porsche in the VK 3001 (P)—the "electricity donor vehicle." *A*

On May 12, 1942, Krupp wrote to the Army Ordnance Office that a follow-up order was urgently needed for the purpose of ensuring the ongoing production of tank hulls. Krupp stated that in addition to the thirty-four hulls completed by the end of April, a further 131 hulls were envisaged by December 1942. According to Program III, organized by the "Panzerwagen Tank Committee," they had again planned 288 VK 4501 (P) tank hulls. This gave a total of 453 tank hulls. Since the previous order size was 200 Type 101 hulls, a follow-up order was still missing for 253 tank hulls. This of course also affected the turret installations. The Army Ordnance Office replied that a decision was to be made about the future of the Porsche or Henschel vehicle by June 15, 1942. Ministerialrat Baier of WuG 6 saw, however, that Krupp could wait no longer to order materials, and for the time being authorized another 100 Porsche vehicles subject to another 253 examples. As to the question of which VK 4501 would ultimately be produced, Ministerial Director Brommer of the Army Ordnance Office stated that this question would not be decided exclusively from a military-technical point of view, but that of course the decision would also be made on the basis of manpower and raw-material requirements.

On May 13, 1942, the Nibelungenwerk announced the following delivery dates for the Type 101 and Type 102:

May 1942	Type 101 = 10 examples	Type 102 = 0 examples
June 1942	Type 101 = 10 examples	Type 102 = 0 examples
July 1942	Type 101 = 11 examples	Type 102 = 1 example
August 1942	Type 101 = 13 examples	Type 102 = 1 example
September 1942	Type 101 = 14 examples	Type 102 = 1 example
October 1942	Type 101 = 14 examples	Type 102 = 1 example
November 1942	Type 101 = 14 examples	Type 102 = 1 example
December 1942	Type 101 = 4 examples	Type 102 = 5 examples

At that time, in addition to the eighteen electric-drive hulls, there were seven modified hulls for the hydraulic drive and one unmodified hydraulic hull in storage at the Nibelungenwerk. Meanwhile, Krupp had confirmed to the Nibelungenwerk on May 15 that this tenth hull, with the number 150 009, could also be sent back for the purpose of modification. On the subject of modifications to turrets 150 001 and 150 002, it had been agreed that the factory would make both turrets ready for loading onto the transport vehicles. At that time turret, number 150 003 was on its way to St. Valentin, and turret 150 007, with barrel 112, arrived in St. Valentin on May 19. After turret 150 003 was placed on hull 150 002, Siemens and Krupp technicians connected the electric traverse mechanism. Changes were also carried out, such as shutdown of the basic excitation of the control apparatus and of the field when the transformer was shut off. The subsequent test drive went well. However, a double fan ran hot due to insufficient oil supply, and as a result the second vehicle could not be transferred to Kummersdorf until days later.

In response to an inquiry from the Army Ordnance Office, on May 19 Porsche listed the manufacturing costs of a Type 101 tank hull. Production time for an autogenous-cut hull was divided into

1. Drawing = 50 hours
2. Autogenous cutting = 80 hours
3. Mechanical processing = 220 hours
4. Assembly and metalworking = 360 hours
5. Welding = 600 hours

A further decrease in working hours was expected for the hulls from number 150 101 onward, which were to be produced using a different version of autogenous cutting. The calculated material requirements for a Type 101 tank hull were

- 28,000 kg for armor plates

- 600 kg for forged parts, bar steel, etc., alloyed

- 3,000 kg for carbon steel

for a total of 31,600 kg of iron and steel material.

In the spring of 1942, drive and idler wheels, including brake drums, for the Type 101 were manufactured in Mechanical Production I in Hall VI. *PA*

According to the list, the machines needed to manufacture thirty Type 101 hulls were

- seven burning cutters

- one planing machine

- four vertical milling machines, one outrigger milling machine, three horizontal milling machines

- one double-column milling machine

- three horizontal boring mills, two radial drilling machines, one column-type boring mill

- four top lathes, two shaping machines, and a hacksaw machine

On May 20, Krupp commented on the points of the May 5 discussion. From turret 150 003 onward, the inner numbers on the number ring of the commander's cupola were recessed. The elevating arc and the control lamp could be moved forward. The Daimler-Benz machine gun mount, like the one

On June 3, 1942, the head of the Army Ordnance Office, General Emil Leeb, visited the Nibelungenwerk. In Hall V, where production of the Tiger was carried out, Otto Zadnik explains to him the driving switch with the two control levers. In the background is a Porsche Type 101 hull with turret.

in the Panzerkampfwagen III, was adopted, and turret 150 002 came back to Essen for inspection. The problem of the emergency exit was reexamined. On the subject of the commander's cupola, the proposed tapered deflector was seen as posing an increased danger to the vision slits. The muzzle brake problem could also not yet be finally clarified and was to be reexamined by Wa Prüf 4. Meanwhile, at the Nibelungenwerk, turret number 150 004, with barrel 111, was delivered on May 21; number 150 008, with barrel 105, on May 23; turret 150 009, with barrel 118, on May 27; and turret 150 010, with barrel 125, on May 28. Until number 150 007, the turrets had a lower roof height. The weight of these turrets was 9,800 kg.

Because of the poor standing height for the loader, the office endorsed a taller turret, which was achieved from turret number 150 008 onward. All the turrets still possessed the shortcoming that the barrel of the coaxial machine gun could be changed only within the elevation range of −8° to +12°. The turrets were also not tested for leaks. Sixteen of the necessary accessory parts were missing per turret. Since there were still delivery problems with vehicle engines, on May 29 the Nibelungenwerk asked Krupp to wait to deliver the next turrets, with the numbers 150 011 to 150 022, stating that it would be satisfactory if these turrets were delivered to the Nibelungenwerk by July 12. If possible, turret 150 011 was not to arrive until the last weeks of June, so that all the

The testing ground often consisted of soft soil, which was difficult for the Panzer IV, but for the heavy tanks, such as the KV I in the background and the Type 101, it was very problematic. The high ground pressure caused the bottom of the Porsche Type 101's hull to touch, and it virtually slid over the ground.

envisaged changes could be made to it and all the following turrets.

When, on May 23, 1942, during a meeting with the führer, the (Ssyms) transport vehicle came up for discussion, Hitler declared that an initial batch of sixty to eighty heavy transport vehicles should be produced for the Tiger heavy tank. He did not regard it as necessary to produce exactly the same number of vehicles and tanks. Hitler considered the ratio of 1:2 to be sufficient. He demanded that these vehicles also be capable of carrying other heavy loads.[38] Hitler did not, however, think that the VK 4501 (H)'s travel tracks belonged with the six-axle

railcars and therefore had to be carried on them constantly. New logistical problems later arose with the arrival of the VK 4503 (H), later called the Tiger B or Tiger II, and its wider travel tracks.

On June 4, at an armaments conference with Speer, Hitler said that it should be investigated whether a Tiger could not be fitted with 120 mm of frontal armor. In this context, Hitler noted that he was in agreement with a slow-moving superheavy tank as a sort of mobile fortress. He was referring to the project for a 100-metric-ton (110 ton) tank, the later Maus.

A Panzer IV hull next to the KV I in front of the steep slope. *PA*

Professor Porsche in conversation with soldiers on the turret replacement weight. *PA*

Driving tests with one of the first chassis and the 10-metric-ton turret replacement weight. *PA*

Since the three Type 101 turrets delivered in May and June 1942 still had to be reworked, testing at St. Valentin was carried out under realistic conditions with a roughly 10-metric-ton (11 ton) turret replacement weight. This replacement weight was encased in sheet steel and filled with concrete (also see chapter 8).

Porsche wanted to explore the chassis' potential in such a terrain and had the vehicle turned around on the spot. The

Professor Porsche attempts a turning maneuver on the spot in the difficult terrain of the test-driving track. *A*

Accomplished! The turning maneuver has succeeded, and the tracks are scarcely still visible because of the soil pushed to the side. *PA*

following series of photos impressively shows the effort involved in turning. The exhaust gases and heated air give some idea of the exertion. Professor Porsche was later to carry out such burrowing experiments frequently, at Döllersheim or Böblingen.

In addition to the vehicle's high ground pressure, the test drives also confirmed the significant weaknesses in the fan cooling of the two gasoline engines, which caused problems for a long time. Starting in June 20, 1942, in addition to the extensive test drives by both types of Tiger, after the turret

PRO and Otto Zadnik were present along with the officers from Wa Prüf 6. The vehicle with the hull number 150 002 has been given the license plate WH 07015, so that it could drive in public traffic areas. *PA*

Numerous sensors were placed on Firing Range West before the first shot was fired from barrel 103, mounted in turret 150 003. In the background is the barracks used for dust and climate experiments by Auxiliary Battery West. *PA*

Behind the reference line is Firing Range West's observation tower and a building of the artillery range railroad. *PA*

had been fitted the second Type 101 vehicle carried out test firing at the Kummersdorf artillery range.

At Krupp, new circumstances had arisen in the production of hulls in June 1942. The first point was already known, since Porsche had demanded that the ratio between electrically and hydraulically powered hulls should no longer be 1:1, but 1:9. The Nibelungenwerk asked that instead of the hydraulic hulls previously envisaged, electric hulls should be delivered effective immediately. As well, all modifications should be carried out immediately upon arrival. The factory was prepared to accept a delay of one month. Krupp reminded that about 200 changes had been introduced since the start of production in December 1941. The large wave of call-ups in May, which hit the staff of the Tiger hull departments particularly hard, was a major problem for Porsche. The Porsche firm requested that starting with the fiftieth hull, some walls, and from the sixtieth hull onward, all remaining walls, had to be made using surface-hardened armor plates. Therefore, the following effects on production occurred:

The old production deadlines envisaged that thirty hydraulic and thirty-one electric hulls would be delivered by the end of May. According to the new demands by the Nibelungenwerk, the figure was forty-four electric hulls. Since twenty-five electric hulls had been delivered previously and another eight hulls would be added by month's end, the shortfall of twelve electric hulls could not possibly be made up. Since the hydraulic hulls had to undergo significant modifications, none of these hulls could be completed in time, especially since the labor shortage made it impossible to take on additional modification work. It was possible only with great difficulty to make the large number of changes requested by the Porsche firm, and further changes could not possibly be accepted. Otherwise, production would have been at risk for the next two to three months. The existing number of installation parts was also far from adequate for the desired number of electric hulls. Krupp was therefore able to substitute only the following delivery dates for the electric hulls:

- by the end of May: 33 examples
- June: 16 examples
- July: 16 examples
- August: 16 examples
- September: 9 examples

as well as the three hydraulic turrets still missing (seven hydraulic hulls had already been delivered).

The other delivery dates for the Type 101 hulls were extended by half a month, to mid-October, beginning with six examples, rising to fifteen by November. According to Krupp, the target price for a Type 101 tank hull with a quantity of 100 examples was 70,000 RM, while for a Type 101 tank turret, also with 100 examples, it was 36,000 RM.

However, the change requests continued. On June 19, the OKH requested that the vehicle be capable of being driven underwater. This request had previously been set back, in the interests of rapid production. But this no longer seemed a priority, since this renewed requirement would force changes in the entire air-routing system. The planned changes could not be implemented until vehicle number 150 016 at the earliest. Plans would have to be made to retrofit the equipment on the first three to fifteen vehicles.

Krupp was also required to provide two welders and two fitters. With the takeover of this work, a further delay in ongoing production was inevitable. Porsche replied that the date for the underwater capability had to be postponed due to the timely connection to the current version, and the current rear engine cover would be installed on thirty Type 101 and ten Type 102 vehicles. Replacement intake gratings made of armor plate were envisaged as replacements from vehicle number 150 003 onward. For twenty-five vehicles, a simple model change should be considered to achieve a better air flow. For the fifteen exit gratings already delivered, a protective grill (mesh size: 750 × 950 × 35 mm, and 4 mm thick) had to be tailored and welded.

Meanwhile, the Army Ordnance Office prepared to take over the vehicles for testing. "Instructions for the Preliminary Implementation of the Acceptance Test for the Pz.Kpfwg. VI" was issued on June 1, 1942. In it stood under

A.) Chassis I. Pz.Kpfwg. VI (P1) and II. Pz.Kpfwg. VI (H1)

a) **Manufacturing Inspection**
1.) Check all lubrication points according to the lubrication plan for thorough lubrication and accessibility.
2.) Check the careful sealing of all gearboxes etc. for excessive penetration of lubricants. There should be only so many traces of oil as required for self-lubrication of the seal.
3.) Check whether entrenching tools, accessories, and equipment fit into appropriate holders and are present, provided they are to be provided by the company.

4.) Check the weld seams after the arrival and test drives for any cracking of the seams and the armor material.

5.) Similar inspection of the vehicle as per the Pz.Kpfw. III or IV.

b) **Vehicle Testing**

1.) During the acceptance drive, ensure that all the tank's operating levers etc. are easy and trouble-free to use.

2.) The driving test has to last at least one hour each, on- and off-road.

3.) The chassis must meet the following conditions:

a) Maximum speed of 40 kph (24.85 mph) for the vehicle, brought to a combat weight of 57 [metric] tons (62.8 tons), on a straight road of medium quality at engine speed of 2,500 rpm [revolutions had been limited to 2,600 rpm for the Henschel Tiger].

b) Climbing ability of 30° in moderate terrain

c) Ground clearance of 480 mm (18.90 in.)

d) Traffic-safe steerability at full speed on the road

e) Traffic-safe braking deceleration from maximum vehicle speed[39]

This list contains an abnormality regarding the maximum engine speed for acceptance. While the Porsche engine was supposed to be checked at the maximum allowable engine speed of 2,500 rpm, the 3,000 rpm maximum speed of the Henschel Maybach HL 210 engine was limited to the above-specified 2,600 rpm. However, this prevented it from achieving its maximum output of 650 hp. Was this a clerical error or a particularly gentle acceptance of the Army Ordnance Office Tiger?

The live firing on July 1 made it apparent that engine ventilation was inadequate to suck the powder gases out of the turret. A roof ventilator therefore had to be installed in the Porsche turret, like the one envisaged for the VK 4501 (H). *PA*

In addition to the acceptance regulations, a preliminary equipment list was compiled in February 1942, detailing which piece of equipment was stored where. Of course, various changes were made in the course of development. To compile this list, representatives of Wa Prüf 6 and Krupp together inspected a hull and a turret. They also checked their accessibility.

Preparations were also made at St. Valentin for training the troops on the Type 101. There the designers from Porsche, Skoda, and Krupp were able to explain their work to those who would later have to repair the vehicles. A very interesting series of lectures under the title "as part of the training on the Pz.Kpf.Wg. VI (4501P) for the troops of the tank arm detached to the Nie-Werk"[40] took place at the Nibelungenwerk in the entourage room in hall V. Two sections were set up for this purpose. As a rule, these consisted of technical personnel and tank drivers from the newly formed schwere Panzerabteilung 501 (501st Heavy-Tank Battalion), which was to be the first to be equipped with the Porsche Tiger. This unit was destined for use in Africa and was to receive the Tiger with air-cooled engines, better suited to the problematic desert climate. They did not yet know that these engines were anything but heat resistant.

Here is the original lecture program:

4/6 Do. Dipl.-Ing. Dr. Judtmann: General lecture on the transmission of power, [and] comparison of mechanical, electric, and hydraulic systems

5/6 Fri. Dipl.-Ing. Reimspieß: Air-cooled gasoline engines

8/6 Mon. Dipl.-Ing. Reimspieß: Air blowers Pz.Kpf.Wg. VI

9/6 Tues. Dipl.-Ing. Reimspieß: Fuel delivery and engine lubrication

10/6 Wed. Dipl.-Ing. Zadnik: General introduction to electrical engineering

11/6 Thurs. Dipl.-Ing. Zadnik: Power transmission in the Pz.Kpf.Wg. VI, general function explanation of the individual devices

12/6 Fri. Dipl.-Ing. Hügel: Generators

15/6 Mon. Dipl.-Ing. Hügel: Electric-drive motors

16/6 Tues. Dipl.-Ing. Schmitt: Electrical-wiring diagram

17/6 Wed. Dipl.-Ing. Zadnik: Interaction of the drive units in the Pz.Kpf.Wg. VI as brief summary of previous lectures

18/6 Thurs. Dipl.-Ing. Fender: Running gear: a) Road wheels with torsion bar suspension

19/6 Fri. Dipl.-Ing. Fender: Running gear: b) Idler wheel and drive wheel

22/6 Mon. Dipl.-Ing. Fender: Running gear: c) Brakes and their operation

23/6 Tues. Krupp Essen N.N.: Operation of the elevating and traversing mechanisms, their design and handling in the Pz.Kpf.Wg. VI

To employ the relatively large number of tank men present, the remainder of the course half day is filled with practical exercises, if possible in connection with production and testing, and plant employees are still to be named to lead them.

The following practical exercises are planned:

1.) Installation of road wheels
2.) Installation of torsion bar suspension
3.) Installation of drive wheels
4.) Installation of idler wheel and brakes
5.) Installation of tracks
6.) Installation of cooling fans
7.) Installation of electric motors in vehicle
8.) Installation and removal of gasoline engine units
9.) Carrying out an oil change
10.) Brake bleeding and operation
11.) Firefighting
12.) Driving technique

The right to change the lecture series on a case-by-case basis was reserved. Herr Leutnant Joschko of the armored forces assembled groups 1 and 2 accordingly. The department heads of the technical departments are invited to attend the lectures and are authorized to appoint one or other employee to participate in the relevant lectures.[41]

The Nibelungenwerk had already made a great deal of effort to bring the complex technology closer to the troops. Requests for further turret changes led to work on a counterbalance for the two turret hatch covers, to create additional vision opportunities for the loader in the form of periscopes in the turret roof, and to lower the gunner's seat by 40 mm (1.57 in.). The turret's standing height was determined by the lowest possible height of the turret platform in the vehicle, combined with the turret height dictated by the weapon. It was possible, however, to lower the edge of the platform by 10 mm (0.39 in.). In the meantime, they also began working on the vehicle's underwater-driving capability. This also affected the required equipment, such as an auto foot air pump with check valve for sealing the turret ring with a rubber hose, and a 2 m long hose and a so-called moment pump nipple connection. The equipment also included an Edco air pressure gauge for 0.7 to 3 atm, and a special wrench with universal joint for tightening the spindles for the mounting frame.

Hitler between Gauleiter Eigruber and Director Judtmann during the tour of Hall V. The close-up inserted at the top of the image shows the parked hull and turret of the Porsche Type 101. *Below right*, the driving switch with the two driving and steering levers. *BSB*

Here, too, the Type 101 tank hulls are stacked one on top of another, in part tipped on end. The factory's space problems were becoming clearly evident. *BSB*

Wa Prüf 6 then stipulated that two foot pumps, two air pressure gauges, and two universal joints should be carried by the battle train for each ten Tiger vehicles (Porsche or Henschel). For the air shaft, in April Porsche proposed the creation of a standard air shaft for the Porsche Type 101 and Porsche 180 with an inner diameter of 664 mm. As well, from turret 150 031 onward, the desired solution of a standard air shaft should be possibly by machining the otherwise unchanged hatch cover frame to a diameter of 660 mm (25.98 in.).

Because Hitler had a very great interest in the Porsche Tiger, at eight in the morning on June 20, 1942, he visited the Nibelungenwerk in St. Valentin unannounced while on his way to Munich. In addition to hall VI, where the Panzer IV was made, he was also shown hall V and the Porsche production line. On June 23, 1942, Speer subsequently presented to Hitler the planned production numbers for May 12, 1943: 285 examples of the Tiger tank, with which Hitler was satisfied. However, at this point in time he focused on future engine development of air-cooled diesel engines especially for the Panther and Tiger series, so that another field of activity opened up for Professor Porsche. As well, a new committee under the leadership of Professor Porsche, Oberbaurat Augustin of the Armaments Ministry, and Oberstleutnant Holzhäuer of Wa Prüf 6 was established. The project for the air-cooled diesel engine ran under the internal Porsche designation Type 220 and later also had an impact on the Porsche Type 180.

The next day, at Krupp in Essen, Kniepkamp gave his opinion on the Porsche Tiger. He announced that the Porsche vehicle now weighed 60 metric tons instead of the planned 45 metric tons and reached a speed of just 35 kph (21.75 mph). Fuel consumption of its air-cooled engines on the road was one and a half times higher than that of the Henschel vehicle, while off-road it was even two or three times as high. He named the electric drive's poor efficiency in the partial load range as the reason. The air cooling of the gasoline engines was also insufficient, so that the engines were already worn out after driving just 100 km (62 mi.). This was also associated

with increased oil consumption of 98.5 liters (26 gal.) by one engine and 55 liters (14.5 gal.) by the other.

In contrast, the electric steering worked well. This statement must be put into perspective, however. Efficiency in the partial load range was certainly poor, and cooling was insufficient. In evaluating these results, however, one must consider the instruction that the test vehicle was to be tested under the harshest conditions at Kummersdorf in order to reveal its shortcomings. The vehicle was to be subjected to extreme loads on the obstacle course to determine which parts would fail, and when. One can get the impression that the Porsche

As head of the Tank Committee, Professor Porsche not only had to worry about his own tank project but also had to demonstrate the prototype from his competitor, the Army Ordnance Office, to Speer. This vehicle also had a turret replacement weight. In the right background, a so-called VK Sport is ready to go. *SB*

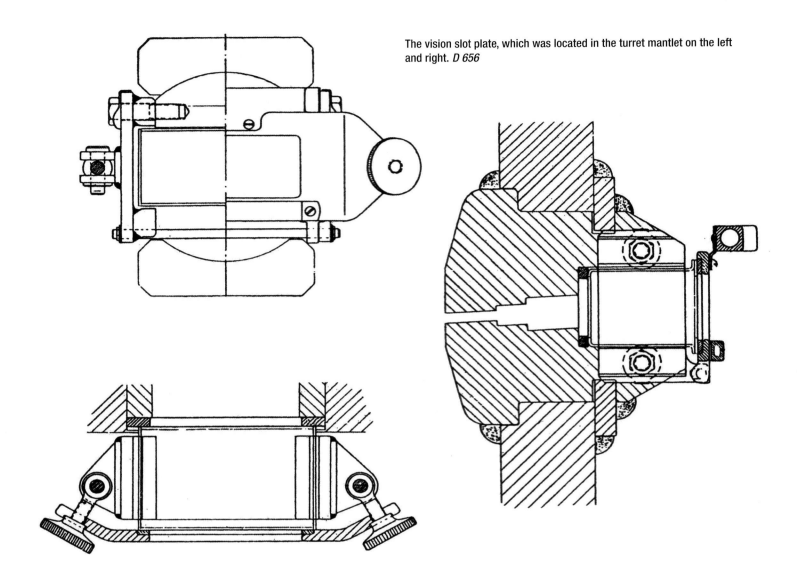

The vision slot plate, which was located in the turret mantlet on the left and right. *D 656*

vehicles were purposely worn out to prove their inadequacy. The ongoing changes and the loss of workers due to call-ups forced Krupp on June 27, 1942, to again change the delivery deadlines for the hulls. So far, including the end of June, Krupp had delivered fifty-three electric and seven converted hydraulic hulls to the Nibelungenwerk, while the new planning that had become necessary called for the following:

July: twelve electric hulls
August: ten electric hulls
September: ten electric hulls
October: five electric hulls and three hydraulic hulls

Delivery of the VK 4502 (P 2) (Type 180) would then take
place:

end of November: six examples
December: ten examples
January 1943: fifteen examples, etc.

This increase to fifteen examples was, however, possible only if the requested replacement workers were assigned and trained more quickly.[42]

On the occasion of a meeting of the Weapons Committee with Minister Speer on June 24, 1942, point 1 on the priority list stated that the necessary chassis for the self-propelled carriage based on the Tiger chassis had to be made available from Tiger production. This clearly shows that at this early date there were plans to produce an assault gun, and that it was not the result of later emergency use of the Porsche tank hulls.

The vehicle with the hull number 150 001 on the factory road at the Nibelungenwerk. Because of the gun barrel, which protruded far in front, the turret was usually turned to the six o'clock position (facing to the rear) when being driven. *PA*

Turret 150 011, with barrel 120, was delivered to the Nibelungenwerk on June 25. Krupp announced delays in the deadlines for delivery of turrets 150 012 to 022, which had been caused by the call-up of twenty-seven skilled workers and four key personnel, as well as by the subsequent addition of the emergency exit. The estimated shipping date of turret number 150 022 was therefore postponed to July 31, 1942. At this point, in late July, it was possible to complete the missing accessory parts for the ten turrets already delivered, such as the eight machine gun covers, five crates with spare breech parts, ten breech covers, ten adjusting wrenches for impact fuses, twenty shoot-through muzzle caps, ten muzzle caps, ten unloaders, ten pockets for muzzle caps, six covers for the TZF 9b telescopic sight, and eleven tins of grease via the Army Ordnance Office.

The Army Ordnance Office stipulated that as of August, all turrets were to be equipped with the smoke grenade launcher made by the Gebr. Müller firm, one on each side of the turret, and with two switch boxes for this equipment.

Referring to the command vehicle version of the Tiger, on June 30, 1942, the Nibelungenwerk advised Krupp that only those turrets with the new overall height should be used. Hull 150 006, with the first turret with the higher roof, number 150 008, was to be built as a command vehicle. To do so, the Nibelungenwerk required from the Krupp firm the necessary parts as well as tools and fitters to install the exit hatch and the antenna bushing in the turret. Due to elimination of the coaxial machine gun, the necessary plug for the mantlet, which had to be bulletproof, was also absent.

The vehicle with turret number 150 005—still with the old single-piece 640 mm track and old idler wheel—during a test drive on the factory road

Turret 150 012, with barrel number 107, was delivered to the Nibelungenwerk on July 1. Prior to that, the turret was checked for leaks for the first time. It was found that water penetrated mainly through the vision slit inserts. Changing the barrel of the coaxial machine gun still was possible only with an elevation of −8° to +12°. Due to the delayed deadline, the turret was shipped anyway. Dr. Judtmann of the Nibelungenwerk asked Krupp about further delivery dates, since the factory in St. Valentin planned to deliver two test vehicles and ten production vehicles in July, twelve vehicles in August, and, starting in September, fifteen vehicles per month. However, it was completely unclear whether the backlog from May and June, a total of eighteen vehicles, could be made good at all. Dr. Judtmann was of the opinion that Herr Krömer of the Armaments Ministry might have to put up with it. Regarding the second Porsche production batch, the deadline of delivering the same number of these vehicles from December 1942 was still valid. Construction of the VK 4502 test vehicle on a provisional chassis, for which the new turret was to be delivered by mid-October, depended on delivery of the necessary drawings.

Meanwhile, discussions continued on the subject of the emergency exit in the turret. Porsche stated in a letter to Krupp on July 4 that the submachine gun opening in the emergency hatch cover was missing from the Krupp turret drawings. Krupp explained that this previous opening could not be accommodated in the jettisonable hatch cover. Wa Prüf 6 had also not commissioned it. Krupp wanted to provide the necessary hatch opening beginning with turret number 150 013. Krupp regarded the retrofitting of turrets 150 001 to 012, as requested by Wa Prüf 6, as very difficult, since subsequent modification work at the Nibelungenwerk was scarcely possible, and transporting the turrets back to Essen was too time consuming.

Wa Prüf 6, however, wanted to have the emergency escape hatch as a permanent feature of the command vehicle. On July 14, Krupp listed the problems with the new requirement: because of the curvature of the turret, this hatch's straight locking clamp had to be replaced by a curved locking clamp. Since the hatch cover weighed about 100 kg (220 lbs.), the danger existed of crushing injuries, especially when entering

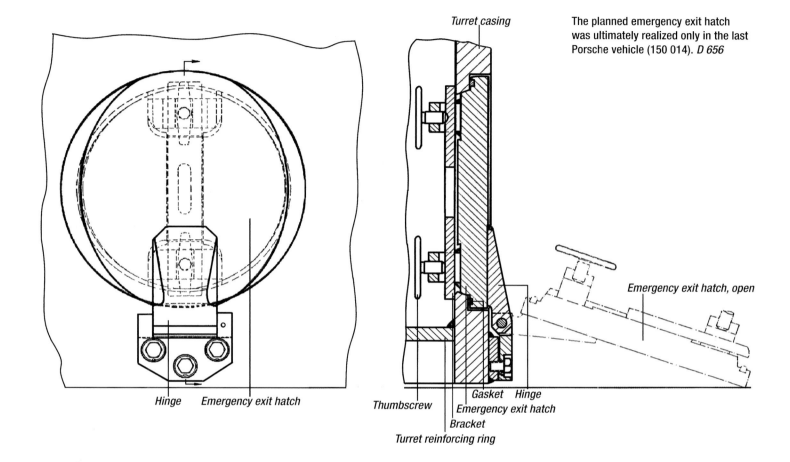

Turret casing

The planned emergency exit hatch was ultimately realized only in the last Porsche vehicle (150 014). *D 656*

Emergency exit hatch, open

Hinge   Emergency exit hatch

Thumbscrew   Gasket   Hinge
Emergency exit hatch
Bracket
Turret reinforcing ring

or exiting with the tank in a sloping position. This made it necessary to install a spring balancer. Since the turret's maximum pivot radius was 1,215 mm (47.83 in.), the planned installation of a hinge was still possible, since the intake gratings had a contact radius of about 1,400 mm (55.12 in.).

Concerning the problem of stowage bins, the Nibelungenwerk advised Krupp that the stowage bin had to be water resistant to 0.4 atm for underwater travel. The desired water resistance could not be achieved under the specified pressure with the BW stowage bin (Panzerkampfwagen IV), with a sheet thickness of 2 mm. The stowage bin would have to be made of 4 mm sheet metal. Since the Pz.Kpf.Wg. IV stowage bin was only an interim solution for the Tiger, Krupp recommended designing a new stowage bin, especially since the Pz.Kpf.Wg. IV turret's angle of inclination was different than that of the Tiger turret (therefore, the inclined hanging of the first bins). It was to be noted, however, that if submerged travel was required, the stowage bins could be removed in a few minutes and sent back to the train. The effort did not

justify the benefit. Since turret 150 013 was not required until August 10, it was to already have the fittings for track links and stowage bins. It was also expected that the hatch with side hinge would already be installed. After the arrival of this turret, turret 150 001 was to be sent back to Krupp. Due to the delays that had occurred, 150 013 and 150 014 were now to be furnished as command vehicle turrets. Oberst Fichtner, on the other hand, suggested to Krupp that the Nibelungenwerk should undertake the incorporation of the openings for the emergency exits in the turret itself, so that Krupp needed to deliver only the hatch covers to St. Valentin. The factory could make the necessary hinges itself in the shortest possible time. This would make it possible for a considerable percentage of the turrets stored in the Nibelungenwerk to be provided with emergency escape hatches without having to transport them back to Essen.

On July 23, the Porsche firm announced its new type classification. According to this classification, from the thirty-first vehicle onward, the VK 4501 (P) was to receive the

Porsche type designation 103. That means in detail that in the future there would be thirty Type 101 vehicles, ten Type 102 vehicles, and sixty Type 103 vehicles. The basic design of all three types was the same, but the Type 103 was to receive the new air intake and air exhaust screen because of the new engine air ducting. This resulted in thirty-one new individual drawings under this name. The next day, the Porsche firm also informed Krupp AG that the Porsche **Type 130**—VK 4501 (P) with liquid-cooled engines—had been dropped from the Tiger program. The delivery of the center-left and center-right air outlets for the twenty-five planned vehicles of this type was thus canceled.

The development team (*left to right*: Professor Porsche, Xaver Reimspieß, Emil Rupilius, Otto Zadnik, and Ferry Porsche) during a heated debate. *PA*

Long debates about the engine at the entrance to the test-driving area at the Nibelungenwerk. *PA*

Engine and cooling problems had
to be solved, whether at the rail
crossing on the way to the
test-driving area . . . *PA*

. . . or in the area itself. Here is the Tiger with the turret number 150 004. The chassis is one of the first five made, with the large track stops and missing side track shields. *A*

Checking the drive in the chewed-up terrain. *PA*

Testing of the two Tigers at Kummersdorf since July 10 had meanwhile revealed problems with the Porsche vehicle's electric turret traverse. The electric traverse time of the turret was twenty-seven seconds (from three o'clock to nine o'clock via twelve o'clock). The turret could be traversed manually from twelve o'clock to three o'clock in sixty seconds. Because of its sluggishness, however, manual traverse was possible only up to a slope of 7°. The biggest problem with that was that when the turret was traversed electrically, from 7.5° downslope the clutch slipped, causing the turret to run back to twelve o'clock. After readjusting the clutch in the traverse motor's switching device, at an upslope of 12° the lines began to overheat, and it became necessary to abandon the attempt.

Electric Turret Traverse

Gradient	Traverse Range			Current Consumption in amperes	Remarks
	from	via 12 o'clock	to		
Downslope					
4°	5^{00}		7^{00}	40	
5°	5^{00}		7^{00}	50	
7°	5^{00}		7^{00}	110	
7.5°	10^{00}		2^{00}	80	} clutch slipped
8°	13^{00}		13^{00}	80	} turret could not be held in intermediate position
11°	11^{00}		11^{00}	80	} ran back to 12 o'clock position
Downslope	from	via 5	to	130	cables began to overheat; turret could not be held at 2:30. The turret held at 3:30 and 4:15.

The measurement with an upward gradient of 12° took place after the clutch in the traverse motor's switching device had been readjusted. Further measurements could not be taken as a result of cable faults.

Manual Turret Traverse

Gradient	Traverse Range				Remarks
	from	via 12 o'clock	to		
Downslope					
4°	5^{00}		7^{00}		
5°	5^{00}		7^{00}		
7°	5^{00}		7^{00}		too difficult
7.5°					not possible
12.5°					not possible
Downslope					
12°					not possible

Zadnik, who was at Kummersdorf for the testing, asked Krupp to send a specialist to the Nibelungenwerk, since the test drives at Kummersdorf were interrupted for some time.

When on July 23 Hitler had read the report on the testing of the Tiger tanks at Kummersdorf, in consultation with Speer he determined the following:

a) The Tigers must be ready for use at the front in 1942, by September at the latest.

b) The Tigers could be operated only with a sparing driving style, since the vehicles could be rendered unusable in a short time by overuse.

c) The Tigers were initially envisaged for use in France, thus avoiding the harsh Russian conditions. Therefore, these less strenuous operational conditions could be used when testing the vehicles.

d) The Russian 52-metric-ton (57.3 ton) heavy tank (KV-I) was to be subjected to the same demands in endurance testing, to determine if the Russian tank was also unable to cope with the highest demands.

e) With increasing vehicle weights, such as the 100-metric-ton (110 ton) tank currently being developed, an unsparing driving style was impossible. These vehicles had to be driven with care.

f) These standards were to be used to assess the two Tiger models.[43]

It should be noted that regarding point c, hours earlier Hitler had declared that deployment of the first Tiger company to the Leningrad area was to be expedited.

Further comparison drives between Porsche and Henschel Tigers took place at Kummersdorf on July 27, 1942. Both prototypes covered 200 to 300 kilometers (km) on the test courses there. Various deficiencies were revealed with respect to the drive wheels, road wheels, and engines; however, most could be rectified. Nevertheless, further difficulties were anticipated. For this reason, the planned departure date for a Tiger company with ten vehicles was set back from August 8 to the end of August. On the basis of Hitler's instructions, Wa Prüf 6 stipulated that the current trials should not be carried out at maximum speed and maximum stress in the long term; otherwise the completion date could not even come close to being met. These tests had to be planned for

On August 27, 1942, Armaments Minister Speer visited the Nibelungenwerk for the first time. He was shown through the premises by President Meindl and Director Dr. Judtmann. Also present were representatives of the Army Ordnance Office, Professor Porsche, and Director Hacker of Steyr. Despite all the improvements, Speer remained skeptical about the Porsche design. *PA*

the later months. That same day, there was a meeting at Simmering-Pauker-Graz in Vienna. In addition to the Porsche leadership, Directors Hacker and Walter and General Radlmeieer were present. The content of the discussion also included the new types. The next day, all drove to the Nibelungenwerk in St. Valentin. In addition to a meeting on the Tiger assembly line, an off-road drive in a Tiger was carried out, which made a great impression on the Porsche engineers. On July 29, there was also a tour of Steyr-Motorenbau, and the Daimler-Benz aeroengines produced there were of interest, especially for the Maus project.

Speer was known to have had an aversion to Professor Porsche and his tank design from the beginning. It was clear to him, however, that Porsche had direct contact with Hitler, and so he had to protect himself on all sides. How was he to safely degrade Porsche to loser of the design competition? He set up a committee of experts that could deliver the desired result without Speer being seen as the guilty party. However, this committee was to deliver an expert opinion of the Porsche Tiger only. The Henschel Tiger was another matter. Interestingly, the committee was under the leadership of the Army Ordnance Office and the Army High Command, and in this instance Speer deviated from Todt's line of industrial self-responsibility. As a result, the Army Ordnance Office was finally able to fully demonstrate its aversion to Professor Porsche's special position. In Oberst Thomale, Speer placed at the head of the decision-makers a tank soldier who was particularly interested in a robust tank. This was not the Porsche Type 101; therefore,

further events could be foreseen. At that time, however, the Henschel vehicle was also anything but reliable. But that was not Oberst Thomale's concern.

In August 1942, extensive tests were carried out at the factory into dust resistance and its filtering, in order to track down the cause of the engine problems. The designers had found that the high wear of the Type 101 engine had to do with poor filtering of the intake air. To address this, the vehicle was fitted with additional intake filters and revised air baffles. It was notable that this vehicle already had the new two-part track with star-shaped idler and drive wheels.

Meanwhile, production of the Porsche had been halted on account of the continuing engine problems. At that time, the four Porsche Tigers assigned to troop trials were at the training camp at Döllersheim. After schwere Panzerabteilung 501 was withdrawn for retraining, this time from the Porsche to the Henschel Tiger, starting on August 10, 1942, elements of the likewise newly formed schwere Panzerabteilung 503 were sent to the training camp at Döllersheim in Austria. Their objective was training on the Porsche Tiger.

Franz-Wilhelm Lochmann, then a young tank soldier, provided an interesting description of events: "It was a great tank, which immediately inspired me. The two sides of the running gear were each powered by a gasoline engine, a generator, and an electric motor. The vehicle drove like a streetcar. The drives for the two sides of the running gear were started separately; two levers regulated forward and reverse travel as well as the desired speed. The running gear seemed

Speer during a test drive in tank chassis 150 005 at the Nibelungenwerk. He drove this Porsche Tiger without turret as well as a Panzer IV with turret replacement weight. *PA*

On this occasion the minister is test-driving the complete vehicle, made up of chassis 150 007 and a turret with high roof. Here the tank is driving through the empty pool at the end of the test-driving track. Since the vehicle already has the tall turret with the brackets for smoke grenade launchers and a turret ventilator, the turret can be only 150 011 or 150 012. *PA*

Driving and climbing experiments were also carried out in the gravel pit with a turret replacement weight. The vehicle in this photo is probably the hydraulic Tiger. It should come as no surprise that the significantly lighter Panzer IV had a better performance, since the difference in ground pressure between the two vehicles was too great. *PA*

President Meindl, Minister Speer, and Professor Porsche look a little perplexed. *PA*

The professor and Ferry in front of
Hall IV at the Nibelungenwerk. *PA*

clearly better to us than that of the Henschel Tiger, which we would get to know later. The 88 mm gun was all the rage to us. The turret was located very far forward; therefore the driver and radio operator had no upward-facing hatches. Usually the entire crew had to climb in and out through the turret. It quickly became obvious to us that the driver and radio operator, in particular, would have very bad cards in an emergency, although both could exit the vehicle through floor hatches. I got to know this tank relatively well, because I carried out radio-training sorties in it almost constantly. Unfortunately, the technology of this ingenious tank was not yet ready for series production. There were daily complications with our exercises. I especially remember vehicles stuck in difficult terrain and frequent engine fires."[44]

Driving in dusty conditions with the special baffles and additional dust filters. *PA*

The subject of engine fires was a constant companion of the Porsche Type 101 engine, since engine sealing was never resolved satisfactorily. The crankshaft seal on the flywheel side in particular caused problems. The escaping oil bound the dust and contaminated the cooling fins of the cylinders. Engine overheating made the problem worse, thinning the engine oil and making it easier for it to leak out. A vicious circle. If the leaking oil came into contact with the hot engine parts, such as the exhaust system, the result could be an engine fire. The engine problems also affected the Henschel Tiger's Maybach

Vehicle 150 023, which has the turret replacement weight and modified track shields, being used for driver training. The driver's visor and machine gun ball mount are still missing. *A*

engines, which was revealed during testing at the Kummersdorf artillery range. The Type 101 engines were still running on the test bench on August 10. The new Mahle pistons still gave cause for concern. In September the Porsche engineers compared the comparative figures from the engine endurance runs in Stuttgart and at Simmering-Pauker-Graz. The problems seemed to lie in the routing of the engine-cooling air.

The following series of photos illustrates the already well-known recovery exercises involving Porsche Tigers. They were taken at the training camp at Döllersheim on August 26, 1942, in the presence of Porsche engineers and tank soldiers of schwere Panzerabteilung 503. The four troop-training vehicles still had the low turret with central rise in the turret roof (for the gun at maximum depression). Some were later fitted with the taller turret to improve the loader's standing height.

Krupp delivered turret number 150 013, fitted with barrel 112, to the Nibelungenwerk on August 15. The turret was again checked beforehand for leaks. The ingress of water was about 2.5 liters in ten minutes. This turret was to be installed on the first vehicle issued to the troops, which still had the older turret with the lower roof. At the same time, Krupp specialists dealt with the problem of the intermittent traverse mechanism encountered during the test at Kummersdorf on July 23, carrying out driving and shooting experiments with two vehicles at a gunnery range near the Nibelungenwerk. Military officers were present, as was engineer Schmidt of Porsche. The turret was tested in various traverse positions to an inclination of 16°, without complaints. This exceeded the target figure of 15°. The turret was easily traversed all around with the engines shut down (no battery charge). The complaints were inexplicable to the experts. On the other hand, the fact that the turret could not be traversed manually at minor inclinations was felt to be disadvantageous. The previous type of turret lock was also untenable, since even normal vehicle vibrations caused the lock to disengage, and the turret immediately began to swing. A counterbalance spring was to be fitted to production vehicles, one each for the commander's and loader's hatches.

The vehicle in the lower photo with the turret number 150 005 is parked in the shed. The placement of external equipment differed from vehicle to vehicle. In the upper photo is the vehicle with the turret number 150 007. *SB*

On August 20, the Wa Prüf 6 issued instructions to the Krupp firm that turrets were no longer to be designated VK 4501 and VK 4502 but, effective immediately, Tiger 1 and Tiger 2. On August 25, Krupp wrote to the ministry that while the dates for the first sixty vehicles of the first series had been clarified, planning for the remaining forty vehicles had not yet taken place. Since, on the other hand, Krupp had found out that the Wegmann firm had received a contract for an additional forty turrets for the Henschel vehicle, the assumption was that the forty Porsche vehicles would fall under the table and forty Henschel vehicles were to be produced in their place (about which Krupp wasn't wrong).

The ministry disagreed with the claim that the forty Porsche vehicles were not to be built. The contract for the forty Henschel vehicles had been issued only because the dates for the Porsche vehicles were not clear. They agreed to meet with Krömer to sort the matter out. Concerning the problems with the stowage bins, Wa Prüf 6 was able to determine that the waterproofing requirement no longer existed.

They were already sufficiently rainproof and dustproof. The office established the required volume as 50 to 60 liters (1.77–2.12 ft.³) per man. As far as was possible, the shape of the bin was to be the same for Porsche and Henschel. Consideration was to be given to the different spare tracks links used by the two types.

On September 1, a consultation took place between the Nibelungenwerk and Krupp on sending the offending turret from the Kummersdorf vehicle back to Essen for repairs. All turrets were now to receive a friction clutch on their elevating and traversing mechanisms. Furthermore, as previously described, a counterbalance was installed for the commander's and gunner's hatches. Krupp asked that this first be used in delivery of the newest turret, number 150 013. Turret number 150 014 was also to be delivered in time, so that roughly three

Driving to the troop-training area. *PA*

The crew of the tank selected for the recovery experiment, which has the turret number 150 007, receives its instructions. Present in addition to the Porsche people were officers from schwere Panzerjägerabteilung 503, such as the battalion commander, Oberstleutnant Post, and the commander of the 1st Company, Oberleutnant Förster. *PA*

The vehicle is slowly guided to the trench. *PA*

The tank that is to be "shipwrecked" has spare track links on its turret, here located under the so-called Rommel bin, which is sitting at an angle to the turret. The two tow cables have been attached to the front as a precaution, in order to be better able to recover the tank after it has sunk into the marshy trench. The turret was again turned to the six o'clock position. *PA*

Tank expert General Radlmeier watches the recovery exercise attentively. *PA*

The two Porsche Tigers with the turret numbers 150 005 and 150 006 stand ready to recover the bogged-down vehicle. In order to use the towing lugs on the back of the tank, the spare track links on the rear had to be removed. *PA*

PA

Above right: Zadnik and Porsche standing in front of the bogged-down Porsche Tiger. The exercise called for it to be recovered by two other Porsche Tigers. *PA*

The crew of the recovery vehicle put away the tow cables, and Zadnik is in conversation with the tank soldiers of the 503rd Heavy-Tank-Destroyer Battalion. Professor Porsche, who walked back to the starting point, often encouraged getting his tanks stuck, in order to draw conclusions for the running-gear and drive systems. *PA*

The recovery of the bogged-down vehicle by two other tanks went without a hitch. *PA*

Reverse recovery with just one recovery vehicle was also tried. In this case the stuck vehicle was 150 005, with antenna and tow cable positioned on the right. *PA*

The vehicle without antenna, with turret number 150 006, also had to go into the trench for subsequent recovery. This time the tow cable was attached to the left tow hook. *PA*

of the latest turrets could be delivered to the Nibelungenwerk by the end of September. Should the turrets not arrive in time, turrets 13, 12, and 11 were to be mounted sequentially on production vehicles 1, 2, and 3. The smoke grenade launchers could not yet be delivered and had to be requested directly by the Nibelungenwerk.

Krupp was advised that the four troop-training vehicles, which had gone to Döllersheim, were still equipped with the old turrets with lower roofs. After they were returned to the factory, these turrets were to be made available for conversion. On the subject of the emergency exit, information was given that installation of the hatches was to begin with turret number 150 013. Hatches for turrets 150 008 to 012 were to follow later, and the Nibelungenwerk had to "spindle in" the round opening in the turret casing. Turrets 001 to 007 did not receive an emergency exit hatch, since the turret walls were 80 mm lower and thus could not accommodate so large an opening.

On the occasion of a meeting between Panzerabteilung 502 and Wa Prüf 6 on August 21, the troops expressed the wish that, in addition to raising the elevation handwheel, its recommended speed also be reduced. By limiting the elevation field to 15° as in the VK 4502, it was possible to move the handwheel upward 45 mm (1.77 in.) and 65 mm (2.56 in.) to the rear. The 0.5° per rotation reduction in the recommended speed of 0.95° per rotation reduced maximum directional force from about 7 to about 4 kg.

At an armaments conference on September 9, 1942, Hitler requested that in addition to the newly developed Type 41 88 mm Flak, the first Porsche Tiger series should also be sent immediately to Africa, since he considered the Porsche vehicle's air-cooled engines particularly well suited to African conditions. So that the new antiaircraft gun could also be used in an armored vehicle as quickly as possible, on September 20, Hitler directed that some of the Porsche Tigers be planned as assault guns with 200 mm (7.87 in.) of frontal armor and this 88 mm gun with a length of L/71 (the later Ferdinand tank destroyer).

Hitler was aware that the new Porsche Tiger 2 (Type 180) with its 88 mm L/71 tank gun would not be ready for service before mid-1943, and probably therefore preferred this variant, which could be implemented more quickly. Furthermore, the installation of a 210 mm heavy howitzer on a Tiger chassis was also to be examined. The required armor plates were to be taken from Kriegsmarine stocks. In this regard Hitler expressed that he had received information that the Porsche Tiger's fuel capacity was sufficient for a range of just 50 km in difficult terrain, which he found tactically unacceptable. Hitler demanded a range of at least 150 km (93.2 mi.).[45] It should be noted that while the Porsche Tiger had a fuel capacity of 520 liters (137.37 gal.), that of the Army Ordnance Office's Tiger was 534 liters (141 gal.) (including reserve tank), which, with a fuel consumption of 900 to 935 liters (237.75–247

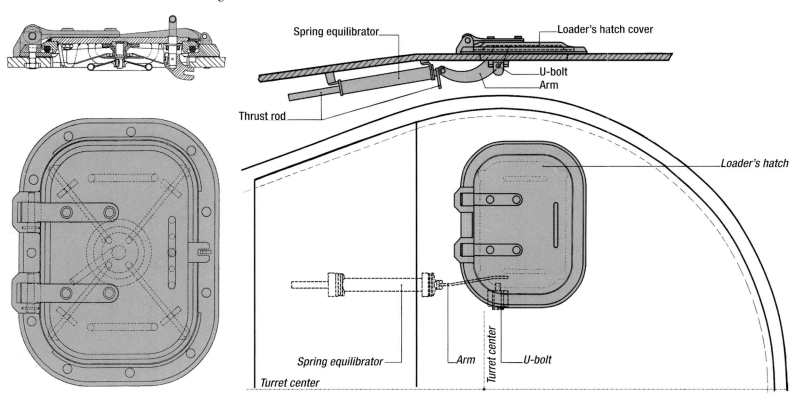

Principle of the loader's hatch weight balancer. *D 656*

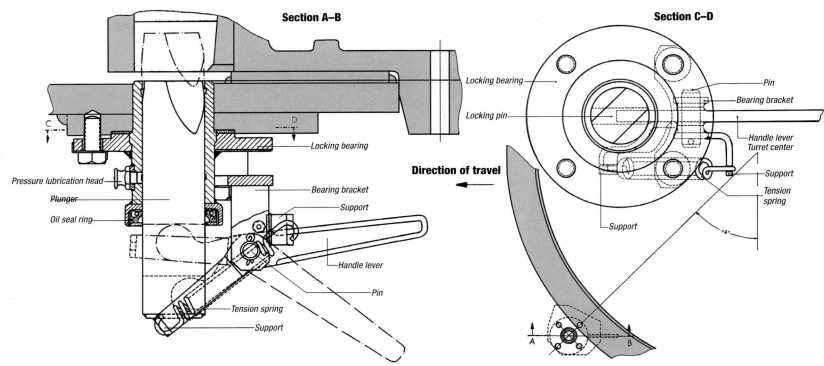

Section A–B

Pressure lubrication head
Plunger
Oil seal ring
Locking bearing
Bearing bracket
Support
Handle lever
Pin
Tension spring
Support

Direction of travel

Section C–D

Locking bearing
Locking pin
Pin
Bearing bracket
Handle lever
Turret center
Support
Tension spring
Support

The first-series turret traverse lock, which was criticized by the troops, as used on the Porsche Tigers. *D 656*

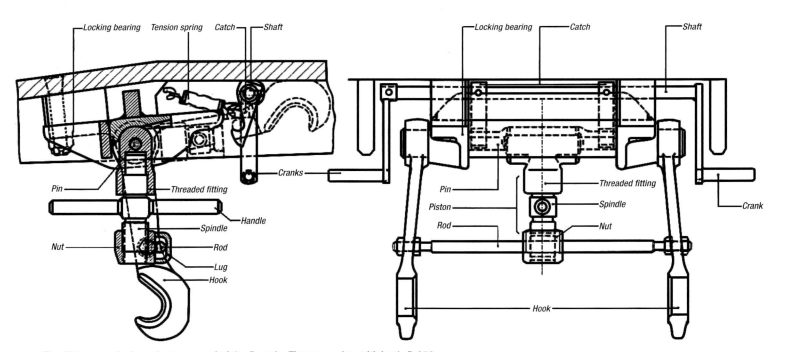

Locking bearing   Tension spring   Catch   Shaft
Pin
Threaded fitting
Cranks
Handle
Spindle
Nut
Rod
Lug
Hook

Locking bearing   Catch   Shaft
Pin
Piston
Rod
Threaded fitting
Spindle
Nut
Crank
Hook

The 0° traverse lock on the turret roof of the Porsche Tiger was also criticized. *D 656*

138

Lifting lug

Tank commander's cupola with bulletproof-glass inserts

Lifting lug

88 mm KwK 36

Mounting bracket for baggage bin

Loader's seat (stowed)

Emergency exit hatch, opened

The emergency exit hatch in the turret of the Henschel version, with hydraulic gearbox. *D 656*

Foot lever for firing machine gun

Turret platform

Hydraulic gearbox

Gunner's seat

gal.) of gasoline per 100 km (62.14 mi.) in difficult terrain, also yielded a range of just 50 to 80 km (31–49.7 mi.).[46] The army's data sheets specified a range with full tanks of about 110 km (68.35 mi.) in moderate terrain for the Tiger I Ausführung E. Hitler was apparently not given these figures by Speer and the Army Ordnance Office, resulting in the creation of a one-sided picture.

Meanwhile, schwere Panzerabteilung 502, with four Henschel Tigers, had seen its first action near Leningrad on September 22, 1942, and in the prevailing marshy terrain it had turned into a disaster. Prior to this, however, there had been considerable problems with the tank's Maybach engines and Olvar gearboxes. About this, Oberst Thomale said literally that "he refuses to send Germans into combat in such a tank." A representative of the Maybach firm responded by saying that they had always been told that the vehicles did not have to be absolutely ready for use by the troops. The firm was only to strive for their dispatch to the front with all means, so that they could be checked for usability in the field.[47] One tank was knocked out and the other three became bogged down. The element of surprise had been lost, because the Red Army later recovered one of the bogged-down Henschel Tigers and was able to evaluate it.

On October 1, Oberstleutnant Holzhäuer took over the leadership of Wa Prüf 6 from Generalmajor Fichtner. On October 2, 1942, the 1st Company of schwere Panzerabteilung 503, which had been sent to Döllersheim for training at the beginning of August, carried out trial shooting with a Tiger (P). The objective was to test ventilation conditions after the gun was fired. Among those who took part in addition to Porsche engineer Schmidt were Oberstleutnant Post,

commander of schwere Panzerabteilung 503, and Oberleutnant Förstner, commander of the battalion's 1st Company. *Wa Prüf* 6 had granted only ten shots for the trial, however. The first three shots were fired with hatches closed, engine ventilation switched on, and turret ventilators switched off.

One shot was fired with hatches open and engine ventilation switched on; single shots were fired with hatches open as well as an opened commander's cupola hatch and closed entry hatches, with the engine ventilation switched off and turret ventilator switched on. This resulted in afterflaming and heavy smoke buildup in the fighting compartment. The test sequence was repeated, with the difference that additional fresh air of about 10 m³/min. was blown in via a hose with a diameter of 50 mm (1.97 in.). This time there was **no** afterflaming, and the smoke nuisance was also minor. It was realized that a ventilation unit polarized for ventilation with a performance of more than 12 m³/min. (423.77 ft.³/min.) in place of the ventilator produced a better result. This meant that the crew was also independent of the airflow from the vehicle's engines. On October 15, the Henschel Tiger with the number 250 017 also arrived at the training camp at Döllersheim for comparative trials.

On October 5, there was a meeting at St. Valentin with Krupp, Porsche, and the Nibelungenwerk on the topic of turret changes. The revised friction clutches on the elevation and traverse mechanism, the counterbalance on the commander's hatch cover, and the drip pan under the traverse motor had already been installed from turret number 14. It was thought that if possible, the air hose for the new type of ventilation should also be fitted, as well as the hooks for hanging submachine gun magazines and machine gun tool bags. Krupp still had not received the smoke grenade launchers, and these would therefore be installed at the unit level. The drawing of the smoke signal basket, which was to be attached in the blind spot behind the commander's cupola, was to be sent first to the Army Ordnance Office and from there to Krupp. The following shortcomings were eliminated:

- the loader's seat swiveling out beyond the permissible level

- the self-loosening turret lock, which was secured by means of a snap spring

- Mounting of the turret was to be carried out by trained personnel only. The two guide pins were supplied firmly screwed in.

- The holders of the vision blocks (protective glass blocks) had to be capable of proper opening and closure

- The footrests had been changed so that the storage of the collapsible grenade containers could not be moved.

- The retaining brackets for the stowage bin were still welded on, since it was the simplest version.

- Three wire ropes of the same length were sufficient for installing the turret. However, the chute had to be installed in the turret before it was put on.

- The scissors telescope, with which every second tank was to be equipped, should be attached to the coupling ring by means of a clamping screw, making it possible to swivel it around.

- From the twenty-fifth turret, a prism mirror will be installed in front of the loader's hatch. A kit should be carried as a spare and added to the equipment list.

- Turrets 25 and 26 were envisaged as the first command turrets. In these turrets, the gunner's viewing slot on the right-hand side of the turret had to be closed, and the parts protruding into the interior of the turret had to be burned off.

- The stowage bin design should be worked out so that there is 300 mm (11.81 in.) (200 mm high track link + 100 mm holder) of space for attachment of the track link on the rear of the turret. But since every second track link was made without teeth, there was the

possibility of mounting these track links on the rear of the turret and thus reducing the gap to 200 mm.

- The instructions for sealing the vehicle should be attached above the machine gun opening behind the commander's seat.

- The turrets previously delivered to the Nibelungenwerk, including chutes and screws, were to be sent back to Krupp when new turrets were delivered, using the same railcars.

- The quick travel lock in the steepest possible gun position desired by the troops was omitted due to the corresponding friction clutch.

- In the case of the Type 180, the question of changing the driver's visor holder by installing a corner mirror was settled; in the case of the Type 101, a change was no longer possible.

- The adjustable commander's seat was envisaged for turret 14.

- Some of the provided hatch keys were not cut and did not fit past the retaining bracket on the hatch cover.

On October 5, the Nibelungenwerk wrote to the Krupp firm, informing it that a demonstration of Tiger vehicles was to take place at Berka near Eisenach on October 20, 1942. The latest turrets were envisaged for these two vehicles. Krupp was therefore asked to do everything it could to ensure that the two turrets with the numbers 150 014 and 150 015, which were conceived for armored command vehicles, were dispatched to the Nibelungenwerk by October 15. A special feature of these turrets was that they were designed for a second set of radio equipment. This included closure of the opening for the coaxial machine gun as well as the loader's vision flap. In addition, the commander's hatch was equipped with an opening for a scissors telescope and, behind it, a basket for smoke signals. To accommodate this, the hatch hinge was moved back and a spring balancer was added for weight compensation. The commander's seat was designed to be foldable. The emergency exit was first to be added to production vehicles.

On October 14, during a meeting at Krupp, Oberbaurat Kniepkamp announced that the Henschel test vehicle had covered 3,000 km (1,864 mi.) and the steering had been very easy (after two engine and steering gearbox changes). Two hundred examples of this model (VK 4501 H) were to be built by mid-1943. Start-up of the Tiger 3 (VK 4503 H) was to follow, but probably not before September 1943. The engine (Maybach HL 230) and cooling system from the Panther were supposed to be installed in this new Henschel model. Wa Prüf 6 envisaged that a variety of gearboxes would be tested—a Maybach Olvar, a ZF-Allklauen, an electromagnetic one, and a fully automatic AEG three-speed liquid transmission.

The running gear was to be double instead of triple interleaved. Because of the vehicle's greater weight, an additional road wheel was installed. A 1,000 mm wide (39.37 in.) track was planned, in order to reduce the vehicle's high ground pressure to an acceptable 0.7 kg/cm^2 (9.95 psi) (which never happened). The Porsche Tiger 2 was not going to be built (VK 4502 P). The construction of 100 Porsche Tiger 1s had also been canceled for the time being. A comparative driving test between the two Tiger models was supposed to be carried out at Berka near Eisenach at the end of October.[48] In his own way, Kniepkamp was already anticipating the decision that was to come.

Krupp subsequently announced on October 19 that it was already working on the contract it had received for 100 turrets for the Porsche Tiger. By the time that work on the Porsche Tiger 1 (Type 101) was halted, the company had already sent fifteen turrets to the Nibelungenwerk. Because the delivery of tank parts and the guns had gone according to plan, at that time there were eighty-five guns and the same number of tank parts in the workshop. Since there was the danger of a stoppage, the turrets were supposed to be sent without design changes, since it was impossible to store the entire second series in the second mechanical workshop. It should also be noted that turrets for the new VK 4501 (P 2) were already in production preparation.

Krupp named the planned production numbers for the Type 101 (P 1) turrets:

- delivered: 15 examples
- November 1942: 15 examples
- December 1942: 15 examples
- January 1943: 15 examples
- February 1943: 15 examples
- March 1943: 5 examples
- April 1943: 5 examples
- May 1943: 5 examples
- June 1943: 5 examples
- July 1943: 5 examples
- August 1943: 3 examples
- Total: 100 examples

Krupp assured that the first new turret for the Type 180 would be completed by the end of December 1942. Meanwhile, turrets 150 014 and 150 015 had arrived at the Nibelungenwerk.

On October 29, 1942, the Army Ordnance Office replied with an express telegram that production of the VK 4501 (P 1) tank was to be halted immediately, and that of the VK 4501 (P 2) after completion of the three test casings (three hulls and three turrets) that had been ordered. The Krupp firm received the follow-up order for the delivery of ninety complete VK 4501 (Henschel) armored shells. The still-existing tank turrets for the Type 101 (P 1) were to be used for this order. Thus the Army Ordnance Office had made the decision to halt production of the Porsche Tiger before the Tiger Committee, which had been created for that purpose, had made a decision. The whole thing, therefore, was nothing but a farce. Despite this, one of the most elaborate demonstrations ever by Wa Prüf 6 followed at Berka.

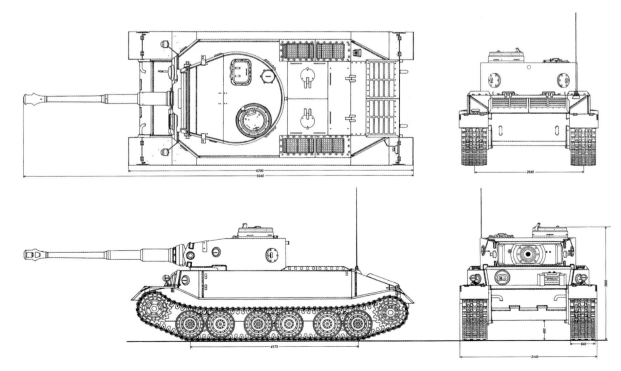

The Tiger (P 1) with tall turret and roof ventilator. The emergency exit is still absent. *SB*

CHAPTER 3

The "Decision" at Berka vor der Hainich

First, the reader must be introduced to this relatively unknown military training area, which was also used postwar by the Red Army and the National People's Army. The Berka training area is located on the southern ridge of the Hainich, a chain of forested hills in Thuringia, and beginning in 1936 the Wehrmacht used it as the training area for Panzerregiment 2, based at Eisenach. The Hainich's military history began much earlier, however. The Duchy of Weimar-Eisenach established a military training area there in 1871–72. In 1933–34, a grass airfield was secretly established south of the Kindel (country south of the Hainich) for Kampfgeschwader 253.

Furthermore, the Gebrüder Thiel (Thiel Brothers) firm from Ruhla set up a testing station there for the shells and bomb fuses it produced. In 1936, the Wehrmacht acquired further wooded areas for the 7. Panzerdivision Thüringen.[49] These covered an area of 85.6 hectares (211.5 acres) with the forest locations Hazelwurzel, Seeberhof, Galilea, Vier Winde, and Trockene Kutte. At the same time, work began on a Wehrmacht shooting range in the Long Valley, near Berka-Sulzrieden.[50] The military used the Bufleben to Großenbehringen rail line, used by so-called Nessel Valley Rail, to transport equipment and armored vehicles to the testing station.

Movement of the vehicles from the railway station to the base was by road over the 6 km stretch on Reichsstraße 84. Two tracks in the Großenbehringen station were upgraded for a Culemeyer transport system, in which the complete railway car could be loaded onto multiaxle trailers via a ramp and thus transported directly to the Kindel.[51]

Since the possibilities for tank testing in the area of the Kummersdorf artillery range were not adequate to conduct sufficient trials under service conditions, in 1939, planning was begun for a testing area for the Verskraft (Motor Vehicle Testing Center) in the base training area. Tank testing by the Verskraft must have been moved to the Hainich area in 1938,

however. A photo with the caption "Großenlupnitz 1938" shows an Austrian Fiat-Ansaldo CV-35 tankette there.

The testing area was located on very difficult and stubborn loessial soil. It therefore made sense to lay down special routings so that endurance trials could be carried out under demanding conditions. As well, part of the base testing area was set aside for the Verskraft. This was followed by the surveying of corresponding routes, in order to establish wide lanes and create the necessary infrastructure.

In addition to the driving routes, the Verskraft also required an infrastructure for vehicle maintenance and the inspection and repair service. This resulted in the building of a sentry box plus a large workshop, a barracks with communal rooms and offices, and washbasins for cleaning the vehicles. The unusually heavy soil, which dried out very quickly in wind and weather, demanded special equipment for cleaning the vehicles. In addition to pressure washers, washbasins with concrete thresholds were built for softening the dirt that had hardened and for better loosening of the sludge by moving the running gear.

Berka was primarily used to the test the practicality of the Wehrmacht's tracked vehicles in the most-difficult terrain. The test tracks laid out in the Großlupner Forest had the great advantage of being protected from the wind and sun; thus there was little variation in their degree of difficulty. Berka was also chosen for demonstrations and comparisons, when testing under particularly difficult conditions was required. This included the herein-described comparison of the two Tiger types on 1942 and a demonstration of recovery and towing equipment to a large gathering of frontline officers in 1943–44.[52] From September to October 1944 there was also extensive testing of a Type 276 VW Kübelwagen, a Type 82, and a Steyr 1.5-metric-ton truck with limbered 37 mm Pak 37 plus ammunition trailer on circuit no. 1 at Berka.

According to Oberst Esser's files, one of the biggest demonstrations by Wa Prüf 6 took place in the first weeks of November 1942. Willi Esser was head of the Verskraft at the Kummersdorf artillery range from February 1938 until the end of the war.

And so a demonstration of the two competing Tigers took place before both the Tiger and the Tank Committees at Berka in front of the Hainich Hills. This comparison was supposed to officially decide on the further construction of the Porsche series. Internally, however, as previously described, the decision in favor of the Army Ordnance Office vehicle had already been made.

The tank demonstration is a very controversial topic in the literature. Authors such as Karl Pawlas maintain that this demonstration most probably never took place at all, since no documents were available at the time of his writing. In his book *Panzer II und seine Abarten*, Wolfgang Spielberger wrote: "The committee met at Eisenach and Berka in the period from October 26 to 31, 1942, to examine the Tiger tanks." According to his account, the participants were the two chairmen of the Tiger Committee, Professor Eberan von Eberhorst (Dresden Technical University) and Oberst Thomale (head of army equipment and commander of the replacement army). Representing the Army Ordnance Office were Oberst Esser, Oberst von Wilke, and ten other officials from the office. The only representatives from the tank industry were staff from the Alkett and Krupp firms. Also present were Oberstleutnant Post and Major Lueder, the commanding officers of the 501st and 503rd Heavy-Tank Battalions, respectively.[53]

In his book *Panzerfahrzeuge im Zweiten Weltkrieg*, Hartmut Knittel makes reference to MAN documents[54] that state that extensive demonstrations and driving tests took place at Berka,

near Eisenach, from November 8 to 14, 1942, under the direction of Speer, Fichtner, and Holzhäuer. The found files of Oberst Esser confirm these demonstrations by about thirty vehicles and give a detailed picture of what took place, even if they are unfortunately incomplete. The documents found could be augmented well with Esser's handwritten notes.

This postwar photo shows a Culemeyer transport carrying a Reichsbahn tank car, just as it could have happened from Großenbehringen to the Kindel. *BA*

According to this report, the following vehicles participated:

- two Henschel Tigers (250 011 and 250 013, later also the Kummersdorf Tiger 250 001)

- a Henschel Tiger with electric ZF 12 E 170 manual gearbox (probably 250 018)

This photo was probably taken in the area of the airfield on the Kindel, below the Hainich. *F*

- two Porsche Tigers (150 014 and 150 015)

- a MAN Panther, later joined by a second MAN Panther

- a Daimler-Benz Panther without turret

- a Panzer II with electric gearbox

- a VK 3601 Henschel without turret

- a Panzer III with Olvar gearbox

- two Soviet tanks, a T-34 and a KV-I

- a Panzer III with wider tracks

- a Panzer III with interleaved running gear

- a Panzer III with rubber-saving road wheels

- two Panzer III flamethrower tanks

- two armored cars equipped with flamethrowers[56]

The Verskraft's Berka field office on the Kindel. *Above left*, the washbasin, coming right at the entrance from the test site, was used for the first cleaning of the track drive. In the center was a stream, whose water was either let into the wash bay by a dam or could be diverted through a hose. With it, the mud could be washed away with the help of the Treisbach (a local stream). The concrete rises also created a vibrating effect that shook off the soaked mud. *Below*, the barracks immediately after entering the road. It housed the social areas and the rooms for the testing service right the workshop building.

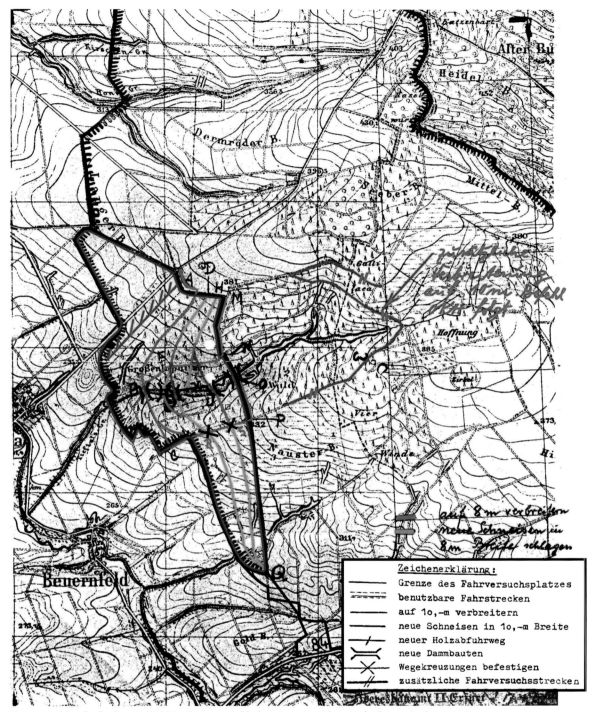

The map of the Großenlupner Wald testing area, with the necessary changes in the marked-out routes

The first demonstration took place on November 2 under the direction of General Fichtner. The participants were to arrive for the demonstration at noon. It was also anticipated that the following would also take part:

- one 1-metric-ton (1.10 ton) and one 3-metric-ton (3.3 ton) prime mover

- one Raupenschlepper (Ost) caterpillar tractor

- two Radschlepper (Ost) wheeled tractors

- one Latil tractor with two Anhänger *(Ost)* trailers

- plus several 3-metric-ton (3.3 ton) trucks with SS-, Opel-, and Luftwaffe-type track drives

The two competing Tigers had been undergoing comparison since November 2. The first event was a drive on the closed Eisenach to Erfurt Reichsautobahn. Fuel consumption was measured on the outward and return journeys. Measurements were taken on the two Henschel Tigers 250 011 and 250 013 and the Porsche Tiger 150 015.[57] The results were as follows:

	Max. speed	Liters per 100 km	Liters per metric ton over 100 km
1. Outward Drive			
H 11	24.2	314	5.6
H 13	26.6	288	4.66
P 15	27.35	466	7.55
2. Return Drive			
H 11	0	314	5.6
H 13	26.9	288	4.66
P 1	28.45	466	7.55

		Average	Quantity	Distance	Assuming Easy Terrain		
	l/100 km	liters per metric ton over 100 km	liters	km RAB	l/100 km	travel range	l/tg
H	288	5.13	570	198	432	134	~10
P	456	7.74	525	115	684	77	~8.85

Oberst Esser's information in the bottom list, stating that the Henschel vehicle's fuel capacity was 570 liters (150.58 gal.),[58] is, however, incorrect, since all later documents list a fuel capacity, including reserve, of 534 liters (141 gal.), made up of one 88-liter (23.25 gal.), one 98-liter (25.89 gal.), and two 174-liter (45.97 gal.) tanks. Possibly another 36-liter (9.5 gal.) tank was originally planned but could not be realized because of its unfavorable position in the fighting compartment. The greater quantity of fuel also resulted in different ranges, which did not make Porsche Tiger 150 015's very high fuel requirement look any better.

Interestingly, this confirmed the statement by Henschel engineer Pertuss, cited below, that the Porsche vehicle traveled faster, which of course, in addition to higher fuel consumption, also placed greater loads on the drive units. Oberst Thomale had, however, demanded an average speed of 30 kph (18.64 mph) for both competitors. Concerning Oberst Esser's list, it is also interesting that the second Henschel vehicle was no longer present on the return drive! Had it broken down instead of the Porsche vehicle? This would, however, place Mr. Pertuss's notes in a different light. Or had the second Porsche Tiger not been included in the list because of the previously mentioned engine fire?

Anyway, the next day, the third of November, the Tigers went into the difficult terrain of the Hainich. The Porsche vehicle 150 015 and the Henschel vehicle 250 013 each completed six circuits. Each lap had a length of 7.925 km (4.9 mi.). Once again, the Henschel vehicle's fuel consumption was clearly better. On average, the Army Ordnance Office vehicle required 800 to 1,000 liters (211.34–264 gal.) of fuel per 100 kilometers (62.14 mi.) at an average speed of 11 to 12 kph (6.8–7.5 mph). The Porsche tank, on the other hand, required an average of 1,800 liters (475.5 gal.) per 100 kilometers (62.14 mi.) at a lap speed of about 10 kph (6.2 mph). A considerable difference. The poorer efficiency of the electric drive very probably came into play here, especially in the partial load range. The 534-liter (141 gal.) fuel capacity of the Henschel Tiger thus translated into a range of 60 km (37.28 mi.) in Berka's difficult terrain, while the Porsche vehicle's 525 liters (138.7 gal.) was sufficient only for about 30 km (18.64 mi.). In detail, the values looked like this:

In addition to the enormous fuel consumption, noticeable in this list is the slightly higher lap average for all vehicles at the end of the comparison, combined with slightly lower fuel consumption.

Berka Terrain 1st Lap: 7.924 km	250 013						250 011			
3 Nov. 1942	1st Drive	2nd Drive	3rd Drive	4th Drive	5th Drive	6th Drive	1st Drive	2nd Drive	3rd Drive	4th Drive
Average kph	12.3	11.6	11.3	11.25	11.46	10.78				
l/100 km	985	912	932	920	925	972				
4 Nov. 1942	1st Drive	2nd Drive	3rd Drive	4th Drive	5th Drive	6th Drive	1st Drive	2nd Drive	3rd Drive	4th Drive
Average kph	12.8	13.6					15.12	15.12	14.42	14.6
l/100 km	835	790					828	820	883	984
5 Nov. 1942	1st Drive	2nd Drive	3rd Drive	4th Drive	5th Drive	6th Drive	1st Drive	2nd Drive	3rd Drive	4th Drive
Average kph	12.97	14.15					13	15.7	16.1	
l/100 km	807	807					990	855	832	
Average fuel consumption	870 liters / 100 km						884 liters / 100 km			
Resulting possible range	61 km						60 km			
Total km driven	88						56			

	150 015						150 014			
3 Nov. 1942	1st Drive	2nd Drive	3rd Drive	4th Drive	5th Drive	6th Drive	1st Drive	2nd Drive	3rd Drive	4th Drive
Average kph	9.96	8.64	9.44	9.55	9.91	9.51				
l/100 km	1,836	1,795	1,780	1,816	1,816	1,792				
4 Nov. 1942	1st Drive	2nd Drive	3rd Drive	4th Drive	5th Drive	6th Drive	1st Drive	2nd Drive	3rd Drive	4th Drive
Average kph	10.15						9.66	9.52	9.7	
l/100 km	1,785						1,583	1,710	1,722	
5 Nov. 1942	1st Drive	2nd Drive	3rd Drive	4th Drive	5th Drive	6th Drive	1st Drive	2nd Drive	3rd Drive	4th Drive
Average kph	10.60						9.74	9.54	9.89	
l/100 km	1,650						1,800	1,742	1,685	
Average fuel consumption	1,783 liters / 100 km						1,707 liters / 100 km			
Resulting possible range	29 km						30.5 km			
Total km driven	64						48			

Meanwhile, the Tiger Committee held a meeting in Eisenach on the same day. The evening before, the participants had already thought about comparability. The content of the November 3 meeting included a comparison of the technical data of both candidates and weighed their advantages and disadvantages. This was based on the evaluations of the testing of both vehicles at Kummersdorf. The committee members noticed, however, that the Henschel vehicle had driven 3,100 km (1,926.25 mi.) at Kummersdorf, the Porsche vehicle just 300 km (186.4 mi.). A reason was not given, only that the existing shortcomings in the Henschel vehicle could be eliminated more quickly.

■**The first point of the comparison was the dimensions:**

Hull length was to be about 7 meters [therefore without gun]:
Henschel: 7.87 m (25.8 ft.)
Porsche: 7.77 m (25.5 ft.)

*The maximum **Specified Height** was to be 2.99 m (9.8 ft.):
Henschel: 2.83 m (9.3 ft.) (?) [was 2.99 m]
Porsche: 2.80 m (9.18 ft.) [with tall turret]

*The prescribed **Width** was the allowable transit limit of 3.30 m (10.8 ft.):
Henschel: with 525 mm (20.7 in.) travel track:
             3.14 m (10.3 ft.)
          with 725 mm (28.5 in.) operational track:
             3.57 m (11.7 ft.)
The Henschel vehicle thus exceeded the limit with the operational track.

Porsche: with 640 mm (25.2 in.) track:
             3.30 m (10.8 ft.) without track shields
             3.38 m (11.09 ft.) with track shields
          with 700 mm track (27.6 in.):
             3.42 m (11.2 ft.) without track shields
             3.50 m (11.5 ft.) with track shields

*The prescribed **Ground Clearance** of 450 to 500 mm (17.7 to 19.7 in.) was met:
Henschel: 470 mm (19.5 in.) [according to specification,
             445 mm (17.5 in.) in front,
             455 mm (17.9 in.) in rear]
Porsche: 480 mm (18.9 in.)

*The required **Wading Ability** of 1,250 mm (49.2 in.) was achieved:

Henschel: 1,800 mm (70.9 in.)
Porsche: 1,700 mm (67 in.)

■**The second point was the weight of ±48 metric tons (52.9 tons):**

Both types exceeded this to a considerable degree:
Henschel: 56.7 metric tons (62.5 tons)
Porsche: 59.3 metric tons (65.4 tons)

■**The third point was engine performance:**

Henschel: the 650 hp HL 210 engine gave a power-to-weight ratio of 11.4 hp / metric ton
Porsche: two 311 hp Type 101 engines gave a power-to-weight ratio of 10.6 hp / metric ton

The required target driving range with five hours at full power gave the need for the following:
Henschel: 222 g/PSh × 660 hp; degree of efficiency of 0.765 gave 191.5 l/h; 960 liters of fuel were required for five hours
Porsche: 225 g/PSh × 2 × 254 hp; degree of efficiency of 0.765 gave 169.5 l/h; 850 liters of fuel were required for five hours.

None of the vehicles met the requirements.
But with this data, inconsistencies stand out. On the one hand, the figure given for the HL 210's specific fuel consumption, 222 g/PSh, is too low. Professor Eberan had specified an optimum value of 276 g/PSh for the Maybach HL 230 engine and an average value of 25% to 100% of Nmax of 325 g/PSh. According to his calculations, the Porsche 101/4 engine had an optimum value of 217 g/PSh and an average value of 25% to 100% of Nmax of 257 g/PSh. The values are based on clutch performance. Fan power had already been deducted for both engines.[59] The horsepower figure of 2 × 254 hp for the Porsche vehicle, compared to 660 hp for the HL 210, also confused Oberst Esser's calculations, especially since the correct figures are present as given above.

■**The fourth point concerns the still-existing difficulties with the engines.**

Henschel HL 210:
Had sufficient performance. There were, however, the following difficulties:
(a) Heavy oil loss at the flywheel bearings, resulting in oil consumption of 20 to 25 liters (5.3–6.6 gal.) per 100 km

(62 mi.), which led to range restrictions. The target was 7 liters (1.8 gal.) per 100 km (62 mi.).

(b) The various cylinder head gasket defects.

Porsche Type 101:

The engine was currently unusable. According to the Porsche firm, the engine was not yet fully developed; therefore an experiment with the Maybach HL 210 and electric drive was to be carried out. [This also brought no improvement, as would later be shown by the Ferdinand assault gun.]

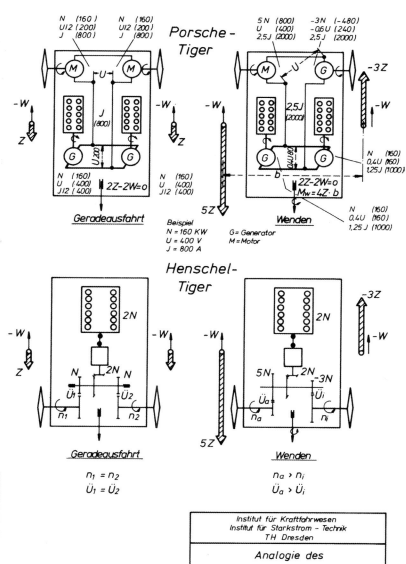

Blowers:

Henschel: There were no disengageable clutches for the blowers. Furthermore, there were leaks in the lubrication system caused by defective hoses and their fittings.

Cooling Performance:

This should be sufficiently dimensioned to withstand +45°C temperatures in the tropics.

Henschel: The requirement was to be met by adopting a higher fan speed (+47%).

Porsche: No additional measures were needed to meet this condition. However, the first prototype vehicle developed several oil leaks, and the leaking oil contaminated the cooling fins. The associated reduction in cooling performance caused major problems during testing.

There were, however, general problems with both engines.

The Gearboxes:

Prescribed for the Henschel Tiger was an Olvar gearbox from Maybach with speeds of 2.8 kph (1.74 mph) in first gear and 45 kph (28 mph) in the highest gear. The total reduction range was 1:16. Operation was simple and easy to learn; shift times were acceptable. The Olvar gearbox was not yet sufficiently reliable, however, and could also not be repaired by the troops. The gearbox's automatic mechanism was very sensitive to contamination. Further difficulties arose in the insufficient durability of the brake cone. A total of 1,507 kilometers (936 mi.) were covered on the flat, and about 750 kilometers (466 mi.) in the parabolic dunes at Kummersdorf. The service life of the gearbox was then around 300 km (186 mi.). The Maybach firm had not yet allowed fitters from outside the company to repair the gearbox.

Steering:

Henschel: The system's durability had not yet been proven. The vehicle steered very easily. Operation in winter was viewed as possible. The planetary gearing caused trouble (hot running) and was caused by poor lubrication. Auxiliary steering was available. The gearbox and steering system could be removed only together, which Oberst Thomale regarded as a disadvantage.

Porsche: Steering was easy. Suitability for operation in winter had not yet been demonstrated.

Running Gear:

Henschel: The running gear was heavily loaded. Overall, the design was satisfactory. The durability of the solid rubber tires, however, was regarded as questionable. Rubber-saving road wheels, which enabled a continuous speed of 40 kph (24.85 mph), were therefore desired.

Porsche: The running gear was simple in design, easily accessible, and easy to maintain. It could therefore be easily repaired. Durability was still questionable.

The **Specific Ground Pressure** of both vehicles was extremely poor:

Henschel: 1.09 kg/cm2 (15.5 psi) (with track width of 725 mm, or 28.54 in.) or
1.14 kg/cm2 (16.2 psi) minus the perforations

Porsche: 1.13 kg/cm2 (16 psi) (with track width of 640 mm, or 25.2 in.)
1.03 kg/cm2 (14.65 psi) (with track width of 700 mm, or 27.6 in.)

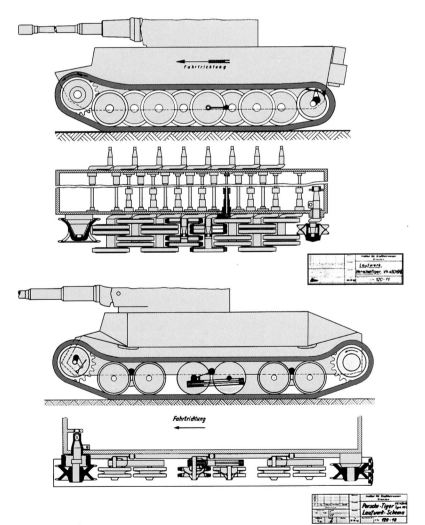

Comparison of the running-gear systems of the two Tigers. *TU*

Track Guidance, Soiling, Override:
Henschel: Track guidance was good, and there was no unbearable overriding. The problem of soiling first had to show itself at Berka.

Porsche: When steering, the track lashed out against the armored hull.

This problem had to be checked after the change made at Berka.

The Suspension:
Henschel: Had simple torsion bars, four with a diameter of 58 mm (2.3 in.) and twelve with a diameter of 55 mm (2.2 in.) (369 kg/cm or 298 kg/cm). Compared to the Panther tank, the Tiger had a harder suspension. The internal shock absorbers could not yet be examined. The compressive stress on the Henschel was 3,790 kg (8,355 lbs.) or 3,230 kg (7,121 lbs.).

Porsche: The suspension was even harder (428 kg/cm) and more vulnerable to shellfire than that of the Henschel vehicle. The compressive stress of the Porsche was 4,330 kg (9,546 lbs.).

Both types were vulnerable to mines.

Road Wheels:
Henschel: Rolling resistance was 14,500 kg (31,967 lbs.), and the solid rubber tires were not yet durable. The Continental firm recommended a fatigue loading of 20 kph (12.4 mph); however, after the experiment at Kummersdorf, Wa Prüf 6 regarded 30 kph (18.6 mph)as the duration maximum.

If the solid-rubber tires, bearings, or torsion bars were damaged, disassembly of the running gear was very involved, which was a major drawback. The rubber-saving road wheels for the Henschel Tiger were already in development and were to enable a continuous speed of 40 kph (24.85 mph).

Porsche: Rolling resistance was 16,000 kg (35,274 lbs.), and the durability of the steel tires on the road wheels still had to be checked. It was noticeable that the rim and hub had too-little play.

Idler Wheel Adjustment:
Henschel: This was regarded as suitable.
Porsche: Adjustment was still very labor intensive. The change made still had to be checked on the prototype.

Maximum Speed:
Henschel: 45 kph (28 mph); however, continuous speed was 20 kph (12.4 mph) on account of the Continental solid-rubber tires.

Porsche: 40 kph (24.85 mph) according to company information
35 kph (21.75 mph), on the basis of tests with the first vehicle

The minimum speed of both tanks was about 4 kph (2.5 mph).

Gradeability was specified as 30°.
Both types were capable of greater than 35°.

Climbing Ability was specified as 800 mm (31.5 in.):
The drive and idler wheel average was

Henschel: 792 mm (31.2 in.)
Porsche: 800 mm (31.5 in.)

Armament was to consist of a 75 mm tank gun with eighty rounds of ammunition, or a 105 mm tank gun with forty rounds:
Both types had an 88 mm KwK L/56 with sixty to eighty rounds of ammunition.

Immersion Capability was supposed to be 4 meters.
Henschel: An air pipe was envisaged in the rear. There were still concerns about problems with the sealing of the damper flaps, which were intended to ventilate the engine compartment, two on the left and two on the right. The air duct in the jacket pipe of the exhaust was also seen as problematic, as was the control device for the switch to submersed travel. The coupling of the fan clutch with the damper flaps was unacceptable.
Porsche: Vulnerability to shellfire was greater because of the larger surface area of the two pipes. On the other hand, the possibility of escape by the crew in the event of an accident was advantageous. The sealing of the air duct and the exhaust was still unclear.

Total **Space Usage** (driving and fighting compartments):
Henschel: 10.20 m³ (360 ft.³)
Porsche: 7.40 m³ (261 ft.³)

Available Space:
Henschel: 7.75 m³ (273.7 ft.³)
Porsche: 6.10 m³ (215 ft.³)

Excess Pressure in the fighting compartment:
Henschel: negative pressure
Porsche: 1. Excess pressure, 2. Negative pressure, better protection against gases and chemical agents

Recovery of Wounded:
Henschel: acceptable
Porsche: poor

Armor Shape:
With regard to slope, this was poor on both types of Tiger. The plate thicknesses were equal and sufficient for both tanks.

Maintenance: Interchangeability with other armored vehicles was absent in both.
Henschel: Easier maintenance was possible.
Porsche: Maintenance planning was still missing.

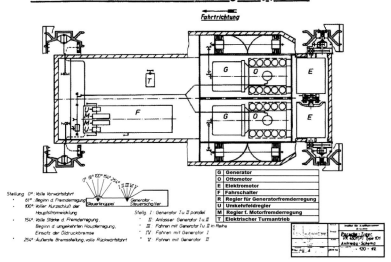

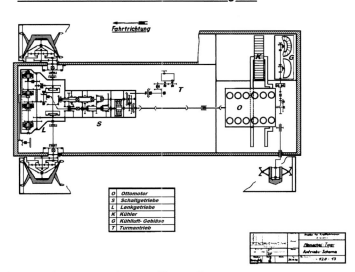

The different drive systems of the two Tigers. *TU*

Noise Generation should if possible be 70 to 80 phon, less if possible:
Henschel: has been classified as normal.
Porsche: From the outside, the blowers and the exhaust were very loud, from inside the tracks.

Oberregierungs-Baurat Röwere (Wa Chef Ing. 4) of the Army Ordnance Office subsequently compared the material and manufacturing requirements of both Tiger types:

Steel and Iron			
Material	VK 4501 H	VK 4501 P	
		with electric drive	with hydraulic drive
Armor material	28,150 kg	30, 360 kg	30,360 kg
Alloyed steel	4,047 kg	9,844 kg	10,766 kg
Nonalloy steel	25,141 kg	17,280 kg	13,913 kg
Gray cast iron	5,802 kg	10,368 kg	11,648 kg
Steel and iron total	63,150 kg	67,852 kg	66,687 kg

Nonferrous Metals			
Copper	21 kg	1,335 kg	40 kg
Copper alloy	72 kg	427 kg	330 kg
Aluminum and aluminum alloy	228+270 kg*	1,186 kg	1,807 kg
Lead	141 kg	115 kg	115 kg
Other	70 kg	66 kg	49 kg
Nonferrous metals total	802 kg	3,129 kg	2,341 kg

* Engine nonferrous metals total.

The statements made in these compilations about the expenditure of material and labor clearly spoke in favor of the Army Ordnance Office vehicle, primarily due to the high use of copper in the electric version of the Porsche Tiger. Why, however, the amount of armored and alloyed steel used in the Porsche vehicle was so high, although its volume was smaller with the same armor thickness, could not be determined.

As previously described, Krupp gave the Army Ordnance Office the estimated material requirements for a hull:

Armor plates:	28,000 kg
Forgings, steel bars, billets, etc. alloyed:	600 kg
Nonalloy steel:	3,000 kg
Total:	approx. 31,600 kg of iron and steel material

The Porsche firm stated a requirement for armor steel for a hull with a raw weight of 26,400 kg (58,202 lbs.) and 18,200 kg (40,124 lbs.) for a complete hull. For the turret, Porsche planned a raw weight of 10,500 kg (23,149 lbs.), and for the finished turret, 6,545 kg (14,429 lbs.). For the turret, there was also the cast-steel armor, with a raw weight of 1,500 kg (3,307 lbs.) and a completed weight of 1,200 kg (2,645 lbs.), plus copper with a raw weight of 55 kg (121 lbs.) and a finished weight of 44 kg (97 lbs.).

The production time for an autogenous-cut VK 4501 (P) hull, including all loose and installed parts, was structured as follows, according to Krupp:

1. Drawings:	50 hours
2. Autogenous cutting:	80 hours
3. Mechanical processing:	220 hours
4. Assembly and metalworking:	360 hours
5. Welding:	600 hours
Total:	**1,310 hours**

Comparison of Production Numbers for the VK 4501 (H) and VK 4501 (P) Chassis (without tracks)

Running No.	Group	VK 4501 H	VK 4501 P		Remarks
			electric	hydraulic	
1	**Armored Hull** With additions and installations (e.g., track shields) a) Hull with associated parts, scope of delivery of steelwork b) Scope of work of the assembly plant	**1,759 hrs.** Henschel **400 hrs.** Henschel	**1,594 hrs.** Krupp **230 hrs.** Nibellg.*	**1,594 hrs.** Krupp **230 hrs.** Nibellg.	
2	**Running Gear** Road wheels with mounting and springing, return rollers and shock absorbers, but without idler and drive wheels	**1,230 hrs.** (1)	**1,100 hrs.** (2) Skoda	**1,100 hrs.** (2) Skoda	1) During the transition of pressed metal wheels, to reduction to about 600 hours 2) During the transition of pressed metal wheels, to reduction to about 750–900 hours
3	**Track Drive and Track Adjustment** Drive wheel with side drive, idler wheel with track adjustment, track brake	**670 hrs.**	**1,000 hrs.** Skoda	**1,000 hrs.** Skoda	
4	**Steering Gear** From the gearbox flange to the side drive including existing intermediate shafts, the actuation linkage, lines, and the steering device, respectively, the corresponding units for the electric or hydraulic drive	**700 hrs.** (1) ZF	**3,100 hrs.** Siemens-Schuckert	**790 hrs.** Voith	1) For new 2 gear, radius steering, reduction to about 400 hours
5	**Manual Gearbox** From the engine flywheel to the drive flange of the gear unit including any intermediate shafts, the operating linkage and the switching devices or the corresponding units for electric or hydraulic drive	**450 hrs.** Maybach		**725 hrs.**	**725 hrs.**
6	**Engine(s)** Without the finished parts not manufactured in the factory, such as carburetor, ignition, starter, etc.	**395 hrs.** (1) Maybach	**700 hrs.** (2) Simmering of Wag.-Fa.	**700 hrs.** (2)	1) Assuming; 2) Time for 2 engines assuming production of 400 engines per month
7	**Cooling System** Including blower and blower drive	**185 hrs.** ?	**120 hrs.** Voith	**200 hrs.** (1) Voith	1) Oil cooling in addition
8	**Fuel and Compressed-Air Systems** Reservoirs and pipes for oil, water, air and exhaust system air extraction	65 hrs.	65 hrs.	65 hrs.	

Running No.	Group	VK 4501 H	VK 4501 P		Remarks
			electric	hydraulic	
9	**Throttle, Starter, and Clutch Linkages** Electrical equipment	**36 hrs.** (1)	**50 hrs.** (2)	**50 hrs.** (2)	(1) 1 engine (2) 2 engines
10	**Other** Seats, racks, ammunition storage, cover, etc.	**160 hrs.**	**155 hrs.**	**155 hrs.**	
11	**Final Assembly**	**550 hrs.**	**340 hrs.**	**340 hrs.**	
	Total: **Plus approx. 50% for turret, gun, weapons**	**6,600 hrs.** **3,500 hrs.**	**8,454 hrs.** **3,500 hrs.**	**6,959 hrs.** **3,500 hrs.**	
	Ratio	1	1.28	1.05	

On November 4, 1942, the Siemens-Schuckert firm was given the opportunity to explain to the committee the advantages of the electric drive. The Siemens representative emphasized the drive's stepless adjustment. He explained that this drive principle was too large and heavy for smaller vehicles, and that an acceptable ratio could be expected from a vehicle weight of 25 metric tons (27.55 tons). A certain additional weight was considered a disadvantage. Space and weight did not increase proportionally. With twice the tank weight, the additional gain was 25%. With the installed drive power of 2 × 310 hp at 2,500 rpm, Siemens hypothesized a weight of 45 metric tons (49.6 tons). The higher weight meant that the maximum tractive force also had to be increased from 42 to 52 metric tons (46.3 to 57.3 tons). Siemens therefore proposed raising the final drive's gear ratio from the then-current 1:15 to 1:18.

This would, however, result in a reduction in cruising speed from 35 to 30 kph (21.75 to 18.6 mph). According to studies, it was possible to increase the performance of combustion engines by increasing the speed, since the generators could produce 430 hp at a speed of 3,600 rpm. Asked about use in the tropics, Siemens indicated a maximum allowable overtemperature of 105°C (221°F) with a continuous load or a continuous current. Electrical efficiency was 82%. The Henschel vehicle's drive, on the other hand, had an efficiency of 90%.

The next day, November 5, the Tiger Committee held another meeting in the Hotel Kaiserhof in Eisenach. This time the development firms Porsche and Henschel (not Wa Prüf 6!) had the opportunity to defend or to explain their products and to respond to the questions submitted in writing the previous day.

The Hotel Kaiserhof in Eisenach

The first to appear before the committee was Xaver Reimspieß as representative of the Porsche firm. He stated the following key design aspects:

1. All units were housed in the engine compartment, separated from the fighting compartment.

2. The rear drive required as a result had fewer disadvantages than was generally assumed.

3. In accordance with the führer's wishes, air-cooled engines developed in-house were used.

4. Two engines were used for safety and design reasons.

5. The turret was positioned far forward, so that machinery could be removed without raising the turret.

6. Installation of a suspension with rocking-lever compensation, which did not require any shock absorbers and was maintenance free.

7. The track shape was made according to specifications from the Army Ordnance Office.

8. Rubber-sparing road wheels were used because of the rubber shortage and expected longer running life.

Reimspieß also explained the anticipated improvements:

1. New, more-powerful engines

2. New blowers with lower power requirements and less noise

3. Sloping of the armored hull. 35° in front and 75° on the sides. This resulted in an increase in ammunition capacity to 60 to 65 rounds of the larger armor-piercing ammunition for the 88 mm L/71 gun.

4. Creation of emergency exits for the driver and radio operator

5. The new blower arrangement resulted in an increase in fuel capacity from the former 520 liters (137.4 gal.) to 820 liters (216.6 gal.), which made possible greater range.

6. Thicker floor and roof armor from the previous 25 mm (0.98 in.) to 40 mm (1.6 in.)

Chief designer Erwin Ader of Henschel was the next to be given the opportunity to explain his design:

1. Construction of the vehicle was carried out according to the task set by the Army Ordnance Office in consistent pursuit of previously proven designs.

2. The choice of an interleaved suspension reduced track wear thanks to its larger road wheels and lower driving resistance. The subsequent weight increase made asymmetrical road wheels necessary. The topic of saving rubber was not topical when design began; however, the transition to rubber-saving road wheels, which was possible in principle, had already been examined.

3. The in-house development of the engine and gearbox was consciously avoided.

4. Henschel also adopted the completely developed brakes from the Argus firm.

5. Despite the difficult arrangement of interior compartments, ninety-two rounds of ammunition for the gun and 4,000 rounds of machine gun ammunition could be accommodated.

6. Since the blower drive was not controllable by means of V belts, the drive consisted of a bevel gear and coupling.

Ader envisaged the following improvements for the Henschel vehicle:

1. For the Henschel Tiger 2, side plates sloped at 83°; for the Henschel Tiger 3 a front plate sloped at 40° and side plates at 65°. As a result, however, just seventy rounds of the larger cartridge ammunition could be accommodated.

2. Use of symmetrical road wheels each with four rubber bands

3. Use of the Panther engine, including cooling system, for the Henschel Tiger

The next step was to respond to the committee's previously written questions: the committee wanted to know the extent to which an increase in speed would be possible with the existing chassis. Ferry Porsche, speaking for the Porsche KG, answered that there was no concern since the running gear was regarded as adequate. Engineer Aders of Henschel, on the other hand, was uncertain if the durability of the solid-rubber tires would allow this. There was still no experience with the rubber-saving road wheels. They wanted to stick with the solid-rubber tires for as long as possible, to keep driving resistance low.

The next question concerned the maximum achievable engine performance: Ferry stated that the engines in the current Berka vehicle were not of the latest version, and each produced 265 hp, since the blowers currently being used required 45 hp. Porsche expected 350 hp from improved engines and a lower power requirement of just 32 hp from the new blowers. Despite this, tropical suitability was guaranteed. However, the engine was not yet fully developed; therefore Porsche was planning to experiment with two Maybach HL 210 engines.

For the Henschel vehicle, Erwin Ader stated that the more powerful Maybach HL 230 engine, producing 750 hp, was planned in place of the HL 210. The two blowers in the tropical version required 55 hp. The necessary experience with the switchable fan clutch was still lacking. The turret fan also had a power requirement of about 2 horsepower.

Oberst Thomale then turned to the subject of fuel requirements. On the state autobahn he expected a range of 250 km (155 mi.) at an average speed of 30 kph (18.6 mph). Both candidates were still a long way from that. He calculated that on the basis of its determined fuel consumption, the Henschel vehicle would require 720 liters (190 gal.) of fuel for the specified range. It had just 570 liters (150.6 gal.) (?) on board; therefore, bottom line, 150 liters (39.6 gal.) were missing. According to his calculations, however, the Porsche vehicle required 1,140 liters (301 gal.) for this distance, of which just 525 liters (139 gal.) were available. Its fuel capacity therefore fell short by 615 liters (162.5 gal.).

This was followed by a statement by Ferry Porsche. He attributed the current high consumption to the poor engine. The current vehicle could accommodate another 200 liters (52.8 gal.) of fuel in addition to the 525 liters (139 gal.), which gave a total of 725 liters (191.5 gal.). In the new Porsche Tiger 2, 820 liters (216.6 gal.) were available, and side tanks next to the crankcases enabled a total of 1,020 liters (269.5 gal.) to be carried. The requested radius of action could thus be achieved, especially since the later engine's (the Porsche Type 101/3's) fuel consumption would drop because of the reduced blower power consumption, improved cylinder heads, and the two-stage carburetors.

Designer Aders, however, expected no reduction in fuel consumption with the Maybach engines being used. He did not think accommodating the shortfall of 150 liters (39.6 gal.) of fuel in the Henschel Tiger was possible, but the requirement might possibly be met in the later Henschel Tiger 2.

Both companies were subsequently asked about their vehicle's diving capabilities. The designers explained their systems on the basis of the schematic drawing from the Institute for Automotive Engineering.

In the discussion that followed, attention was drawn to the increased vulnerability to fire of the large pipes in contrast to buoys. With its two pipes, the Porsche vehicle showed itself to be more vulnerable; on the other hand, there was an escape option for the crew. There were still concerns about the high

air speeds in the Porsche vehicle's pipes, created by the air cooling of its engines.

Director Freyberg of Alkett offered the experience his company had already gained on this topic (planned Operation Sea Lion). Regardless, the participants agreed that the Porsche firm's original submersed-travel solution, supplying the drivetrain by means of an electric cable from a second Porsche Tiger positioned on the other bank, should be tested immediately. Ferry promised to prepare the experiment as quickly as possible so that it could be carried out in early 1943. For its part, the Henschel firm wanted to undertake the preparatory pressure and carbon monoxide measurements for the diving experiments in about ten days.

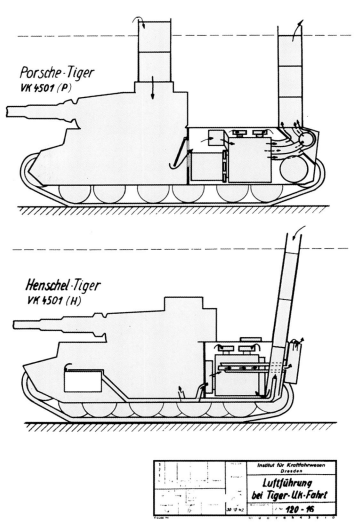

The different air routings for the planned underwater travel. *TU*

The next topic was the subject of dust filtration, which presented a problem in Africa, for example. Aders announced that the additional Feifel cyclone filter would be properly installed on six vehicles by the beginning of the following week.

The Porsche company, on the other hand, was of the opinion that on the basis of its own tests at Naples, the dry filters of the latest design were sufficient. This probably meant the Army Ordnance Office testing in the Balkans in August–September 1941, where a VW Type 87 had achieved very good results with an eddy current filter combined with a felt bellows dry filter. Oberst Esser contradicted and referred to the Verskraft's negative experiences with this type of filtering.

Another question was aimed at an opposite topic; namely, the tanks' cold-weather performance and the countermeasures by both firms. Erwin Ader declared that with use of the Fuchsgerät (literally "flue device," a device that allowed a cold engine to be heated for starting), no starting problems in severe cold were expected. Oberstleutnant Holzhäuer confirmed the maturity of this procedure for other vehicles.

Ferry Porsche did not expect the Porsche vehicle to have any starting problems with the starting fuel used in cold weather. The electric drive was able to fully exploit its advantages, especially in low temperatures. To the question of condensation and the entry of powder snow, the Siemen representative answered that suitable filters were available.

Henschel wanted to ensure the function of the preselector gearbox when it was very cold by means of gas oil additives. Oberst Esser and Professor von Eberan pointed out, however, that not only the starting behavior should be tested, but also the lubricity in the oil load transmission due to the dilution of the oil. A certain heating-up of the steering gear oil could result from the constantly rotating gears after starting the engine.

On the subject of heating, Aders referred to the planned-but-as-yet-untested ventilation of the Henschel Tiger. Porsche had envisaged a 10-horsepower, two-cylinder unit for this. This unit would preheat the engines and charge the batteries. Furthermore, the crew compartment could also be heated electrically. The unit's exhaust and cooling warmth could also be used to heat the engine compartment.

This ended the question round with the designers. The Tiger Committee then proceeded to deliberate. On the subject of fuel consumption, Oberst Esser determined that consumption on the autobahn would diverge further than the test bench values at Kummersdorf. Oberbaurat Röwer asked that values from the current testing at Berka be included in the minutes, to which Oberst Thomale agreed. However, he demanded that in the future, the Henschel vehicle's steering gear and the manual gearbox would have to be capable of being replaced independently of each other.

Chief engineer Aders assured that as of the future Henschel Tiger 2, it would be possible to remove the bevel gear on the manual gearbox without disassembling it. On the topic of solid-rubber tires, he stated that those of the Panther had been much more simply made, and that consideration should be given to adopting these for the Tiger. Oberst Esser pointed out, however, that it was difficult to remove the Panther's solid-rubber tires in a short time. Ministerialrat Baier was of the opinion that the durability of the solid-rubber tires had nothing to do with their design. At the time, these solid-rubber tires were lasting for a distance of just 30 kilometers. Oberst Esser suggested that the rubber-sparing road wheels be included in development for the Henschel Tiger.

Oberstleutnant Post, battalion commander of s.Pz.Abt. 503, criticized the Porsche running gear, because he found it too hard. The amount of noise it generated was too great, especially for radio traffic. Professor von Eberan asked whether mechanical parts of the drive had ever been defective, and if this could be the cause of the noise, and Oberstleutnant Post replied that the answer was no.

Oberst Thomale asked Oberstleutnant Post to comment on experiences with troop trials with the Porsche Tiger. He was largely in agreement with the design but complained about poor accessibility. There were no problems with power transmission. The vehicle's cardinal fault was its engine. Professor von Eberan asked Oberst Thomale how the Henschel vehicle had looked after 300 km (186 mi.). Eberan admitted that the Porsche tank had an immature engine at that time. A decision had to be made as to whether these defects were due to design principles. Oberst Thomale agreed that he was right, that two tanks were being compared, one of which had 300 km (186 mi.) of testing behind it and the other 3,000 km (1,864 mi.). The prerequisites were the same for both: both had the same development time, and both had undergone no factory testing. Both Tigers had come to Kummersdorf for testing after a driving time of about 20 kilometers.

The difference in the number of kilometers traveled by the two tanks was not due to lack of time. In the case of the Henschel vehicle, the defects could be eliminated more quickly than in the case of the Porsche vehicle. Oberregierungs-Baurat Röver added that at the very beginning of production of the Porsche vehicle, the changes were so extensive that production at the Nibelungenwerk factory had slowed or, as at the current time, had to be stopped completely. Director Freyberg of Alkett finally summarized again that in the end, neither vehicle was ready for production.

The meeting in Eisenach continued on November 6. This time the Maybach company was available to answer questions. The first topic was the HL 210 engine's high oil consumption. The loss of engine oil was 2.2 kg/hr. (4.85 lbs./hr.) at a speed of 3,000 rpm. Maybach planned to lower oil consumption to an acceptable 1.5 kg/hr. (3.3 lbs./hr.) with an improved oil control ring. The company continued to work hard to eliminate the problems with the crankshaft bearings. Asked about the blower power requirements, Maybach confirmed the power loss of 48 hp with normal gearing. Blower efficiency could be improved from 30% to 70%. Blower power for the new, larger Maybach HL 230 engine was not significantly greater and was 50 hp at most. The problem of afterflaming of the exhaust gases in the exhaust was still being worked on.

As to the problem with the Olvar gearbox, the Maybach representative expressed himself as follows:

(a) The wear on the brake cone was due to shifting of the second to sixth gears. As a countermeasure, Maybach planned to lock the fifth and sixth gears.

(b) The required interchangeability of the bevel gears still had to be examined by the factory. Oberst Thomale made it a condition that the gearbox was not extended, and only an extractor was needed for this work.

(c) Maybach had no concerns about the oil dilution planned for winter operation, provided the oil dilution was chosen in such a way that at −20°C the viscosity of the oil was equal to that of a temperature of +20 to +30°C. A special winter gear oil was also possible. Oberst Esser had planned related experiments at Kummersdorf, to check the effects of this dilution of the oil on ease of shifting, wear, functioning of the gearbox, and seals. Oberst Thomale attached great importance to the good inter-changeability of the gearbox. A further requirement was that the manual gearbox had no adverse effect on the efficiency of the engine. A good ability to assemble and repair the Olvar gearbox was also important to him.

So much for the discussions by the Tiger Committee in Eisenach on the basis of the surviving documents. Concerning the Maybach HL 210 engine, there was still harsh criticism from elements of the Army Ordnance Office of the manipulation of the test resorts and the stubborn use of these sophisticated gasoline engines. So it was tried hard, including by Kniepkamp, to push the use of available diesel engines, such as the MB 507. However, this page-filling topic is not part of the content of this book. Concerning the demonstration on the testing grounds at Berka—in conclusion to this subject—here is another interesting report by a participant from the MAN company:[60]

After the other tracked vehicles mentioned above were unloaded at the Großbehringen train station on November 8, 1942, these vehicles were inspected by Oberstleutnant Holzhäuer and other officers at the station. There the participants were informed that a first demonstration in the field would take place in the afternoon. The vehicles should be available on the site so that the demonstration could begin at 14:00. Minister Speer, accompanied by General Fichtner, Oberst Thomale, Oberstleutnant Holzhäuer, and other officers, arrived at the site at 15:30. All of the tracked vehicles took part in the driving tests on this day and in some cases drove through the difficult and swampy terrain. The VK 3601 became stuck at an especially difficult place and therefore had to be pulled out.

At about 10:00 the next day, November 9, the inspection by Minister Speer and the other participants was continued. The vehicles drove one after the other to the Mittelberg. The climbing ability of a selected vehicle was to be checked in a deep, muddy trench. The VK 3601 was the first to go. Despite several attempts, it was unable to drive through the above-named trench. It then managed to pass through a less difficult piece of terrain.

Next up were the two Henschel Tigers, which, however, were also unable to drive through the difficult section. They were followed by the two Porsche Tigers. These succeeded in crossing the difficult section, albeit with their turrets turned to face the rear. Meanwhile, the ground had become very chewed up by the time the MAN Panthers began their drive. But despite this, both MAN Panthers unhesitatingly drove through this section. The next vehicle in line was the Daimler-Benz company's Panther. Despite repeated attempts, it failed to get through the problematic section and subsequently had to be towed out. During this attempt, the Daimler Panther had sustained damage to its power transmission system. It drove about two more kilometers over undisturbed ground before the vehicle finally completely broke down. As a result of this defect, it was unable to take part in any of the remaining driving tests.

Minister Speer asked that the two MAN Panthers should again drive through this section. But the ground was so torn up because of the recovery efforts that the two vehicles were unsuccessful in crossing this difficult area. The two Panthers tried it at another spot and then overcame the slope to the left and right of the torn-up section of terrain.

The two Porsche Tigers, which likewise made another attempt, were also unable to cross this terrain. After the chewed-up muddy trench, the drive proceeded over a likewise very muddy forest road and a grassy area. From then on, Panther number two had to dispense with further driving tests that day, since an engine problem forced it to return to base. Speer next took the controls of the VK 3601 himself. All of the remaining vehicles subsequently had to form up on the open field in front of Mittelberg. There followed a speed comparison over a small rise. Speer in his turretless VK 3601 drove about 10 meters in front of the MAN Panther. All of the other vehicles were about 50 meters (164 ft.) behind. The second Panther also broke down due to a blower failure and finally had to be towed back by a Porsche Tiger.

On November 11, the vehicles were inspected by selected frontline officers. The tanks were driven back up to the Mittelberg and lined up there. On this day, however, none of the subjects managed to drive through the problematic section from the previous day. The VK 3601, this time being driven by Oberst Thomale, broke down during this attempt. Since the resulting damage could not be repaired on the spot, the vehicle could not be used for further driving tests. The next invited industry representatives were given the opportunity for a demonstration the following day. And again all vehicles failed on the drive to the Mittelberg because of the mud sink that was the "church ditch." Both Henschel Tigers then had to look for a less demanding route. The two Porsche Tigers also got stuck and had to be pulled out again. Then they went back to the starting point, which was in the Verskraft grounds.

On the last day, November 13, the vehicles were demonstrated to maintenance officers. The drive took the vehicles up to the familiar hill again in the direction of Mittelberg. However, no attempt was made to pass through the problem

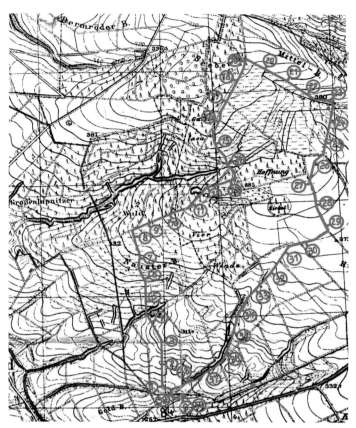

This is how Oberst Esser planned the circuit. Start and finish was the object of the Verskraft. The vehicles were to line up again at the level of the Mittelberg.

The VK 3601 with Minister Speer at the wheel, and sitting to his right is Professor Porsche. This problematic depression on the Mittelberg was fed by the "church ditch," which made the shell limestone soil greasy. *BPK*

section again. Since a more favorable position was taken, all of the vehicles still taking part were able to cross the "church ditch." There was no prescribed order on the way back to base, As a result, the MAN Panther drove away from the other vehicles, which arrived ten minutes later. And at the end there were one Henschel and one Porsche Tiger, two Panzer IIIs, and one Panzer II left. All of the other tanks had broken down.

So much for this detailed report. Speer personally took the wheel of these tanks, and it has to be noted that he had made a habit of driving the test candidates himself. He did so probably as much for fun as anything else. How else can it be explained that Speer drove around in the VK 3601, the forerunner of the VK 4501 (H), at a time when the two Tigers were already being put through their paces. Ferry Porsche later complained that Speer often used a so-called test bed: "It was a tank without a turret. We called this vehicle the

In the background are two Henschel Tigers. The Tiger in the foreground is the Kummersdorf vehicle 250 001, recognizable by its license plate. The Tiger (H 1) behind it is still carrying the turret replacement weight. *Kobierowski*[51]

The Porsche Tiger with chassis 150 014 and turret 150 014 was subsequently loaded for transport to Kummersdorf. In the background is a Panzer III with narrow tracks. It is either the vehicle with interleaved road wheels or with rubber-saving road wheels. *SB*

The Henschel Tiger 250 001 with the Kummersdorf license plate WH 013896 next to the Panzer III, with wide Ost-Kette (east track), on its way up to the Mittelberg. *BSB*

'sports car,' because of course without the tremendous weight of the turret with its heavy armored cupola and gun, it could be driven almost like a sports car off-road. Speer obviously enjoyed driving the test bed off-road, while he didn't even bother to test-drive the Porsche Tiger a single time."[62] That wasn't entirely true, however, since, as can be seen in the photos taken on August 27, Speer drove the Porsche Tiger at the Nibelungenwerk. Ferry was probably unaware of this, since it can be proven that he was not at the factory at that time.

A letter by Fritz Holzhäuer, which the latter wrote after the war, creates further confusion regarding what happened at Berka. In it, Holzhäuer wrote that with the best will in the world, he couldn't remember a tank demonstration at Berka on November 2, 1942. He says he definitely wasn't in Berka at that time. He would also never have seen the Porsche Tiger and would know it only from the files. This couldn't actually be true, since his predecessor, General Fichtner, had to bring the Tiger development to a close, but, according to Oberst Esser, Holzhäuer had already taken over all the dealings of an office manager of Wa Prüf 6 by October 1, 1942. The list of participants also proved something else. Therefore, Holzhäuer's statement cannot be assessed.

There is another report on this event, from the estate of one Robert Pertuss, who was then employed by Henschel as an engineer taking part in development of the Tiger H. This report, which can be read in the book *Tiger im Kampf III*,[63] gives a subjective picture of the comparative trials at Berka, which will be reproduced verbatim for the sake of completeness: "Professor Porsche had—as always—proceeded based on himself and his connections to Hitler and was so self-opinionated that he believed that he could do without contact with the head office experts. The result was then shown at Berka. During the test drive on the autobahn to Eisenach [the mentioned date of October 26, 1942, was incorrect], Porsche accelerated [Professor Porsche could not have been present for the autobahn drive, since he did not arrive at Berka until November 6, and that day the test subjects drove the off-road circuit] and, driving as fast as he could go, disappeared on the horizon. I myself was sitting on the Henschel Tiger, and I was urgently advised by Herr Knie[p]kamp, who explained that the autobahn was the worst thing for tracks, and that,

under all circumstances, only "driving slowly" would bring the prospect of making it through. [This comment raises the question as to whether this was a fair comparison between the two vehicles, if one of them drove extra slowly to protect its technology]. We—I as yet had no experience in this area—therefore drove slowly, sweating with excitement, left behind by all the other conference participants, who drove away in a considerable wave of automobiles to catch up to Porsche. When he saw no more of us, Herr von Heydekampf stayed behind and energetically urged me to finally show that we could at least keep up. I was thinking that Heydekampf and I were pulling in the same direction. We wanted to win, but as automobile builders neither of us knew anything about tracked vehicles, and therefore Knie[p]kamp was probably right. I therefore continued driving slowly. Heydekamp was furious and drove ahead to the Porsche vehicle.

So we drove on alone, left behind by everyone but Knie[p]kamp, until the Wartburg appeared on the horizon and a pillar of smoke became visible in front of us. By now I was soft-boiled. Then when we drove over a hill, which had previously blocked our view, the Porsche tank suddenly appeared on the autobahn. It was burning and was surrounded by a good fifty officers and other participants in this show. Knie[p]kamp looked up at me from his automobile and grinned. They made room for us and we drove on alone, back on the opposite lane and always with spectators in our wake. For the last few kilometers before the exit, Knie[p]kamp, waving and laughing, turned us loose and we shifted into eighth gear and showed what we could do.

The next day we had difficulty in the off-road area. Heavy rain had softened the loamy soil and showed us where the limits of our specific ground pressure of about 1 kg per cm^2 lay. But the participants were knowledgeable tank men and just laughed. They knew how to handle such ground. Then in the afternoon [of October 31; Ferry did not arrive until November 3] there was a final meeting of all participants, led by Oberst Thomale. Herr Professor Porsche was no longer present. His son spoke and explained in detail the merits of his father's design. Herr Dr. von Heydekampf was then asked to finally comment on the Henschel design. But he deferred to me, who after this sort of request from Thomale had no choice but, though unprepared, to say something, that the vehicle could be built, that it could drive and could shoot, and that it cost money; how much, no one knew at that moment. More I did not know. It seemed to suffice, for everyone laughed, and I sat back down again. That was practically the end of the investigation. While we were still sitting at the table, Oberst Thomale had gone to the telephone in the next room, from where he was then called by Heydekampf. The latter came back, red faced, and then told me that he had just spoken briefly with Hitler and that the decision had been made in our favor."

This report has the appearance of an abbreviated summary of the fourteen-day event at Berka. The reason for this is probably the interval between when the report was written and the events, which caused details to become blurred.

In his diary, Karl Otto Saur wrote that the Tank Committee met on the Wartburg near Eisenach on November 8, 1942, and that the decision on the planned successor, the Tiger (P 2), was made on November 9. Another meeting took place on November 10, on the Wartburg. This corresponds exactly to the contents of Karl Rabe's diary. The following brief entries about the events at Berka are found there:

03/11/42, Tuesday: Ferry (Porsche) goes early to Berka.

06/11/42, Friday: Prof. P. (Porsche) is in Berka. Georg Rupprecht traveled to Berka to meet Prof. P. and took with him two models (type 205) from the Klein firm in Esslingen.

07/11/42, Saturday: Prof. P. is in Berka.

10/11/42, Tuesday: Ferry returned from Berka with Martin at 16:00; the test drives there went well on the whole.

11/11/42, Wednesday: Prof. P. arrived from Eisenach at 12:00 and explained the Tank Committee's decisions of yesterday:

> Type 101 has been halted. Further vehicles are to be built as assault guns: Type 131.
>
> Type 180, three vehicles with turret in rear, no production until after demonstration.
>
> Type 205 will be changed, turret moved to rear[64]

This means that work on the Porsche Tiger 1 was stopped definitively. The Porsche KG subsequently concentrated on the Porsche types 131, 180, and 205, which was understandable since the Type 101 was long out of date in terms of design. In a long-distance call with Ministerialrat Baier and Oberst von Wilke on December 8, 1942, it was determined that in addition to the chassis for the ninety assault guns to be produced from the first series of Tiger (P 1), Wa Prüf 6 required the following vehicles:

(a) a complete Type 101, electrically powered with the air-cooled Porsche engines. This was the former Berka vehicle (150 014), which at that time was at Kummersdorf. This piece of equipment was assigned to the department Wa Prüf 6/III.

(b) Two vehicles with Porsche engines, meaning the complete Type 101. Specifically, it concerned the two vehicles that were still on their way to schwere Panzerabteilung 503 for gunnery exercises. One vehicle was allocated to Wa Prüf 6/II; the other went to Wa Prüf 6/II b.

(c) Three electric chassis, but with Maybach HL 120 TRM (Type 130) liquid-cooled engines, and the hydraulic chassis of the Type 102 (150 013) with Porsche engines and a hydraulic reserve system. Wa Prüf 6/III received this vehicle.

(d) A complete vehicle (electric or hydraulic) for gunnery experiments for the Wa Prüf 6/II group (probably 150 015 from Berka).

(e) Two tank hulls with the additional strengthening for ballistics tests by the Wa Prüf 6/II b group.

This total of ten vehicles were the tanks from the prototype series. The ninety remaining Porsche Type 101 tank hulls were renumbered after conversion into Type 131 88 mm assault guns or tank destroyers.

At the end of 1942 a request from Hitler resulted in the design of a so-called Ram Tiger. Impressed by the fierce in the built-up areas of Stalingrad, Hitler was seeking a tank capable of knocking down houses. This maneuver posed a great risk to a tank like the one in the picture below, since debris could plug the engine-cooling system and the superstructures might also be affected. Likewise, the forward track wheels could be damaged when they struck the wall. The possibility of becoming stuck in debris also had to be considered.

Therefore, on January 1, 1943, Professor Porsche designed a sort of "ram hood" for the armored chassis of the Type 101.

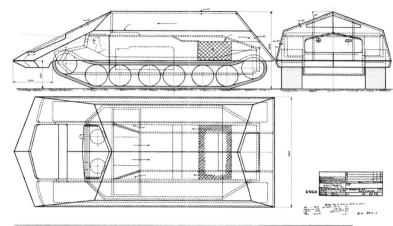

Based on the 59-metric-ton (65-ton) tank, after removing 11 metric tons (12.1 tons) for the turret and 1.33 metric tons (1.5 tons) for equipment, the chassis had a total weight of 46.67 metric tons (51.44 tons). The armored hood, which was between 30 and 50 mm thick (1.18 to 1.97 in.), caused the vehicle's weight to rise to 60.47 metric tons (66.7 tons) but remained within the set framework of 61 metric tons (67.2 tons). On January 5, 1943, Hitler inspected a model of this curious vehicle, without making a decision to convert three Porsche chassis. The armaments industry had other problems to solve, and Stalingrad was history.

On the occasion of an armament conference on January 3, 1943, Hitler demanded the calculation of the theoretical weight of the Porsche Tiger and its speed, if this were brought to the armor strength of the Maus in all areas. Also envisaged was an armament of one 88 mm tank gun with a length of L/100.

Obviously, this would require the design of a new running gear. Hitler requested this review again on January 18. This time only the frontal armor was to equal that of the Maus (200 mm). The side armor was to be 100 mm (3.94 in.) in thickness, and the roof and floor armor were to be reduced accordingly. Armament options were to be an 88 mm KwK L/100 or 88 mm KwK L/71. Hitler believed that much time would pass before the Maus finally entered service, and that until then, an interim solution of a superheavy but slow Tiger had to be found.[65]

The Porsche Tiger Rammhaube existed only as a model. *PA*

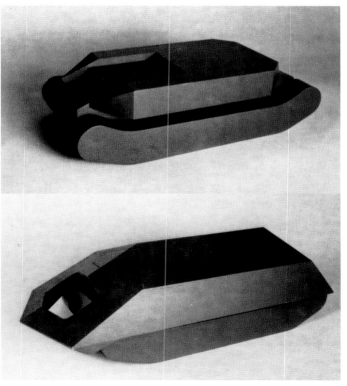

A really superfluous demonstration of a Porsche Tiger breaking through a wall. The photo was probably taken at Berka vor dem Hainich in one of the many deserted towns. *PA*

The wooden model of the Porsche Tiger Rammhaube. *PA*

On January 15, 1943, a meeting was held between Wa Prüf 6 and AK Krupp. The topic was the Tiger I turrets that had been ordered. For uniformity of execution, Krupp asked that a prototype H 1 turret be provided by the Wegmann company. This company was responsible for manufacturing the Henschel turret. Furthermore, Wa Prüf 6 determined that of the one hundred Tiger P 1 turrets, just ninety-two were to be converted into the H 1 model. The eight missing turrets consisted of the seven turrets of low design, which were not needed for the project, and the single command turret no. 150 014, which was being used for trials at Kummersdorf. Of the ninety-two turrets, Krupp was ultimately to convert just forty Porsche 1 turrets, with the remaining individual parts to be delivered to Wegmann. The ninety-two turrets retained the previous commander's cupola with the glass blocks. Regardless of this delivery, Krupp had to deliver a batch of 230 version H 1 armored casings with the new prism cupolas developed for the Porsche Tiger 2.

In the end, the only Porsche Tiger of the first series left was the hydraulic variant, the Type 102, with the hull number 150 013 and the turret replacement weight. At the end of August 1943, the vehicle was still at Kummersdorf, where it was being used for towing and recovery experiments in combination with a towing triangle. An additional towing lug was fitted at Kummersdorf, similar to that of the Ferdinand. Towing experiments were carried out with the assault gun, also referred to as the Ferdinand tank destroyer or, at that time, number 150 011, which was still located at Kummersdorf.

On March 1, 1944, in addition to the two Ferdinand tank destroyers at Kummersdorf (chassis nos. 150 010 and 150 011), schwere Panzerjäger-Regiment also requested the Porsche Type 102 hydraulic tank chassis for use as a recovery vehicle.

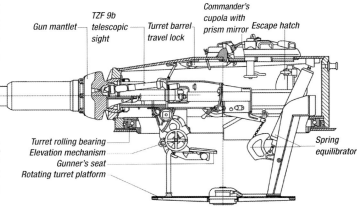

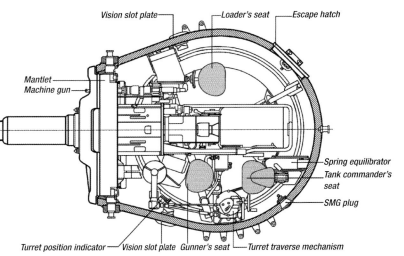

The improved Tiger turret with new commander's cupola. *D 656*

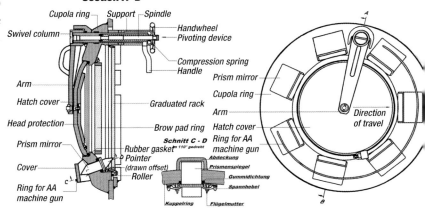

The new cupola with prism periscopes for the Tiger (H 1) turret. It was based on the cupola of the Porsche 2 turret. *D 656*

Towing experiment by a Ferdinand tank destroyer (P) with Porsche Tiger 150 013 at the Kummersdorf artillery range. *SB*

At a meeting of the Tank Committee on January 26, 1943, Porsche proposed the use of the Porsche Tiger with the hydraulic Voith drive as a tank recovery vehicle; however, this was rejected in favor of the Berge-Panther. But instead of being used as a turretless recovery vehicle, in 1944 the last hydraulic chassis at Kummersdorf was fitted with the Porsche turret with the number 150 014, which was in storage there. This turret had the emergency escape hatch in its right rear. As well, unlike the basic version, it had an opening for a scissors telescope in the hatch cover in the commander's cupola, and behind this cupola there was a basket for signal ammunition. Unlike that of the production version, the cupola hatch cover was hinged at the rear.

The two upper front plates were reinforced analogous to those of the assault gun, and the planned deflector strips were welded onto the front and sides of the hull roof. Unlike the basic type, two driver's optics were installed above the driver's position, similar to those of the heavy tank destroyer. The smoke grenade launchers on the left and right of the turret were left off, on account of the negative experiences encountered to date. Enemy fire had often caused the grenades to ignite, blinding the crew. The engine covers that were present and the structure over the hydraulic gearbox allow the reasonable presumption that, contrary to claims made in the literature, the vehicle still had the two Simmering air-cooled engines.

The liquid-cooled Maybach HL 120 engines would have required a modified engine ventilation system. So, at the end of May 1944, "schwere Panzerjägerbteilung 653 was supplied for its use a Porsche Tiger VK 4501 (88 mm KwK L/56) with hydraulic power transmission."[66] Having been removed, the turret replacement weight remained behind at the Verskraft in Kummersdorf (see chapter 8).

Interestingly, the battalion commander's command vehicle had two 2-meter mast antennas, which could give rise to speculation, since the right VHF antenna was envisaged as normal equipment for the Fu 2 and Fu 5 SE 10U sets (a 10-watt transmitter and two VHF receivers)—standard in German

The command vehicle with the tactical number 003 had an opening in the cupola hatch cover for a scissors telescope. This enabled the commander to observe the battlefield through the closed hatch cover. It was attached to the cupola ring and could thus be rotated 360°. The hatch hinge was attached behind the cupola. Behind the cupola was a basket for smoke signal cartridges. *SM*

It was conspicuous that the towing lug in the center of the rear plate was changed again, compared to the photo taken at Kummersdorf. Note the unchanged original gratings and the *Zimmerit* coating. *M*

tanks. Now, as a command vehicle, the vehicle required the second antenna on the turret roof, since the additional radio equipment as per service regulation D 9023/1 was to be located in the right front of the turret.

For this, the opening for the turret machine gun had to be closed, just like the viewing window of the loader or second radio operator, which did not happen on turret 150 014. In a command Tiger, this space in the turret was occupied by the standard Fu 5 VHF radio set. The first radio operator, located at right front, was provided either with a Fu 7 VHF radio set, which was intended for communication with supporting aircraft, or, as was more often the case, the Fu 8 medium-wave transceiver for communication with higher-level staffs.

Instead of the 2-meter VHF antenna, these vehicles had the corresponding antennas in the right rear. Externally, this radio suite was identifiable by the Sternantenne D star antenna with a length of 1.8 meters, while the Fu 7 air-ground radio, because of its different frequency, had a 1.4-meter-long (4.6 ft.) mast antenna. The reason for the second 2-meter VHF antenna can only be guessed at. A conceivable use would be

Visible in this photo are the smoke signal cartridge basket and the opening for the scissors telescope in the cupola hatch cover. *SM*

Apart from that, this vehicle had all of the final changes in this series. *M*

an additional Fu 2 VHF receiver in the tub under the commander's seat. As a rule, only command vehicles of assault gun units had two 2-meter VHF antennas, since their radio frequency differed from that of the tank units. The variant as a reconnectable spare antenna, like that envisaged for the Maus tank, could also be eliminated, since both antennas were on the rear hull and thus would be moved less frequently by the gun barrel when the turret rotated.

This last Porsche Tiger was lost by Army Group North Ukraine after the Red Army's great offensive at the end of July 1944 and burned out. On July 26, 1944, Krupp asked the Army Ordnance Office what it should do with the six completed "Ausführung A," or low design, turrets stored at the factory. Due to the acute space problems, a quick decision had to be made. Since the turrets had no interior fittings and were also without pivot bearings, the Army Ordnance Office's department responsible for fortifications also had no interest in the turrets, and so in August 1944 the OKH approved the scrapping of the six low turrets. However (as the photo below shows), events prevented this from happening. One can only speculate as to what happened to the seventh turret. Perhaps this turret, like the two missing Porsche chassis, ended up being used as a hard target on the gunnery range.

Not all of the shells were scrapped, as this photo taken in 1945 shows. It shows a low-type turret shell and three low turret walls stacked atop a turret shell of the Maus tank. *PA*

The trigger for this new development was Hitler's persistent urging for the installation of the more powerful 88 mm Flak 41 in the Tiger tank. There were many designations for this project, which ranged from "VK 4501 verstärkt" (enhanced VK 4501) through "second series VK 4501 (P)" and "VK 4501 (P 2)," to "VK 4502 (P)." Ultimately, it was named Porsche Tiger 2 or Tiger 2. At Porsche the vehicle had the internal designations "Special Vehicle III" and "Porsche Type 180" or "181." The latter designation applied to both the chassis and turret.

On July 23, 1941, Oberst Fichtner declared to Professor Porsche that he was not happy with the Krupp turret of the VK 4501 and was seeking a better solution for later. However, as a result of Hitler's demand for heavier frontal armor of 150 mm (5.9 in.) and side armor of 80 mm (3.15 in.), plus the necessity of a greater turret ring diameter, a heavier chassis also had to be created that met these requirements. The planned second series of 100 VK 4501 (P) seemed an obvious choice. The Soviet T-34, which as we know Professor Porsche became familiar with in November 1941, had a major influence on the shape of the vehicle.

Two documents exist, both dated January 23, 1942. The first deals with the delivery of the second series of Tiger turrets. It unrealistically requests delivery of the welded turrets by the sheet metal press shop to the 2nd Mechanical Workshop by mid-June 1942. In the second document, Krupp orders a hundred each of the no. 5c tank boxes (turret junction boxes for 12-volt systems and intercom), no. 21 (intercom,

The powerful 88 mm Flak 41 on the Type 202 special trailer. The gun barrel was withdrawn onto the cradle for transport. *SL*

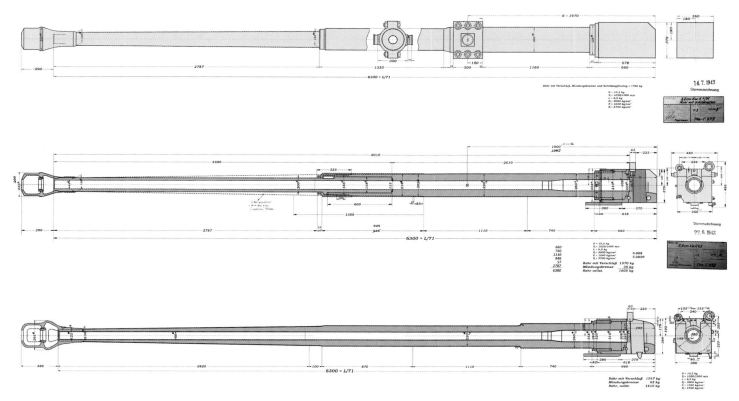

Above, the later two-piece 88 mm KwK L/71 with small muzzle brake; *below*, the monobloc barrel with larger muzzle brake

commander), and no. 22 (intercom, gunner) for the radio and intercom systems. As a result, the order to manufacture these turrets was already in place in 1941.

As previously described, on January 18, 1942, Hitler requested a review to determine the weight of the Porsche Tiger with the frontal armor thickness of the Mäuschen (little mouse) and 100 mm (3.94 in.) side armor, since much time was going to pass until completion of the Maus. The tank was to be armed with the 88 mm L/100 or L/71 gun. The review showed an unacceptable weight increase, for which the existing chassis would not have been adequate. As well, the 88 mm L/100 gun not only would have been clumsy in action but would also have been susceptible to vibration and sagging of the barrel. Even with the shorter 88 mm KwK L/71 with its 5.6-meter-long (18.37 ft.) freestanding barrel, later measurements revealed 3.5–5.5 millimeters (0.14–0.22 in.) of sag at the muzzle when the vehicle was moving.[67] Of course, this was at the expense of accuracy. Therefore, later the 88 mm KwK L/71 never matched the accuracy of the 88 mm KwK L/56.

As previously mentioned in the chapter on the Type 101, on January 27 and 28, 1942, a meeting took place between the Porsche company and representatives of Krupp and Daimler-Benz. As Porsche KG's representative, Reimspieß informed those present that in the future, the Porsche Type 101's front plate was to be sloped from 45° to 30°. As well, a new driver's visor was to be installed, analogous to the Soviet T-34 tank, which as it was known also had no hatches for the driver and radio operator in the hull roof. The driver's visor was to be large enough that it could also serve as an escape hatch. The Type 101's great disadvantage, the lack of a forward exit, was to be remedied, at least for the driver. For the radio operator, an emergency escape hatch in the floor was in the planning. The suggested dimensions of the free opening for the driver's hatch were 450 × 350 mm (17.7 × 13.8 in.). Daimler-Benz then presented a series of designs for driver's visors. These included designs for periscopes in the hatch cover and a block visor. Daimler-Benz also assured a design for a ball mount for 30° of deflection.

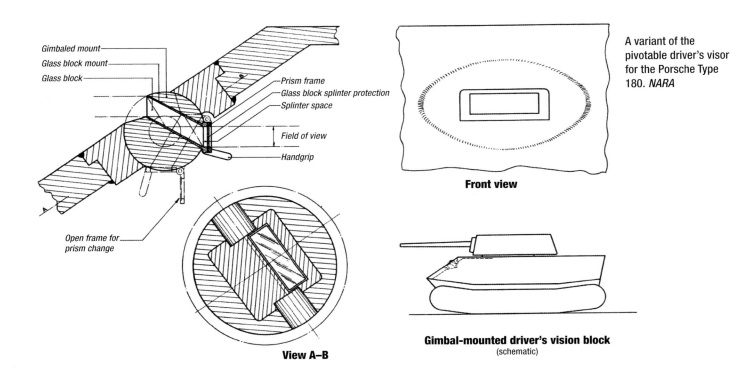

Gimbaled mount
Glass block mount
Glass block
Prism frame
Glass block splinter protection
Splinter space
Field of view
Handgrip
Open frame for prism change

View A–B

Front view

Gimbal-mounted driver's vision block
(schematic)

A variant of the pivotable driver's visor for the Porsche Type 180. *NARA*

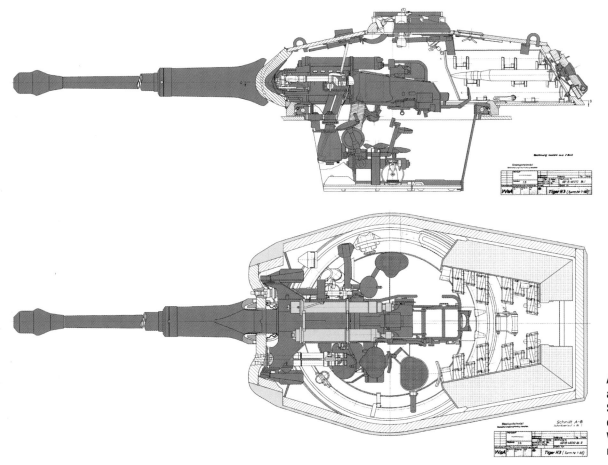

A Porsche 2 turret, also referred to as reinforced, weighed 12,500 kg. Shown here, however, is the converted version for the Henschel VK 4503 with hydraulic traverse mechanism.

Krupp's first task was to produce a hull for ballistics tests, with extensive use of autogenous cutting, incorporating this new front-plate slope. The new driver's visor and associated ball mount were also to be fitted. Krupp was to receive the new drawings in good time. However, the Krupp company did not see itself in the position to carry out these fundamental changes on the first 100 Type 101 hulls, which were already in production. Because time was pressing, materials for the next hulls, 150 101 to 150 150, had already been ordered.

Therefore, a decision had to be made by February 7, 1942, and the corresponding drawings had to be available to Krupp by February 11. Furthermore, the hulls were to be made with extensive use of autogenous cutting. The Porsche company asked Krupp to take over the design work for the new hulls[68] based on the Porsche design. Porsche sent the necessary drawings of the superstructure with the front plate sloped 30° to Krupp on February 2.

In return, Krupp sent a telegram to the Porsche KG on the same day with the material requirements in homogeneous armor plates for the new shape with 30° sloped front plate. Among other things, the planned front plate now consisted of just one "plate-under 1,960 × 900 × 80" (old) and the "front plate 3,100 × 1,500 × 140" (new). The front wall plates 105 and 109, the sidewalls 121 and 122, and the roof walls 139 and 140 were dropped without replacement. The effort to improve the unfavorable shape of the Type 101 vehicle was clearly there.

Two different vehicle layout designs were created, differing mainly in turret arrangement. Version A had a rotating turret in the front and the complete drive system in the rear, while on Version B the turret was placed in the rear and the engine-generator unit between the driver and the fighting compartment. In this version the electric motors were beneath the fighting compartment. This breakdown was similar to that of the later Porsche Type 131, the Ferdinand tank destroyer. The vulnerable driver's visor was no longer needed for this version, since the hatches for the driver and radio operator fit in the hull roof.

At the Porsche company, this VK 4502 (P) project ran as the Type 180 A with the Type 101/3 engine, and the Porsche Type 180 B with the Type 101/4 engine. The hydraulic variant of the vehicle, which was again part of the plan, bore the designation Porsche Type 181 A with the Type 101/4 engine. The Porsche Type 181 B was to have one or two Deutz engines

	Device 18/36	Device 41
Barrel length	L/56	L/71
Barrel protrusion over front of vehicle	2,500 mm	3,820 mm
Barrel weight	1,465 kg	1,900 kg
Shell weight	15 kg	23 kg
Shell length	930 mm	1,200 mm
Shell diameter	112 mm	147 mm
Turret weight, including weapon	9.7 t	13.5 t
Servicing diameter	1,820 mm	2,100 mm
Outer diameter	2,320 mm	2,600 mm
Brake pressure	7 t	10 t
Muzzle brake effect	35%	60%
Rate of fire	±12 shots/min.	±8 shots/min.

Comparison of the main characteristics of the 45-metric-ton tank armed with the 88 mm KwK L/56 and the 88 mm KwK L/71, dated December 1942.

on a trial basis. Concrete work under the type designation 180 began in early 1942. In principle, therefore, the Porsche Type 101 project was obsolescent even before its first test drive. The gross weight of the new Porsche Type 180 was 64 metric tons (70.5 tons), with an overall length of 8,345 mm (328.5 in.), an overall width of 3,400 mm (133.85 in.) and a height of 2,740 mm (107.9 in.). The turning circle was put at 2.15 m (7.05 ft.). The circular cutout in the hull roof for the turret ring was to be 2,400 mm (94.5 in.), and its thickness was to be increased from 40 to 45 mm (1.6 to 1.77 in.). Krupp strengthened the all-around protective strips on the hull roof, which were designed to shield the turret from hits between the turret and hull roof and prevent turret jamming when under fire, from 25 to 40 mm (0.98 to 1.57 in.). Fuel capacity was increased to 640 liters (169 gal.).

On February 7, 1942, the Krupp company received the official "war order" for the building of one hundred armored hulls and one hundred armored turrets for the VK 4501 (P 2). The delivery schedule for the hulls demanded eight for August 1942. Fifteen hulls per month were to follow from

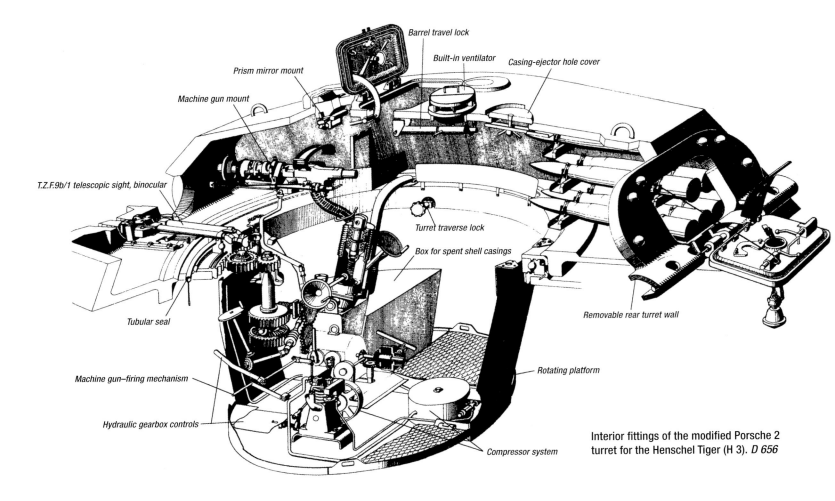

Barrel travel lock

Built-in ventilator   Casing-ejector hole cover

Prism mirror mount

Machine gun mount

T.Z.F.9b/1 telescopic sight, binocular

Turret traverse lock

Box for spent shell casings

Removable rear turret wall

Tubular seal

Rotating platform

Machine gun–firing mechanism

Hydraulic gearbox controls

Interior fittings of the modified Porsche 2 turret for the Henschel Tiger (H 3). *D 656*

Compressor system

September onward. Turret production initially foresaw six examples for November and fifteen per month from December 1942 onward. These components were to be delivered to the Nibelungenwerk. The one hundred turrets were to be completely assembled by Krupp.

On March 3, Krupp sent a reminder that the delivery dates for fifty rolling bearings for the turret traverse had to be ordered from the Kugelfischer company as quickly as possible, if assembly of the second series was to begin on time. On March 23 and 24, 1942, the Krupp officials met with Professor Porsche and Ferry Porsche at Zuffenhausen for discussions. In addition to the Type 101, which was in production, they also discussed the Type 180, especially the first hulls with the numbers 150 101 to 150 165. A larger cutout 500 mm (19.7 in.) in diameter was decided on for the driver's visor. It was located 570 mm (22.4 in.) from the center of the vehicle and 400 mm (15.75 in.) from the upper edge of the front plate. Krupp agreed to manufacture the complete hatch and the connections to the ball mount itself. Krupp wanted to extend the upper side plates, with their upper edges over

the top edge of the roof, as far as the already rolled plates made it possible. Strips made of nontempered material were sufficient for covering the roof.

The drill holes for the running gear and the idler and drive wheels were exactly the same as those in the hull of the VK 4501 (P). Single trunnions were to be attached to the rear wall of the hull, left and right. Furthermore, there were to be no openings for the exhausts in the hull walls. At that time, the engine compartment was unchanged from that of the VK 4501 (P). The hull bottom also remained the same, with the single difference that the opening for the spent casing chute was eliminated. The fuel tank filler openings were likewise not to pass through the hull but instead were to be covered by separate caps. The same was planned for attachment of the antenna. Only the openings for the cables for the left and right headlamps and the taillight had yet to be determined.

Due to the lack of time, the individual drawings of the hull produced by Krupp were approved by Porsche without examination. The dates were the minimum to keep up with the delivery of the Type 101. Following the fifteen hulls already

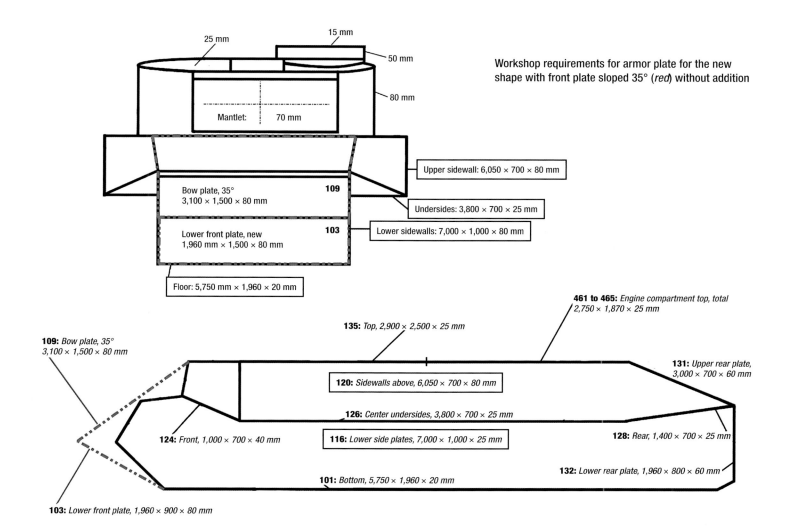

25 mm
15 mm
50 mm
80 mm
Mantlet: 70 mm

Workshop requirements for armor plate for the new shape with front plate sloped 35° (*red*) without addition

Upper sidewall: 6,050 × 700 × 80 mm

Bow plate, 35°
3,100 × 1,500 × 80 mm
109

Undersides: 3,800 × 700 × 25 mm

Lower front plate, new
1,960 mm × 1,500 × 80 mm
103

Lower sidewalls: 7,000 × 1,000 × 80 mm

Floor: 5,750 mm × 1,960 × 20 mm

461 to 465: *Engine compartment top, total 2,750 × 1,870 × 25 mm*

135: *Top, 2,900 × 2,500 × 25 mm*

109: *Bow plate, 35° 3,100 × 1,500 × 80 mm*

131: *Upper rear plate, 3,000 × 700 × 60 mm*

120: *Sidewalls above, 6,050 × 700 × 80 mm*

126: *Center undersides, 3,800 × 700 × 25 mm*

124: *Front, 1,000 × 700 × 40 mm*

116: *Lower side plates, 7,000 × 1,000 × 25 mm*

128: *Rear, 1,400 × 700 × 25 mm*

132: *Lower rear plate, 1,960 × 800 × 60 mm*

101: *Bottom, 5,750 × 1,960 × 20 mm*

103: *Lower front plate, 1,960 × 900 × 80 mm*

ordered, a further forty-five hulls were to be immediately laid down. The next day it was agreed that the slope of the front plate would have to be 35° with a projecting upper edge, instead of the 30° originally planned.

An exit hatch with driver's visor and ball mount were envisaged in the front plate for at least the first fifteen hulls. For the ballistics test, Krupp planned to adopt a front wall with bow section. A reinforcement of homogeneous armor steel was to be welded over the upper and lower bow plate joint. Furthermore, armor thickness of the forward part of the hull bottom was to be doubled to 20 mm (0.79 in.). To also be able to meet the turret production deadlines, Krupp asked the Army Ordnance Office to order fifteen sets per month, consisting of the complete gun, the fixed machine gun, the optics, etc., as of August 1, 1942. The provision of fifteen flexible machine guns was to follow, starting on August 20, and fifteen antiaircraft machine guns from September 1, 1942. The Army Ordnance Office regarded providing the machine guns as unnecessary, since this was a task for the Army Ordnance Depot.

Further meetings concerning this new tank project followed at Krupp on April 19, 1942, and in Stuttgart on April 21. The affected Krupp officials met to internally finalize the turret deadlines on April 24. The target dates for the production start for the VK 4502 (P) series, following the VK 4501 (P), were as follows:

- For the first turret, the delivery from the metal presses to the 2nd Mechanical Workshop was to take place on July 31, 1942. Completion in the 2nd Mechanical Workshop on October 15, 1942.

- For the second to sixth turrets, running deliveries to the 2nd Mechanical Workshop were planned until the end of August. They were to be completed in November 1942

- Deliveries for another fifteen turrets was envisaged by the end of September, and their completion for December 1942. The production of a further fifteen turrets per month was also planned

To make assembly easier, it was suggested that the first and second turrets be completed together by October 15. For the necessary individual parts, with the help of a special meeting with Dr. Walter, the delivery of steel castings to the 2nd Mechanical Workshop was to be shortened from the previous 2.5 months to just six weeks. Krupp ordered fifty ball bearings from VKF and fifty from Kugelfischer. However, the problem was that the 2nd Mechanical Workshop needed the first ball bearing from August 20, but the rings ordered here from Krupp went to VKF only from the end of June.

VKF needed 3.5 months for processing; therefore, delivery could not take place until October 15, 1942. Kugelfischer, on the other hand, required just 2.5 months for delivery; however, it did not begin receiving the raw material until the end of August, which meant that the ball bearings were ready for delivery until mid-November. As an alternative, Krupp tried to expedite delivery of the tubular rings by the end of May and press VKF to also reduce its production time to 2.5 months. Should this not succeed, the placement of the turrets on a simulator without the ability to traverse had to be investigated.

Problems also arose with regard to the delivery date for the gun. The Army Ordnance Office had promised the date of September 1, 1942, for this. The gunmaker DHHV, however, did not figure on a delivery until the end of November at the earliest, and therefore the 2nd Mechanical Workshop's schedule could not be kept. As well, because of the existing quota rules, Krupp anticipated difficulties in the short-term procurement of iron and steel.

As a consequence, at a meeting in Kummersdorf on May 4, the delivery date for the first four Type 180 vehicles was postponed to October 1942. Also problematic was the planned delivery date for the swiveling transformer by Siemens-Schuckert. The "Conz" transformer envisaged by Reimspieß could not be accommodated in the VK 4502 on account of its size. Only the transformer of the earlier VK 4501 (P) fit in the new vehicle. Despite the immediate order of one hundred transformers and one hundred contactors and the adoption of "special measures," the earliest possible delivery date by Siemens would be the beginning of January 1943.

On May 12, Porsche handed the necessary drawings for the driver's visor and superstructure to Heerlein of Krupp. The agreement was made to execute the rear upper sidewalls with a slope of 15°. The upper crease line was to be shifted from 2,400 mm to 2,900 mm (94.5 to 114 in.). This enabled the entire engine compartment to be covered with a single

large cover. This cover's dimensions were 2,700 mm × 2,400 mm (106.3 × 94.5 in.), and it weighed 1,300 kg (2,866 lbs.). The bulkhead between the fighting compartment and the engine compartment moved 60 mm rearward. A travel lock for the gun barrel was envisaged on the rear of the tank. It was to have two positions: one for when the vehicle was driving and the other for underwater travel. This enabled the required air shaft to be placed in the middle of the engine cover. Furthermore, the Army Ordnance Office requested that the designation for the Type 180 be standardized as VK 4502 (P) and that the designation VK 4501/2 (P) be dropped. To avoid reworking the hull and built-in parts as much as possible, Professor Porsche asked Heerlein to initially produce just thirty Type 180 hulls and to only make preparations for the remaining hulls. According to Heerlein, the requested proposed emergency exit in the turret was possible only in the bulged right sidewall, which was just 80 mm (3.15 in.) thick. However, this exit seemed not very practical and was difficult to make. Heerlein expected the Porsche company to provide the necessary drawings to determine the cross section of the front deflector strip and the connection of the   air shaft above the turret and the turret hatch. Further groundwork with information on lifting capacity, radius, and swivel range was also required from Porsche for the arrangement on the turret of a crane rail or a boom, in order to be able to install and remove the running gear with the help of a pulley system. The thickness of the rear beams was to be reduced from 40 to 25 mm (1.6 to 0.98 in.), since these beams were less exposed to fire, and the bevel at the back was only half as great. The rear towing lugs were extensions of the trunnions from the lower sidewalls, which penetrated the rear wall. The opening in the front wall was also dimensionally fixed. This clarified the final shape of the hull. VKF had already stated that it could deliver the first three turret traverse bearings by August 15. Kugelfischer, on the other hand, regarded the August 15 deadline for the first three rolling bearings as endangered and gave the end of August as the earliest delivery date. Krupp therefore asked the Army Ordnance Office to exert the necessary pressure to ensure that the planned deadline could be met. Kugelfischer ultimately agreed, on condition that Krupp deliver the raw materials in time.

Schmitt (Porsche's electrical engineer) had a meeting with Heerlein of Krupp concerning the turret traverse mechanism on June 5, 1942. At this meeting, both stipulated that the planned transformer in the turret of the Type 180 was, if possible, to be installed under the gunner's seat, which roughly corresponded to the hydraulic drive of the Henschel vehicle.

The question of battery power supply had to be clarified in a further test. In this, the high currents were to be conducted through copper blocks under high pressure onto a slowly rotating, massive copper cylinder. On the basis of the knowledge gained, the new slip-ring transformer would then be designed. The upper part was based on the seven-part transmitter provided by the office for signals purposes. Cables with a gauge of 95 mm^2 (0.15 in.^{2}) were to be attached to the lower part for the transmission of the high battery currents.

Since the heavy cable could cause problems in assembly due to its stiffness, Schmitt envisaged four cables with a gauge of 25 mm^2 (0.04 in.^{2}) per terminal. In addition, they wanted to investigate a turret traverse mechanism without any transformer as soon as possible. Either a 24-volt DC motor that could be switched and reversed at three speed levels, similar to that of the T-34, or a reversible motor running at constant speed with mechanical step gearing would be used, whose lowest gear would make possible a turret traverse rate of about 1° per second and whose highest gear would enable a traverse rate of about 15° per second. The first detailed construction design of the Porsche Type 180 was discussed with representatives of the Nibelungenwerk on June 8, 1942.

The next day, Dr. Loppert and engineer Wegemann met with the leading Porsche engineers in Stuttgart for further discussions about the Type 180. On June 18, 1942, the Army

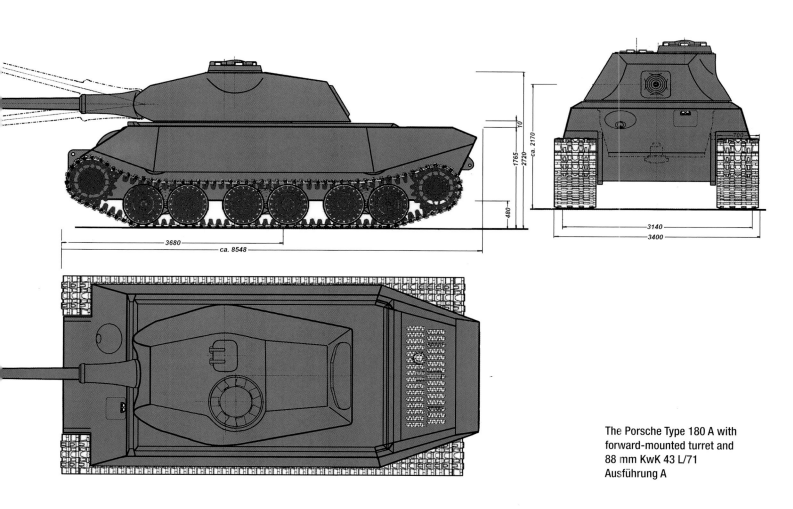

The Porsche Type 180 A with forward-mounted turret and 88 mm KwK 43 L/71 Ausführung A

Ordnance Office increased the order for the VK 4501 (P 2) from one hundred examples of each to two hundred tank hulls and two hundred turrets. These hulls and turrets were to be given consecutive numbers from 150 001 to 150 300. The armaments ministry informed Director Müller of Krupp that for reasons of secrecy, the designation "VK" was to be dropped and replaced by the cover designation Tiger.

In July 1942, Wa Prüf 6 wrote to Krupp that during a demonstration of a commander's cupola with a rotating inner ring, it had decided in favor of an antiaircraft machine gun or a scissors telescope, and that the new tank would dispense with the rotating ring on the basis of simplified production. A simple retaining pin on the outer edge of the cupola was to suffice. For the new turret being developed, they asked Krupp to delete the rotating band in the commander's cupola. The twelve-hour turret position ring was to remain, however.

Directors Walter and Hacker plus General Radlmeier and the leadership of Porsche gathered at the Nibelungenwerk on July 27, 1942, for a major conference on the planned new types—the Type 131, the Type 180, and the Type 205—and on August 3, it was possible to discuss more-concrete dates concerning the Type 180 with the representatives of the Armaments Ministry, the Krupp company, and the Nibelungenwerk. Consequently, on August 5, 1942, chief engineer Rabe received a visit from General Fichtner and Oberstleutnant Holzhäuer of Wa Prüf 6 from Kummersdorf, who in turn presented their own ideas about the project. This development was closely linked to that of the Maus battle tank.

Concerning the planned 88 mm KwK L/71, the question still had to be clarified whether the barrel should have conical or cylindrical grooves. Both types would therefore undergo firing tests. As well, Wa Prüf 1/7 regarded the twist rate, with a constant 5°, as too small for the planned 88 mm sabot shells. For conical grooves, a twist rate of 4.5°–5.5° was regarded as sufficient. On the basis of a drawing dated September 28, 1942, the twist rate of the twenty-four grooves was subsequently increased to 6°.

At a meeting in Essen on August 18 and 19, Heerlein of Krupp and Biersack of Wa Prüf 6 determined that because of the brevity of the time available for design, the turret was not sufficiently optimized in terms of production technology. The workload was still too great. The mounting of the optics was

to be simplified. They also wanted to simplify the direction indicator, deleting the scale for indirect firing with its 6,400° division, since Wa Prüf 6 did not consider indirect firing from the tank to be necessary. Also regarded as unnecessary were the needle bearings in the pinions for the turret drive, which could easily be replaced by composite or sintered iron bushings.

The main problem, however, was production of the turret shell. The pressed front wall required a considerable amount of work in the steelworks. This was clearly evident from the crack sensitivity of the pressed part. The mechanical and autogenous processing effort was enormous. A further review by the tank production specialists was urgently needed.

On September 8, the Krupp company wrote to the Army Ordnance Office, advising it that because of processing errors on the front plates of turrets 5 to 8, in some cases major dimensional deviations had occurred. This was still tolerated for the first four turrets. Since the time-consuming production of the special sidewall for turret number 8 had led to a three-week delay, changes to turrets 6 and 7 would cause further delays and bring assembly to a halt. Krupp therefore made a request that it be allowed to assemble turrets 5, 6, and 7 in the same way as turrets 1 to 4. The Army Ordnance Office ultimately approved this request.

On October 6, 1942, there were further discussions with Krupp and Porsche about the new turret with the long 88 mm KwK L/71. Krupp once again stated that the design of the turret was in no way suitable for large-scale production. Production of the turret shell required a great deal of effort. In particular, it recommended that the pressed bulge in the left sidewall, envisaged to accommodate the commander's cupola, should be deleted. Krupp presented a design with a smooth sidewall. This modified shape, however, caused an asymmetrical tenoning with the turret's front plate and a reduction in its slope angle of about 15°.

For a further development of the turret, Krupp wanted to change the position of the commander's cupola to allow a more favorable angle of slope for the turret side. Furthermore, the dovetailing of the turret sidewalls with the turret front was to be carried out so that as little adjustment work as possible was required. Matching and grinding three surfaces with thicknesses of 80 mm with a handheld grinder was regarded as unacceptable. This also applied to the other plates with their joints. The design of the turret's rear wall, with its

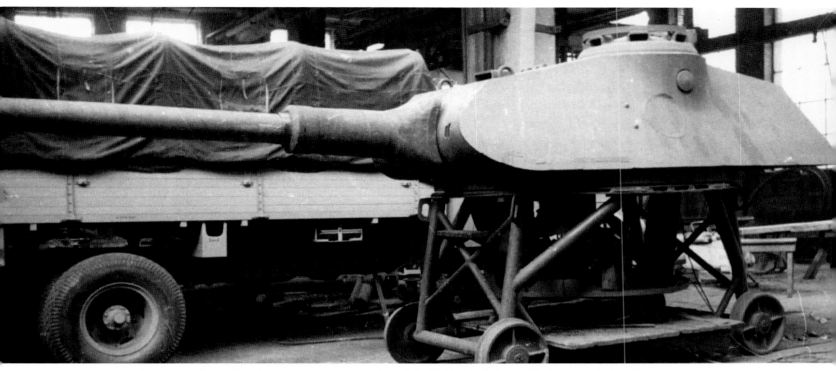

The new ventilation scheme for the Type 103/1 engine, as it was to be installed in the initial phase of the Type 180 design. *TU*

processing surfaces for the gun hatch and the gun armor with its complicated holes and fitting surfaces, also had to be revised.

The Army Ordnance Office, however, disagreed with the new design and insisted on the symmetrical shape with the pressed bulge as a jutty for the commander's cupola. The thickness of the bulge's vertical surface was to be increased from 80 to 100 mm (3.15 to 3.9 in.) for safety reasons. The office left it up to whether the reinforcement should be applied on the interior or exterior. In any case, on the exterior the transition from the sloped surface to the vertical bulge had to be made curved and not angular.

Meanwhile the Siemens-Schuckert company had declared itself ready to deliver the first eight transformers by the beginning of November 1942. Twenty transformers would be delivered each month beginning in December, so that the entire order could be filled by April 1943.

On September 27, 1942, the special representative for Tiger production, Diplom-Ingenieur Krömer of the Krupp company, received the abovementioned letter concerning tank production. Concerning the Tiger (P 2), Krupp announced the following production manufacturing deadlines:

- The first hull on November 21, 1942 (previous deadline October 1942 = 1 example)

- The second hull on December 8, 1942 (previous deadline November 1942 = 10 examples)

- The third hull on December 15, 1942 (previous deadline December 1942 = 16 examples)

None of the three hulls had surface hardening; the cut-to-size installation parts were to be supplied loose without processing. The further delivery of eight hulls was promised for January 1943 (previous deadline for January 1943 = 15 examples). The next fifteen hulls were to follow in February 1943 (previous deadline for February 1943 = 15 examples). In addition, fifteen hulls per month were to follow from March onward. For the finished Porsche turrets, the result was ten examples for March 1943, and from April, fifteen examples monthly.

While an increase to twenty-eight to thirty examples was envisioned by the end of 1943, this required the immediate assignment of the required twelve German machine fitters. By this point in time, however, these ideas had already been fulfilled.

The Army Ordnance Office's response of October 29, 1942, known from the previous chapter, contained only the demand for the production of three hulls and three turrets for the VK 4501 (P 2), and afterward the discontinuation of Porsche Tiger production. On November 9, there was a large meeting at the Armaments Ministry chaired by Hauptamtleiter Karl Otto Saur on the topic of the Porsche Type 101 and Type 180. In the end, the participants decided that the previous Porsche Type 101 should be equipped with two Maybach engines instead of the Porsche power plants. As for the Porsche Type 180, only the three test vehicles were to be built by mid-December 1942. In Stuttgart, meanwhile, the new double blower of the Type 101/3 engine ran on the test bench for the

first time on November 3. This was necessary to be able to carry out measurements of the temperature behavior and the air flow rate on the new engine.

For the second version, the Porsche Type 181, according to a letter of October 23, 1942,[69] the Voith company had envisaged a NITA four-speed torque converter transmission for the Sla 16 sixteen-cylinder diesel engine then in planning and development.

After the previously described comparison of the two competitors at Berka on November 11, 1942, Professor Porsche came from Eisenach to Stuttgart and shared with his engineers the decisions made by the Tank Committee the previous day. There the Tank Committee had favored the Type 180 B with

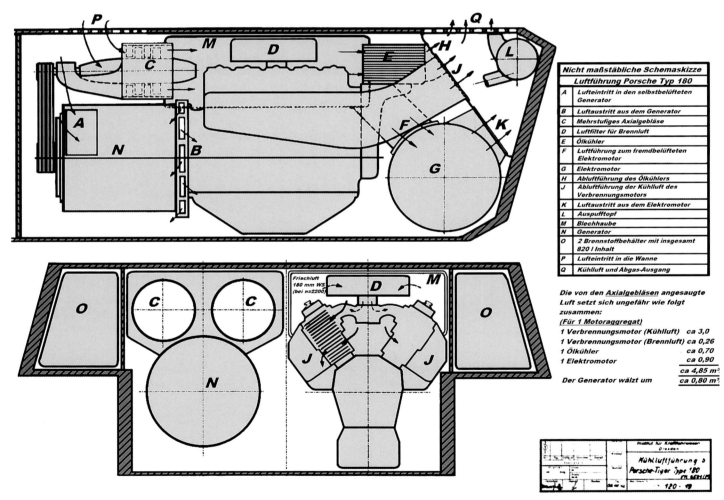

Nicht maßstäbliche Schemaskizze	
Luftführung Porsche Typ 180	
A	Lufteintritt in den selbstbelüfteten Generator
B	Luftaustritt aus dem Generator
C	Mehrstufiges Axialgebläse
D	Luftfilter für Brennluft
E	Ölkühler
F	Luftführung zum fremdbelüfteten Elektromotor
G	Elektromotor
H	Abluftführung des Ölkühlers
J	Abluftführung der Kühlluft des Verbrennungsmotors
K	Luftaustritt aus dem Elektromotor
L	Auspufftopf
M	Blechhaube
N	Generator
O	2 Brennstoffbehälter mit insgesamt 820 l Inhalt
P	Lufteintritt in die Wanne
Q	Kühlluft und Abgas-Ausgang

Die von den Axialgebläsen angesaugte
Luft setzt sich ungefähr wie folgt
zusammen:
(Für 1 Motoraggregat)

1 Verbrennungsmotor (Kühlluft)	ca 3,0
1 Verbrennungsmotor (Brennluft)	ca 0,26
1 Ölkühler	ca 0,70
1 Elektromotor	ca 0,90
	ca 4,85 m³
Der Generator wälzt um	ca 0,80 m³

The new ventilation scheme for the Type 103/1 engine, as it was to be installed in the initial phase of the Type 180 design. *TU*

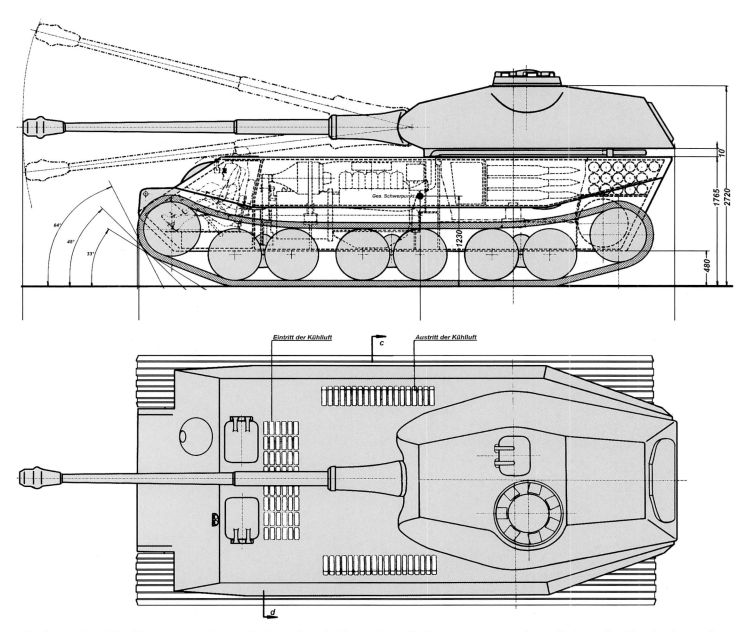

The Porsche Type 180 with rear-mounted turret. The internal-combustion engines with their generators were located between the driver / radio operator compartment and the fighting compartment. The air circulation was changed accordingly. The resulting lack of contact between the two crew member groups was a disadvantage. This design was used in the Ferdinand tank destroyer. *PA*

rear-mounted turret. Initially, only three vehicles were to be built. Quantity production would be possible only after successful testing. So Wa Prüf 6 had achieved what it wanted. Porsche was basically out of the running in the tank project, and the gentlemen of the Army Ordnance Office hoped that the professor's 189-metric-ton (208-ton) Maus tank project would be unsuccessful and that he would finally fail as a builder of tanks.

On November 20, the Krupp company received an inquiry from Wa Prüf 6 as to the production status of the three Tiger P 2 turrets. The Army Ordnance Office had stopped series production of these turrets for the time being. Only those parts of the turrets that could be used to make the Henschel Tiger 2 were to be delivered to the Wegmann company. Krupp reported that the three Porsche 2 test turrets were about 70% complete. They were missing only the 88 mm Kampwagenkanonen

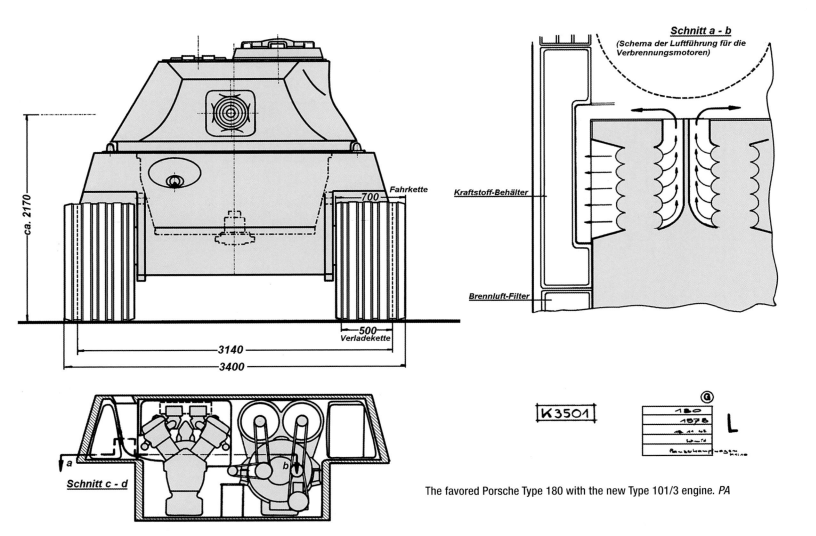

The favored Porsche Type 180 with the new Type 101/3 engine. *PA*

43, Ausführung A guns, which were supposed to be supplied by the office (Wug 2/VI), since the guns of this type already produced were finding use primarily in the 88 mm Pak 43/2 Ferdinand. Also still missing were the direction indicators, the twelve-hour pointer drives, and the seats. Details also had to be clarified, such as the installation of the smoke grenade launchers (Nebelwerfer), the spent-casing ejection, the ventilator, the ring for the antiaircraft machine gun, etc. The TZF 9 turret telescopic sights were also required to complete the work.

On January 11, 1943, Krupp inquired of the Army Ordnance Office whether the written order for the three Tiger (P 2) test turrets and hulls had been clarified. According to the telex dated December 14, 1942, the entire contract was to be awarded to Alkett. But when Krupp asked Alkett about the order on January 7, the answer came back that it knew nothing about three test pieces with the designation VK 4501 (P 2). Alkett had received the order from the Army Ordnance Office to make only two VK 4501 (P) vehicles mounting an 88 mm gun as assault guns. This was a reference to the Type 131, the Tiger (P) heavy tank destroyer.

The Army Ordnance Office (WuG 6) had not even informed Oberstleutnant Crohn of Wa Prüf 6 about the placement of the order. After reviewing the documents relating to

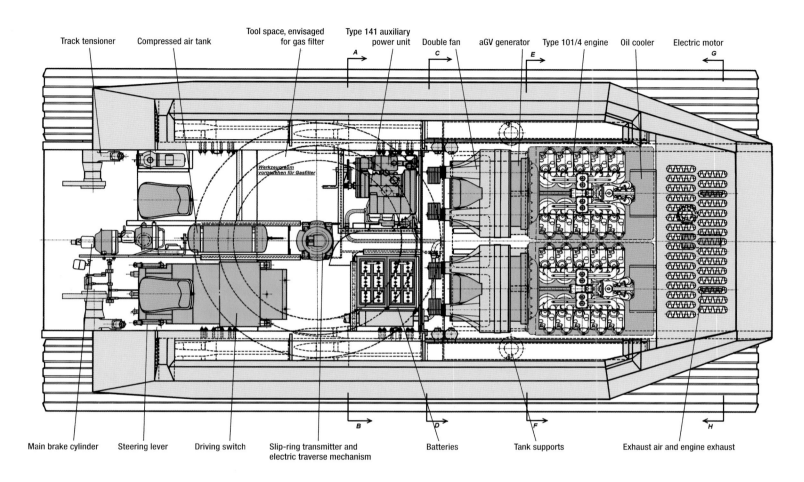

Track tensioner — Compressed air tank — Tool space, envisaged for gas filter — Type 141 auxiliary power unit — Double fan — aGV generator — Type 101/4 engine — Oil cooler — Electric motor

A — C — E — G

Werkzeugraum vorgesehen für Gasfilter

B — D — F — H

Main brake cylinder — Steering lever — Driving switch — Slip-ring transmitter and electric traverse mechanism — Batteries — Tank supports — Exhaust air and engine exhaust

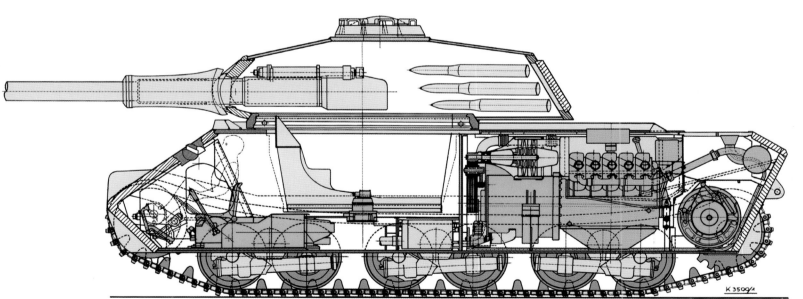

K 3500/4

The interior fittings of the Type 180 B were adopted from the Type 101 and differed mainly in the new engine-cooling system. *PA*

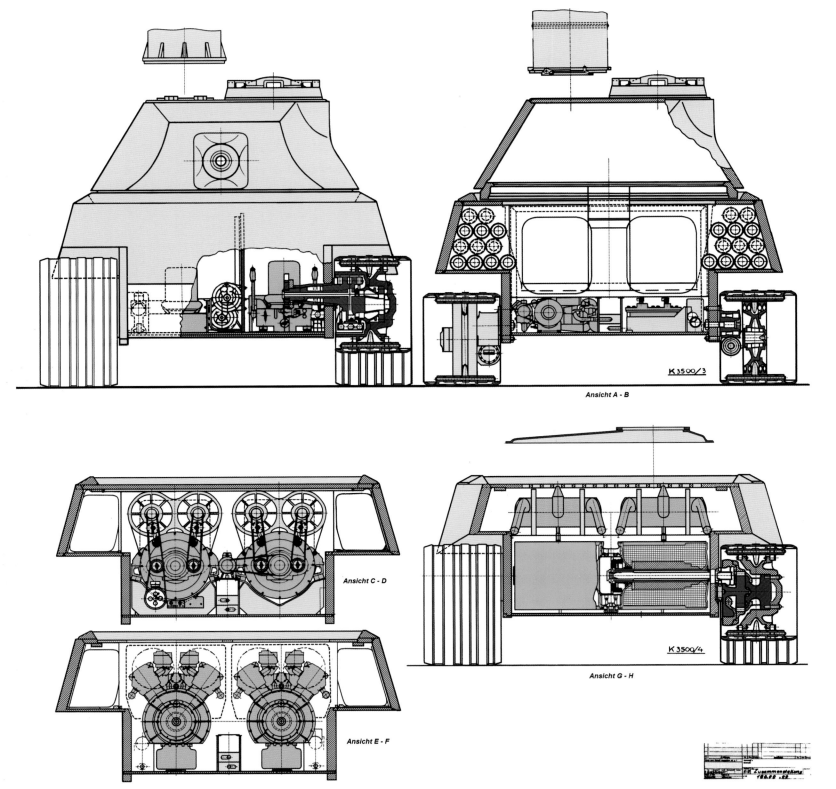

Ansicht A - B

Ansicht C - D

Ansicht E - F

Ansicht G - H

K 3500/3

K 3500/4

Composition of the Porsche Type 180 A from December 9, 1942, with forward-mounted turret. This design was no longer current at that time. Because of the new type of double fan used by the 101/3 engine, the fans in the side overhangs were replaced by larger fuel tanks in these projections. Installation of the two air pipes for underwater travel is still indicated. *PA*

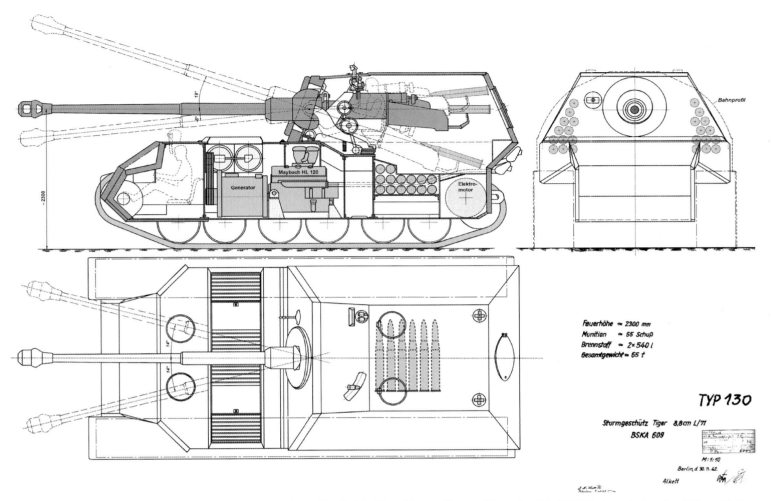

Feuerhöhe ≈ 2300 mm
Munition ≈ 55 Schuß
Brennstoff ≈ 2× 540 l
Gesamtgewicht ≈ 65 t

TYP 130

Sturmgeschütz Tiger 8,8cm L/71
BSKA 609

M: 1:10
Berlin, d 30. 11. 42.
Alkett

The Alkett drawing of the Ferdinand tank destroyer, then still called the Tiger (P) assault gun, of November 20, 1942. The type designation 130 used here was not correct and should have read Type 131. The Type 130 was the planned liquid-cooled chassis of the Porsche Tiger. *PA*

the intended purpose, he was able to formally confirm to Krupp this order for the three Type 180 test vehicles. Krupp, however, insisted on an immediate official order, since some items, the three hulls for example, had already been delivered to the Nibelungenwerk. Due to the missing order, the associated delivery notes were not recognized by the army acceptance point. In addition, Krupp had to point out to Wa Prüf 6 that the official provision of the guns, the optics, etc. had to take place immediately, so as to avoid delays in completion. It was also necessary to provide the required slip ring assemblies as quickly as possible. Krupp referred to the order of September 26, 1942, for two hundred slip ring assemblies for the two hundred turrets ordered. Since only three examples

of these current turrets were to be completed, only three slip ring assemblies were required. The cables for the signals section were to be tied into junction box number 5 c. On January 15, 1943, a meeting also took place between Wa Prüf 6 and AK Krupp. The experimental turret with gun and cupola with prism periscopes for the Henschel Tiger 3 was to be sent to Kummersdorf by February 1, so that the interior layout and functionality could be checked. The second Henschel turret was to be delivered with full interior fittings, but with a gun stub instead of an actual gun, for use as a ballistics test turret. Wa Prüf 6 had to contribute a gun without barrel, a turret telescopic sight, periscope, machine gun, ammunition belt bag, etc.

It was to be decided in Kummersdorf whether a lifting device was necessary for the ammunition. Krupp still had to change the handle and move the lifting device for the commander's swing-type hatch cover and his footrests, as well as raise the handwheel for the manual turret traverse.

With regard to the armor, Krupp pointed out that the reinforcement of the gun mantlet to 150 mm (5.9 in.) of rolled or pressed material in the course of further development would result in a weight gain of about 300 kg (661 lbs.). A further reinforcement to about 180 mm sloped at 40° could even result in an additional 500 kg (1,102 lbs.). For this, both shield bearings had to be moved directly to the gun, whereby the bulge for the previously external trunnion mount was no longer necessary.

The final discussion point again concerned the so-called pressed bulge for the commander's cupola. It could be removed only if the slope of the turret side was changed from 60° to 69°, thus moving the commander's cupola 500 mm (19.7 in.) farther toward the center of the turret. Retaining the side plate thickness of 80 mm (3.15 in.) would result in a weight increase of about 400 kg (882 lbs.). Increasing the armor thickness to 90 mm (3.54 in.) on account of the smaller 69° slope would have meant a weight increase of about 500 kg (1,102 lbs.). The decision as to whether the pressed bulge was to remain and, if so, in which form, was therefore a matter of great urgency.

Of the previous P 2 turrets, at that time twenty shells were already in mechanical processing. A further number was in the tank workshop, and so forty to fifty turret shells could be expected in a short time. Individual metal sheets were already on hand for another fifty turrets. Therefore, a decision was urgently needed whether to produce fifty turrets according to the previous pattern with 100 mm (3.94 in.) of frontal armor, or immediately transition to production of a turret with a reinforced front with or without the pressed bulge.[70]

On January 18, a meeting was held at the Armaments Ministry on the topic of support for the Porsche 2 turrets. Wa Prüf 6 guaranteed the necessary optics; however, Baurat Biersack of Wa Prüf 6 was not entirely clear as to what the three vehicles that were to be completed would be used for. If the plan was to use them for training, then obviously they had to be complete. The ministry pointed out that it would be impossible to complete the turrets at the right time if

provision of the guns could not be ensured. It was planned to deliver the three test vehicles by February 1943.

On January 21, Wa Prüf 6 responded that information was still missing:

1. Would raw materials still be needed for the turrets and hulls? If yes, the required material had to be taken from unused subscription rights and from any existing material for the canceled P 2 series.

2. When should the gun and optics be made available?

3. What was the current production status of the turrets?

It was pointed out that the three turrets, which were to be equipped with the 88 mm KwK 43, should not be confused with the three Tiger H turrets being built, since these were also to be equipped with the KwK 43.

On January 25, 1943, Crohn finally submitted the written order (the so-called War Order) to the Krupp firm for the three turrets and three hulls for the three Panzerkampfwagen Tiger (P 2) test vehicles. The recipient of the three complete turrets and three hull shells was the Nibelungenwerk in St. Valentin.

Three days later Krupp answered Wa Prüf 6, informing it that the three hulls for the test vehicles were already at the Nibelungenwerk. Krupp had also taken the required raw materials for the three turrets, which were also complete, from the canceled P 2 order. Additional small quantities of raw materials could be required for any changes to be made to the turrets, and would be requested if necessary. Krupp needed the guns and optics as well as other provisions for the turrets immediately, because the guns in particular would have to be available for main assembly. It was also emphasized that the work on the **two** Henschel Tiger turrets (a test turret and a ballistics test turret) was proceeding separately.

At the sitting of the Tank Committee in Berlin on February 17, 1943, the Tiger (P 2) and Tiger (P 3) were discussed in addition to other topics, such as the Maus and Löwe. Oberst Thomale wanted to know the state of work on the Tiger (P 2) vehicle. Professor Porsche reported that the three prototype Tiger (P 2) vehicles were primarily test vehicles for the new

The first prototype Tiger (H 3) (Tiger B) with the so-called Porsche turret. The vehicle had many similarities to the final variants of the planned Porsche Type 180. *SB*

running gear envisaged for the Maus tank. Production of the three vehicles at the Nibelungenwerk had to be temporarily postponed at Saur's direction in favor of accelerated production of the Ferdinand assault gun. Porsche reported that in addition to development of the Tiger (P 2) and the Maus tank, the Tiger (P 3) was being worked on as a further design. The Porsche internal designation was Type 181. The tank was to be equipped with a hydraulic drive and the new air-cooled diesel engine of about 900 hp. By this Porsche meant the sixteen-cylinder Sla 16 diesel engine from Simmering-Graz-Pauker, which was under development. This engine had been developed on behalf of the "Joint Stock Company for

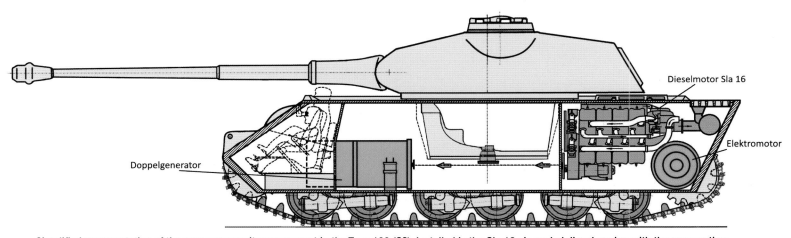

Simplified representation of the new power unit arrangement in the Type 180 (C?). Installed is the Sla 16 air-cooled diesel engine with the new grating. The planned arrangement of the two generators behind the driver's compartment, lengthwise or crosswise, is not known. A double arrangement of the generators analogous to the Maus tank was conceivable.

Air-Cooled Diesel Engines" and was supposed to replace the Maybach HL 230 engine of the Panther and Tiger (H 3) tanks. Porsche wanted to present the technical data to the Tank Committee at the next meeting in order to take further action. Of the three Tigers (P 2) from Porsche, only one vehicle was supposed to be completed with a turret. The other two vehicles were to be completed as chassis with turret replacement weights. The remaining two turrets were to be used elsewhere (on the Tiger [H 3]). All questions relating to turret construction, gun mounting, and delivery of ammunition were to be tested and evaluated by the Army Ordnance Office.

Since the Panzerjäger (P) tank destroyer conversions were almost completed, they met at the Nibelungenwerk with Porsche and Reimspieß to discuss the design of the future Type 180 vehicles in detail. It was decided that the three Type 180 test vehicles, whose turrets had long been in the factory, would be completed according to the latest designs by Reimspieß. The turret of this new design was positioned roughly in the middle of the vehicle. In the rear was the new

Sla 16 sixteen-cylinder diesel engine from Simmering. Design work on this engine was largely complete, and it was supposed to begin running in early August 1943. The generator was mounted longitudinally in front of the turret. The gearbox previously envisaged by Reimspieß could be abandoned and replaced by a slightly oblique driveshaft. On the basis of this decision, Reimspieß had to draw up a detailed draft, since the existing 1:10-scale draft did not yet show all the details of the placement of the individual power units.

As a result, the Porsche Type 101/3 and 101/4 engines were completely eliminated from the program for the Porsche Type 180. The ten engines ordered were not to be canceled, however, since this engine type was to be used, not only for the hydraulic vehicle (Type 102) but the existing Tiger vehicles as well. Beyond the scope of the three Type 180 test vehicles, talks were to be held with the Voith company about a hydraulic drive. Above all, the question of the steering gear had to be clarified, since no satisfactory solution had yet been found in the Type 102, with its pneumatically controlled clutch steering.

The Sla 16 sixteen-cylinder diesel engine had two BBC turbochargers and two fans, which have been removed here. *PA*

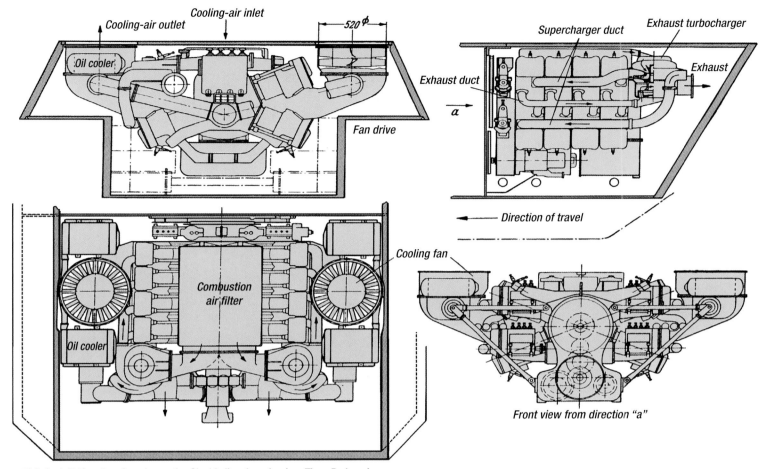

This installation drawing shows the Sla 16 diesel engine in a Tiger B chassis.

The execution of the plan was again delayed, because in August 1943 the Simmering-Graz-Pauker company of Vienna had just one order from Wa Prüf 6 for three Sla 16 engines. A new application had to be submitted for the five Sla 16 engines desired by Porsche, including the necessary materials. An amended order was also necessary for the Sla 16 engines without the transmission gearing. The purpose of this gearing was to adjust the maximum engine speed of 2,000 rpm to the 3,000 rpm required for the existing Olvar gearbox when replacing the Maybach HL 210 engines with the Sla 16.

The Votih NITA hydraulic turbo transmission was to be connected to this diesel engine by means of a so-called Bibby coupling. There was also a need to talk about ordering an economical number of Sla 16s. Simmering envisaged a figure of six engines for the Porsche Type 180, while the remaining four engines were intended for Wa Prüf 6's test Panthers. However, Professor Porsche did not want to accept more than

five engines. He hoped that a decision would be made in Berlin in a week's time. At a meeting on August 22–23, 1943, Porsche stated that due to the delayed production of the Sla 16 at Simmering, they should fall back on the first Type 180 B project with the air-cooled 15-liter engines. Simmering-Graz-Pauker had, however, already scrapped the remaining engine parts after long negotiations, and the company refused to resume production of the Type 101 engine. At this point, Reimspieß was to continue working on the Type 180 as a vehicle with the sixteen-cylinder diesel engine from Simmering, and the new hydraulic Voith gearbox in the rear as well as the turret positioned forward of the engine.[72]

On September 10, 1943, Krupp wrote to Porsche that, as was known, completion of the three test turrets with the 88 mm KwK 43 L/71 had been delayed several times due to various incidents during the intervening period. Meanwhile, the original turret design had been extensively modified in cooperation with the Army Ordnance Office (the later production turret for the Henschel Tiger [H 3]). Therefore, Porsche was asked if it could use the upgraded turret for its vehicle. Krupp wanted to avoid having to produce two different turrets.

Despite this, Reimspieß's work on the Type 180 project with the Sla 16 diesel engine and the central turret continued. The aim was to complete the three test vehicles as quickly as possible. Porsche expected an in-depth report from Reimspieß on the question of the vehicle's brakes. However, work on the Maus tank was urgent, and the Porsche engineers were tied to this project, a favorite of Hitler's. On December 1, 1943, Krupp again inquired about the delivery of the three P 2 tank turrets, since Porsche KG had until then failed to answer. This and the required drive for the chassis got no further, because other tasks were more urgent.

At the end of 1943, the Nibelungenwerk was commissioned to produce the Jagdtiger (Sd.Kfz. 186) tank destroyer, developed from the Tiger (Sd.Kfz. 182), since Henschel, the development company, was unable to transport the heavy 34-metric-ton hulls into its factory. To simplify production, the Nibelungenwerk, together with Professor Porsche, proposed the installation of the Type 180 knee-lever running gear from the Type 180. The Porsche KG also referred to this running gear as a universal running gear.

A discussion concerning the installation of the Porsche running gear on the 128 mm Tiger tank destroyer took place at the Nibelungenwerk on September 23, 1943. Because of a breakdown in deliveries from Skoda, there was the problem that after the first six to eight vehicles, the tank destroyer would again have to be equipped with the Henschel running gear. Hacker declared this measure unacceptable because, after the temporary introduction of the Henschel running gear, there would no longer be any possibility of reintroducing the Porsche running gear. As a result, Hacker arranged for design, purchase, and operation to be expanded to allow the first nine vehicles to be equipped with the running gears produced by Skoda, and the subsequent production vehicles with the Porsche running gears produced at the Nibelungenwerk. In his view, a precondition for this was a redesign proposed by Reimspieß in order to save large forgings and reduce the number of necessary dies to three or four. Hacker emphasized that he had assumed a very great responsibility toward his company as well as to the Tank Committee. For this reason,

he asked Professor Porsche to have the design of this running gear thoroughly checked by the calculating department in Stuttgart and to personally check the control analysis again.

On November 26, however, Professor Porsche was informed that Blaicher, the new chairman of the Central Tank Committee, had sent a copy of a letter from the Army Ordnance Office to Director Judtmann of the Nibelungenwerk, in which it was pointed out in the strongest possible terms that the Porsche running gear should not be introduced until it had been thoroughly tested. The factory management was

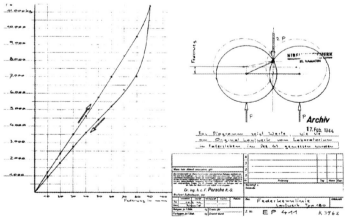

The spring characteristic curve of the Porsche Type 180 suspension indicates values for spring pitch and roller load. These values were measured in Fallersleben in December 1943 on the test bench illustrated above. *PA*

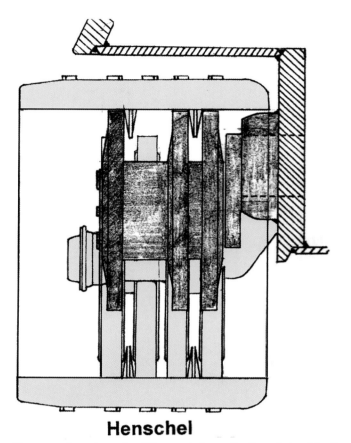

Henschel

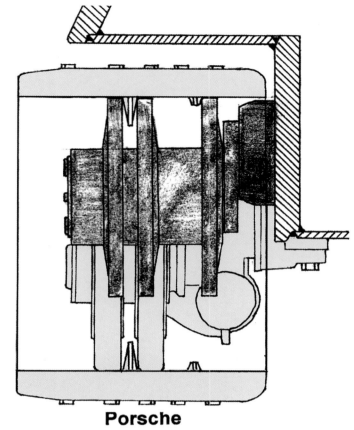

Porsche

The comparison shows the difference between the Henschel and the Porsche running gear.

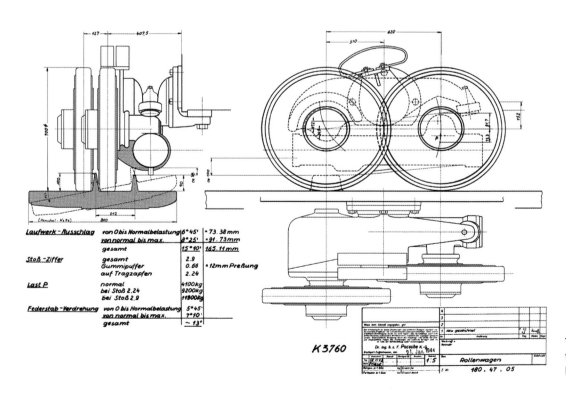

K 3760

The Porsche Type 180 bogie for the Henschel Jagdtiger, drawn on November 18, 1943. *PA*

threatened with the harshest consequences if it were to circumvent the arrangement in any way.[73] This of course had an impact on further production of the Jagdtiger. Due to the higher tare weight of the Jagdtiger, Porsche reduced the axial spacing of the bogies from 750 to 620 mm (29.5 to 24.4 in.). Professor Porsche promised Hitler a saving of 450 hours of production time per vehicle as well as 5.2 metric tons (5.7 tons) of raw materials and complex machine tools. At this very moment of the shortage economy, the Army Ordnance Office was unable to deny this enormous advantage. But Wa Prüf 6 wanted to test both running gear variants beforehand. One Jagdtiger was therefore built with a Porsche running gear and one with a running gear by Henschel.

Comparative trials were carried out at Kummersdorf in March 1944. It turned out that the Porsche chassis, due to its great weight of 70 metric tons (77 tons), was sprung even harder than the Ferdinand assault gun. In addition, the Henschel track, with its division of 152 mm (5.98 in), did not harmonize with the Porsche chassis, resulting in very disturbing resonances. The Ferdinand's finer 130 mm (5.1 in.) track significantly improved running behavior in the test. However, with a width of 640 mm (25.2 in.), the track was far too narrow for the high ground pressure, since the Henschel track, with a width of 800 mm (31.5 in.), provided a barely tolerable ground pressure value of 1.06 kg/cm^2 (15 psi). In principle, the Ferdinand's track could be compared to the Henschel vehicle's 660 mm wide (26 in.) travel track. Designing a new, wider track for the vehicle was out of the question at that time. As a result, just ten Jagdtiger with the Porsche Type 180 running gear were delivered, before production at the

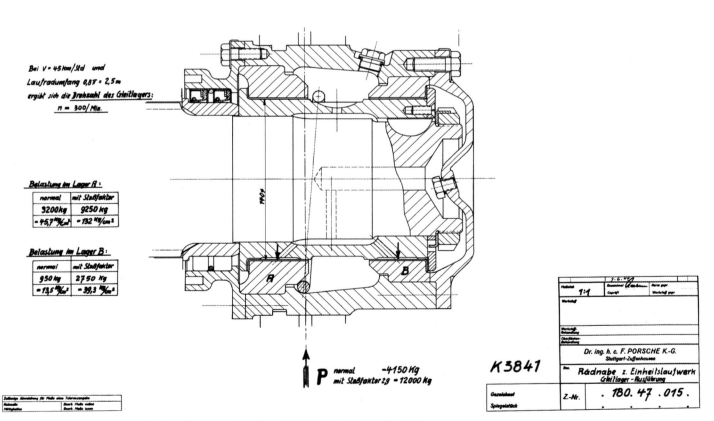

The wheel hub of the later standard running gear of the Type 180 (slide-bearing version). *PA*

The Jagdtiger prototype made by the Nibelungenwerk, with the Porsche Type 180 running gear and the 800 mm wide Henschel track. *PA*

Nibelungenwerk was switched to manufacture of the more complicated Henschel running gear.

In a letter dated May 6, 1944, it was stated that the materials for the Porsche Tiger 2 project, which were no longer needed, were released as 100,805 kg (222,237 lbs.) of scrap armor plate. On August 26, 1944, Wa Prüf 6 requested information from Krupp as to whether the finished Porsche 2 turret had been handed over to Wegmann and when the remaining two Porsche 2 turrets would be completed or also sent to Wegmann. Krupp replied that the three Porsche 2 turrets had already been delivered to Wegmann in Kassel at the end of May 1944. As far as Krupp was aware, Wegmann had already carried out the conversion to the shape of the Henschel 3

production turrets 1 to 50 and delivered the finished turrets to Henschel.[74]

The story of the Porsche Type 180 was not quite over, however. As early as August 1943, Hauptamtsleiter Saur had demanded of the turret maker Wegmann that it equip a Tiger H 1 turret with an 88 mm KwK L/71 as quickly as possible. Krupp delivered the required turret to Wegmann at the end of September 1943. Assembly was delayed, however, because the required gun could not be delivered until October 10, 1943.[75]

Meanwhile, a Porsche Type 180 hull had been delivered from the Nibelungenwerk to Kummersdorf. On March 6, 1944, Wa Prüf 1 wanted to carry out a lifespan shoot at the

Taken in 1945, this photo shows the dug-in VK 4502 with the Tiger 1 turret and the tactical code K 01 at the Kummersdorf artillery range. The gun can clearly be seen to be an 88 mm KwK L/71. This first version of the gun had a monobloc barrel and was equipped with the light muzzle brake. The turret has the cupola with prism periscopes for the commander. *SP*

Meppen gunnery range, using an 88 mm KwK 43 barrel with conical grooves. For this purpose, Wa Prüf 1 provided the 88 mm test barrel RV 1 L/71. According to the report, this test barrel was installed in a Tiger 1/VK 4502,[76] which was still at the Kummersdorf artillery range. The designation is rather confusing. It must be said that the original name of the Porsche Type 180 Tiger was "Tiger 2." When its development was halted, the "Tiger 3" (i.e., the former VK 4503 from Henschel) was given the designation "Tiger 2" or "Tiger B."

This Type 180 (VK 4502) chassis supplied by the Nibelungenwerk was probably the experimental vehicle intended for a gun turret. Since all the turrets, including the three test turrets of the VK 4502, were converted and delivered to Wegmann for production of the Tiger B, this chassis did not initially have a turret. For this reason, Wa Prüf 6 used the Henschel-type turret, which was completed at the end of 1943, with the long 88 mm KwK 43 and placed it on the VK 4502 chassis at Kummersdorf.

Since the hull was still without an engine, because the Sla 16 diesel, as was known, was still not ready for use, the chassis at least acted as a carrier for the turret so that gunnery trials could be carried out. However, since the VR 1 barrel had already been fired many times, it was not suitable for the planned lifespan shoot by Wa Prüf 1, and so the vehicle and turret apparently remained at the Kummersdorf artillery range until 1945.

The fact that this prototype had to have been built was also shown toward the end of the war by a list compiled by the inspector general of armored forces for a speech by the führer on March 31, 1945, in which, among other units, the Kummersdorf Panzer Company was listed, with an "armored train (immobile)," in which there was a Porsche Tiger with an 88 mm L/70 gun. The assumption that this referred to a Porsche Tiger tank destroyer can be refuted by the strength report submitted by schwere Panzerjäger-Kompanie 614 (614th Heavy-Tank-Destroyer Company), since the remaining four Tiger (P) tank destroyers were in the area of Wünsdorf/Zossen.

According to eyewitness accounts on April 21, 1945, on the orders of the battle commander of the Kummersdorf artillery range, a "Tiger" that had been abandoned due to "vehicle damage" was towed to the road in the direction of Horstwalde. Then there was an exchange of gunfire in which several Soviet T-34s were knocked out.[77]

When a British officer interrogated Professor Porsche in 1945, he also asked him about the Porsche Tiger: "There is one thing we don't understand. We were very well informed about the experiments you carried out with new tanks. We knew what was going on at Berka and Kummersdorf. Above all, we knew what performance your tanks achieved during the test drives. We had, to be honest, great respect for the first use of the new Porsche Tigers. We made appropriate preparations. And then German tank models came to the front, but they weren't the Porsche models that had achieved such excellent results. We waited. We thought the Germans would pick up these tanks to use them with the element of surprise and then in large numbers. We became nervous. None of these tanks came. I do not understand that. Professor Porsche, why were these models not built, and it they were built, why were they not used in large numbers? We were faced with a mystery. We would like to hear what was behind it."

"Yes," said Professor Porsche. "Actually I don't know. I can only tell you about the internal intrigues and disputes that took place."[78] Although the British officer had exaggerated, in addition to the material problems and intrigues by the Army Ordnance Office, construction of the Porsche Tiger suffered, above all, due to time constraints. If the time frame for development of the Porsche Type 100 was still about two and a half years from the first stroke of the pen to the first test drive, for the Porsche Type 101 it was only eleven months. The Porsche Type 131, the Ferdinand, was only about four months, even though almost everything was changed except for the chassis. One can, of course, question why the Army Ordnance Office contributed so little to the elimination of the Porsche Tiger's teething problems. The reason was that the office pushed its own design with all its strength. Since it also found support from Armaments Minister Speer, the Porsche Tiger had no real chance.

Finally, a quote made by the former head of the Army Ordnance Office, General der Artillerie Emil Leeb, about this development in 1958: "A second development by a prominent engineer close to the party proceeded parallel to the Army Ordnance Office's Tiger development tank, and it took a great deal of effort to prevent the Army Ordnance Office's development tank from being canceled while still in its infancy."[79]

This ends the story of the Porsche Tiger, since none of the vehicles survived the war. Its gasoline-electric-drive concept was also no alternative in tank design for the future. The disadvantages of the hybrid drive, such as poor efficiency, high weight, and great material expenditure, could not outstrip the mechanical drive in tank design. More on this appears in chapter 7.

CHAPTER 5

Technology in Detail

The Wooden Model

As with any weapons engineering project at the time, a 1:1-scale wooden model was created prior to production in order to be able to realistically check operating and access options.

The model of the Tiger (P) consisted of a mix of original and wooden components.

The driver's seat with the two steering levers. At the top of the photo is the left track tensioner, and in front of it the accelerator pedal and the brake pedal. In the middle between the driver's and radio operator's seats are the compressed-air tanks for operation of the brakes. A cover was placed over them, and on it was the switch box. The instrument panel was in the niche to the driver's left. Under the driver's seat was the driving switch. *PA*

View of the driver / radio operator compartment from the rotating turret platform. The two seats are missing. The driving switch is partly visible under the driver's seat base. *Above left*, the KFF 2 driver's optic combined with the Fahrersehklappe 100 driver's visor, and to the right, in the radio operator's station, the mount for the bow machine gun in the ball mount. Forward, *left and right*, are the adjusting devices for the track tensioners. These were later criticized because they were difficult to reach. *PA*

Part of the turret with the folded gunner's seat. The seats for the driver and radio operator and the ball mount for the bow machine gun have been fitted. On the far right and at the bottom of the photo is the planned ammunition stowage for the 88 mm shells, located in the spaces above the two tracks. *PA*

The carousel-shaped shell storage fixture in the right projection. *PA*

This look backward reveals the two access doors to the generators. Below is the compressor for the compressed-air supply, which was later located right in the engine compartment. The opening in the center was meant to accommodate the exhaust pipe of the Type 141 auxiliary power unit, which, though not present here, was located on the right side in the direction of travel. *PA*

The seat in the foreground was merely posed there, since otherwise it would have been mounted much too low on the rotating turret platform for the commander. The gunner had a folding seat, in order to enable the driver to exit the turret to the rear. *PA*

View from the rotating platform upward toward the mockup of the breech of the 88 mm KwK 36, without breechblock. On the two sides are reproductions of the recoil brake and recuperator. On the left is the binocular Turmzielfernrohr 9b telescopic sight, and, *above right*, the coaxial 7.9 mm Maschinengewehr 34 machine gun. In the rear left of the turret roof is the commander's cupola and, *at right*, the narrow loader's hatch. The turret essentially reflects the design of the Porsche Type 100 turret. *PA*

Armament

The 88 mm KwK L/56 was created from the 88 mm Flak 36 from Krupp and cost 18,000 RM. The sole manufacturer of the gun was the Buckau R. Wolf AG machine factory in Magdeburg. Production time was about six months, with an effort of 2,500 working hours.

Maximum recoil energy was 3 MT and resulted in a normal recoil length of 550 mm (21.65 in.). The recoil brake's piston stop was at 600 mm (23.6 in.). The average brake pressure was 6,400 kg (14,110 lbs.) and was able to bring the 5.1 liters (1.35 gal.) of fluid to a pressure of 100 kg/cm^2 (1,422 psi). The gun also had a pneumatic recuperator, which had a counterrecoil force of 1,040 kg (2,293 lbs.) with 4.4 liters (1.16 gal.) of fluid and 2.85 liters (0.10 ft.^{3}) of airspace. A compensator was also installed, which had to compensate for the barrel's weight moment about the trunnions. The gas pressure

in the barrel was 2,800 kg/cm^2 (39,825 psi), exceptional gas pressure was 3,200 kg/cm^2 (45,515 psi), and muzzle gas pressure was 625 kg/cm^2 (8,890 psi).

The elevation range extended from −8° to +20°. The weapon weighed 1,310 kg (2,888 lbs.), with the tube weighing 676 kg (1,490 lbs.); the jacket, 310 kg (683 lbs.); the muzzle brake, 62 kg (137 lbs.); the breech, 50 kg (110 lbs.); and the wedge-type breechblock with interior equipment, 30.5 kg (67.24 lbs.). Barrel length was 4,928 mm (194 in.), which was equal to a caliber length of about L/56. The tube length was 4,690 mm (184.65 in.), which consisted of the rifled section of 4,093.5 mm (161 in.) and the chamber of 596.5 mm (23.5 in.). The stated life of the barrel was about 6,000 shots. The muzzle energy of 330 MT made possible a range of about 12 km (7.5 mi.) at maximum elevation of 20° and a muzzle

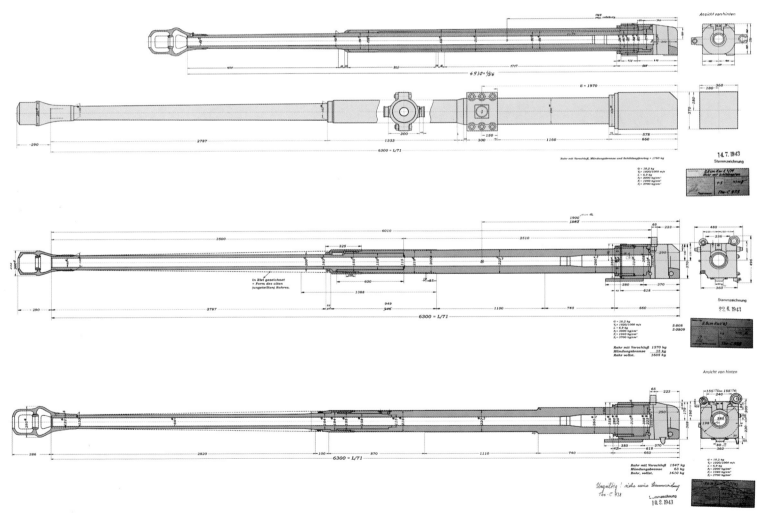

Comparison of the 88 mm L/56 and L/71 guns, the latter with the early and late muzzle brakes

The 88 mm KwK 43 with monobloc barrel, without muzzle brake and recoil cylinder. The barrel was bent in an attempt to destroy the gun. *SF*

velocity of 820 m/sec. (2,690 ft./sec.). The possible rate of fire was about ten rounds per minute.[80] The 88 mm KwK 43 of the Porsche Tiger 2 had a caliber length of L/71, was 6.28 m (20.6 ft.) long, and weighed 1,605 kg (3,538 lbs.). A firing range of 9,350 m (5.8 mi.) could be achieved with the maximum barrel elevation of 15°, with a muzzle energy of 537 MT. Firing rate was six to ten rounds per minute.

The ammunition used by the 88 mm KwK 36 was in general similar to that of the 88 mm Flak 18/36, and that used by the 88 mm KwK 43 L/71 to that of the 88 mm Flak 41.

Only the threaded percussion primers had to be replaced for the tank gun. The high-explosive shell weighed 9 kg (19.8 lbs.) and achieved a muzzle velocity of 800 m/sec. (2,625 ft./sec.). The Panzergranate 39 armor-piercing round weighed 9.65 kg (21.3 lbs.). The Hohlladungsgranate HL hollow-charge antitank shell weighed 7.65 kg (18.9 lbs.), and the Panzergranate 40/43 7.3 kg (16.1 lbs.). The ammunition of the 88 mm Flak 18, 36, and 37 underwent certain changes, especially for manufacturing reasons. Using the armor-piercing round as an example, iron, KPS (copper-plated soft iron), and FES

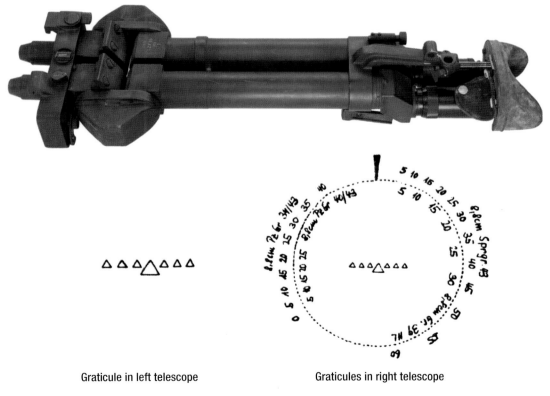

Graticule in left telescope

Graticules in right telescope

The Turmzielfernrohr 9b telescopic sight was used in the first series of turrets.

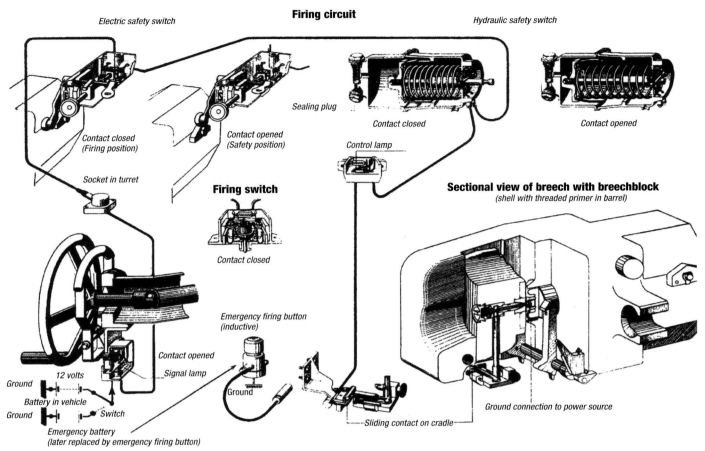

Firing circuit

Electric safety switch

Hydraulic safety switch

Sealing plug

Contact closed
(Firing position)

Contact opened
(Safety position)

Contact closed

Contact opened

Socket in turret

Firing switch

Control lamp

Sectional view of breech with breechblock
(shell with threaded primer in barrel)

Contact closed

Emergency firing button
(inductive)

Contact opened

12 volts

Signal lamp

Ground

Battery in vehicle

Ground

Switch

Ground

Emergency battery
(later replaced by emergency firing button)

Ground connection to power source

Sliding contact on cradle

As was common in German tanks, the gun was fired electrically.

(sintered powder metal) driving bands were used. The improved Panzergranatpatrone 39-1 had increased penetration performance, the Panzergranatpatrone 39 A*I* used an explosive charge incorporating a granular aluminum flash producer, and the Panzergranatpatrone 39 AI-1 had increased penetration performance and an explosive charge incorporating a granular aluminum flash producer.

In addition, the Panzergranatpatrone 40, with hard core (tungsten) and further improved penetration performance, and the Granatpatrone 39 HI, a hollow-charge antitank shell in several versions (performance levels), were produced. Penetration performance with the Panzergranate 39 and 39 AI, with a muzzle velocity of 773 m/sec. (2,536 ft./sec.) at a range of 1,000 meters (3,281 ft.), was 100 mm (3.9 in.) of armor steel; with the rare Panzergranate 40, with a muzzle velocity of 930 m/sec. (3,051 ft./sec.), 135 mm (5.3 in.) of armor steel; and with the Granate 39 HI, with a muzzle velocity of 600 m/sec. (1,969 ft./sec.), 90 mm (3.5 in.) of armor steel at any range.

The standard shell casing length was 570 mm (22.4 in.), and the external diameter of the cartridge case rim was 111.5 mm (4.4 in.). The empty casing weighed about three kg (6.6 lbs.). The weight of the charge was as follows:

- for the Panzergranatpatrone 39 = 2.500 kg (5.5 lbs.) Digl. RP-8 [diglykol, smokeless propellant based on diethylene glycol, *translator*]

- for the Panzergranatpatrone 40 = 2.850 kg (6.3 lbs.) Digl. RP-8

- for the Sprenggranatpatrone L/4.5 = 2.950 kg (6.5 lbs.) Digl.RP-8

The ready-to-fire shell thus weighed between 15.1 and 15.3 kg (33.3 and 33.7 lbs.).

Shell length for the Sprenggranatpatrone was 931 mm (36.65 in.); for the Panzergranatpatrone 40, 871 mm (34.3

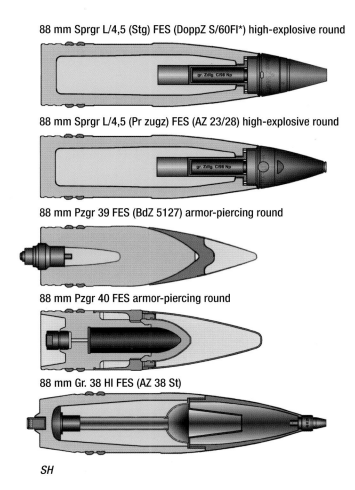

88 mm Sprgr L/4,5 (Stg) FES (DoppZ S/60Fl*) high-explosive round

88 mm Sprgr L/4,5 (Pr zugz) FES (AZ 23/28) high-explosive round

88 mm Pzgr 39 FES (BdZ 5127) armor-piercing round

88 mm Pzgr 40 FES armor-piercing round

88 mm Gr. 38 HI FES (AZ 38 St)

SH

From left to right:
88 mm HE shell, HE shell, Pzgr Patr 39 AP Shell, Pzgr Patr 40 AP Shell, Gr.Patr 39 HI. *SH*

in.); and for the Granatpatrone 39 HI, 923 mm (36.3 in.). Ammunition capacity was sixty-four rounds. Still under development in January 1942, was an 88/65 mm sabot projectile for the VK 4501's 88 mm KwK L/56, for which Prüf 4 had to design a cage for the muzzle brake. Development dragged on, however, and projectiles of this kind were not produced until the end of the war. The penetration performance of the later 88 mm KwK 43 L/71 was more than sufficient, however; consequently there was no longer a need for the sabot projectile.

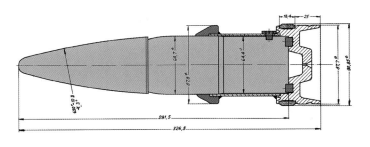

Gesamtgewicht _____ ≃ 6,100 kg
Fluggewicht _____ ≃ 4,800 "

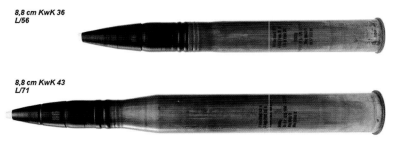

8,8 cm KwK 36
L/56

8,8 cm KwK 43
L/71

In the picture for comparison, *above*, the ammunition for the 88 mm KwK L/56, and, *below*, the Panzergranatpatrone 39 armor-piercing round of the 88 mm KwK L/71 from the planned Porsche Type 180

The ammunition used by the 88 mm KwK 43 L/71 was identical to that of the 88 mm KwK 36 L/56. Its improved performance was attributable to its greater barrel length, but primarily to its larger propellant charge, enabling it to achieve a muzzle energy of 536 MT compared to the KwK 36's 349 MT. The muzzle velocity of the high-explosive round was 700 m/sec. (2,297 ft./sec.), while that of the Panzergranate 39-1 was 1,000 m/sec. (3,280 ft./sec.). The armor-piercing round was thus able to penetrate 165 mm (6.5 in.) of armor steel at a range of 1,000 meters (3,280 ft.). With this ammunition the life of a

barrel was about 1,200 shots. The less common Panzergranate 40/43 even achieved a muzzle velocity of 1,130 m/sec. (3,707 ft./sec.), enabling it to penetrate 192 mm (7.6 in.) of armor steel at a range of 1,000 m.[81] With the larger propellant charge, the armor-piercing round's cartridge length rose to 1,128 mm (44.4 in.), while that of the high-explosive round increased to 1,183 mm (46.6 in.). Depending on the type, cartridge weight ranged from 16 to 22.8 kg (35.3 to 50.3 lbs.).

Furthermore, the Porsche Tiger was armed with two 7.92 mm MG 34 (with armored barrel protection), one being

The MG 34 with armored barrel, standard equipment in German tanks

The turret machine gun was mounted next to the main gun and was aimed with it. *D 656*

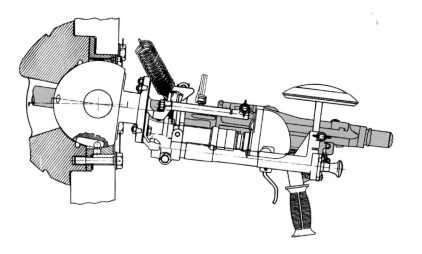

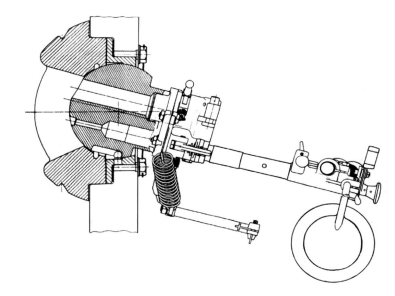

The bow machine gun, operated by the radio operator, and the associated Kugelzielfernrohr 2 telescopic sight. Because of the thicker armor plate, the Kugelblende 100 ball mount was used instead of the initially planned Kugelblende 50. *D 656*

Lfd. Nr.	Benen-nung	Bemerkungen
1	Geber	mit Druckknopfschaltern
2	Werfer	
3	Stecker	Bosch, LEA 19/4 z
4	Steckdose	Bosch, RS 155/3 (im Turm)
5	Schutz-element	25 DIN 72581 (im Kasten Pz Nr. 5c)

Leitgs. Nr.	Quer-schnitt	Bemerkungen
L 207	1,5²	vom Geber zur Steckdose im Turm
L 202	1,5²	vom Geber zum Werfer 1, vorn links
L 203	1,5²	v. G. z. W. 2, vorn rechts
L 204	1,5²	v. G. z. W. 3, mitte links
L 206	1,5²	v. G. z. W. 5, hinten links
L 207	1,5²	v. G. z. W. 6, hinten rechts

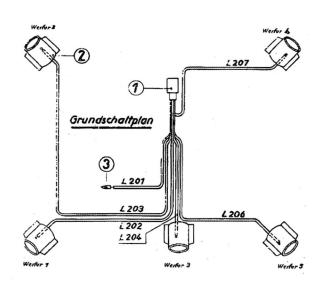

Grundschaltplan

Zeichnung-Nr.
021 D 2758 –1

In addition, the planned smoke grenade launcher system must be mentioned, although in practice the Porsche Tiger was never equipped with this system. *D 656*

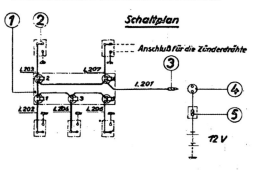

Schaltplan

Anschluß für die Zünderdrähte

12 V

Abb. 71
(siehe Seite 81)

Schaltplan d. S-Minenwerfer-
Anlage (Kampfwagen)
Für Befehlswagen fällt Werfer 3 weg

a coaxial machine gun to the right of the main gun and the other in an armored ball mount in front of the radio operator as a bow weapon. The prescribed locked position of this machine gun was such that in its outermost position the muzzle pointed to the far left.

The Porsche Engine

Since the engines of the Porsche Tiger Type 101 were the main problem, this engine will be discussed in greater detail here. After the successful testing of the 10-liter gasoline engines of the Porsche Type 100, it became necessary to design a more powerful engine for the new and heavier Porsche Type 101.

On September 5, the new engine was handed over to Simmering-Graz-Pauker AG Vienna (SGP AG Wien), specifically to Herr Michelmeier. The assertion made in some books that the Type 101 engine came from Steyr-Daimler-Puch is not true. At that time, in addition to the 10-liter (610 in.^{3}) engine for the Type 100, this company mainly produced aircraft engines under license from Daimler-Benz.

The new ten-cylinder gasoline engine was an air-cooled 72° V engine with a displacement of 15 liters (915 in.^{3}). It was a long-stroke engine with a bore of 115 mm (4.5 in.) and a stroke of 145 mm (5.7 in.). In the center of the "V" was a 50 JFF 2 two-barrel off-road carburetor made by the Solex company of Berlin. Contrary to what has been written in the literature, this engine was no "highly sensitive,

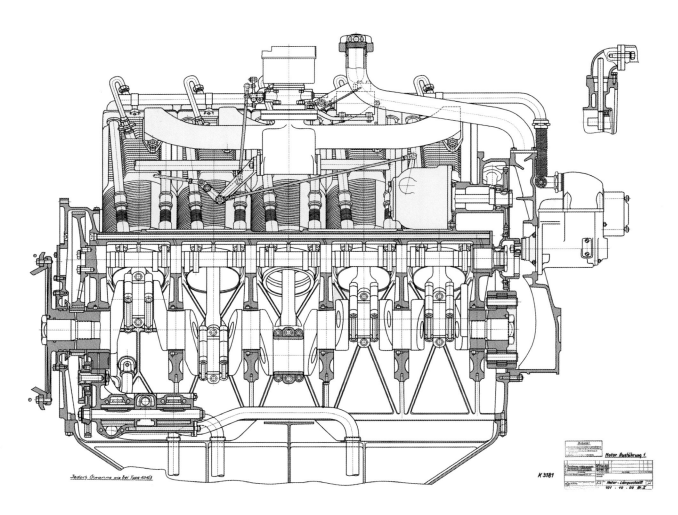

The Type 101/1 engine in cross section. *PA*

high-maintenance Arab from the House of Porsche."[82] The 15-liter engine produced 320 hp at 2,400 rpm.

By comparison, the Maybach HL 120 TRM high-performance engine later used in the Ferdinand assault gun had a displacement of 11.9 liters (726 in.[3]) and produced 300 hp at 3,000 rpm. This was a specific output of 25.2 hp per liter, in comparison to 21.3 hp per liter of the Porsche Type 101. This liquid-cooled engine had a maximum torque of 80 m/kg and a compression ratio of 1:6.5. With this engine concept it was possible to speak of a high-performance engine. With its 650 hp, also at 3,000 rpm, the Henschel rival's Maybach engine, the HL 210, had an even-higher specific output of 30.5 hp per liter. What is considered positive in racing was not the optimum for a robust tank engine. The maximum torque of the Porsche Type 101 engine, on the other hand, was higher, at 105 m/kg at a speed of 1,900 rpm. It had a compression of only 1:5.6 and an average working pressure of 8.3 atm. All of this spoke for better durability, theoretically! The engine was relatively light due to its air cooling, weighing between 420 and 450 kg (926 to 992 lbs.). By comparison, the Maybach HL 120 weighed 940 kg (2,072 lbs.). The ignition consisted of a magneto, an encapsulated distributor, and ten spark plugs. Starting was initiated by means of the generators. A battery-independent inertia starter was planned.

The lateral double blowers were driven by a secondary drive of the generator (Type 101) or a hydraulic gearbox (Type 102). The latter was in two stages due to the hydraulics. The drawing on page 209 illustrates the right fan drive. Fan power consumption per vehicle was 2×40 hp, which was sufficient for an air output of 2×5.8 m[3]/sec. This corresponded to an air flow rate of 50,000 kg/hr. (110,231 lbs./hr.).

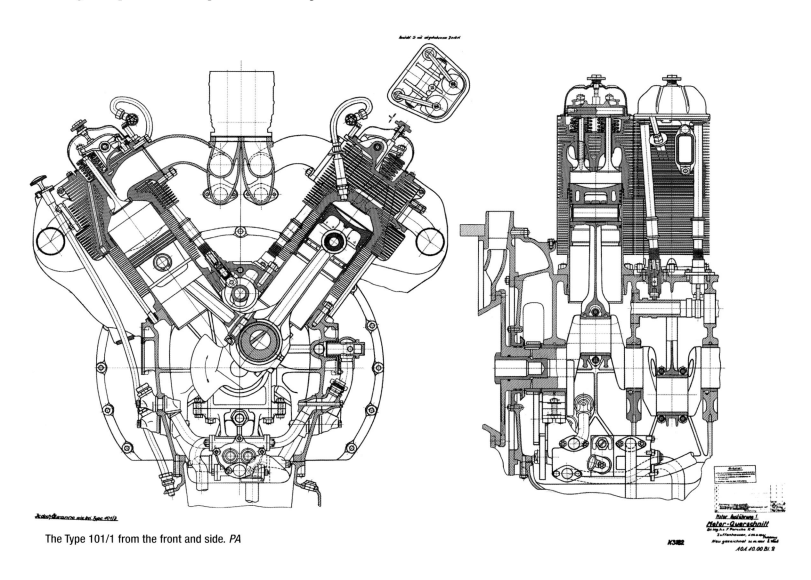

The Type 101/1 from the front and side. *PA*

The open engine compartment during dust trials in August 1942. The fan's exhaust opening can be seen on the extreme outer right edge. Due to their limited space, one can easily imagine the problems with cooling the inner cylinder banks. *PA*

The thermal difficulties as well as the problems with stability first led to the redesign of the cylinder heads. A Porsche Type 117 was replaced by the cylinder version B Porsche Type 119. In the new cylinder head, with its spherical combustion chamber, the valves, arranged in a V shape, had a larger diameter. The new inlet valve had a diameter of 61 mm (2.4 in.) (previous diameter was 54 mm, or 2.1 in.), and the hollow outlet valve, which was filled with sodium for better cooling, had a diameter of 52 mm (2 in.) (previous diameter was 44 mm, or 1.7 in.). Porsche had retained the conventional pushrod drive, since the crank drive remained the same. Further measures for better filling with the fuel mixture led to more favorably shaped channels to and from the valves. This measure and the combustion chamber with its improved shape made possible a more favorable combustion process. The new Mahle pistons no longer had a bulge in the piston bottom. The cylinder head had more-generous ribbing,

The side-mounted (in this case, the left) fan completely assembled in the assembly hall, ready for installation. It was made by Voith. *PA*

and the valve covers were split and smaller. Access to the valves could be opened without screws for the purpose of adjusting the valves. The cylinder head–cylinder connection was again made via a shrink thread, preventing head seal problems.

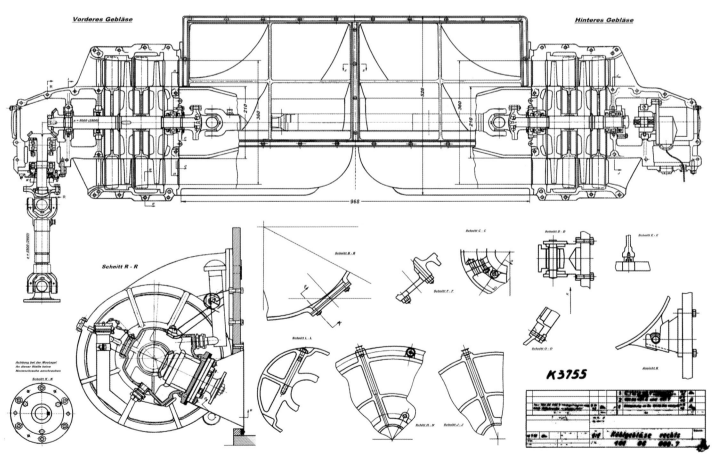

The right side-mounted fan of the Porsche Type 101. *PA*

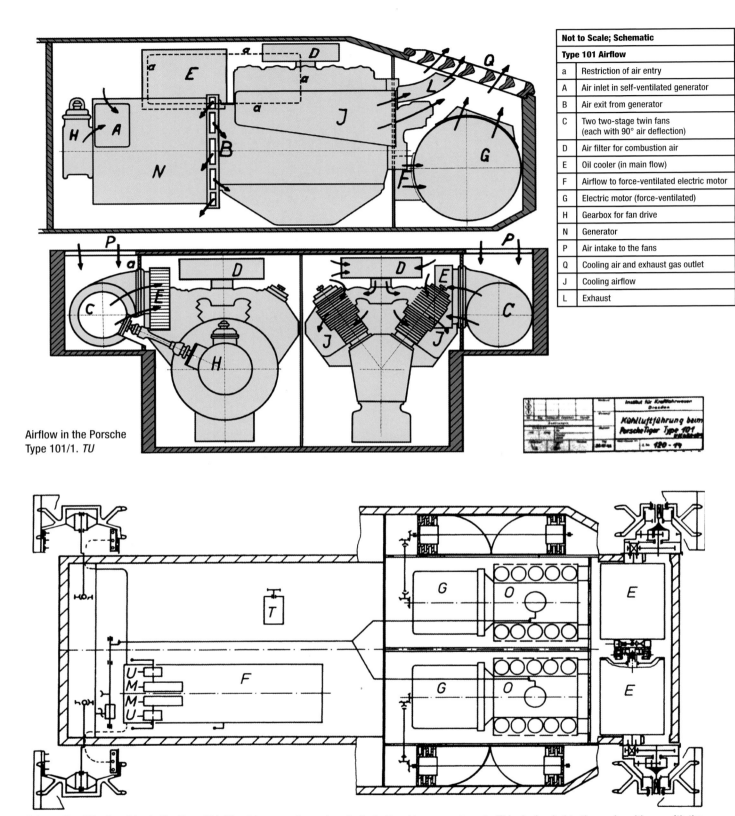

Not to Scale; Schematic	
Type 101 Airflow	
a	Restriction of air entry
A	Air inlet in self-ventilated generator
B	Air exit from generator
C	Two two-stage twin fans (each with 90° air deflection)
D	Air filter for combustion air
E	Oil cooler (in main flow)
F	Airflow to force-ventilated electric motor
G	Electric motor (force-ventilated)
H	Gearbox for fan drive
N	Generator
P	Air intake to the fans
Q	Cooling air and exhaust gas outlet
J	Cooling airflow
L	Exhaust

Airflow in the Porsche
Type 101/1. *TU*

Schematic of the fan drive in the Type 101. The drive was via cardan shafts to the side compartments. This design led to thermal problems with the inner banks of cylinders. *TU*

212

The remaining cooling problems and associated lubrication problems led to a further major development of the engine, which had a major impact on cooling and mixture formation. Its performance data rose slightly to 350 hp at 2,600 rpm, with 104 mkg (752 lb.-ft.) of torque. Maximum torque of 115 mkg (832 lb.-ft.) was achieved at a speed of 1,900 rpm. The internal designation for this engine was Porsche Type 101/3.

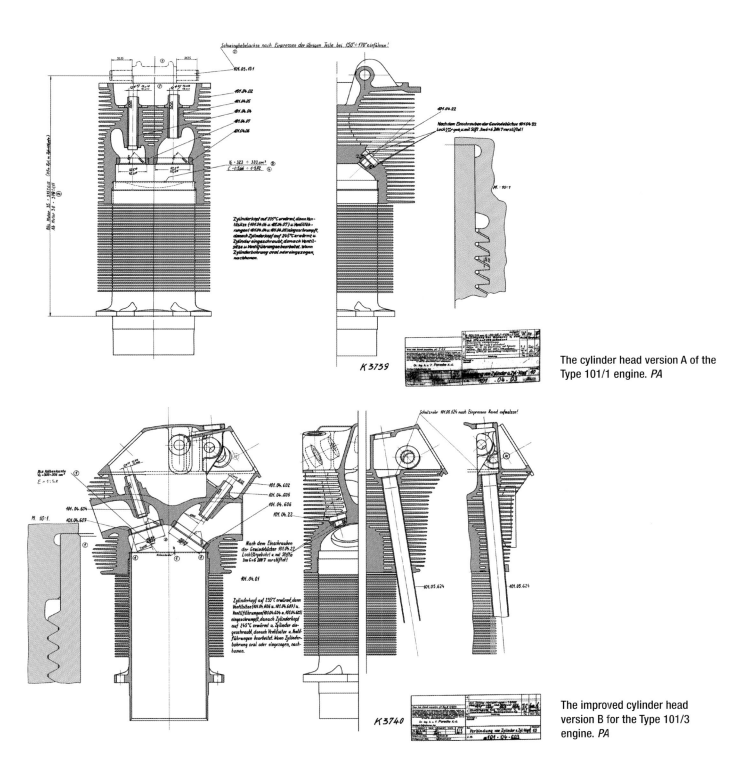

The cylinder head version A of the Type 101/1 engine. *PA*

The improved cylinder head version B for the Type 101/3 engine. *PA*

The mixture was now formed with the help of two Solex 40 JFF2 two-barrel off-road carburetors. Between the two carburetors was the speed limiter. New Mahle pistons as well as the previously mentioned new cylinder heads were used.

For better engine oil cleaning, the designers replaced the previous magnetic filter with an oil centrifuge driven by the camshaft. In the course of further development, the Type 104/4 engine was developed for the Porsche Tiger 2.

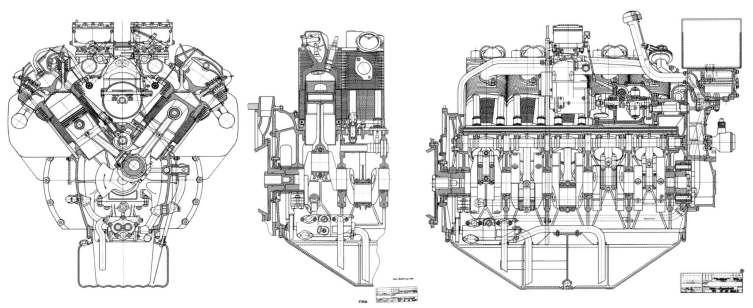

The Type 101/3 engine from the front and side. *PA*

The improved Type 101/3 engine in side section

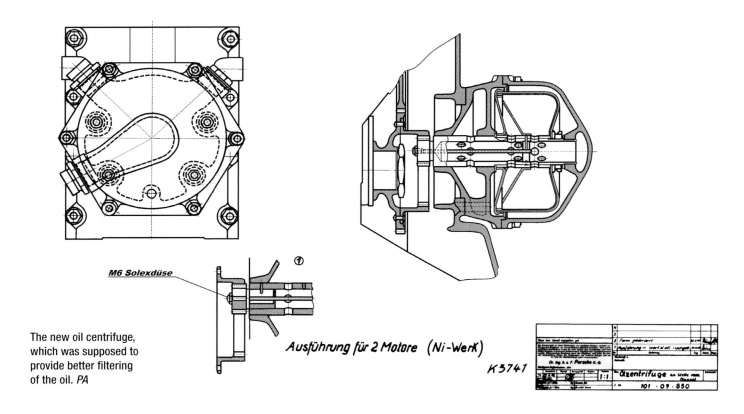

The new oil centrifuge, which was supposed to provide better filtering of the oil. *PA*

M6 Solexdüse

Ausführung für 2 Motore (Ni-Werk)

K 3741

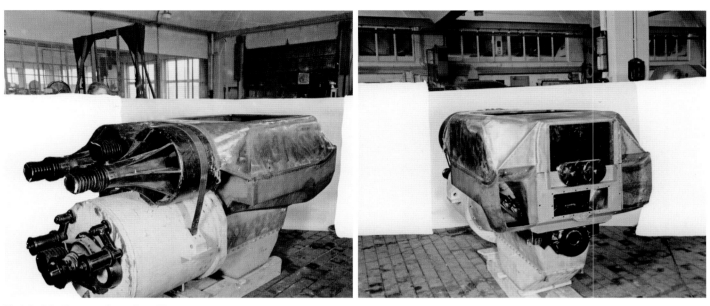

Model of the Type 101/3 engine. *PA*

The new Porsche Type 101/3 engine with generator mockup and the new twin fan made of wood. The oil cooler is also missing. *PA*

215

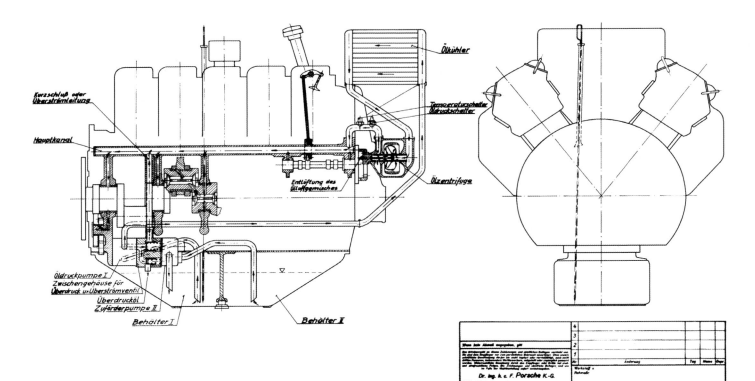

Lubrication chart of the redesigned engine. Note the position of the oil cooler in front of the engine. *PA*

K 3639

Cooling was provided by twin fans directly in front of the engine. The airflow now ran from front to rear instead of crosswise as before, which of course required new fan screens (gratings) for the vehicle. The oil cooler, located in the air stream, was between the cylinder banks of the 101/3 engine. The fans were each driven by six Continental V belts. It proved possible to reduce the fans' power consumption from 2 × 40 hp to 2 × 35 hp. The sole difference between the left and right engines was the external hose connections (flow and return) to the oil cooler. *PA*

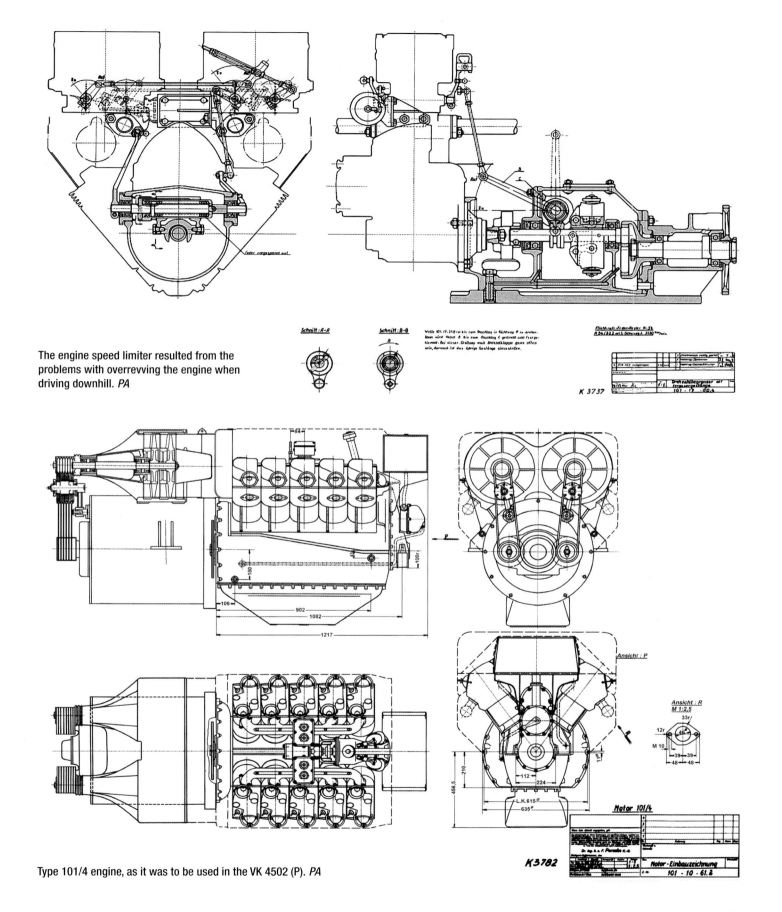

The engine speed limiter resulted from the problems with overrevving the engine when driving downhill. *PA*

Type 101/4 engine, as it was to be used in the VK 4502 (P). *PA*

217

The last variant of the engine built was created as the Type 101/3A. On October 15, 1943, Karl Rabe wrote to Oberbaurat Augustin, the armaments representative in Berlin: "In addition to the development of the [air-cooled] diesel engines, work was also continued on the 101/3A gasoline engine of the Dr. Porsche KG company, the drive engine for the Pz.Kpfw. Tiger P. In particular, gasoline injection pumps were added instead of carburetors, which significantly improved performance and fuel consumption. The supercharging conditions were clarified using the single-cylinder engine. Today, the engine has a shaft power of 370 hp without supercharging and is expected to achieve a continuous power of 500 hp with

supercharging. For this reason, it seems necessary to complete this work at an accelerated rate, to create the engine of about 500 hp, which we currently lack."[83] This means that at least one ten-cylinder gasoline engine was built (derived from the 1.5-liter [91.5 in.^{3}] single-cylinder Type 193). Only one 1.5-liter engine was completed with supercharging, however.

This was the conclusion of the joint development of air-cooled ten-cylinder engines by Porsche, Steyr, and Simmering-Graz-Pauker. Interesting engine developments appeared during the war, in which Porsche also participated, out of the need to increase the power-to-weight ratio of heavy tanks. While the Maybach tank engines were liquid-cooled, Porsche's

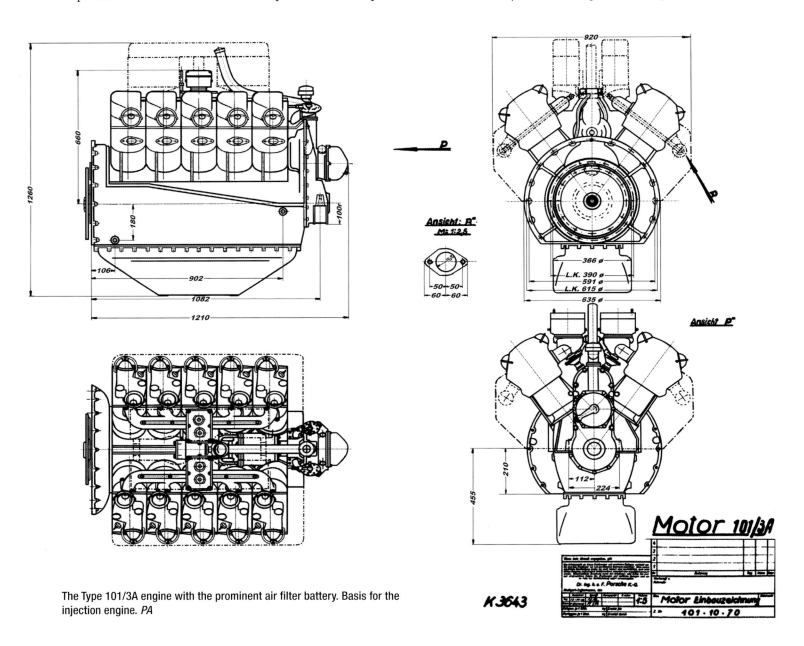

The Type 101/3A engine with the prominent air filter battery. Basis for the injection engine. *PA*

Photos of the ten-cylinder Porsche Type 101/3 carburetor engine, on the basis of which the gasoline injection engine was later created. The new air filter on the two twin carburetors is a prominent feature. *PA*

tank engines were based on air-cooled units. The German army command initially wanted only carburetor engines for armored vehicles, as relevant German industry realized that production of synthetic diesel fuel was scarcely possible. These concerns became irrelevant in mid-1942, because from then on, synthetic diesel fuel could be produced in sufficient quantities. From that point on, the development of diesel tank engines was accelerated.

In 1942, Porsche had begun developing an air-cooled diesel engine capable of producing 650 hp, which was interchangeable with the Maybach HL 230 engines and could be installed in existing tanks. Two prototype engines were built and tested by Simmering-Graz-Pauker AG. This company in Vienna had developed test benches for these large engines and taken over the entire experimental development program. Together, Porsche and the Simmering company examined the following single-cylinder test engines to assess potential use in armored vehicles:

- Type 117: single-cylinder tests for the Type 101, cylinder head version 1, fuel-gasoline, system: carburetor, displacement 1.5 liters (91.5 in.^{3})

- Type 119: single-cylinder tests for the Type 101/3, cylinder head version 2, fuel-gasoline, system: carburetor, displacement 1.5 liters (91.5 in.^{3})

- Type 158: single-cylinder tests for the Type 101 as diesel engine, system: direct injection, displacement 1.5 liters (91.5 in.^{3})

- Type 159: single-cylinder tests for the Type 101 as diesel engine, system: Simmering front chamber, displacement 1.5 liters (91.5 in.^{3})

- Type 191: single-cylinder tests for the Type 190, the diesel version of the Type 180, system: direct injection, displacement 1.64 liters (91.00 in.^{3})

- Type 192: single-cylinder tests after conversion from the Type 191 for the Type 205, fuel-diesel, displacement 2.3 liters (140.36 in.^{3})

- Type 193: single-cylinder tests for the Type 101/4 with gasoline injection, displacement 1.64 liters (91.00 in.^{3})

- Type 212: single-cylinder tests for the air-cooled 16-cylinder engine in X configuration, fuel-diesel, displacement 2.3 liters (140.36 in.^{3})

- Type 213: single-cylinder tests for the air-cooled 16-cylinder engine in X configuration, fuel-diesel, displacement 3.0 liters (183.07 in.^{3})

The Sla 16 diesel engine in X configuration, without the baffles and turbochargers. *PA*

The Sla 16 sixteen-cylinder diesel engine complete with air filter, baffles, and turbochargers. *PA*

The 2.3-liter (140 in.^{3}) Type 192 formed the basis of the design of a sixteen-cylinder diesel engine in X or double-V configuration with a cylinder angle of 135°. At the end of the war, this development ended in the 36.8-liter (2,245.7 in.^{3}) Sla 16 diesel engine (Simmering air-cooled, supercharged sixteen-cylinder engine), with an output of 720 to 800 hp at 2,000 rpm. The Sla 16's air cooling was achieved by two fans, each of which was capable of discharging 6,000 liters (212 ft.^{3}) of air per second at 4,100 rpm. In this air stream there were two oil coolers on each side. The fans' power requirement

The shrink-fitted cylinder head and the welded engine housing of the Sla 16. *PA*

was 80 hp. As a novelty, the engine had two exhaust-driven turbosuperchargers based on the Buechi/Brown-Boveri system. Their maximum speed was 28,000 rpm. This enabled a maximum charge pressure of 1.33 atm and a maximum output per turbocharger of 510 liters/sec. (1,080 cfm). The air filter, a vortex filter, consisted of 144 cells. The combustion system operated according to the Simmering-Graz-Pauker AG's patented prechamber process. This engine was designed to replace the Maybach HL 230 gasoline engine of the Panther and Tiger (B) tanks, whereby the engine speed of the Sla 16 had to be adjusted to the 3,000 rpm of the Maybach engine by means of gearing. Porsche also planned to use this engine in the Porsche Type 180. The Porsche Type 213 engine, with its increased displacement, became a 48-liter (2,929 in.[3]) version of the Sla 16 diesel engine, with an output of 1,500 hp at 2,500 rpm. Porsche thus had an alternative for the Maus tank and the E-100. This chapter is supplemented by the Porsche Type 141 generator set. The waste heat from the two-cylinder engine, which was developed from the Volkswagen engine, was used to heat the fighting compartment. The 3 kW generator, driven by V belts, had to charge the batteries when the main engines were not running. In addition to starting the main engines, the two main batteries made it possible to traverse the turret when the tank was stopped. The 24 volts generated were also necessary to supply the excitation voltage for the generators and electric motors.

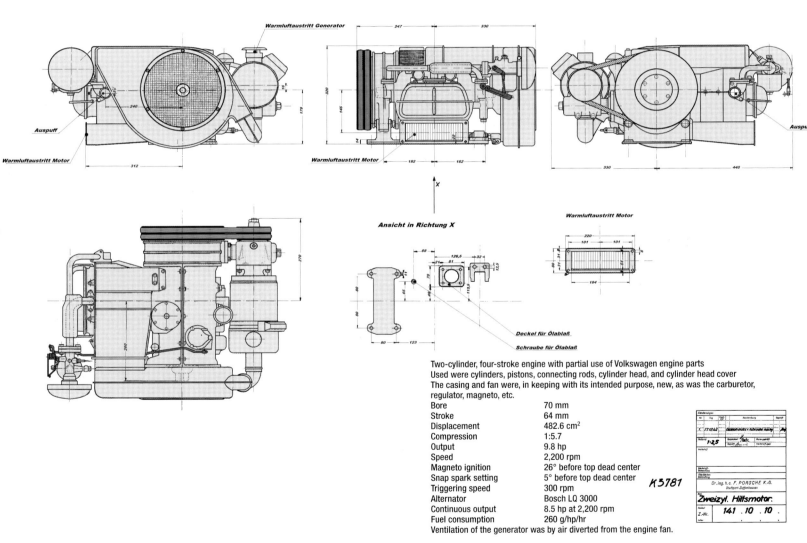

Two-cylinder, four-stroke engine with partial use of Volkswagen engine parts
Used were cylinders, pistons, connecting rods, cylinder head, and cylinder head cover
The casing and fan were, in keeping with its intended purpose, new, as was the carburetor, regulator, magneto, etc.

Bore	70 mm
Stroke	64 mm
Displacement	482.6 cm²
Compression	1:5.7
Output	9.8 hp
Speed	2,200 rpm
Magneto ignition	26° before top dead center
Snap spark setting	5° before top dead center
Triggering speed	300 rpm
Alternator	Bosch LQ 3000
Continuous output	8.5 hp at 2,200 rpm
Fuel consumption	260 g/hp/hr

Ventilation of the generator was by air diverted from the engine fan.

The Type 141 auxiliary power unit, which in principle was half a VW engine

The Electric Drive

The electric drive required about 940 kg (2,072 lbs.) of strictly rationed copper per vehicle. The two DC generators were self-ventilated and had a fan wheel on the rotor shaft. The possible continuous generator power was 250 kW at 2,500/3,000 rpm, which corresponded to 385 volts at 650 amperes. At 325 volts and 650 amperes, a continuous output of 210 kW was

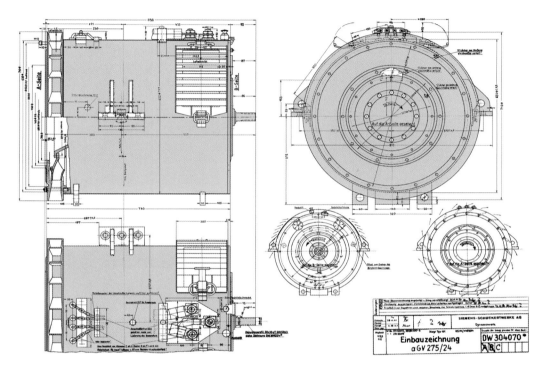

Installation drawing of the aGV 275/24

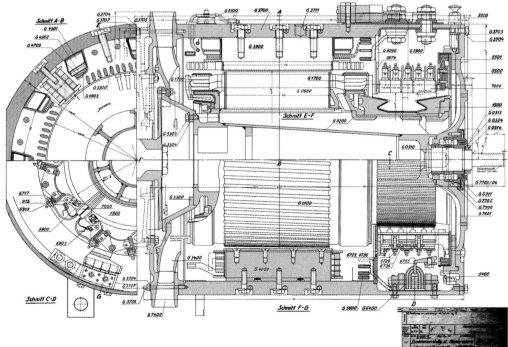

Composition of the generator

achieved. A generator designated aGV 275/24 had a diameter of 650 mm (25.6 in.), was 825 mm (32.5 in.) long, and weighed about 914 kg (2,015 lbs.).

The two Type D 1495a DC electric motors each had a diameter of 650 mm (25.6 in.) and were 850 mm (33.5 in.) long. Maximum power was 230 kW at 1,300 rpm. Both motors were one unit, with an external shoe brake in the middle

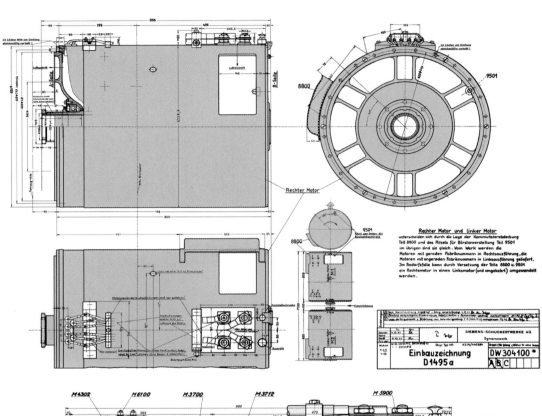

Installation drawing of the D 1495a motor

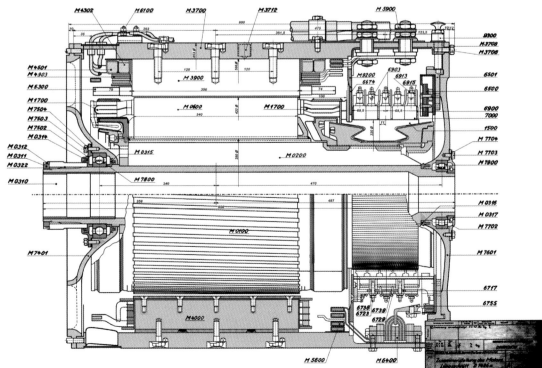

Composition of the 1495a electric motor

Both electric motors installed in the rear of the Tiger (P) chassis. In principle, both engines were interchangeable, and only the fittings had to be changed. In the middle is the vehicle's parking brake. *B*

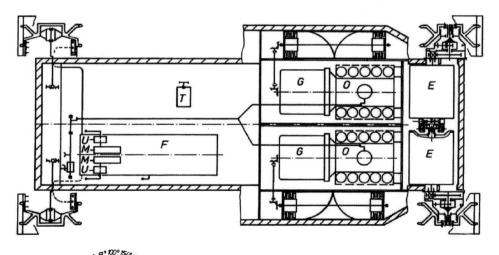

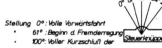

Stellung 0° : Volle Vorwärtsfahrt
    "   61° : Beginn d. Fremderregung
    " 100° : Voller Kurzschluß der
            Hauptstromwicklung
    " 154° : Volle Stärke d. Fremderregung,
            Beginn d. umgekehrten Haupterregung,
            Einsatz der Öldruckbremse
    " 254°: Äußerste Bremsstellung, volle Rückwärtsfahrt

Stellg. I : Generator I u. II parallel
    " II : Anlasser Generator I u. II
    " III : Fahren mit Generator I u. II in Reihe
    " IV : Fahren mit Generator I
    " V : Fahren mit Generator II

G	Generator	R	Regler für Generatorfremderregung
O	Ottomotor	U	Umkehrfeldregler
E	Elektromotor	M	Regler für Motorfremderregung
F	Fahrschalter	T	Elektrischer Turmantrieb

Institut für Kraftfahrwesen Dresden	
VK 4501(P) Typ 101	
Porsche - Tiger	
Antriebs - Schema	
30.10. 42	120 - 12

The drive scheme of the Type 101 Porsche Tiger. *TU*

225

acting as a parking brake. One motor weighed about 1,130 kg (2,491 lbs.). Like the generators, the electric motors had to be excited by 24 volts. The motors were ventilated by the airflow from the internal combustion engines.

The heart of the drive control was the drive switch, located under the driver's seat. The main switch and generator switch

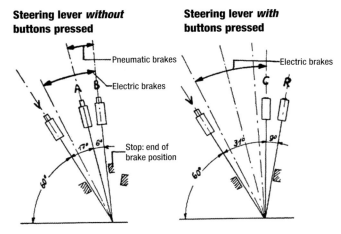

Steering lever *without* buttons pressed

Pneumatic brakes
Electric brakes
Stop: end of brake position

Steering lever *with* buttons pressed

Electric brakes

B = Stopped brake position
brake

C = Gradient brake position

Driving switch

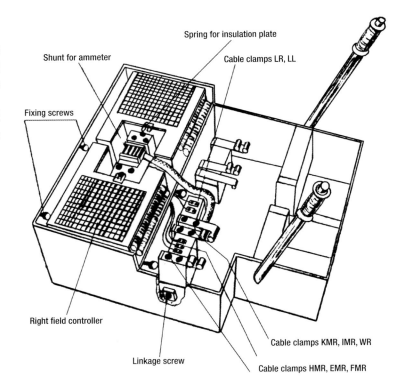

Spring for insulation plate
Shunt for ammeter
Cable clamps LR, LL
Fixing screws
Right field controller
Linkage screw
Cable clamps KMR, IMR, WR
Cable clamps HMR, EMR, FMR

Driving switch, opened

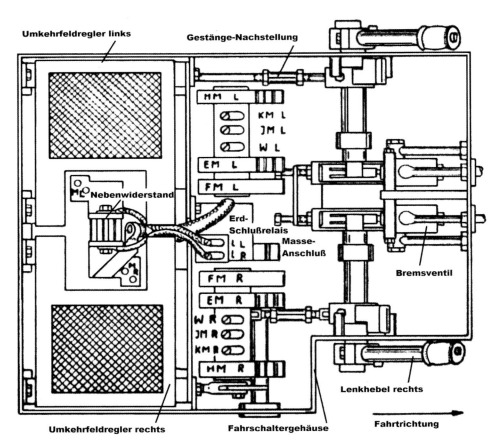

Umkehrfeldregler links
Gestänge-Nachstellung
HM L
KM L
JM L
W L
EM L
FM L
Nebenwiderstand
Erd-Schlußrelais
L L
L R
Masse-Anschluß
FM R
EM R
W R
JM R
KM R
HM R
Bremsventil
Lenkhebel rechts
Fahrtrichtung

The linkage acted on the two field controllers, depending on whether the vehicle was being driven or braked. Driving in reverse was also controlled by the position of the steering levers. D 656

Umkehrfeldregler rechts
Fahrschaltergehäuse

Klemmen am Fahrschalter

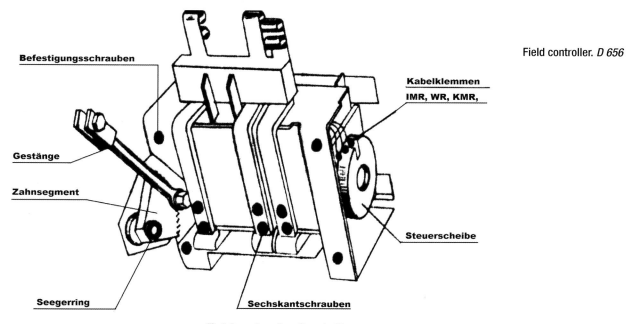

Field controller. *D 656*

Befestigungsschrauben

Kabelklemmen
IMR, WR, KMR,

Gestänge

Zahnsegment

Steuerscheibe

Seegerring

Sechskantschrauben

Feldregler im Gestell

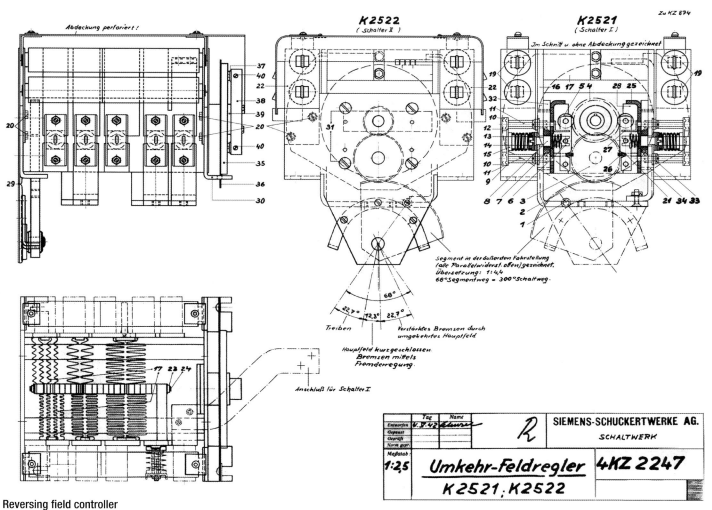

Reversing field controller

weighed about 228 kg (503 lbs.). It consisted of the left and right reverse field controllers, the two steering levers with rods, and the brake valves.

If both steering levers were forward, the vehicle drove forward at maximum speed. From the lever position of 61°, foreign excitation and thus deceleration took place. Reverse main excitation began from the 154° lever position, which means the motors were switched into reverse. At the same time, the pneumatically assisted hydraulic driving brake was used. The maximum rear position was 254° and was the extreme braking position. By pressing the buttons on the steering levers, reverse drive was also possible in this position. The control box, with speed switch, the rotary switch, the preselector switch, and the controller for external excitation, was

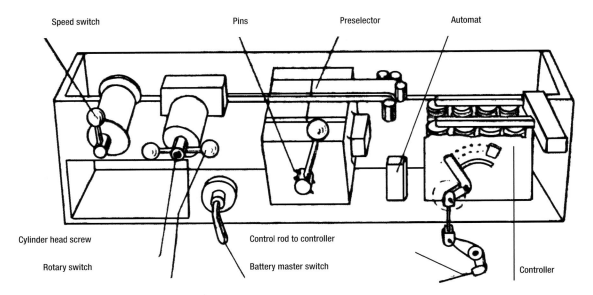

Speed switch   Pins   Preselector   Automat

Cylinder head screw   Control rod to controller

Rotary switch   Battery master switch   Controller

Switch box. *D 656*

Switch box

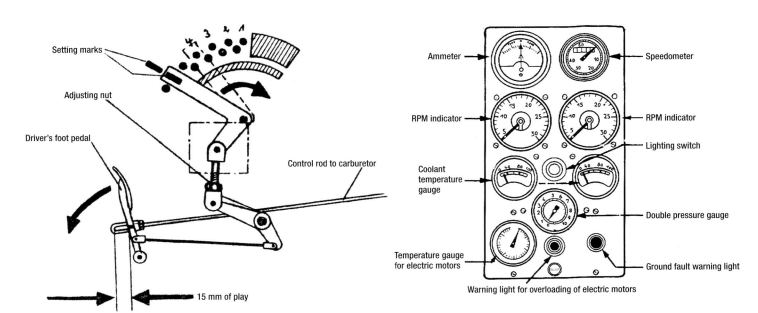

Setting marks
Adjusting nut
Driver's foot pedal
Control rod to carburetor
15 mm of play

Ammeter   Speedometer
RPM indicator   RPM indicator
Lighting switch
Coolant temperature gauge
Double pressure gauge
Temperature gauge for electric motors
Ground fault warning light
Warning light for overloading of electric motors

The controller lever arrangement. The Porsche tank destroyer's instrument panel could be identified by the two coolant temperature gauges for the two Maybach HL 120 engines. The panel was located in the niche to the driver's left.

located to the right of the driver. The speed switch was used to adjust the driving load. Position 1 was intended for heavy terrain, Position 2 for medium terrain, and Position 3 for light terrain or road travel. The rotary switch could be switched on or off only for start-up. The third switch was the preselector for the generator control switch. The last switching element was the controller. This was connected to the driving pedal and transmitted the driving commands, on the one hand, to the two generators as a foreign excitation, and on the other hand, via the throttle linkage to the carburetors. In addition, there were the main battery switch and the elements of the low-voltage system, such as the power outlets, the alternator charging controls, and the dimming and rear light switches. On the back of the switch box were the fuses for the 12-volt

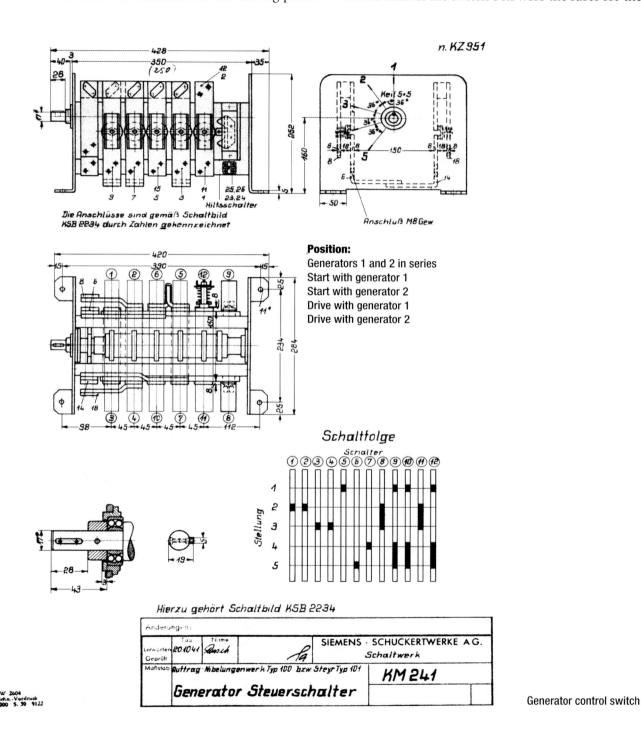

Position:
Generators 1 and 2 in series
Start with generator 1
Start with generator 2
Drive with generator 1
Drive with generator 2

Generator control switch

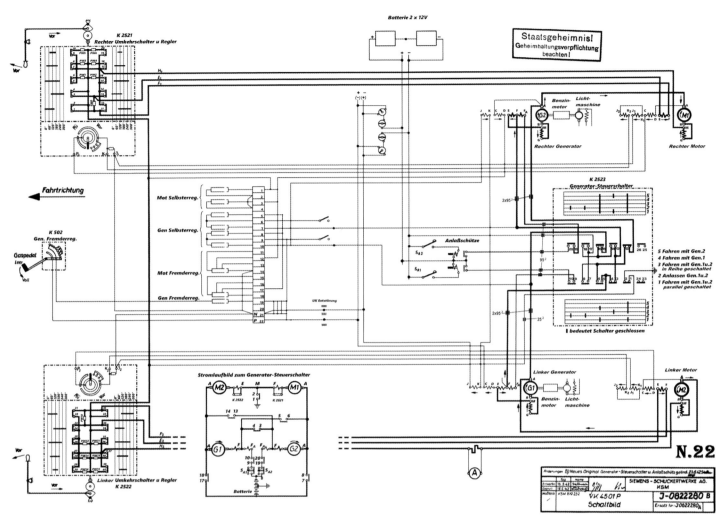

The electric-driving circuit diagram of the Porsche Type 101 (VK 4501 P). The control switch was later changed in the Porsche Ferdinand tank destroyer. The new position 1 was the driving position, position 2 was idle, position 3 was driving with the left engine only, and position 4 was driving with the right engine only. *PA*

system. The dashboard was next to the driver, to the front right. The switching sequence or position of the generator control switch was changed on June 23, 1942, in contrast to the above plan dated October 1941. In position 1, generators I and II were switched, not in parallel, but in series. In position 2 the internal combustion engine was started by both generators instead of by generator I only. In position 3 the function of the start-up of generator II was omitted and both generators were thus connected. Position 4 retained the function of driving with generator I, just as position 5 meant driving with generator II. This meant that in case of damage, the vehicle could be driven on just one internal-combustion engine. This

of course meant driving at half power. Porsche used a so-called Leonhard set for the Siemens aG 56n turret traverse system. The onboard voltages of 12 and 24 volts were insufficient for the 10-metric-ton (11-ton) turret, since the required amperage necessitated large cable cross sections. The voltage had to be increased in order to use manageable cable cross sections and to be able to better control the speed of the traverse motor. Given the state of the art at that time, a Leonard set was used to help transform the voltage and control speed. The 24-volt direct-current motor (control motor) drove a foreign-excited DC generator (control generator) sitting on the same shaft. On the same shaft was a direct-current secondary-circuit generator, the so-called exciter. With this circuit, an adjustable armature voltage was supplied to the DC control motor, and thus the speed was changed, with torque remaining the same. The process took place completely independent of the load on the control motor. The required foreign excitation was provided by the exciter.[84] The radio system consisted of the standard Fu 5 radio set. This set included a VHF receiver and a 10-watt transmitter. Three transformers provided the voltage required by the devices. These rotating voltage converters had the task of transforming the necessary voltage from the 12 volts of the two vehicle batteries to 130 volts for the two receivers and 350 volts for the 10-watt transmitter. The single-armature converter used for this was similar in principle to the Leonard turret traverse system.

A sample image of a three-machine unit as a Leonard transformer. *ETW*

The two elements of the Fu 5 radio set, the Ukw.E.e (receiver) and the 10W.S.c (transmitter). Both are "yellow-stripe devices," which meant that the receiver was used as an amplifier and the transmitter as a supplier of power to the throat microphones of the Bordsprechanlage Z intercom system used by the commander and the driver / radio operator.

Radio and intercom system in the Pz.Kpfw. VI P₁.

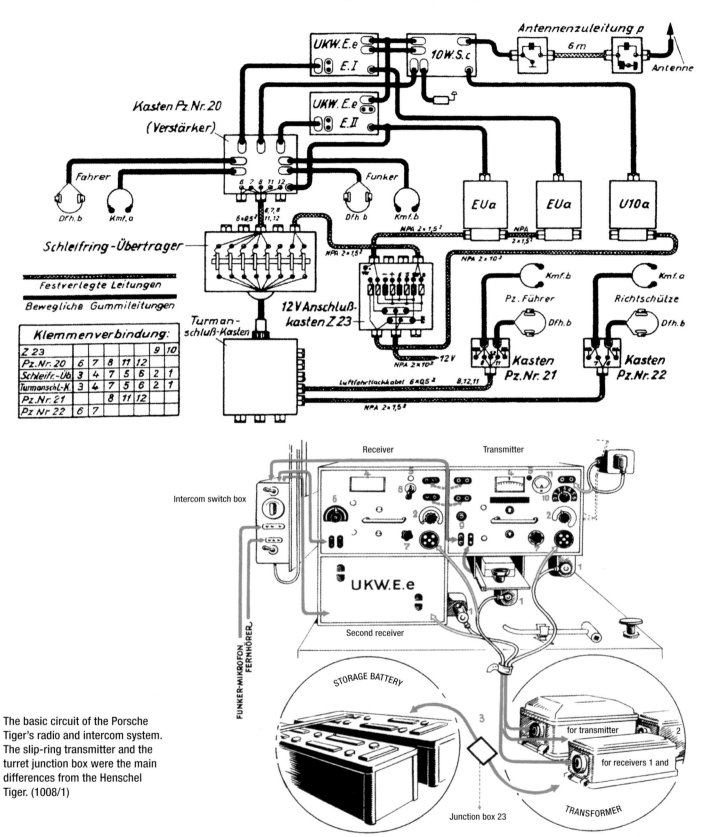

The basic circuit of the Porsche Tiger's radio and intercom system. The slip-ring transmitter and the turret junction box were the main differences from the Henschel Tiger. (1008/1)

The Hydraulic Drive

As described at the beginning, Professor Porsche saw not only the preferred electric drive but also the hydraulic drive as a means of propelling a heavy armored vehicle without interruption of traction, even in difficult terrain. Hydraulic engineering had made remarkable progress in the late 1930s. The efficiency of 85%–90% was similar to that of the electric drive at that time. In contrast to the electric drive, the hydraulic drive had the advantage of better cooling. Medium hydraulic fluid could be used to dissipate heat loss via oil coolers, which could easily be integrated into the engine cooling circuit. Electrical windings lacked such a capability. On the contrary, the windings still had to be surrounded by an insulator, which prevented rapid head dissipation. For better heat dissipation through the air flow, the surface had to be enlarged, which in turn drove up the amount of copper and the weight. This

meant that there were very tight limits to the heat dissipation of electrical power transmission. This was a very big problem, especially in the tank; because of the all-around armor protection, few ventilation openings were available. Another problem was that at low speed, particularly high currents flowed through the windings, which limited the power to be transmitted. In the case of hydraulic transmission, it was possible to use full engine power continuously at low speeds. Provided that the hydraulic system was properly encapsulated, another point in favor of hydraulics emerged, because the system, unlike the electric drive, was insensitive to external influences such as moisture and dust. Professor Porsche therefore included the hydraulic drive in his tank project. Two types of hydraulic drive were considered. The first system was the hydrostatic drive. On February 2, 1942, there was a

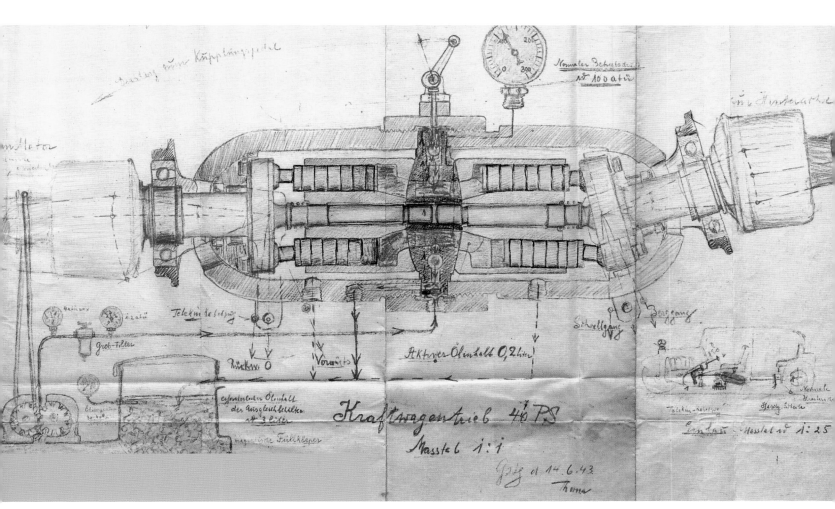

Function drawing of the hydrostatic drive by Professor Thoma. *BAMA*

The vehicle with the hydrostatic drive still exists at Fort Lee, Virginia, in the United States.

meeting with Professor Thoma from Karlsruhe, who presented his design of an axial piston transmission with swiveling cylinders. He emphasized the advantages of this tandem gearbox over the hydrodynamic gearbox, since the efficiency factor of his hydrostatic transmission was much flatter, thus resulting in a larger and more favorable range of use. In practice, this meant that high speed and engine power were required to travel with the hydrodynamic system, while for the hydrostatically powered vehicle it was child's play to start in idle with low engine rpm.

This system made possible, at minimal cost in materials, stepless driving with great drive power, whereas economic use of the hydrodynamic drive over a wide speed range was impossible because of its steep efficiency curve. For example, two or three torque converters with different gear ratios had to be built side by side to enable sensible driving. Unfortunately, it is not known why Professor Thoma was unable to win over Ferdinand Porsche. Professor Thoma was later able to test his system in practice, when the SS-Führungshauptamt (SS

operational headquarters) gave him the opportunity to install the drive in a Panzerkampfwagen IV. However, Professor Porsche famously opted for Dr. Voith's hydrodynamic drive. The first discussions about a hydraulic version of the Porsche Type 101 took place on July 12, 1941. However, Porsche and Voith had already been able to gather initial insights during discussions on the Type 100 project. The designs for the project, now known as the Type 102, were created in January and February 1942. The basic vehicle design of the Type 101 project was maintained. Instead of two generators, Porsche used a Voith NITA turbo transmission for each engine. At the beginning of 1942, at Voith's suggestion, the design was changed to include a G24 twin turbo gearbox with a common steering gear instead of two individual converters. However, this led to significant changes in the hydraulic hulls already under construction at Krupp. As previously described, the entire hull production process at Krupp and the Nibelungenwerk was disrupted, and this caused considerable delays.

On the hydraulic gearbox, which weighed 800 kg, were the two auxiliary drives for the alternators, for the compressor, and for the two side fan drives. Since the hydraulic unit, in part due to the central Cardan drive, was very tall, the improved engine cooling with the double blowers could not be used later. The Type 102 retained the conventional blowers, which were located only on the outside of the two engines, front and rear, and thus directed the airflow from outside to inside. The drive took place via cardan shafts. Porsche had envisaged another auxiliary drive as an option for connecting a coolant pump for possible Porsche Type 130 liquid-cooled engines. The gearing of the two-stage hydraulic gearbox was 1:0.797. The 60-metric-ton (66-ton) heavy tank's maximum speed was the same as that of the version with electric drive at 35 kph (21.75 mph).

The Type 101 ten-cylinder engine transmitted its power via the input shaft and a pair of gears to the intermediate shaft. In addition to the output for the fan and the V-belt disc for the alternator and compressor, the input shaft powered the hydraulic pumps via bevel gears. These three pumps, which sat on a shaft, were the main pump, the return pump, and the control pump on the input side. On the following intermediate shaft were the two equally large hydraulic converter units. The necessary different gearing of the two converter units was achieved with the help of gear pairs. At the end of the intermediate shaft was the exit-side control pump. Both control pumps compared the engine speed (input speed) with the output speed. If the output speed dropped despite high engine speed, the control pumps ensured that the lower-geared converter was filled and the higher-geared converter was emptied. Of course, this also happened the other way around. The gear pairs of both converters were constantly in engagement with the output shaft. From this shaft the force was transferred to a cardan shaft. Instead of the electric motors, as in the Type 101, there was a final gearbox in the rear of the Type 102. This gearbox was also made by the Voith company. It was manufactured by the Böhmisch-Mährische Maschinenfabrik AG company.

The cardan shaft connected the Voith turbo transmission with this gearbox. The cardan shaft passed the power on to the transverse main shaft via an input shaft with bevel gears. There was another sliding piece on this input shaft in front of the bevel gears, with which the speed could be reduced again via a planetary gearbox. This slow gear allowed for

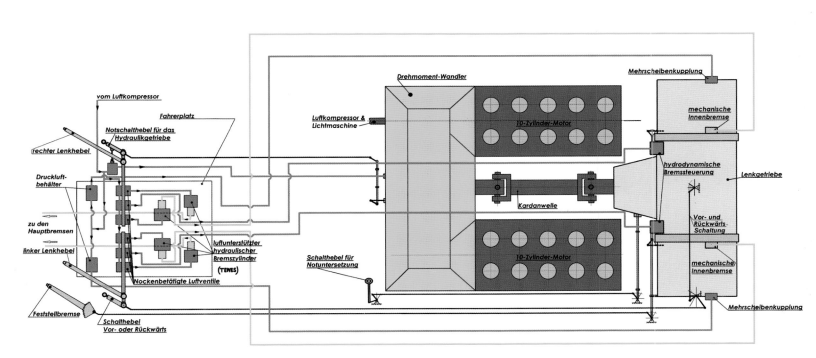

The schematic function chart of the hydropneumatically controlled Porsche Type 102

Voith-Zeichnung G01-0001
schematischer Kontrollplan

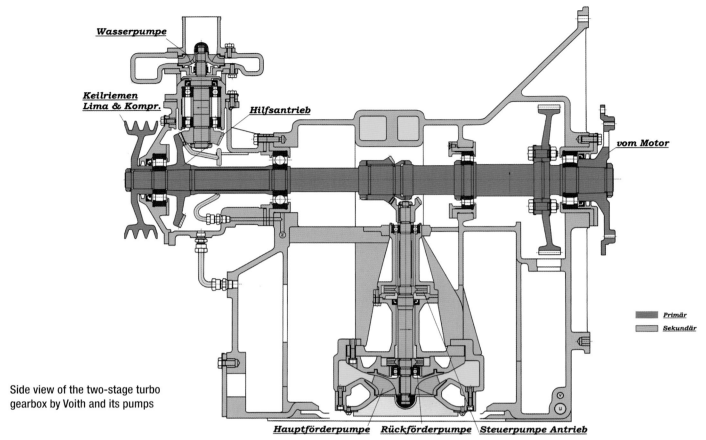

Wasserpumpe

Keilriemen
Lima & Kompr.

Hilfsantrieb

vom Motor

Primär
Sekundär

Side view of the two-stage turbo
gearbox by Voith and its pumps

Hauptförderpumpe   Rückförderpumpe   Steuerpumpe Antrieb

Schnitt A - B Voith-Turbogetriebe   GG. 24-0700.

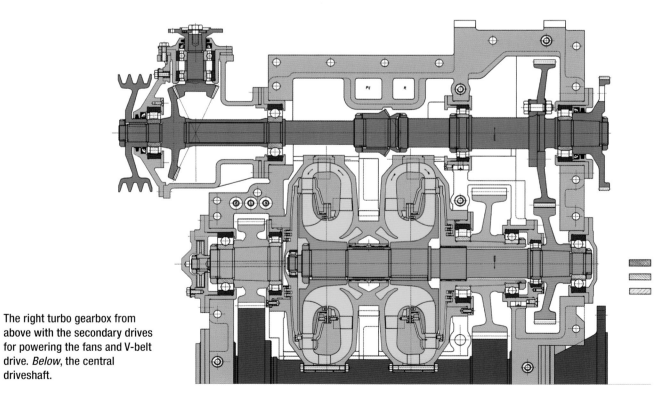

The right turbo gearbox from
above with the secondary drives
for powering the fans and V-belt
drive. *Below*, the central
driveshaft.

GG 24-0800.

greater torque on the drive wheels and was intended to allow continued movement in the event of a failure of the hydraulic torque converter. For this purpose, the converter units could

be switched mechanically without pressure in the event of a hydraulic defect. The steering gear also contained the direction of travel. The direction of travel (i.e., forward and backward)

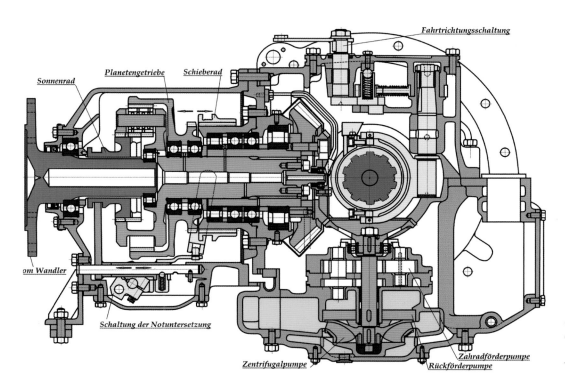

Center profile through the final drive with the switchable "emergency or recovery gear" and the hydraulic feed pumps

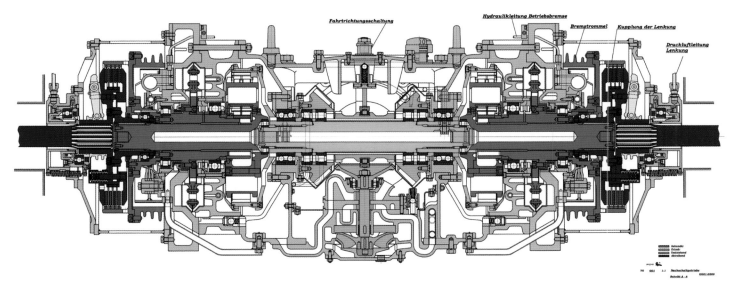

Front view of the final drive with the reverse gearshift. In addition to the hydraulic eddy current brake, there was also the hydraulically actuated service brake and the mechanical parking brake. Outside the air-controlled clutch steering.

View of the steering gearbox and the hydraulic module in the background. The two combustion engines between them are missing. The engines transmitted the power to the torque converter via gears. The mounting brackets on the sides were envisaged for the Bosch AL/SED electric starters, since no starting with the help of the hydraulics was planned. *PA*

could be switched mechanically to the respective left or right bevel gear only when the vehicle was stopped via a sliding wheel.

In the middle position, the gearbox was in idle. The flow of power continued via one planetary gearbox on each side. The bevel gears also provided the drive for a hydraulic pump. This centrifugal pump supplied the hydrodynamic vortex brakes. Together with the hydraulically operated brakes, these supported steering depending on the steering radius, by means of the multidisc clutches on the left and right. They were controlled by means of cam-actuated compressed-air valves, and brake actuation was transmitted by air-assisted hydraulic brake cylinders. Power transmission of the parking brake, which was also integrated in the final drive, took place mechanically. In March 1942, the chassis was assembled in the Nibelungenwerk; however, the missing internal-combustion

Visible in the foreground on the torque converter are the auxiliary drives for the fans and the V-belt pulleys for the alternator and compressor. Beneath the covered outlets are the drives for the optional coolant pumps of the Type 130. *PA*

engines caused the work on the chassis to stop. Fifty electric and fifty hydraulic vehicles were initially planned. Later, the requirement was famously reduced to ten hydraulic vehicles, with only one chassis ultimately completed for testing. The completed hydraulic hulls with the numbers 150 004, 150 009, 150 010, 150 012, 150 016, 150 017, 150 019, 150 020, and 150 021 were converted into gasoline-electric chassis at Krupp.

Problems arose during the 2,000 km (1,243 mi.) test at the factory due to considerable oil loss and difficulties with the compressed-air control for the steering clutches. The latter reacted very sluggishly to the steering command, and isolated accidents are said to have occurred at higher speeds. It was not until March 1944 that the Type 102 vehicle with chassis number 150 013 and the turret replacement weight came from the Nibelungenwerk to the Verskraft at Kummersdorf. Due to the lack of interest in the hydraulic drive on the part of Wa Prüf 6, the vehicle covered just 200 to 500 km (124–311 mi.) during the brief test at the army testing station at Kummersdorf. Voith reacted with disappointment that they were not given any opportunity for further development. As previously described, in addition to the two Ferdinand tank destroyers, on March 1, 1944, schwere Panzerjäger-Abteilung 653 also requested the hydraulic tank chassis from Kummersdorf for use as a recovery vehicle. Thus, at the end of May 1944, "a Porsche Tiger VK 4501 (88 mm KwK 36 L/56) with hydraulic **power transfer was sent for use by the 653rd**

Heavy-Tank-Destroyer Battalion."[85] On March 7, 1944, engineer Müller of the Porsche company drove to the Kummersdorf artillery range. Instead of being delivered as a recovery vehicle, this Porsche Tiger was fitted with turret 150 014. In its final configuration this turret had been intended for a Tiger command vehicle. Unlike the standard production turret, it had an opening in the commander's hatch cover for a scissors telescope, and behind the cupola there was a basket for signal ammunition. After its removal, the turret replacement weight remained behind at the experimental station at Kummersdorf (see chapter 8).

Refueling in the factory testing area. Looking on are Porsche, Hacker, and engineer Kugel of Voith. *PA*

The intensive testing of the Type 102 in the Nibelungenwerk's testing area, the limited fuel capacity of about 520 liters, and the hydraulic system's limited effectiveness made refueling in the field necessary. Standing on the turret replacement weight, Porsche, Hacker, and Oberingenieur Kugel of Voith discuss technical matters. The oil stains on the layer of dust below the special exhaust hood attest to the oily engines or hydraulic drive. *PA*

The Running Gear

The Porsche Type 101's running gear was basically based on that of the Porsche Type 100. Of course, due to the higher weight, such parts as torsion bars, drive wheels, and road wheels had to be strengthened. The road wheel diameter rose

from 600 to 794 mm (23.6 to 31.25 in.), and the three return rollers were dispensed with.

There were three torsion bar bogies on each side, with the two front pairs installed with the bearer arm in front of

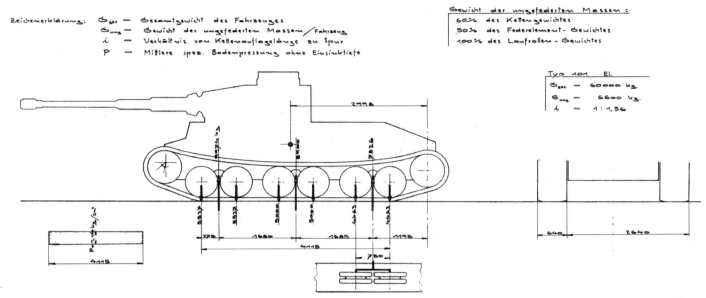

The weight distribution list showed the center of gravity in the middle of the vehicle. The steering ratio (track contact length to track) was 1:1.56. With a gross weight of 60 metric tons, this gave an average ground pressure of 1.16 kg/cm². This high value, which was achieved only on a firm surface, rose on softer ground to an unacceptable figure of 0.9 kg/cm² with a sink depth of 100 mm. *PA*

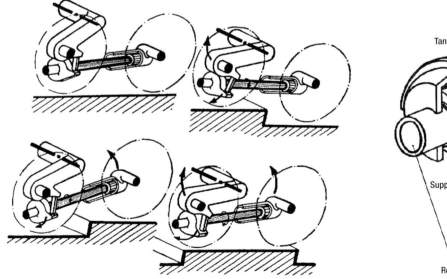

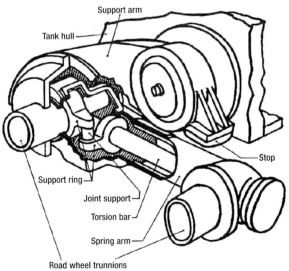

Support arm
Tank hull
Stop
Support ring
Joint support
Torsion bar
Spring arm
Road wheel trunnions

Drawings showing how the suspension operated. *D 656*

the wheels, and the rear pair installed with the bearer arm behind the wheels. A complete suspension unit without road wheels weighed 402 kg (886.25 lbs.). Since each road wheel weighed 219 kg (483 lbs.), the complete suspension element had a weight of 840 kg (1,852 lbs.).

Problems with the running gear mainly concerned the trunnions, which were bolted to the chassis. These gradually developed cracks, which were caused by additional vibration loads on the trunnions due to repercussions of the torsion bar springs while driving, as well as lateral thrust forces on

An example of the simple repair technology for the changing of road wheels and torsion bar units. A small lifting device was planned, which was necessary given the weights specified above. *PA*

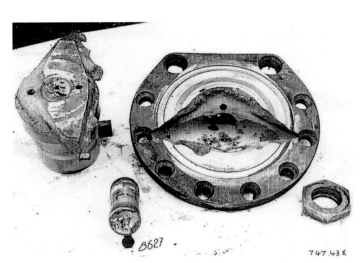

A broken-off trunnion, to which the bogie was attached, from a Porsche tank destroyer. *PA*

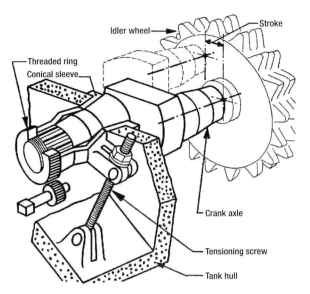

Functional diagram of the track tensioner. *D 656*

the tracks when steering. These cracks began to appear on the Tiger (P) at about 1,400 km (870 mi.) and on the Panzerjäger Ferdinand, which was roughly 10 metric tons (11 tons) heavier, at about 900 km (551 mi.).

The reason was an unfavorable transition in the mechanical processing carried out after the forging. This was problematic because of the six trunnions on the Tiger (P), two (or, in the case of the Ferdinand, three) of them could be changed only after the removal of the engines and generators or driving switch. For this reason, Wa Prüf 6 proposed a constructive change in the forging treatment, the insertion of a relief notch in the flange, and the enlargement of the fillet.

The tracks and sprockets, in particular, were subject to some changes in the course of development of the Tiger. In contrast to the Leopard's 500 mm (19.7 in.) track with 160 mm (6.3 in.) spacing, while the Porsche Tiger was also given a

The old version of the hub had a spoke-shaped appearance. The drive hub was mounted with twelve bolts. *PA*

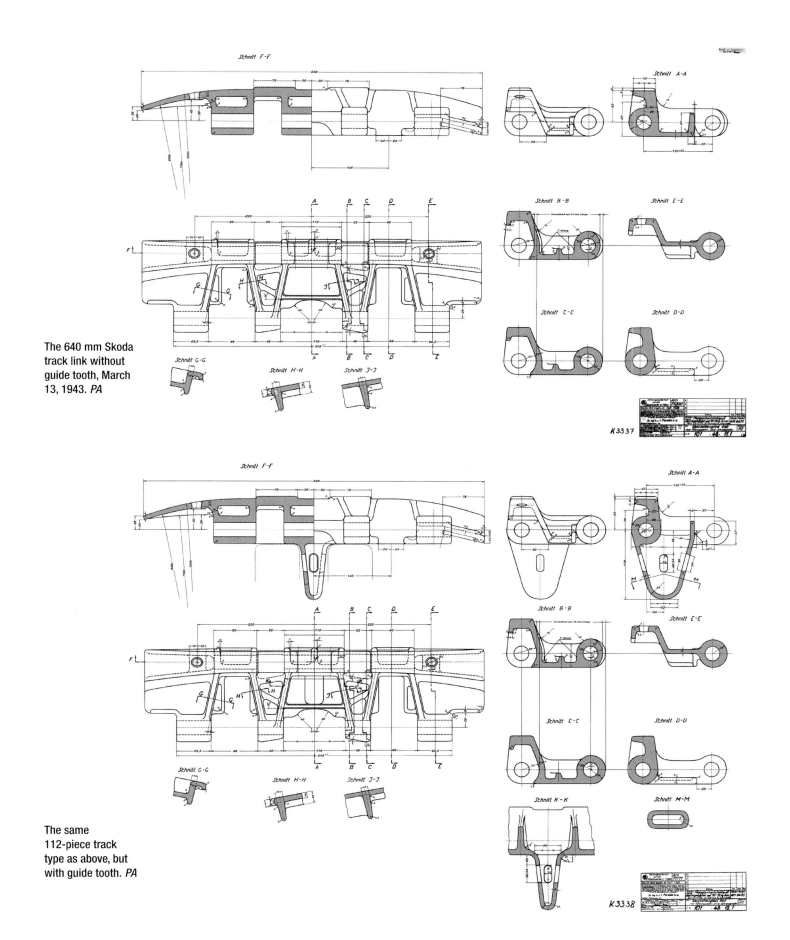

The 640 mm Skoda track link without guide tooth, March 13, 1943. *PA*

The same 112-piece track type as above, but with guide tooth. *PA*

CHAPTER 6

The SSyms Railcar
by Joachim Deppmeyer

In addition to Henschel & Sohn, in 1941 the Nibelungenwerk in St. Valentin (Steyr-Daimler-Puch AG) was commissioned to design a Panzerkampfwagen VI tank and build 100 examples together with the Porsche company. The project was designated VK 4501 (P) Tiger. Construction began at the end of 1941. The first Tiger tanks produced by Henschel and Porsche had, under all circumstances, to be demonstrated at the Wolfsschanze Führer Headquarters, Görlitz station (East Prussia), on the Rastenburg to Angerburg line, on April 20, 1942. Hitler wanted to use this opportunity to decide which of the two Tigers would be produced in quantity.

The Deutsche Reichsbahn (DRB, or German State Railway) had already commissioned a series of trial railcars (the official railway designation), but in April 1942 they were not yet

The VK 4501 (P) Tiger on an SSt wagon. Here the tank still has the narrow 500 mm tracks, however. *PA*

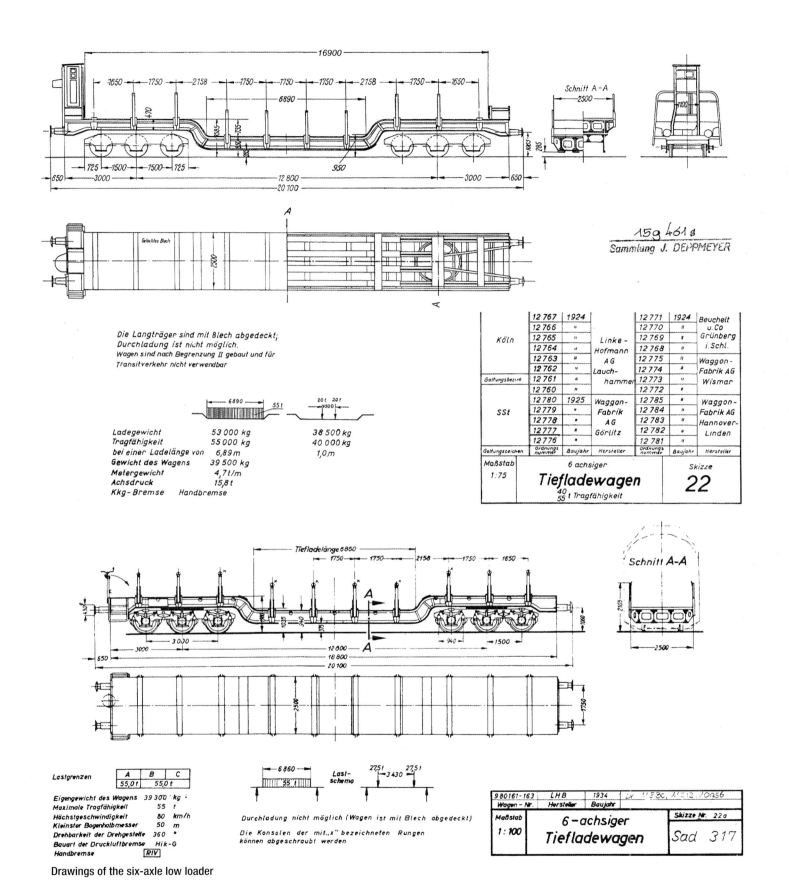

Drawings of the six-axle low loader

available. A low-loading car (SSt) with a cranked bridge (drawing 22a) and a low loading length of 6,860 mm (270 in.) was selected as a replacement. The side rails were removed for carriage of the tanks, and carrying capacity was 55 metric tons (60.6 tons). The combat weight of the VK 4501 (P) Tiger was 57 metric tons (63 tons). The SSt came from a series of twenty cars, partly conceived to carry the first planned 150 and 170 mm guns for the Reichswehr. The funds came from the Reinhardt job creation program, which the new Reich government had established. At the instigation of the Reich, for reasons of secrecy Krupp signed the vehicles as private cars with the Reichsbahn Essen Division (506155-506174 P Esn). The railcar numbers changed later. The heavy tanks could not drive onto the SSt over an end-loading ramp, however. Loading and unloading instead had to be carried out by crane, with the turret turned to the 180° position. The DRB also had six-axle low-loading cars with a cranked bridge for exceptional transports in its own fleet of railcars, as seen in drawing 22, with a carrying capacity of 55 metric tons, which were broadly similar to those described above.

After the demonstration of the first two different examples of Tiger on April 20, 1942 (Hitler's fifty-third birthday), a committee finally decided in favor of the Henschel tank. The Altmärkische Kettenfabrik GmbH in Spandau presented a design for an assault gun based on the Porsche chassis, which was accepted. The Nibelungenwerk was commissioned to complete the ninety chassis originally planned for the Porsche Tiger, while Alkett assumed responsibility for the fixed superstructures. The Sd.Kfz. 194 was armed with an 88 mm Pak 43/2. Deliveries began in April 1943 with thirty vehicles, and the remaining sixty examples followed in May 1943. In addition to schwere Panzerjäger-Abteilung 654, the Ferdinand also equipped the newly formed schwere Panzerjäger-Abteilung 653 at Bruck/Leitha. It was an army unit and was attached to the OKH, which made the unit available to subordinate command authorities on a temporary basis on the basis of task requirements.

The photo of the Ferdinand assault gun driving onto an access ramp could have been taken during testing of a dismountable railroad loading ramp. It served as a replacement for fixed ramps at places where these were not present, as well as between stations if there was a malfunction or if, for tactical reasons, immediate loading or unloading appeared necessary.

The Ferdinand assault gun with the number 234 driving up a loading ramp. Standing in the foreground is Professor Porsche with two designers, critically observing the loading procedure. *A*

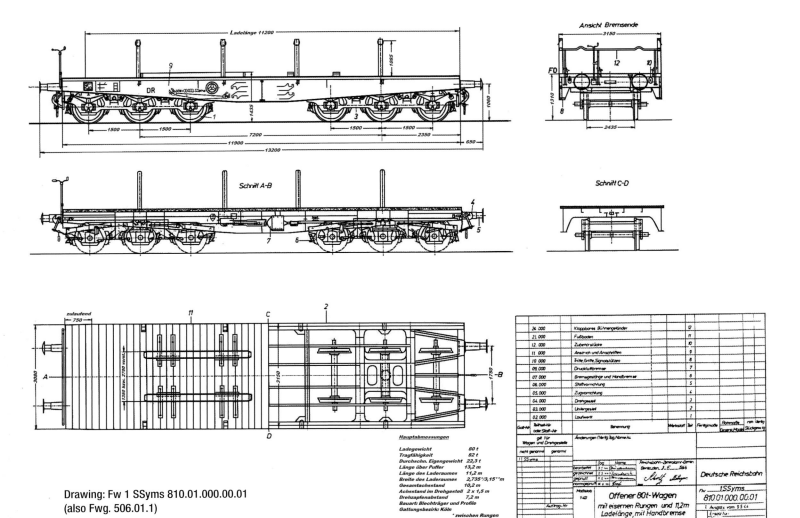

Drawing: Fw 1 SSyms 810.01.000.00.01
(also Fwg. 506.01.1)

A brand-new SSyms (Cologne 14
436) on the grounds of the
Westwaggon factory in Cologne.
SD

The car had a simple device in the first floorboard on the head pieces, in order to be able to place ramps of a special design. Unfortunately, details are not available. It is not known whether it was the ramp shown.

In September 1941 the Ordnance Office reported the need for a six-axle railcar for transport of a Wehrmacht "special device" (in plain language, the Tiger heavy tank) with a carrying capacity of 72 metric tons (79.3 tons) for lines with 16-metric-ton (17.6-ton) axle pressure and 84 metric tons (92.6 tons) for ones with 18-metric-ton (19.8 tons) axle pressure. The Army Ordnance Office estimated the required number at 250 vehicles. So far, the German State Railway had not owned a heavy car for these load capacities, since there was insufficient demand for this type of transport. The four-axle SSy covered the range to a load weight of 50 metric tons (55 tons). The question arose whether the desired new railcars would be available for public transport or should be used as private cars by the army. The main railcar office decided to abandon these 250 cars, and the German State Railway took over the procurement and costs.

The RZA Berlin suggested the Westwaggon wagon factory for the design and construction of this new model and asked the factory for a statement as to when the first railcars could be delivered if an SS quota was immediately allocated. With an immediate start, the factory believed that it could complete design work by the end of 1941, but the required materials could be requested immediately and thus be possible for the fourth quarter of 1941. The breakdown by dimensions took place at the beginning of November. The delivery of the railcars was scheduled to begin in July 1942, and delivery was scheduled for the end of 1942.

The total load of 83 metric tons (91.5 tons) could be accommodated over a length of 8 m, whereby the load could be driven from either end, including from the next car without overloading bridges. The bridge railing could be completely folded down. On the basis of this information, the German State Railway ordered the RZA to negotiate the price for fifty examples with the DWV and to place the order with a delivery date of August 1. The Wehrmacht asked that one car be left available for it to purchase. After its delivery, it received railcar number Bln 919 050 P, operator "Army Experimental Station Heegesee," home station Rehagen-Klausdorf.

Transfer traffic could be set up only by changing the bogies, however. In such cases the shipper had to procure and retain the necessary bogies himself. This also included suction air brake lines, in order to at least be able to run the vehicles as cable trolleys. The head pieces of tall, six-axle, heavy railcars therefore received an additional four holes for the buffer-fastening screws, which allowed the buffers to be moved to a greater distance.

In fact, on November 12, 1942, the Army Ordnance Office placed an order with the Wggf. Uerdingen for 220 three-axle interchangeable bogies in the Spanish rail gauge of 1,674 mm for SSyms (work order S 5334). Deliveries were to begin with twenty examples in August 1943. After Spain repeatedly refused to enter the war on the side of Germany, an attack on Gibraltar leading to the severing of the straits, which had repeatedly found its way into Hitler's War Directives as Operations Felix and Isabella, was no longer feasible. The Army Ordnance Office therefore canceled the interchangeable bogie contract.

During loading of the Tiger heavy tank, there were at first difficulties securing the vehicles to the railcars. The adjustable support bars proved too weak, and the keys also bent easily. From this point of view, in February 1943 it was determined that during the war these vehicles would be used only to transport tracked vehicles, and that therefore the support bars should be designed as adjustable longitudinal stanchions and that the stanchions could be done away with. It has not been established whether the head of Division 30 in the Reich Ministry of Transport complied with this requirement.

Westwaggon delivered the first heavy railcar on schedule at the beginning of June 1942. The follow-up orders in the various vehicle programs can be found in the appendix. Because of its importance, the design was even included in the war program. The German State Railway ordered a total of 1,511 SSyms six-axle railcars, but only about 1,250 were completed. In mid-1944, there was a renumbering, and the four- and six-axle SSy(s) and SSyms railcars each received different number groups.

FPR	De	Numm	WgNumv	WgNr+Gattung+Verw		Stück	Bauartbezeichnung	U WgNr+Gattung	Fa-Zeichnung	Plz	Zeichnung	Kennzi	Lfw	Lfj	Wa-Nr	zus Bemerkung
420	28	036	14435-	14484	Köl DRB	50	1SSyms	61435- 61484Köl	11045/01.1 VWW	Fwg	506.01.1	15336	WWk1	194206-08	11045	urspr.als SSkmras gepl.
420	28	038			Köl DRB	100	1SSyms		11045/01.1 VWW	Fwg	506.01.1	15336	Sim1	verl.		n.Uerdingen verlagert,fr.150x geplant
420	28	040	14485-	14584	Köl DRB	100	1SSyms	61485- 61584Köl	AX 1080 Uer	Fwg	506.01.1	15336	Uer1	1942/43	2583	v.Sim übernommen
430	28	092	14585-	14824	Köl DRB	240	1SSyms	61585- 61824Köl	AX 1080 Uer	Fwg	506.01.1	15336	Uer1	1943/44	2588	
430	28	092	19266-	19375	Köl DRB	110	1SSyms	60266- 60375Köl	AX 1080 Uer	Fwg	506.01.1	15336	Uer1	1943/44	2588	zusätzlich
430	28	092	19376-	19675	Köl DRB	300	1SSyms	60376- 60675Köl	11045/01.1 VWW	Fwg	506.01.1	15336	Beu1	1943/44		
430	28	092	19676-	19696	Köl DRB	21	1SSyms	60676- 60696Köl	AX 1080 Uer	Fwg	506.01.1	15336	Uer1	1943/44	2588	zusätzlich
440	28	412	19697-	20026	Köl DRB	330	1SSyms	60697- 61026Köl	143.01.1 SAE	Fwg	506.01.1	15336	Beu1	1944/45		nur 230 Wg.ausgeliefert?
440	28	412	20027-	20386	Köl DRB	360	1SSyms	60027- 60265Köl+	143.01.1 SAE	Fwg	506.01.1	15336	Uer1	1944/45	2599	+61266-386Köl,199Wg.geliefert+bezahlt

1SSyms
Maßstab 1:100

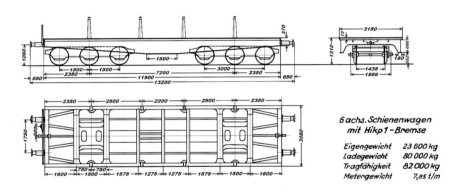

6 achs. Schienenwagen
mit Hikp1 - Bremse

Eigengewicht	23 600 kg
Ladegewicht	80 000 kg
Tragfähigkeit	82 000 kg
Metergewicht	7,85 t/m

Hauptausschuß Schienenfahrzeuge beim Reichsminister für Rüstung und Kriegsproduktion - Sonderausschuß Eisenbahnwagen   Görlitz, den 2.3.44

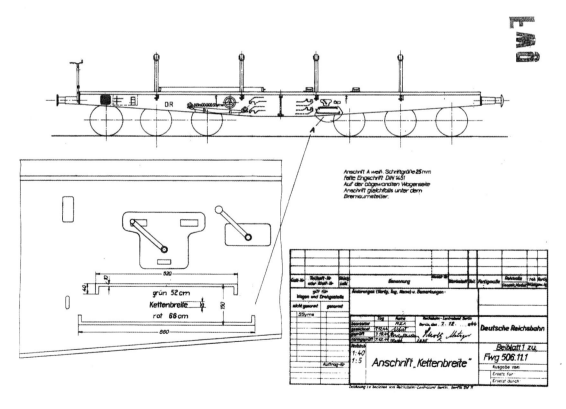

The track marked "grün 52-cm" (green 52 cm) was the travel track of the Tiger 1, and the track marked "rot 66-cm" was the travel track for the Tiger 2, which were always carried on the railcars.

CHAPTER 7

Possibilities and Limits of an Electric Drive for Tracked Vehicles

by Rolf Hilmes, scientific director (ret.) / Dipl.Ing.

1. Motivation for the Electric Propulsion of Tracked Vehicles

Its relatively high efficiency, optimal traction distribution, and controllability aroused interest in an electric drive for motor vehicles at the beginning of the last century. We must recall the battery-powered Lohner-Porsche electric car of the year 1901 or the Austrian army's gasoline-electric-powered "militia trains" from the year 1910. If a generator driven by a combustion engine is available, the problem of carrying along storage media (batteries) is eliminated. This was probably what prompted French engineers to equip the St. Chamond tank (photo 01) with a gasoline-electric drive in 1917.

Several years later the Russians and Americans also began working on an electric drive for tracked vehicles. At the

Photo 01: Assembly of a French St. Chamond tank; one can see the installation of the four-cylinder in-line engine (66 kW) with the flange-mounted generator (1917). With a modest generator output of about 54 kW (the vehicle's maximum speed was 4 kph), the level of the total loss and the thermal problems of the rudimentary design (from today's point of view) of the electrical system were obviously manageable. *Hilmes archive*

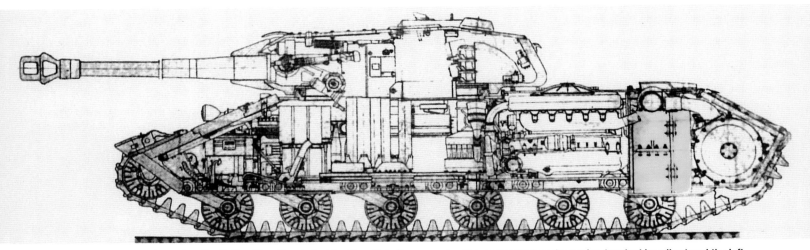

Photo 02: Object 253 (based on the IS 6), with a diesel-electric drive. Note the generator flange-mounted on the engine (marked in yellow) and the left drive's electric motor. *Hilmes archive*

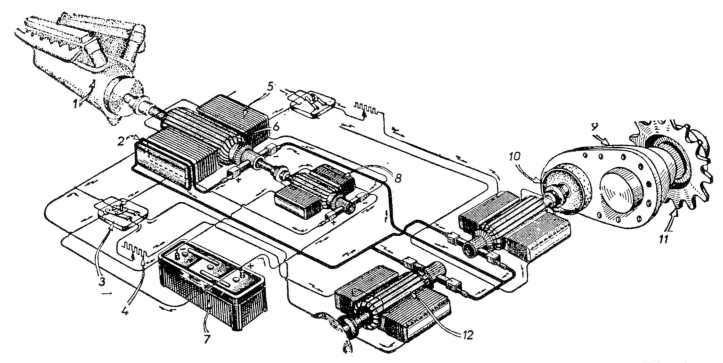

Photo 03: Diagram of a diesel-electric power transmission system from a Russian reference work from the 1940s. The system's overall efficiency is likely to have remained within narrow limits. *Hilmes archive*

beginning of 1944, the Soviets produced the Object 253, an experimental vehicle based on the IS-6 with a diesel-electric drive (photos 02 and 03). And in autumn 1943, the Americans equipped the T 23 heavy tank with a gasoline-electric drive. In both cases, however, they went no further than experimental vehicles/

The activities undertaken in Germany in the 1940s by the Porsche company, which led to the VK 4501 (P) Tiger, the Ferdinand/Elefant, and the Maus superheavy tank, became more popular. Despite this, electric propulsion in motor vehicles failed to make a major breakthrough by the end of the Second World War.

2. New Attempts in the Postwar Period

After the Second World War, the topic of electric propulsion of vehicles, exploiting available technologies, was taken up again by all the relevant nations. The test bed vehicle Marder DEA (photo 04) was created in Germany in 1985.

The generator (440 kW) on the diesel engine and the electric motors (2 × 750 kW) on the drive wheels were equipped with permanent magnets made from cobalt samarium. Static converters with power transistors were used in the power electronics, which enabled four-quadrant operation. The vehicle fulfilled the required functions; however, the construction expenditure (especially the volume required) was significantly higher than that of a comparable mechanical drive. In the period that followed, further demonstrators emerged in Germany; for example, an 8×8 wheeled vehicle (30 metric tons, or 33 tons) with a 600 kW generator and eight wheel hub motors in 1987.

In 1996, a Wiesel 2 armored weapons carrier was fitted with a diesel-electric drive (65 kW generator), resulting in the Wiesel LLX (photo 05).

Photo 04: A look into the engine compartment of a Marder armored personnel carrier with diesel-electric drive. Beneath the metal box is the generator; a drive motor can be seen on the right. The empty space was later filled by an element of the power electronics. *Hilmes archive*

Photo 05: Wiesel LLX (light armored air-transportable experimental vehicle) from the year 1990; the electric motor was integrated into the rear return roller. *MaK Company*

Photo 06: The VTE 4×4 test bed from the year 2006. Two radiators (for the engine and power electronics) had to be installed in the front of the vehicle. The wheel hub motors (each 50 kW) are clearly visible. *Hilmes archive*

As the last activity in this field, in 2006 the 12.6-metric-ton VT-E heavy 4×4 experimental vehicle, with a 200 kW generator and four 50 kW wheel hub motors, was produced in Germany. Trials were successful, and the vehicle was even issued MOT approval (photo 06).

As part of the preliminary investigations for the Puma infantry-fighting vehicle, a detailed comparative investigation was carried out between

- a purely electric drive

- an electromechanical drive

- and a purely mechanical drive carried out at an input power of 800 kW (photos 07 and 08)

The result of this meaningful study was that conventional power transmission with modern components could be expected to result in minimal expenditure in terms of weight and volume. Hence the Puma infantry-fighting vehicle was subsequently also equipped with the HSWL 256 hydrostatic-hydrodynamic superimposed steering system from the Renk company.

In the postwar period, in the US, France, South Africa, and also Russia, there were also test beds, sometimes several, that were used to investigate diesel-electric drives for military vehicles. None of these many programs resulted in quantity production, however.

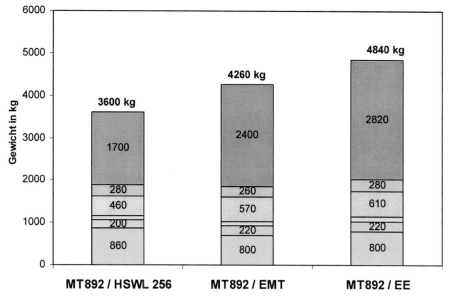

Photo 07: Result of a weight comparison for a mechanical, electromechanical, and electric drive (800 kW) from the year 2002. The conventional drive system showed the most-favorable results. *Hilmes archive*

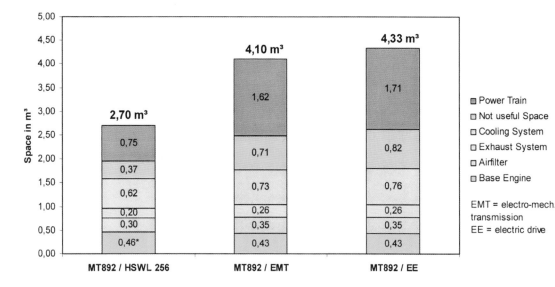

Photo 08: Result of a volume comparison for a mechanical, electromechanical, and electric drive (800 kW) from the year 2002. The conventional drive system showed the most-favorable results. *Hilmes archive*

3. Possibilities of a Diesel-Electric Drive for Tracked Vehicles

In the 1980s, numerous advantages were expected from a diesel-electric drive in military vehicles, such as

- provision of the high power requirements for future combat vehicles

- more flexible integration of the drive components possible

- lower weights and volumes

- greater reliability, self-diagnosis capability, lower operating costs

- operation of the diesel engine at the most efficient level

- maximum torque could be supplied to the drive wheels at the starting point

- energy recovery possible during braking

- stepless driving and steering

- low vulnerability of the overall system

The hype reached its climax with the unveiling of an "all-electric vehicle" (AEV) at the beginning of the 1990s. The power to be provided for this would have made it possible for numerous other components (traction drive, electrical armor, and numerous consumers) to be supplied with power difficulty.

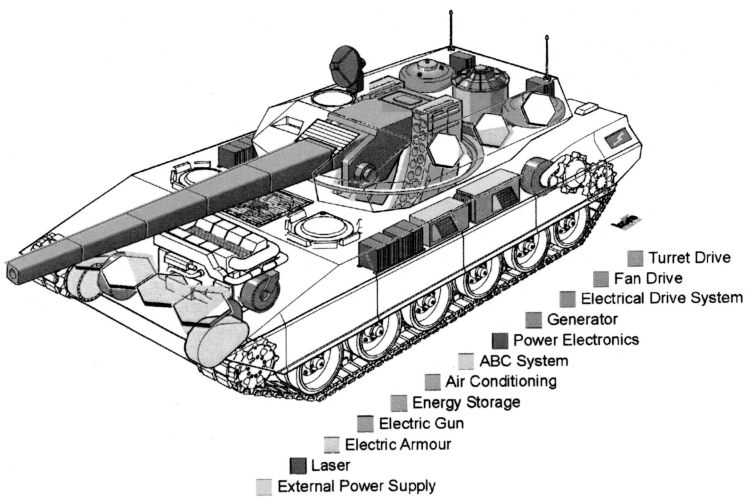

Turret Drive
Fan Drive
Electrical Drive System
Generator
Power Electronics
ABC System
Air Conditioning
Energy Storage
Electric Gun
Electric Armour
Laser
External Power Supply

Visionary idea of an "all-electric vehicle," in which virtually all functions (including weapon and armor) are to be realized by electric energy. *Hilmes archive*

4. Limits of the Diesel-Electric Drive for Tracked Vehicles

As we know, in tracked vehicles, turning and steering are achieved by producing a speed difference between the two drive wheels. In principle the drive wheel on the inside of the turn must turn more slowly than the one on the outside of the turn. If tighter turning radii are required, the drive wheel on the inside of the turn must be braked, because the tracked vehicle basically displays the tendency to drive straight ahead. In this state, the drive wheel on the inside of the curve takes up power ($P = M \times w$) from the ground and guides it into the steering gear. In older steering gears (clutch-brake steering gears or single differential steering gears), this power is converted into heat and wear in slipping steering brakes, which sometimes led to high steering losses. The invention and introduction of the overlay steering gear (first used in 1921 in the French Char I B tank) enabled so-called regenerative steering to be established in tracked vehicles. With this type of gearbox, the reduction in the speed of the drive wheel on the inside of the curve is not converted into heat and wear by slipping steering elements; rather, it is produced by a speed difference generated in the gearbox. The power consumed by the drive wheel on the inside of the curve, also known as "reactive power," is, among other things, transferred by the so-called zero wave to the drive wheel on the outside of the curve (photo 10).

This creates additional tension in some gear parts, but this is predictable and controllable. Due to the transfer of reactive power to the drive wheel on the outside of the curve, there is no additional wear and no components are significantly heated (so no additional cooling is required). For electrical power transmission, the (reactive) power consumed by the inner drive wheel must be transferred to the outer drive wheel by electrical means via the power electronics. In order to reduce the speed on the inside drive wheel, the electric motor becomes a generator in this driving state. The electric motor on the drive wheel on the outside of the curve must thus receive the drive power produced by the generator on the main engine, as well as the reactive power transferred from the side on the inside of the curve. Thus the electric motors on the drive wheels have to be significantly oversized. A quantitative consideration regarding the layout of the components of a 55-metric-ton (60.6-ton) vehicle with drive power of 1,100 kW shows that the electric motors on the drive wheels must be designed to receive up to 1,900 kW of power (photo 11).

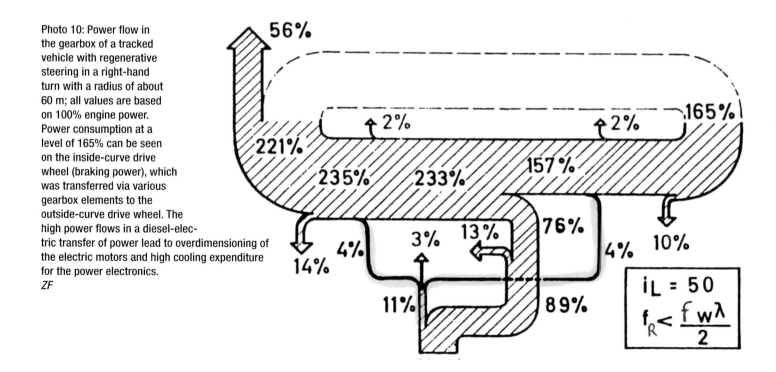

Photo 10: Power flow in the gearbox of a tracked vehicle with regenerative steering in a right-hand turn with a radius of about 60 m; all values are based on 100% engine power. Power consumption at a level of 165% can be seen on the inside-curve drive wheel (braking power), which was transferred via various gearbox elements to the outside-curve drive wheel. The high power flows in a diesel-electric transfer of power lead to overdimensioning of the electric motors and high cooling expenditure for the power electronics.
ZF

$$i_L = 50$$
$$f_R < \frac{f w \lambda}{2}$$

In addition to oversizing the two electric motors, electrical heat loss in the power electronics proved to be another problem in the electric transmission of power. For example, with an assumed efficiency of 95%, during a transfer of 1,000 kW of reactive power there occurs a power loss of 50 kW (that corresponds to an immersion heater with a power of 50,000 watts). In reality, it is not just the active power that occurs in power electronics; rather, electrical reactive and apparent power components also circulate in the components with a corresponding phase shift, which leads to further losses or an increased accumulation of heat. Thus, with the electrical transmission of power—in addition to the cooling of generators and electric motors—there is another, considerable cooling effort required for the power electronics for the two electric motors and the main generator.

Because today's components (semiconductors) in power electronics can endure a maximum temperature of only about 70°C (158°F), the vehicle cooling system must be split into a low-temperature and a high-temperature part. Until the industrial and series application of SiC semiconductor elements (which are to allow an operating temperature of about 110°C, or 230°F), in tracked vehicles a diesel-electric will always be

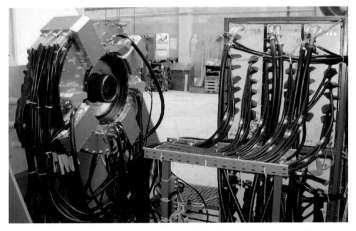

Picture 11: View of an electric motor on WTD 41's test bench in Trier. A complete diesel-electric power transmission system for a heavy tracked vehicle (50 metric tons, 1,100 kW) was set up there. The picture shows one of the two electric motors. The electric motor had a diameter of 1,040 mm and weighed 800 kg. With an operating voltage of 750 volts and currents of up to 3,000 amps, the motor is capable of developing a short-duration maximum power of about 2,500 kW. On the right, next to the oil-cooled motor, are the associated (liquid-cooled) power electronics. Note the amount of cable. *Hilmes archive*

larger in volume and heavier than a comparable mechanical drive. In addition, higher development and procurement costs are to be expected with a diesel-electric drive (factor of approximately 1.6).

Wheeled vehicles avoid the problem of regenerative steering and thus the transfer of reactive power from the drive wheel on the inside of the curve to the one on the outside. The use of wheel hub motors can eliminate driveshafts and differentials. The advantages of a diesel-electric drive are obvious here. Despite this, in the last twenty years no nation has produced in quantity and put into service a military wheeled vehicle with a diesel-electric drive. This state of affairs leaves many questions unanswered.

Conclusion

Even with the use of modern technologies for the electrical and electromechanical components, the electrical transmission of power in a tracked vehicle still leads to a higher weight and volume expenditure. In this respect there is absolutely no reason to accept these disadvantages in an electrical transmission of power, especially since the conventional mechanical transmission of power does not have any capability deficits in meeting military requirements. The transition to a new, risky technology, which presumably leads to higher costs and higher development and procurement expenditures, as well as the necessary changes in the area of material maintenance (e.g., training of the maintenance staff), is therefore neither necessary nor required. After the brief flare-up of the idea of the "all-electric vehicle" at the beginning of the 1990s, on closer examination and after the performing of reliable analyses—as so often happens when revolutionary technologies appear—there quickly followed a phase of disillusionment. Today this topic has vanished into thin air. Even more: barely 120 years after the appearance of the Lohner-Porsche car, apart from laboratory curiosities (technology platforms), nowhere in the world has a single military vehicle with diesel-electric drive been produced in quantity.

CHAPTER 8

In the Footsteps of the Porsche Tiger

If the interested historian goes to the historical places where the Porsche Tiger was tested, he will still find traces of this story. The Nibelungenwerk was located in St. Valentin. After the war the Steyr company used the property with the surviving buildings for the construction of agricultural machinery.

Another track leads to what is now the Kummersdorf Estate, where the Verskraft, Wa Prüf 6's army motor vehicle

The former Nibelungenwerk now belongs to the Canadian company MAGNA. The eastern, still-surviving Hall IV is used by the company for the production of vehicle parts. The former Halls II, III, and VI are used by the Case IH company (with Steyr) to manufacture tractor cabs and for final assembly. The entrance area (1), the workshops (2), the canteen (3), and the railroad buildings (4) are still in use today. The former testing area was revamped and is now a modern testing area of the Steyr Engineering Center of Magna Power Train.

testing center, was located. The 8 km long, circular forest course comprised tracks 1 to 4. Tracks 5 to 8 were used when the first course had to be repaired. The purpose was to surmount a gradient of 7 to 10 m. The course was used by the Verskraft to test the Porsche Tiger and the Ferdinand.

The site of the former Firing Range West, where Porsche Tiger 150 002 was tested and adjusted in the presence of Professor Porsche and Otto Zadnik, is today dense forest. However, debris testifies to the former structures in this area.

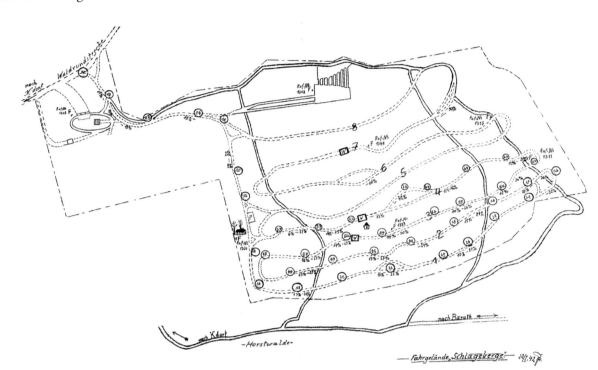

Map of the Schlageberge driving area

Anfahrtstraße

1. Steigung = 11% (6°)
   Gefälle = 9% (5°)
2. Steigung = 14% (8°)
   Gefälle = 18% (10°)
3. Steigung = 15% (8°)
4. Steigung = 25% (14°)
   Gefälle = 9% (5°)
5. Steigung = 19% (11°)
   Gefälle = 12% (7°)

Bahn 1

1. Steigung = 17% (10°)
   Gefälle = 15%
2. Steigung = 13% (7°)
   Gefälle = 22% (12°)
3. Steigung = 15% (8°)
   Gefälle = 21% (12°)
4. Steigung =
   Gefälle = 32% (18°)

Bahn 2 (von unten)

1. Steigung = 36% (20°)
   Gefälle =
2. Steigung = 24% (13°)
   Gefälle = 11% (6°)
3. Steigung = 24% (13°)
4. Steigung = 27% (15°)
   Gefälle = 17% (10°)
5. Steigung = 25% (14°)
   Gefälle = 13% (7°)

Bahn 3

1. Steigung = 12% (7°)
   Gefälle = 24% (13°)
2. Steigung = 14% (8°)
   Gefälle = 25% (14°)
3. Steigung = 14% (8°)
   Gefälle = 30% (17°)
4. Steigung = 10% (6°)
   Gefälle = 26% (15°)
5. Steigung = 12% (7°)
   Gefälle = 36% (20°)

Bahn 4

1. Steigung = 21% (12°)
   Gefälle = 12% (7°)
2. Steigung = 32% (18°)
   Gefälle = 12% (7°)
3. Steigung = 42% (23°)
   Gefälle = 12% (7°)
4. Steigung = 15% (8°)
   Gefälle = 11% (6°)
5. Steigung = 27% (15°)
   Gefälle = 6% (3°)

Bahn = 1 Schleife
Bahn 1 bis 4 zus. ca. 8000 m
Höhenunterschied 7 bis 10 m

The former Verskraft driving area with incline tracks as they appear today. It belongs to the Federal Institute for Materials Research and Testing (BAM) and today calls itself Test Site Technical Safety (TTS).

In the former "new Verskraft" there is still a remnant of a turret replacement weight from a Porsche Tiger. That was a minor sensation for me! Over the years, some of the iron sheets had been removed and a kind of profile frame had been welded on. The weight has sunk deep into the ground. It originally weighed about 10 metric tons, made up of about 8.5 metric tons of concrete and 1.5 metric tons of steel sheet. It is probably the turret replacement weight from the hydraulic Porsche Tiger with the chassis number 150 013, which until

it was delivered to schwere Panzerjägerabteilung 653 in April 1944 was the last vehicle to still carry this weight. It was subsequently fitted with Tiger turret 150 014 in storage at the Verskraft.

There are still several more or less well-preserved factory and storage halls in the new Verskraft. It seems, however, that it is only a matter of time until these contemporaneous eyewitnesses collapse, since unfortunately nothing is being done to preserve them.

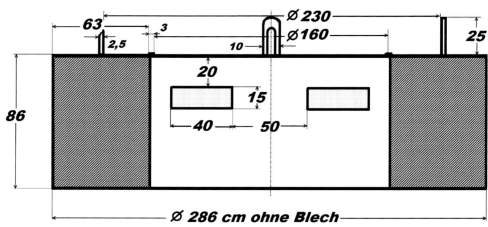

The encasing sheet metal is about 4 mm thick and remains only on the lower and inner parts.

Clearly visible are the prominent vision ports and the four lifting lugs. The attached frame made of pipes and square material was welded on subsequently.

In the upper photo, the turret replacement weight as it once was, compared to the current remains as they were discovered.

Henschel Tiger 250 001 WH 013896 is demonstrated to General Guderian. With him are Oberst Esser and Oberstleutnant Holzhäuer. The vehicle is sitting in front of Factory Building (West) for fully tracked vehicles (*lower photo*).

Jagdtiger 350 001 with the running gear of the Porsche Type 180 in front of the garages at the new Verskraft

The Verskraft's test company during a muster in front of a factory building

Another photograph shows the spot where the Porsche Tiger VK 4502 stood in April 1945. According to an account by Kummersdorf resident Willi Klär, he was supposed to repair the gun of the dug-in Porsche Tiger, because the barrel did not run forward after it was fired. The recuperator was no longer under pressure. Klär was unable to reach the tank since the area was under heavy fire. This Tiger and an antitank gun had knocked out several Soviet tanks before the Red Army bypassed this point of resistance to the east, using a lane created in the forest.[87]

Another important part of the history of the Porsche Tiger took place at Berka vor der Hainich in the area of the

Direction of fire of the dug-in VK 4502 with its 88 mm KwK L/71 on April 21, 1945. Its location was the bridge to the exit from the town of Kummersdorf in the direction of Horstwalde.

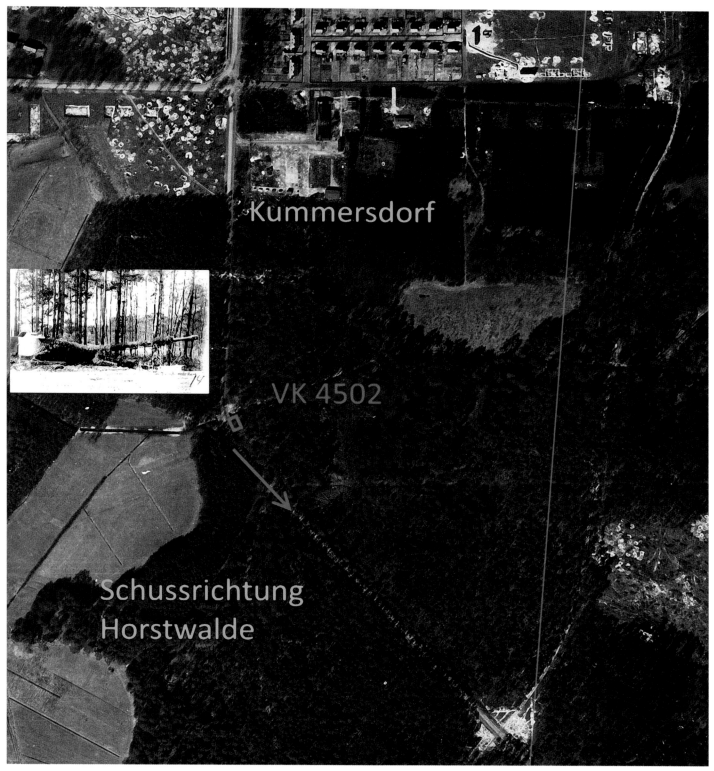

Kummersdorf

VK 4502

Schussrichtung
Horstwalde

The VK 4502's location at the bridge in the direction of Horstwalde in April 1945, where several T-34s were knocked out. The Red Army tanks ultimately bypassed the point of resistance to the right (east) in the direction of the "Sprenggarten" (clearing). *LBD*

Kindel (country south of the Hainich). Internally it was also spoken of as the Großenlupnitz Forest. The name "Berka" for the testing grounds is misleading because, on one hand, there are several villages with the name Berka (for example, Bad Berka with the Army Munitions Institute), and, on the other hand, the village is relatively far away from the site of the Verskraft. The nearest village is Beuernfeld, 2 km away. All that was in Berka vor der Hainich was a local Wehrmacht firing range.

Leading from the present-day B 84 is the entrance to the Verskraft field office. The aerial photo was already shown in the chapter concerning Tiger testing in 1942. Apart from concrete footpaths, all that remains is concrete rubble from the workshop and the two washbasins. Several of the overgrown washbasins on the exit from the testing grounds still exist intact today.

Ehemaliger
Truppenübungsplatz
Kindel
✈ 14.05.2009 – 17:11 Uhr

The ground at Berka in front of the Hainich as it appears today. The Hainich is an extended, wooded ridge, whose southern area is now part of a national park. The Kindel area is in the southern part of the Hainich.[88] *VR*

Only one thing is almost completely preserved: the washbasin at the entrance from the testing area. Visible on the right is the weir, which could dam up the brook. A pipeline is embedded in the middle so that the water could be diverted if necessary. The stream was dry when this photo was taken.

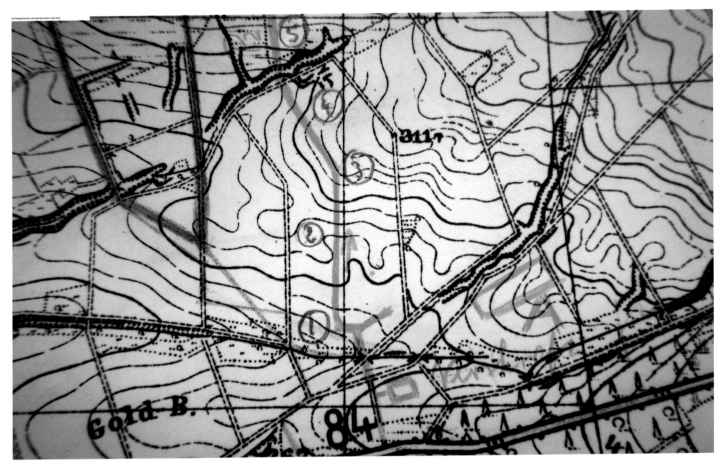

Starting point 1 of the circular route in the direction of Mittel-Berg as it appears today. The rectangles with the designations A, B, and C drawn on the above map indicate the locations where the vehicles were to park.

The former parking area for tanks and flamethrower vehicles in front of the Mittel-Berg in 2018. Curiously, part of the track on the Mittel-Berg, where Panther and Tiger tanks once did their laps, is now called the "Wildcat Trail."

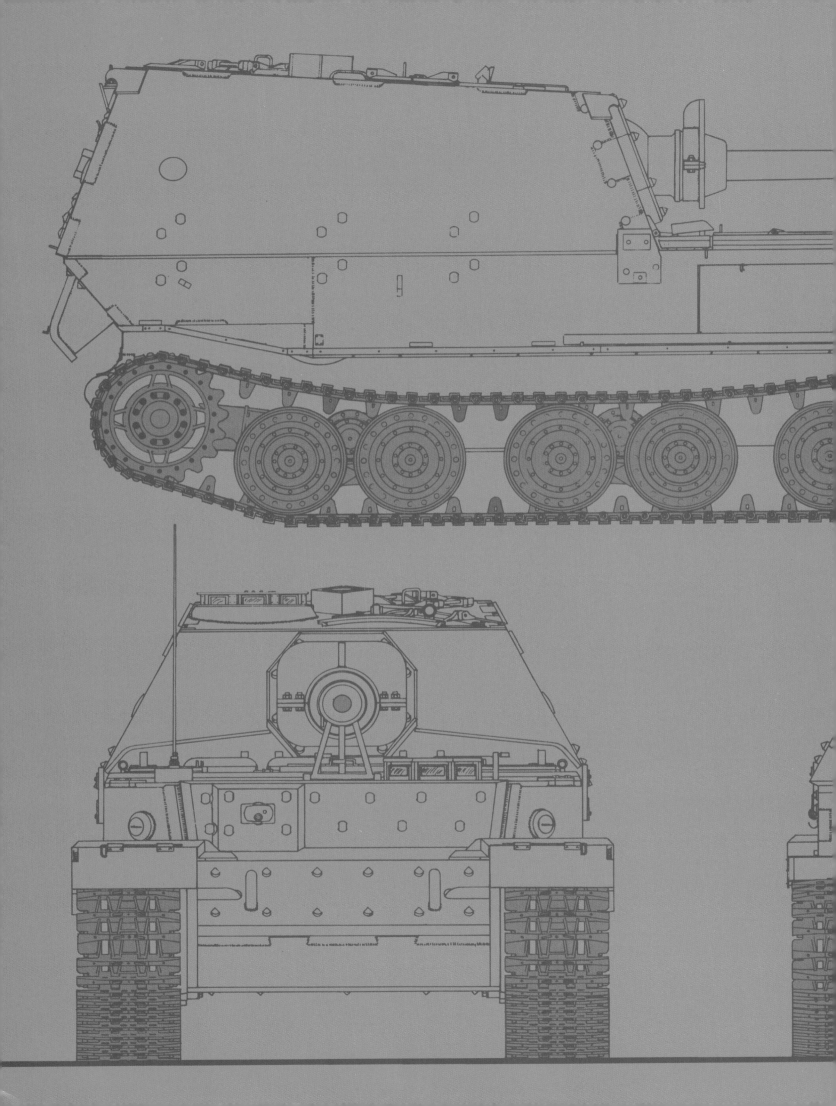

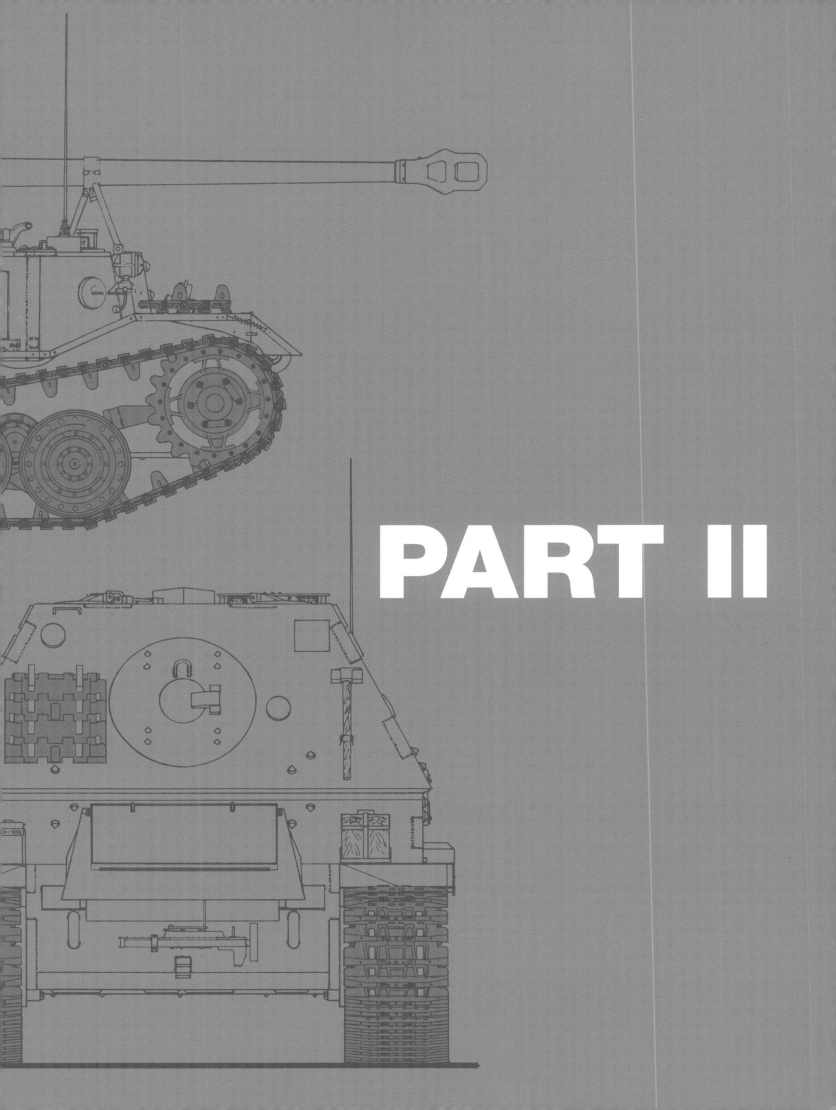

PART II

CHAPTER 9

The Panzerjäger Tiger (P): Porsche Type 131

The development of a battle tank with the long 88 mm KwK L/71 was going to take too much time for Hitler, however. At an armaments conference in Berlin on September 20, 1942, under point 15 he demanded that the Porsche Tiger be developed into a self-propelled gun with the long 88 mm L/71 gun and 200 mm of frontal armor. The possible installation of a 210 mm howitzer in a self-propelled gun based on the Porsche Tiger was also to be examined. In addition to the 200 mm of frontal armor, the hull's side and top plates were to be made thicker. Hitler agreed that the required armor steel plates could be taken from navy stocks held at the shipyards. Hitler saw the heavy self-propelled gun as an opportunity to quickly get the 88 mm Flak 41, a weapon he very much favored, into service as a mobile antitank weapon.

Since the Porsche Type 101 Tiger was undergoing testing at that time, the chassis of the Porsche Tiger, which was already in production, was available for this urgently needed heavy self-propelled gun. While initially only some of the Porsche vehicle chassis were to be diverted for production of the self-propelled gun chassis, a complete conversion offered further advantages. Hitler now faced the problem of having to decide on just one version of the VK 4501 as a heavy

armored vehicle, since the German armaments industry was in no position to mass-produce two heavy armored vehicles in parallel.

When on November 10, 1942, following competitive trials at Berka, the Tiger committee decided to halt production of the Porsche Tiger in favor of the Henschel Tiger, at Eisenach it was further decided that the chassis of the Porsche Type 101 should be converted into a self-propelled gun with the Porsche designation Type 131. The committee further decided that of the one hundred chassis ordered from Krupp, the ninety as-yet-unmodified armored hulls were to be converted into self-propelled guns, ten Porsche Tigers having already been completed.

One week later, on November 18, there was a major meeting with Hauptamtsleiter Saur at the Armaments Ministry on the topic of "the Porsche Tiger as self-propelled carriage for the 88 mm L/70 assault gun." The participants, including General Radlmeier and Professor Porsche, with his chief engineer Karl Rabe and his electrical specialist Otto Zadnik, drove to the Alkett Company in Berlin, which had received the design contract. They were later joined by Steyr's general manager, Meindl.

The 88 mm Flak 41 in traveling configuration with gun barrel withdrawn

Porsche Tiger 150 014 during the comparative trials at Berka in November 1942. *Hoff-45722*

The talks continued the next day in the presence of Karl-Otto Saur, Krömer—commissioner of the "Tiger program"—and representatives of Wa Prüf 6, Krupp and the Nibelungenwerk. It was established that the Alkett Company of Berlin would be responsible for the conversion's design and that special representative Krömer would ensure that deadlines were met by the main suppliers and subcontractors. Further, it was arranged that Krupp would resume production of the new armored components in their previous shape with the same thicknesses. Since the superstructure and the thicker frontal armor had caused the vehicle's weight to rise, consideration had to be given as to whether the drive's existing transmission ratio could be retained. For safety's sake, gears for a revised transmission ratio were also produced.

Replacement was to take place later. Calculations and partial weight measurements by Alkett revealed a combat weight of 63.475 metric tons (70.25 tons). Completion of the first vehicle was to be accelerated to the extent possible through the use of manual labor. So as not to interrupt ongoing production of the Panzerkampfwagen IV by Krupp, it was also decided that the hulls would be modified by the Oberdonau Ironworks. For this purpose, as of January 1, 1943, Krupp was to dispatch a foreman, a fitter, and four qualified German welders to the factory in Linz to weld on the additional armor plate and the stiffeners (see table below for the delivery dates envisaged by Krömer).

The Alkett Company of Berlin specialized in the production of assault guns and had already amassed experience in special designs for the HWA. Alkett was therefore to carry out the conversions. The company had previously designed assault guns and self-propelled guns based on the Panzer IV, as per Hitler's order. However, the existing chassis of the Panzerkampfwagen III/IV would be overloaded with the long 88 mm Pak 43 or a 210 mm howitzer. Then in October 1942, a self-propelled soft-steel carriage for the 88 mm Pak 43/1 L/71 was demonstrated to Hitler. Although Hitler regarded this lightly armored tank destroyer, which was open at the top and rear, as an interim solution, the vehicle remained in production until 1945, first as the Sd.Kfz. 164 Hornisse (Hornet) and, from February 27, 1944, as the Nashorn (Rhinoceros). Building on experience gained with the Panzer-Selbstfahrlafette V mounting the 128 mm Kanone 40, a fighting compartment in the rear was seen as the best solution for the new self-propelled gun. This provided the gun crew with sufficient space and kept the long gun barrel from projecting too far past the front of the vehicle, since in addition to barrel recoil considerations, there also had to be adequate space for loading the long rounds of ammunition. Separation of the

Deadlines for Main Suppliers and Subcontractors of the Tiger P as Sfl. 8.8 Stu.-Gesch. L 70

Unit	from	by	to 12/31	Jan 05	Jan 10	Jan 15	Jan 20	Jan 25	Jan 31	Feb 10	Feb 15	Feb 20	Feb 28	Mar 10	Mar 15	Mar 20	Mar 25	Mar 31	Apr 10	Apr 20	Apr 25	Apr 30	May 12
Complete vehicles	Alkett												5	8		10		12	12	14		14	15
Superstructures	Krupp	Alkett								5		5	5	10		15		15	15	15	10		
Guns	Krupp	Alkett								5		5	10	10		15		15	15	15			
Chassis	Nilwerk	Alkett								5		5	5	10		10		15	15	15		10	
Engine cover and grating	Krupp	Alkett								5		5	5	10		10		15	15	15		10	
Gusset and floor armor	Krupp	Oberdonau	5			10			35			40											
Frontal armor	Krupp	Nilwerk	1	9		10		15			15			10		15		15					
Radio equipment	HZA	Alkett								5			8	10	12	12		14	14	15			
Optics	HZA	Alkett								5			8	10	12	12		14	14	15			
Engines	Maybach	Nilwerk			10		10			10	20		20	30	30			30	20				
Electrical equipment	Siemens	Nilwerk			10		10			10	20		20	30	30			30	20				
Gun base	Ried	Alkett								5		10	10	10	11			11	11	11			

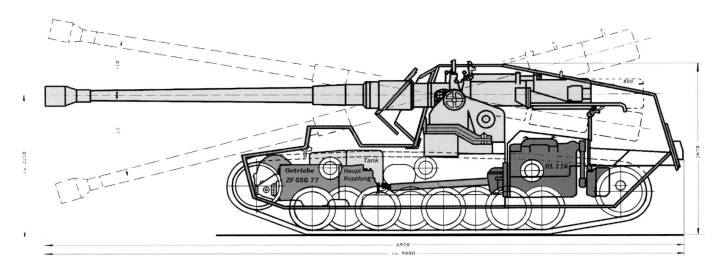

The Panzer-Selbstfahrlafette V armed with the 128 mm Kanone 40, developed from the 128 mm antiaircraft gun

fighting compartment from the driver / radio operator's position caused by the vehicle's structural shape was a disadvantage, as was its serious tail-heaviness. There was also very limited access to the drive compartment in the center of the vehicle. In addition, it had to be anticipated that assault gun crews would be exposed to increased thermal stress due to heat from the engines and generators. In contrast to the Panzer-Selbstfahrlafette K 40, however, the two Maybach engines with generators of the new assault gun, which had been designated the Porsche Type 131, were located forward of the vehicle's center of gravity, which in part compensated for its tail-heaviness. The advantages of this structural configuration ultimately outweighed its disadvantages.

The weight determination presented by Alkett on November 18 generated an argument from the Nibelungenwerk. On December 11, therefore, Krupp presented a newly calculated estimated weight for the assault gun:

This photo depicting a crewman of a Nashorn tank-destroyer holding an 88 mm high-explosive round illustrates the space required by this ammunition and the vehicle's relatively unprotected fighting compartment.

The total weight of the old version of the Porsche Tiger:	59 metric tons	(65 tons)
less the old, lower turret with 88 mm L/56 gun:	– 10 metric tons	(11 tons)
gave a chassis weight of	49 metric tons	(54 tons)
added was the new gun shield superstructure:	+ 15 metric tons	(16.5 tons)
the new 88 mm L/71 gun with gun mantlet:	+ 3.5 metric tons	(3.85 tons)
plus the angled hull superstructure:	+ 1.5 metric tons	(1.65 tons)
This gave a total weight of	72 metric tons	(79 tons)

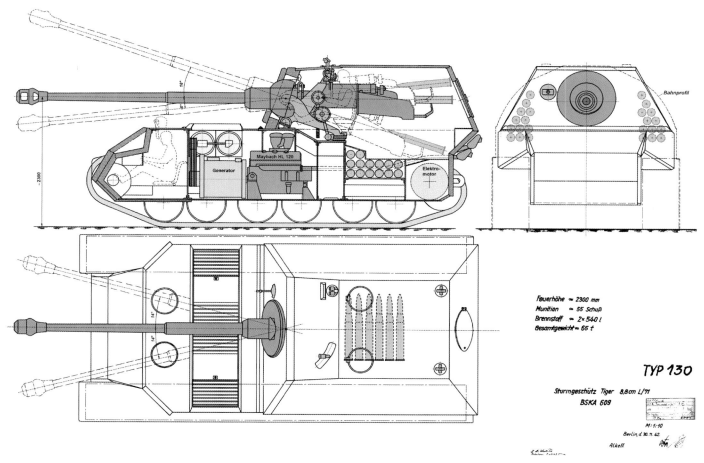

Feuerhöhe ≈ 2300 mm
Munition ≈ 55 Schuß
Brennstoff ≈ 2× 540 l
Gesamtgewicht ≈ 65 t

TYP 130

Sturmgeschütz Tiger 8,8cm L/71
BSKA 609

M: 1: 10
Berlin, d 30. 11. 42
Alkett

In addition to "straightened" supplementary armor on the front of the vehicle, the Alkett design of November 30, 1942, also had a machine gun in the superstructure. The HWA, however, thought it unnecessary, which later proved to be a serious error. The Type 130 designation in this drawing is in error, since the Porsche Type 130 was the designation for a planned Porsche Tiger with liquid-cooled engines.

The vehicle was officially weighed during the demonstration at Berka, revealing a gross weight of 59 metric tons (65 tons) for the Porsche Tiger and a turret weight of 10 metric tons (11 tons), and the results provided the basis of computation for the above figures. On December 28, 1942, Alkett again weighed the chassis without cover plate, hull superstructure, and track shields, and with 350 liters (92.5 gal.) of fuel. This revealed a weight of 40.68 metric tons (44.84 tons). Alkett estimated the weight of the angled hull superstructure, at 1.5 metric tons (1.65 tons), the track shields at 0.2 metric tons (0.22 tons), the remaining 650 liters (171 gal.) of fuel at 0.5 metric tons (0.55 tons), the engine cover plates at 3.6 metric tons (4 tons), the armored superstructure at 13.55 metric tons (14.9 tons), the gun at 3.53 metric tons (3.9 tons), the additional frontal armor at 2.13 metric tons (2.35 tons), the ammunition and storage racks at 1.25 metric tons (1.38 tons), the equipment and crew at 0.83 metric tons (.91 tons), and the tools and spare parts at 0.8 metric tons (0.88 tons). The total gave a combat weight of 68.57 metric tons (75.58 tons). The vehicle's weight had thus reached a limit. The running gear and the drivetrain had originally been designed for a vehicle weight of 45 metric tons (49.6 tons). In the course of development of the Porsche Tiger, weight had risen to the above-cited figure of 59 metric tons (65 tons). The most recent weight increase not only exceeded the maximum weight of 65 metric tons (71.6 tons) specified by Professor Porsche, it also negated the expected advantage of the improved power-to-weight ratio resulting from the installation of the Maybach engines. As well, it exceeded the 65-metric-ton capacity of the pioneer equipment required for river crossings by the vehicle.[1]

The hull shell of the Porsche Type 101 Tiger prior to conversion. The side boxes originally housed the blowers for the air-cooled gasoline engines. *WS*

The first 88 mm Porsche Sturmgeschütz L/71 assault gun. This is very probably the handmade preproduction vehicle with the number 150 010. *WS*

Converting the completed Porsche Tiger hull shell into a Type 131 assault gun was a considerable task. Not only did numerous armor plates have to be removed, but the conversion also involved new partitioning of the hull (the engines and generators were now arranged in the center of the vehicle), modified maintenance openings, and transverse panels. Only the electric motors (not in photo) remained in their previous position in the rear. In the center of the hull floor is the mounting for the two alternators and their tensioners (*arrow*).

Since the Porsche Tiger hulls delivered for the assault gun chassis could not be used in their existing form, they were modified to requirements by the Eisenwerke Oberdonau GmbH in Linz. Fifteen hulls were delivered to the Nibelungenwerk, followed by twenty-six in February, thirty-seven in March, and finally twelve in April.

When the Tank Committee held a meeting at the Armaments Ministry on January 28, 1943, on the subject of the "Assault Gun on Tiger P," Porsche reported that the vehicle's weight was 69 metric tons (76 tons) and that its speed had to be limited to 20 kph (12.4 mph). The unsuitable suspension was blamed for the track failures that had occurred. The tracks

and suspension would therefore have to be modified. It remained to be decided where the ballistic tests, which had to be completed before this was done, should be carried out. This remained to be decided by the responsible persons at Wa Prüf 6. The potential candidates were the artillery ranges at either Kummersdorf or Hillersleben. On the subject of the vitally important tank recovery vehicle, Porsche proposed the use of a Porsche Tiger with the hydraulic drive developed by Voith. The committee, however, decided in favor of a recovery vehicle based on Panther components.

On February 6, 1943, Hitler demanded the accelerated production of ninety assault guns on the Porsche Tiger chassis with the long 88 mm gun and 200 mm of armor. Though advised of the continued shortcomings of the vehicle's suspension and the necessary driving tests, Hitler demanded that all available resources be dedicated to completing the required testing and supporting production, so that vehicles could be sent to the front in numbers in the shortest possible time.[2]

On February 16, Porsche sent his electrical specialist Otto Zadnik to Alkett in Berlin to deal with the assault gun, even though the Porsche Company's focus of development at that time was the Porsche Type 205, the Maus battle tank. There are just thirteen entries concerning the Type 131 assault gun

Air intake

Air exhaust

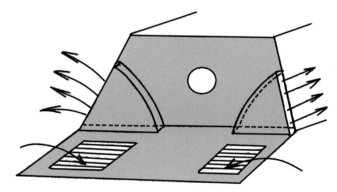

Proposal for an improved exhaust air conduction system designed to avoid excessive heating of the fighting compartment; however, it was not possible to implement it.

in the diary of Porsche's chief designer Karl Rabe, while just under two hundred entries regarding the Type 205 can be found there. This clearly illustrates the relative importance of the work being done on the assault gun and that on the Maus. Only Porsche's senior engineer Xaver Reimspieß was involved to a greater extent in work on the Ferdinand at the Nibelungenwerk.

On February 10, members of the Verskraft carried out the first measurements and tests with the Alkett test vehicle on the Alkett Company grounds. It was probably chassis 150 010, since according to a report by the Nibelungenwerk dated March 23, the test vehicle with the chassis number 150 011 later used at Kummersdorf was still in the configuration of a Porsche Tiger.

The initial temperature measurements taken during the one-hour drive revealed critical levels. Cooling air for the generators was drawn from the compartment for the driver and radio operator. The engine compartment was ventilated by two cooling fans housed in the floor of the fighting compartment. A special fan was installed on the front of the generators to cool the electric motors. The cooling air was fed by this fan to the electric motors through two lateral air ducts. The exhaust air exited the vehicle in the rear center. To shield the fighting compartment against unnecessary thermal loads, the exhaust pipes exited the sides of the hull instead of its rear, as originally planned. As a result, however, a planned muffler had to be eliminated due to lack of space.

The thorough investigation of the elevated coolant temperatures brought to light a flaw in the tensioning device for the cooling fan's V belt. The V-belt tension pulley was skewed, as a result of which the belt was often shed. The V belt's dimensions were abnormal, and therefore standard-size belts had to be synthetically stretched to a usable size. This was of course done at the cost of the service life of these overstretched belts. This also raised the question of how to guarantee the delivery of spares. As well, the insufficient distance between the V-belt pulley and the partition (to the driver's compartment) made replacing these belts extremely difficult. The drive's bevel gears were also inadequately sized, which later led to their premature failure. This drive had no overflow plug, necessary for checking the oil level. There was thus no way to determine how much oil was present. This faulty design later led to the failure of 75% of the drives after a mileage of about 200 km (124.25 mi.).

Additional problems were encountered, specifically the following:

- The Bowden cables used instead of throttle linkage rods were poorly routed and caused variations in resistance, which led to unequal engine speeds.

- The poorly insulated fuel line from the left tank passed too close to the exhaust pipe. The installation of a protective strip was proposed to shield the lines and shutoff valves on the forward partition in the radio operator's compartment.

- The reliability of the Pallas electric fuel pump was found to be inadequate. It was therefore suggested that a fuel tank with a downpipe should be installed, which could also be used to provide fuel to the starter.

- A modified installation of the so-called fox device, for warming of the coolant, was required because of the expected circulatory problems and inadequate freedom of operation.

- The coolant hoses were likely abrasion points because of poor connections and routing.

- The coolant drain outlet was very complex because of the use of forty-eight screws (forty according to photo?). A proposal was therefore made to design a cover that was simpler to open. The drain screw of the "fox device," to which access was poor, was also worthy of replacement.

- Because of a cover plate in the fighting compartment held in place by screws, the compressed air system's ATE compressor was difficult to access for the purpose of checking its oil level.

- The oil filter actuator was very difficult to access because it was located behind the driver's seat mount.

- Protruding screws made it impossible to remove the cover on the driving switch. The switch-box cover had been made of metal that was too thin; therefore, stepping on it created the danger of short circuits.

- The water pump V belts for the Maybach engines ran too close to the exhaust pipe. Even minor retightening caused the alternator tension rollers to touch the guide rollers. It was recommended that the tensioning device be modified.

- The absence of a muffler on the exhaust system was criticized for tactical reasons. The use of flexible pipe ends on the exhaust pipes was also problematic, since these had led to constant problems when used on the Panzer Ia. This error should not have been repeated.

- Elimination of the starter switch meant that the generators' starting coils could not be used. The loss of this reliable starting method was very regrettable when the available electrical and the inertia starters were overloaded

by the high inertia of the rotors. The probable reason for this was that the Maybach HL 120 engines had a higher compression ratio of 1:6.5 and, because of their greater compression, were more difficult to turn over.

- A power outlet was very desirable for starting with an external power source, especially since the required cables were already present.

- There were problems tuning the electrical system. Under heavy loads the speed of the combustion engines was so reduced that only a fraction of engine power was available. A drop in rpm of 1,300 to 1,500 was recorded during tests, equivalent to about half maximum power.

- The existing tow hooks did not enable the vehicle to be towed using tow bars. Installation of a horizontal tow hook centrally on the rear plate had therefore been suggested. It was thought that this hole should make it possible to use the Henschel Tiger's tow fork. The tow hooks on the front of the vehicle should likewise have holes suitable for the tow fork's bolts.

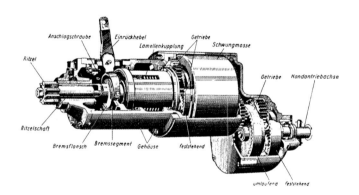

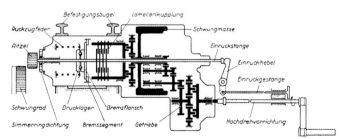

The mechanically operated inertia starter was standard equipment on German tanks. *WS*

Porsche and Zadnik on chassis 150 012 during a test drive on the company test grounds. The old chassis number, 150 067, can still be seen on chassis 150 012. *PA*

- The attachment of the inertia starter actuator rod was too weak. As well, it was recommended that the mounting of the driveshaft guide sleeve and the winding up of the inertia starter should be checked by two men with the gun installed and superstructure in place.

- Development of a disassembly device for the running gear was recommended for repairs. How the engine-generator packs, the electric motors, the cooling-fan set, the gun, and the superstructure were to be removed in the field was unclear. According to Wa Prüf 6, a gantry crane made by the Fries Company (a "Strabokran" gantry crane with up to 16 metric tons [17.6 tons] of lifting force) was necessary for these workshop tasks.

The next meeting of the Tank Committee on February 17 included, among other things, that the three "Tiger P 2 or VK 4502" prototype vehicles were to be regarded primarily as test vehicles for testing the new running gear, also to be used by the Maus. By order of Hauptdienstleiter Saur, the manufacturing work (on the Maus) would have to be set back temporarily in favor of accelerated production of the Tiger assault gun.[3] Furthermore, on the subject of the "Tiger P assault gun," the question arose as to how to supply the units with necessary spare parts and special tools so that they could carry out fieldwork on the assault guns. The committee therefore decided that Oberstleutnant Stollberg, director of the repair course at the Nibelungenwerk, should compile a list of the necessary equipment and tools and arrange for their production by the Nibelungenwerk (power train and chassis) and Alkett (superstructure and armament). Professor Porsche pointed out that it was absolutely necessary to produce the required spares.

He regarded the HWA's original intention, to take spare parts from damaged vehicles in the field, as unacceptable. Exactly what was to be included in the first batch of spare parts was to be determined in cooperation with Oberstleutnant Stollberg. Oberst Thomale also made reference to the required driver training, whereupon the participants decided that chassis nos. 150 004, 005, and 006 would be made available at St. Valentin for this purpose.[4] These chassis numbers were, however, the numbers of Porsche Tiger hulls, since the chassis numbers of the assault guns had been changed and ran from 150 011 to 150 100.

General function testing of the 88 mm gun took place at the artillery range at Hillersleben on March 2, 1943. A total of fifty rounds were fired, covering the entire azimuth and elevation ranges. The frequent jams were blamed on a defective recoil brake, since this problem had appeared only rarely at Meppen when the gun was first fired. The gun's recoil had little effect on the vehicle. When the gun was fired, the vehicle moved back just 30 to 50 mm (1.2–2 in.). Removal of the smoke gases by a ventilator installed over the floor plate with a conveying capacity of 12 m³/min. (423 ft.³/min.) was also regarded as satisfactory. Ten rounds of rapid fire were twice loosed off with five persons in the fighting compartment and hatches closed.

No breathing difficulties were encountered. A rather larger roof opening was envisaged to improve suction effect. Since the sliding armored cover over the optical sight opening had not yet been installed, its effect on lateral sighting ability could not be evaluated.

The following points were later discussed step by step:

- The complete vehicle with equipment weighed 65 metric tons (71.6 tons).

- Driving speed was 28 kph (17.4 mph) on road, 10 kph (6.2 mph) off-road.

- The vehicle buried itself on a 30° slope and sandy soil.

- Current strengths of from 800 to 1,000 amperes were measured during the tests with the Porsche Tiger at Berka. During testing of the Ferdinand, current strengths rose to 2,000 amperes, and the cause for this was not discovered.

- The troops complained that the 15-metric-ton (16.5 ton) superstructure had to be removed in order to carry out an engine change.

- Twenty-six rounds of ammunition were carried in fixed storage; another fourteen rounds were supposed to be carried loose.

On March 19, 1943, a weapons demonstration was carried out in Hitler's presence at the Rügenwalde artillery range. The focus of attention was the Gustav 800 mm gun (after the Dora, the second gun of this type). Also present was a Ferdinand assault gun and a Panzer IV with armor skirts. Guderian, who had been the inspector general of armored forces since February 28, 1943, wrote of the Ferdinand that, apart from its long gun, it was unarmed and therefore defenseless in close combat. In his opinion this was the vehicle's Achilles' heel, despite its heavy armor and its good gun. As it had been built, it would have to be used, even though for tactical reasons Guderian could not share Hitler's enthusiasm for this vehicle.[5] Since assault guns were normally attached to the artillery and were envisaged as infantry support weapons, in his directive Hitler specified that the heavy-assault guns were to be placed under the inspector general of armored forces. The Ferdinand assault gun therefore became the Panzerjäger auf Fahrgestell "Tiger P" (Tank Destroyer on Porsche Tiger Chassis), or Sd.Kfz. 184. So Guderian, as a person newly authorized to issue directives, decreed that "the new heavy-assault guns are to be employed only for special tasks on main battlefronts. They are primarily tank destroyers."[6] Guderian had thus prevailed against the artillery generals, since in December 1942 the OKH had

One of the vehicle chassis assigned to the driver-training program. *KHM*

decided in principle to equip three heavy-assault gun battalions (the 190th, 197th, and 600th) with thirty vehicles each under the command of the General der Artillerie. On February 28, Guderian redesignated the 190th and 600th Battalions as light-assault gun battalions. On January 21, 1943, he transferred Sturmgeschütz-Abteilung 197 to Bruck an der Leitha in Austria and subsequently renamed it schwere Panzerjäger-Abteilung 653 (653rd Heavy-Tank-Destroyer Battalion). The unit was thus officially transferred from the Sturmartillerie to the Panzertruppe.

Krupp was relieved of the task of converting the Porsche Tiger hulls, since Saur insisted that Krupp should concentrate all its resources on construction of the Maus battle tank. Since Alkett was later to take over assembly of the Maus, only the factory at St. Valentin was left. The Nibelungenwerk, which had already assembled some of the Porsche Tigers, became the sole conversion and assembly plant for this new assault gun. Workers had been sent from Alkett to St. Valentin in

The firing trials at Hillersleben also included firing the gun at maximum barrel elevation. *WS*

During the demonstration at Rügenwalde, the Ferdinand sits in the shadow of the huge Gustav 800 mm gun. *Hoff-47511*

Hitler, Porsche, and Speer during inspection of the Ferdinand at Rügenwalde on March 19. Standing on the vehicle (*far left*), Oberst Holzhäuer explains the driver's position. Hitler was extremely impressed. *Hoff-47547*

Oberst Holzhäuer, head of the Wa Prüf 6, shows Hitler the fighting compartment through the open rear hatch. Standing below him is Karl-Otto Saur, and behind him Porsche and Speer. *Hoff-47512*

February to help out. Nevertheless, this was not quantity production in the true sense; rather, it was "stopgap production." This caused great difficulties at the Nibelungenwerk, especially since Alkett was unable to deliver the design drawings on time, and later the problems resulting from the necessary changes to the production process again caused major disruptions at the factory.

The Tank Committee held its next meeting at the Nibelungenwerk on March 23, 1943. The subject was of course the Tiger assault gun. Saur was first to make reference to the demonstration before Hitler and the absolute necessity of making the assault guns ready for frontline service as quickly as possible. Criticisms were to be expressed only if they would

also be useful in the future. Hitler had ordered that the ninety vehicles were to leave the factory ready for operational use. All production therefore had to take place at the Nibelungenwerk. For this reason, a significant part of the Alkett factory was to be transferred to St. Valentin. The next day, some of the production equipment and 120 workers from Alkett were moved to St. Valentin with the help of thirty-six railcars. As stated previously, criticisms were to be forborne in the general interest.

Saur entreated both factories to display "iron comradeship." Foreman Hahne of Alkett was in charge, and therefore the work would be carried out according to his program. Hahne, who had been named plant manager, was highly decorated, having received the Knight's Cross of the War Merit Cross. His men were responsible for installing the superstructures on the chassis from the end of March to the beginning of May.[8] Saur stressed that he and Professor Porsche had promised Hitler that the vehicles, with the exception of the shortcomings that might yet arise, would be operational as soon as possible, even if with limitations. Hitler was thus aware of the vehicles' restricted operational capabilities. The vehicles were not supposed to be used in mountainous areas,

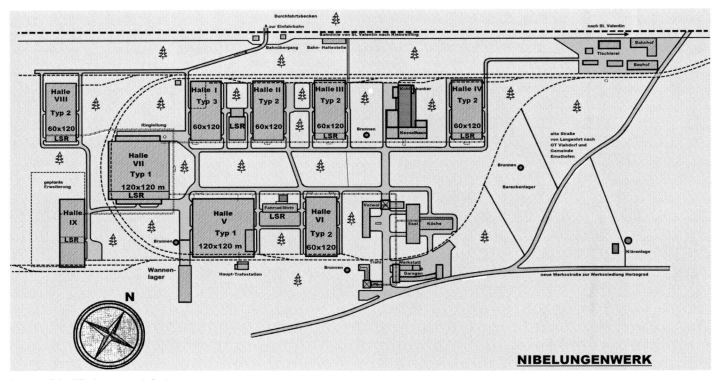

Layout of the Nibelungenwerk factory

and there were no special demands of the design. The ninety vehicles were to be deployed together, and therefore the entire personnel-training program could be seen as a whole.

Saur emphasized that the ninety vehicles must be operational by May 12, 1943. After that date, nothing more could be changed, and this was to be ruthlessly adhered to, no matter what happened. Siemens had the job of forming another committee and monitoring and directing the work on-site. Saur rejected Porsche's suggestion to initially update the basic features of the first thirty vehicles. This work was not supposed to take place until after all ninety vehicles had been completed, to avoid exposing the entire effort to any risk.

Saur also emphasized that this entire action was both a reward and a test for the Nibelungenwerk. A factory that was capable of successfully carrying out such a combined action would be capable of even-greater feats. In particular, Saur was referring to a potential significant rise in production of the Panzerkampfwagen IV at the Nibelungenwerk.

Director Judtmann was next to report on the production status of the assault gun:

150 011 was still in the Porsche Tiger design configuration.

150 012 had not yet been accepted by the army.

150 013 to 018, 019 to 023, and 025 to 030 were being handed over to the military command.

150 024, 031 to 033, and 035 to 036 were being released by the factory.

150 034 and 037 were still being test-driven.

150 038 to 060 were still in production.

The February and March deliveries were supposed to consist of fifty vehicles. The first fifteen chassis were delivered in February as planned. Because of problems, some of which have been mentioned previously, in March the factory was able to deliver only twenty vehicles instead of the anticipated thirty-five. When

Top: In this photo the 88 mm Pak 43/2 has been installed; however, the armored enclosure in front of it has not. *Below*, the vehicles parked in Factory Building VII just prior to completion. The windows are covered in this part of the building. *PA*

Vehicles 150 051 and 150 053 in the foreground shortly before completion of assembly. Assembly of the assault guns required half the building's capacity. Building VII was actually envisaged for final assembly of the Panzer IV; therefore work on the Ferdinands interrupted production of the Panzerkampfwagen IV. *PA*

The 88 mm guns for the Ferdinands laid out in the center of Building VII, and behind them their armored enclosures. *PA*

the director of the Nibelungenwerk tried to explain the reasons for the delay, he was told that no report was required. Difficulties arose, for example, in tuning the equipment packs and the checking of the generators by Siemens, the cooling system, and the fuel pumps. The conversion required approximately four hundred hours work per vehicle.

The 65-metric-ton vehicles were no problem for the factory cranes in Building VII. *PA*

On he subject of training, it was reported that the first ten vehicles had been delivered to the troops for training. One of these was assigned to Siemens for testing at the Kummersdorf artillery range. The experimental vehicle was to remain at the factory.

The training command now consisted of two Panzerjäger (tank destroyer) battalions, which were to be stationed at Döllersheim. This gave the troops the opportunity to immediately identify any defects that might arise. Oberstleutnant Below was responsible for this. The entire command received orders to move from Jüteborg to Döllersheim. Since the Nibelungenwerk was supposed to deliver all completed vehicles to Döllersheim, a factory team with Alkett employees was to be prepared for Döllersheim. Only the tank mechanics were able to remain at the Nibelungenwerk for training. Oberstleutnant Stollberg interjected that the 1st Battalion's driving instructors had not yet completed training at St. Valentin. Saur, however, insisted that driver training take place at Döllersheim. Zadnik pronounced himself in favor of also sending the incomplete vehicles there, so that the troops could also become familiar with the defects that still remained.

There followed a list of the design's problems and defects. Oberst Esser reported that the sandy soil at Kummersdorf was causing the carbon brushes to become very dirty, and they therefore had to be cleaned. This was not possible in the current condition, however. He proposed turning the brush carrier rings so that replacing the carbon brushes was possible in installed condition. Saur demanded that there must first be a precise determination, since there would be no time for a later modification. All of this had to be defined precisely with the factory. A significant part of the training was to be extended to cover precisely these things. Therefore, in addition to the employees from the Nibelungenwerk and from Alkett, the Siemens Company also had to be represented at Döllersheim.

Alkett further reported that the cooling-fan drive had to be strengthened, so that only vehicles with this new belt drive left the factory. The vehicle's driving characteristics had to be adapted to operational-readiness requirements. The troops had to know how far the vehicle could be stressed.

Siemens determined that the electric drive was not sufficiently powerful, and therefore aftereffects were to be expected. The company was already dealing with this problem. The party from Siemens consisted of twelve employees and was deployed with the troops in the form of individual teams to pass on the knowledge they had acquired.

Zadnik and Judtmann spoke next about installation shortcomings, as a result of which five machinery packs had to be replaced because of electrical flashovers. Their cause had not been fully explained, but they could not be explained by overloading. The director was of the opinion that it might be related to braking currents. The motor defects were caused by the main driving switches, which were satisfactorily modified little by little. Saur saw this as a job for Siemens and demanded that its team be augmented. Siemens also blamed the problem on excessively high braking currents.

The changes to the main driving switch were supposed to prevent the driver from causing excessive braking currents, usually unintentionally. During test drives with the new switch, the vehicle was able to negotiate a gradient without difficulty. The duration of the 1,200-ampere load was limited to about ten minutes. In soft sand, on the other hand, the current rose to 2,000 amperes, which could be permitted for only one minute. If the uphill resistance was deducted, there still remained a traction resistance of 800 kg/ton (1,600 lbs./ton). In that situation, traction resistance rose to the point that the available current was no longer sufficient.

Saur emphasized that concerning this point, Siemens must determine the permissible load. The driver had an ammeter; however, he was unable to see it from his seat. The indicator definitely had to be moved into the driver's field of view. According to Professor Porsche, a fuse against overcurrent as demanded by Oberstleutnant Holzheuer was impossible. In response, Porsche requested operating instructions in

which the precise load limits were laid down. According to Saur, these questions should be discussed internally. Referring to slides, Oberstleutnant Stollberg once again graphically described to the participants the defects that had been encountered to date.

To the named and already known defects, such as the routing of pipes, coolant drain, chafing pipes, radiators and cooling fans, steering levers, foot brake rods, changing torsion bars, special tools, track tensioner, etc., Michaels of Alkett responded that most of these problems had already been addressed. Notification of these defects had been given too late, however. With this the most-important topics had been discussed. The representative of WaPrüf 6 could not pass up pointing out that his department was not supposed to be brought in after construction was complete, but from the very beginning of design work.

Saur cited Speer, who rejected the ongoing modifications and stressed that more consideration must be shown to production of the vehicles: "Basically the following is true: 100 vehicles with 80% met demands are better than thirty vehicles with 100% met demands. In agreement with Herr Generaloberst

Vehicle 150 096 beside a completed chassis in front of the factory building. *PA*

Speer at the controls during his "customary" test drive at the Nibelungenwerk. *BA*

Guderian, it has been determined that the ninety vehicles can see action with the shock troops as soon as possible. We must make the most of these five weeks before the delivery date!"

On the subject of spare parts, Saur emphasized that the production of the ninety vehicles had to take precedence over everything else. For this reason, it had been determined that the vehicles would remain together in their unit, "because sooner or later they will have to devour each other!" (meaning that some would eventually have to be cannibalized to provide spare parts for the others).[9]

Albert Speer inspected the Nibelungenwerk again on March 31, 1943, and undertook a test drive in a completed Ferdinand on the factory grounds. After the test drive he spoke very approvingly about the vehicle.

Hitler and Speer subsequently visited the Nibelungenwerk on April 4, 1943, in part to see for themselves production of the Ferdinand assault gun. All sorts of leading people were present, including Professor Porsche and his son Ferry.

On April 4, 1943, the Verskraft (Research Center for Motor Vehicles) of the Kummersdorf artillery range received a research contract from Wa Prüf 6/3 to carry out service trails with the 88 mm Sturmgeschütz 43/1 (Ferdinand). It was envisaged that the Ferdinand with the chassis number 150 011, which was to be delivered in May, would be used for these trials.

On April 23, 1943, Professor Porsche criticized the work of Siemens-Schuckert. He had hoped for radical measures to address the deficiencies found on April 21. He saw the company's decisions as no more than stopgaps and expected, for example, a more robust resistance element capable of dealing with operating and installation conditions in the armored vehicle. Switching devices with contacts and other sensitive devices, comparable to the Bosch magneto, were to be shielded, so that any tank mechanic could handle them. Porsche also regarded the brush holders in the armored vehicle as unreliable, since even a minor degree of friction in the lever of the carbon brush holders could bring the vehicle to a stop and cause its loss in combat. He expected Siemens to make relevant proposals. The professor expressed his disappointment that the lessons learned by Alkett about cable routing and protection against water, oil, and dirt had not been fully exploited. He also regarded radio interference suppression, which had been surprisingly good in the old Porsche Tiger, as still unresolved in the current project. He regarded a proposal to

Hitler was of course particularly interested in the 88 mm Pak 43/2 L/71, a weapon which he favored. *Hoff-47538*

Hitler touring Building VII. Between Hitler and Speer is Obermeister Hahnke of Alkett. On the left are plant director Judtmann and Gauleiter Jury. *Hoff 47530*

Standing beside the assault gun in this photo are Hahne, Jury, Hitler, and Speer. *Hoff-47521*

dispense with radio communications while on the move on account of the scarcity of time as unacceptable.[10]

During a meeting between Hitler and Speer on May 4, Hitler declared himself very happy that the delivery deadlines could be met. He expressed his thanks with these words: "The führer recognizes the outstanding achievement by the Vienna

Army Ordnance Office in building the Sturmpanzer and in completing the Ferdinands. He wishes his thanks conveyed to the Vienna Army Ordnance Office and its men."[11]

Though officially designated Sd. Kfz. 184, Panzerjäger Tiger (P), called "Ferdinand" by the army, the designation "Sturmgeschütz mit 8,8 cm Pak 43 auf Fahrgestell Tiger P"

The last converted chassis with the number 150 091 leaves the line on April 23. *WS*

It is finished. The last assault gun with the number 150 100 leaves the factory building. Written on the superstructure next to the wrench and hammer inside the wreath: "Many busy hands brought a job to completion, May 8, 1943."

May 8, 1943: The Ferdinand leaves the production line, adorned with greenery and covered in slogans. Written on the left side of the superstructure is "We came from Greater Berlin and joined hands with Ostmark [Austria] to create this 'beast.' Now the job is finished; now the Ferdinand rolls to the front, to defend our Fatherland, and our wishes go with it: 'Forward to victory! That is what Berlin desires! And Vienna too!'"

also existed. The last vehicle, with the number 150 100, was completed in Building VII on May 8, 1943. The deadline to deliver the last vehicles to the Wehrmacht by May 12 had thus been met. The HWA, more precisely the Vienna Army Ordnance Office, first accepted thirty and then, in May, the remaining sixty Ferdinand tank destroyers. Of these, four vehicles were initially made available for crew training.[12] During initial trials the 88 mm Pak's unprotected ball mantlet was criticized, since it allowed small fragments to enter the fighting compartment. On May 6, therefore, Krupp received a rush order to produce a mantlet that could be bolted on by the troops. These mantlets were sent to the units by rail on May 13.

March saw the formation of the second unit to be equipped with the Ferdinand tank destroyer, schwere Panzerjägerabteilung 654 (654th Heavy-Tank-Destroyer Battalion). As part of the likewise newly formed Panzerjäger-Regiment 656, the unit was also designated II. Abteilung/Panzerjäger-Regiment 656, and on April 28 it was moved to Rouen in France. Its three companies were designated the 5th, 6th, and 7th Companies. Their vehicles were numbered accordingly. The 5th Company consisted of the two staff vehicles numbered 501 and 502, while the four vehicles of the 1st Platoon had the numbers 511 to 514, those of the 2nd Platoon 521 to 524, and those of the 3rd Platoon 531 to 534. This system was repeated in similar fashion in the remaining companies. The numbers of the battalion battle staff's vehicles were II 01 to 03. On May 5, the unit received its first five Ferdinands from its sister battalion for training.

The last vehicles at the factory shortly before final acceptance by the Army Ordnance Office. *PA*

The vehicles still lack the antifragment plate in front of the ball mantlet. *PA*

The first five Ferdinands during transport to s.Pz.Jg.Abt. 654 at Rouen for training. *WS*

The remaining forty vehicles were handed over by the personnel of schwere Panzerjäger-Abteilung 653 by May 10. This was followed by comprehensive training of the tank destroyer crews. A large exercise was held in early June in the presence of Generaloberst Guderian. During the debriefing after the exercise, he stated the heavy tank destroyer's mission: "The main purpose of the Ferdinand is to act as a battering ram and smash open a well-fortified continuous front and thus clear the way for the following tank units deep into the enemy rear."[13]

As the I Battalion of the 656th Heavy-Tank-Destroyer Regiment, the 653rd Heavy-Tank-Destroyer Battalion moved from its base at Leitha to Neusiedl am See for training. Officers, vehicle commanders, and drivers received several weeks of training at the Nibelungenwerk. Some of the crews helped with the final assembly of the tank destroyers. During this time, the participants were quartered at Camp Ennsdorf, near Enns/Donau, or in Haag. The crews subsequently began combat training at Training Camp Bruck, while the workshop and repair echelon worked to overcome the Ferdinand's "teething troubles."

On the occasion of a visit by Generaloberst Guderian to schwere Panzerjäger-Abteilung 653 at Neusiedl am See on May 24, after a shooting-exercise demonstration there was a lengthy discussion with Zadnik, representative of the Porsche

KG. In addition to the heavy tank destroyer, they also discussed general questions relating to tank design. Guderian commented that the vehicle's service introduction had gone quite smoothly so far; however, he criticized the inadequate protection against the entry of water and dirt and its inadequate close-combat weaponry.

With respect to the first point, Zadnik declared that tarpaulins and metal rain gutters were envisaged for protection against water. As well, on the basis of their combat experience, the troops wanted to fit metal guards over the gratings, so as to be forearmed against hand grenades and Molotov cocktails. Protection against dust, however, was difficult, especially since the exhaust air exited downward almost vertically at the rear of the vehicle, producing meter-high clouds of dust. Alkett and the Nibelungenwerk were well aware of the problem, but there was still no suitable solution.

In Guderian's opinion the second point could be solved only by installing one or two machine guns. It was possible to retrofit flexibly mounted machine guns in front in the radio operator's position and in the rear in the gun superstructure. Flexibly mounted machine guns were needed in the front and rear, and for the sides at least openings for submachine guns. Guderian's requests for close-combat weaponry were followed by a discussion about antiaircraft defense and the use of flamethrowers. Guderian thought that the use of the Flak 43

This photo illustrates the enormous amount of dust produced by the Ferdinand. *KHM*

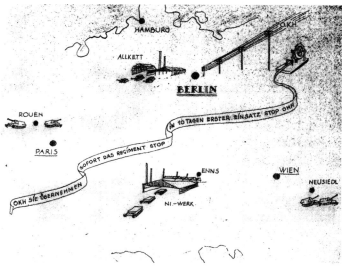

Oberingenieur Reimspieß was well known for his topical caricatures. This one shows schwere Panzerjäger-Abteilung 654 at Roeun and the schwere Panzerjäger-Abteilung 653 at Neusiedl for acceptance of their vehicles and training. The drawing includes the Alkett Company in Berlin and the superstructures it made, plus the Nibelungenwerk, which manufactured the tank destroyer's chassis. *PA*

Prototype No. 150 with the chassis number 150 011, with the Verskraft at the Kummersdorf artillery range. *PA*

as a paired weapon was at least worth looking into, especially for the Maus. As to the Ferdinand's 88 mm gun, Guderian thought that this gun represented the limits of antitank defense; otherwise the 75 mm L/71 gun of the Panther tank would be completely adequate. Despite the effectiveness of the latest antitank guns, Guderian thought that a Panzerdämmerung (twilight of the tank), as suggested by Hitler, was unthinkable. The tank remained the best antitank defense. The important thing to him was mass production. If the standard Panther production tank was sufficiently capable, then consideration could be given to halting production of the Panzer IV.[14]

When the demonstration was over, the tank drivers succeeded in returning all of the Ferdinands to Neusiedl over the 42 km (26 mile) course, including the exercise, with no breakdowns. Guderian had to be convinced of this seemingly improbable fact by his aide-de-camp.[15]

The initial interim report by the Research Center for Motor Vehicles (Verskraft) on the Sturmgeschütz 43/1, based on chassis no. 150 011, was tabled on June 8, 1943.

The vehicle, which was finally delivered from Alkett-Borsigwalde to Kummersdorf by using a SSyms special railcar, was actually the last tank destroyer delivered, and it underwent testing by the Verskraft at the Kummersdorf artillery range until May 31.

The total of 538 km (334 mi.) driven by the vehicle was broken down into 408 km (253 mi.) with Alkett and 130 km (81 mi.) with the Verskraft. Of this, the testing unit drove 26 km (16 mi.) on roads, 44 km (27 mi.) on the old forest circuit, and 60 km (37 mi.) on the test course in the parabolic dunes.

The open engine compartment of a knocked-out tank destroyer. On the forward partition are tight-fitting tension pulleys. The hit passed through the driver's space into the engine compartment. In the foreground, somewhat askew, is the 88 mm Pak's splinter guard. Below is the damaged vehicle's right radiator space. Clearly visible are the remains of the cooling fan with Cardan shafts. In the center is the right coolant filler pipe. *WS*

The following deficiencies revealed themselves:

- The already familiar stiffness of the throttle Bowden cable with subsequent breakage after 493 km (306 mi.). Operation of the gas pedal was at the limits of the possible when the second carburetor stage was engaged. In addition to the sticking Bowden cables, the control unit return spring in the switch box was too strong.

- The twin oil pressure gauge was difficult to read because of its low-contrast color scheme.

- The right fuel tank held just 348 liters (92 gal.), while the left one held 503 liters (133 gal.).

- The left valve cover seal on the right engine was leaking.

- Both alternator V belts on the right alternator failed after 493 km (306 mi.). In addition to the floor plate in the fighting compartment, the driveshaft to the rear cooling fan for the electric motors had to be removed in order to replace the belts.

- Adding oil to the left engine was difficult without an angle funnel or hose, since the filler point was under the center engine flap, which because of the additional frontal armor could be opened only slightly.

- The left engine's coolant temperature gauge was faulty, since it was indicating about 20°C (68°F) too high.

- This engine's V belts could not be retensioned and, as previously described, were difficult to access because of the proximity between the belt pulley and the partition.

- Faulty assembly in the switch box hampered steering. Self-excitation of the left generator was short-circuited. The vehicle could be turned to the left only by using the air brake.

- When the gun was fired, the circuit breaker for the separate excitation of the generators and motors tripped independently.

- The protective strainers for the generator air baffles were missing. This resulted in the possibility of the entry of foreign objects; for example, while refueling or when installing the radiator and carburetor.

- When driven in wet sand, the track overrode the drive sprocket, which caused the track to become wedged on the guide shoes (limit stops on the hull superstructure). As a result, the electric motors' friction clutch slipped, the clutch became unusable, and the vehicle therefore had to be towed away. Because of the loss of the friction clutches, only the air brakes were available for steering and braking. To maintain sufficient compressed air, however, the engine, which powered the compressor, had to be started at regular intervals. Nevertheless, the vehicle was limited to large turning radii.

- To remove the electric motors, the upper part of the armored superstructure had to be unfastened and slid forward. Removal of the air baffles over the engines was very time-consuming because of the large number of screws. The electric motors had suffered badly on account of the slipping clutches. The insulation of the windings had burned because of the high electric currents. The insulation resistances of all windings were still perfect, however. The reason for this was the unacceptably high speeds of the motors, which ran continuously because of the slipping clutches. The brush boxes and the collectors were burned by the brushes sparking in places. Because of the dust that had entered, the carbon brushes' pressure fingers had lost contact pressure. Because of the increased play of the carbon brushes, these were not jammed, however. It was considered necessary to use hingeless brushes without pockets, so that this problem did not reappear as quickly. This made it possible to simplify the complex servicing of the difficult-to-access electric motors.

- The left band brake with coating was worn out, and the clutch casing was discolored. The right clutch, on the other hand, exhibited neither wear nor stress. As a consequence, Professor Porsche determined that the friction clutch could be eliminated and the connection could be made rigid by means of a geared ring. The new electric motors were equipped with it. Installation of the drive motors and assembly of the vehicle were tedious on account of the large number of fixing bolts and the air ducts' felt seals. The time requirement for these tasks added up to seventy-seven working hours. Required here were at least a 15-metric-ton (16.5 ton) crane and special tools for the Sturmgeschütz 43/1.

- The cooling system was a source of problems. As a result of the shape of the rear cooling-air exhaust, when on the move or while stationary off-road, there was a stream of air blowing forward at an angle under the hull. This resulted in the formation of a cloud of dust in front of the driver, which made driving extremely difficult. A remedy was a curved baffle plate extending the entire width of the vehicle. On the other hand, the unpleasant whirling up of dust caused by the exhaust gases blown from above onto the upper halves of the tracks from the existing exhaust openings could not be avoided.

- The arrangement of the center grating was seen as unfavorable. It was screwed in place so that the air guide vanes faced the rear, allowing fragments from shells striking the front of the superstructure to enter the cooling fan compartment. Changing the grating's position by 180° remedied the situation. To do this, however, a cutout had to be added for the radio operator's hatch support.

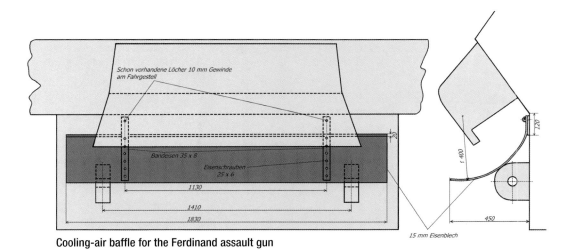

Cooling-air baffle for the Ferdinand assault gun

- Moving the exhaust pipes negatively affected the warming of cooling air for the electric-motor compartment. These exhaust pipes were separated from the air ducts by just 50 mm where they passed, and were therefore supposed to receive thermal insulation.

- There was inadequate spacing between the suction compartment for the four radiator fans and the engine compartment, allowing hot air from the engine compartment to enter the cooling circuit. Thermal problems could result, especially at high temperatures. At the time of the check, the coolant temperature was 90°C (194°F) with an outside temperature of 20°C (68°F). Another weakness that was identified was that the stop valve for the coolant circuit, necessary for the conveyance of engine coolant, was not secured. Shaking during off-road driving caused this valve to gradually close.

- The running gear still had the old final drive with the gear ratio of 1:15. A rubber block on the left rear limit stop had to be replaced after 413 km (256 mi.). Another shortcoming that was discovered was that off-road, minor steering movements caused the drive sprockets and idler wheels to become completely clogged, since these lacked sufficient open areas for the dirt and mud to escape.

- Criticisms of the superstructure included the driver's hatch, which required a great deal of effort to open from the inside. The assist spring was therefore definitely in need of improvement. As well, a handhold for the radio operator was seen as necessary.

On May 30, vehicle 150 011 was made drivable again with Alkett's help, and on June 3, 1943, it was loaded onto a railcar for transport to Hillersleben, where ballistic tests were subsequently carried out. Afterward the vehicle was to be transported from there to Friedrichshafen. Maybach was to carry out further tests involving the Maybach HL 120 TRM engine on behalf of the Verskraft. The abovementioned baffle was meanwhile accepted by Alkett, and the Nibelungenwerk was tasked with producing it and sending it after the vehicles. The troops were then to install the baffles on the spot.

The 2nd Platoon of the 2nd Company of schwere Panzerjäger-Abteilung 653 began entraining at Parndorf on June 8, 1943, and the process was captured in the following

Front and side views

Ferdinand assault gun. *PA*

Right: Professor Porsche and two of his engineers watch a Ferdinand being loaded over what was called a "mobile Tiger ramp." *PA*

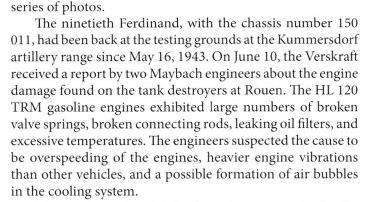

PA

PA

series of photos.

The ninetieth Ferdinand, with the chassis number 150 011, had been back at the testing grounds at the Kummersdorf artillery range since May 16, 1943. On June 10, the Verskraft received a report by two Maybach engineers about the engine damage found on the tank destroyers at Rouen. The HL 120 TRM gasoline engines exhibited large numbers of broken valve springs, broken connecting rods, leaking oil filters, and excessive temperatures. The engineers suspected the cause to be overspeeding of the engines, heavier engine vibrations than other vehicles, and a possible formation of air bubbles in the cooling system.

Meanwhile, on June 16, Ferdinand 150 011 arrived at the Maybach-Motorenbau factory in Friedrichshafen, where instruments to measure rpm, temperatures, and vibrations were installed. The new final drives with the gear ratio of

1:16.8, which had arrived the day before, were installed at the same time. The old final drives with the gear ratio of 1:15 were sent back to Skoda on June for conversion on the eighteenth. The experiments were thus able to take place under the same conditions as experienced by the vehicles in France. As a result of the new gear ratio, the final speed was lowered and off-road performance improved. The tests were expected to continue until June 24. The measured maximum speeds with the new gear ratio were

- in speed switch setting 3 and fully opened second carburetor stage 33 kph (20.5 mph)

- in speed switch setting 2 and fully opened second carburetor stage 19 kph (11.8 mph)

The chimney sweep in the photo brought Ferdinand 231's crew luck, since they and their vehicle survived the Battle of Kursk. Just one of the vehicles on this train was lost in the battle! *PA*

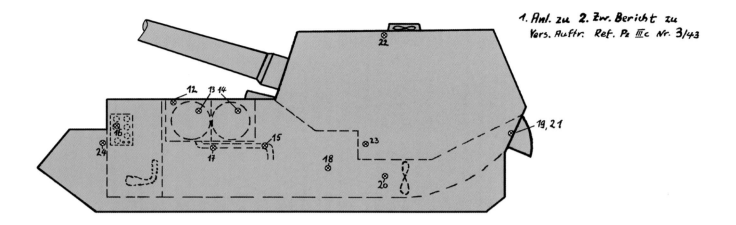

1. Anl. zu 2. Zw. Bericht zu
Vers. Auftr. Ref. Pz IIIc Nr. 3/43

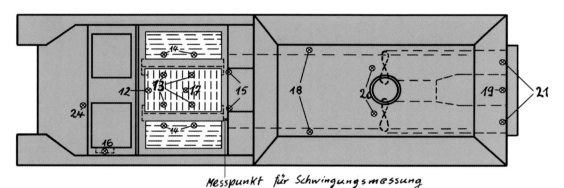

Messpunkt für Schwingungsmessung

Anordnung der Temperatur-Messtellen
im Stu. Gesch. Ferdinand Fg. Nr. 150011.   9.7.43

Measuring points. The original caption reads: "Arrangement of temperature measuring points in Ferdinand assault gun chassis no. 150011."

- in speed switch setting 1 and fully opened first carburetor stage 14 kph (8.7 mph). In this case the second carburetor stage could not be engaged, since the maximum speed of the gasoline engines of 3,000 rpm had already been reached

The primary objective of the trials was off-road testing over long, continuous gradients, such as the local Pfänderstrasse. The engine engineers also wanted to take advantage of the presence of the vehicle to create guidelines for the repair and replacement of individual engine parts and complete engines. Siemens asked Maybach for permission to take part in the trials, since it was interested mainly in cooling conditions in and around the drive engines. The test drives were supposed to begin on June 21, but the experimental vehicle developed a problem with the left cooling-fan drive—made by Alkett. A new cooling fan with triangular driving flange had to be urgently procured. Maybach immediately sent a telex to Alkett; however, Alkett referred it to the spare-parts warehouse at the Nibelungenwerk. Only if there was no other possibility was Alkett prepared to remove the necessary parts from the preproduction machine with the chassis number 150 010, which was in the factory. According to a letter dated June 18, the complete cooling fan with triangular flange was to be sent by rail so that the tests could continue. If shipment by courier was not possible, it would be brought to Stuttgart by the head waiter of the dining car and from there taken to Friedrichshafen by a Porsche employee.

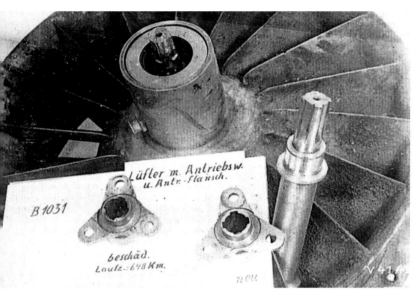

The defective cooling fan clearly shows the broken-out wedge profile of the part on the left. *PA*

Since Major Hoffmann of the Verskraft, who was on the scene, wanted to have some additional parts sent, such as two heat shields, a crank for the inertia starter, a remote-reading thermometer system for the drive engine developments, and a circuit diagram for the electrical system, it was suggested that they be transported by a Verskraft truck, which at that time was at the Simmering Company in Vienna and was supposed to deliver replacement engines to St. Valentin.

However, the spares were not available at the Panzer Ordnance Depot (HZA, or Army Ordnance Depot) in Magdeburg, and therefore the Nibelungenwerk was to deliver the required parts. It was envisaged that the previously mentioned Verskraft truck transport would be used, coming from Vienna via the Nibelungenwerk in St. Valentin. In order to fully exploit the truck's 4.5-metric-ton (5 ton) cargo capacity, additional Ferdinand spares were to be sent along from the Army Ordnance Depot Magdeburg. This was dependent, however, on approval from Wa Prüf 6. If all went according to plan, the truck was expected to arrive in Magdeburg on July 2. On July 8, however, approval from Wa Prüf 6 to take materials from the Army Ordnance Depot had still not been received. To save time, it was suggested that the truck should be redirected straight to the Research Center for Motor Vehicles (Verskraft) at the Kummersdorf artillery range. Since this was not possible, probably because of the existing bureaucracy, a Porsche fitter finally picked up the vitally needed spares from the Nibelungenwerk and transported them to the Kummersdorf artillery range.

Meanwhile, at Hillersleben on June 19, a single armored superstructure of the Ferdinand, which was designated Stuk (Sturmkanone) 43/1, underwent firing trials. Firing at the chassis was unnecessary, since it had already undergone firing trials as the Tiger chassis, but without the additional frontal armor. It had been planned to carry out the firing trials together with parts of the Maus battle tank at the artillery range at Kummersdorf; however, the crane at Kummersdorf was not capable of unloading the 50-metric-ton (55 ton) Maus turret. The decision was therefore made to carry out the firing trials at the army experimental station at Hillersleben, where cranes capable of unloading the turret were available. The homogeneous armor plate on the front of the Ferdinand's armored superstructure was 204 mm thick and was made of type 7690 steel. The side armor was 84 mm thick and was made of type E 22 steel. The exact composition is shown in the table below.

An 88 mm Panzergranate 39-1 armor-piercing round was fired at the front of the superstructure from a distance of 100 m. This produced coarse eruptions on the front plate and its reverse and cracks in the weld seams. A 75 mm armor-piercing round was fired at the side plates from an angle of 48°, and a 120 mm (4.7 inch) diameter hole was punched through the armor plate. A 150 mm high-explosive shell striking the side plates produced longitudinal cracks over one-half to

Name	Steel Type	Plate Thickness	Tensile Strength	C	Mn	Si	Cr	Mo	Ni	V	P + S
Front	PP 7690	204 mm	074 kg/mm^2	0.36	0.37	0.34	2.3	0.12	2.73	Spr.	0.29
Side, left	E 22	083 mm	092 kg/mm^2	0.38	0.7	0.33	1.71	0.11	0.8	0.15	0.21
Side, right	E 22	085 mm	094 kg/mm^2	0.38	0.7	0.33	1.71	0.11	0.8	0.15	0.21
Rear	E 22	084 mm	097 kg/mm^2	0.4	0.74	0.38	1.79	0	0.57	0.13	0.21
Roof	E 32	032 mm	116 kg/mm^2	0.41	0.81	0.5	1.45	0.09	1.61	0.1	0.31

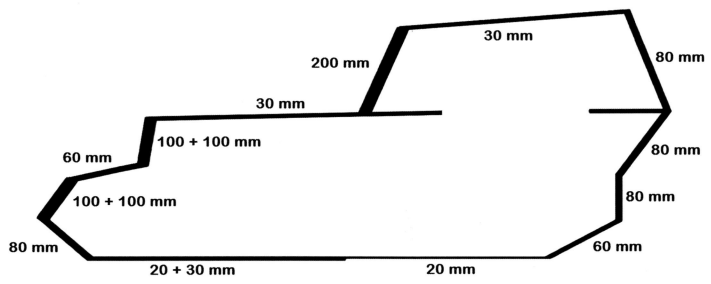

Ferdinand assault gun armor plate thicknesses

three-quarters of the length of the superstructure. It was suspected that the cracks in the left and right weld seams would not have occurred if the plates had fit together better, their poor fit being apparent from the unequal cross sections of the weld seams.

The test vehicle's first test drive took place at Friedrichshafen on June 23, having been delayed by the cooling-fan problem. The cooling fan's rejected spline shaft was replaced with the spare parts taken from the Alkett vehicle 150 010, since as we know, the attempt to quickly procure replacement parts had failed.

A drive on the Friedrichshafen-Bregenz road and the 19% Bregenz-Fluh (elevated mound) was used to check the cooling system. In consideration of the running gear, the gasoline engines were not fully loaded. They ran at a speed of 2,000 rpm, which in field switch setting 3 was sufficient for a speed of about 22 kph (13.7 mph). The lower speed of the right cooling fan (−25%) stood out. The Maybach engine was fully loaded during the hill climb. An average speed of 5 kph (3.1 mph) was achieved on the hill at an engine speed of 2,300 rpm.

The electric motors' power consumption was about 600 amperes. In the curves in field switch setting 2, the value rose to 1,200 amperes. The cooling fans worked properly, and the cooling effect was regarded as satisfactory, with an external temperature of up to 40°C (104°F). The coolant circulation, with 46 liters (12.15 gal.) in the cooling circuit, was found to be extraordinarily low, however. It was further determined that because of the arrangement of the cooling system for the drive engines and the engine compartment, heating of the fighting compartment was unavoidable, since the discharged hot air, with a temperature of about 80°C (176°F), passed under the fighting compartment. With hatches closed and exhaust fan running, temperatures of about 60°C (140°F) were measured in the area of the gunner's feet and 41°C (105°F) at the roof ventilator, with an outside temperature of 21°C (70°F).

The additional findings concerned the installation conditions of the Maybach HL 120 TRM engines:

- When working on the forward part of the engines there was no retaining device for the center and right hatch covers, and the opening angle of the central engine hatch was too small (*because of the gun, which was directly above it*). As a result, changing the valve springs, spark plugs, etc. in the center of the engine was possible only under the most-difficult conditions. To disassemble the cylinder heads it was necessary to first remove the entire superstructure.

- It was found that the two engine oil filters had never been used, since the Bowden cables were hopelessly jammed. Since the filters could not be used, the engine oil was not cleaned as prescribed and, by way of the bypass valve, returned uncleaned to the engine lubricating points.

- The markings on the flywheels were so obscured by the generator cooling fans that they could not be used to adjust the ignition or the control shaft.

- The inertia starters could not be used, since the installed starter mechanisms were not usable on account of their poor placement.

- The cooling-fan drive by Alkett was so poorly designed in some places that the failure of a cooling-fan drive had to be expected. By that time the drive on the other side would already be in very poor condition.

- The alternators were separate and not installed on the engine and powered organically. After the failure of an alternator during the test drive, after driving about 3 km (1.8 mi.) the engine could not be started again, since the batteries were quickly drained by the field and braking currents. The reason for this was that the V belts were overstretched and had to be retensioned. Afterward, however, further tensioning was not possible.

Examination of the problem of potential overspeeding of the HL 120 engines revealed that the danger was greatest when the driver started on the road in field switch setting 1. At a speed of 14 kph (8.7 mph) and activation of the first carburetor stage, the engine very quickly reached 3,000 rpm. If the driver fully depressed the accelerator pedal, the engine had to greatly overspeed. This was particularly dangerous because overspeeding was not possible in the other driving conditions and field switch settings. This led the driver to stop paying attention to the rpm indicator. A certain risk posed

Test vehicle 150 011 at the Kummersdorf artillery range. A vehicle registration number was regulation there, since vehicles were also driven on public roads. The Verskraft's red registration numbers always began with WH 0. *PA*

315

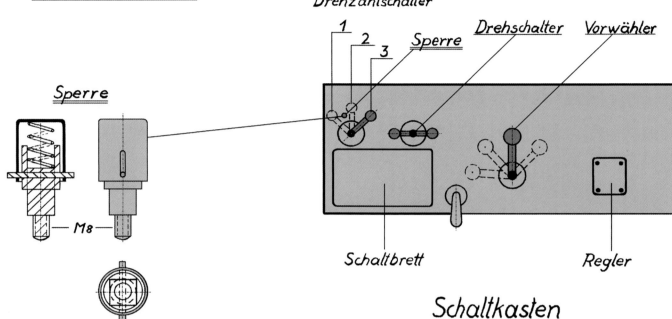

Federstiftsperre für Drehzahlschalter auf Schaltkasten

Drehzahlschalter

1 2 3 *Sperre* *Drehschalter* *Vorwähler*

Sperre

M8

Schaltbrett *Regler*

Schaltkasten

A spring pin lock for the first field switch stage was suggested as a measure to prevent overspeeding of the gasoline engines, a solution that, judging by the photos of Elefant 102 at Aberdeen, was never implemented. The original caption reads: "Spring pin lock for the speed switch on the switch box." *PA*

by insignificant overspeeding was at best possible when descending a slope or during heavy braking. It was proposed that field switch setting 1 be locked and the drivers be instructed to use this setting only in the most difficult terrain.

Vibration measurements were compared with the values from the VK 3601 tank. At a speed of 5 kph (3.1 mph) there was a very great difference. Despite its significantly higher weight, the tank destroyer experienced a very high level of high-frequency vibrations, and these appeared most strongly when the vehicle slid. The resulting load on the engines was minimal on account of the relatively supple engine mounts. Negative effects on the other components could be expected, however. It was determined that the primary causes of these vibrations were the relatively firm suspension and the track pitch.

A normal off-road drive was subsequently carried out to check the entire cooling system. The route consisted of a mix of winding level road, a moderately steep hill road (15%), and finally an off-road circuit on moderately difficult ground and a maximum gradient of about 20%. During the hill drive,

power consumption on the steepest section (15% gradient) was 900 to 1,000 A. Off-road, while on the steep slope a pause had to be taken to cool the windings because of overheating of the drive engines (power consumption of 1,000 to 1,200 A at gasoline engine speed of 2,000 rpm). The subsequent attempt to negotiate a 22% gradient had to be abandoned, since the tracks began spinning because of the vehicle's serious tail-heaviness. The ground conditions were similar to those at Berka (greasy, sticky clay). The experiments were therefore concluded after 106 km (66 mi.).

On June 28, the vehicle was loaded and sent back to the Kummersdorf artillery range. The defects were subsequently investigated by the Verskraft. It was thought that the high air outlet temperatures of 98°C (208°F) behind the drive engines were caused by the parallel arrangement of the exhaust pipes and air ducts, which resulted in heating of the latter. Heat-insulating shielding plates were supposed to solve the problem. Improved efficiency of the drive engine cooling fans and improved duct sealing were also envisaged.

The second defect involved the left steering lever, which after the off-road drive at Friedrichshafen was stiff and difficult to operate. A detailed examination revealed that two parallel resistances had caused the left motor's stabilizing winding to partially melt, and during the off-road drive, parts of it had fallen onto the drum switch shaft. Both reverse field controllers were subsequently replaced.

The schwere Panzerjäger-Abteilung 653 was transported to Russia from June 9 to 12. The transport required eleven trains. Detraining took place 35 km (22 mi.) south of Orel. The schwere Panzerjäger-Abteilung 654 departed for Russia on June 15, on fourteen trains. Its destination was Smiyevka station near Orel, the first train unloading there on June 24.

Meanwhile preparations had begun for schwere Panzerjäger-Abteilung 653, with forty-four Ferdinands, and schwere Panzerjäger-Abteilung 654, with forty-five Ferdinands, to take part in the battle of the Kursk salient. Professor Porsche was less than enthusiastic about this hasty deployment of the Ferdinand tank destroyer, since he rightly expected numerous teething troubles.

The attack by schwere Panzerjäger-Regiment 656 began early on July 5, 1943, in the 9th Army / XXXI Panzer Corps sector north of Kursk. Also attached to the regiment were Sturmpanzer-Abteilung 216 and two remote-control tank companies, Panzer-Funklenkkompanien 313 and 314. The armored attack force was bolstered by two assault gun brigades,

View of the opened driving switch under the driver's seat. In the foreground (*at left of photo*) are the steering lever shafts. In the background (*below right in photo*) is the opened reversing-field regulator with melted resistors. *PA*

Parked and ready to go: a Ferdinand of schwere Panzerjäger-Abteilung 654 at Rouen. *KHM*

The 2nd Company of schwere Panzerjäger-Abteilung 653 at Neusidel am See. *KHM*

The enormous vehicle was naturally an attention getter. *KHM*

Rear view of one of the first training vehicles at Neusiedl am See. *KHM*

A towed 88 mm Flak 18 passes a waiting Ferdinand. *KHM*

After arriving at the front near Orel, the Ferdinands caused a stir wherever they went. This vehicle of the 1st Company of the schwere Panzerjäger-Abteilung 653 already has rain gutters on the front of its armored superstructure. *KHM*

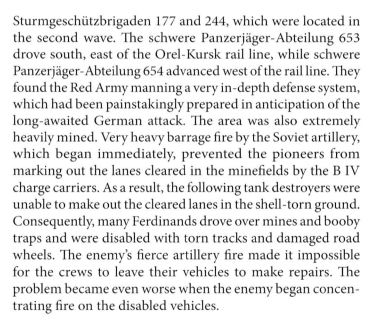

Sturmgeschützbrigaden 177 and 244, which were located in the second wave. The schwere Panzerjäger-Abteilung 653 drove south, east of the Orel-Kursk rail line, while schwere Panzerjäger-Abteilung 654 advanced west of the rail line. They found the Red Army manning a very in-depth defense system, which had been painstakingly prepared in anticipation of the long-awaited German attack. The area was also extremely heavily mined. Very heavy barrage fire by the Soviet artillery, which began immediately, prevented the pioneers from marking out the lanes cleared in the minefields by the B IV charge carriers. As a result, the following tank destroyers were unable to make out the cleared lanes in the shell-torn ground. Consequently, many Ferdinands drove over mines and booby traps and were disabled with torn tracks and damaged road wheels. The enemy's fierce artillery fire made it impossible for the crews to leave their vehicles to make repairs. The problem became even worse when the enemy began concentrating fire on the disabled vehicles.

The radio vehicle (Steyr 1500 A/01) of Oberleutnant Wegelin, commander of 3rd Company, schwere Panzerjäger-Abteilung 653. He was able to maintain contact with the company's combat vehicles by using the Fu 5 radio, and with the senior staffs by means of the Fu 8 (the larger set with star antenna). The Ferdinands were apparently seldom used as command vehicles. *KHM*

The Ferdinands of the schwere Panzerjäger-Abteilung 654 move into the battalion's assembly area. *KHM*

Ferdinands of schwere Panzerjäger-Abteilung 653 east of the rail line, advancing in the direction of Ponyri. *KHM*

The claims in the relevant literature that the Ferdinands were a preferred target of tank-killing teams cannot be verified by members of the two battalions. Hauptmann Henning, commander of the 653rd, commented: "The initial fear that the Ferdinand would be seriously threatened by enemy infantry proved unfounded in practice. The loud report when it fired its gun and the powerful emotional effect of the Ferdinand ensured that no enemy infantrymen came near the Ferdinand during all our days in action."[16]

Unteroffizier Neunert also said, "I never saw enemy tank-killers approaching our gun. Moreover, the infantry following us knew that they had to protect us against such attacks."[17] The problem of the absent machine gun in the front of the vehicle did not reveal itself until after the tank destroyers had broken through and the light escorting Panzer IIIs and the infantry of the 86th Infantry Division were held up by the very heavy defensive fire. The Ferdinands were then left on

their own and had no other option but to clear the enemy trenches with their 88 mm guns alone. The schwere Panzerjäger-Abteilung 653 reached its objective for the fifth of July with twelve vehicles still serviceable. The schwere Panzerjäger-Abteilung 654 had worse luck, however, and one of its platoons lost about a third of its vehicles in several minefields.

On July 7, the schwere Panzerjäger-Regiment 656 gave the following status report on its eighty-nine Ferdinands: seven total losses, forty-six vehicles under repair, and thirty-six serviceable. As well, it had requested that seventy 12-volt batteries be immediately flown to Orel. The many cases of mine damage had taken their toll. Despite this, employment of the Ferdinands was characterized as successful. On the following day, in addition to seven total losses (8%), fifty-four vehicles were reported in need of repairs (54%) and thirty-four serviceable (38%). On the other side of the coin, the two tank-destroyer battalions destroyed forty enemy tanks on the

A vehicle of the 1st Company's 3rd Platoon photographed while en route to Karachev. *KHM*

Ferdinand 511 passing a broken-down Panzer IV. *KHM*

third day. However the vehicles were in serious need of repairs because of the continual pressure and intense fire. There was no time for the necessary repairs, however, due to the desperate situation at the front. As a result, wear rose disproportionately. The vehicles were employed in small groups or even individually to fend off the attacking Red Army, and as time went on, they more frequently became saviors in the hour of need.

On July 8, the schwere Panzerjäger-Regiment 656 reported abnormal lubricant consumption to the higher-ranking department responsible for fuels. About 15 kg (33 lbs.) of lubricating grease was needed to lubricate one Ferdinand a single time. The high stress on the running gear caused abnormal heating, which caused the grease to leak out. The fifth road wheel was also subject to additional heating due to the exhaust pipe, which exited the hull above it. To ensure that the running

gear remained serviceable, it had to be greased daily or at the latest after 50 km (31 mi.). For the eighty-nine Ferdinands, each requiring 15 kg (33 lbs.) per day, daily consumption totaled 1,335 kg (2,943 lbs.) of grease. The regiment's III Battalion, Sturmgeschütz-Abteilung 216 with its Sturmpanzer IVs, also experienced increased demand caused by its vehicles' running gear, which was overloaded by four metric tons (4.4 tons). Because there were always Ferdinands undergoing repair, this battalion's requirements could be covered by the regiment's daily requirement of 1,335 kg. The second point was the need for motor oil.

Because of the great strain on the two Maybach engines in the Ferdinand, an engine change was regarded as absolutely necessary after 100 km (62 mi.) at the latest. This also took into account the fact that while in action the vehicles' engines had to be kept running even when they were stationary, so that the tank destroyers could be turned at any time. The requirement for a single Ferdinand oil change was 54 liters (14.25 gal.), which resulted in a total requirement of 4,806 liters (1,270 gal.). The Maybach engine in the Sturmpanzer IV had to endure twice the strain of one in a Panzer IV. The weapon's use in action was similar to that of the Ferdinand, and an oil change was necessary after 400 km (248 mi.) at the latest.

With 27 liters (7.1 gal.) required for an oil change, the III Battalion's total requirement was 1,215 liters (321 gal.) of motor oil. Included in this calculation was the Ferdinand's daily consumption of 15 to 20 liters (4 to 5.3 gal.) and that of the Sturmpanzer at 4 to 6 liters (1 to 1.6 gal.). The schwere Panzerjäger-Regiment 656's daily requirement for lubricants, assuming 25 km (15.5 miles) of travel, was thus 868 liters (229 gal.) of motor oil, 300 liters (79 gal.) of gear oil (Sturmpanzer), and 1,335 kg (2,943 lbs.) of lubricating grease.

The status report of July 14, 1943, revealed that the two battalions had suffered nineteen total losses, which by August 1, 1943, rose to twenty. These numbers are in conflict with those of the Red Army's investigating committee of July 15 (see below), which later examined the captured Ferdinands.

Guderian wrote of the use of the Ferdinand in Operation Citadel in mid-July: "My fears concerning the Panther's readiness for combat were confirmed. The ninety Porsche Tigers that were deployed with Model's army also failed to meet the requirements of close combat, because they did not carry sufficient rifle ammunition, which was made even worse by the fact that this tank had no machine guns and, after entering the enemy's infantry battle zone, literally had to shoot at sparrows with cannon. . . . On reaching the enemy's artillery position, they found themselves alone."[18]

This opinion probably arose from the report to the general staff on operational experience involving schwere Panzerjäger-Regiment 656, which stated that the very heavy artillery fire smashed the attack by the infantry, resulting in the tank destroyers being left alone in the open and drawing artillery fire. The absence of machine gun armament was making itself felt. The majority of the resulting heavy losses of nineteen Ferdinand tank destroyers were blamed on direct artillery hits on their gratings. This claim is open to skepticism, since the previously cited Red Army committee had closely examined the Ferdinands abandoned on the Ponyri battlefield on

This Ferdinand of the schwere Panzerjäger-Abteilung 654 was abandoned after sustaining mine damage. This vehicle, 501, was later put on display at Kubinka. *KHM*

July 15, after the Wehrmacht's retreat. It found that several tank destroyers had been set on fire; however, the bailed-out crews had destroyed their own vehicles. According to the committee, twenty-one Ferdinand tank destroyers were left behind on the battlefield. Of these, sixteen vehicles had been disabled with damaged tracks and road wheels. Ten of these vehicles had been disabled by mines, and six by hits from enemy guns on their running gear. Of these, fourteen Ferdinands were subsequently set on fire by their crews. Just one Ferdinand was directly knocked out, by a 76 mm shell that penetrated its side armor. Another Ferdinand took a direct bomb hit, while another tank destroyer took a direct hit on the roof of its fighting compartment from a 203 mm shell. Another vehicle became bogged down, and just one vehicle was set on fire by close-range weapons.

Two Ferdinands were repaired by the Soviets and used for testing or displays. Another Ferdinand was destroyed in gunnery trials. Following the German retreat, several unserviceable and cannibalized Ferdinands were also left behind at the maintenance bases of the repair battalions, since there were often no recovery vehicles or SSyms wagons available during the retreat. Most of the photos of abandoned Ferdinands usually show only chassis and fire damage. The described artillery hits would have inflicted a different level of destruction on the vehicles. As well, there was no reason for the Soviet committee not to mention these direct hits.

According to the German experience report, mine damage caused forty Ferdinand tank destroyers to be put out of action temporarily by July 11, the majority of which had damage to several track links, while some others also had damaged swing arms and road wheels. Despite the high rate of loss, the Ferdinands and Sturmpanzers always reached their assigned objectives. These gains often had to be abandoned, however, since no tank units were sent to back up the regiment's tank destroyers and Sturmpanzer, and the infantry lacked the strength to follow the tank destroyers. Against such an in-depth defense system and the enemy's great superiority in artillery, a breakthrough would have been possible only by coupling a panzer division with infantry in armored troop carriers, with significantly lower losses.[19]

A typical sight at the beginning of the Battle of Kursk. A significant number of the vehicles were lost due to mine damage. Once immobilized, the tank destroyers were exposed targets for the Soviet artillery. *KHM*

Members of the heavy-tank-destroyer battalions later said "that the Ferdinand had proved itself in action and was very popular with the troops. Its appearance often caused panic among the enemy and in places caused him to retreat in panic."[20] The war diary of the 9th Army contains the following entry under July 9: "Especially noteworthy is a successful attack by the XXXXI Panzer Corps in which the Ferdinand tanks again proved themselves as the driving force of the attack." Two days later the XXIII Panzer Corps reported: "The action by seven Ferdinands, which followed up the attack by the infantry and was escorted by assault guns, proved very successful in breaking up the enemy's system of positions and repulsing repeated counterattacks."[21]

A number of other experience reports were written at that time, which may be familiar to many readers. Here, however, we will cite the reports that, in keeping with the character of the book, reflect the Ferdinand's technical problems at that time.

On July 19, 1943, an Unteroffizier Böhm wrote to General Hartmann of the Armaments Ministry: "The Ferdinand has proved itself. It was decisive here, and nowadays one cannot get by against the masses of enemy tanks without such a weapon; assault guns are insufficient. The electric drive has completely proved itself, coming as a pleasant surprise to the drivers and crews. Motor and electrical failures few. Somewhat underpowered for its weight, tracks rather narrow. If it is improved based on experience, it will be outstanding! . . . They came somewhat late and there are too few of them. We need ten times as many; then we could move forward."[22]

There was also a report dated July 25, 1943, by Porsche employee Heinz Gröschl to Professor Porsche. Gröschl had been attached to the schwere Panzerjäger-Abteilung 653 to analyze on the spot the vehicle's remaining shortcomings and if possible remedy them: "Our vehicles have been in action for three weeks now, and with the mileage previously driven by them have now logged an average of 500 km (310 mi.). I have amassed sufficient experience to be able to paint a picture of the success or the failure of our vehicle. In agreement with the relevant officers of the battalion, I can say that the weapon was a success and that there was general regret that only the small number was available. With an average number of fifteen enemy tanks destroyed per vehicle, it is entirely justifiable to speak of it as a success. It must be emphasized, however, that this number could have been far higher. Unfortunately the majority of all vehicles were almost always under repair. This situation deteriorated from day to day, because, with increasing wear of all parts, the supply of spares, which was far from adequate in any case, was quickly used up. To date there have been practically no deliveries of spare parts. Of the original complement of forty-four vehicles, seventeen are missing as of this date. Of these, seven were given to the other battalions by order of the regiment, and the remaining ten must be written off as total losses. Below I am reporting to you the most-common damages and malfunctions:

Running Gear (Bogie Suspension):
Contrary to expectations, no damages were caused by overloading. The soft ground may have played a significant role in this. The wastage of rubber pads (especially on the rear two bogies) and rubber rings (usually on the fifth road wheel beneath the exhaust) was very high. Locknuts did not become detached; nevertheless a large percentage of the vehicles used the old metal safety devices. Replacement of curled road wheel rings must now be carried out on a large scale. Until now about twenty bogies (swing arm with spring housing) and a larger number of road wheels have been rendered unusable by enemy action. Damaged swing arms, burst spring housings, and road wheels that were torn off with the locknuts and often deformed were most common, mainly attributable to mines. Unfortunately, replacements were and are not available in sufficient quantities. Where possible, parts from knocked-out vehicles were used.

Final Drives (Reduction Boxes):
Apart from one case at Neusiedl, which was surely discussed by Herr Zadnik, no issues until now. You are sufficiently familiar with worn track attachment screws.

Working on the final drive of vehicle 133. The drive wheel has already been removed. *KHM*

This Ferdinand of the schwere Panzerjäger-Abteilung 654 was cannibalized due to lack of spares on the road to Briansk during the retreat. *KHM*

Steering Gear with Brakes:

Herr Zadnik is aware of several cases of brake damage at Neusiedl. Since then, no difficulties. Two vehicles remained in action for one or two days despite being damaged. In each case one brake drum was shot through. The internal parts were of course completely destroyed.

Tracks:

One of the most difficult problems as of late. On most vehicles a third to a half of all links have broken one or two times. There are no replacements. Mines and gunfire have left a large number of links unusable.

Hull:

Has proved to be almost impervious to shellfire. Apart from numerous pits, everything has remained intact except for one penetration (76.2 mm caliber) of the side armor in the area of the rear cooling fan driveshaft. By chance, this penetration also had no adverse consequences. On the other hand, practice has shown that the gratings are a vulnerable spot, for in addition to gasoline bombs, an artillery or bomb hit on or near the grating can set the vehicle on fire. The splinters enter the fuel tanks or damage other important parts, such as coolant hoses. The temperature in the engine compartment is so high that in some cases the fuel in the tanks began to boil. The arrangement of winches, tools, and cables on the outside of the hull was wrong. It was foreseeable that these items would be destroyed in a very short time.

Superstructure:

Was also penetrated from the side in two cases. The sealing of the superstructure and the gratings on the hull is extremely poor or is completely absent. Very fine but still dangerous splinters enter through the gun barrel's ball mantlet. Crewmen were wounded. The temperature inside the fighting compartment is still too high. It has occurred that ammunition for the flare pistol self-ignited. According to drivers and gunners, heating of shells lying on the floor has led to long shots.

Gasoline Engines:

Engine failures have been very numerous as of late. The following damages are seen: bent or broken valves, which result in wrecked pistons, bent or broken connecting rods, ruptured cylinder heads. In my opinion these phenomena are caused by capacity being excessively on the short side. Cracks in the cylinder head and leaking cylinder liners are surely a result of overheating. Experience has shown that a loss of 10 liters [2.6 gallons] of coolant is unbearable. The seals of the exhaust collector pipe almost always last only a short time. This is a constant fire danger. The installation of new seals is an

The acute spares shortage made it necessary to bring in the urgently needed replacement engines by aircraft. *WS*

Example of a tank workshop in the field. In this photo the scene is dominated by the HL 120 TRM engines.

extremely difficult and time-consuming job given their known inaccessibility. At present it is almost impossible to completely **replace defective engines, because there are no** replacements.

Cooling System:

Leaking radiators and rejected cooling fans have already caused us a great deal of work. The radiators usually channel into the soldered joint of the lower support. I assume that the short, rigid tube connection between the lower supports of the two radiators is the cause. On rejected cooling fans the drive flange was welded to the cooling-fan shaft. There are no replacement parts for this.

Generators, Electric Motors:

We had the last failure of a generator at Neusiedl. It was again the known connection at the downward-facing blade contact. Since then the systems have been working perfectly. It must be emphasized, however, that until now we have had primarily

dry weather and that only rarely do the vehicles completely cool down. On the other hand, the accretion of dust, especially in the generators, is very considerable, although operating reliability does not seem to be suffering.

Driving Switch:

There have been no noteworthy problems. The reversing field regulator has been replaced on three vehicles. Here, too, dust-tightness leaves much to be desired.

Alternators, Storage Batteries:

The alternator with reverse direction of rotation has given rise to major complications. It is responsible for the total loss of one vehicle. There were several vehicles daily with blown fuses and therefore discharged batteries. Herr Zadnik will have already reported about this to you. We have now gone over to installing the alternators with their previous direction of rotation and have already carried out this work on nine vehicles. This has put an end to the complaints. Herr Scharpf of the Bosch Company, who was assisting us in this matter, has unfortunately been killed. The mounting of the collectors [120-volt batteries] is poor. The first day of the attack alone cost us thirty batteries. Each vehicle that hit a mine lost at least one and not rarely all its batteries. In each case the case was ruptured or completely wrecked. Gunfire sometimes had the same effect. The two radio batteries are subjected to very heavy loads and therefore must often be charged outside the vehicle. (As described previously, on July 7, the schwere Panzerjäger-Regiment 656 urgently requested that seventy batteries—12 volt, 105 ampere—be delivered by air to Orel.)

Bowden Cables, Tachometer:
Problems were also encountered with the Bowden cables, which could be repaired only with the greatest difficulty, for not even the smallest spare part made it into our hands. The tachometers of many vehicles failed. The vehicles were driven without a tachometer. Such instruments, especially ones that are so difficult to access, must function with great reliability, for in action there is no time to replace them.

Guns:
The cannon was very effective but was almost always in need of repair. For reasons as yet unexplained, the lands broke out of the barrel, and the shell-casing ejector did not work. The casings often had to be removed with a hammer and chisel. Driving in combat with the barrel unlocked caused the elevation and azimuth mechanisms to deflect, causing up to 20 cm of play to be detected at the muzzle. Heating of the entire vehicle often caused the elevating and traversing mechanism to jam. The gun had to be boresighted again after a brief period of operations. In several cases the forward barrel support was shot away. Stabsfeldwebel Brunnthaler has submitted a more detailed report to the commander of Battalion 653."[23]

The problem with the batteries described above requires further examination. The Ferdinand had four 12-volt batteries with a rating of 105 amperes. Pairs of batteries were connected in parallel and both groups in series. Also, 12 volts was required for the onboard voltage. The excitation of the electric drive, the two starters, and the two alternators operated with a voltage of 24 volts. These four batteries were located in the right front, directly beneath the radio operator's seat. While the detonation of mines or other explosive charges did not penetrate the floor armor, the shock effect of the explosion was so great that in some cases the battery case cracked and

was thus destroyed. Thanks to their magneto ignition, the gasoline engines could continue running without battery voltage, and the direct-current alternators continued to deliver current for excitation and for the electrical firing of the gun, but because the running gear or at least one track was as a rule damaged, the assault gun was initially disabled.

There is also a technical report by a T.T.V.-Rat* Schwarz (schwere Panzerjäger-Abteilung 654) submitted to designer Xaver Reimpieß dated August 8, 1943: "The running gear, for which we have your personal skill to thank, has proved its worth. As I wrote to you, almost all cases of running-gear damage could be quickly repaired. This running gear is far superior to a running gear such as that found today on the Panther and Tiger. For one, the Ferdinand has what is probably the shortest conceivable replacement time for a road wheel on such a heavy vehicle. As well, none of the rubber rings on any of the vehicles, which have traveled an average of 500 km, are worn, with the exception of the one on the fifth road wheel, which is directly exposed to the exhaust gases. I regard this running gear as arguably ideal for so heavy a tank, and it would also be possible to install it on the hull if the side armor was

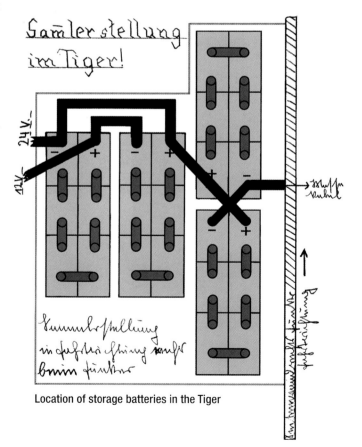

Location of storage batteries in the Tiger

not as thick. In terms of design, with an eye toward possible towing, thought should be given to placing small chain rings around the running gear, as can be seen on the Ferdinand sent back to the Ni-Werk [Nibelungenwerk], which incidentally represents a conglomeration of spare parts from several Ferdinands. The electric drive has actually stood up well; only the new version of the electric motor must be even more technically attuned to the gasoline engine.

"The arrangement of the removable superstructure and grating plates has proved itself to be very advantageous for repairs. In the workshop we can repair almost any damage sustained in action in two working days, and make the vehicle serviceable again in this disproportionately short time. According to statements by Tiger and Panther units, they require two to three days for the removal of a single rear road wheel [!]. From a war technology point of view, the 200 mm [7.9 in.] of armor is excessively thick. Even twenty to thirty direct hits by Russian antitank guns up to 102 mm in caliber have inflicted wounds on the Ferdinand with a maximum depth of just 5 cm [1.96 in.]; thus they could probably have gotten by with 12 to 14 cm [4.7 to 5.5 in.] of frontal armor. The side armor does not seem to me to be overly thick, since the relatively slow Ferdinand can easily take flanking fire from fast Russian tanks.

"Even at that time, it was even clear to you that the tracks had to be strengthened, and if I remember correctly, deliveries of stronger tracks for the Ferdinand are supposed to begin in August. But even the current tracks have, in fact, demonstrated outstanding running life and proved too weak only if several mines were struck simultaneously."[24] (*Translator*: A civilian official of the armed forces with the function of technical officer.)

Concerning the problem of the tracks, there had in fact already been a new development. At an internal meeting on August 26, 1943, Professor Porsche was extremely impatient that Skoda was still delivering the old tracks to the Nibelungenwerk, even though the new track possessed major advantages. Fender, the Porsche representative at Skoda, blamed the Nibelungenwerk, since it would accept no interruptions and demanded that Skoda continue delivering the old tracks. Not until September were only the new tracks to be delivered to the Nibelungenwerk.[25]

Measurements of different gratings had been taken at the Verskraft at the end of July, but the results were not compiled until the end of the following month. The Windhoff Company had sent the results of its experiments with the most effective

grating shape for the VK 4501 P assault gun to Alkett on May 26. The proposed new type of grating was tested alongside the one currently in use on the Ferdinand. Air resistance measurements revealed that the grating currently in use had by far the worst shape of any grating tested to date. For example, on one of the new grating shapes, air resistance was 40 mm WS (392 pascals) at an air speed of 15.5 m/sec. (50.8 ft./sec.), while an air resistance of 200 mm WS (1,961 pascals) was measured on the Ferdinand grating. The Verskraft was concerned not only about the low flow resistance necessary for the cooling system, but also about the grating's vulnerability to fragments. The new gratings also had to be easy to produce, so that they could be manufactured and delivered quickly.

Combat experience had shown that with their aperture width of 11 mm (0.4 in.), the gratings already in use were too easily penetrated by fragments (sketch 1). As a result of this,

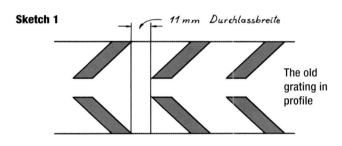

Sketch 1 *11 mm Durchlassbreite*

The old grating in profile

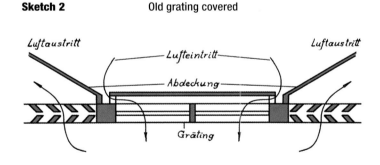

Sketch 2 Old grating covered

Luftaustritt *Lufteintritt* *Luftaustritt* *Abdeckung* *Grating*

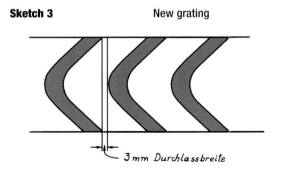

Sketch 3 New grating

3 mm Durchlassbreite

the generators, the gasoline engines, and the fuel tanks were often so damaged that total losses resulted in practice. There were two possible avenues to avoid this. The first was a cover over the previous grating proposed by the troops (sketch 2). The second proposal envisaged a new grating with an aperture width of just 3 mm (0.12 in.) (sketch 3). To quickly achieve the final values in the relatively low outside temperatures of 19°–26°C (66°–79°F), tracks 1 and 2 in the parabolic dunes were used to take measurements.

Furthermore, measurements were to be taken to determine to what degree the temperature rise caused by the proximity of the exhaust pipe to the air duct was responsible for the self-ignition of ammunition. Measurements were carried out at the ammunition racks, which were located on the floor of the fighting compartment, below the exhaust pipe. The results revealed that with a covered grating, as suggested by the troops, temperatures were on average 6°C (42°F) higher than with the standard version. With the new Alkett grating, however, temperatures were about 9°C (48°F) lower than with the old grating. The numbers clearly favored the new style of grating, which represented a significant improvement compared to the gratings previously found on operational vehicles.

Measurements at the ammunition racks, however, produced values that seemed questionable. Even with the unfavorable grating, these were no higher than 50°C (122°F).

On August 6, Alkett presented its cost breakdown to the Army Ordnance Office. The factory in Spandau calculated the cost of procuring the necessary materials and carrying out the work for the conversion of the ninety Porsche Tigers into assault guns at 607,624.60 reichsmarks. However, this estimate did not include the Maybach engines or the armaments and equipment, since these were provided by the HWA.

Meanwhile the poor technical state of the armored vehicles led Oberst von Jungfeld, commander of schwere Panzerjäger-Regiment 656, to report the problematic situation to the army headquarters on July 24. In his report he indicated that the regiment had been in action continuously since July 5. Only the I Battalion had once had twenty-four hours for technical maintenance. Both the Ferdinands and the Sturmpanzer had an extraordinary number of technical defects, and after three to five days in action the vehicles had to spend two to three days in the workshops to be made serviceable again.

Excessive use of the vehicles, which were actually supposed to undergo technical repairs every fourteen to twenty days,

The air baffle over the electric-motor exhaust air vent can be seen clearly on the rear of vehicle 534. *KHM*

The 1st Company of the schwere Panzerjäger-Abteilung 653 on the move

resulted in a rise in the number of cases of repaired vehicles breaking down again while on their way back to their units. The Oberst therefore advised the army headquarters that in a very short time the regiment would no longer be operational. At that time the regiment had fifty-four Ferdinands and forty-one Sturmpanzers. Twenty-five Ferdinands were operational (four of them only conditionally), as were eighteen Sturmpanzers. The regimental commander therefore suggested that the vehicles be withdrawn from the front. Just three groups were to be left in readiness behind the front as a mobile reserve, while all remaining Ferdinands were to go into the workshop for maintenance and repairs.

On August 26, the two heavy-tank-destroyer battalions, the 653rd and 654th, had a total of fifty Ferdinand tank destroyers. By the end of July 1943, schwere Panzerjäger-Regiment 656, to which the two battalions belonged, had alone destroyed **502 Soviet tanks and 300 guns, and schwere**

Panzerjäger-Abteilung 653's share alone was 320 tanks for the loss of thirteen Ferdinand tank destroyers written off. The regiment's loss–kill ratio was thus 1:20, while the latter battalion had an even better ratio of twenty-four enemy tanks destroyed for every tank destroyer lost. By comparison, schwere Panzer-Abteilung 503, with its Henschel Tiger Is and IIs, destroyed 1,700 tanks and 2,000 guns during its entire service life while losing 252 tanks written off as total losses, resulting in a loss–kill ratio of 1:15, while schwere Panzer-Abteilung 503 had a loss–kill ratio of just 1:1.28. Of course these results depended on many factors, which were not always influenceable. Nevertheless, it could hardly be said that the Ferdinand heavy tank destroyers were a failure.

Since the beginning of August, schwere Panzerjäger-Abteilung 653 had been in rest position at Briansk. The schwere Panzerjäger-Abteilung 654 also arrived there with its remaining vehicles. By order of Führer Headquarters, it was directed to

Ferdinand crew posing with the impressively large shells for the 88 mm Pak L/71 gun. *KHM*

hand its remaining nineteen Ferdinands over to its sister battalion and was sent to the Orleans area of France to reequip on the Jagdpanther. On Hitler's order, schwere Panzerjäger-Abteilung 653 and Sturmpanzer-Abteilung 216 were moved to Dnepropetrovsk for repairs to their vehicles. There, with the help of Porsche, Alkett, and Siemens, they were to be brought up to the latest equipment standard.

The task of transporting the vehicles ran into major difficulties, however. Locating a suitable factory building led to further delays. The first workshop elements and the first four Ferdinands arrived at Dnepropetrovsk on August 26. It was not until the twenty-ninth, however, that the building could be set up to accept the heavy vehicles. Procurement of the necessary cranes also took more time than anticipated. The Ferdinand battalion was entitled to three 6-metric-ton (6.6 ton) and two 3-metric-ton (3.3 ton) slewing cranes. Just one

3-metric-ton and one 6-metric-ton cranes were available for ongoing repairs, however, since one Sd.Kfz. 100 (3-metric-ton crane) was destroyed in a rail accident, and one 6-metric-ton crane had gone missing during rail transport after the evacuation of Orel. The work groups therefore had to wait for each other due to the lack of lifting capacity.

As a result, not a single crane was available for the repair echelons near the front. A four-to-six-week repair period per vehicle had been planned, since the bulk of the vehicles required thorough maintenance after three weeks of uninterrupted action. A pause for repairs every five to six days would have been more appropriate. All additional configuration changes also had to be implemented. Work on the Ferdinands was supposed to be carried out by the workshop companies of schwere Panzerjäger-Abteilungen 653 and 654, and the work on the Sturmpanzer by Workshop Companies 545 and 552, which had been sent in addition.

The tank destroyers fought in individual battle groups, acting as mobile "fire brigades" at the front. *KHM*

The following changes were necessary for the Ferdinand tank destroyers:

A. Fire Prevention and Firefighting

- alteration of gratings for better protection against splinters and fragments

- shielding of the fuel line against the exhaust

- alteration of the exhaust collector pipe connections

- oil drip protection for the valve covers

- steps to prevent leaf deposits on the exhaust pipes

- improved engine compartment accessibility from the fighting compartment

- installation of a fire-extinguishing system consisting of two 5-liter carbonic acid snow extinguishers

B. Remedies against Mine Damage

- elastic mounting of the batteries

- removal of the mounting feet on the generator casings

- improvement of the alternator mounting

C. Elimination of Fault Sources in the Low-Voltage System

- installation of the alternators with new armatures prepared by Bosch

- supplying the separate excitation of the generators with 12

In December, unserviceable Ferdinands and Sturmpanzer are gathered by the road in preparation for transport to Nikopol. At the top right, above the prime mover, can be seen a Ferdinand recovery vehicle. Beginning in September 1943, the Nibelungenwerk began delivering one vehicle of this type per company. *KHM*

volts instead of 24 volts (improvement of radio conditions, reduced interference)

- radio interference suppression of superstructure and hull

- protection for ammeter to prevent damage

D. Drive

- rigid closure of friction clutches on the electric motors

- installation of the larger gear ratios in the final drives

- delivery of the new tracks

- removal of the rubber pads on the running gear

E. High-Voltage System

- stagger K 58/8 resistors as protection against vibration

- replace rigid groundings with ones with high-ohmic resistors

- thorough cleaning of electrical machines and switching devices

- removal of the bath below the air baffle on the generators

F. Superstructure

- install rain gutters on the front

- seal joint between hull and superstructure

- install screens on gratings

- increase pre-tension of compensating spring on driver's and radio operator's hatches

- weld probes onto the hull in front of the superstructure

Engine change after removal of the superstructure. *KHM*

Here a 16-metric-ton mobile gantry crane removes Ferdinand 102's superstructure. *KHM*

- mount spare track links, tools, and tool boxes on the rear of the superstructure

- install rain and glare shields over periscopes

- install air flow units under rear protective hood

- better weld joints on the cover over the engine compartment

G. Other Changes

- modify shape and slope of gun mantlet

Ferdinand 513 (chassis number 150 036) is prepared for its overhaul. *KHM*

After removal of the superstructure and engine cover, all of the work assemblies are accessible. *KHM*

- improve defense against splinters behind the ball mantlet by turning the gun mantlet

- reinforcement or strengthening of the superstructure roof plate

- emergency exit through installation hatch in rear wall of superstructure

- cupola with periscopes for the commander

- proposal for a machine gun for insertion into the gun barrel

- activation of forward gun support (*barrel travel lock*) from the driver's position

- periscope for the radio operator

- machine telegraph between commander and driver

- better rubber bearing for the periscope

- improve cooling system and cooling-fan drive

- improve screw fitting of the water-filling funnels and attach the screw cap with chain to the socket

- improve attachment of the rear protective hood

- change nuts for stub shafts, operation by Allen key

- alter exhaust pipe exit, requiring a stronger track deflector

There followed a detailed list of the damages sustained by the fifty Ferdinands. Almost all of the vehicles required repairs to their cooling systems and the new alternators. The Maybach engines of twenty-two of the Ferdinand tank destroyers were so worn out that they were in urgent need of replacement; however, there were only twenty-four gasoline engines available as replacements. Another fifty-four gasoline engines were therefore required for a general overhaul of all Ferdinands, but since a maximum of ten gasoline engines were in storage

at the Nibelungenwerk and their immediately allocation could not be guaranteed, the delivery of thirty Maybach HL 120 TRM engines from ongoing Panzer III and IV production was requested. Twenty-six worn-out gasoline engines had been sent from Dnepropetrovsk to Panzer Spare Parts Dump B in Magdeburg for accelerated repair on September 25.

The repair of these engines was therefore especially urgent, since the Ferdinands awaiting overhaul at Dnepropetrovsk had already covered 400 km (248 mi.) in action, and the Maybach engines were good for a maximum running time of 800 hours. A greater demand for gasoline engines was therefore expected in a short time, since the allowable running time was reached very quickly. The regiment therefore suggested that the units overhaul the engines themselves. To do so, the two workshop companies needed the required spare parts such as cylinder liners, pistons, rings, etc. needed for the complete overhaul of fifty engines. They also needed special tools such as engine stands, cylinder liner extractors, etc. for about six engine overhaul teams. An urgent request was submitted to the inspector-general of armored forces for the immediate delivery by air of twenty sets of pistons and cylinder liners, including four sets of tools, since not a single replacement engine was left. Because of the almost daily engine damage, these vehicles were now finally out of service.

The plan for general repairs was frustrated by the situation at the front. A battle group of fifteen Ferdinand tank destroyers and twenty-five Sturmpanzers had to be formed, and a seven-day "quick repair" program was launched to make them operational. New old-type tracks and new gasoline engines were installed. The fitters worked twelve hours a day. The Ferdinands received no improvements at all but were partially overhauled. The results of these quick repairs showed themselves during entraining, when three Ferdinands and two Sturmpanzers broke down again. After the vehicles for the battle group had been completed, work resumed on fourteen other Ferdinand tank destroyers, which were now to receive a general overhaul with all the configuration changes. Since completion of this work was more than questionable, a call was made to use old components to at least make the vehicles mobile, so that they could at least be loaded onto trains at short notice.

The regiment was transferred into the Zaphorozhye bridgehead for future employment. The withdrawal of the

For the planned refurbishment at Nikopol, the tank destroyer's superstructure was first to be removed by means of a 16-metric-ton *Strabokran* (*Straßenbockkran*, or mobile gantry crane). The crane must have been working at the limits of its capacity, since according to Alkett the superstructure alone weighed 13.55 metric tons. To this was added the gun, which weighed 3.53 metric tons, for a total of 17.08 metric tons. The superstructures seen in this photo have already been fitted rain gutters on the front of their superstructures. *KHM*

entire German front in mid-September must also have interrupted the major repair program at Dnepropetrovsk, which had already begun, and the workshop units were moved to Nikopol with all their materiel. As anticipated, transporting the forty-two Ferdinand tank destroyers by rail from Dnepropetrovsk to Nikopol was seriously hindered by heavy rail congestion. As a precaution, in case of emergency those responsible planned to move the entire column by road to Zaphorozhye and from there by rail to Nikopol. Since the railways in the entire army area were more than overburdened, as a further precautionary measure it was envisaged that the valuable spares could be transported in the regiment's own trucks to a previously selected warehouse in Zaphorozhye. The best-case scenario was for the repairs to begin on about

October 1, so that the vehicles could be made cold resistant before winter, since as of yet no decision had been made about their use in winter.

The relocation of the spare-parts dump also proved to be problematic, since this caused deliveries of spares and conversion parts to grind to a halt. The trains carrying the parts necessary to carry out the repairs, which had been intercepted and wrongly redirected by the Reichsbahn, absolutely had to be passed through to Nikopol. It had also become evident that the trains from Vienna and Magdeburg absolutely had to have escort detachments, which in the event of delays were to turn directly to Army Group South.

Another cause for concern was the retrofitted tracks of the new type, since the track links were more susceptible to

A tank maintenance unit's improvised repair of Maybach 120 TRM engines, including self-made test stand

Ferdinands waiting to entrain at Nikopol. *KHM*

breakage on account of cavities in the castings. In action it was also found that the enemy was concentrating his fire on the tracks. Since no more new tracks were available in the unit, delivery of the remaining 180 sets of tracks was to be accelerated. As well, 6,000 ice cleats had to be sent for the improved tracks, since the ice cleats from the Panzer IV used on the older tracks no longer fit. Other equipment required for winter use was also missing, such as hot-air blowers and hot-water trailers. A very high requirement for Glysantin antifreeze also had to be expected, since when under fire the Ferdinand tank destroyer tended to lose a great deal of coolant.

The supply of conversion parts for the Skoda final drive with the 1:16.38 gear ratio was also exhausted. Thirty vehicles had previously been equipped with it. Skoda claimed to have delivered conversion sets for seventy-five vehicles to Magdeburg. It was not known where these conversion parts were, since at least twenty-five more sets were required for the Ferdinand. Having realized that it was pointless to shoot at the Ferdinand from the front, the enemy was now concentrating his fire on the vehicle's running gear, and the need for running-gear parts was acute.[26] Of fifteen Ferdinand tank destroyers, ten were under repair because of running-gear damage.

By the end of November 1943, just four Ferdinands remained operational. Eight vehicles were in short-term and thirty in long-term maintenance. Of the Sturmpanzers, just two were operational, and the remaining forty-three vehicles were in long-term maintenance. This vehicle situation forced the army command to make the decision to pull out the entire tank-destroyer regiment and send it back to St. Valentin for general refurbishing.

On December 10, schwere Panzerjäger-Regiment 656 received orders to rest and reequip. Even as it was in the midst of entraining, the regiment had to leave a battle group behind in the Nikopol bridgehead to once again lend support to the threatened infantry divisions. The scattered battle groups from schwere Panzerjäger-Regiment 656 had to plug gaps in the front's antitank defenses until December 25. Nevertheless, the eight operational Ferdinands and ten Sturmpanzers in the bridgehead destroyed large numbers of enemy tanks.

Meanwhile, at the Kummersdorf artillery range, the Verskraft continued testing Ferdinand 150 011. The necessary conversion parts for the new equipment state were listed in a letter to the Nibelungenwerk dated September 7, 1943:

- The new gratings should be delivered from Brandenburg in four weeks.

- The Nibelungenwerk was to produce the air baffles for the floor-cooling fan (electric motors).

- Fuel tanks, mounting brackets for the resistors, support brackets for the water pump air vents, the splash guards in the valve cover, the peepholes for the engine compartment, and the battery boxes were also ordered from the Nibelungenwerk.

- The rubber pads for the battery boxes were to be procured with Alkett's help, since they were made by a manufacturer in Berlin.

- The rain deflector for the driver's hatch cover and the sealing rubbers for the hull cover and for the driver's and radio operator's hatches were also to be procured by Alkett.

- The exhaust pipes with their mounting springs came from Stuttgart. Slotted flanges had to be produced to ensure that the exhaust pipes also had freedom of movement. Alkett had to deliver appropriate templates for cutting out the openings in the hull.

- Strengthened cooling-fan shafts and the associated trunnions and 9 mm (0.35 in.) of armor protection for the fuel tank beneath the exhaust air grating were to be delivered simultaneously with the gratings from the Nibelungenwerk.

- Alkett was to contribute a stand-up collar strainer in front of the engine compartment air intake grating.

Furthermore, the vehicle's weight with tools and accessories (not including crew, radio equipment, and twenty-six rounds of 88 mm ammunition [weighing 545 kg, or 1,201 lbs.]) was listed as 64,370 kg (141,911 lbs.). Because of the worn engines, it was possible to make only an interim calculation of fuel consumption. On the forest circuit this was between 867.9 and 933.9 liters per 100 km (0.27 and 0.25 mpg), while on the parabolic dunes, consumption rose to between 1,380 and 1,620 liters per 100 km (0.17 and 0.14 mpg). Excessive oil consumption figures of 20.5 and 36.3 liters (5.4 and 9.6 gal.) caused the Verskraft to measure engine compression at a mileage of 818 km (508 mi.).

In the process, the previously noted poor accessibility of the engines was confirmed. For example, it required 1.5 hours to remove the twenty-four spark plugs. Compression, which was measured after the change, was still only between 2 and 6 atm (29 and 88 psi), which pointed to worn engines. The

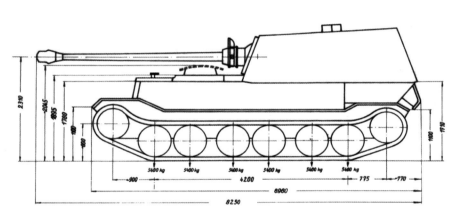

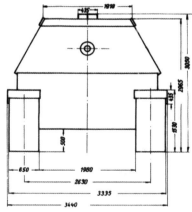

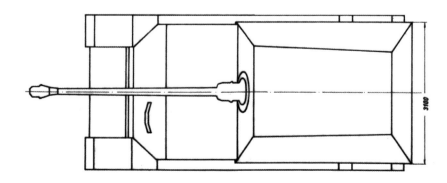

8,8 cm Pz.Jäger 43/2 (L/71) Tiger P.

Sd. Kfz. Nr. 184

Scale drawing by Wa Prüf 6 dated September 1, 1943

The Ate compressor, worn out after barely 800 km, and the left generator, damaged after 960 km

air filter, which was cleaned after every 100 km, had a roughly 2 cm (0.8 in.) thick layer of dirt and sand, which was attributable to severe dustiness in the battle zone. The heavy dust buildup also affected the braking system's air compressor, which after 764 km (475 mi.) no longer conveyed air because of excessive wear.

The problematic oil filter control was moved to the right steering lever. The issue of varying cooling-fan revolutions, as was suspected, was due to worn cooling-fan drives and the lengthened 1,900 mm (75 inch) V belts. After 227 km (141 mi.) the right 24-volt alternator failed after the 1,075 mm (42 inch) V belt broke. After 720 km (447 mi.) the left alternator's fuse failed. A new final-drive gear ratio of 1:21.6 was installed for the purpose of an experiment by Siemens-Schuckert.

As expected, the tests resulted in a thermal improvement, since an increase of 36% was achieved with about 840 amperes instead of 1,100. If, however, they wanted to work at higher speeds without high gasoline engine rpm, they had to revert to series-parallel switching of the generators.

This series connection resulted in a reemergence of the difficulties resulting from the divergence of the gasoline engines during driving and especially during braking. For this reason and in view of the fact that the number of Ferdinands had fallen sharply, they wanted to content themselves with the 1:16.8 gear ratio, which because of the weight increase compared to the original Porsche Tiger represented an improvement compared to the earlier gear ratio of 1:15.

Furthermore, they installed one Skoda experimental low-manganese track with a curved shape and one with the standard shape. These came from the hydraulic Porsche Tiger with the chassis number 150 013. The rubber pads on the double swing arms had to be replaced after an average of 700 km (435 mi.).

A further rise in oil consumption to 63 to 90 liters (16 to 24 gal.) per 100 km (62 mi.) and a water leak into the right engine made it necessary to remove both engines after they had driven 911 km (566 mi.). The running gear was also closely examined. Cracks were found in the trunnions that established the connection from the hull to the double swing arms.

The same cracks appeared on the Porsche Tiger, which was 9 metric tons (9.9 tons) lighter, after it had traveled 1,395 km (866 mi.). These cracks appeared to be the preliminary stage in a process leading to the complete failure of the trunnion. These trunnions were left on the vehicle to determine runtime values. In view of the importance of these trunnions on the Porsche running gear that was being used, a design change was seen as necessary, especially since the replacement of several trunnions was particularly difficult and time consuming. It was possible to remove two trunnions from the Porsche Tiger and three of a total of six trunnions from the Ferdinand only after the engines and generators or the driving switch had been removed.

Two measures were proposed:

- introduction of a relief notch in the flange and enlargement of the chamfer

- change in the forging treatment, so that the fiber flow in the highly stressed transition from the trunnion to the flange was not so severely interrupted

The checks on the electric drive revealed a heavy dust buildup in the armature gap, on the brush cases, and on the

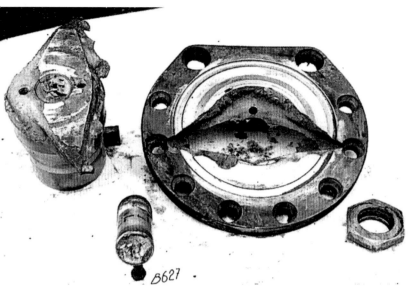

New towing lugs on Ferdinand 150 011 at Kummersdorf. *BA*

A broken-off trunnion, which on the Porsche Tiger occurred at 1,153 km

Below: Here one of the few Tiger recovery vehicles towing a broken-down vehicle with a tow cable; here, however, the recovery vehicle required help from a second tank destroyer while towing in the mud. *KHM*

brush holders. This resulted in heavy brush wear, since the brush springs no longer built up sufficient pressure.

On October 25, on behalf of the Verskraft, the Schüler-Motoren AG disassembled and checked the worn-out Maybach engines. The water penetration was a result of the left cylinder head, which was cracked right through to the valve seat. On the second engine the left cylinder head was also cracked. Almost all of the wet cylinder liners in both engines were too conical from bottom to top and had worn oval. The abnormally heavy oil consumption displayed by the engines could be explained by this high cylinder liner wear.

A common sight at the overhaul sites: an unserviceable Ferdinand like this one, missing the center bogie on its left side. *KHM*

The improved towing installation, as requested in February, was also worked on. At Kummersdorf in early September, the Verskraft conducted experiments with a new tow coupling that made it possible to use the standard tow fork. A new hitch coupling was installed on the Ferdinand and on Porsche Tiger 150 013. The triangle-shaped tow bar made it possible for the tow vehicle to steer and brake the damaged vehicle, which was not possible with a tow cable and simple tow bar. This resulted in considerably enhanced safety during a recovery.

On November 12, 1943, the Verskraft submitted its comments on the report on increased lubricants consumption submitted by schwere Panzerjäger-Regiment 656 of July 8:

- The Verskraft calculated that 40 kg (88 lbs.) of grease was required per vehicle for the first lubrication, consisting of 2 kg (4.4 lbs.) of grease per road wheel and trunnion bearing and 4 kg (8.8 lbs.) of grease for cooling-fan and other bearings. Also, 15 kg (33 lbs.) of grease per vehicle was required for relubrication after every 100 km (62 mi.). The abnormal heating and the subsequent running out of grease when the vehicle was driven were not observed by the Verskraft. The additional heating to which the fifth road wheel was subjected by passing exhaust gases was considerably reduced by changing the shape of the exhaust stub.

- As regards engine oil consumption, it was confirmed that the nature of the weapon made it necessary to keep the engines running to turn the vehicle. The Verskraft therefore thought it useful to change the oil on the basis not of kilometers driven, but instead of hours of operation. The dimensioning of the electric drive required the Maybach engines to maintain a constant, high operating speed, which made it necessary to change the oil after about forty hours of operation. This was all the more important because the inadequate air filtering resulted in greater wear on the gasoline engines.

- A total of 12 liters (3.2 gal.) of gear oil were required for the first fill (2 × 4 liters for the final drives and 4 × 1 liters for the cooling-fan drive). During vehicle testing over 900 km (559 mi.) by the Verskraft, about 3 liters (0.8 gal.) of gear oil had to be topped up. No damage to the final drives was experienced during this test.

- Fuel consumption on the forest circuit was approximately 900 liters per 100 km (0.26 mpg), and in the dunes, 1,400 to 1,600 liters per 100 km (0.17 to 0.15 mpg). In summary the Verskraft determined that on the basis of its experience, the consumptions reported by the units were too high.

Since testing of the Ferdinand tank destroyer by WaPrüf 6 was declared ended, after servicing and completion of the necessary configuration changes the vehicles were supposed to be handed over to the troops. On December 5, 1943, the Verskraft reported the two Ferdinands with the chassis numbers 150 010 and 150 011 as ready to entrain. At short notice, however, the HWA ordered that both vehicles should receive a full complement of weapons, radios, and vehicle equipment, including antiskid gear and ammunition. The Verskraft was at first overstretched. As an experimental station, it was incapable of such a task at such short notice. To prevent the railroad's transport wagons from being blocked unnecessarily, it was decided to set the vehicles aside. The HWA also did not see this delay as problematic, since schwere Panzerjäger-Abteilung 653 was being pulled back to Austria to rest and reequip anyway.[27]

In addition to the familiar Ferdinand with the chassis number 150 011, the letter also mentioned a Ferdinand with the chassis number 150 010. The latter vehicle was apparently tested by Alkett over roughly 400 km (248 mi.), and it was briefly mentioned on June 16, 1943, at Friedrichshafen, where 150 011's cooling-fan drive had broken loose, and out of necessity the decision was made to use the cooling-fan driveshaft from 150 010.

The vehicle number is therefore unusual, since the surviving documents always speak of ninety Ferdinand tank destroyers, beginning with chassis number 150 011 and continuing to chassis number 150 100. The Kummersdorf Ferdinand was always characterized as the ninetieth and last Ferdinand. Ferdinand 150 010 would therefore be the ninety-first tank destroyer and thus the largely manually produced preproduction vehicle made by Alkett. Unfortunately it is not possible to completely clarify this issue on the basis of surviving documents.

The Verskraft reported the condition of both surplus vehicles to the responsible Army Motor Vehicle Workshop Vienna on December 12:

1st Vehicle Chassis No. 150 010:
Mileage on discharge, about 450 km (279 mi.). The vehicle was transferred to the Panzer Ordnance Depot Magdeburg with a mileage of 392 km (243 mi.), without equipment, and from there was entrained for transport to Putlos for comparative shooting trials. Subsequently delivered to the Verskraft. Condition:

- The odometer was defective, probably because of a defective transmitter.
- The running gear's steel wheels were badly crimped, and as a result the rubber suspension travel was seriously limited; replacement seems necessary.
- Coolant antifreeze was added in a 50:50 ratio.

2nd Vehicle Chassis No. 150 011:
Mileage at discharge, 960 km.
Condition:

- Both gasoline engines were overhauled at 911 km (566 mi.).
- Last oil change was also carried out at 911 km.
- Running gear underwent general overhaul at 911 km.
- New carbon brushes were installed for the right generator at 911 km, and for the left generator at 948 km (589 mi.).
- New low-manganese tracks were mounted at 948 km.
- The left generator was replaced with a new one at 960 km (596 mi.).
- Cooling-fan drive, compressor, etc. were overhauled and lubricated at 911 km.
- The intercom system was checked.
- New-type antiskid cleat was installed on every eighth and tenth link only.
- Coolant antifreeze was added in a 50:50 ratio.

KHM

On December 28, both vehicles were finally handed over to the Army Motor Vehicle Workshop in Vienna.

The transfer of schwere Panzerjäger-Regiment 656 to the Nibelungenwerk began on December 16, and the last of twenty-one trains arrived there on January 10, 1944. The regiment's Sturmpanzer IVs went to the army arsenal in Vienna for general repairs. At first the Nibelungenwerk refused to accept the Ferdinands, since this would cause a major disruption in the ongoing production of the Panzer IV. By order of the OKH, however, the factory had to make one of its buildings available for the general refurbishing of the Ferdinands.

And so the Nibelungenwerk took charge of the forty-eight Ferdinand tank destroyers and two Ferdinand recovery vehicles to carry out the requested modifications to improve their combat effectiveness. Initially it was envisaged that the Sturmpanzers should be repaired at the Nibelungenwerk, while the Ferdinands would go to the army arsenal in Vienna. Disassembly of the Ferdinands was already too advanced, however, and apart from about six burned-out vehicles the repair work was carried out at St. Valentin.

These six badly damaged Ferdinands were sent to the Army Motor Vehicle Workshop in Vienna. The configuration changes were those described previously for the planned

Ferdinand 511 (formerly of schwere Panzerjäger-Abteilung 654) during rail transport. *KHM*

Xaver Reimspieß made his opinion known in another of his well-known caricatures, since all of these "new" proposals, such as a machine gun ball mount, improved engine gratings, a new commander's cupola, and new tracks, had long been debated. The caption reads: "For a year now there has been endless debate about periscopes, gratings, and an MG ball mount. Now, after all the ifs and buts, it has them. You can see them in the picture." *BA*

Seit einem Jahr schon gab es Debatten ohne Ende
über Winkelspiegel, Gratings und M.G.-Blende.
Losgelöst von allen Wenn und Aber und Theorie
hat Er sie jetzt. Im Bilde seht ihr sie.

Arriving little by little, the Ferdinands were first parked near Building VIII. Here the vehicles wait on the factory grounds until it is their turn to be overhauled. *History Facts*

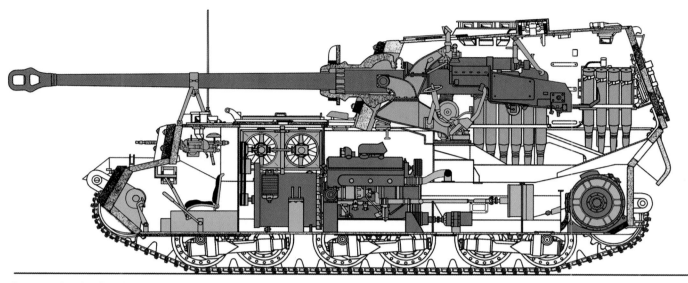

Cross-section drawing showing the ultimate configuration of the refurbished Tiger P tank destroyer. *PA*

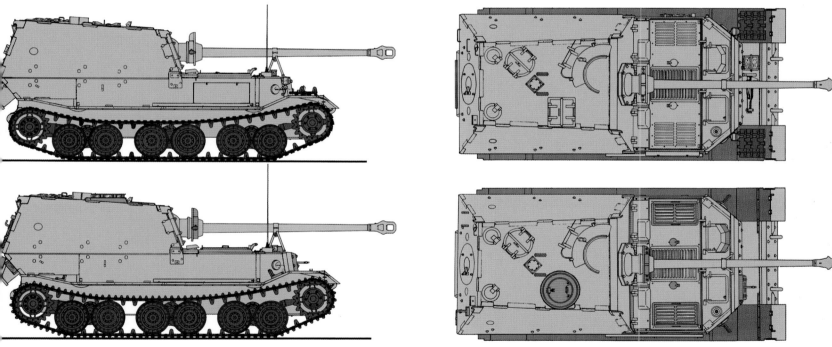

Drawings of the Ferdinand in its original configuration (*above*) and its revised configuration after the refurbishing program at the Nibelungenwerk (*below*). The changes are highlighted in orange.

repair work at Dnepropetrovsk. Instead of the proposed inserted machine gun for the 88 mm gun, a bow machine gun was installed in the radio operator's position. The vehicles also all received a coating of *Zimmerit* for protection against

hollow charges and were painted in a sand-yellow basic finish. It was anticipated that ice cleats from the Panzerkampfwagen IV would be fitted to the tracks. Since these did not fit, according to the troops, considering the extreme strain on the

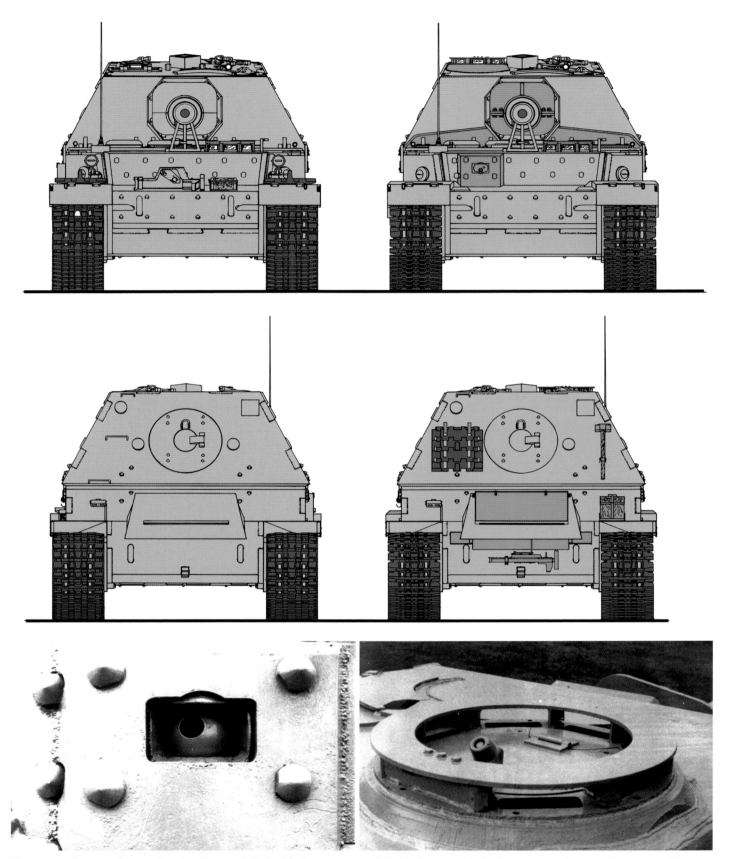

The commander's cupola came from the Sturmgechütz III. A ball mount was installed in the bow plate for the radio operator's machine gun, and it was protected by an additional armor plate. *KHM*

The tank-destroyer refurbishment program began on January 19, 1944. Moving the Ferdinands was no problem for Buidling VIII's 80-metric-ton cranes. *PA*

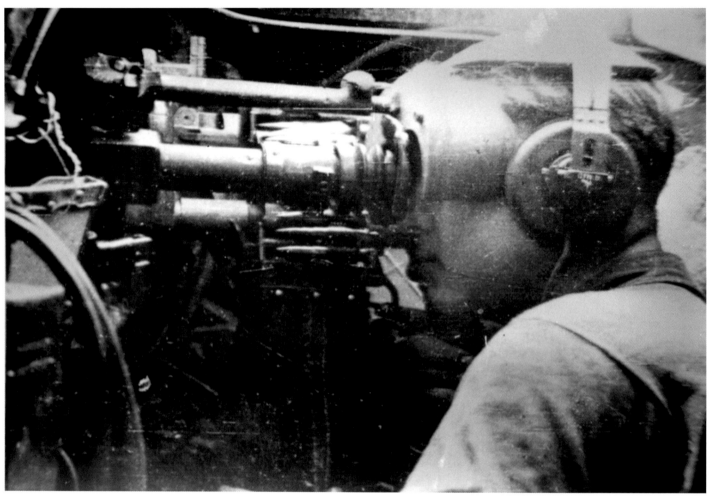

The radio operator in the improved Ferdinand now had the additional task of operating the onboard machine gun. *KHM*

Ferdinand's tracks, Hauptmann Hoffmann proposed a new design on the basis of experience with the Henschel Tiger. The repairs were delayed, however, because the parts from Schutno had not yet arrived, nor were the necessary replacement engines on hand. It was therefore estimated that a maximum of forty-three Ferdinands would be completed by mid-March. This date was also rendered void, since on February 1 orders were received to immediately ready a Ferdinand company. The Americans had landed at Anzio and Nettuno on January 22, 1944. On February 9, the first eight Ferdinands were almost completed. Work on another three vehicles was accelerated to ensure their completion in time. The quality of the refurbishment suffered considerably as a result.

On February 15, the 1st Ferdinand Company, with eleven Ferdinand tank destroyers, left for Italy together with a Sturmpanzer company. With it went a complete workshop platoon with gantry crane, an Sd.Kfz. 9/1 (Kfz. 100 crane truck), and a Ferdinand recovery vehicle. The battle group took part in the German counterattack on February 28, 1944, and it immediately became obvious that the terrain around Cisterna was completely unsuitable for the heavy tank destroyers.

The vehicles could move only on the narrow, hard-surfaced roads, since the terrain on both sides was very marshy. The first two Ferdinands became bogged down and sustained mine damage, and they could not be recovered under heavy

An Elefant on the road to Cisterna in March 1944. *KHM*

In Italy, too, because of the constant retreat, mine damage often meant the end of the tank destroyer. *BA*

In the repair workshop in Rome. Innovations such as the bow machine gun and commander's cupola, as well as the Zimmerit coating, can be seen here. *KHM*

The modified Ferdinands were again available for training at the Nibelungenwerk. *KHM*

American fire. By order of Führer Headquarters on May 1, 1944, the designation "Ferdinand" for the Porsche tank destroyer (Sd.Kfz. 184) had to be removed from all files and replaced by Elefant (Elephant).[29] The reason for this is not known, but on February 27, 1944, Hitler had already ordered that the Hornisse (Hornet) 88 mm tank destroyer should be renamed Nashorn (Rhinoceros).

After costly fighting and the protracted retreat in terrain unsuitable for the heavy tank destroyers, what was left of the company—three Elefant tank destroyers and one Elefant recovery vehicle—entrained at Piadena on August 2. The transport arrived in Vienna on August 6, 1944.

Meanwhile at the Nibelungenwerk, the refurbishment of the remaining vehicles was considerably delayed as a result of the earlier outfitting of the 1st Company. There were still thirty-two Ferdinands under repair in the Nibelungenwerk. The next eight Ferdinands were not completed and handed over to the 2nd Company until February 26. On March 1, there were still twenty-one Ferdinands and two Ferdinand recovery vehicles undergoing repairs.

Furthermore, the battalion asked for the allocation of the two Ferdinands at Kummersdorf for testing and the hydraulic Porsche Tiger for use as a recovery vehicle. It appears that the battalion had not yet been informed that the two vehicles at Kummersdorf had been handed over to the army ordnance depot. The Porsche Tiger stationed at Kummersdorf was the sole Porsche vehicle with a hydraulic torque converter transmission, made by Voith, instead of the electric drive.

Since WaPrüf 6 had no real interest in the hydraulic drive, this Porsche Tiger was only half-heartedly tested. As well, instead of a tank turret with the 88 mm KwK L/56, it had only a weight to compensate for the turret. The Verskraft also had in storage a single Porsche Tiger turret for a command vehicle (no. 150 014). This turret was placed on the requested hydraulic chassis with the number 150 013, and the two additional armor plates were installed on the frontal armor analogous to the Elefant tank destroyer, along with periscopes for the driver. The new command vehicle was turned over to schwere Panzerjäger-Abteilung 653 at the end of May 1944.

The refurbishment of the vehicles still designated Ferdinand was completed on March 31, 1944, to the extent that the 2nd and 3rd Companies had almost reached their authorized strengths in tank destroyers, and so on April 2, the loading of thirty Ferdinands and two Ferdinand recovery vehicles began in preparation for transport to Russia.

Until April 18, the unit took part in the unsuccessful attempt to relieve Ternopol, and it was still possible to make

This Elefant with the tactical number 124 after it was destroyed by its crew in Soriano. The vehicle was apparently used as a source of spare parts, since various items are missing. On the bow plate is a torsion bar bogie from the right side. *KHM*

good vehicle losses with the repaired vehicles that had not been sent previously. Among them were four tank destroyers, after May 1 called Elefant, on which the rear hatch was hinged to make it easier to install and remove the gun.

The closable hatch could also be used as an entry and exit. On July 1, the two companies had thirty-four Elefant tank destroyers on strength. According to "Overview of the Army's State of Armaments," the last report in July 1944 showed that forty-one vehicles were still on hand.

The following counteroffensive by the Red Army forced the Wehrmacht units to fight delaying actions as they retreated.

The hydraulic Porsche Tiger was the only one of its kind to see action. *KHM*

This photo illustrates a command vehicle of the schwere Panzerjäger-Abteilung 653. Externally it is recognizable as such only by the mast or star antenna at the top right on the rear of the vehicle. After the modifications at the Nibelungenwerk, most of the equipment was stowed on the rear of the vehicle, since any items on the front were vulnerable to the intense fire to which exposed Ferdinands or Elefants were as a rule subjected, and were lost. *KHM*

Loading ammunition into the fighting compartment of Elefant 332 through the small rear hatch. *KHM*

This Elefant of the 3rd Company has sunk to the bottom of its hull in a meadow. *KHM*

Rail was the best way to transport the heavy tank destroyers. The SSyms transport wagons that were used always carried the narrower Tiger I or Tiger II loading tracks. *KHM*

Taken in July 1944, this photo shows a completed Elefant at St. Pölten after undergoing repairs at the Army Ordnance Office Vienna. It was one of four vehicles that received a reclosable rear hatch. *KHM*

Here the pneumatic brake's brake lining can be seen following removal of the brake drum. *KHM*

Since this meant that vehicles could not as a rule be recovered, losses rose. The beginning fuel shortage and the absence of bridges able to accommodate the Elefant forced the crews to abandon their vehicles and blow them up.

By the end of July 1944, the heavy-tank-destroyer battalion had lost nineteen of its Elefant tank destroyers in this way, and both recovery vehicles. The single Porsche Tiger was also lost during this period. Because of its heavy losses, the battalion was transferred back to Austria to reequip on the Jagdtiger tank destroyer. The remaining twelve Elefant tank destroyers were combined into a single company and remained in the east.

After a period of rest and refit, during which it received two more Elefant tank destroyers from the Nibelungenwerk, the 2nd Company of schwere Panzerjäger-Abteilung 653 remained in the Kraków area. The unit, also called the Elefant Company, was renamed the schwere Heeres-Panzerjäger-Kompanie 614 (614th

Heavy Army Tank-Destroyer Company) on December 15, 1944. The unit, with its fourteen tank destroyers, was further decimated during the continued fighting withdrawals.

At times not a single Elefant was serviceable. By the end of January 1945 the company had just four Elefant tank destroyers. The retreat led it via Frankfurt/Oder into the southern metropolitan area of Berlin. A final refit took place in the Stahnsdorf area in early February 1945. There the company was supposed to be equipped with ten Elefant or Jagdtiger (Porsche running gear) tank destroyers; however, the latter did not arrive. On February 25 the unit had four Elefant tank destroyers, all of which were in serious need of repair. According to a letter of March 3, 1945, spares were en route from Linz, but on the basis of the situation, this was an illusion. The company occupied its last defense line in the Wünsdorf area near Zossen on April 21.

One Elefant was left behind, broken down, on a head ramp at Mittenwalde Station. A second Elefant was abandoned in firing position in Klein Köris on the branch road to Löpten. The confusion of the retreat enabled the other two tank destroyers to reach the inner city of Berlin, and on May 1 they were captured by the enemy near the Holy Trinity Church after fighting in Karl-August Square.

The vehicles had thus done their job. Despite inadequate supplies of spare parts, the tank destroyer had not completely exhausted themselves by the end of the war. There were still four tank destroyers, now officially called Elefant, in March 1945. For the small production run of ninety or ninety-one vehicles, this was a significant number. Of course the heavy vehicle also had one major disadvantage; namely, its poor power-to-weight ratio. Its great weight of 65 metric tons (71.5 tons) and the associated high ground contact pressure made

it difficult for the overloaded chassis, which had actually been designed for a 45-metric-ton (49.5 ton) vehicle, to cope. With its Maybach engines the vehicle was underpowered, causing fuel consumption to increase beyond measure. As a result, the internal combustion engines wore out very quickly.

While being interrogated after the war, Saur spoke positively about the Ferdinand tank destroyer: "Porsche proposed the electric drive as a revolutionary innovation. Unfortunately, it did not go into mass production, losing out to the Henschel vehicle, since its timely start-up could not be assured. His ninety preproduction examples were later converted into assault guns (Ferdinand) with 200 mm of frontal armor and 88 L/71 gun capable of penetrating 167 mm of armor. These vehicles survived the difficult campaigns in Russia to such an extent that after a year had passed, we still had fifty-seven vehicles of this type at the front."[31]

One of the last photos of an abandoned Elefant, probably the one at Klein Köris. *WS*

CHAPTER 10

The Tiger (P) Bergepanzer (Recovery) Vehicle

In the literature there is talk of three or five Tiger recovery vehicles. Unfortunately, the true number cannot be confirmed. Of the one hundred chassis that were completed for the Porsche Tiger, ninety were converted into tank destroyers. Alkett also used the ninety-first chassis (150 010) as a preproduction vehicle. Two chassis, ninety-two and ninety-three, were used up in firing trials. The ninety-fourth chassis was the hydraulic vehicle. One chassis (the ninety-fifth) is missing from the list (Ramm-Haube). The remaining five chassis were probably the planned recovery vehicles.

Since the planned Panther recovery vehicle was not available in sufficient numbers, in August 1943 the Nibelungenwerk initially converted three vehicles, similar to the Ferdinand tank destroyer, powered by two Maybach HL 120 TRM engines and converted to liquid cooling. According to the table of organization of March 9, 1944, the combat train of each company included one Ferdinand recovery vehicle. Instead of the casemate superstructure, the vehicles were fitted with a smaller armored hood, which unlike the Ferdinand tank destroyer was equipped with an MG 34 machine gun in a ball mount.

An entry hatch from the Panzerkampfwagen IV was fitted at the rear of the hood. Low walls were welded onto the sides so that various items of recovery equipment could be stored on the deck. A two-metric-ton auxiliary crane, a tow fork, and the recovery beams completed the vehicle's equipment.

A Ferdinand has broken through a 24-metric-ton bridge. Due to a lack of recovery vehicles, other tank destroyers are being used to extract the tank destroyer. The excessive strain placed on the tow vehicles often affected their serviceability. *KHM*

Famo prime movers were officially earmarked for the workshop company's recovery platoon. As this photo impressively testifies, depending on the nature of the terrain, as many as five prime movers could be required to recover a single Ferdinand in an adventurous way. *KHM*

There was no capstan, however. The supplementary armor present on the Ferdinand tank destroyer was deleted. This benefited vehicle weight, which was about 50 metric tons (55 tons).

It is documented by strength reports that Ferdinand recovery vehicles were delivered to schwere Panzerjäger-Abteilung 653 in September 1943, one per company. Of the three Ferdinand recovery vehicles, two returned to the Nibelungenwerk at the end of 1943 and were refurbished by March 31, 1944. Another Porsche chassis with the number 150 005 had previously been converted into a recovery vehicle, and at the beginning of 1944 it went to the 1st Company in Italy. As of May 1, the vehicle's official designation became "Recovery Elefant," analogous to the tank destroyer.

The two vehicles modernized at the Nibelungenwerk were sent back to the 2nd and 3rd Companies in Russia in April 1944. The Elefant recovery vehicle from Italy returned slightly damaged to the Nibelungenwerk in August 1944. The two Elefant recovery vehicles and the previously mentioned last Porsche Tiger were lost in the East in July 1944. The fate of the Elefant recovery vehicle from Italy and the possible fifth recovery vehicle cannot be determined. They were probably sent to the unit while it was resting and reequipping.

One of the first three Ferdinand recovery vehicles, still with old tracks. On its deck are recovery beams. The photo was taken at the Nibelungenwerk. *PA*

Towing of a tank destroyer by several prime movers required a very high degree of coordination and skill when it came to start-up and braking by the recovery vehicle. *KHM*

The Panther recovery vehicle, as here at Kursk, was available to the armored forces only in inadequate numbers. *KHM*

Side view of a Ferdinand recovery vehicle on the factory grounds. The upward-pointing exhaust pipe can be seen between the superstructure side plates. In front of it is the mounting lug for the auxiliary crane. *PA*

A Ferdinand recovery vehicle after the configuration changes, photographed at St. Pölten in March 1944. *KHM*

Late Ferdinand recovery vehicles could be identified by their *Zimmerit* coatings. A second Ferdinand recovery vehicle can be seen in the garage behind. The vehicle also has a second machine gun in the rear on the superstructure in a rotatable mount taken from an assault gun. The swivel range of the integral ball mount was probably insufficient for self-defense by the recovery troops. *KHM*

The opening for the Porsche Tiger's bow machine gun has been closed. This vehicle lacks the *Zimmerit* coating. It is still wearing the old-version tracks. The driver has the vision block from the Porsche Tiger. *PA*

Elefant recovery vehicle in action in Russia. It has the later convex tracks. *KHM*

An Elefant recovery vehicle is demonstrated to members of the 100th Jäger Division. *KHM*

An Elefant recovery vehicle negotiating a slope in May–June 1944. The lighter (50 metric ton) recovery vehicle was preferred for driver training. *KHM*

This photo gives a good impression of the recovery vehicle from above. *KHM*

This photo illustrates the Elefant recovery vehicle with the chassis number 150 005 in Italy in 1944. Clearly visible are the new convex Skoda tracks, which were always installed back to front. The track shields have suffered badly. Under tow is a broken-down Elefant. *KHM*

CHAPTER 11

In Museums

Two tank destroyers, one Ferdinand and one Elefant, survived the war and will be described in detail here.

Ferdinand 501

This vehicle of the schwere Panzerjäger-Abteilung 654 survived the war. The Ferdinand with the tactical number 501 and the chassis number 150 072 was in the Russian tank museum at Kubinka when it was photographed. During the Battle of Kursk it drove over a mine and lost a track. The crew apparently set off an explosive charge inside the fighting compartment before abandoning the disabled vehicle. The vehicle was a command vehicle with additional radios. The tank destroyer was later restored to drivable condition by the Red Army and tested at Kubinka.

The crew of Ferdinand 501 before the Battle of Kursk. *KHM*

The vehicle after its capture by the Red Army . . .

. . . and during trials at the testing grounds at Kubinka

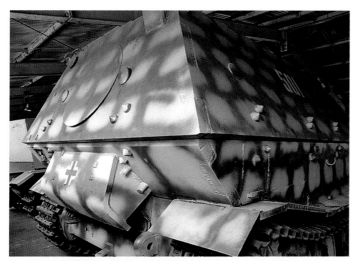

These images show Ferdinand 501 in the Kubinka Tank Museum in 2007.

The interlocking armor plates can be clearly seen on the rear and sides of the vehicle. On the track shield is the tube for the barrel-cleaning equipment.

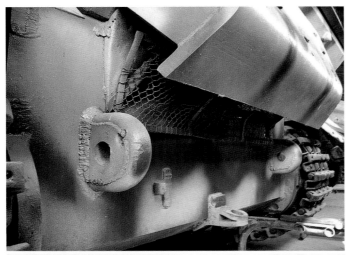

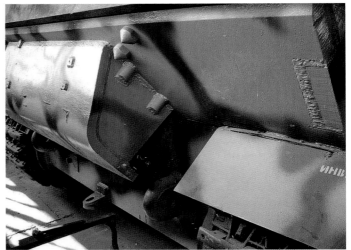

The exhaust air duct, which was responsible for churning up large amounts of dust

The left sloped side of the outer superstructure

Idler wheel (*above*) and drive sprocket. The latter had received a hit.

The jettisoned rear hatch cover on the roof of the superstructure

The jettisoned rear hatch cover on the roof of the superstructure

View into the driver's position. The left vision port is welded shut, since the instrument panel was located in the niche. At the top is the driver's hatch compensating spring. Below it is the fireproof bulkhead with a view of the V-belt tensioning device for the 1,900 mm long cooling-fan belt.

377

One of the three periscopes in the driver's hatch is still present.

The sealed vision holes for the Porsche Tiger driver's periscope can be seen in the driver's visor. The crosspieces are the fittings for the supplementary armor.

Behind the driver's position can be seen the left generator with the cooling-fan V belts. Above is the V-belt tensioning device. Below it was the driving switch, and on it the driver's seat. Next to it is the fuel connection with the left tank's shutoff valve.

The right generator with its four-part V-belt drive

The track tensioner on the driver's side and the brake pedal

379

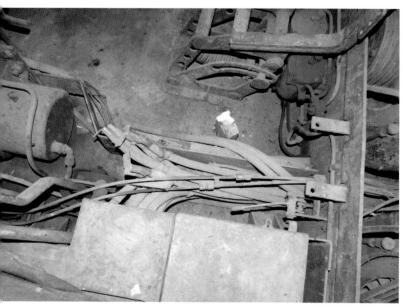

View of the air lines and electrical cables between the driver's and radio operator's positions. The switch box, which is missing, was mounted here.

Located in front are the compressed-air chamber for the brake system, the brake cylinder and the right steering lever, the hand brake lever, and both pedals.

The two assist springs for the driver's and radio operator's hatches

The radio operator's seat, and behind it, the two fuel filters

The radio operator's station. On the sidewall are the screw plates for mounting the FuG 5 radio.

A set of batteries were housed under the seat. The second set was to the right of this seat, under the radios.

The right vision slot and the radio operator's grab handle

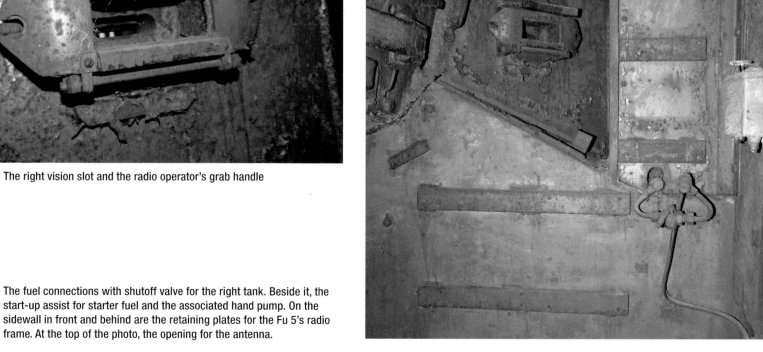

The fuel connections with shutoff valve for the right tank. Beside it, the start-up assist for starter fuel and the associated hand pump. On the sidewall in front and behind are the retaining plates for the Fu 5's radio frame. At the top of the photo, the opening for the antenna.

The fighting compartment, looking aft from the gunner's hatch. Lying on the floor is the self-propelled gun telescopic sight. The cover over the electric-motor air exhaust is missing.

The right rear corner of the fighting compartment, where the second radio set was located

The hatch cover seen here is a sheet metal replacement. The original was jettisoned by the crew when it bailed out at Kursk and is lying on the roof of the superstructure.

View of the breech with recuperator (*left*) and recoil brake (*right*)

The front of the fighting compartment. The gunner sat on the left, the commander on the right.

The gunner's position with azimuth and elevation handwheels. At the bottom of the photo, beneath the crossbeam, is the left Maybach HL 120 engine.

The kidney-shaped opening without cover for the gunner's angled telescopic sight for self-propelled guns

The box for the gunner's headset and throat microphone. On the right, the remains of the left engine's four air filters.

The barrel recuperator and recoil damper in the extended position suggest that the crew attempted to destroy the vehicle, which is supported by the missing rear hatch cover.

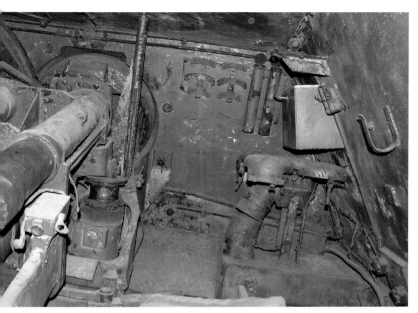

On the right side is the commander's position, with box for the headset and throat microphone, the necessary connection box (Pz. Kst. Nr. 21), the container for the breathing tubes, and, below it, the bracket for the right Maybach engine's air filter.

In the roof is the loader's hatch (also without cover) with cutout for the fan, which is missing here. To the left and right of it are the remains of the bracket for the gun's locking hooks, which are also missing. The photo illustrates well the limited access to the Maybach engine from the fighting compartment.

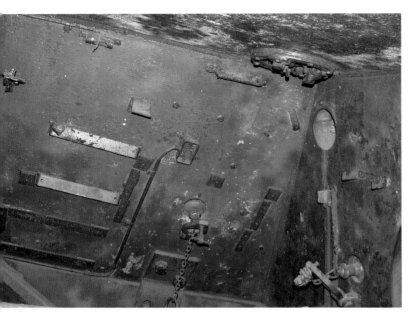

In the center of the photo is the plug for the machine gun opening, and next to it, on the left, the bracket for the additional radio set of a command vehicle. In the corner is an ammunition rack for the shells fired by the main gun.

A periscope opening without periscope in the rear left corner of the roof

Ferdinand 501 is now in Patriot Park near Moscow.

Elefant 102

The Americans captured this Elefant, number 102 of the schwere Panzerjäger-Abteilung 653, in Italy in May 1944. It had previously seen action at Kursk with the schwere Panzerjäger-Abteilung 654 bearing the tactical number 511. *KHM*

This photo clearly shows the probable reason for the abandonment of Elefant 102: a shell struck the vehicle's left front, jamming the brake drum.

Elefant 102 at Aberdeen Proving Grounds, in the US state of Maryland, before restoration. *KHM*

The Elefant, with the number 102 and chassis number 150 071, after its exterior was refurbished

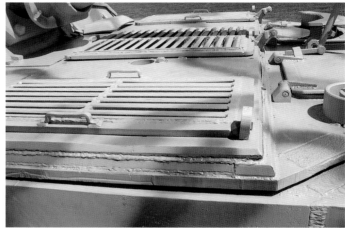

The three narrow engine covers in front of the rear plate provided the only access to the Maybach engines from the outside, since the radiator compartment was sealed off from the engine compartment. There was also limited access from the fighting compartment after the floor plates had been removed, as shown in the photos of the interior. One can easily imagine the resulting maintenance problems.

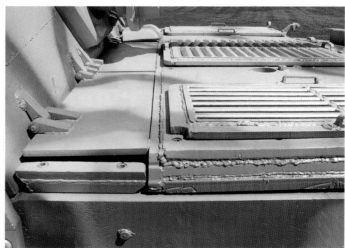

The interlocking joint between the armor plates can be seen clearly above the right mounting bracket.

Curiously, the 640 mm Skoda track seen here was assembled somewhat randomly (link with guide tooth–tooth–no tooth–no tooth). The banana-shaped track deflectors can be seen well above the track, as they can in the next photo as well.

The dirt deflectors in front of and behind the drive sprocket can be seen well in this photo. In this case the arrangement of the track links is correct.

The Aberdeen vehicle, 102, on loan to the Bovington Tank Museum

The retrofitted machine gun ball mount with additional armor plate. The radio operator's right vision slit was sealed.

Behind the engine cover, it can be seen that the rain gutter on the right side of the frontal armor was torn off.

In front of the center radiator grating is the retaining device for the radio operator's hatch cover.

The restorers used silver paint to highlight the hit taken by the vehicle.

Close-up of the gun mantlet

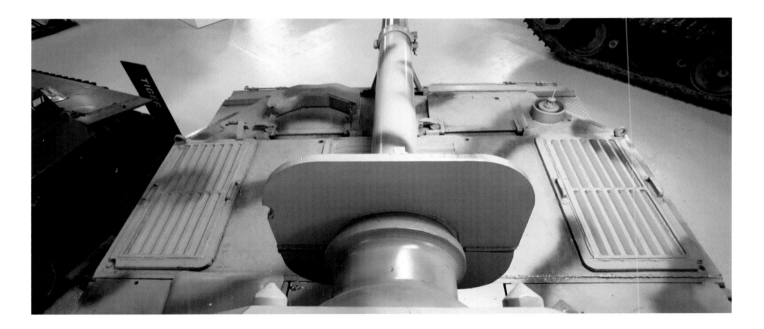

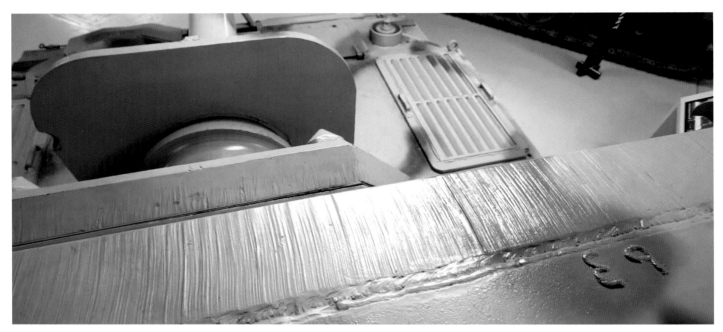

This image provides a good impression of the thickness of the front plate.

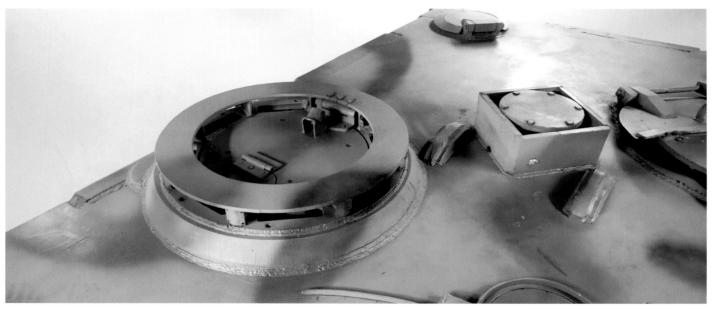

The retrofitted commander's cupola and the shielded ventilator atop the superstructure

All of the periscopes are missing from the commander's cupola.

The stop for maximum deflection attached to the spring arm is clearly visible in this view.

Interior shot of the driver's position. On the right is the complete control box. On the left was the instrument panel, of which all that remains is one strand of cable. *TM*

This enlargement, looking right toward the radio operator's position, shows the remains of the Kst. Pz. Nr. 20 intercom box. The Fu 5 VHF radio set was located under it, in front of the radio operator. To the right of the radio operator, the two mounting brackets with butterfly nuts testify to the mounting of the radio system's two EUa and U10a1 transformers. The arrow on the left points to the chassis number 150 071. Right above is the bell of the machine telegraph, with which the commander passed instructions to the driver if the intercom failed. *TM*

Interior photos showing Elefant 102's fighting compartment in its current unrestored condition. Comparing them with older photos of the interior reveals that several components have been removed. *TM*

Early photos of the commander's side of the fighting compartment. The complete Mahle air filter is still present. *KHM*

The gun, seen from the right. *KHM*

The closed breech shows that
the firing pin was removed.
KHM

The right side with the ammunition and radio equipment racks
(command vehicle). *KHM*

Next to the box for the headset and throat microphone is the commander's lever for the machine telegraph. With it he could transmit instructions to the driver after the loss of the intercom system. Under it is the connection box (Kst. Pz, Nr. 21) for the commander's headset and throat microphone. *KHM*

Four racks for the main gun's ammunition are still present on the floor. *KHM*

View of the left side of the fighting compartment. In addition to additional ammunition racks, boxes for flare cartridges and spare parts for the main gun can be seen. *KHM*

Among the items in front of the gunner's seat are two containers for the breathing hoses. *KHM*

View under the gun in the direction of the gun base. *KHM*

The floor brackets for six rounds of main gun ammunition are still present. The shells were stored with their tips facing down. This made it easier for the loader to pick up a shell and load the gun. *KHM*

The center ammunition rack . .

. . . and the rear left rack. Floor brackets for nine rounds can be clearly seen. *KHM*

This view looking up to the roof reveals the assault gun telescopic sight and its mount. *KHM*

It is obvious that the commander's cupola was fitted retroactively. *KHM*

CHAPTER 12

Technical Features in Detail

Of the detailed technical features, only those components that differed from those of the Porsche Tiger will be examined here. In addition to the gun, these include the Maybach engines. The official designations for this vehicle were varied:

Sturmgeschütz 8.8 cm K (auf Fahrgestell Tiger P) (Ferdinand): Summary of Equipment 1 April 1943

Panzerjäger Tiger (P): Equipment Description D 656/1–3, 1/5/1943

8.8 cm Stu.Gesch. mit 8.8 cm Pak (auf Fahrgestell Tiger P): Summary of Equipment 1 December 1943

8.8 cm Pz.Jäger 43/2 (L/71) Tiger P: Book of Armaments, 1 December 1943

8.8 cm Panzerjägerkanone 43/2 (L/71): Armaments Designations, 28 January 1944

Elefant (8.8 cm Stu.Gesch. mit 8.8 cm Pak 43/2) (Sd.Kfz. 184): Summary of Equipment 1 July 1944[32]

Specification as per the spec sheets for army weapons, vehicles, and equipment, 1944 (in brackets as per spec sheet of 25 August 1943)

Stu.Gesch. m. 8.8 cm Pak 43 (auf Fgst. Tiger P) (Elefant) (Sd.Kfz. 184)

Vehicle combat weight	65 metric tons (64.37 metric tons) [71.6 tons (70.9 tons)]
Power plants	two Maybach HL 120 TRM 530 hp (2 × 300 hp)
Power-to-weight ratio	8.16 hp /metric ton
Maximum speed	39 kph (road: 20 kph, off-road: 10 kph) 24 mph (road: 12 mph, off-road: 6 mph)
Fuel capacity (including reserve)	950 liters (503 + 348 = 851 liters) 251 gallons (133 + 92 = 225 gallons)
Range on one fuel fill-up	road: 150 km (93 mi.), medium terrain: 90 km (56 mi.)
Fuel consumption in medium terrain	1,000 liters / 100 km (264 gal. / 62 mi.)
Trench-crossing capability	2.64 m (8.7 ft.)
Specific ground pressure	1.23 kg/cm² (1.08 kg/cm²) 17.5 psi (154. psi)
Climbing capability	0.78 m (2.6 ft.)
Wading capability	1.0 m (2.0 m) 3.3 ft. (6.6 ft.)
Crew	6 men (5 men)
Length	8.14 m (26.5 ft.)
Width	3.38 m (3.34 m) 11 ft. (10.95 ft.)
Height with superstructure	2.97 m (9.7 ft.)
Height of muzzle	2.31 m (7.6 ft.)
Ammunition capacity: for main gun for MG for SMG	50 rounds (2 × 12 + 2 × 18 = 60 rounds) 600 cartridges 384 cartridges
Armament: (a) forward-firing weapons (b) in fighting compartment	1 × 88 mm Pak 43/2 (L/71) 1 × MG 34 loose, 2 SMG (entry was not corrected)
Optical equipment	1 × Sf 14 Z; 1 × Sfl. ZF 1a, 2 × periscopes, 3 × prism mirrors
Radio Equipment (standard equipment)	1 × Fu 5 or Fu 2 set, Kst. Pz. Nr. 20 intercom system
Armor	Hull front 100 + 100 mm (3.9 + 3.9 in. / 80°, side 80 mm / 60°; 80 mm (3.1 in.) / 90°, superstructure 200 mm (7.8 in.) / 70°, roof 30 mm (1.2 in.) / 0°, floor 20 + 30 mm (0.8 + 1.2 in.) / 0° in front, floor 20 mm (0.8 in.) / 0° in rear
Tracks	right: 110 links, left: 109 links, track weight 2,440 kg (5,379 lbs.), contact area 4.115 m (13.5 ft.), track width (center of each track) 2.68 m (8.8 ft.), track spacing 130 mm (5.1 in.), track width 640 mm (25.1 in.)
Running-gear weights	each road wheel 219 kg (483 lbs.), each drive wheel 506 kg (1,115 lbs.), each idler wheel with 19 teeth 554 kg (1,221 lbs.), each final drive 544 kg (1,199 lbs.), each idler wheel crank with brake 438 kg (965 lbs.), each swing arm with torsion bar 402 kg (886 lbs.), each torsion bar 38 kg (84 lbs.).
Tractive resistances	±45 kg / metric ton (90 lbs./ton) on concrete road, ±55 kg / metric ton (110 lbs./ton) on cobblestones, ±90 kg / metric ton (180 lbs./ton) on unpaved road with thick layer of sand and dust

The 88 mm Pak 43/2 L/71 Gun

The 88 mm Pak 43/2 (L/71) consisted of a one-piece barrel, carriage, and accessory and supply items. The gun had an elevation/depression range of +16° (+14° according to other sources) to −8°, azimuth range of 15° in both directions (14° according to other sources). Maximum range with 16° of barrel elevation was given as 9,700 m (31,824 ft.). Barrel length with a caliber length of L/71 was 6.298 m (20.66 ft.) without muzzle brake, with muzzle brake 6.686 m (21.93 ft.). The complete gun weighed 2,200 kg (4,850 lbs.) and had an average life of 1,200 shots. Rate of fire was six rounds per minute. The gun was made by the Dortmund-Hoerder-Hüttenverein, Lippstadt factory. Its price was 20,000 RM, and the average production time was eight months.[33]

	Type 18/36	Type 41
Barrel length	L/56	L/71
Barrel protrusion over	2,500 mm (98.4 in.)	3,280 mm (129.1 in.)
Front of tank Barrel weight	1,465 kg (3,229.8 lbs.)	1,900 kg (4,188.8 lbs.)
Cartridge shell weight	15 kg (33 lbs.)	23 kg (50.7 lbs.)
Cartridge shell length	930 mm (36.61 in.)	1,200 mm (47.24 in.)
Cartridge shell diameter	112 mm (4.40 in.)	147 mm (5.78 in.)
Turret weight including weapon	9.7 metric tons (10.7 tons)	13.5 metric tons (14.9 tons)
Servicing area diameter	1,820 mm (71.65 in.)	2,100 mm (82.67 in.)
Outer diameter	2,320 mm (91.33 in.)	2,600 mm (102.36 in.)
Brake pressure	7 metric tons (7.7 tons)	10 metric tons (11 tons)
Muzzle brake performance	0%	0%
Rate of fire	approx. 12 rounds/min.	approx. 8 rounds/min.

Based on the relevant manual D 2030

The Gun Barrel

The one-piece monobloc gun barrel tapered toward the front and consisted of a muzzle brake that was unscrewed counterclockwise and the clamping bolt for the easily removable breech. The bore consisted of the chamber, the forcing cone, and the rifled part of the barrel. This rifled part had thirty-two grooves with a constant right-hand twist of 6° 30'.

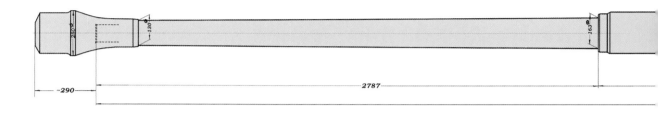

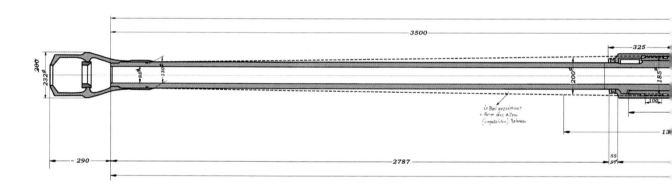

Above, the two-piece barrel with small muzzle brake; *below*, the one-piece barrel used in the Ferdinand with larger muzzle brake

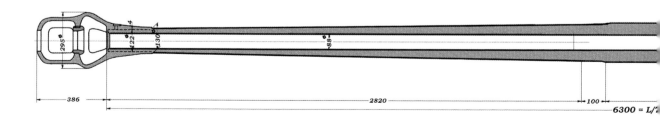

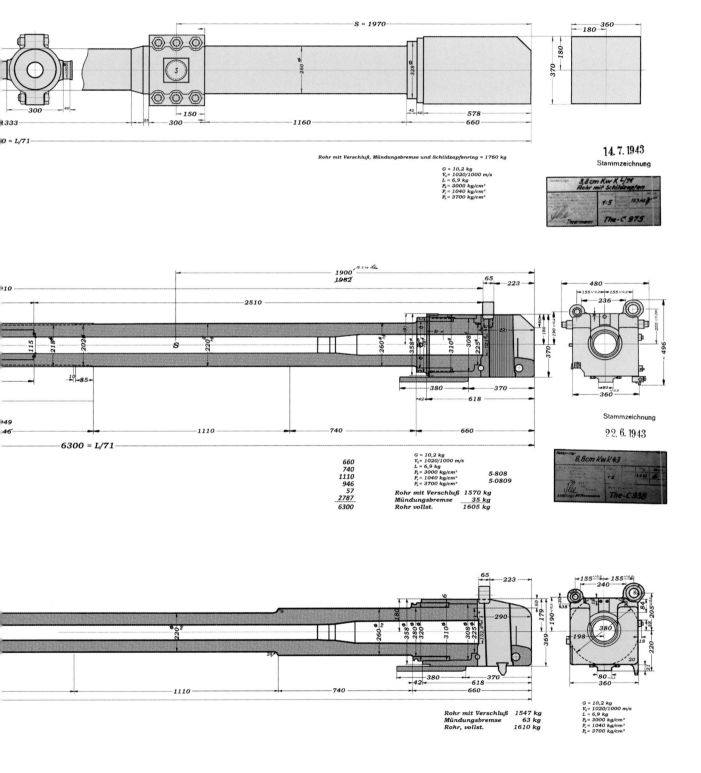

S = 1970

360
180

180

370
260

328

300
40
150
42 40
578
660

333
300
300
25
1160
660

0 = L/71

Rohr mit Verschluß, Mündungsbremse und Schildzapfenring = 1760 kg

G = 10,2 kg
V_0 = 1020/1000 m/s
L = 6,9 kg
P_g = 3000 kg/cm³
P_e = 1040 kg/cm³
P_k = 3700 kg/cm³

14. 7. 1943
Stammzeichnung

8,8 cm KwK L/71
Rohr mit Schildzapfen
1:5
The-C 975
Thermann

1900
1982

65
223

480
155 +/0,2 155 +/0,2
236

10

2510

180
190
370

496
205 +/0,3

115
218
2024
260
220
358
308
310
225
22

10
85

380
370

80
360

618

949
46

1110
740
660

6300 = L/71

660
740
1110
946
57
2787
6300

G = 10,2 kg
V_0 = 1020/1000 m/s
L = 6,9 kg
P_g = 3000 kg/cm³
P_e = 1040 kg/cm³
P_k = 3700 kg/cm³

5-808
5-0809

Rohr mit Verschluß   1570 kg
Mündungsbremse   35 kg
Rohr vollst.   1605 kg

Stammzeichnung

22. 6. 1943

8,8 cm KwK 43
1:5
The-C 938

65
223

155 +/0,2 155 +/0,2
240

180
290
179
190

369

220
260
358
280
320
310
308
225
132,4

198
380

42
380
370

80
360

618
660

25

1110
740
660

Rohr mit Verschluß   1547 kg
Mündungsbremse   63 kg
Rohr, vollst.   1610 kg

G = 10,2 kg
V_0 = 1020/1000 m/s
L = 6,9 kg
P_g = 3000 kg/cm³
P_e = 1040 kg/cm³
P_k = 3700 kg/cm³

413

The Breech

The breech accommodated the breechblock and recuperator. The piston rods were fixed in the barrel brackets by the recoil brake and recuperator. Also part of the breech are the retainer plate to prevent twisting of the monobloc barrel, the gun slide, the stop for the recoil marker, the insert for the breech pawl, the plate for the ejector shaft, and the cams of the electric safety switch.

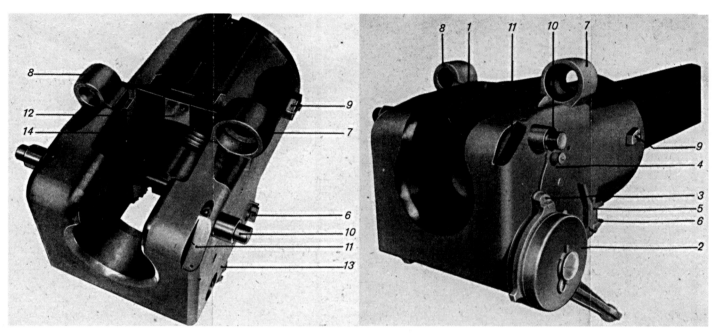

1. Breech block
2. Reciprocator
3. Locking pin
4. Safety
5. Ejector claw pressure lever
6. Ejector shaft plate
7. Bearer for recoil brake piston rod
8. Bearer for recuperator piston rod
9. Cam for electric safety switch
10. Trunnion for cradle lock
11. Quadrant plate
12. Safety plate
13. Bushing for pawl
14. Threads for threaded breech hoop

The Breechblock and Recuperator

The breechblock is a semiautomatic falling breechblock with electric firing. Prior to being fired for the first time, it is opened manually. After it is loaded for the first time, it closes automatically. After the gun is fired, the breechblock opens briefly automatically shortly before the counterrecoil movement is completed and ejects the empty shell case. For manual closure the spring housing handle is pulled back and the ejector shaft push handle is pushed forward.

1. Breech block
2. Ejector
3. Reciprocator
4. Slider crank
5. Cocking lever
6. Locking pin
7. Safety

The Carriage

The carriage consists of the gun cradle with recoil guard, the ball mantlet and the cradle lock, the recoil brake with hydraulic safety switch, the recuperator, the balance weights, the top carriage with trunnions and traverse bar, the elevating and traversing mechanisms, the sighting mechanism, and the electric firing system.

The cradle lock is located under the roof of the super-structure. When the vehicle is being driven, the gun is locked at 0°. For this purpose the cradle lock frame is placed over the trunnions on the breech and the bearings on the vehicle roof. By rotating its sleeve, the pressure plug is squeezed against the breech. In order to fire, the lock is removed and the lock plug is folded away and fastened under the roof.

The recoil brake sits on the right side of the barrel cradle, and its purpose is to brake the barrel's recoil and regulate its counterrecoil. It consists of a brake actuator, the actuator base, the gland, the piston with piston rod, the control rod, and the counterrecoil rod tube. The recoil brake holds about 5.4 liters (1.4 gal.) of recoil cylinder fluid (*braun ark*; *translator's note*: a mixture of fluids for use in temperate and cold climates) and has an average braking power of 6,300 kg (13,889 lbs.). Recoil length is between 550 mm (21.65 in.) and a maximum of 580 mm (22.8 in.). On the recoil brake is the hydraulic safety switch, whose purpose is to interrupt the electric firing system if hydraulic pressure falls as a result of a leak.

The recuperator is found on the left beside the recoil brake, and its purpose is to move the barrel forward into firing position once more after the recoil. It consists of an air res-ervoir with base, the cover and the cap of the compression cylinder, the gland, and the piston with piston rod. The latter enters the compression cylinder. In it is about 5.3 liters (1.4 gal.) of recoil cylinder fluid (*braun ark*). Air pressure in the air reservoir is from 5 (71.1 psi) to 50 kg/cm^2 (711 psi).

1. Barrel cradle
2. Recuperator
3. Top carriage
4. Trunnion bearing
5. Sighting-mechanism bearing
6. Sighting mechanism
7. Elevating mechanism
8. Traversing mechanism
9. Traverse bar

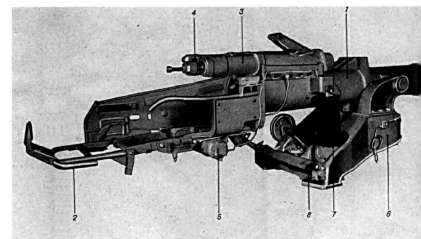

1. Barrel cradle
2. Recoil guard
3. Recoil brake
4. Recuperator
5. Hydraulic safety switch
6. Top carriage
7. Elevating mechanism
8. Traversing mechanism

The Gun Cradle with Recoil Guard

The purpose of the gun cradle with recoil guard and ball mantlet is to guide and support the barrel. The recoil guard protects the crew from the recoiling barrel, while the ball mantlet shields the gun cradle against fire from the front.

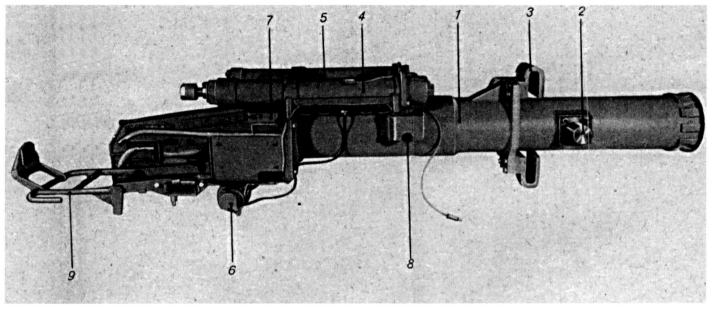

1. Top carriage
2. Traverse bar
3. Trunnion bearing
4. Sighting-mechanism bearing
5. Elevating mechanism
6. Elevating-mechanism handwheel
7. Traversing mechanism
8. Traversing-mechanism handwheel

The Top Carriage

In its trunnion bearings it carries the gun cradle with barrel and ball mantlet. At the front it is mounted on a ball stud—which is bolted to the vehicle's platform—and a ring bolted to the bottom prevents it from lifting. At the rear the top carriage is connected to the traverse bar with the aid of two sliding shoes. On the left trunnion bearing is the mount for the sighting mechanism. In front of the elevating-mechanism handwheel is the mounting flange for the backup (emergency) firing mechanism. On the right side is the bearing block, on which the sliding cover for the roof opening is hinged. Also on the right side are both bearings for the elevating mechanism. Its range of elevation is from −8° to +15°. Also on the elevation mechanism's handwheel is the firing mechanism's spring-loaded trigger.

On the rear part of the top carriage is the traverse mechanism's threaded spindle. The traverse range is 15° to either side of the center position. Provision is also made for a traverse lock in the rear part of the top carriage, in which a fitting for locking the carriage can be mounted in the existing holes in the traverse bar.

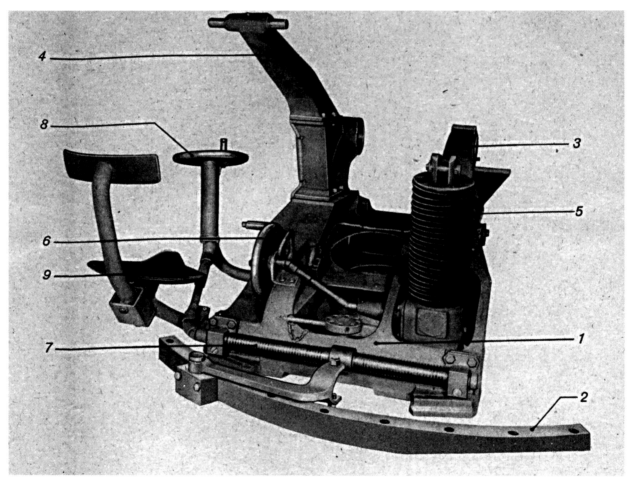

1. Top carriage
2. Traverse bar
3. Trunnion bearing
4. Sighting-mechanism bearing
5. Elevating mechanism
6. Elevating-mechanism handwheel
7. Traversing mechanism
8. Traversing-mechanism handwheel

1. Top carriage
2. Ball studs
3. Traverse bar
4. Trunnion bearing
5. Aiming-mechanism bearing
6. Elevating mechanism
7. Elevating-mechanism handwheel

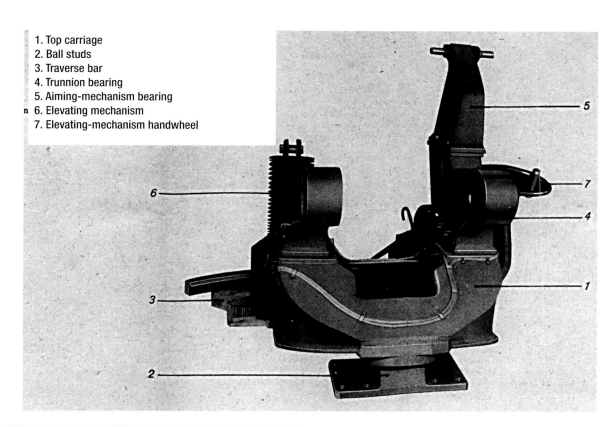

The jackscrews of the elevating and traversing mechanisms can be seen clearly here. *WS*

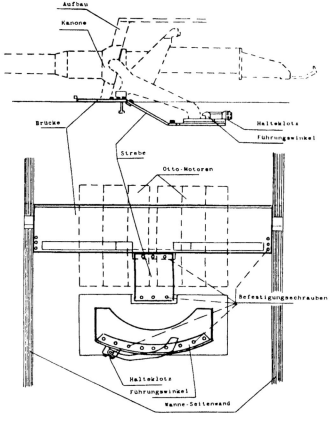

D 656/3

The sighting mechanism (*1*) with measurement plane on the cradle (*7*)

The Telescopic Sight for Self-Propelled Carriages (Sfl. Zf. 1a) installed and in action. *KHM*

Ammunition

The cartridge ammunition used was similar to that of the 88 mm Flak 41. Only the cartridges' threaded primers were different, since German tanks, in contrast to the artillery, had an electric firing device. The standard ammunition load of the Ferdinand tank destroyer consisted of Panzergranate 39-1 or 39/43 armor-piercing rounds and high-explosive shells:

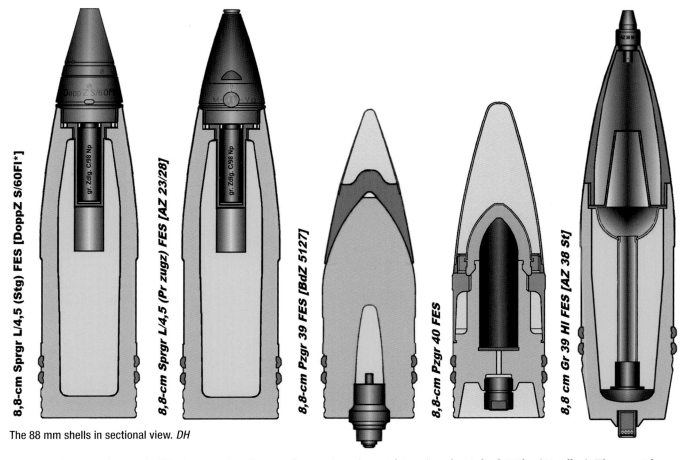

The 88 mm shells in sectional view. *DH*

- The L 4.5 high-explosive shell had a muzzle velocity of 700 m/sec. (2,296 ft./sec.) and weighed 9.4 kg (20.7 lbs.). The cartridge length was 1,183 mm (46.6 in.), and it weighed 18.8 kg (41.4 lbs.).

- The Panzergranate 39-1 had a muzzle velocity of 1,000 m/sec. (3,280 ft./sec.) and weighed 10.2 kg (22.5 lbs.). It was capable of penetrating 165 mm (6.5 in.) of armor steel at a range of 1,000 m (3,280 ft.) at an impact angle of 30°. At 2,000 m (6,560 ft.) it was still capable of penetrating 139 mm (5.47 in.). Cartridge length was 1,128 mm (44.4 in.).

- The Panzergranate 39/43 had similar performance data to the 39-1, but as a cartridge round it weighed 23 kg (50.7 lbs.) and was 1,125.4 mm (44.3 in.) long. Like all /43 shells, unlike earlier rounds it had wider rotating bands. It was thus also suitable for ensuring accurate shooting from worn gun barrels with greater than 500 rounds fired.

- The Panzergranate 40/43 had a muzzle velocity of 1,130 m/sec. (3,707 ft./sec.) and weighed 7.3 kg (16 lbs.). The cartridge was 1,108.2 mm (43.6 in.) long. It was capable of penetrating 192 mm (7.55 in.) of armor steel at a range of 1,000 m (3,280 ft.) at an impact angle of 30°. At 2,000 m (6.560 ft.), performance fell to 136 mm (5.35 in.). This heavy projectile was seldom used because of the acute shortage of tungsten.

- With its lower muzzle velocity of 600 m/sec. (1,968 ft./sec.), the Granate 39 HL had become less important, since the penetrative ability of the Panzergranate 39-1 in the 88 mm Pak 43/2 was clearly better. The hollow charge was capable of penetrating 90 mm (3.5 in.) or armor steel regardless of firing range. The projectile weighed 7.65 kg (16.9 lbs.), the complete cartridge round 16 kg (35.3 lbs.).

421

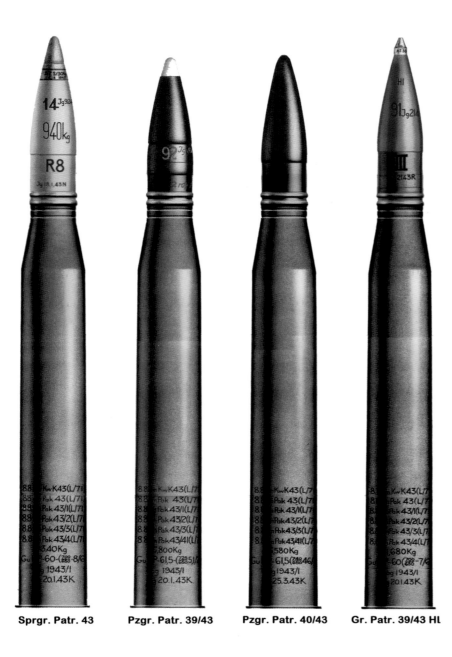

Sprgr. Patr. 43	Pzgr. Patr. 39/43	Pzgr. Patr. 40/43	Gr. Patr. 39/43 HL

The ammunition supply is described differently in various documents. In one case it is listed as fifty 88 mm cartridge rounds; then, in another, as two sets of twelve cartridge rounds and two of eighteen cartridge rounds in fixed racks, and therefore a total of sixty rounds of ammunition; and, finally, as twenty-six cartridge rounds in fixed racks and fifty loose cartridge rounds, for a total of seventy-six rounds. In practice the amount of ammunition loaded into the tank destroyer varied from crew to crew. Unfortunately, no ammunition racks are still present in Ferdinand 501 at Kubinka; therefore the quantity of ammunition it carried cannot be verified. In Elefant 102, on the other hand, six racks can be seen on the right side. Farther below, however, there is a larger area, which could accept more than the six on the sidewall. The racks in the rear right, rear left, and left sidewall of the fighting compartment reveal exactly the same picture. Racks for nine shells can be seen on the floor at the rear left. Thus, in addition to the twenty shells on the walls, another forty shells could be mounted in front of them as ammunition at the gun. There were probably additional shells under the gun.

The Maybach HL 120 TRM Engine

The Maybach HL 120 TRM engine was the standard engine of the German tank arm and was used in the Panzerkampfwagen III and IV, among others. The twelve-cylinder gasoline engine had a 60° V configuration. Cylinder bore was 105 mm (4.1 in.), and the piston stroke 115 mm (4.5 in.). This gave a displacement of 11,867 cm³ (724 cubic inches). Compression ratio was between 6.2 and 6.6:1. According to the operating manual of September 17, 1942, engine output during continuous operation was 265 hp at 2,600 rpm. The engine's maximum output was 300 hp at 3,000 rpm, and fuel consumption was 235–255 g/hp per hour. Short-term overspeed was 3,200 rpm, and maximum torque was 80 kgm (578.6 lb.-ft.). The engine

weighed about 1,000 kg (2,204 lbs.), depending on completion. The crankshaft was mounted on seven roller bearings, and the overhead valves were controlled by an overhead camshaft in each bank of cylinders, driven by spur gearing. The liquid cooling system was pump-operated. The fuel-air mixture was produced by two Solex 40 JFF II double-downdraft off-road carburetors. The engine was started either by a Bosch BNG 4/24 4 hp electric starter or by an AL/ZMD/R9 mechanical-inertia starter. Power for the batteries was provided by a 600-watt Bosch GTLN 600/12-1500 RS alternator driven by three V belts. Sources indicate that a 24-volt alternator was originally used for separate excitation of the generators and

The HL 120 with round exhaust manifolds, modified oil cooler connection, and three alternator V belts. The free double-belt pulley on the water pump was envisaged for a separate cooling-fan drive. *WS*

electric motors. Since the vehicles equipped with these engines had different alternators, the number of alternator V belts varied, probably because of the higher power transfer. The Panzerkampfwagen III and IV had different alternators; for example, the GQL 300/12-900 RS, which at 12 volts in continuous operation produced 300 watts and a maximum of 450 watts. The abovenamed GTLN 600/12/1500 RS alternator required three V belts for its output of 600 watts or a maximum of 900 watts, while the GTLN 700/12/1500 B1 alternator, with an output of 700 watts or a maximum of 1,050 watts, probably had four V belts.

In contrast to the normal arrangement, the Ferdinand's alternator was not attached to the engine, instead being attached reversed to the hull floor, as can be seen in the photo of the hull shell at the beginning of the book. The measurements of the V belts (1,075 mm [42.3 in.]) and their tensioning mechanism for this engine were unusual compared to other vehicles equipped with this engine. As a result, the standard alternator rotated in the opposite direction, which according to the documentation was the reason for the premature failure of the alternators in the Ferdinand at Kursk. The problem was solved when Bosch modified the rotor.

Both the superstructure and the gun had to be detached and moved back. The unit was lifted out horizontally, using a special sling. Unfortunately, there was not as favorable an alternative for removing the electric motors. To remove them, the superstructure had to be detached in the field, raised with a ratchet winch from the outside or two hydraulic jacks from inside, and pushed forward about 1.3 m. To prevent the superstructure from slipping off, guide plates were mounted on the now-open holes on the hull sides.

The following are detailed drawings made by Obergefreite Rolf Sabrowsky (3./656), which were made during conversion training on the Ferdinand.

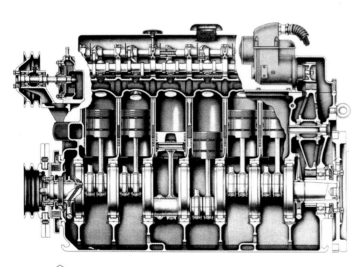

Maybach-Motor Typ HL 120 TRM

4249

The Maybach HL 120 TRM with one belt pulley for two V belts. The engines that powered the Panzerkampfwagen III (ZW) and Panzerkampfwagen IV (BW) differed only in having different oil tanks and—due to the different fan drives—water pump pulleys.

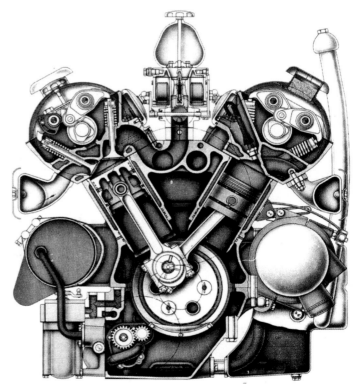

An opened-up Maybach HL 120 TRM photographed during the refurbishment process. In the left foreground, on the engine is the inertia starter, and on the right, the oil cooler. Above are the two Solex double carburetors. *WS*

The HL 120 with flattened exhaust manifolds and two alternator V belts. *WS*

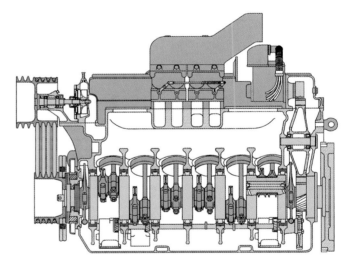

The Maybach HL 120 TRM with four alternator V belts. The two oil scavenge pumps and the oil-circulating pump can be seen at the bottom of the engine.

425

View from the gunner's seat, looking under the gun base. The two carburetors can be seen beneath it. Above it is the azimuth handwheel. The elevation handwheel is missing, probably as a result of the hit. The cooling fan for the electric motors can partly be seen on the right.

View from the loader's position on the right (*behind the commander*) looking in the direction of the engine. The valve cover is missing. Missing from the intake manifold is the pipe to the air filter, which was on the inside of the front plate. On the gun are the jackscrew for the vertical-elevation mechanism, and below it, the horizontal azimuth mechanism jackscrew and the electrical supply to the gun. *WS*

Preparations for an engine change on Elefant 334, using an Sd. Kfz. 100 with a 3-metric-ton Bilstein crane on a Büssing NAG. The engine cover was removed first. *KHM*

Here the engine cover is being removed by an Sd.Kfz. 9/1 (18-metric-ton prime mover with a 6-metric-ton crane). *KHM*

The next photo provides good details of the Maybach engine installed in the same vehicle. The water pump's pulley is missing. The lower water hose from the oil cooler was modified for use of a "fox device" (coolant heater). The flat exhaust manifold has a straight manifold connection. The close-up also clearly shows the new alternator-tensioning device on the engine. *KHM*

Changing the gasoline engine-generator unit. It is interesting that the superstructure was not repositioned as prescribed, as revealed by the bolted retaining plate, The men thus spared themselves a great deal of additional work. The inclined position was probably made possible through the use of a simple wire cable. The flange-mounted 385-volt aGV 275/24 generator weighed 900 kg and produced 250 kW. *KHM*

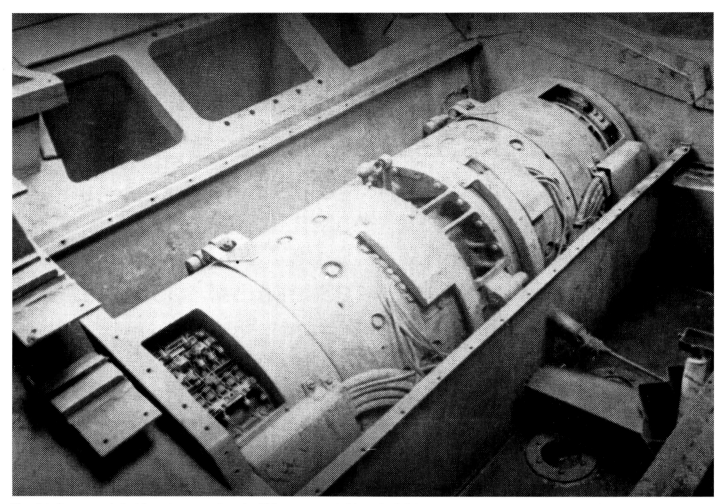

View into the exposed electric-motor compartment, which was separated from the fighting compartment by a metal sheet held in place by a large number of machine screws. A type D 1495a electric motor weighed 1,130 kg and produced 230 kW at 1,300 rpm. In the background are the vent openings for the electric-motor cooling system. Between the two motors was the mechanical parking brake in the form of a band brake. *WS*

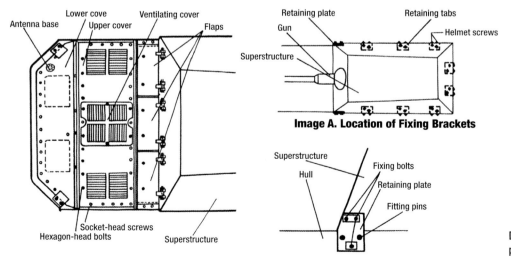

Image A. Location of Fixing Brackets

Drawings from the D 656/3 describing preparatory work for changing assemblies

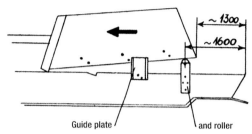

Image E. Superstructure in Forward Position

Now raise evenly with two ratchet jacks (image F) until the roller can be positioned between the hull and superstructure on each side at a distance of about 1,600 mm (images E and F).

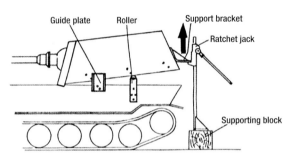

Image F. Raising the Superstructure

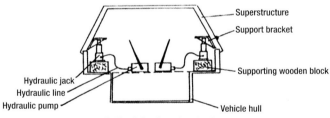

Image G. Positioning the Jacks

These drawings illustrate the instructions for raising the superstructure.
D 656

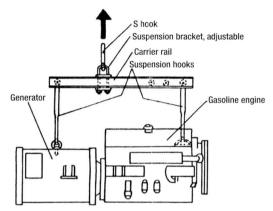

Image J. Suspension Device for Gasoline Engine-Generator Unit

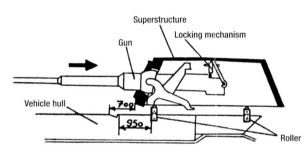

Image K. Removal of the Superstructure

This is how D 656/2 envisaged the proper changing of the engine-generator.

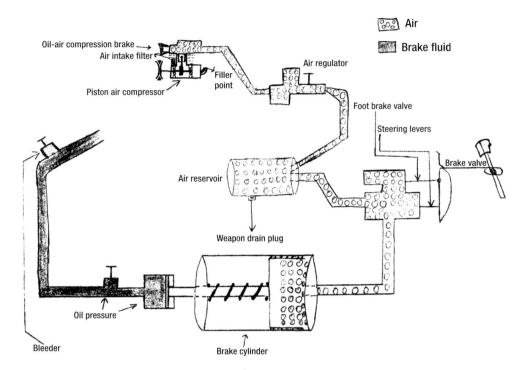

Air

Brake fluid

Oil-air compression brake

Air intake filter

Filler point

Piston air compressor

Air regulator

Foot brake valve

Steering levers

Brake valve

Air reservoir

Weapon drain plug

Oil pressure

Bleeder

Brake cylinder

Sketch of the pneumatic braking system. *KHM*

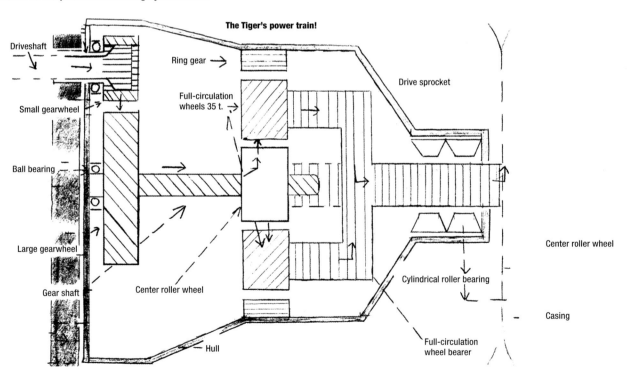

The Tiger's power train!

Driveshaft

Ring gear

Drive sprocket

Full-circulation wheels 35 t.

Small gearwheel

Ball bearing

Center roller wheel

Large gearwheel

Cylindrical roller bearing

Casing

Gear shaft

Center roller wheel

Full-circulation wheel bearer

Hull

Cross-section drawing of the final drive. *KHM*

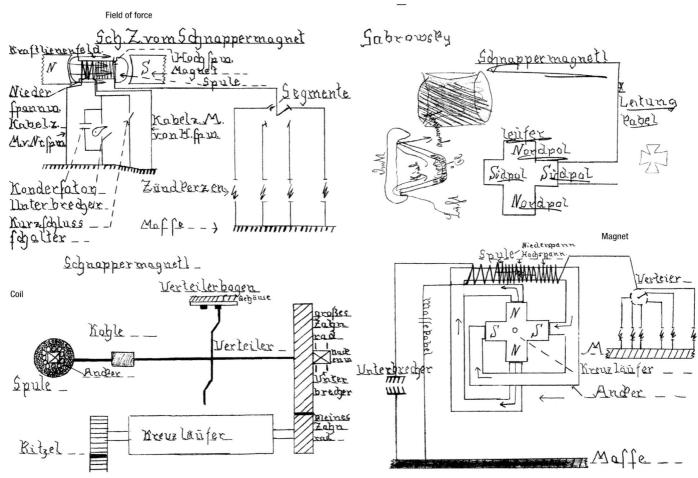

Drawings of the magneto ignition, at the time called *Schnappermagnet* (literally "snapper magnet"). *KHM*

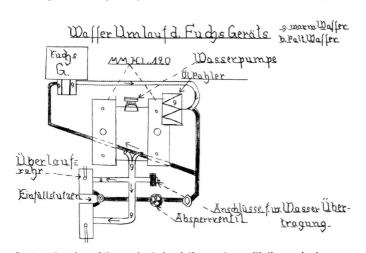

System drawing of the coolant circulation system with the coolant preheater called the "fox device." *KHM*

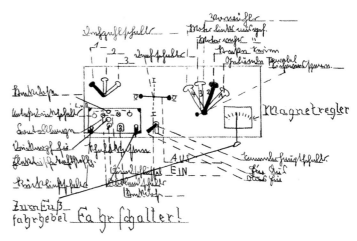

Labeling of the driving-switch control elements. *KHM*

Summary

Herr Hilmes kindly contributed a segment about the "Potential and Limitations of an Electric Drive for Tracked Vehicles" for my book about the Porsche Tiger, in which it was determined that the increased weight and volume expenditures were the main disadvantages of electric power transfer in tracked vehicles. Development and procurement costs for this drive were also one and a half times higher than for a mechanical drive.

To conclude my work on the Porsche tank destroyer, however, I would like to express my personal opinion about the electric drive used by the Porsche armored vehicles developed in the Third Reich. In my opinion the three armored vehicles developed by Porsche were not bad designs; rather, they were misdevelopments.

The designs of the Porsche Tiger, the Porsche tank destroyer, and the Maus battle tank were well thought through, but they went in the wrong direction. The concept of the electric drive for a tank had several advantages. The vehicles were popular with the troops since they could be driven like a tram, and the running gears of the first two types were very maintenance friendly. In addition to ease of operation, the electric drive made it possible to achieve an infinitely variable force output, even in these very heavy vehicles. This is illustrated by the fact that the main cause of breakdowns in most German tanks, final drive damage, was not a problem at all in the Porsche vehicles.

In addition to the electric drive's poorer degree of effectiveness, the main problem of these Porsche developments was the very high level of mechanical wear of their gasoline engines. In these cases the electric drive's thermal loads, touched on by Herr Hilmes in the previous book, did not appear or were marginal, probably because of the vehicles' low driving speeds. The very short operating life of the gasoline engines was the basic problem. This affected both newly developed engines from Simmering and the proven engines from Maybach and Daimler-Benz:

- The Porsche Tiger with the air-cooled ten-cylinder engine had a 320 hp Simmering gasoline engine, which produced its maximum output at 2,400 rpm. At a speed of 1,900 rpm, maximum torque was 105 m/kg (156 lb.-ft.). With a compression ratio of 1:5.6 this gave an engine output per unit of displacement of 21.33 hp. The newly developed combustion engine caused serious thermal problems from the beginning. As well, in the test vehicles the engines were already worn out after about 300 km

(186 mi.). Wa Prüf 6 suspected that inadequate filtering of the intake air was the caused for the increased wear. Unfortunately the developed version of the engine was not used.

- The second project, the Porsche tank destroyer, used the twelve-cylinder, liquid-cooled Maybach HL 120 TRM. As indicated by the "HL," this was a high-performance engine. It produced 300 hp at a speed of 3,000 rpm. Maximum torque was 79 m/kg (117 lb.-ft.). With a compression ratio of 1:6.5 the engine had an engine output per unit of displacement of 25.21 hp. This was actually a tried-and-tested engine that had been in use in the Panzerkampfwagen III and IV for some time. Approximately 40,000 HL 108/120 engines were produced during the war. The engine established the good reputation enjoyed by Maybach engines and was regarded as reliable and long lasting. In the Panzer III, even in sandy North Africa, the HL 120 TRM still had an average life of 2,000 to 3,000 km (1,242–1,864 mi.).[34] The engine life of 5,000 front km (3,107 mi.) demanded by the inspector-general of armored troops could be achieved only if the tank engines were limited to medium rpm. In the Porsche tank destroyer, however, the maximum operating life of these Maybach engines was just 800 km (497 mi.). In addition to poor air filtering by the Mahle filters being used, the Verskraft also cited the constant high rpm as the reason. It must be added that the air filters were the same in design and function as those of the Panzer III and IV. These vehicles did not have this problem with the cleaning of intake air. Only vehicles destined for use in Africa were also fitted with felt bellows filters.

- The third project was the Maus battle tank, the first prototype of which had a liquid-cooled, twelve-cylinder Mercedes-Benz MB 509 engine. This gasoline engine, derived from the DB 603 aeroengine, initially produced 1,200 hp at 2,300 rpm without supercharging and with reduced compression (because of the lower-octane Wehrmacht fuel), which was later reduced to 1,080 hp because of high engine wear. This was sufficient for an engine output per unit of displacement of 24.27 hp. The running performance of the engine, which was changed on July 10, 1944, on account of wear, can only be estimated at about 100 km (62 mi.), since the course of

432

testing was partially calculated in operating hours. An operating hour was roughly equal to a mileage of 1.1 km or 0.68 mi. (from January 14 to March 10, 1944, the Maus logged fifty-five operating hours, which was equivalent to a mileage of about 60 km, or 37 miles).

The combustion engines of all three projects, from a variety of manufacturers, became worn out remarkably quickly. This was probably due to the constant high revolutions combined with insufficient horsepower for vehicle weight, which quickly brought the engines to their operating limits. The constant high rpm was necessary for the electric drives being used, in order to deliver sufficient electrical power. In contrast, in a tank with mechanical drive, a combustion engine as a rule operated at low and medium rpm, which of course benefited engine life.

Professor Porsche probably recognized this problem in 1944, since he generally preferred a hydraulic drive for his final tank projects. Examples of this include the Panzerkampfwagen Porsche Type 181 (Tiger II), with an Sla 16 sixteen-cylinder, X-configuration diesel engine and a four-speed Voith hydraulic transmission, and the light Panzerkampfwagen Porsche Type 245 and 250, with Voith hydraulic torque converter.

Appendixes

Appendix A
Equipment List for the Porsche Tiger

Provisional Equipment List for the Pz.Kpfw. VI P (8.8/56)

4501—Superstructure for 8.8 cm KwK. Krupp Turret
Status: February 1942

Consec. No.	Name	No.	Drawing No.	Provided by	Type of Installation
1	88 mm KwK 36 L/56	1	5 Gr. 38	Wa J Rü	installed in mantlet
2	Box of parts for 88 mm	1		(WuG 6)	
Contents:	Empty box	1			
	Table of contents	1			
	Thrust bearing (firing pin)	1			
	Firing-pin springs	2			
	Firing pin, complete	2			
	Return bolt	1			
	Power supply, complete (to breech)	1			
	Spring split pin (to thrust crankshaft)	1			
	Ejector halves, right with:	1			
	Claw	1			
	Countersunk screw (for claw)	1			
	Space brush (for ignition hole)	1			
	Standard test lamp with 12 V bulb (to test the firing)	1			
3	Wiper with 6-piece rod	1	5 Stg. 980 lg. na.	(WuG 6)	on track
			5D2899-37U1		shield
			1 Stg. 919 lg. na.		
			5D2899-37U2		
4	Wiper cover	1	5C6899-205	(WuG 6)	carried loose
5	Breech cover canvas for 88 mm KwK 36	1	5B3899-2	(WuG 6)	on weapon
5a	Adjusting wrench for AZ 23	1	1,7977E + 308		
	Strap for adjusting wrench	1	8353		
6	Muzzle cap canvas or imitation	1	5C3899-6		on weapon
6a	Muzzle cap (shoot-through)	10	5B3899-5	(WuG 6)	in warehouse
	Bag, canvas (for 10 muzzle caps)	1	605C490		
	Sealing caps (only for weapons in UK vehicles	1	4/VI E 03479		
	Wiper piston	1	5D6899-115 U4		loose
	Casing extractor	1	5E6899-40		loose
	Grease gun (for 140 cm^3 with tube)	1	U 547		loose
	Grease can (for 0.05 kg of lubricating grease)	1	J9441/3E1099-210		loose
7	Spent-casings bag	1	(for Henschel only)		loose

Consec. No.	Name	No.	Drawing No.	Provided by	Type of Installation
8	Bracket for counterbalance spring	1			
11	Casing extractor	1		(WuG 2)	in warehouse
12	Sealing plug for MG	1	021D869	manufacturer	
13	Sealing plug for SMG	1	021R875	manufacturer	
13a	Sealing hood for external fan	1	021R860U51	manufacturer	
14	Boxes for MG tools	2	021St7614	manufacturer	rigidly mounted
15	Cover for MG 34	1	021C37499-230	Wa J Rü	loose
16	Muzzle guard for gun mantlet	1	021C39099-80	(WuG 6)	loose
17	Muzzle guard for mantlet for MG 34	1	4StAKF31441		loose
18	Belt bags	29	021St39150		2 on weapon, 27 stowed
19	Belt bag holder frame	1	021St37462	manufacturer	on weapon
19a	Belt bag holder frame	1			
20	Container for MG accessories (bipod, butt, and front sight holder)	1	021B7622	manufacturer	buckled to frame
21					buckled up
22	T Z F 9 b	1	027Gr.265	(WuG 2)	turret mantlet
23	Cover for T Z F 9 b	1	021 37489-255	(WuG 6)	loose
24	Driver's KFF 2 telescope (1 set = 2 pieces)	1 set	027Gr. 3539	(WuG 6)	in warehouse
25	Dust cap cover for KFF 2	2	021St33999-21	(WuG 2)	loose
26	KZF 2 ball telescopic sight	1	027Gr,5075	(WuG 2)	in ball mount
27	Cover for ball mount "100"	1	new type Wa Prüf 6	(WuG 2)	
29	Prism insert	12	as per VGB sample	(WuG 6)	(8 pieces + spares)
30	Protective glass 70 × 240 × 94	1+2	021St9296	(WuG 6)	(1 piece + spares)
31	Protective glass 70 × 150 × 94	9+13	021St9280	(WuG 6)	(9 pieces + spares)
32	Cover for SMG	1	021C37499-255	(WuG 6)	rigidly mounted
33	SMG magazine bag	1	01B3321	(WuG 6)	on holder
34	Prism insert	2+1	021D2746-1	(WuG 6)	(parts plus spare)
36	External fan 12–13 m^3/min.	1	Friedrich August-Hütte company	(WuG 6)	installed in turret
Parts for Communications Equipment					
37	Insertion device Morse key	1	024bSt95201	(WuG 7)	permanently installed
38	Slip-ring assembly 8-part (with hollow shaft) Model C, only for Henschel and pz.Kpfw. VI P2	1	024b93027 Ausl.	(WuG 7)	
39	Resting sockets for 5-prong plugs 3	24bSt14030	manufacturer		
40	Base plate EU a	2	24BSt3701	(WuG 7)	permanently installed
41	Base plate U 10a	1	24bSt3101	(WuG 7)	permanently installed
42	Mast antenna (2 m)	2	24bSt3670	(WuG 7)	1 installed
43	Antenna base no. 1, movable for mast antenna (2 m)	1	024bSt14101	(WuG 7)	permanently installed
	Protective cover for antenna base 1	24bD93062			

Consec. No.	Name	No.	Drawing No.	Provided by	Type of Installation
44	Rubber holder (Fu) 60	8	024bSt14029	(WuG 7)	permanently installed
45	Suspension system (P 10 EU)	1	024bSt3669	(WuG 7)	permanently installed
46	Suspension system (P 10 UES)	1	024bSt3415	(WuG 7)	permanently installed
47	Mass connection cable for suspension system	3	024bSt14018	(WuG 7)	permanently installed
48	Antenna lead P	1	24bSt40344	(WuG 7)	permanently installed
49	Cable box no. 20 with RV 12 P 2000 tubes	1	024b96007	(WuG 7)	permanently installed
50	Cable box no. 21	1	024b96008	(WuG 7)	permanently installed
51	Cable box no. 22	1	024b96009	(WuG 7)	permanently installed
52	Cable box no. 5 c	1	024bD21803	(WuG 7)	permanently installed
53	Z 23 12-volt junction box	1	024bSt10703	(WuG 7)	permanently installed
54	Dfh.b headphones	2	24bSt602	(WuG 7)	permanently installed
55	Kmf. a throat microphone	2	24bSt612	(WuG 7)	permanently installed
56	Kmf. b throat microphone	2	24bSt611	(WuG 7)	permanently installed
57	Double elbow plug, 20 mm, interchangeable with rest	6	024bD3849	(WuG 7)	permanently installed
58	Double elbow plug, 20 mm, not interchangeable with rest	5	024bD3777	(WuG 7)	permanently installed
59	Distributor piece	1	024bD3713	(WuG 7)	permanently installed
60	NPA cable, 2×1.5^2	3 m		manufacturer	
	NPA cable, 2×10^2			manufacturer	
	Varnished aviation cable 6×0.5^2			manufacturer	
	Varnished aviation cable 3×0.5^2			manufacturer	
64	Out-of-action flag (yellow & black)	1	024D33477	manufacturer	in container
68	Hatch key	2	024D33477	manufacturer	
68a	5-prong T-plug	1	024bD3715		
68b	5-prong elbow plug	1	024bE3815		
68c	Special rubber hose line, 5 lines	1.5 m			
Permanently Installed Mounting Brackets:					
69	Mounting brackets for gas masks (3 in turret, 2 in hull)	5	21St7604	manufacturer	permanently installed
70	Mounting brackets for canteens (3 in turret, 2 in hull)	5	21St7602	manufacturer	permanently installed
71	Mounting brackets for mess kits (3 in turret, 2 in hull)	5	21St7603	manufacturer	permanently installed
72	Mounting bracket for first-aid kit	1	21St7601	manufacturer	permanently installed

Consec. No.	Name	No.	Drawing No.	Provided by	Type of Installation
73	Mounting bracket for SMG	1	021D7607	manufacturer	permanently installed
74	Mounting bracket for SMG magazine bag	1	01B3321	manufacturer	permanently installed
75	Mounting bracket for flare pistol	1	21St7609	manufacturer	permanently installed
76	Mounting bracket for MGbarrel container	1	21St7605	manufacturer	permanently installed
77	Mounting bracket for directional gyro	1	021D37454U7	manufacturer	permanently installed
78	Mounting bracket for directional gyro transformer	1	021D9249U83	manufacturer	permanently installed
79	Mounting bracket for MG ammunition box	3		manufacturer	permanently installed
80	Mounting bracket for MG accessories	1	021C39021U38	manufacturer	permanently installed
81	Mounting bracket for first-aid kit, fire extinguisher	1		manufacturer	permanently installed
82	Mounting bracket for headphones	2 + 2	24bGr23901	manufacturer	permanently installed
83	Box for 12 flares	2	21St7613	manufacturer	permanently installed
84	Flag container	1			
85	Container for lubricator	1	21St7618	manufacturer	permanently installed
86	Container for spare KFF 2	1	21St7612	manufacturer	permanently installed
87	Container for breathing tube (3 in turret, 1 in hull)	3 + 1	21St7617	manufacturer	permanently installed
88	Container for 27 belt bags			manufacturer	permanently installed
89	Container for 88 mm ammunition ($\frac{1}{2}$ AP and $\frac{1}{2}$ HE)			manufacturer	permanently installed
90	Container for 2 pieces of protective glass 70 × 240 × 94	1	21St7610	manufacturer	permanently installed
91	Container for 3 pieces of protective glass 70 × 150 × 94	1	21St7624	manufacturer	permanently installed
94	Container for gun and cradle book	1	21St7620	manufacturer	permanently installed
95	Container for telescopic	1	21St7634	manufacturer	permanently installed sight accessories
96	Container for muzzle caps (shoot-through)	1		manufacturer	permanently installed
97	Container for 4 prism inserts	1	new type	manufacturer	permanently installed
xx+)	Accommodated in the armored hull				

Appendix B
The Porsche Types until 1945

Type 60	VW KdF ("Strength through Joy")
Type 61	narrow-version Type 60
Type 62	prototype VW Kübelwagen
Type 63	
Type 64	sports car based on Type 60
Type 65	VW driving-school equipment
Type 66	VW right-side steering
Type 67	VW invalid vehicle
Type 68	VW Reichspost mail delivery car
Type 70	Steyr
Type 81	VW van with 286 superstructure
Type 82	VW Kübelwagen
Type 83	VW "Kreis" power transmission system
Type 84	VW "Dr. Hering" power transmission
Type 85	VW all-wheel study
Type 86	VW Kübelwagen with all-wheel drive
Type 87	VW KdF with all-wheel drive
Type 88	VW bus on Kübelwagen chassis
Type 89	VW experimental automatic Beier BBC system
Type 92	Command vehicle or flatbed truck
Type 93	Limited slip differential
Type 94	DB racing engine
Type 95	Bus crawler suspension

Type 96	Hydraulic power transmission
Type 97	DB heavy truck
Type 98	VW Schwimmwagen Type 128 with Type 62 CL superstructure
Type 99	Study for Type 91 and Type 95
Type 100	Special Vehicle I VK 3001 Leopard
Type 101	Special Vehicle II–VK 4501 (P)
Type 102	VK 4501 (V) Tiger tank hydraulic
Type 103	VK 4501 (P) Tiger tank improved cooling, double fan
Type 104	VK 4501 (P) tank
Type 106	VW experimental PIM power transmission
Type 107	VW exhaust turbocharger
Type 108	DB double-compressor engine
Type 109	two motorcycle engines
Type 110	Small Tractor A with 1938–39
Type 111	Generator system or tractor with 2 two-cylinder engines
Type 112	Tractor I, improved Type 111
Type 113	Small Tractor III with carburetor and generator
Type 114	Sports car with V-10 twin cam engine, 72 hp
Type 115	VW engine with compressor, overhead camshaft and hemispherical combustion chamber
Type 116	VW study racing car on Type 114
Type 117	Experimental single-cylinder engine with old Type A head
Type 119	Experimental single-cylinder engine with new Type B head

Type 120	Stationary engine (emergency) power KdF with magneto ignition for RLM
Type 121	VW stationary engine for HWA
Type 122	Stationary VW engine with battery ignition
Type 123	Mobile electrical device with 1943 VW engine, rotary current 15 kWA
Type 124	Type 82 for rail operation
Type 125	Study for wind turbine
Type 126	Fully synchronized gearbox KdF study for VW
Type 127	VW sleeve-valve engine, Wankel system
Type 128	Schwimmwagen A large
Type 129	Type 128 VW short chassis
Type 130	Type 101 liquid-cooled engine
Type 131	Vehicle with liquid-cooled Type 101
Type 133	Hydraulic drive or self-priming carburetor
Type 135	130-watt wind turbine
Type 136	736-watt wind turbine
Type 137	4,500-watt wind turbine
Type 138	Schwimmwagen B large
Type 139	Type 138 Schwimmwagen without center frame
Type 141	½ VW engine for Type 101
Type 142	3-axle road tractor
Type 145	Steyr Type 70, automobile
Type 146	Steyr Type 170
Type 147	Steyr Type 170 all-wheel drive

Type 151	VW experimental gearbox, Puls system
Type 152	VW experimental gearbox, Stieber system
Type 153	Skoda Ost wheeled tractor with 6-cylinder engine
Type 155	Snow cleat system for Type 82
Type 156	Rail operation system for Type 166
Type 157	Rail operation system for Type 82
Type 158	1.5-liter single-cylinder diesel engine with direct injection
Type 159	1.5-liter single-cylinder diesel engine with Simmering prechamber
Type 160	VW self-supporting body study
Type 162	Self-supporting off-road vehicle
Type 164	VW light 6-wheel off-road type with two VW engines
Type 166	Schwimmwagen C small
Type 168	Running gear and suspension
Type 170	Assault boat
Type 171	Assault Boat II
Type 174	Assault boat engine with normal VW engine
Type 175	Ost wheeled tractor with steel wheels
Type 177	5-speed gearbox for a VW off-road vehicle
Type 178	5-speed gearbox for VW housing
Type 179	VW engine with fuel injection
Type 180	Special Vehicle III with electric drive
Type 181	Special Vehicle III with hydraulic drive
Type 182	Off-road vehicle, 2-wheel drive with universal superstructure

Type 187	Off-road vehicle, all-wheel drive with universal superstructure
Type 190	Type 101 engine converted to diesel operation
Type 191	Single-cylinder test engine for Type 190 diesel 120 × 145
Type 192	Diesel prechamber, Simmering
Type 193	Single-cylinder experiments for Type 101/103 with fuel injection
Type 197	Starting device for VK Kübel Type 82
Type 198	Steyr starting device for Type 82
Type 200	10-liter air-cooled diesel engine for Type 100
Type 205	Maus tank
Type 209	DB 44.5-liter V-12 diesel engine
Type 210	Air-conditioning systems for armored vehicles
Type 212	16-cylinder air-cooled diesel engine for Type 205
Type 213	Single-cylinder experiment for Type 212
Type 215	Single-cylinder experiment 135 × 160 with direct injection
Type 220	Air-cooled engines, also 16-cylinder diesel engine, biturbo
Type 224	Copy of captured Merlin engine
Type 225	VW electric power transmission by Brown, Boverie & Cle.
Type 226	Copy of captured Cyclone engine
Type 230	Wood-generator system for VW
Type 231	with gas generator (acetylene)
Type 235	VW with electric drive
Type 236	Stove insert for wood burning operation, Imbert generator for Type 230
Type 239	Type 82 powered by wood generator

Type 240	powered by bottled gas
Type 241	Auxiliary power unit for Type 205
Type 245	18-metric-ton Special Vehicle V small
Type 247	Aeroengine for all-wing-powered glider, based on VW
Type 250	Tank destroyer with 105 mm gun
Type 252	VW "PIV" power transmission system
Type 255	Special Vehicle IV with mechanical drive
Type 258	Running gear study for tracked vehicles
Type 260	Cooling system for Panzer IV
Type 261	Heating system for Panther 1 G
Type 262	HL 120 exhaust cooling
Type 263	38-tonne cooling system
Type 267	Consultation Maybach HL 230 engine
Type 276	VW Type 82 with limber hook for Pak 37
Type 280	Project M, preparatory work for Type 300
Type 283	Version of Type 82 for wood gas
Type 285	3.5-hp water turbine
Type 287	All-wheel-drive chassis for command vehicle based on Type 87
Type 288	13-hp water turbine
Type 289	15-hp water turbine
Type 290	Development SAG device. Project S Telefunken self-supporting
Type 291	600 mm wind tunnel
Type 292	300 mm wind tunnel
Type 293	SS wheeled tractor, road and rail
Type 294	Ski binding

Type 298	Further developed AS 014 pulse jet for V 1 or radio for VW
Type 300	Aircraft gas turbine of the cheapest type
Type 305	Gas turbine for tanks
Type 307	Heavy fuel carburetor
Type 309	Two-stroke diesel engine for VW or off-road vehicle with all-wheel drive
Type 312	Tractor with gasoline engine
Type 313	Type 312 with 17 hp air-cooled diesel engine
Type 320	Weapon "Berta" I
Type 321	Weapon "Berta" II
Type 330	with HoKo generator drive
Type 331	with wood-burning generator drive
Type 332	with AK generator drive
Type 82/1	3-seat Kübelwagen body
Type 82/2	Siren car body
Type 82/3	Tank and armored car superstructure
Type 82/5	Flatbed version of Type 82 and 92
Type 82/6	Tropical flatbed truck
Type 82/7	3-seat command vehicle based on Type 82
Type 82/8	Open off-road vehicle based on Type 820 wooden construction
Type 87/0	Off-road vehicle, 4-seat, self-supporting
Type 87/1	Off-road vehicle, 3-seat, self-supporting
Type 87/7	Command vehicle based on Type 287

Appendix C
Equipment Description and Instruction Manual
for the Chassis D 656/1 Panzerjäger Tiger (P)

Panzerjäger Tiger (P)

Porsche Tiger Tank Destroyer
Chassis Description and Operating Instructions

May 1, 1943

Contents

Introductory Remarks

A. Description of the Chassis
1. Main Components of the Chassis
2. General
3. Armored Hull, Cover Plate, and Superstructure
4. Partitions
5. Gasoline Engines
6. Generators
7. Electric Motors
8. Power Transmission from Electric Motor to the Track Drive
9. Engine/Motor Controls
10. Driving Switch
11. Foot Brake
12. Hand Brake
13. Running Gear
14. Electric Light and Starter Systems
15. Tools and Auxiliary Equipment

B. Instructions for Driving the Vehicle
16. Putting into Operation
17. Check the Tank Destroyer Each Time before Driving
18. Driving the Tank Destroyer
19. Driving the Tank Destroyer Off-Road
20. Ten Commandments for the Driver

C. Maintenance Instructions
21. Jobs after Completion of Driving
22. Installation of the Track

D. Lubrication Instructions
23. Oil Lubrication
24. Grease Lubrication

Introductory Remarks

A. Description of the Chassis of the Panzerjäger Tiger (P)

1. Main Components of the Chassis

The chassis consists of the following main components:

Armored hull
2 gasoline engines with flange-mounted generators
2 electric motors
Driving switch
Switch box with switchboard for low-voltage system
Cooling system
Final drives
Running gear
Track
Brake system
Forward and rear partitions

2. General

The armored hull in illustration 1 is designed to be the chassis. Installed in it are the gasoline engines with generators, the electric motors, the running gear, the 88 mm gun, and the superstructure.

Illustration 1. Superstructure of the Tiger (P) tank destroyer (outline)

Two engine packs, each consisting of a gasoline engine and a flange-mounted generator, are housed in the engine compartment in the center of the hull. Fuel tanks are mounted on both sides of the engines in the hull side extensions. Two radiators and cooling fans are installed on both side panels over the generators.

A forward partition separates the engine compartment from the driver and radio operator's compartment in front, and a rear partition from the fighting compartment behind it.

The electricity produced by the two generators is supplied to two electric motors, which are located in the rear of the vehicle. These power the drive sprockets by means of a friction clutch, a stub shaft, and a final drive. The drive sprockets are mounted on the two final drives, which are bolted to the outside on the hull's side panels. The parking brake engages the friction clutches.

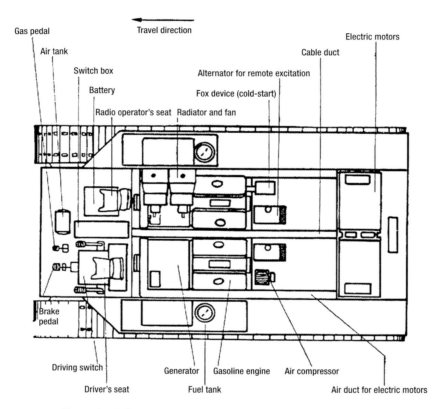

Illustration 2. Superstructure of the Tiger (P) tank destroyer (layout)

In the front part of the vehicle, the driver's seat is located on the left, and the radio operator's on the right. Under the driver's seat is the driving switch, with steering levers; to the right of the driver's seat is the switch box with operating switches for the electric drive, as well as the hand brake lever and the pressure gauge for the pneumatic brake system. To the driver's left is the instrument panel, and the accelerator pedal and brake pedal are installed on the front wall.

The idler wheels with sprockets are mounted on adjustable crank axles in the hull front and are slowed by the steering brakes. The drive wheels, each with two sprockets, are mounted on the final drives at the rear of the vehicle and are powered by the electric motors. Between the idler wheel and drive sprocket on each side of the vehicle are six road wheels, which are mounted in pairs, each sprung by a torsion bar.

The tank destroyer rides on two caterpillar tracks, which give it excellent off-road capability. The 88 mm gun is swivel-mounted on a top carriage. The fighting compartment is covered by a superstructure, in whose front panel the gun is shielded by a ball mantlet and whose rear is equipped with an exit hatch.

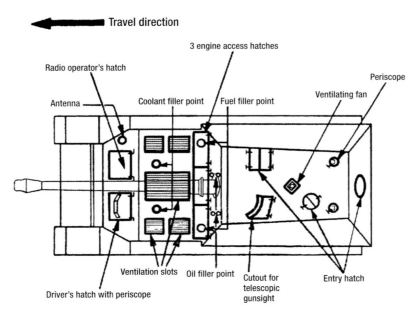

Illustration 3. Location of hatches in the cover plate and superstructure

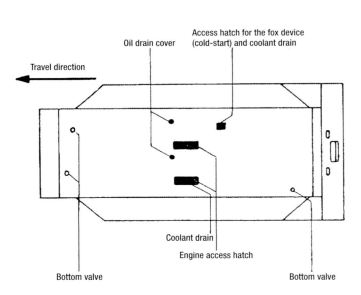

Travel direction

Oil drain cover

Access hatch for the fox device
(cold-start) and coolant drain

Coolant drain

Engine access hatch

Bottom valve

Bottom valve

Illustration 4. Position of hatches in bottom of hull

3. Armored Hull, Cover Plate, and Superstructure

Hatches, covers, and valves are mounted in the armored hull, cover plate, and superstructure, whose location and purpose are shown in illustrations 3 and 4.

4. Partitions, Illustration 5

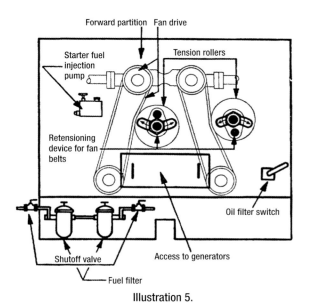

Forward partition Fan drive

Starter fuel
injection
pump

Tension rollers

Retensioning
device for fan
belts

Oil filter switch

Shutoff valve

Access to generators

Fuel filter

Illustration 5.

A forward partition separates the engine compartment from the compartment for the driver and radio operator. On it are found

2 belt tensioners for V belts
2 fuel filters with 2 fuel pumps
1 operating lever for the oil filter
1 starter fuel injector pump

A rear partition separates the engine compartment from the fighting compartment. Installed behind it are

2 alternators
2 alternator belt tensioners
2 alternator controllers
1 control valve
2 cooling fans for the engine compartment.

5. Gasoline Engines, Illustrations 6 and 7

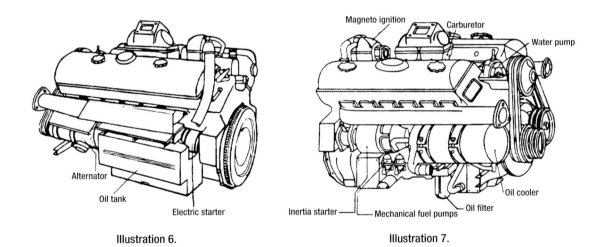

Illustration 6.

Illustration 7.

Two gasoline engines (Maybach HL 120 TRM) are installed in the Porsche Tiger tank destroyer, and these power two generators, which provide the electricity to drive the two electric motors. Each of the two gasoline engines is bolted together with a generator and, with it, is installed in the hull.

The casing of the gasoline engine consists of four parts:

the engine block with two banks of cylinders assembled in V configuration, the two cylinder heads, and the crankcase bottom.

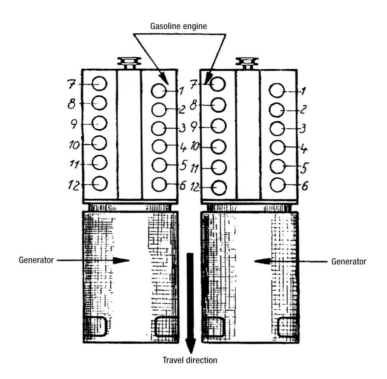

Gasoline engine

Generator

Generator

Travel direction

Illustration 8. Arrangement of the cylinders

The twelve cylinders are arranged in two rows; see illustration 8.
They are numbered:

Left back to front: 1–6
Right back to front: 7–12
The ignition sequence is 1–12–5–8–3–10–6–7–2–11–4–9.

Between the engine block and the crankcase bottom is the crankshaft, with six cranks, seated in seven ball bearings. Two connecting rods sit on a crank pin.

Twelve cylinder liners are inserted into the engine block. Coolant flows around their outsides; they are sealed by two rubber rings against the crankcase, and a collar presses their surface against a stepped ring face.

The valves are arranged suspended in the two cylinder heads. They are controlled by the camshafts, which are seated on seven bearings in each cylinder head, by means of rockers. Both camshafts and the magneto ignition with impulse coupling between the cylinder heads are gear-driven. The pistons are made of a lightweight alloy and have three compression rings and two oil control rings. The piston pins are floating pins and are secured by two Seeger rings.

Installed in or on each gasoline engine are
2 oil sump pumps
1 hydraulic oil pump
1 oil filter
1 water pump—driven by the crankshaft by
1 alternator—common V belt
2 mechanical fuel pumps, driven by the oil pump shaft
2 Solex two-stage downdraft cross-country carburetors
1 electric starter
1 inertia starter
1 oil tank
1 oil cooler

Furthermore, within the engine compartment are
2 fuel tanks
4 radiators with cooling fans

Outside the engine compartment are
8 air filters
2 cooling fans

To reduce height and taking into account possible sloping positions by the Porsche Tiger tank destroyer, it is equipped with a dry sump lubrication system (illustration 9).

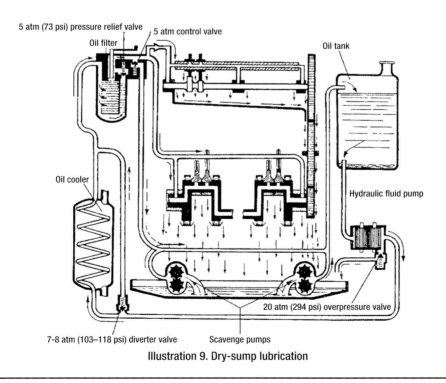

Illustration 9. Dry-sump lubrication

A hydraulic oil pump, which together with the two sump pumps is driven by a spur gear and shaft drive, pushes the oil stored in the oil tank on the right side of the engine via an oil cooler and oil filter out to the lubrication points in the engine. In the oil cooler, the coolant cools the engine oil, and any contaminants are removed by the oil filter. The oil is conveyed via a lubrication oil line through two oil introduction bearings at the ends of the crankshaft, and the hollow camshaft to the individual big end bearings. The crankshaft ball bearings and the small end bearings are lubricated by splashed oil. The oil is pumped through two more oil lines into both cylinder heads by way of the rocker arm shafts to the rocker arm bearings with rocker arm rollers, and to the camshaft bearings. Two sump pumps pump the oil flowing from the bearings into the crankcase back into the oil tank.

The hydraulic oil pump has a 20 atm (294 psi) pressure relief valve to protect against overloads. A second 7–8 atm (103–118 psi) valve makes it possible to bypass the oil cooler if oil thickened by the effects of cold encounters strong resistance in the oil cooler. A 5 atm (73 psi) valve is located in the oil filter, as seen in illustration 10, and opens if the filter becomes clogged.

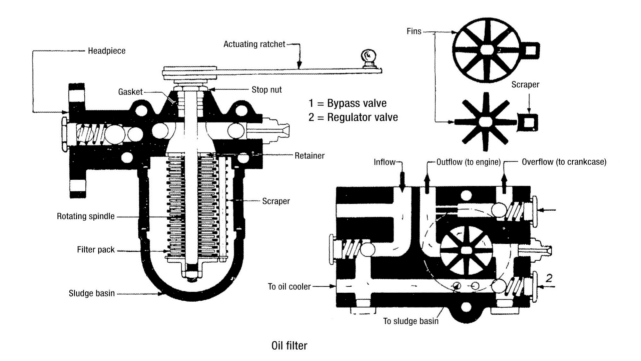

Oil filter

The subsequent oil control valve regulates oil pressure to 5 atm (73 psi). The oil filter is cleaned by operating a lever on the front partition behind the driver, which engages the actuator ratchet by means of a cable.

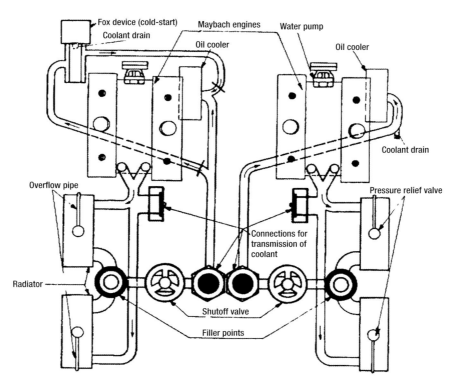

Illustration 11. Arrangement of the cooling system
(Fox device is installed only in some of the tank destroyers)

Coolant circulation in each engine is achieved by means of a centrifugal pump, which together with the alternator is driven by two V belts. Above each generator are two radiators, which are connected by equalizing pipes. The pipes between the gasoline engines and the radiators can be closed by means of valves, so that during cold starts and coolant transfer, the liquid coolant can circulate only in the cooling areas of the gasoline engines.

Connections make it possible to transfer the warm coolant from another tank or tank destroyer into the tank destroyer being started. Pressure control valves open if the coolant temperature exceeds 195°C (383°F). Steam vented from these valves is discharged through pipes.

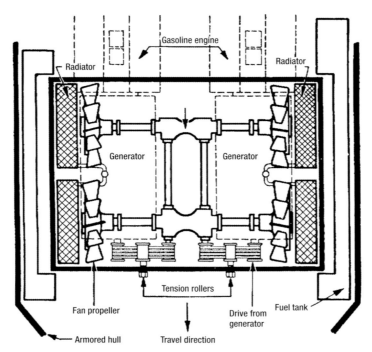

Illustration 12. Fan drives

The two cooling fans of each gasoline engine, seen in illustration 12, are each driven by four V belts on pulleys on the free end of the generator shaft and two bevel gears. The V belts are tensioned from the driver's position by adjusting a tension pulley mounted on a crank arm.

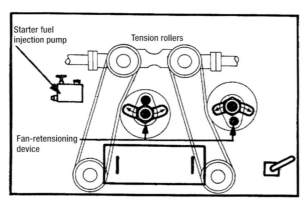

Illustration 13. Fan belt tension

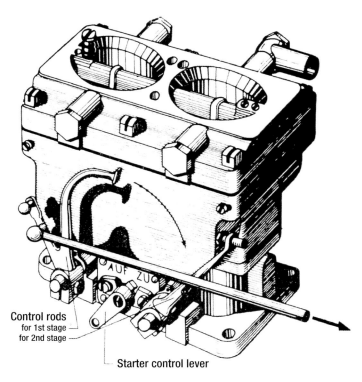

Control rods
for 1st stage
for 2nd stage

Starter control lever

Illustration 15. Carburetor

The fuel-air mixture for each gasoline engine is produced in two Solex two-stage-down-draft, cross-country carburetors, each of which works on the intake line of one bank of cylinders.

Each two-stage carburetor consists of two individual carburetors, the second of which becomes effective only when the accelerator pedal is fully depressed. The starter mechanism in the same housing makes it possible to start the gasoline engine easily. This starter mechanism is controlled by a hand lever behind the driver's seat on the right, which is connected to it by a control rod. The fuel level in the carburetor is controlled by two float needle valves, which are operated by one balance shaft for each two floats. The fuel flows from the float chambers into two main jets, which are inserted into the nozzle holders with their flanges facing up. The air, which flows past the nozzle holder through a venturi, draws fuel from the jet, atomizes it, and combines with it to form an ignitable fuel-air mixture. A throttle valve regulates the quantity of aspirated fuel-air mixture and thus engine output.

At low engine revolutions the air flow in the venturi is insufficient to draw sufficient fuel from the jet.

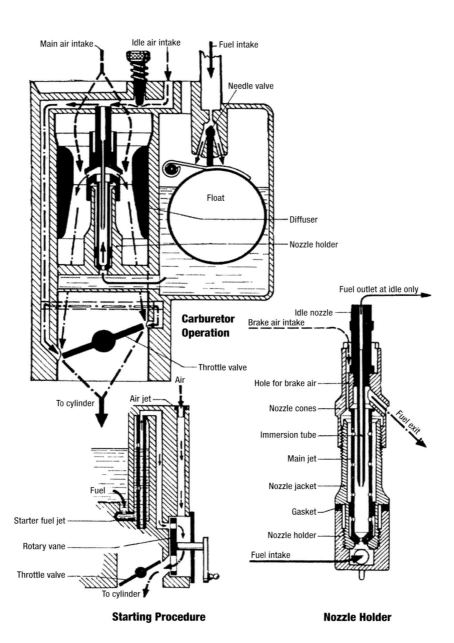

Main air intake — Idle air intake — Fuel intake

Needle valve

Float

Diffuser

Nozzle holder

Carburetor Operation

Brake air intake

Idle nozzle

Fuel outlet at idle only

Throttle valve

Air

Air jet

To cylinder

Fuel

Starter fuel jet

Rotary vane

Throttle valve

To cylinder

Hole for brake air

Nozzle cones

Immersion tube

Main jet

Nozzle jacket

Gasket

Nozzle holder

Fuel intake

Fuel exit

Starting Procedure

Nozzle Holder

Through the narrow air duct of the idle mechanism (illustration 14), which exits on the throttle valve, which is almost closed at idle, the fast-moving intake air sucks fuel through the idle jet from the main jet. This produces an ignitable fuel-air mixture, which is regulated by an adjusting screw at the top of the carburetor. A rich fuel-air mixture with a high percentage of fuel is produced in the starter mechanism (illustration 14), which enables the engine to be started even in cold conditions. When the starter mechanism is activated, a channel to the intake pipe is opened, and air is sucked in through an air jet and fuel through a fuel jet and dip tube. Fuel and air mix in a mixing chamber and pass under the throttle valve, which is closed during starting, into the intake pipe.

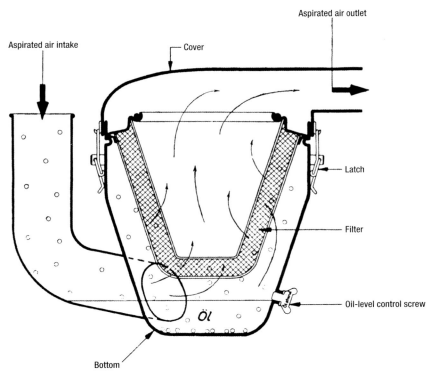

Illustration 16. "Mahle" air filter

The purpose of the eight air filters is to clean the intake air. They are connected to the carburetors by a bifurcation. When it passes through the oil-wetted inserts of the air filters, dust and particles of dirt are removed from the air, and it arrives clean at the carburetors.

There is one electric starter and one inertia starter for starting each of the gasoline engines. The electric starters on the right sides of the gasoline engines are engaged by two push buttons on the switchboard. The inertia starters in illustration 17 are on the left sides of the gasoline engines and are wound via a Cardan shaft from the drive dog in the partition by inserting a hand crank.

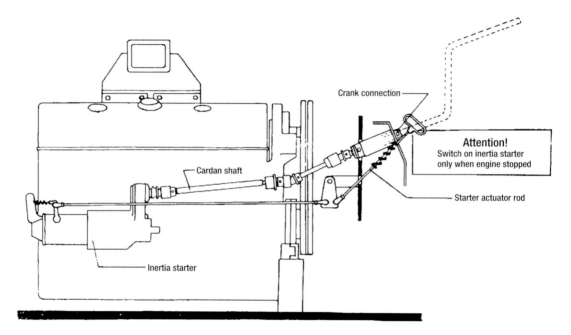

Crank connection

Attention!
Switch on inertia starter
only when engine stopped

Starter actuator rod

Cardan shaft

Inertia starter

Illustration 17. Inertia starter

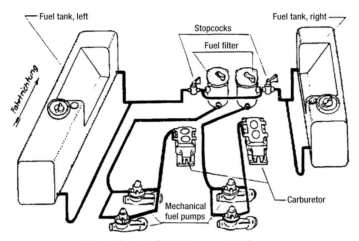

Illustration 18. Fuel storage and delivery

The fuel is housed in two tanks that are located in the extensions over the tracks on both sides of the engine compartment. The filler openings are accessible through doors in the engine cover. The fuel flows through two lines, which can be shut off by fuel cocks, to the fuel filters (illustration 19), in front of the forward partition in the driver's compartment.

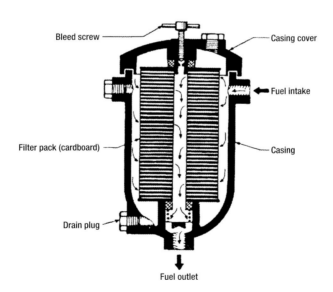

Illustration 19. Fuel filter

During operation, four mechanical fuel pumps (illustration 20) driven by the gasoline engines deliver fuel to the carburetors.

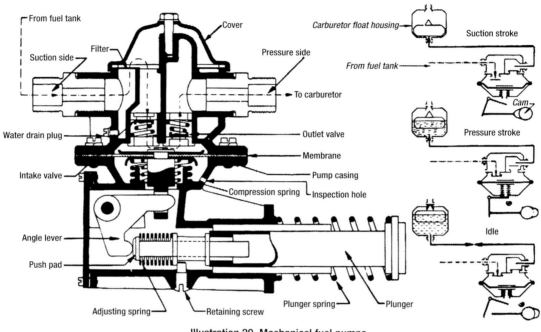

Illustration 20. Mechanical fuel pumps

A freewheel device in these fuel pumps automatically shuts off the flow of fuel if the carburetors are full.

A starter fuel injection pump is installed on the forward partition behind the radio operator's seat to facilitate cold-weather starting of the gasoline engines. It conveys starter fuel to the intake line, where it is atomized by jets.

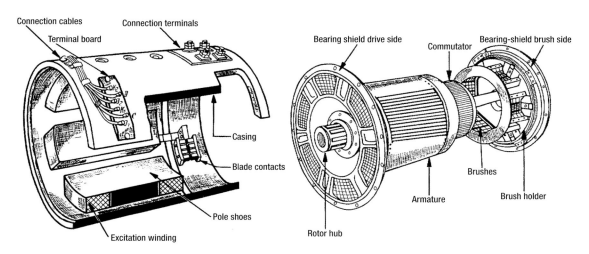

Illustration 21. Generator and electric-motor casing

Illustration 22. Generator and electric-motor armature

The output of the two gasoline engines is converted into electricity by two generators and fed to the electric motors that power the vehicle. A generator is flange-mounted to each gasoline engine. Installed in the generator casing are coils on poles with pole shoes, which produce the magnetic field, and a terminal board. Inside the casing, an armature rotates between the poles. It is mounted on the one side on the gasoline engine's flywheel and on the other side in ball bearings in the end shield. It has coils that are attached to the commutator. When the gasoline engine sets the electric motor's armature turning, a current is produced in the armature's coils, which flows into the commutator and is picked up by the power transmission brushes. The power transmission brushes are held in groups of ten in six brush holders. The brush holders sit on a rotating brush ring, which is mounted on the end shield. From the brushes, the electric current flows via a terminal board, cable, and driving switch to the electric motors, actuates them, and drives the vehicle. Generator cooling air is provided by a cooling fan mounted on the armature. A second cooling fan mounted on the armature delivers cooling air to one of the electric motors via an air duct. A belt pulley is mounted on the free end of the shaft and powers the cooling fan for the gasoline engines' radiators.

7. Electric Motors

Two electric motors, similar in design to the generators, are installed in the rear of the tank destroyer and power the vehicle. The engine casings are secured by tension bands in the hull beneath the fighting compartment. They contain the coils, which produce the magnetic field, on poles and pole shoes, and a terminal board. The power transmission brushes are held in groups of ten in six brush holders. The brush holders sit on a rotating brush ring, which is mounted on the end shield. In the casing an armature rotates between the poles. It is supported by roller bearings in two bearing seats. It has coils that lead to the commutator. The electricity fed to the electric motors from the generators via the terminal board produces in the coils a magnetic field, flows via the power transmission brushes and the commutator into the armature coils, and sets the armature rotating.

8. Power Transmission from Electric Motor to the Track Drive

A. Friction Clutch, Illustration 23

A friction clutch is installed on the armature shaft of each electric motor, protecting the motor against damage in case of overload. Inside the friction clutch, clutch discs are pressed together by springs. If a predetermined load is exceeded, the discs slide apart, interrupting the flow of power.

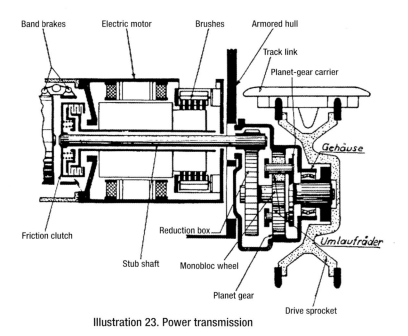

Illustration 23. Power transmission

B. Stub Shaft, Illustration 23

The rotation of the electric motor is transmitted by a stub shaft to the final drive. It engages the clutch and the final drive's drive pinion with splines and is run by the armature's hollow shaft.

C. Final Drive, Illustration 23

In the final drive there is reduction gearing, and a planetary gearbox reduces the electric motor's revolutions to that of the drive wheel. Each drive wheel is supported on roller bearings in the final drive casing and has two sprockets that engage and power the track.

9. Engine/Motor Controls

The power that moves the tank destroyer is produced by the gasoline engines, converted into electricity by the generators and fed to the electric motors, which drive the vehicle.

Changes in the tank destroyer's speed and direction of travel are achieved by strengthening or weakening the flow of current to the electric motors.

The accelerator pedal, with which the driver controls the vehicle's speed, operates the throttle valves on the carburetors by means of cables and, at the same time, a control unit for the generators. The position of the throttle valve controls the output and speed of the gasoline engines, and operation of the control unit controls the electric current.

The control unit is built into the switch box next to the driver's seat on the right (illustration 24).

In position 1, a preselector housed in the switch box (illustration 24) switches on both generators, and positions 3 and 4 make it possible to switch off a damaged generator.

Switch position 2 has been disabled.

The speed of the gasoline engines, which should be high off-road and low when driving on roads, is regulated by a rotary switch (illustration 24) in the switch box (positions 1, 2, 3).

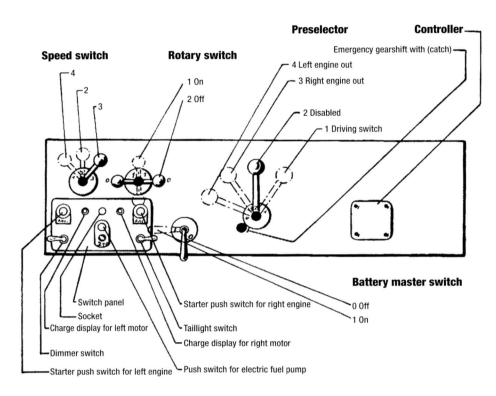

Illustration 24. Control box

10. Driving Switch

The tank destroyer is steered by changing the speed of its two caterpillar tracks. When driving a curve, the electric motor on the inside of the curve drives the track with less power than the electric motor on the outside of the curve. Consequently the track on the inside of the curve turns more slowly, and the vehicle carries out a steering movement. When making a tight turn, the inside track is slowed down even more.

The driver, who while steering pulls one of the steering levers, hereby adjusts the control unit built into the driving switch under his seat (illustration 25). On the other hand, when braking, the driver pulls back on both steering levers.

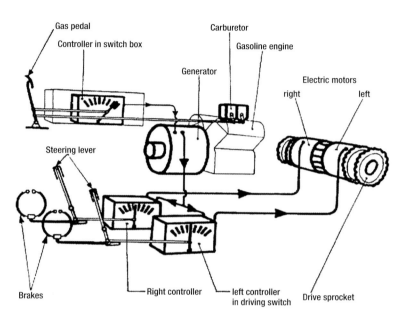

Illustration 25. Power transmission

Hereinafter the driving switch's mode of action will be examined in more detail, using illustrations 26 a and b.

Pulling back the steering lever initially switches on the electric brakes, and the farther back the levers are, the greater the braking effect. From position A the pneumatic brakes are also brought to bear. The maximum effect is achieved when the steering lever is against stop B. The push buttons on the brake levers are not pressed. The electric brakes alone are preferably used to brake on gentle gradients. In combination with the pneumatic brakes they are used primarily to stop the vehicle. The steering levers can be moved rearward past the stop if the buttons on the steering levers are depressed; see illustration 26 b. The electric brakes are hereby augmented significantly, while at the same time the pneumatic brakes are switched off. In the process the steering levers must be moved back only to position C, which can be clearly felt as an intermediate position because of a detent. This type of braking is preferably used to brake in steep, longer gradients (gradient brake).

Air compressor
Pressure regulator
Steering lever
Brake shoes
Air reservoir
Entlüfter
Brake valve
Hydraulic brake cylinder
Oil pressure cylinder
Brake cylinder
Oil pressure transmission
Pneumatic

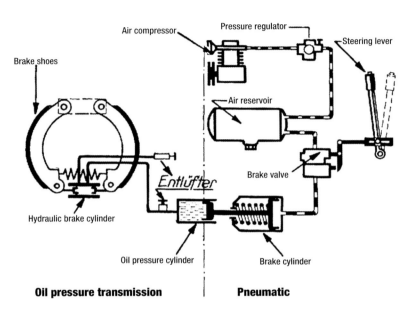

Illustration 26. Brakes

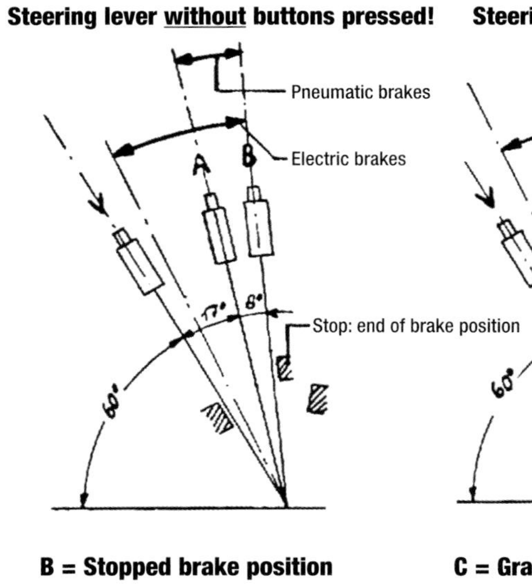

Steering lever without buttons pressed!
Pneumatic brakes
Electric brakes
A
B
17°
8°
60°
Stop: end of brake position
B = Stopped brake position

Illustration 26a

Steering lever with buttons pressed!
Electric brakes
C
R
31°
9°
60°
C = Gradient brake position

Illustration 26b

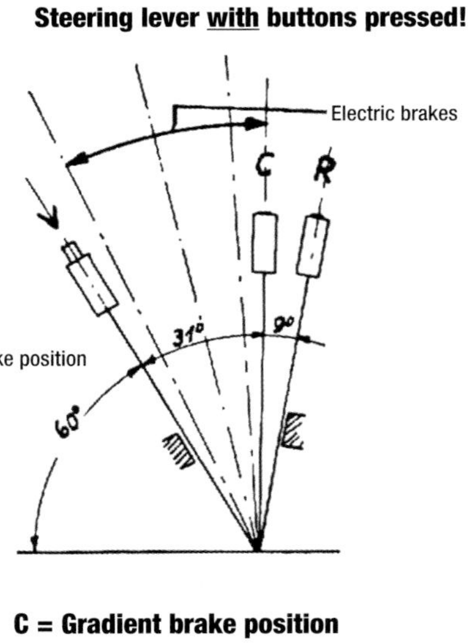

Pulling or snatching back both levers back to the rear stop R is fundamentally to be avoided when braking. Position R is used only for driving in reverse at full power and in exceptional cases for steering by pulling back just one lever.

When turning, only the steering lever on the inside of the curve is pulled back. The resulting braking forces are the same as those during braking, except that they affect the track only on the inside of the curve. The second steering lever must always remain forward when turning.

A compressor produces the compressed air required for the pneumatic brakes. It is collected in an air bottle and kept at a specific pressure by a pressure regulator. Two brake valves in the driving switch box, which are operated by the steering levers during part of their travel, pipe the compressed air into the brake cylinder of the track to be braked. The braking cylinder's piston acts on a hydraulic oil cylinder, which forces hydraulic fluid through a line into three hydraulic brake cylinders and presses the three pairs of brake shoes against the brake drum. Bleeders at the end of the hydraulic brake cylinder and at the entry into the shaft of the idler wheel make it possible to bleed the brake system.

11. Foot Brake

A rod from the foot brake opens the two pneumatic brake valves installed in the driving switch and brakes both tracks.

12. Hand Brake

The parking brake's brake band acts on the outer ring of the friction clutch. The driver operates the parking brake with a hand brake lever by means of a pawl, a pulley with steel band and a rod.

13. Running Gear

A. Drive Wheel

The drive wheel is mounted on the final drive at the rear of the assault guns and is powered by the electric motor. It has two replaceable sprockets, whose teeth engage and drive the track.

B. Idler Wheel, Illustration 27

The idler wheel turns about a crank axle that is mounted on the front of the armored hull. Skewing the crank axle changes the position of the idler wheel and affects track tension. To swivel the idler wheel, a threaded ring is screwed back by means of a pinion, and as a result the clamping of the crank axle in the conical sleeve is released.

After the clamping bolts, which are set in an adjusting arm, are loosened, with the aid of engine power the crank axle with idler wheel is swiveled with brakes set. The idler wheel has two interchangeable sprockets, whose teeth engage the track. A brake slows the idler wheel.

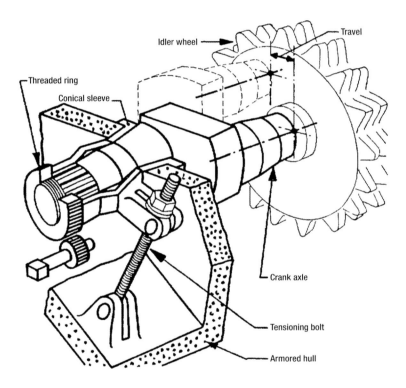

Idler wheel

Travel

Threaded ring

Conical sleeve

Crank axle

Tensioning bolt

Armored hull

Illustration 27. Crank axle with idler wheel

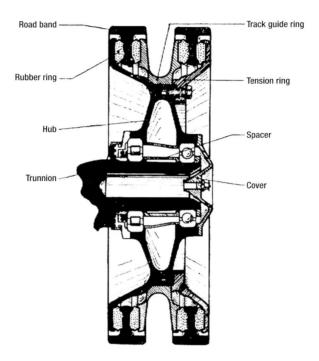

Illustration 28. Road wheel

Installed in each brake drum are three pairs of brake shoes, which are spread by the hydraulic brake cylinder.

C. Road Wheels, Illustration 28

The road wheels are designed as dual wheels, with two tires made of steel and a track guide ring. The tires are each held by two rubber rings between notches. The rubber rings allow the road wheels running on the tracks to be sprung. After the retaining bolts have been unfastened, the clamping rings, rubber rings, tires, and track guide rings can be removed in sequence.

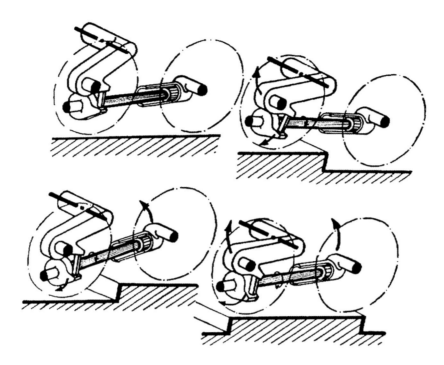

Bilder 29 : Arbeit der Federung
Illustration 29: Suspension operation

D. Double Swing Arms, Illustration 30

Two road wheels are mounted on each double swing arm, which is made up of a support arm and a spring arm. The support arm is mounted in ball bearings on a trunnion attached to the hull sidewall. On its free end it has one road wheel and the spring arm.

The second road wheel is mounted on the spring arm. A torsion bar—a round rod of spring steel with two spur-gear heads—engages the free end of the spring arm with one head. The other head engages a sleeve on the spring arm mount, which carries a ring with a cleat, the support ring. By way of an articulated support with ball sockets, this ring's cleat rests against the cleat of a second support ring, which is attached to the support arm trunnion. When the vehicle crosses uneven ground, a wheel is raised and the spring arm is pressed against the support arm (illustration 29). The spring arm's deflections relative to the support arm are cushioned by twisting the torsion bar and limited by rubber bumpers.

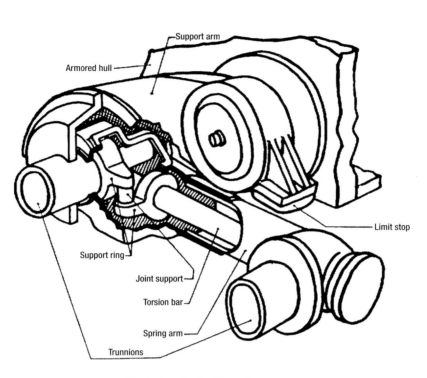

Illustration 30. Double swing arm

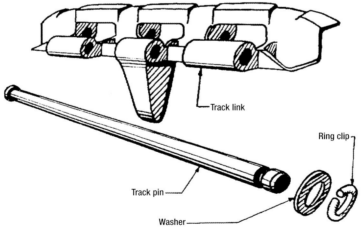

Illustration 31. Track link

E. Tracks, Illustration 31

The tracks consist of individual interlinked track links, which are connected to one another by pins. The track is not lubricated. The pins are secured by circular clip retainers.

14. Electric Light and Starter Systems

The electric lighting system of the Panzerjäger Tiger (P) has a voltage of 12 volts, and the electric sliding armature starter a voltage of 24 volts. Four 12-volt batteries installed under the driver's seat are charged by two alternators located beneath the fighting compartment. The entire system can be switched off by using the battery master switch (illustration 33). The system is controlled from the control panel. The fuse cartridges, seen in illustration 32, are mounted on the rear wall of the switch box and are accessible from the radio operator's seat.

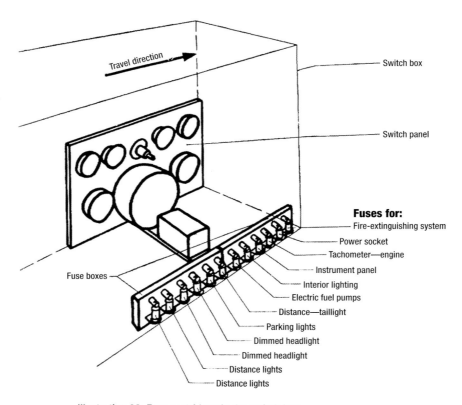

Illustration 32. Fuse cartridges in the switch box

The individual electrical devices are toggled using the switching key as follows:

Key Position	Switched On	Switched On with Special Switch
0 Key removed		Starter, distance taillight, sunset light
0 Key inserted	Instrument lighting, interior lighting, power outlet, ignition	Starter. distance taillight, sunset light
1 Key removed	Parking light	Starter, distance taillight, sunset light
1 Key inserted	Parking light, instrument panel lighting, power outlet, ignition	Starter, distance taillight, sunset light
2 Key removed	Driving beam	Starter, distance taillight, sunset light
2 Key inserted	Driving beam, instrument panel lighting, power outlet, ignition	Starter, distance taillight, sunset light

15. Tools and Auxiliary Devices

Tools, spare parts, and auxiliary devices are carried for conducting minor repairs. The tools and spare parts are kept packed in two boxes in the interior of the vehicle. The auxiliary equipment is carried in part inside and in part outside the assault gun. This consists of

2 crowbars, 800 and 120 mm diameter
1 wooden support block
2 wire cables, 8 and 32 mm diameter
1 sledgehammer
2 power cables
1 drift punch
1 track-connecting tool
1 antenna mast container
2 coolant hoses
1 box wrench for track adjustment
1 ratchet wrench for adjusting idler wheel
1 stud for removing track pins
2 couplings for power transfer cables
1 20-metric-ton trolley jack
4 shackles, 75 mm
1 12-meter tow cable, diameter 12 mm
8 track links
1 blowtorch
1 signaling disc
1 fire extinguisher

B. Driving Instructions for the Panzerjäger Tiger (P)

16. Putting into Operation

Driver:
Check and top off coolant, open fuel cock, insert ignition key. Switch on cold-start device in cold weather.

Gunner and Loader:
Wind inertia starter of one gasoline engine. Gunner and loader insert the starter crank and turn it to the left, slowly gathering speed, never jerkily, and remove it when a sufficient rotation speed (60 rpm) has been achieved. The gunner then pulls hard on the starter actuator rod handle and releases it immediately when the engine starts.

    Note: Under no circumstances should the *gasoline engine* be **allowed to run without coolant**. Otherwise, rubber sealing rings in the cylinder liners will melt immediately. Start second gasoline engine in same way.

Driver:
When starting with the electric starter, always start just one gasoline engine and then the other. Switch off cold-start device. When one gasoline engine is running, the second can be started with the help of the generator in the following way:

    Set preselector to position 1,
    move both steering levers forward,
    place rotary switch in vertical position,
    apply throttle.

    Oil pressure must rise to at least 4 atm (58.8 psi) after several revolutions of the engine.
    Switch off engine after one minute of running time. Unscrew plug from oil filler neck (illustration 6) and remove dipstick. Fill to the upper mark with "Wehrmacht Tank Engine Oil" or "Wehrmacht Engine Oil." Oil measurements on an engine that has not been run will provide an incorrect value.

17. Check the Tank Destroyer Each Time before Driving

A. Engine
1. Listen to the sound of the engine and observe the exhaust gases. (If the engine is running irregularly with black exhaust smoke, check spark plugs and carburetor.)
2. Is the engine losing oil? Fuel? Coolant?

B. Pedal System
1. Operability of the accelerator pedal

C. Electrical System
1. Condition of lighting
2. Proper operation of the alternator (Red charging indicator light goes out at higher revolutions.)

D. Running Gear
1. Track pin spring clips all present and undamaged?
2. Track pins undamaged?
3. Track links undamaged?
4. Correct track tension? (The track is properly tensioned if the track sagging over the road wheels is in full contact with the third and fourth road wheels and hangs freely over the second and fifth road wheels at a distance of one finger width.)
5. Cracks in idler or drive wheels?
6. Road wheels damaged?

E. Pneumatic Brakes
1. Check pressure in the brake system. The gauge must indicate a pressure of 6 atm (88 psi).
2. Every time before driving and at least once every 50 km (31 mi.) during longer drives, check to ensure that the pneumatic brakes are properly set, meaning forcefully enough. For this reason, slowly begin driving, first without and then with the brake pedal depressed. The difference between the two currents should be 500 to 800 A. 500 A is the lowest acceptable value; otherwise the brake must be readjusted.

F. Gun
Elevating and traversing mechanism and barrel locked?

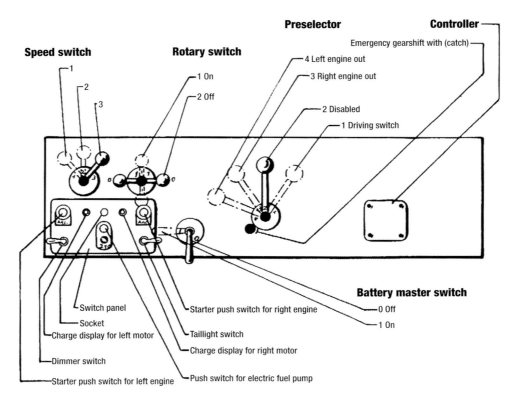

Preselector

Controller

Emergency gearshift with (catch)

Speed switch

Rotary switch

4 Left engine out

3 Right engine out

1 On

2 Off

2 Disabled

1 Driving switch

1

2

3

Switch panel

Starter push switch for right engine

Battery master switch

0 Off

1 On

Socket

Charge display for left motor

Taillight switch

Dimmer switch

Charge display for right motor

Starter push switch for left engine

Push switch for electric fuel pump

Illustration 33. Control box

18. Driving the Tank Destroyer

A. Starting Up and Operating the Generator
The vehicle is operated as follows:

Forward Travel:
Push both steering levers forward to the stop.
Set preselector to position 1.
Place rotary switch in the vertical position.
When the throttle is opened, the vehicle begins to move.

Reverse Travel:
Both steering levers, press the push buttons downward and move levers back to the stop.
Set preselector to position 1.
Place rotary switch in the vertical position.
When the throttle is opened, the vehicle begins to move backward.

If a gasoline engine or generator fails, the tank destroyer can be driven with just one gasoline engine. Switch positions 3 and 4 are designed for this.

Position 3:

Emergency position in the event of failure of the right gasoline engine or generator.

Position 4:

Emergency position in the event of failure of the left gasoline engine or generator.

Switching to emergency positions 3 and 4 is to be carried out as follows:

Throttle back, move both steering levers forward to the stop, turn rotary switch to the horizontal position, turn lock under the preselector lever to the left, place preselector lever in position 3 or 4, turn rotary switch to vertical position, step on the gas.

B. Engine Speed

Keep gasoline engines at a speed between 1,500 and 2,600 rpm while driving, and do not exceed 2,600 rpm. Allow engine speed to briefly rise to 3,000 rpm only when turning or covering difficult routes. Adjust speed of gasoline engines to traction resistance by flipping speed switch (illustration 33) and varying acceleration. When traction resistance is high, when turning in difficult terrain and on inclines, move speed switch forward or vertically to position 1 or 2. The high revolutions will fully exploit maximum engine power. When traction resistance is low, on the road, in easy terrain, and on downhill gradients, move speed switch back to position 3. The low revolutions will spare the gasoline engines and save fuel.

C. Oil Pressure and Coolant Temperature

The oil pressure gauge, seen in illustration 34, must be monitored regularly while driving. A gauge indicates the pressure for each gasoline engine. The colder the oil is, the higher the oil pressure, and with the engines warm (coolant temperature at least 50°C [122°F]) and 2,000 rpm, not lower than 4 atm (58.75 psi).

Coolant temperature while driving should be 80°C (176°F). If the coolant temperature rises and exceeds 95°C (203°F), check in the following sequence:

1. coolant level
2. tension of the V belts to the cooling fans
3. fouling of the exterior of the radiator
4. fouling of the interior of the radiator
5. proper functioning and cleanliness of the pressure relief valve
6. Ignition timing
7. Carburetor adjustment

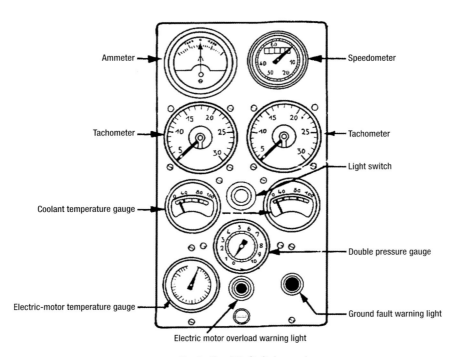

Ammeter

Speedometer

Tachometer

Tachometer

Light switch

Coolant temperature gauge

Double pressure gauge

Electric-motor temperature gauge

Ground fault warning light

Electric motor overload warning light

Illustration 34. Switch panel

D. Driving, Steering, and Braking

1. The tank destroyer's speed is controlled by use of the gas pedal.
2. When driving straight ahead, both steering levers remain in their rest positions at the forward stop. This enables the electric motors to develop their full tractive force.
3. When steering, the inside-curve steering lever is moved backward only rapidly, not jerkily, while the outside-curve lever fundamentally remains in the forward final position. Always try to get by in position A (electric brake only); this is quite possible when driving on roads and straight ahead in gentle terrain and in flat curves. The steering effect is enhanced if the steering lever is pulled back to position B (electric and pneumatic brakes). This position should, however, be used as little as possible for steering.

Reason: To spare the pneumatic brakes and avoid unnecessary losses.

4. An even-greater enhancement of the steering effect is achieved without utilization of the pneumatic brakes, if the button on the steering lever is pressed and the lever is pulled farther backward past position B, if necessary to the limit stop position R. The second lever **must** remain in the fully forward position (important!). This steering method is to be used mainly in difficult, winding terrain.

5. For rapid braking, use either the electric and pneumatic brakes to stop B or the foot brake. It is **strictly forbidden** to brake the vehicle purely electrically **with buttons pushed** and pulling back on both steering levers, since the machinery can be damaged by overcurrents and rendered unserviceable.

6. In summary, there follows a listing of the cases in which the push buttons on the steering levers may be pressed:

   (a) **Both** push buttons may be pressed only
      1. when driving backward
      2. when driving on a gradient with the gradient brake; vehicle must first be slowed to a walking pace with the pneumatic brakes.

   (b) **One** push button may be pressed if the second steering lever is fully forward.

E. General Steering Guidelines

In contrast to wheeled vehicles, steering consumes a great deal of additional power. Difficult terrain and the use of incorrect steering techniques can lead to the vehicle becoming stuck, and to dangerous loads on the electric motors and running gear. In such cases, steering movements are to be carried out only if unavoidably necessary. The driver should seek out a solid point in the terrain, which is in his primary direction, and drive straight toward it. Curves are to be avoided (illustration 35).

Steering is to be carried out only in positions that offer minor resistance to the steering movement (illustration 36). Off-road, the driver must drive with foresight, searching out gentle slopes and firm ground and steering toward these positions.

Do not turn on bridges or railroad tracks, since these can be destroyed and the running gear damaged by turning on railroad tracks (illustration 37).

Avoid driving in deep ruts, since the tank destroyer's hull can easily contact the ground, and driving out of a rut places heavy loads on the running gear and motors (illustration 38).

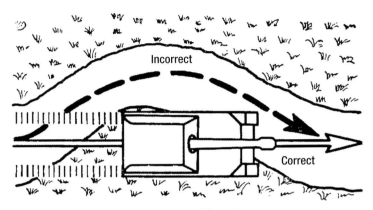

Illustration 35. Driving off-road

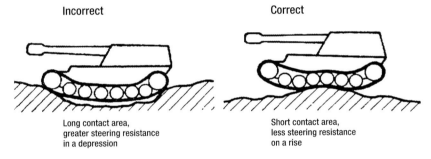

Incorrect

Correct

Long contact area,
greater steering resistance
in a depression

Short contact area,
less steering resistance
on a rise

Illustration 36. Steering off-road

Drive over thick tree stumps slowly with the tracks, since otherwise the hull will become stuck (illustration 39). Vertical obstacles (broken walls, barricades, etc.), are to be taken with the help of logs placed under the tracks (illustration 40).

All changes of direction are to be made using the widest-possible turns. Sharp turns or turns in place are to be made only if it is absolutely necessary (illustration 41). Pull the steering lever back only as far as necessary for the vehicle to carry out the steering movement. Leave the lever in this position to the maximum degree possible, and make minor improvements in the lever's position only if the vehicle leaves the curved path.

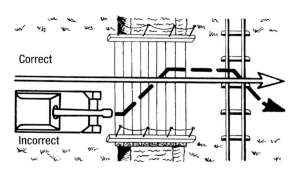

Illustration 37. Driving over bridges and tracks

Illustration 38. Driving in a rut

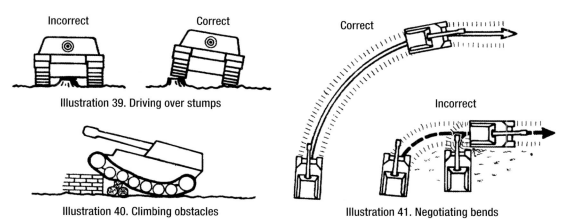

Illustration 39. Driving over stumps

Illustration 40. Climbing obstacles

Illustration 41. Negotiating bends

19. Driving the Tank Destroyer Off-Road

A. Driving Up Steep Slopes

1. Position the tank destroyer perpendicular to the slope.
2. Do not turn if it can be avoided.
3. If the tracks slip, apply only sufficient throttle to keep the motors pulling.
4. Apply only sufficient throttle to prevent the red warning light from illuminating.

B. Driving Down Steep Slopes

1. Position the tank destroyer perpendicular to the slope. Do not accelerate on the slope.
2. If necessary, use the foot brake to reduce the vehicle's speed to less than a walking pace.
3. Then drive down the slope, using the gradient brake (purely electric braking to spare the pneumatic brakes).
4. Avoid turns as much as possible. If necessary, move the steering lever on the outside of the desired curve forward.

C. Stopping and Parking the Tank Destroyer on an Uphill Slope

1. Avoid parking on a slope whenever possible.
2. Hold both steering levers against the forward stop (do not pull).
3. Ease off on the gas pedal until the tank destroyer stops.
4. Release the brake pedal until the tank stops. (The tank destroyer cannot be held in position on a slope by using just the throttle for longer than ten seconds. In any case, immediately step on the brake pedal.)
5. Place rotary switch in horizontal position.
6. Allow gasoline engines to continue running at high rpm for some time, in case the electric motors should be very hot (in excess of 100° C [212° F]).
7. Shut off engines.

D. Stopping and Parking the Tank Destroyer on a Downhill Slope

1. Avoid parking on a slope whenever possible.
2. Use gradient brakes to come to a halt and fully depress the brake pedal until the vehicle stops.
3. Apply parking brake.
4. Place both steering levers against forward stop.
5. Shut off motors/engines; turn rotary switch to horizontal.

E. Pulling Away on an Uphill Slope

(Parking brake is engaged; steering levers against the forward stop.)
1. Start engines; place rotary switch in vertical position.
2. Fully depress brake pedal; release parking brake.
3. Apply throttle; release foot brake.

F. Pulling Away on a Downhill Slope
(Parking brake is engaged; steering levers against the forward stop.)
1. Start engines; place rotary switch in vertical position.
2. Fully depress brake pedal; release parking brake.
3. Hold down push buttons and pull both steering levers back to the rear stop.
4. Release foot brake and slowly move steering levers forward until the tank destroyer moves forward slowly (gradient brake).

G. Surmounting Obstacles
Surmount very difficult terrain and obstacles, trenches, broken walls, tree stumps, etc. with sharply reduced speed. If, while on an obstacle, the tank destroyer wants to tip and is hanging suspended, apply a little throttle and pull one steering lever (turn the tank destroyer). This will cause the vehicle to touch down with no heavy jolts. Drive slowly on bumpy roads, and do not allow the vehicle to stop on the middle of a bump. When driving in wooded terrain, ensure that the hull does not become lodged on tree stumps.

H. Parking the Tiger (P) Tank Destroyer
At the end of the drive, the driver releases the throttle and allows the tank destroyer to roll to a stop before setting the parking brake. The gasoline engines are turned off by removing the ignition key and placing the rotary switch in the horizontal position. The steering levers should be placed in rest position against the forward stops. In any other position, the batteries will be discharged. Select a parking location where the tank destroyer cannot roll away. Because of the tank destroyer's great weight, placing stones in front of the tracks cannot reliably prevent it from rolling off.

20. Ten Commandments for Drivers

1. Parking Brake
Before pulling away, depress the hand brake button to release the brake, then push hand brake lever forward forcefully, causing the linkage to release the band brake!

2. Maximum Speed
20 kph (12.4 mph)

3. Tachometer
1,500 to 2,300 rpm, briefly higher!

4. Ammeter
(a) to 700 A: continuous
(b) to 1,000 A: 15 min., then turn off remote excitation. Cool down electric motors at 1,300 rpm.
(c) over 1,300 A: 10 sec. (red flickering light)

5. Ground Fault Light
If the ground fault light comes on, immediately stop and park the vehicle. Disconnect ground cable (left of driving switch) from the wall and isolate.

6. Driving and Steering:
(a) While driving, place both steering levers in the most forward position!
(b) When steering, always keep the outside-curve steering lever in the forward position!
(c) Move inside-curve steering lever quickly, not jerkily!
(d) In difficult terrain, on winding roads, and when turning in place, press buttons.

7. Braking
Braking by pulling back on both steering levers with the buttons depressed is strictly forbidden. Use foot brake for rapid braking.

8. Driving Down a Slope
Bring vehicle to a walking pace, using the foot brake, then move both steering levers to the rear with buttons pressed, to first noticeable rest.

9. Stopping or Halting on a Slope
(a) Hold vehicle with engine power for 10 sec. at most!
(b) For longer stops, apply foot brake, reduce throttle, and apply parking brake.

10. Parking the Vehicle
Rotary switch to 0, cool motors for a few minutes at 1,300 rpm, turn off battery master switch, and place both steering levers in the most forward position!

C. Care instructions for the Panzerjäger Tiger (P)

21. Jobs after Completion of Driving

A. Thoroughly Clean Vehicle Outside and Inside.

B. Engines
1. Top off fuel, coolant, and engine oil.
2. Is it losing engine oil? Fuel? Coolant?
3. Clean air filter elements, check oil level, and if necessary, add engine oil and, if very dirty, replace.

C. Running Gear
1. Check road wheels, steel tire rings, and track guide rings.
2. Replace missing or damaged track pin ring clips. Place washer on end of track pin. Place ring clip in the recess of the ring clip driver. Place clip driver on free end of pin and drive ring clip on with hammer (illustrations 42, 43).
3. Replace damaged track pins.
   (Let track run until the damaged pin is on the front side of the idler wheel. Position track-connecting tool, insert track pin in bottom hole of track-connecting tool, and, using the sledgehammer, drive in the track pin, causing the ring clip and washer to come off. Position drift punch and push out the old track pin. Drive in new track pin from the inside and drive on ring clip as in 2. Remove track-connecting tool.
4. Replace damaged track links (illustration 44).
   (Remove two track pins as in 3. With track tensioner positioned, during which the crowbar can be held in place by inserting a second track pin, remove the damaged link from the track. Install new link. Drive in both track pins again and secure [with disc clips]; remove track-connecting tool.)

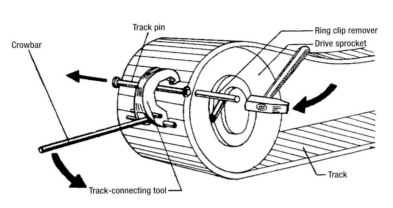

Illustration 42. Changing a track pin

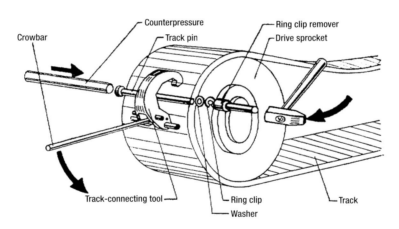

Illustration 43. Changing a track pin

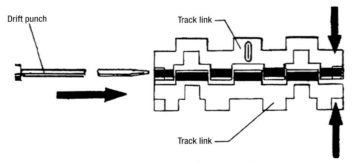

Illustration 44. Changing a track link

D. Electrical System
Repair damage that occurs while driving.
1. Replace damaged fuse cartridges and bulbs.
2. Repair loose connections, fasten loose wires, repair abrasion points. Turn off master switch before starting this work.
3. Refill contents of electrical supply box.

E. Accessories and Tools
1. Repair or replace damaged or lost accessories and tools.
2. Check accessories and tools to verify completeness and pack in their prescribed locations.
3. Refill oil can and grease gun.

22. Installation of the Track
1. Position the track-connecting tool on the front of the idler wheel, tension the track with it and a crowbar, and knock out the track pins with stud and drift pin.
2. Move the tank destroyer forward until the track is lying free on the ground.
3. Lay out the new one behind the vehicle, in the same direction as the old one, and attach the two track ends with a track pin driven in halfway.
4. Back up the tank destroyer until the drive sprocket is over the free end of the track, in a position to allow the first track link to be attached to the drive sprocket.
5. Insert the drift pin into the last track link, and with it, lift the end of the track onto the teeth of the drive sprocket.
6. Drive the tank destroyer forward again.
7. Using the drift pin, pull the end of the track that is past the drive sprocket over the road wheels, until the free end of the track can be attached to the idler wheel.
8. Remove the track pins between the old and new track.
9. Turn the idler wheel with a crowbar, until the free end of the track is hanging down over the front of the idler wheel.
10. Depress the brake pedal, move the steering levers with depressed push buttons to the rear stop, and allow the electric motors to run until the upper end of the track is tensioned.
11. Pull the hand brake lever.
12. Bring the two track ends together with the crowbar, align the links with the drift punch, and join them with a track pin.
13. Place a washer on the track pin and secure it with a disc clip.

D. Instructions for Lubrication

To function well and have a long life, the tank destroyer requires proper lubrication.
As necessary, the oil must be topped off sooner or the lubrication points cleaned and relubricated, as determined by the vehicle's condition and operating conditions (damaged seals or muddy ground, loose sand, heavy rain).

23. Oil Lubrication

A. Engines
The level of oil in the oil tank must be checked daily, using the oil dipstick. The engraved identification marks indicated the highest and lowest oil levels. Engine oil should always be filled to the highest mark.

When changing the oil, after removing the hatch in the hull bottom, with the engines warm, drain the old oil from the oil tank and crankcase bottom through the drain holes. To ensure that the oil also drains from the oil lines, turn the engine over several times, using the inertia starter with the ignition key removed.

Fill with fresh oil, and to ensure that the empty oil lines are again filled, turn the engine over briefly once more. Return oil level to the highest mark.

The oil filter is to be cleaned when the oil is changed.

B. Final Drives, Fan Drives, and Double Swing Arms
Gear oil is added to the final drives and fan bevel-gear drives through the filler necks. Oil is to be added until it flows out of the tap-threaded overflow holes. In the most-extreme cases, the oil level can be allowed to fall to the lowest thread of the overflow hole. A drain plug is used to drain the gear oil during an oil change. In the double swing arms, the flap that is located on the swing arm on the upper side of the joint is filled to the bottom edge with gear oil. Changing the oil in the swing arm is not required. However, care should be taken to ensure that following repairs of any kind, such as replacement of a torsion bar, that oil that was lost is replaced.

24. Greasing

For lubrication points that are greased with a grease gun, after thoroughly cleaning the grease nipples the fresh grease is to be injected until all of the used grease has oozed out of the lubrication point and the fresh grease is visible. The grease collars must remain standing.

The following are to be kept free of oil and grease:

the rubber V belts for alternators, water pumps, fans, and air compressor
the coolant hoses
the electrical lines (cable duct)
all electrical switches and regulators
the generators and electric motors
the rubber rings in the road wheels and stop blocks
the paint finish

Berlin, May 1, 1943

Army High Command
Army Ordnance Office
Office Group for Development
and Examination

under the authority of
Holzhäuer

Glossary

A.K.	Krupp department for artillery design ("Kruppaka" in teletype messages)
A.Z.	Impact fuse
Bd.Z.	Base-detonating fuse
D.Z.	Combination fuse
Digl.Bl.P . . .	Diglycol flake powder and the measurements
Digl.R.P . . .	Diglycol tube powder and measurements
FES	Sintered-iron guide rings
FEW	Soft-iron guide rings
(HK)	Hard core
HI	Hollow-charge antitank shell
HL	High-performance engines
HI/C	Type C hollow charge
HWA	(Heereswaffenamt) Army Ordnance Office
In 6	Inspectorate of Transport Troops
Kgs 64/640/130	K = high-speed track, g = cast steel, s = floating bolts, 64 = design, 640 = track width in mm, 130 = spacing in mm
KPS	Guide rings made of copper-coated steel
KwK	(*Kampfwagenkanone*) tank gun
L/5	Shell length is five times the caliber
L/55	Barrel length is 55 times the caliber
L/71	Gun barrel length is 71 times the caliber
Nz.Man.N.P.	Nitrocellulose powder with stick propellant
Pzgr.	*Panzergranate* (armor-piercing shell)
Simulaker	Simulator, mockup
Sprgr.	*Sprenggranate* (high-explosive shell)
St.K.	Steel core
Stg.	*Stahlguss* (steel casting)
TS	*Treibspiegel* (sabot)
Verskraft	Army Ordnance Office, Research Center for Motor Vehicles
VK	Experimental design with planned operational weight
Vo	Muzzle velocity
Wa Prüf	Army Ordnance Office, office group for development and testing
Wa Prüf 1	see above; Ballistics and Ammunition section with four branches of service and nine groups (as of 1943)
Wa Prüf 2	see above; Infantry section at Kummersdorf
Wa Prüf 4	see above; Artillery section with ten groups
Wa Prüf 5	see above; Pioneer and Railroad Pioneer section
Wa Prüf 6	see above; Motor Vehicle and Motorization section with three main sections: vehicles, tanks, and motorization
Wa Prüf 7	see above; Signals section
Wa Prüf 8	see above; section for Optics, Survey, Army Meteorology, Mapmaking, Artillery Fire Control
Wa Prüf 9	see above; Gas Defense section at Spandau
Wa Prüf 10	see above; section for special equipment—small-caliber rocket projectiles (late 1944)
Wa Prüf 11	see above; section for special equipment—large rockets (late 1944) at Peenemünde
Wa Prüf 12	see above; Proving Grounds
Zt.Z. S/ . . .	Time-delay fuse

Endnotes

Foreword

1. Werner Oswald, *Kraftfahrzeuge und Panzer der Reichswehr, Wehrmacht und Bundeswehr* (Stuttgart: Motorbuch-Verlag, 1977), 349.

2. Karl R. Pawlas, ed., "Den Porsche-Tiger 'Ferdinand,'" *Waffen-Revue* 65 (1987): 29.

3. Nachlass Saur, IfZ., ED 442, p. 47.

4. Nachlass Saur, IfZ., ED 442, box 1.

Part I

1. Oswald, *Kraftfahrzeuge und Panzer*, 349.

2. Pawlas, "Den Porsche-Tiger 'Ferdinand,'" 29.

3. Saur estate, Institute for Contemporary History Munich, ED 443, p. 47.

4. PA, house note subject: Porsche Type 100: Leopard of 27 November 1940.

5. Saur estate, Institute for Contemporary History Munich, ED 442, box 1.

6. BAMA RH 8/2640.

7. BAMA RH 8/2641.

8 Stefan Zima, *Entwicklung schnelllaudender Hochleistungsmotoren* (Düsseldorf, Germany: VDI-Verlag, 1987), 231.

9. Saur estate, Institute for Contemporary History Munich, ED 442, box 1.

10. Porsche Museum, *Ferdinand Porsche: Pioneer of the Hybrid Drive*.

11. Hartmut H. Knittel, *Panzerfahrzeuge im Zweiten Weltkrieg* (Herford, Germany: Verlag E. S. Mittler & Sohn, 1988).

12. The later name, Leopard, did not come from the Army Ordnance Office and was also unknown to the office.

13. Saur estate, Institute for Contemporary History Munich, ED 442, box 1.

14. Walter Rohland, *Bewegte Zeiten: Erringerungen eines Eisenhüttenmannes* (Stuttgart: Seewald Verlag Stuttgart, 1978), 75.

15. *Kriegstagebuch des OKW* ("OKW war diary"), vol. 1, part 2 (Augsburg, Germany: Verlag Weltbild, 2007), 1,004.

16. BAMA RH 8/1642.

17. Estate of Eberan von Eberhorst, TUD, B-178b-I and IV.

18. Porsche Archive: Die Panzerentwicklung bei Porsche of 18/07.1964.

19. Saur estate, Institute for Contemporary History Munich, ED 442.

20. Document, memorandum of 26/05/41.

21. Saur estate, Institute for Contemporary History Munich, ED 442.

22. Document, circular from the Reich minister for armaments and munitions.

23. Saur estate, Institute for Contemporary History Munich, ED 442.

24. Todt document of September 23, 1941.

25. Wa Prüf 6 document of September 27, 1941.

26. Saur estate, Institute for Contemporary History Munich, ED 442, box 1.

27. Michael Winninger, *Das Nibelungenwerk, OKH Spielwaren: Die Panzerfabrik in St. Valentin* (Andelfingen, Switzerland: Müller History Facts, 2011), 185.

28. Ibid., 195.

29. BAMA RH 8/2793.

30. BAMA RH 8/2793, p. 145.

31. BAMA RH 8/2795.

32. BAMA RH 8/2795.

33. Saur estate, Institute for Contemporary History Munich, ED 442, box 1.

34. Ibid.

35. BAMA RH 8/2797, p. 152.

36. Porsche Archive, *Diary of Karl Rabe, Porsche Chief Designer: 1940–1945*.

37. Walter Spielberger and Hilary R. Doyle, *Der Panzer-Kampfwagen Tiger und seine Abarten* (Stuttgart: Motorbuch-Verlag, 1998), 76.

38. Willi A. Boelcke, *Deutschlands Rüstung im Zweiten Weltkrieg* (Stuttgart: Akademische Verlagsgesellschaft Athenaion, 1969), 125.

39. BAMA RH 8/2791, p. 67.

40. BAMA RH 8/2791, p. 27.

41. BAMA RH 8/2791.

42. BAMA RH 8/2792, p. 22.

43. Boelcke, *Deutschlands Rüstung im Zweiten Weltkrieg*, 156; and Saur estate.

44. Franz-Wilhelm Lochmann, Richard Freiherr von Rosen, and Alfred Rubbel, *Erinnerungen an die Tigerabteilung 503* (Würzburg, Germany: Verlagshaus Würzburg, 2015), 131.

45. Boelcke, *Deutschlands Rüstung im Zweiten Weltkrieg*, 186.

46. *Instandsetzung*; and Lochmann et al., *Erinnerungen an die Tigerabteilung 503*.

47. Spielberger and Doyle, *Der Panzer-Kampfwagen Tiger*, 94.

48. BAMA, RH 8/2803.

49. Günter Groth, *Die Chronik der Gemeinde Behringen am Hainich in Thüringen—1920 bis 1945* (Bad Langensalza, Germany: Verlag Rockstuhl, 2008), 49 and 69.

50. Paul Botzum and Rainer Lämmerhirt, *Wüstungen im Hainichgebiet* (Mihla, Germany: Heimat- und Verkehrsverein, 1995), 21.

51. Harald Rockstuhl, *Nesseltalbahn und die Kindelbahn* (Bad Langensalza, Germany: Verlag Rockstuhl, 2005), 140 and 150.

52. Esser, *Die Kraftfahrversuchsstelle des HWA*.

53. Spielberger and Doyle, *Der Panzer-Kampfwagen Tiger*, 89.

54. MAN WA 315.1-4.9 (12-4).

55. BAMA, MSG 224/27.

56. Knittel, *Panzerfertigung im Zweiten Weltkrieg*, 88.

57. BAMA, MSG 224/27.

58 Wa Prüf 6 data sheet of March 5, 1944.

59. Speech by Eberan: "Gasoline or diesel engines in tanks," 1944.

60. Thomas L. Jentz and Hilary L. Doyle, *Germany's Tiger Tanks, DW to Tiger I: Design, Productions & Modifications* (Atglen, PA: Schiffer Military History, 2000), 189.

61. *Die Woche* 17 (April 28, 1943).

62. Ferry Porsche and Günther Molter, *Ferry Porsche, mein Leben* (Stuttgart: Motorbuch-Verlag, 2004), 132.

63. Wolfgang Schneider, *Tiger im Kampf III* (Uelzen, Germany: Schneider Armour Research Uelzen, 2013), 55.

64. Porsche Archives, Karl Rabe diary, 1940–1945.

65. Saur estate, Institute for Contemporary History Munich, ED 442.

66. Karlheinz Münch, *Combat History of schwere Panzerjäger-Abteilung 654* (Winnipeg, MB: J. J. Fedorowicz, 2002).

67. BAMA, RH8/2820.

68. BAMA, RH8/2793, p. 130.

69. WABW, B 123, Bü 1346.

70. BAMA, RH8/2816.

71. PA.M.K1.4.4-102tlw.

72. PA.M.K1.4.8-186tlw.

73. PA.M.K1.4.11-244.

74. BAMA, RH 8/2830.

75. Spielberger and Doyle, *Der Panzer-Kampfwagen Tiger*.

76. Tiger 1, therefore, because the designation Tiger 2 had already been issued for Henschel's Tiger B (former Tiger 3).

77. Wolfgang Fleischer, *Die Heeresversuchsstelle Kummersdorf* (Wölfersheim-Berdstadt, Germany: Verlag Podzun-Pallas, 2000), 179.

78. Herbert A. Quint, *Porsche: Der Weg eines Zeitalter* (Stuttgart: Steingrüben-Verlag Stuttgart, 1952), 266.

79. Emil Leeb, *Aus der Rüstung des Dritten Reiches (Das Heereswaffenamt 1938–1945)*, Wehrtechnische Monatshefte-Beiheft 4 (Berlin: Mittler & Sohn, May 1958), 47.

80. Karl R. Pawlas, W 127, Datenblätter des Heeres 1944.

81. Karl R. Pawlas, W 127, Datenblätter des Heeres-Waffen, Fahrzeuge, Gerät.

82. Wolfram Pyta, Nils Havemann, and Jutta Braun, *Porsche: Vom Konstrultionsbüro zur Weltmarke* (Munich: Siedler-Verlag, 2017), 268.

83. Porsche Archives, Memorandum of October 15, 1943.

84. VEB Elbtalwerke Heidenau, three machine units.

85. Münch, *Combat History of schwere Panzerjäger-Abteilung 654.*

86 BAMA, RH 8/1567, p. 151.

87 Wolfgang Fleischer, documents.

88 Harald Rockstuhl, *Hainich under der Nationalpark aus der Luft* (Bad Langensalza, Germany: Verlag Rockstuhl, 2014), 41.

Part II

1. BAMA: RH 8-1567.

2. Boelcke, *Deutschlands Rüstung im Zweiten Weltkrieg*, 288.

3. PA. M. K1.4.2-59.

4. PA. M. K1.4.2-60.

5. Heinz Guderian, *Erinnerungen eines Soldaten* (Stuttgart: Motorbuch-Verlag, 2003), 271.

6. Ibid., 269.

7. Winninger, *Das Nibelungenwerk, OKH Spielwaren*, 207.

8. Ibid., 212.

9. PA.M. K1.4.3-86.

10. PA.M. K1.4.7.

11. Boelcke, *Deutschlands Rüstung im Zweiten Weltkrieg*, 254.

12. Winninger, *Das Nibelungenwerk, OKH Spielwaren*, 213.

13. Manfred Dörr, *So kämpfte die schwere Panzerjäger-Abteilung 654* (Zweibrücken, Germany: VDM, 2011), 19.

14. PA.M. K1.4.5-124.

15. Karlheinz Münch, *Einsatztgeschichte der schweren Panzerjäger-Abteilung 653, 1943–1945* (Schwetzingen, Germany: Münch, 1996), 35.

16. Roman Töppel, *Kursk 1943:Die größte Schlacht des Zweiten Weltkrieg*s (Paderborn, Germany: Ferdinand Schöningh, 2017), 128.

17. Ibid.

18. Guderian, *Erinnerungen eines Soldaten*, 283.

19. BAMA: RH 10/58.

20. Töppel, *Kursk 1943*, 29.

21. Ibid., 224.

22. Münch, *Einsatzgeschichte der schweren Panzerjäger-Abteilung 653*, 46.

23. PA.M.K1.4.8.

24. PA.M. K1.4.9.

25. Ibid.

26. BA/MA RH 10/58.

27. BAMA RH8-2865.

28. BAMA RH8-1567.

29. Münch, *Einsatzgeschichte der schweren Panzerjäger-Abteilung 653*, 106.

30. Ibid., 141.

31. lFZ, Saur Estate, ED 442, box 1m, vol. 2, Interrogation of August 8, 1945.

32. Pawlas, "Den Porsche-Tiger 'Ferdinand,'" 29.

33. Datenblätter, Heeres-Waffen, Fahrzuge, und Gerät.

34. Walter J. Spielberger, *Panzer II und seine Abarten* (Stuttgart: Motorbuch-Verlag, 2003).

Bibliography

BAMA Freiburg, Files: RH 8 I/ 449, 473, 820, 883, 1053, 1567, 1631, 1642, 1668, 1673, 1905, 1911, 2639, 2641, 2645, 2646, 2647, 2648, 2669, 2777, 2790, 2791, 2792, 2793, 2794, 2795, 2796, 2797, 2798, 2799, 2800, 2801, 2802, 2803, 2804, 2805, 2806, 2815, 2816, 2817, 2818, 2819, 2820, 2821, 2822, 2823, 2865, 3127, 3206, 3280, 3883, 3920, 3951, 3952, 4609, RH 10/58, 349, RH 21/2/244, RW 19/560, 882, 1919, 1924, MSG 224/1, 2, 7, 8, 11, 12, 13, 14, 17, 18, 27, 28, 29, 30, 31, 42, 46, BV 5/4285, 1183

WABW Stuttgart, B 123, Büchel 1346.
Institute of Contemporary History, estate of Karl-Otto Saur.
Porsche Archive, including diary of Karl Rabe, 1931–1945, and *Pioneer of the Hybrid Drive*.
University archive of the Dresden University of Technology, estate of Eberan von Eberhorst.

Anderson, Thomas. *Ferdinand and Elefant: Tank Destroyer*. Oxford: Osprey, 2015.
BAMA Freiburg. Holding: RH 81.
Boelcke, Willi A. *Deutschlands Rüstung im Zweiten Weltkrieg*. Frankfurt: Akademische Verlagsgesellschaft Athenaion, 1969.
Botzum, P., and R. Lämmerhirt. *Wüstungen im Hainichgebiet*. Bad Langensalza, Germany: Verlag Rockstuhl, 2005.
D 656/1 Panzerjäger Tiger (P) Gerätebeschreibung und Bedienungsanweisung, 1943 ("Porsche Tiger tank destroyer equipment description and operating manual").
D 656/2 Panzerjäger Tiger (P) Instandsetzungsanweisung zum Fahrgestell, 1943 ("Porsche Tiger tank destroyer chassis repair instructions").
D 656/3 Panzerjäger Tiger (P) Instandsetzungsanweisung zum elektrischen Teil, 1943 ("Porsche Tiger tank destroyer electrical-equipment repair instructions").
D 656/22 Tiger E und Turmbeschreibung ("Tiger E and turret description").
D 656/23 Pz.Kpfw. Tiger Ausführung E, Handbuch für den Panzerfahrer, 1944 ("Tiger Ausf. E, handbook for tank drivers").
D 656/24 Fristen Tiger E ("Tiger E maintenance schedule").
D 656/27 Die Tigerfibel, . . . so'ne schnelle Sache, 1943 ("The Tiger primer, crew manual").
D 656/30 b und 30 c Instandsetzungsanleitung für Panzerwarte ("Repair instructions for tank mechanics").
D 9023/1 Die Funk- und Bordsprechanlage im Pz.Kpfw. Tiger als Befehlswagen, 1943 ("The radio and intercom system in the Tiger command vehicle").
D 1008/1 Die Funk- und Bordsprechanlage im Pz.Kpfw. VI (H) und (P), 1942 ("The radio and intercom system in the Pz.Kpfw. VI (Henschel) and (Porsche), 1942").
D 2030 8,8-cm-Panzerjägerkanone 43/2 (L/71).
Dörr, Manfred. *So kämpfte die schwere Panzerjäger-Abteilung 654*. Zweibrücken, Germany: VDM, 2011.
Fleischer, Wolfgang. *Die Heeresversuchsstelle Kummersdorf*. Wölfersheim-Berdstadt, Germany: Verlag Podzun-Pallas, 2000.
Friedli, Lukas. *Die Panzerinstandsetzung der Wehrmacht*. Uelzen, Germany: Schneider Armour Research, 2005.
Groth, Günter. *Die Chronik der Gemeinde Behringen am Hainich in Thüringen—1920 bis 1945*. Bad Langensalza, Germany: Verlag Rockstuhl, 2008.
Guderian, Heinz. *Erinnerungen eines Soldaten*. Stuttgart: Motorbuch-Verlag, 2003.
Institute of Contemporary History. Estate of Karl-Otto Saur.
Jentz, Thomas L., and Hilary L. Doyle. *Germany's Tiger Tanks, DW to Tiger I: Design, Productions & Modifications*. Atglen, PA: Schiffer Military History, 2000.
Knittel, Hartmut H. *Panzerfertigung im Zweiten Weltkrieg*. Herford, Germany: Verlag E. S. Mittler & Sohn, 1988.
Kriegstagebuch des OKW ("OKW war diary"). Vol. 1, part 2. Augsburg, Germany: Verlag Weltbild, 2007.
Leeb, Emil. *Aus der Rüstung des Dritten Reiches (Das Heereswaffenamt 1938–1945)*. Wehrtechnische Monatshefte-Beiheft 4. Berlin: Mittler & Sohn, May 1958.
Lochmann, Franz-Wilhelm, Richard Freiherr von Rosen, and Alfred Rubbel. *Erinnerungen an die Tigerabteilung 503*. Würzburg, Germany: Verlagshaus Würzburg, 2015.
Möller, Eberhard, and Werner Brack. *Einhundert Jahre Dieselmotoren für fünf deutsche Marinen*. Hamburg, Germany: Verlag E. S. Mittler & Sohn, 1998.

Mommsen, Hans. *Das Volkswagenwerk und seine Arbeiter im Dritten Reich.* Düsseldorf, Germany: ECON-Verlag, 1997.

Münch, Karlheinz. *Combat History of schwere Panzerjäger-Abteilung 653.* Winnipeg, MB: J. J. Fedorowicz, 1997.

Münch, Karlheinz. *Combat History of schwere Panzerjäger-Abteilung 654.* Winnipeg, MB: J. J. Fedorowicz Publishing, 2002.

Münch, Karlheinz. *Einsatzgeschichte der schweren Panzerjäger-Abteilung 653, 1943–1945.* Schwetzingen, Germany: Münch, 1996.

Pawlas, Karl R., ed. "Den Porsche-Tiger 'Ferdinand.'" *Waffen-Revue* 65 (1987): 29–76.

Pawlas, Karl R., ed. "Porsche-Tiger 'Ferdinand' Teil 2." *Waffen-Revue* 66 (1987): 63–100.

Pawlas, Karl R., ed. "Porsche-Tiger 'Ferdinand' Teil 3." *Waffen-Revue* 67 (1987): 81–104.

Porsche, Ferry, and Günther Molter. *Ferry Porsche, mein Leben.* Stuttgart: Motorbuch-Verlag, 2004.

Pyta, Wolfram, Nils Havemann, and Jutta Braun. *Porsche: Vom Konstruktionsbüro zur Weltmarke.* Munich: Siedler-Verlag, 2017.

Quint, Herbert A. *Porsche: Der Weg eines Zeitalters.* Stuttgart: Steingrüben-Verlag Stuttgart, 1952.

Rauscher, Karl-Heinz. *Steyr im Nationalsozialismus: Industrielle Strukturen.* Gnas, Austria: Weishaupt-Verlag, 2004.

Rockstuhl, Harald. *Nesseltalbahn und die Kindelbahn.* Bad Langensalza, Germany: Verlag Rockstuhl, 2005.

Rohland, Walter. *Bewegte Zeiten: Erinnerungen eines Eisenhüttenmannes.* Stuttgart: Seewald Verlag Stuttgart, 1978.

Saur, Karl-Otto, and Michael Saur. *Er stand in Hitlers Testament.* Berlin: ECON-Verlag, 2007.

Schneider, Wolfgang. *Tiger im Kampf III.* Uelzen, Germany: Schneider Armour Research Uelzen, 2013.

Schwarzmann, Peter. *Panzerketten.* Königswinter, Germany: Brandenburgisches Verlagshaus, 2013.

Spielberger, Walter J. *Panzer II und seine Abarten.* Stuttgart: Motorbuch-Verlag, 2003.

Spielberger, Walter J., and, Hilary L. Doyle. *Der Panzer-Kampfwagen Tiger und seine Abarten.* Stuttgart: Motorbuch-Verlag, 1998.

Spielberger, Walter J., and Hilary L. Doyle. *Schwere Jagdpanzer.* Stuttgart: Motorbuch-Verlag, 2003.

Svirin, Michael. *Das Schwere Sturmgeschütz Ferdinand.* Zurich, Switzerland: Armada, 2002.

Töppel, Roman. *Kursk 1943: Die größte Schlacht des Zweiten Weltkriegs.* Paderborn, Germany: Ferdinand Schöningh, 2017.

Treue, Wilhelm, and Stefan Zima. *Hochleistungsmotoren: Karl Maybach und sein Werk.* Düsseldorf, Germany: VDI-Verlag, 1992.

WABW Stuttgart, B 123, Büchel 1346.

Winninger, Michael. *Das Nibelungenwerk, OKH Spielwaren: Die Panzerfabrik in St. Valentin.* Andelfingen, Switzerland: Müller History Facts, 2011.

Wirtgen, Rolf, and Frank Köhler, eds. *Kampfpanzermotoren in Deutschland 1939 bis 1990—Ein Überblick anhand ausgewählter Typen.* Koblenz, Germany: Bundesamt für Wehrtechnik und Beschaffung, 2008.

Zima, Stefan. *Entwicklung schnelllaufender Hochleistungsmotoren in Friedrichshafen.* Düsseldorf, Germany: VDI-Verlag, 1987.

Image Credits

(PA) Porsche Archive
(SH) Hilmes Collection
(SB) Spielberger Collection
(SF) Fleischer Collection
(SM) Münch Collection
(SP) Pasholok Collection
(SH) Henschel Collection
(SL) Lüdeke Collection
(BPK) BPK Photo Agency (h_30014347)
(BSB) Bavarian State Library Munich (Photo Archive), hoff-45722, hoff-45721, hoff-43202, hoff-43197
(BAMA) Federal Archives Military Archive Freiburg
(BA) Federal Archives, Koblenz, 183-15005-0003, 101I-313-1004-25
(TU) Estate of Everan von Eberhorst, University Archive of the Dresden Technical University
(LBD) Aerial Photo Data Bank Dr. Karls GmbH
(VR) "Hainich Illustrated Book and the National Park from the Air," Verlag Rockstuhl
(Steyr) MAGNA-St. Valentin
(WB) Wolfgang Spielberger
(KHM) Karlheinz Münch
(DH) Dirk Hensel
(Hoff) Bavarian State Library, Munich, Photo Archive, 45722, 47511, 47512, 47521, 47530, 47538, 47547
(TM) Tank Museum
(HF) History Facts
(DV) Service Manuals
(no identifier) author's collection

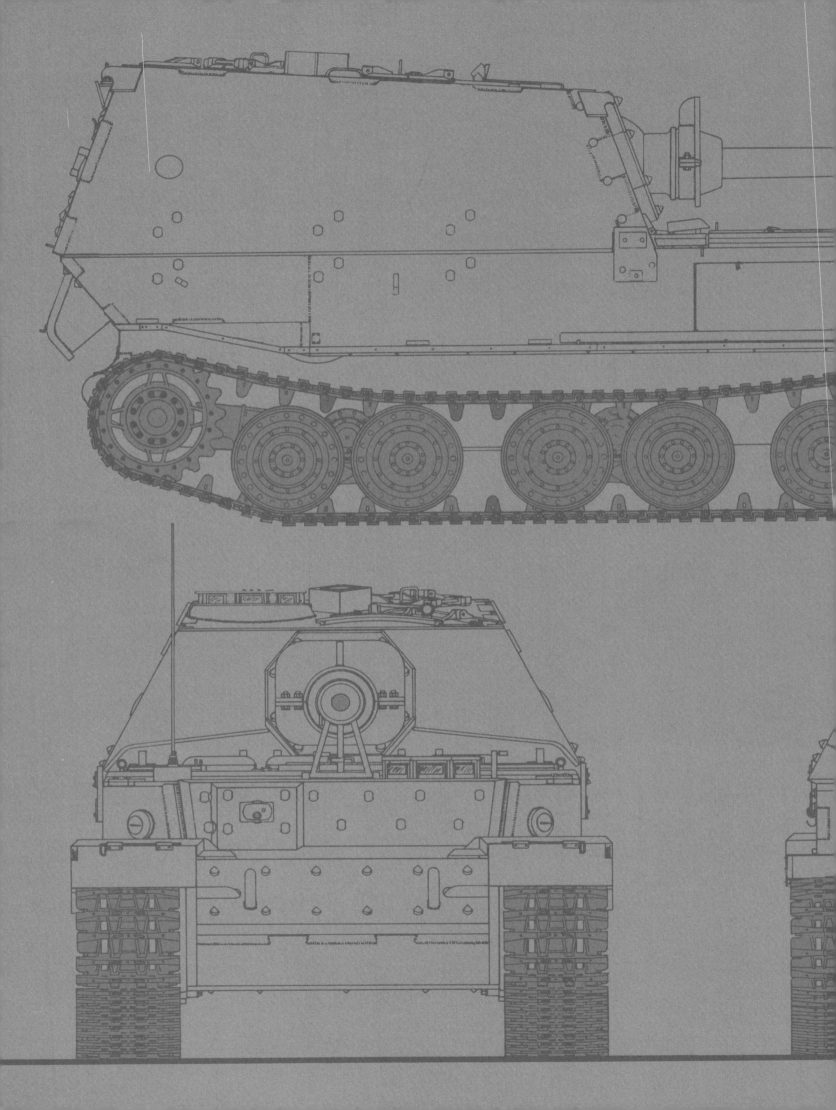

ITALIAN FILM POSTERS

DAVE KEHR

ITALIAN FILM POSTERS

Produced by the Department of Publications,
The Museum of Modern Art, New York

Edited by Joanne Greenspun
Designed by Gina Rossi
Production by Christina Grillo
Printed and bound by Conti Tipocolor s.p.a., Florence, Italy
Printed on 150 gsm Perigord

Library of Congress Control Number: 2003109319
ISBN 0-87070-692-6

Published by The Museum of Modern Art, New York
11 West 53 Street, New York, New York 10019 (www.moma.org)

Distributed in the United States and Canada by D.A.P., New York

Distributed outside the United States and Canada by
Thames & Hudson Ltd., London

All photographs of posters from the Museo Nazionale del Cinema,
Turin, are by Roberto Goffi; all others are by Thomas Griesel
and John Wronn.

Front cover: Anselmo Ballester. Detail of *Il grande caldo (The Big Heat)*.
1954 poster for the 1953 American film directed by Fritz Lang.
See p. 111 for whole image

Back cover: Ercole Brini. *Ladri di biciclette (Bicycle Thieves)*. Poster for the 1948
Italian film directed by Vittorio De Sica. Collection Nazionale del Cinema, Turin

Title page: Anselmo Ballester. Detail of *Il Frutto del peccato
(The Restless Years)*. Undated poster for the 1958 German film
directed by Helmut Kautner. See p. 80 for image

Printed in Italy

CONTENTS

PREFACE / Mary Lea Bandy

Other than the original films themselves, few works in the vast international history of film production are more appealing to archivists and collectors than the poster. Variations in design and color, style and wit, and images of glamour, intrigue, and sex appeal all make the film poster fascinating to study and delightful to view again and again. While thousands of these posters survive, they are fragile, often damaged from use in theaters, or stored clumsily on rolls, or folded or torn. Those that are intact can be breathtaking in their freshness and boldness, conveying to us today why poster artists are so special.

Unfortunately, film studios and distributors have not always retained the materials they produced. The International Federation of Film Archives, or FIAF, was established in 1938 to assist organizations intending to collect and preserve such materials. At that time, the cinema was nearing middle age and had passed through various critical phases. Sound and color, valued from the inception of the motion picture, were achievable: the talking picture had been around for nearly a decade in the United States, for example, and Walt Disney was making Technicolor cartoons in dazzling tones. What, therefore, should be collected and preserved from the gigantic worldwide wardrobes and closets of cinema's family? First and foremost, the films themselves needed to be located, gathered, identified, catalogued, reassembled in the right order, exhibited, redistributed, and conserved in vaults.

Such tasks, daunting in themselves, were but one part of the effort to preserve film history. Behind the films were scripts and storyboards, budgets and contracts, screen tests and outtakes, costumes, props, set designs, and stage sets. In the public forum, in theater lobbies, on the screen, and in newspapers and magazines, massive amounts of press and publicity materials were generated. There were newsreels, short subjects, and photographs of the sets and portraits of the stars. Glamorous press books and giveaways showed famous faces on cigarette boxes, bottle caps, fans, lunch boxes, etc. But the best of the promotional materials were those made by often nameless artists, who created posters of color and line that conveyed all the passion and allure promised in the ad copy, indeed far better than words could deliver.

Never mind if the film was black and white, the poster artists used colors to powerful effect. And none knew how to do this better than the Italian designers. They understood their subject, the narrative film; they grasped the marketplace, a highly competitive network of theaters in cities and towns throughout Italy; they knew their audience, the people who crowded the cinemas several times a week; and they were expert at posing the famous faces and bodies of actors they never would meet. These designers had wit and flair; they possessed a mastery of design and of printing techniques; and they knew what they were selling: the romantic and sexual attraction of screen gems.

Archives from the 1930s on understood that poster images were key to preserving the history of a country's national production. Italian archives have assembled impressive collections of film posters, thanks to the energies and talents of their staffs and of individuals whose holdings were subsequently acquired to form the basis for research and exhibition. Italy has film archives in Bologna, Cagliari, Gemona, Milan, Rome, and Turin, and at the Vatican. The Turinese collection of posters is outstanding, deriving from the collection of Maria Adriana Prolo, who in the 1930s began assembling a comprehensive selection that grew to 300,000 posters. Subsequently Signora Prolo founded the Museo Nazionale del Cinema, Fondazione Maria Adriana Prolo, and the poster collection is an important part of this museum. Our thanks go to Alberto Barbera, Donata Pesenti Campagnoni, Maria Grazia Girotto, and in particular to Nicoletta Pacini at the Museo Nazionale del Cinema for their collaboration on this book, and for taking the lead in restoring one of the world's finest collections of poster art. Film companies and individuals have also assembled noteworthy collections. We particularly thank Martin Scorsese, whose appreciation of Italian cinema knows no peer.

The Department of Film and Media at The Museum of Modern Art wishes to thank Dave Kehr, *un uomo del cinema*, a cinephile in the best sense of the word, as writer, critic, collector, whose breadth of knowledge of world cinema, and keen eye for the art of the poster as for that of the moving image, make him the perfect author for our first publication of film posters.

ACKNOWLEDGMENTS

It would be impossible to thank all of the people who, knowingly or unknowingly, have helped me with this project over the years. In New York, I owe a particular debt to Mary Lea Bandy of The Museum of Modern Art for nurturing this book through thick and thin; to Michael Maegraith, Joanne Greenspun, Christina Grillo, and Gina Rossi in the Museum's publications department for managing the complicated logistics of this project; and to Mikki Carpenter and Erik Landsberg in the Museum's imaging department for overseeing the creation of the magnificent reproductions to be seen in the following pages. The restoration team at J. Fields Studio performed several miracles in the course of preparing this book, transforming scraps of yellowed paper into highly displayable pieces. Martin Scorsese generously lent posters from his collection, and Jane Bay of Lucasfilm rode to a last-minute rescue. Melinda Hunt took some additional photos and provided invaluable support.

In France, I must thank Jean-Louis Capitaine of Ciné-Images for introducing me to the work of Anselmo Ballester many years ago, and to Dominique Besson of Dominique Besson Affiches for helping me to locate many rare pieces.

In Italy, Alberto Barbera, Donata Pesenti Campagnoni, and Maria Grazia Girotto of the Museo Nazionale del Cinema of Turin have been important collaborators on this book. I am particularly grateful to Nicoletta Pacini, who gave most generously of her time and energy in helping to select the posters and in seeing to the restoration of several important pieces. I also wish to thank Luigi Paratella of Jules et Jim, Paolo Barilli of CinemArt, and Francesca Puia of Bolaffi for their great help in finding material. Giulia d'Agnolo Vallan of the Torino Film Festival proved infinitely patient in providing contacts and emergency translations.

—Dave Kehr

NOTE TO THE READER

Some foreign-language films were never released in the United States and are therefore referred to by their original titles only. Those that were released are given in both their original foreign titles and the titles under which they are known in this country. Unless otherwise indicated, all posters reproduced in this book are in private collections.

INTRODUCTION / Dave Kehr

In the final analysis, movie posters are advertisements—in other words, promises made to be broken. But what glorious promises they make! A great movie poster arouses expectations—of romance and mystery, action and excitement, glamour and escape—that few movies can truly fulfill. They are invitations to dream, to sense for a moment the perfect movie that might be made from the materials at hand. And although experience may seldom live up to expectation, we are always ready and eager to be seduced again.

The posters reproduced in this book come from Italy, a country where seduction has long been an art. Though many of the films represented here will be familiar to American readers, most of the images will not. Thanks to a variety of factors, among them a culture uniquely rich in the visual arts, an artisanal pride in fine printing, and, perhaps, a predisposition toward the grand and passionate, Italy produced perhaps the finest film posters in the world for much of the twentieth century. Though the distinctive tradition of Italian film posters is well known to European collectors and cinephiles, and the work of artists such as Anselmo Ballester, Alfredo Capitani, and Luigi Martinati is displayed in museums and commands high prices at auction, these extraordinary artifacts remain largely unknown on this side of the Atlantic.

This book is the first collection of these inventive, colorful, and highly evocative images to be published in English. It attempts to offer an overview of the Italian tradition, as it began with the Art Nouveau-influenced designs of the silent era, developed into the stunning stone lithographs of the 1930s and 1940s, and concluded with the gloriously idiosyncratic creations made possible by offset printing in the 1950s and 1960s. Blending wildly different influences—from the luminous realism of the Renaissance to the furious distortions of the Expressionists—these fascinating works are at once commercial products of our global popular culture and intriguing personal visions of the poster artists.

When I first came across an Italian poster from the early silent era, I was puzzled by the lack of a title, credits, or any other information regarding the film other than the producer's trademark. Nicoletta Pacini, Curator of the poster collection at Turin's Museo Nazionale del Cinema, pointed out to me that these pieces were meant to be used internationally—that, in a time when a film needed nothing but a new set of intertitles to be exported, the distributors in each country would paste a strip of paper over the poster imprinted with the title in the local language.

Vestiges of this early practice survived in Italian poster design long after its origins were forgotten. Though titles and the names of principal cast members had begun to appear on Italian posters by the 1920s, an unwritten law against excessive verbiage remained in effect. While American film posters, after a similarly language-shy beginning, quickly took advantage of slogans, captions, and taglines—"A Sun Play of the Ages!" read the posters for D. W. Griffith's 1916 silent film *Intolerance*—such elements seldom appear on Italian posters. In those rare cases when they do (as on the Italian poster for the 1949 film *La Fonte meravigliosa [The Fountainhead]*, where Gary Cooper warns, "Nessuno me la toglierà!"; see p. 77), they have usually been imported from the American advertising campaign ("No one will take her from me!" proclaims Cooper on the Hollywood poster).

In a sense, Italian film posters remained loyal to the "universal language" of silent film, offering images of emotions rather than the words to describe them. For Anselmo Ballester, who began designing posters in 1911, the silent aesthetic remained at the center of his work until the end of his career, in the 1960s. It was his job to evoke a film's genre, themes, atmosphere, and characters—and often, the ineffable allure of its stars as well—through visual means, without recourse to the press-agent's dictionary of adjectives. It was a job that Ballester, and many of his colleagues, performed brilliantly.

Yet, there is not a single Italian film poster represented in *The Modern Poster*, The Museum of Modern Art's seminal 1988 survey of its poster collection. And, indeed, the work of Ballester, Martinati, and Capitani would seem out of place alongside the modern, highly innovative

Anselmo Ballester
Detail of **CERCATE QUELL' UOMO (KEY WITNESS)**
See p. 11

9

design work for the cinema of Josef Fenneker (see p. 83), Kurt Wenzel, Jan Tschichold, and Schulz-Neudamm (whose chilling image for Fritz Lang's *Metropolis* is one of the world's most sought-after posters) in Germany, or that of Aleksandr Rodchenko and the Stenberg Brothers in the USSR. Although leading Italian designers such as the Art Nouveau master Leopoldo Metlicovitz and the Futurist Enrico Prampolini created occasional work for films, the field was far removed from the avant-garde. Instead, its dominant practitioners drew largely, if not exclusively, on the techniques of nineteenth-century academicism, a visual vocabulary that the public had learned to read and respect. The commercial poster means not to startle, but seduce, and the Italians were masters of the art of aligning sensual contours, beckoning perspectives, and ravishing colors into images that both soothed and suggested, planting a seed of desire that—theoretically, at least—would later blossom into the purchase of a ticket.

Still, long after the opportunity to buy tickets has passed, and long after many of the films illustrated in these pages have been forgotten and in some cases lost, these images retain their appeal. The best of them seem to speak directly to our primal movie-going instincts, conjuring visions of romance, mystery, and adventure that transcend the movie at hand.

Both films and film posters are products of late-nineteenth-century technology. As Thomas Edison and W. K. L. Dickson, in America, were perfecting the Kinetoscope in the late 1880s (the machine, which allowed viewers to see moving pictures through a peephole, was patented in 1891), so Jules Chéret, working in France, was perfecting the lithograph as a means of mass reproduction of brightly colored images, radically different from the woodcut and copperplate engraving methods that had previously been used.

Lithography, invented by the German printer Aloys Senefelder in 1796, was a cumbersome and expensive process based on the mutual antipathy of oil and water. Illustrations were drawn directly on limestone blocks with a grease crayon. The blocks were then moistened with water, which was absorbed by the stone but repelled by the oiled areas. When an oily ink was rolled over the entire block, it would adhere only to the drawing. The print would then be made by pressing a sheet of paper against the block.

Soon attempts were made to reproduce images in color using more than one block, and by the mid-nineteenth century a number of books—including John James Audubon's *The Birds of America*—had been illustrated in this manner. It was left to Chéret, however, to find a way of adapting this process to the large format of public posters, using three stones, inked in red, yellow, and blue and held in perfect registration, to produce a full spectrum of color in different degrees of saturation. Cheret's method allowed him to produce several thousand posters in a single day.

If Chéret had not been such a gifted designer himself, with a delicate color sense and a fine, light line, the medium might not have caught on as it did. But Chéret's cheerful, seductive creations attracted the interest of French artists like Henri de Toulouse-Lautrec, Pierre Bonnard, and Édouard Manet, who began producing advertising posters for theatrical performances, art exhibitions, journals, and the like. With the emergence of the Czech designer Alphonse Mucha, whose dreamy, languorous images of feminine beauty were used to promote everything from cigarette-rolling paper to bicycles, the lithographic poster became central to the design movement known as Art Nouveau.

Both Chéret and Mucha produced early film posters—Chéret for the painstakingly hand-drawn animated cartoons of Emile Reynaud, shown at the Musée Grevin in Paris from 1892 to 1900, Mucha for an educational society, La Société populaire des beaux-arts, founded in 1897 with the noble intention of using cinema to bring images of great art to the common man. The Art Nouveau influence remained strong as the first commercial film posters emerged, produced by companies such as Gaumont in France and Itala Film in Italy.

Gradually, films grew beyond their origins as ten- or twenty-minute comedies and melodramas, and by 1912 the first feature-length films, of sixty minutes or more, were beginning to emerge. In 1913 Giovanni Pastrone directed *Cabiria,* an adventure film set in Imperial Rome that became Italy's first epic. To add prestige to his two-and-one-half-hour film, Pastrone recruited the poet and novelist Gabriele D'Annunzio to write the intertitles and commissioned the Art Nouveau master Leopoldo Metlicovitz to create an eye-grabbing poster (p. 38), depicting the young heroine about to be thrown into a sacrificial fire. The image remains powerful today.

Around this time, a precocious teenager named Anselmo Ballester was creating his first posters for the cinema.

Anselmo Ballester
CERCATE QUELL'UOMO

KEY WITNESS
Tempera on illustration
board, 25 x 16"
(63.5 x 40.6 cm)
Original design for the 1947
American film directed by
David Ross Lederman

The great majority of Ballester's
original designs were donated
to the University of Bologna
by the artist's two daughters.
This is a rare example of
Ballester's work in a private
collection, and it reveals the
precise, minutely detailed
brushwork that allowed a
25-by-16-inch drawing to be
enlarged to 78-by-55. Type,
identifying the cast and filmmaker, would be added later
in the production process.
The movie in question is an
overlooked film noir by
B-movie veteran Lederman.
John Beal played the hapless
hero who awakes after a wild
party to find he has a dead
woman on his hands.

Born in Rome in 1897, son of the Spanish painter and graphic artist Federico Ballester, he studied painting and figure drawing at the Accademia di Belle Arti and the Scuola del Nudo in Rome and is said to have created his first sketches for film posters in 1911. While the majority of the era's graphic artists continued to work in a variety of genres, Ballester quickly came to specialize in film posters, and by 1914 the outlines of his highly personal style had been set, as had his distinctive signature, with a lowercase "a" nestled inside a capital "B." Ballester learned the technique of lithography from his father, and in his early years personally transferred his sketches to the lithographic stones.

In his book *Cinema del Carta: 50 anni de manifesti cinematografici* (1984), Michele Dell'Anno quotes from Ballester's diary: "To become a creator of film posters, it is, of course, necessary to have some of the innate qualities of a painter—to know how to set a pose, to have some skill at drawing, to have a sense of color, to possess some imagination and an ability to appreciate beauty. In your childhood, and continuing through your whole life, you must learn to fill your eyes and your soul with the marvelous nature of things and with the way the great painters have passed them on. And it is necessary to study passionately, to always draw and paint everything from the truth. Then you can let your imagination run free. Whether you are creating a work of art, or a more humble advertising poster, you must be able to attract the interest of the public, to satisfy both the most refined people and the roughest, who are the majority." In his work, Ballester practiced what he preached. He remained active until the early 1960s and died in 1974.

Also working in the Ballester shop in the early teens was Luigi Martinati, a young artist who had studied at the Accademia di Belle Arti in Florence and moved to Rome in 1911. He entered the world of advertising as an apprentice to Federico Ballester, whose designs he transferred to the lithographic stones. At first a technician more than a creator, Martinati became the manager of IGAP agency in Rome, and by 1920 was turning out dramatic, if not terribly polished, designs for films such as *I Rettili della miniera (The Reptiles of the Mine)*. Martinati did not really hit his stride until the early 1930s, when he began creating posters for Warner Brothers (these include *Mystery of the Wax Museum* and *Easy Money)*. He continued to work principally for Warner Brothers through the 1950s. He died in 1984.

Martinati's main contribution to the genre—and it remained his trademark to the end of his career—was the use of a large portrait of the star as the central element of the composition, surrounded by smaller scenic vignettes arranged in imaginatively unreal perspectives (see *Il Terrore dell'ovest [The Oklahoma Kid]* on p. 61). While the central portrait attracted the eye of the passerby, Martinati believed, the details captured it, drawing the potential spectator into the atmosphere and plotline of the film.

The third of the great *cartellonisti* was Alfredo Capitani, born in Ciampino in 1895. After studying at the English Academy in Rome, he began working as a scenic designer for the theater and soon moved into creating decors for films. He met Martinati in 1926 and together they formed an agency called MARALCA (an amalgam of their last names). Capitani continued to design decors as well as advertising posters for a variety of clients. He came to film posters in the late 1930s, when he accepted a commission for a Greta Garbo film from MGM that Martinati was too busy to execute. He, too, continued to work through the 1950s and died in Rome in 1985.

In 1945 Martinati and Capitani invited Ballester to join their agency, MARALCA. The new company was called BCM (for Ballester-Capitani-Martinati), and it effectively dominated film-poster production for the following two decades. Though the trio remained the stars of their profession, many other designers also made names for themselves, including Averardo Ciriello (b. 1918), Ercole Brini (1913–1989), Giuliano Nistri (b. 1923), Sandro Simeoni (b. 1928), Angelo Cesselon (b. 1922), and several others whose work is represented in this volume.

Introduced in Italy in 1940, but not in wide use until after the war, offset printing came to replace the cumbersome lithographic process. Based on a photographic reproduction of a painting, it more accurately reproduced the color and brushwork of the artist, but yielded a less-tactile, less-saturated image. For Ballester, the most painterly of the poster designers, offset printing was a boon; others, however, found their style much diminished with the offset process, and by the late 1950s the film-poster business was thinning out. There was no longer much reason to commission original illustrations when photographs could be reproduced directly on large posters, and by the 1960s, when the Italian New Wave broke with the great films of Federico Fellini, Luchino Visconti, Michelangelo

Antonioni, and other modern-minded directors, the photomontage had come to replace the painting as the basis of film promotion. Photography looked contemporary and cost little; the meticulous styles of Ballester, Capitani, and Martinati had come to seem old-fashioned and pointlessly expensive.

Today, however, it is the painterly work that has come to capture the hearts of collectors. Original Italian posters, even those created as late as 1960, remain quite rare in relation to their American and French counterparts. Even at the height of the poster's popularity, in the early 1950s, a typical print run would consist only of 2,000 copies of the large *quattro foglio* (four sheet) format (approximately 78-by-55 inches) and 3,000 copies of the smaller *due foglio* (two sheet) format (55-by-39 inches). A third format, called the *locandina* (27½-by-13 inches), was produced in larger quantities on thin paper, and was used for display in store windows. (Close observers of the posters reproduced here will be able to see the tiny tax stamps, in two- or three-lire denominations, that were affixed to posters as proof that the appropriate municipal fees had been paid.)

It was standard practice to create a different design for each of the three formats, and even low-budget movies, such as the *Jungle Jim* films produced by Columbia Pictures in the 1950s, were issued with a full range of poster art. And when older films were reissued in Italy—a far more frequent practice in the pre-television past than it is today—they were generally accompanied by new poster designs. However voluminous, this material was considered completely ephemeral, and much of it was destroyed by theater owners after the run of the film was over. Unlike the popular American one-sheet poster format (41-by-27 inches), even the smaller Italian *due foglio* size was too large to be easily displayed in a home or over a bar, a fact that may well have discouraged fans and professionals alike from salvaging used posters for their own enjoyment.

Poster collecting in Italy never enjoyed the vogue it did, and does, in France, where a market developed at the time of the first Chéret prints in the 1890s and has continued to expand to this day. That many Italian film posters have survived at all is a tribute to the tenacity of a few private collectors and museum archivists, who saw what others did not in these instantly disposable items.

Posters have long been the poor stepsisters of film archives, haphazardly acquired and often inadequately stored. Like film itself, posters must be preserved under cool, dry conditions if their original tonalities are to be preserved; most were also printed on cheap paper with a high acid content, which must be chemically removed before the paper literally devours itself. The great majority of posters reproduced in this book come from private collections in the United States, but there are also more than twenty examples from the Museo Nazionale del Cinema of Turin, Italy, home of the largest and best-maintained collection of antique film posters in Italy, if not the world. Under the directorship of Donata Pesenti Campagnoni and poster curator Nicoletta Pacini, the museum's huge collection—over 300,000 individual posters—is being preserved, catalogued, and continually expanded. Many of the museum's finest pieces are on display in the museum's new facilities, inaugurated in 2000, in the city's towering Mole Antonelliana.

This book does not pretend to be the definitive work on the subject of Italian film posters, but rather an eclectic mix of historically important titles and graphically inventive ones, with the emphasis always on the pictorial quality of the poster rather than on the critical importance of the film (indeed, many of the movies represented here have been utterly forgotten).

The sections are organized around genres, the better to give an idea of the basic iconographical elements employed in each form, and to avoid the monotony of a purely chronological approach, which would suggest a "rise and fall" of the form that I do not mean to convey. The functions once performed by these colorful, dramatic compositions are now fulfilled largely by the thirty-second television spots that are the basis of advertising campaigns in the United States and, increasingly, in Europe. It is enough for a contemporary poster simply to provide a reiteration of the typological design of the title, or "title treatment," used in all advertising, and, perhaps, provide a visual clue for spectators desperately trying to find the right theater in their twenty-five-screen local multiplex. We will not see the likes of these titanic posters again, but thanks to the efforts of collectors and curators, we will have these marvelous images to enjoy for centuries to come.

**B**eginning with the worldwide success of Giovanni Pastrone's 1913 silent film *Cabiria,* the historical fantasy—with muscular heroes, treacherous princesses, and lusty serving girls—became the genre most closely identified with Italy (see p. 38). This form grew out of more sober attempts to capture history on film, such as Pastrone's own *Giulio Cesare (Julius Caesar)* of 1909, or the French art film that promised such highbrow diversions as *L'Assassinat du duc de Guise (The Assassination of the Duke de Guise)* in 1908.

But as these early one- and two-reel efforts (ten to twenty minutes in length) grew to larger proportions—and the two-and-one-half hour *Cabiria* made a major contribution to that development—the subjects outgrew simple historical re-creations and became, instead, spectacular visions projected on a safely distant, highly stylized past. The historical fantasy genre became known in Italy and France as peplum, after the leather skirts worn by Roman centurions, and grew to include practically anything set in ancient times, preferably involving imperial legions, persecuted Christians, and natural disasters that could be counted on to wipe evil from the earth in the final reel.

After the Italian film industry lost its international foothold in the wake of World War I, large-scale historical films moved to Hollywood, where D. W. Griffith had been sufficiently impressed by *Cabiria* to imitate it with the Babylonian sequence of his film *Intolerance* (1916). By far the most famous American practitioner of peplum was

Cecil B. DeMille, who molded the genre with his personal brand of fundamentalist Christianity. DeMille is represented here by Anselmo Ballester's poster for the reissue of his 1927 film *The King of Kings,* a typically DeMillian blend of piousness and prurience (see p. 39).

Peplum lost their prominence in the 1930s, as the Italian cinema, under the influence of Benito Mussolini, turned to more contemporary visions of militarism and colonialism, themes that were also popular in American films as the thirties wore on and war again loomed. Not until the war ended was peplum revived, with the triumphant success of Alessandro Blasetti's 1948 film *Fabiola* (p. 17), a spectacular drama about the end of the Roman Empire (complete with Christians being fed to lions) that provided a fresh model for DeMille and led directly to the great boom in Italian "sword-and-sandals" films of the 1950s and 1960s (alas, few of these films have posters graphically interesting enough to reproduce). The "sword-and-sandals" films include such wildly enjoyable works as Vittorio Cottafavi's 1960 *Le Legioni di Cleopatra (Cleopatra's Legions)* and Mario Bava's 1961 *Ercole al centro della terra (Hercules in the Haunted World).*

Included in this section are posters from some much lighter works, such as Ernst Lubitsch's 1943 romantic fantasy *Heaven Can Wait* (p. 23) and the 1936 Shirley Temple vehicle *Captain January,* in which America's favorite moppet is depicted grimly and primly piloting her way out of the great Depression (pp. 18–19). And no survey of the adventure genre would be complete without Luigi Martinati's ravishing posters for *Captain Blood* (1935), which lent actor Errol Flynn's Australian insouciance a touch of Latin passion (pp. 36, 37).

Anselmo Ballester. Detail of **I RIBELLI DELL'ISOLA (SAVAGE MUTINY).** See also p. 24

FANTASY & ADVENTURE

Anselmo Ballester
UNTITLED (IN VECCHIE MEMBRA PIZZICOR D'AMORE [?])
Lithograph, 39⅜ × 27½"
(100 × 70 cm)

Like many early Italian posters, this attractive fantasy image carries no title or date (banners with the title in the local language would be pasted across the poster as the film traveled around Europe and the United States). If the attribution is correct (the title translates as *In Old Limbs, The Stirrings of Love*), the poster dates from 1915, which would make it one of the earliest known works by Ballester. He would then have been eighteen years old.

Tito Corbella
FABIOLA
Offset, 6'6¾" x 55⅛"
(200 x 140 cm)
1949 poster for the 1948
Italian film directed by
Alessandro Blasetti
Collection Museo Nazionale
del Cinema, Turin

Blasetti's 1948 epic was among
the first postwar Italian films
to return to the tradition of
the Italian silent cinema, and is
often regarded as the film that
launched the "sword and
sandals" craze of the 1950s
and 1960s. *Fabiola* was
released in the United States
by Joseph E. Levine, who ten
years later scored a major hit
with his English-dubbed
release of Pietro Francisci's
Hercules. Corbella's busy but
beguiling poster promises an
infinity of pleasures for the
war-weary spectator.

Anselmo Ballester
CAPITAN GENNAIO

CAPTAIN JANUARY
Lithograph, 6' × 6'6"
(182.8 × 198.1 cm)
Undated poster for the 1936
American film directed by
David Butler

One of Ballester's most
imposing posters, this gigantic
stone lithograph—six feet
high and over six feet wide—
presents a definitive image of
Shirley Temple, the immensely
popular child actress (eight
years old at the time of this
film's making) who is credited
with keeping Americans
smiling during the Great
Depression. Though based
on a studio-portrait still,
Ballester's interpretation plays
down the actress's aggressive
cuteness in favor of her
strong-jawed determination.
The brilliantly colored Deco
background evokes the travel
posters of the period.

Anselmo Ballester

IL FIGLIO DI CAROLINE CHÉRIE

LE FILS DE CAROLINE CHÉRIE

CAROLINE AND THE REBELS

Offset, 55 ⅛ × 39 ⅜"
(140 × 100 cm)
1959 poster for the 1955
French film directed by
Jean Devaivre

Brigitte Bardot was actually
rather far down in the cast of
this lurid French historical
drama, part of a series of
"bodice-rippers" that began
with a 1950 vehicle for
actress Martine Carol entitled
Caroline Chérie. By the time
Devaivre's film reached Italy
four years later, Bardot had
become enough of a star to
leap to headline billing.

Anselmo Ballester
LA STREGA DEL RODANO

LE JUGEMENT DE DIEU
Offset, 6'6¾" × 55⅛"
(200 × 140 cm)
1951 poster for the 1949
French film directed by
Raymond Bernard

Bernard, a veteran of the
French silent cinema (*Le
Miracle des loups* [*The Miracle
of the Wolves*], 1924; *Le Joueur
d'echecs* [*The Chess Player*],
1927) and the maker of an
excellent *Les Misérables*
(1933), directed this film on
location in Bavaria. Ballester
neatly balances the horror
elements of the foreground
with the fantasy components
of the background.

Anonymous
HEAVEN CAN WAIT
Offset, 41 × 27"
(119.4 × 53.3 cm)
Poster for the 1943 American
film directed by Ernst Lubitsch

An uncredited American
designer for 20th Century-
Fox created this delightful
image for Lubitsch's romantic
epic, about an aging roué
(loosely based on Lubitsch's
grandfather and played by Don
Ameche) who is called upon
by the Devil to justify a lifetime
of amorous indiscretions.

Anselmo Ballester
IL CIELO PUÒ ATTENDERE

HEAVEN CAN WAIT
Offset, 55 ⅛ × 39 ⅜"
(140 × 100 cm)
1948 poster for the 1943
American film directed by
Ernst Lubitsch

The artist creates an elegant,
romantic variation on the
cartoonish poster created for
the American release of this
late masterwork by Lubitsch
(opposite). The poster depicts
a radiant Gene Tierney, who
played a sort of eternal feminine to the eternal rogue
played by Don Ameche.

Anselmo Ballester
I RIBELLI DELL'ISOLA

SAVAGE MUTINY
Offset, 55 ⅛ × 39 ⅜"
(140 × 100 cm)
1954 poster for the 1953
American film directed by
Spencer Gordon Bennet

A fun pulp image by Ballester
for one of producer Sam
Katzman's Jungle Jim series
adventures. This one finds
some pesky savages rebelling
because, oddly enough, they
don't want their island to be
used for nuclear testing.

Anselmo Ballester
I RIBELLI DELL'ISOLA

SAVAGE MUTINY
Offset, 55 ⅛ × 39 ⅜"
(140 × 100 cm)
Poster for the 1953 American
film directed by Spencer
Gordon Bennet

Even low-budget B pictures
like Sam Katzman's Jungle
Jim series (starring Johnny
Weissmuller, who had become
a little too beefy for the loin-
cloth he wore in the earlier
Tarzan films) could merit two
spectacular designs. In this
sister to the image opposite,
there is less emphasis on jungle life and more on the film's
nuclear theme, evident in the
background.

Anselmo Ballester
EROI DI MILLE LEGGENDE

THIEF OF DAMASCUS
Offset, 55⅛ × 39⅜"
(140 × 100 cm)
1953 poster for the 1952
American film directed by
Will Jason

Ballester essentially ignores
the film he is promoting—a
Columbia Pictures costume
programmer from the inde-
fatigable *schlockmeister* producer Sam Katzman. Why
should the artist even bother
to show the actor Paul
Henreid when a magic carpet
charged with such alluring
companions was available?

Anselmo Ballester
L'UOMO DEL NIGER

L'HOMME DU NIGER
Lithograph, 38 × 28"
(96.5 × 71.1 cm)
Undated poster for the 1940
French film directed by
Jacques de Baroncelli

How many of Old Europe's
imperialist fantasies can you
count in this richly colored
stone lithograph (hint: the
American title was *Forbidden
Love*)?

Alfredo Capitani
L'ISOLA DEI DISPERATI

THE CAMP ON BLOOD ISLAND
Offset, 27½ × 13"
(70 × 33 cm)
Undated poster for the
1958 British film directed
by Val Guest

Capitani's poster for this
prison-camp movie carries
perverse overtones of
Christian iconography.

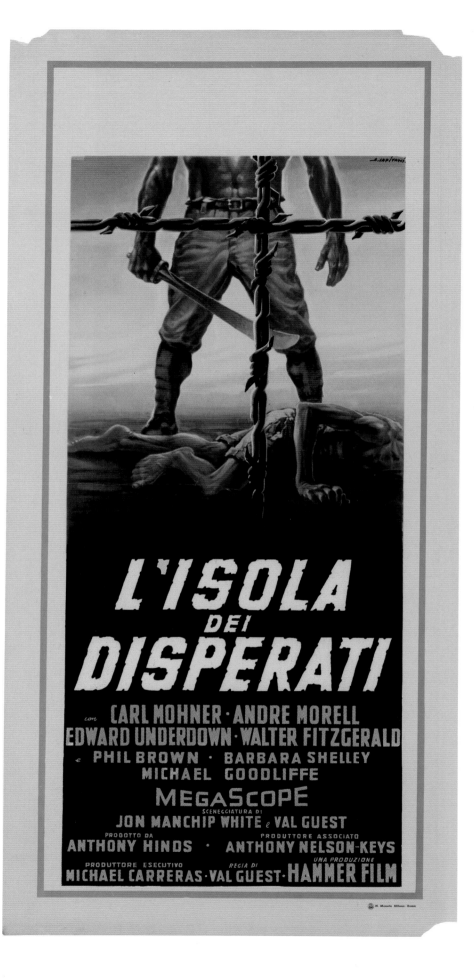

Anselmo Ballester
KASIM, FURIA DELL'INDIA

THE BANDIT OF ZHOBE
Offset, 27½ × 13"
(70 × 33 cm)
Undated poster for the
1959 British film directed by
John Gilling

The unlikely casting of Victor
Mature as an Indian bandit in
rebellion against the British
Raj becomes an occasion for
Ballester to conjure a swirling
cloud of horsemen.

Anselmo Ballester
INVASIONE U.S.A.

INVASION USA
Offset, 55 ⅛ × 39 ⅜"
(140 × 100 cm)
1956 poster for the 1952
American film directed by
Alfred E. Green

This bizarre, low-budget film,
made during the height of the
cold war, consists largely of
newsreel footage from World
War II, rearranged, with a
series of hysterical voiceovers,
into an extremely unconvincing
account of a Soviet invasion of
America, as experienced by six
people hanging out in a New
York bar. Ballester's fantastically
lurid illustration makes no
direct reference to the film,
but seems spun instead
from memories of the anti-
American propaganda posters
turned out by Gino Boccasile
and Dante Coscia as the US
Army made its way through
Italy at the end of the war.

Luigi Martinati
L'ARCIPELAGO IN FIAMME

AIR FORCE

Offset, 55 ⅛ × 39 ⅜"
(140 × 100 cm)
1949 poster for the 1943
American film directed by
Howard Hawks

Hawks's World War II propaganda film, featuring the definitive ethnically balanced bomber crew, was screened in Italy after the armistice. The compact spatial composition is typical of Martinati's stylized approach.

Luigi Martinati
LA SQUADRIGLIA LAFAYETTE

LAFAYETTE ESCADRILLE
Offset, 27 ½ × 13"
(70 × 33 cm)
Undated poster for the 1958
American film directed by
William Wellman

Martinati adapted the contrasting two-panel format he often used for this late, semi-autobiographical film by Wellman, which is loosely based on the director's own experiences flying a fighter plane in World War I. Included in the cast, in minor roles, were David Janssen, Tom Laughlin, and a young Clint Eastwood.

Luigi Martinati
IL PRINCIPE DI SCOZIA

THE MASTER OF BALLANTRAE
Offset, 55 1/8 x 39 3/8"
(140 x 100 cm)
Poster for the 1953
American film directed by
William Keighley

Martinati, who created the
most memorable poster
images of Errol Flynn in his
prime, remained loyal to the
star as the end of his swashbuckling career approached.
This 1953 poster, created six
years before Flynn's death,
finds the actor clearly aged
and in an unusually vulnerable
position, threatened by a
younger man.

Anonymous
MACISTE IN VACANZA
Letterpress, 37 ^{11}/$_{16}$ × 25 ^{13}/$_{16}$"
(95.7 × 65.6 cm)
Poster for the 1921 Italian film
directed by Romano Luigi
Borgnetto
Collection Museo Nazionale
del Cinema, Turin

An attractive example of the
letterpress posters that were
produced for individual cinemas during the silent-film
period. This film is one of the
many featuring Maciste, the
strongman hero who became
a popular favorite in Giovanni
Pastrone's 1913 film *Cabiria*
(p. 38). Here Maciste is taking
a well-deserved vacation.

Luigi Martinati
CAPTAIN BLOOD
Offset, 55⅛ × 39⅜"
(140 × 100 cm)
1948 poster for the 1935
American film directed by
Michael Curtiz
Collection Museo Nazionale
del Cinema, Turin

Martinati's shadowy portrait
of Errol Flynn, for a rerelease
of one of his most famous
films, nicely evokes the
chiaroscuro style of director
Curtiz.

Luigi Martinati
CAPTAIN BLOOD
Offset, 27 ½ × 13"
(70 × 33 cm)
1948 poster for the 1935
American film directed by
Michael Curtiz
Collection Museo Nazionale
del Cinema, Turin

This smaller-format poster for
the 1948 reissue of *Captain
Blood* reunites Errol Flynn
with his costar, Olivia de
Havilland. With Flynn's thrust-
ing sword and the blood-red
background, Martinati deftly
suggests the swashbuckling
thrills in store for the audience.

Leopoldo Metlicovitz
CABIRIA
Lithograph, 6'9½" × 56⅞"
(207 × 144.5 cm)
Poster for the 1913 Italian film
directed by Giovanni Pastrone
Collection Museo Nazionale
del Cinema, Turin

The Art Nouveau master
Metlicovitz created this
astounding image for the
first Italian superproduction,
a highly influential film that
inspired D. W. Griffith to tackle
The Birth of a Nation (1914)
and *Intolerance* (1916). The
Babylonian sequences in the
latter film owe an obvious debt
to Pastrone's reconstructed
Rome. The poster depicts the
title character, a young girl
about to be sacrificed to the
pagan god Moloch but who is
instead rescued by the heroic
slave Maciste, who became
one of the most enduringly
popular characters in Italian
cinema (see p. 35), inspiring
sequels up to the 1960s.

Anselmo Ballester
IL RE DEI RE

THE KING OF KINGS
Offset, 6'6¾" × 55⅛"
(200 × 140 cm)
1950 poster for the 1927
American film directed by
Cecil B. DeMille
Collection Museo Nazionale
del Cinema, Turin

Ballester seems to have
momentarily confused Christ
with Mussolini in this over-
powering image, designed
for a sonorized reissue of
DeMille's silent Biblical epic.

Giulio Ferrari
MADEMOISELLE DOCTEUR
SALONIQUE, NID D'ESPIONS
Lithograph, 6'6¾" × 55⅛"
(200 × 140 cm)
Poster for the 1937 French
film directed by G. W. Pabst
Collection Museo Nazionale
del Cinema, Turin

A specialist in travel posters,
Ferrari also created a few film
posters, including this striking
image for a French spy thriller
directed by visiting filmmaker
Pabst. The film was released in
the United States in 1948 as
Street of Shadows.

Filippo Omegna
CUORE DI MAMMA
Lithograph, 56⅛ × 39¾"
(142.5 × 101 cm)
Poster for the 1909 Italian
film directed by Luigi Maggi
Collection Museo Nazionale
del Cinema, Turin

Omegna, a well-known
Piedmontese illustrator, created
several posters for Ambrosio
Film, a Turin-based company
owned by his brother
Roberto. This wonderfully las-
civious winged Satan is advertising, oddly enough, a silent
film titled *Mamma's Heart*.

Traditionally considered the most problematic genre to export because of the difficulty in dubbing songs, the musical tended to be a domestic product. In Italy that product was often colored by the operatic tradition, either in literal adaptations to the screen like director Flavio Calzavara's *Rigoletto* (1954) or with pop modifications such as director Mario Mattoli's *La Donna è mobile* (1942), a vehicle for the popular tenor Ferruccio Tagliavini (p. 45). Other operas brought to the screen during this period included *Madama Butterfly* (1955), co-produced by Italy and Japan, *Il Trovatore* (1949), directed by Carmine Gallone with Gianna Pederzini, and *Figaro, il barbiere di seviglia* (*The Barber of Seville*; 1955), directed by Camillo Mastrocinque and starring Tito Gobbi.

Many of the major American musicals of the 1930s and 1940s were not released in Italy until after the war, and the posters for them are disappointingly bland. MGM, the major producer of Hollywood musicals in the 1950s, had the most erratic poster-art department in Italy. Few of the works dating from that era are worth reproducing.

More popular in Italy were the biographies of classical composers that Hollywood issued in the 1940s and 1950s. Director Charles Vidor's free-form interpretation of the romance of Frédéric Chopin (played by Cornel Wilde) and George Sand (played by Merle Oberon), included here as *L'Eterna armonia (A Song to Remember;* 1945), is one of many films that found composers dashing off ditties between passionate embraces (such as the one depicted by artist Anselmo Ballester, rising like a spectral vision from Chopin's keyboard; see p. 52).

Ballester's dense style did not lend itself well to the message of lightness and grace that a musical must convey (see his two posters for *Jolson Sings Again* [pp. 46, 47], admittedly as much a melodrama as it is a musical). Rather, this was ripe territory for the artist Ercole Brini, whose graceful, elegant, watercolor compositions can be seen here for two of the most graceful and elegant musicals of the 1950s, Jean Renoir's *French Cancan* and Stanley Donen's *Funny Face* (see pp. 50, 51).

Original Italian musicals from the decade seem to be few and far between. The pop star Luciano Tajoli appeared in a number of 1950s films with titles like *Cantando sotto le stele (Singing Under the Stars), Il Cantante misterioso (The Mystery Singer),* and *Meravigliosa (Marvelous)* without leaving much of an impression on later generations. Marino Giro-lami, who directed several of Tajoli's vehicles, often inserted musical numbers into the many comedies he directed in the 1950s and 1960s, including *Serenate per 16 bionde (Serenade for 16 Blondes),* represented here by a colorful and atypically whimsical poster by Ballester (pp. 48, 49).

Anselmo Ballester. Detail of **NON C'È PASSIONE PIÙ GRANDE (JOLSON SINGS AGAIN).** See also p. 46

THE MUSICAL

Anselmo Ballester
RIGOLETTO
Offset, 6'6¾" × 55⅛"
(200 × 140 cm)
Poster for the 1954 Italian film
directed by Flavio Calzavara

Baritone Tito Gobbi lent his
singing voice, but not his
form, to this 1954 *Rigoletto*,
in which the embittered dwarf
is played on screen by Aldo
Silvani.

Anselmo Ballester
LA DONNA È MOBILE
Lithograph, 27 × 20"
(68.6 × 50.8 cm)
Poster for the 1942 Italian film
directed by Mario Mattoli

The film is an escapist
wartime musical starring the
tenor Ferruccio Tagliavini. Due
to shortages of ink and paper
during the war, Ballester had
to work with a limited lithographic palette and a smaller
format.

Anselmo Ballester
**NON C'È PASSIONE
PIÙ GRANDE**

JOLSON SINGS AGAIN
Offset, 27½ × 13"
(70 × 33 cm)
1950 poster for the 1949
American film directed by
Henry Levin

A touch of Pop surrealism
enlivens Ballester's design for
this small-format image.

Anselmo Ballester
**NON C'È PASSIONE
PIÙ GRANDE**

JOLSON SINGS AGAIN
Offset, 55 ⅛ × 39 ⅜"
(140 × 100 cm)
1950 poster for the 1949
American film directed by
Henry Levin

Columbia Pictures' sequel to
the 1946 film *The Jolson Story*,
starring the soon-to-be-black-
listed actor Larry Parks.
Ballester's two-sheet, medium-
format poster features an
entirely different design from
the smaller one (opposite).

Anselmo Ballester
SERENATE PER 16 BIONDE
Offset, 55 ⅛ × 39 ⅜"
(140 × 100 cm)
1956 poster for the
Italian film directed by
Marino Girolami

This musical fluff about a
group of French schoolgirls
stranded in a ruined castle
was directed by Girolami,
one of the most proficient
manufacturers of such low-
brow entertainment in the
1950s and 1960s. Claudio
Villa was a popular Neapolitan
singer; he is supported here
by the comedy team of
Riccardo Billi and Mario Riva.
Ballester produced an unusually whimsical image for this
romp, conceived in the bright
style of a comic book.

Ercole Brini
FRENCH CANCAN
Offset, 6'6¾" × 55⅛"
(200 × 140 cm)
Poster for the 1955
French film by Jean Renoir

Brini's light, luminous watercolor style finds a perfect
subject in Renoir's tribute to
the Paris of his father,
Pierre-Auguste Renoir.

Ercole Brini
CENERENTOLA A PARIGI

FUNNY FACE
Offset, 55 ⅛ × 39 ⅜"
(140 × 100 cm)
Poster for the 1957 American
film directed by Stanley Donen

A few light strokes of watercolor are enough for Brini to
express the timeless appeal
and elegance of Audrey
Hepburn. The film's formida-
ble costar, Fred Astaire, and
content—a musical set in the
French fashion world—appear
not to have interested the
artist at all.

Anselmo Ballester
L'ETERNA ARMONIA

A SONG TO REMEMBER
Offset, 27 ½ × 13"
(70 × 33 cm)
Undated poster for the 1945
American film directed by
Charles Vidor

Ballester created a swooningly
romantic image for Vidor's
"bodice-ripping" biography of
Frédéric Chopin (played by
Cornel Wilde). Of the three
designs Ballester created for
the film, this small-format
design is the most haunting.

Anselmo Ballester
3 DESIDERI

THREE WISHES
Lithograph, 39⅜ × 27½"
(100 × 70 cm)
1937 poster for the
Italian film directed by
Giorgio Ferroni

Filmed in both Italian- and
Dutch-language versions (the
Dutch film was directed by
Kurt Gerron, who is credited
on the poster for the Italian
version as well), this musical
fantasy places its two young
leads in a fairytale context:
she (Luisa Ferida) dreams of
becoming a radio singer; he
(Antonio Centa) hopes to
invent a new kind of radio.
They are each granted three
wishes to realize their goals.
This solid Deco design by
Ballester emphasizes the text
treatment, which is quite
unusual for him.

Rightly considered the quintessential American genre, the Western also enjoyed a tremendous popularity in Europe. The first American Westerns touched off a craze for "le cow-boy" in turn-of-the-century Paris (and inspired the violent ritual of the "Apache dance" in the louche basement nightclubs of the capital). Not long after, German producers were bringing the works of their homegrown Western author, Karl May, to the screen. But the Italian Western was not born until the late 1950s.

Legend has it that the "spaghetti Western" was born in 1959, when directors-to-be Sergio Leone and Sergio Corbucci were working as assistants on Mario Bonnard's *The Last Days of Pompeii*, an epic being filmed on location in Spain. Corbucci pointed out to his friend and colleague Leone that the vast, desolate plains, and the availability of highly trained horses, would make Spain a convenient double for the American Southwest. Leone agreed, but it was not until 1963, when Corbucci released his Spanish-filmed Western *Massacro al Grande Canyon* that Leone was moved to make a Western himself. The result was the 1964 film *A Fistful of Dollars* (represented here by a first-release poster that tries to pass the film off as American; p. 66). *A Fistful of Dollars* became an instant worldwide sensation.

The Italian poster artists clearly relished the opportunity to design for Westerns, with their rich iconography (boots and saddles and six-shooters) and wide-open landscapes—beautifully conveyed in work such as Anselmo Ballester's poster for the 1941 film *Texas* (which seems to include every visual element the genre had to provide; pp. 62, 63) or Luigi Martinati's *Along the Great Divide* (1951), with its desert that stretches to infinity (p. 59).

When the psychological Western came along in the 1950s, the Italian artists were ready as well. Ballester's two brooding images for Anthony Mann's brutal masterpiece *The Man from Laramie* (1955) communicate much of what was different about these films, which were made for adult audiences and were filled with a violence and bitterness that carried over from postwar film noir (pp. 64, 65). Martinati goes from the delicate pastel portraiture of *The Oklahoma Kid* (1939; p. 61) and *The San Francisco Story* (1952; p. 58) to the neurotic intensity of Arthur Penn's forthrightly Freudian *The Left-Handed Gun* (1958; p. 57),

in which he depicts Paul Newman's Billy the Kid as a sexually charged, borderline psychopath—a figure who heralds the amoral, anti-heroes of the spaghetti Westerns to follow.

The Left-Handed Gun was one of several late 1950s Westerns that suggested the genre was beginning to collapse. The romantic myth of the Western was subjected to furious revisionism, in accordance with the emerging ideologies of the 1960s. The outlaw was no longer an enemy of society but a rebel with a cause, engaged in sustained resistance against a social structure designed to eliminate his individuality. The sheriff was no longer a knightly figure, battling to transform a violent wilderness into a peaceful civilization, but an agent of social oppression, cracking down on heroic non-conformists. Native Americans, treated with ambivalence by the genre from its very beginnings (noble savages in many films; bloodthirsty villains in many others), became symbols of all native peoples oppressed by European and American colonialism.

Leone's Westerns, beginning with *Fistful* in 1964, were the extension and exaggeration of this tendency. His heroes were cynical and self-interested, distinguishable from his villains largely because of their greater sense of style. His establishment figures—assorted sheriffs, generals, bankers, and railroad tycoons—were monsters of greed, far less concerned with nation-building than with building their own bank accounts. The shadow of Vietnam begins to loom over films like *The Good, the Bad and the Ugly* (released in 1966), in which the Civil War is portrayed as an absurd, meaningless conflict—at best, a temporary breach in the social order that allows a few shrewd individuals to enrich themselves.

These attitudes were reflected, with even harsher variations, in the Italian Westerns of Leone's colleagues, Sergio Corbucci (*Il grande silenzio;* 1969) and Sergio Solima (*La Resa dei conti;* 1966), which incorporated Marxist politics into their over-the-top action. The Mexican Revolution of 1910, a popular subject during this period (as in Leone's *Duck You Sucker;* 1972) became a stand-in for the revolution then being dreamed about by many young Europeans and Americans.

As fascinating as these films are, however, they yielded very few posters of note. Most were crude, grisly illustrations of particularly violent moments; only one of the more elegant exceptions, from a late 1960s re-release of Leone's *The Good, the Bad, and the Ugly,* is included here (p. 67).

Anselmo Ballester. Detail of **L'UOMO DI LARAMIE (THE MAN FROM LARAMIE).**
See also p. 64

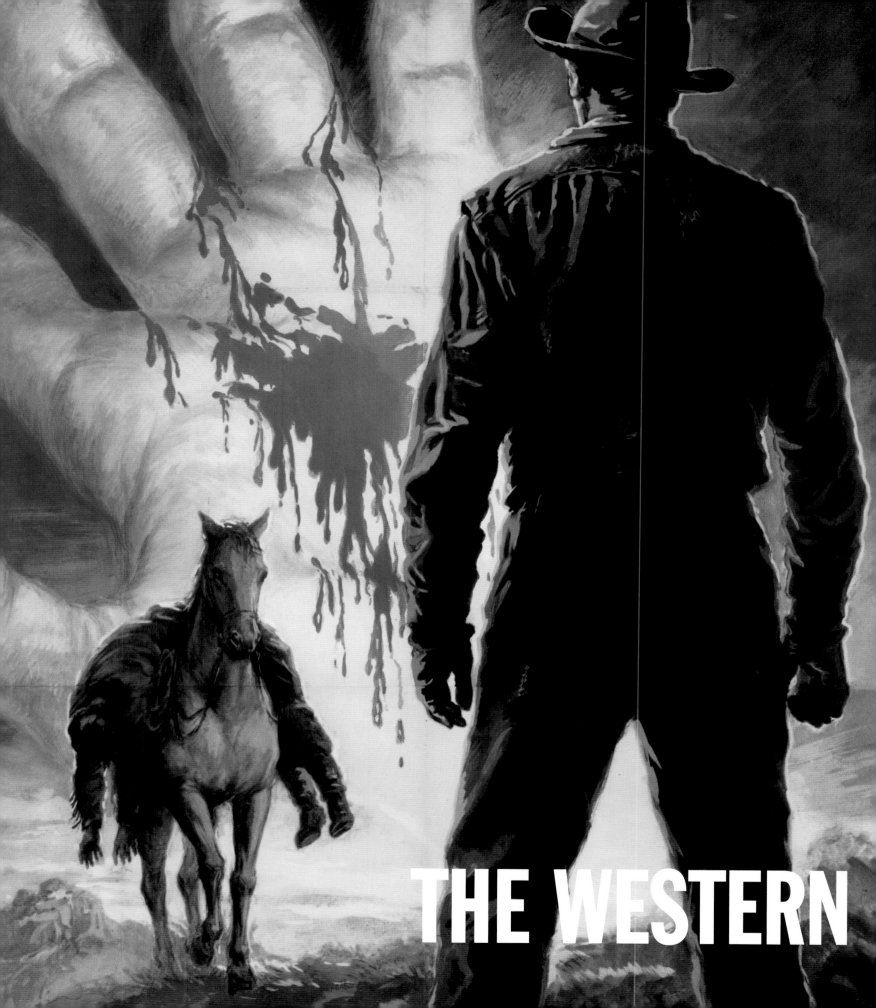

THE WESTERN

Anselmo Ballester
LA LEGGE CONTRO BILLY KID

THE LAW VS. BILLY THE KID

Offset, 55 ⅛ × 39 ⅜"
(140 × 100 cm)
1955 poster for the 1954
American film directed by
William Castle

A dynamic image for this
Columbia Pictures Western,
which was directed by Castle
before his celebrated run of
gimmick-laden horror films,
such as *House on Haunted Hill*
and *The Tingler* (both 1959).

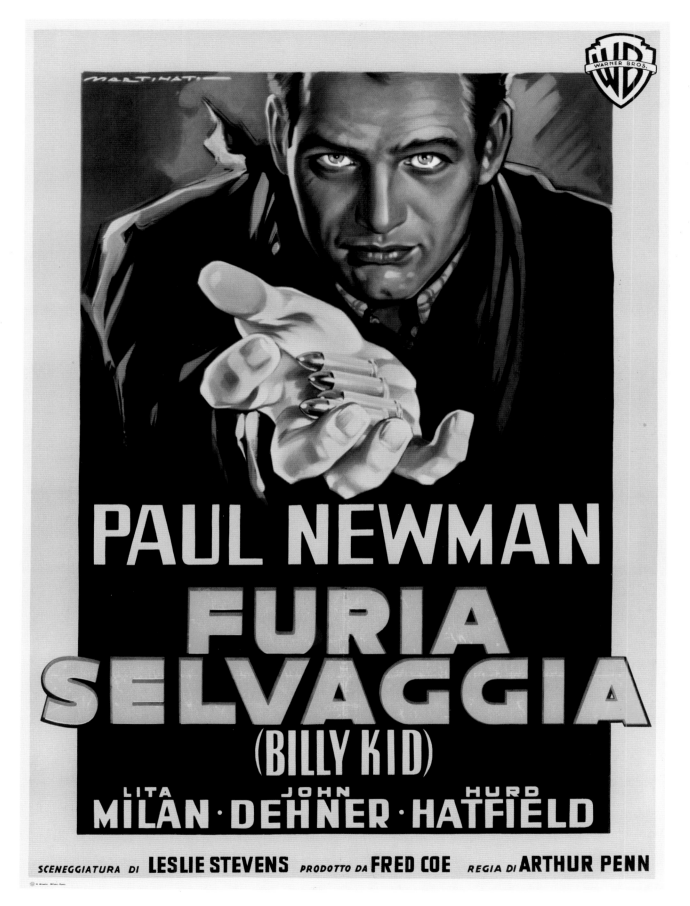

Luigi Martinati
FURIA SELVAGGIA

THE LEFT-HANDED GUN
Offset, 55⅛ × 39⅜"
(140 × 100 cm)
Undated poster for the 1958
American film directed by
Arthur Penn

Penn's pioneering anti-
Western occasions a wildly
dramatic image by Martinati,
one that suggests his posters
for the Hammer horror films
from England.

Luigi Martinati
LA PECCATRICE DI SAN FRANCISCO

THE SAN FRANCISCO STORY
Offset, 6'6¾" × 55⅛"
(200 × 140 cm)
Poster for the 1952 American
film directed by Robert Parrish

A magnificent portrait of
Yvonne De Carlo dominates
this extraordinarily beautiful
poster, made for an unfortunately overlooked Western by
Parrish.

Luigi Martinati
SABBIE ROSSE

ALONG THE GREAT DIVIDE
Offset, 6'6¾" × 55⅛"
(200 × 140 cm)
1952 poster for the 1951
American film directed by
Raoul Walsh

Among the Italian poster
artists, Martinati had the
most sure touch for illustrat-
ing Westerns, as evidenced by
this very expressive image for
Walsh's chase drama.

Anselmo Ballester
IL FORTE DELLE AMAZZONI

THE GUNS OF FORT PETTICOAT
Offset, 6'6¾" × 55⅛"
(200 × 140 cm)
Undated poster for the 1957
American film directed by
George Marshall

Ballester lets his imagination
run wild in this image for an
undistinguished Western from
the late 1950s, to the point of
repressing ostensible star
Audie Murphy in favor of its
all-female supporting cast—
women who must defend
themselves against marauding
Indians while their men are
away fighting the Civil War.

James
CAGNEY
Humphrey
BOGART
ROSEMARY LANE

IL TERRORE DELL'OVEST

Regia di LLOYD BACON

L'AIRONE · ROMA

Warner Bros.

WARNER BROS. WB

Luigi Martinati
IL TERRORE DELL'OVEST

THE OKLAHOMA KID
Offset, 55⅛ × 39⅜"
(140 × 100 cm)
Undated poster for the 1939
American film directed by
Lloyd Bacon

This very elegant image is
loosely based on American
poster art. The film was
Warner Brothers' 1939
attempt to transplant its
gangster stars James Cagney
and Humphrey Bogart into
the Western genre. This is
probably a 1950s reissue of
the film, by which time
Bogart's fame had grown to
equal Cagney's.

Claire **TREVOR**
Glenn **FORD**
William **HOLDEN**

TEXAS

REGIA:
GEORGE MARSHALL

Anselmo Ballester
TEXAS
Offset, 6'6¾" × 55⅛"
(200 × 140 cm)
1947 poster for the 1941
American film directed by
George Marshall

This very busy image suggests
a Brueghelian catalogue of the
Western. Is there any element
missing?

Anselmo Ballester
L'UOMO DI LARAMIE

THE MAN FROM LARAMIE
Offset, 6'6¾" × 55⅛"
(200 × 140 cm)
Undated poster for the 1955
American film directed by
Anthony Mann

Ballester drops the star portraiture he used on the smaller, two-sheet poster (opposite) for Mann's great revenge
Western in favor of a stark,
allegorical depiction of the
film's themes.

Anselmo Ballester
L'UOMO DI LARAMIE

THE MAN FROM LARAMIE
Offset, 55⅛ × 39⅜"
(140 × 100 cm)
Undated 1950s poster for the
1955 American film directed
by Anthony Mann

This medium-size poster,
designed by Ballester for
Mann's scathing revenge
Western, concentrates on
the relationship between the
stars, unlike the more stylized
large format (opposite).

Sandro Simeoni
PER UN PUGNO DI DOLLARI

A FISTFUL OF DOLLARS
Offset, 27½ × 13"
(70 × 33 cm)
Undated poster for the
1964 Italian film directed by
Sergio Leone

Considering the fact that this
was one of the most influential Westerns ever made,
Simeoni created a disappointingly generic poster. This first-
release image uses the
Anglicized pseudonyms adapted by the cast and crew: "Bob
Robertson" is director Sergio
Leone; "John Wells" is the
famous Italian actor Gian
Maria Volonte. These pseudonyms were an attempt to
pass the picture off to unsus-
pecting Italian audiences as an
American production.

Anonymous
IL BUONO, IL BRUTTO, IL CATTIVO

THE GOOD, THE BAD, AND THE UGLY
Offset, 27½ × 13"
(70 × 33 cm)
Undated poster for the
1966 Italian film directed by
Sergio Leone

After using photographic art
for the first release of the
most financially successful of
all "spaghetti Westerns," the
distributors reverted to illustration for this small-format
poster, probably made for the
1968 reissue of the film.

Anselmo Ballester
L'ALBERO DELLA VENDETTA

RIDE LONESOME
Offset, 55 ⅛ × 39 ⅜"
(140 × 100 cm)
Poster for the 1959
American film directed by
Budd Boetticher

Apparently working without benefit of having seen Boetticher's lean, elegant Western, Ballester turns it into a gothic nightmare with this striking, if almost completely irrelevant, image.

Anselmo Ballester
IL SUO ONORE GRIDAVA VENDETTA

GUN FURY
Offset, 27½ × 13"
(70 × 33 cm)
Undated poster for the 1953
American film directed by
Raoul Walsh

Ballester seems to be working
from pure imagination in creating this image for Walsh's
Technicolor Western, released
in 3-D in the United States.

Dismissed by many critics as "women's pictures," melodramas did not achieve respectability until the 1970s, when a new generation of viewers discovered the penetrating social commentary of Douglas Sirk, the transcendent romanticism of Frank Borzage, and the passionate spirituality of Leo McCarey. The recent critical success of the film *Far from Heaven* (2002), Todd Haynes's intelligent and politically pointed pastiche of Sirk's *All That Heaven Allows* (1955), may also help to return this unjustly neglected genre to prominence.

Inherited directly from the nineteenth-century stage, where melodrama (drama with music) had flourished as the middle-class answer to the aristocratic opera, the form appears very early on in films, and was something of an Italian specialty. The so-called diva films—represented here by a very early Anselmo Ballester poster for Francesca Bertini's *Ivonne* (pp. 92–93)—featured strong women defying social convention to get their man (and usually being suitably punished for it). With their grand, operatic gestures and kabuki-like makeup—rings of kohl around their eyes, for example—the divas were monsters of femininity but also role models in a rapidly changing society (Ballester's image of Bertini casually smoking a cigarette would have been shocking in its day).

Melodrama remained central to the Italian tradition through the 1930s and 1940s, as the swirling pastels of Ballester's 1935 poster for the shipboard romance *Aldebaran* attest (p. 74). Though *Aldebaran* has an adoles-cent innocence to it, there is no mistaking the physical passion of artist Luigi Martinati's studies for *The Fountain-head* (1949; p. 77) and *Force of Arms* (a war film, though the poster does its best to hide that fact; 1951; p. 95). Anger is, of course, as important a component of melo-drama as affection, and there is a tense undercurrent of violence in Ballester's images for *Spellbound* (1945; p. 72), *The Marrying Kind* (1952; p. 73), and the 1951 Italian film *Vendetta di zingara (The Gypsy Woman's Revenge;* p. 76). But for all the passionate embraces depicted in the following pages, perhaps the most erotically charged of these images is the two-panel set for Luchino Visconti's *Senso,* with Farley Granger and Alida Valli both looking out haughtily and provocatively from their own separate spaces (pp. 90, 91).

Star portraiture is also very important in the melo-drama genre, which depended so much on the identifica-tion of the audience with the suffering heroine. Ballester gives us an exceptional, tragic portrait of the comedienne Judy Holliday in his poster for *The Marrying Kind* (p. 73), as well as a magnetizing, head-on image of Anna Sten for *We Live Again* (1934; p. 89). But his favorite female subject was Rita Hayworth, whom he painted at least eight times in his capacity as house illustrator for Columbia Pictures. Ballester's Hayworth is an icon of joy and sensuality—head thrown back, red hair streaming, captured in a swirl of motion. For unknown reasons, Ballester was not assigned to Hayworth's biggest hit, the 1946 *Gilda.* In his place, Alfredo Capitani produced a very different Hayworth, a frozen figure in a skin-tight gown, her sexuality commodified into that of the 1940s pin-up girl (p. 100).

Anselmo Ballester. Detail of **LA NEMICA.** See also p. 96

MELODRAMA

Anselmo Ballester
IO TI SALVERÒ

SPELLBOUND
Offset, 6'6¾" × 55⅛"
(200 × 140 cm)
1954 poster for the 1945
American film directed by
Alfred Hitchcock

This classic Ballester poster
transforms Hitchcock's rather
chilly psychoanalytic thriller
into a passionate, erotic
melodrama.

Anselmo Ballester
VIVERE INSIEME

THE MARRYING KIND
Offset, 55 ⅛ × 39 ⅜"
(140 × 100 cm)
Poster for the 1952 American
film directed by George Cukor

Ballester emphasizes the
melodramatic elements in
Cukor's film (heavily influenced
by Italian neorealism) about
the-ups-and-downs of a work-
ing-class marriage.

Anselmo Ballester
ALDEBARAN
Lithograph, 6'6¾ × 55⅛"
(200 × 140 cm)
1935 poster for the
Italian film directed by
Alessandro Blasetti

Blasetti was the quasi-official
filmmaker of the Mussolini
regime (his work includes the
1935 *Le Vecchia guardia [The
Old Guard]*, a heroic tale of
the Black Shirts, and the 1940
celebration of pre-Renaissance
Italy, *La Corona di ferro [The
Iron Crown]*). But he also created a number of lighter,
more modestly scaled films.
One of the latter is this melodrama about a harbor man-
ager who endangers his career
to satisfy his wife's whim.
Ballester uses pastel tones for
this swirling, romantic image.

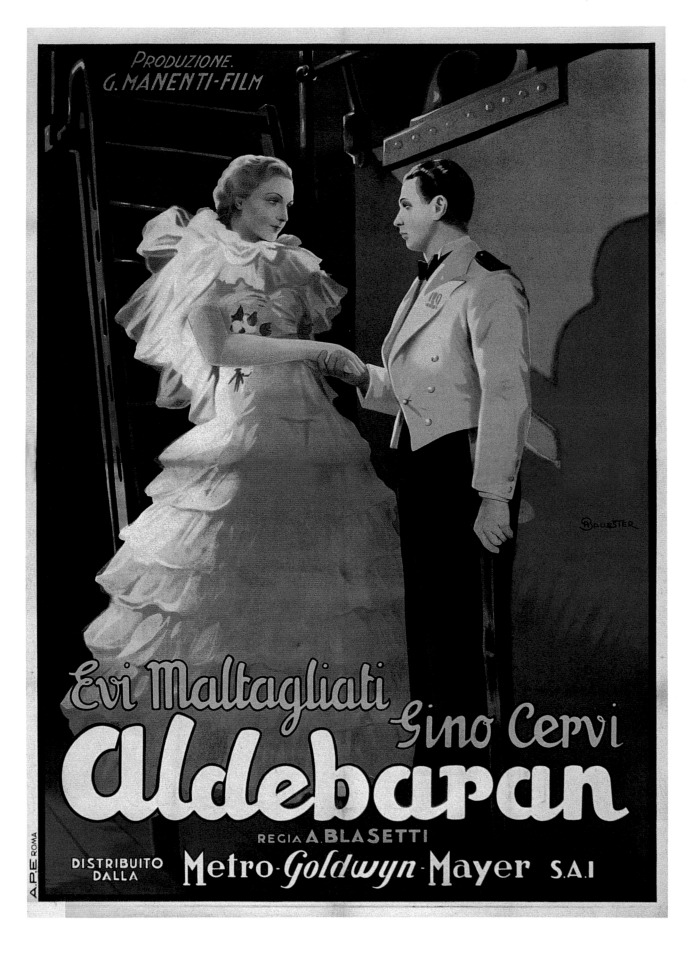

Anselmo Ballester
INCANTESIMO

THE EDDY DUCHIN STORY
Offset, 6'6¾" x 55⅛"
(200 x 140 cm)
1960 poster for the 1956
American film directed by
George Sidney

The artist experiments with
pen-and-ink and a watercolor
wash, creating a moody image
that differs from his usual
painterly style.

Anselmo Ballester
VENDETTA DI ZINGARA
Offset, 6'6¾" × 55⅛"
(200 × 140 cm)
Poster for the 1951 Italian film
directed by Aldo Molinari

A gloriously delirious composition for a little-known film
by the equally obscure Aldo
Molinari. The film was never
released abroad. Its title translates as *The Gypsy Woman's
Revenge*.

Luigi Martinati
LA FONTE MERAVIGLIOSA

THE FOUNTAINHEAD
Offset, 27 ½ x 13"
(70 x 33 cm)
Poster for the 1949 American
film directed by King Vidor

Starting with the same publicity
still used in the American press
campaign, Martinati refines
and reheats the imagery, creating an operatic moment of
willing/unwilling surrender.

Tito Corbella
SGOMENTO

THE RECKLESS MOMENT
Offset, 55 ⅛ x 39 ⅜"
(140 x 100 cm)
1950 poster for the 1949
American film directed by
Max Ophuls

Much of the particular genius
of Italian film poster design
can be seen by comparing
Corbella's graceful yet emotional design to the publicity
photographs from which he
was working (opposite).
Corbella effortlessly enhances
the sense of doom that faces
the unlikely couple of a mid-
dle-aged housewife and the
man who is blackmailing her.
The film itself was remade in
2001 and titled *The Deep End*.

Anselmo Ballester
IL FRUTTO DEL PECCATO

THE RESTLESS YEARS

Offset, 27½ × 13"
(70 × 33 cm)
Undated poster for the 1958
German film directed by
Helmut Kautner

The film's story, sex secrets
of a small town, is a classic
theme of minor American
literature. Here Ballester gives
it a strangely Biblical context
by his choice of iconography.
What is the source of that
hellish red light on the foreground figure?

Luigi Martinati
LA DAMA E IL COWBOY

THE COWBOY AND THE LADY
Offset, 27½ × 13"
(70 × 33 cm)
1956 re-release poster for the
1938 American film directed
by H. C. Potter

Martinati, who created many
memorable images of Gary
Cooper for Warner Brothers,
was apparently recruited to
do the same for this postwar
re-release of a Samuel
Goldwyn production. The
composition and color add
up to a perfect summation of
this lightweight comedy about
a repressed rich girl who dis-
guises herself as a lady's maid
to marry rambunctious cow-
boy Cooper.

Anselmo Ballester
L'IMPOSSIBILE DESIDERIO

AFFAIRS OF A ROGUE
Offset, 11 × 8"
(27.9 × 20.3 cm)
Undated flyer for the
1948 British film by
Alberto Cavalcanti

The front of this one-page
"publicity guide" for a British
costume romance features
some lovely pen-and-ink
sketches by Ballester. His
prominent billing suggests
that his name was not
unknown in the film industry.

Josef Fenneker
MASCHERA BLU

MASKE IN BLAU
Offset, 39⅜ × 27½"
(100 × 70 cm)
Undated poster for the
1942 German film directed
by Paul Martin

The popular Hungarian stage
star Clara Tobody appeared in
this wartime film of her 1932
stage success, as a young
dancer who finds stardom in
Berlin. This curious poster,
which may be a restrike of
a German original, is a late
work by Fenneker, the most
important poster artist during
the great period of the
German silent cinema.

Anselmo Ballester
SCHIAVO DEL PASSATO

THE LATE GEORGE APLEY
Offset, 6'6¾" × 55⅛"
(200 × 140 cm)
1949 poster for the 1947
American film directed by
Joseph L. Mankiewicz

The elusive actress Peggy
Cummins (her few films
include two genre master-
pieces—*Gun Crazy* [1949]
and *Night of the Demon*
[1957]) is given the Ballester
treatment in this image for a
little-seen film by Mankiewicz,
which is based on a novel by
John P. Marquand.

Anselmo Ballester
LA CANZONE DEL CUORE
Offset, 6'6¾" × 55⅛"
(200 × 140 cm)
Poster for the 1955
Italian film directed by
Carlo Campogalliani

Three hard-working artisans of
the Italian popular cinema—
stars Milly Vitale and Alberto
Farnese, and the silent veteran
director Campogalliani—
teamed up for this 1955
melodrama, presented on a
"gigantic panoramic screen"
in hopeful imitation of the
spreading CinemaScope craze.

Anselmo Ballester
AMORE SENZA DOMANI

ALWAYS GOODBYE
Offset, 6'6¾" × 55⅛"
(200 × 140 cm)
1949 poster for the 1938
American film directed by
Sidney Lanfield

Starring Barbara Stanwyck as
a working girl forced to give
up her baby, this Fox Pictures
melodrama was probably
meant as a follow-up to
Stanwyck's immensely successful soap opera *Stella Dallas*—a
connection long lost when the
film was finally released in Italy
eleven years after it was made.
Another of Ballester's magnificent New York skylines
appears in the background.

Anselmo Ballester
SANCTA MARIA
Lithograph, 39⅜ × 27½"
(100 × 70 cm)
Poster for the 1941 Italian film
directed by Edgar Neville

A young Russian girl is diverted from her lifelong belief in Communism when a prayer to the Virgin Mary cures her Italian boyfriend of a fatal disease. This wartime propaganda is dutifully dressed-up by Ballester in appropriate nationalist imagery.

Anselmo Ballester
RESURREZIONE

WE LIVE AGAIN
Lithograph, 55⅛ × 39⅜"
(140 × 100 cm)
Undated poster for the 1934
American film directed by
Rouben Mamoulian

We Live Again was the second
of producer Samuel
Goldwyn's three unsuccessful
attempts to present the stunning Russian-born actress
Anna Sten as his answer to
Greta Garbo. Despite a script
by Preston Sturges and
Maxwell Anderson, this film
was a famous disaster.

Renato Fratini
SENSO
_____

THE WANTON CONTESSA
Offset, 55 ⅛ × 39 ⅜"
(140 × 100 cm)
Poster for the 1954 Italian film
directed by Luchino Visconti

This elegant portrait poster
was created as part of a pair
(see opposite) for Visconti's
sumptuous period romance,
set during the Austrian occu-
pation of Venice. This is a
striking work from an illustrator who did few posters for
the cinema.

Renato Fratini
SENSO

THE WANTON CONTESSA
Offset, 55 ⅛ × 39 ⅜"
(140 × 100 cm)
Poster for the 1954 Italian film
directed by Luchino Visconti

Alida Valli, who had been
pushed toward international
stardom by her appearance in
the 1949 British film *The Third
Man*, seems very much her
haughty onscreen self in
Fratini's stylized portrait.

Anselmo Ballester
IVONNE, LA BELLA DELLA DANZA BRUTALE
Lithograph, 50¾" × 6'2⅞"
(129 × 190.2 cm)
Poster for the 1915 Italian film
directed by Gustavo Serena
Collection Museo Nazionale
del Cinema, Turin

This very early work by
Ballester depicts one of the
great divas of early Italian
cinema, Francesca Bertini, in
a pose that must have seemed
stunningly provocative at the
time of the film's release. The
title, in fact, was subsequently
censored, and appeared *as
Ivonne, la bella danzatrice
(Ivonne, The Beautiful Dancer)*
on release prints.

93

Anselmo Ballester
3 STRISCIE AL SOLE

THREE STRIPES IN THE SUN

Offset, 6'6¾" × 55⅛"
(200 × 140 cm)
Poster for the 1955
American film directed by
Richard Murphy

A Chinese dragon makes a
striking, if culturally insensitive,
design element for this film
about an American GI in
postwar Japan who falls in
love with a local girl.

Luigi Martinati
STRINGIMI FORTE TRA LE TUE BRACCIA

FORCE OF ARMS
Offset, 6'6¾" × 55⅛"
(200 × 140 cm)
1952 poster for the 1951
American film directed by
Michael Curtiz

Martinati has reconfigured a
studio publicity still into a
dynamic composition that
seems to leap from the wall.

Anselmo Ballester
LA NEMICA
Offset, 6'6¾" × 55⅛"
(200 × 140 cm)
Poster for the 1951 Italian film
directed by Giorgio Bianchi

Bianchi's film of a 1917 stage
melodrama by Dario
Niccodemi—a lurid affair
about a noblewoman who
refuses to admit her late hus-
band's illegitimate son to the
family—occasions a riot of
Freudian imagery from the
artist.

Anonymous
DIFENDO IL MIO AMORE!
PRIVATE NUMBER
Lithograph, 6'6¾" x 70⅞"
(200 x 180 cm)
Undated 1930s poster for the
1936 American film directed
by Roy Del Ruth

Most likely this poster is the
work of Anselmo Ballester,
who created other spectacular
posters for the Fox Film
Corporation during this
period (see *Capitan Gennaio*;
pp. 18–19). This is a rare
example of the huge *sei foglio*
(six-sheet) format, sparingly
used during the 1930s and
hardly at all after World War II.
Del Ruth's romantic comedy
pairs working-girl Loretta
Young with poor-little-rich-boy
Robert Taylor.

Anselmo Ballester
TRINIDAD

AFFAIR IN TRINIDAD
Offset, 6'6¾" × 55⅛"
(200 × 140 cm)
Poster for the 1952
American film directed by
Vincent Sherman

Rita Hayworth, never more
radiant than when Ballester
painted her, was reunited with
her *Gilda* co-star Glenn Ford
(see p. 100) for this romantic
thriller that marked the
actress's return to the screen
after her divorce from Aly
Khan. Ford is rendered as
literally colorless by her side.

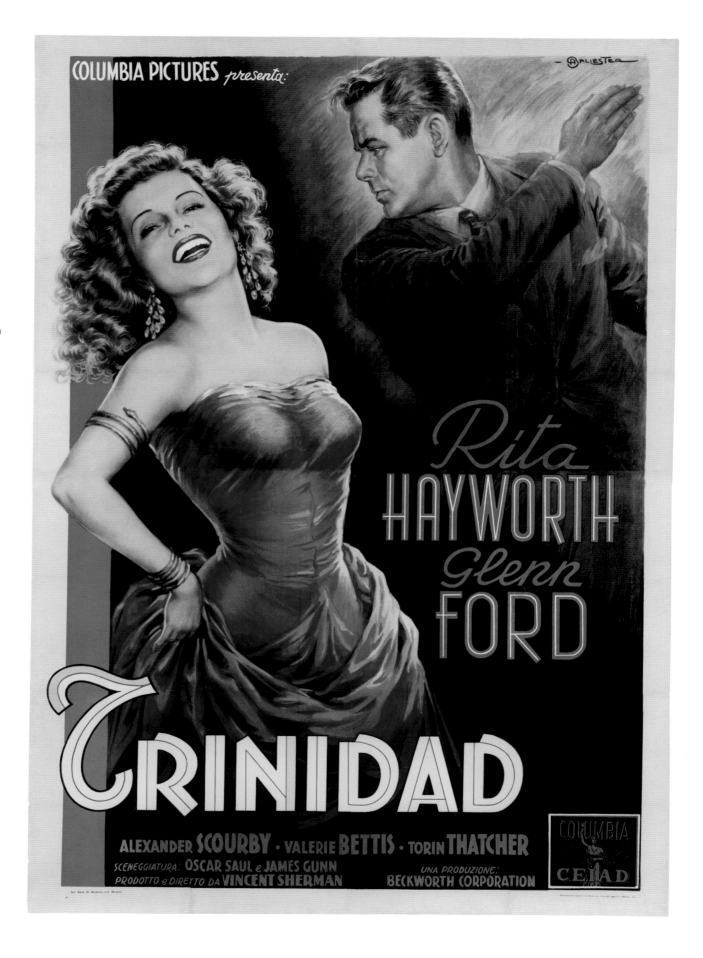

Anselmo Ballester
TRINIDAD

AFFAIR IN TRINIDAD
Offset, 27 ½ × 13"
(70 × 33 cm)
1953 poster for the 1952
American film directed by
Vincent Sherman Collection
Museo Nazionale del Cinema,
Turin

Ballester's small-format poster
for *Trinidad* offers a substan-
tially different design from
the large version (opposite).
These smaller posters, called
locandine, were meant to be
taped to store windows, like
the American window cards,
and are still in wide use in Italy.

Alfredo Capitani
GILDA
Offset, 6'6¾" × 55⅛"
(200 × 140 cm)
1947 poster for the
1946 American film by
Charles Vidor
Collection Museo Nazionale
del Cinema, Turin

Though Anselmo Ballester was
Rita Hayworth's most faithful
interpreter, the poster for her
best-known film, *Gilda*, went,
ironically, to Capitani, who sub-
stituted a chilly sexuality for
Ballester's warm romanticism
(see p. 98). Though based on a
studio portrait also used in
the American press campaign,
Capitani's portrait incorporates
a number of inspired variations, including the recumbent
pose and the satin-latex tex-
ture of Hayworth's famous
strapless gown.

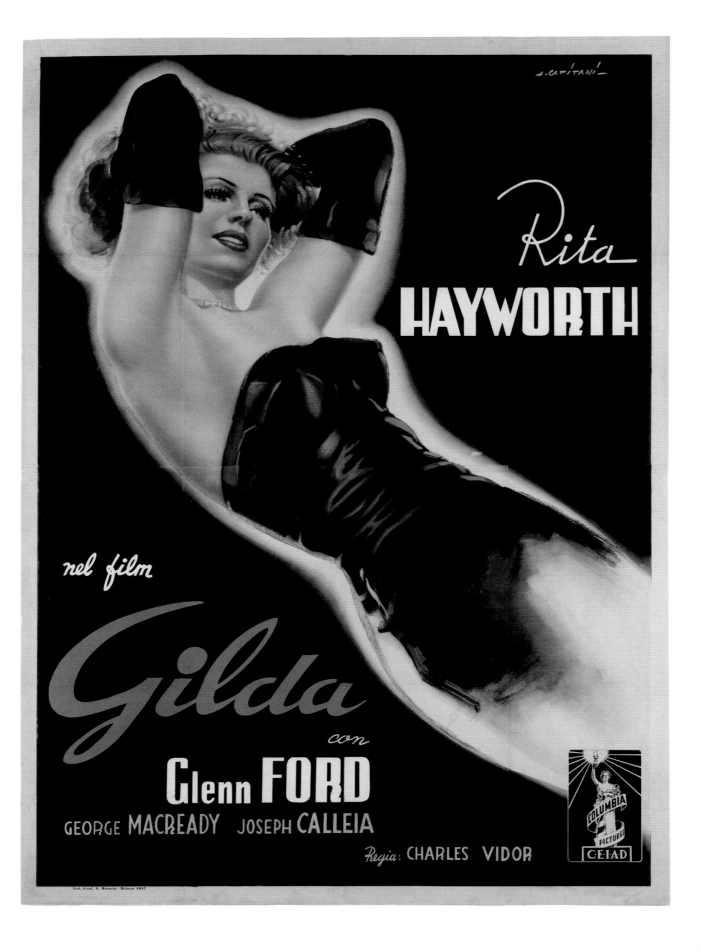

Ercole Brini
VIALE DEL TRAMONTO

SUNSET BLVD.
Offset, 55 ⅛ × 39 ⅜"
(140 × 100 cm)
Poster for the 1950 American
film directed by Billy Wilder

Brini's bright, airy style at first
seems antithetical to Wilder's
brooding, bitter melodrama
about a fading silent-film star
(Gloria Swanson) and her
kept screenwriter companion
(William Holden). But Brini
has beautifully captured one
of Swanson's most characteristic poses—the raised chin,
narrowed eyes, and hand
raised in queenly condescen-
sion, suggesting both defiance
and dread.

Leopoldo Metlicovitz
IL FUOCO
Lithograph, 9'2¼" × 6'9⅞"
(280 × 208 cm)
Poster for the 1915 Italian film
directed by Giovanni Pastrone
Collection Museo Nazionale
del Cinema, Turin

Two years after *Cabiria* (see
p. 38), Metlicovitz illustrated
another film by Pastrone, this
one a domestic melodrama.
The dramatic lighting seems
to anticipate the German
Expressionist cinema, which
was inaugurated four years
later with *The Cabinet of Dr.
Caligari* (1919). The amount of
sheer physical labor that must
have gone into the production of a stone lithograph of
this gigantic scale is impressive
in itself.

HUMPHREY **BOGART** · INGRID **BERGMAN** · PAUL **HENREID**

CASABLANCA

CLAUDE RAINS · CONRAD VEIDT · SYDNEY GREENSTREET · PETER LORRE
Regia: MICHAEL CURTIZ   Warner Bros.

GRAFICHE I.G.A.P. ROMA

Luigi Martinati
CASABLANCA
Offset, 39 ⅜ × 27 ½"
(100 × 70 cm)
Undated poster for the 1942
American film directed by
Michael Curtiz
Collection Museo Nazionale
del Cinema, Turin

World War II's greatest love
story had to wait for the end
of the war to come to Italy,
where it received a worthy
welcome from Martinati,
beginning his long stretch as
Warner Brothers' favorite
Italian artist. Though based on
a studio still, Martinati's rendering of the movies' most
famous couple has a longing
and tenderness all its own;
these are faces that have seen
war, and recently.

**F**ilm noir emerged in Hollywood immediately after World War II, springing from the seeds planted twenty years earlier by German Expressionism and largely shaped by émigré filmmakers who had fled Hitler's Europe. Yet the mood of these films is as distinctively American as the screwball comedies of the 1930s and is tied very tightly to the sense of rupture and disenchantment experienced by war veterans returning to a complacent, uncaring homeland. The basic formula of film noir seems like the screwball comedy set on its ear: instead of harebrained socialites getting out of outrageous scrapes thanks to their innate charm, these films tends to feature working-class males plunged into a nightmarish series of events, often triggered by one tiny moral misstep.

For the poster makers, film noir presents almost as many visual opportunities as the Western, substituting a claustrophobic urban landscape—of skyscraper canyons and shadowy back alleys—for the Western's wide-open spaces. The iconography, too, is similarly well-established: pistols, knives, clutching hands, and icy blondes.

Though the films illustrated in this section may not all fit the strict definition of film noir—there are a couple of thrillers by Alfred Hitchcock here, as well as marginal noirs like Charles Vidor's 1940 *The Lady in Question* (p. 126) and Stuart Heisler's 1950 *Chain Lightning* (p. 130)—the posters that represent them all belong to the same world, where men are frightened or angry, and the majority of women, particularly if they are blonde, are cool and indifferent.

Intriguingly, only one of the films here is by an Italian director—*La Città si difende* (*Four Ways Out*; 1951; p. 123), an early crime drama by director Pietro Germi, who would become famous for social comedies like *Divorce Italian Style*. One wonders if film noir is not a genre that comes naturally to Italian filmmakers. The French, certainly, were producing their fair share during the late 1940s and early 1950s. But much research remains to be done on the Italian popular cinema, and no doubt other titles will come to light. There is always, of course, Mario Monicelli's delightful film noir farce *I soliti ignoti* (*Big Deal on Madonna Street*) of 1958.

Anselmo Ballester. Detail of **CELLA 2455, BRACCIO DELLA MORTE (CELL 2455, DEATH ROW).** See also p. 122

FILM NOIR

Averardo Ciriello
LA FINESTRA SUL CORTILE

REAR WINDOW
Offset, 6'6¾" × 55⅛"
(200 × 140 cm)
Undated poster for the 1954
American film directed by
Alfred Hitchcock

An unusual mixture of painted and photographic images
characterizes this elegant
piece by Ciriello. It is miles
away from his neorealist
poster for *La Terra trema*
(see p. 134).

Anselmo Ballester
IL DIRITTO DI UCCIDERE

IN A LONELY PLACE
Offset, 55 x 35"
(139.7 x 88.9 cm)
1952 poster for the 1950
American film directed by
Nicholas Ray

Humphrey Bogart plays a
screenwriter with an uncon-
trollable violent streak in Ray's
masterpiece, a film that could
be characterized as autobiographical noir. Ballester cap-
tures both the perversity and
the tenderness of Bogart's
relationship with sympathetic
neighbor Gloria Grahame
through contrasting skin tones
and, in the background, a
noirish shadow that fades into
a tattered valentine.

Anselmo Ballester
SPIE!

ACHTUNG! FEIND HÖRT MIT!
Lithograph, 33 × 27"
(83.8 × 68.6 cm)
1941 poster for the 1940
German film directed by
Arthur Maria Rabenalt

This German propaganda film
was released in Fascist Italy in
1941. Director Rabenalt was
an "artistic consultant" on
Leni Riefenstahl's *Tiefland*,
filmed in 1944.

Anselmo Ballester
FRONTE DEL PORTO

ON THE WATERFRONT
Offset, 6'6¾" × 55⅛"
(200 × 140 cm)
Undated poster for the 1954
American film directed by
Elia Kazan

Perhaps Ballester's best-known
poster, this stunning piece
combines the primary visual
themes of Kazan's film into a
surreal allegory of good and
evil, complete with a flight of
pigeons worthy of St. Francis.

Anonymous
THE BIG HEAT
Offset, 41 × 27"
(104.1 × 68.6 cm)
Poster for the 1953 American
film directed by Fritz Lang

The unknown American
poster artist who designed
this violent piece for Lang's
noir masterpiece was working
from some of the same photographic elements that
Ballester used for his poster
for the same film (opposite).
In particular, the tiny portrait
of Lee Marvin in the right
margin of this poster becomes
a towering demonic figure in
Ballester's version.

Anselmo Ballester
IL GRANDE CALDO

THE BIG HEAT
Offset, 6'6¾" × 55⅛"
(200 × 140 cm)
1954 poster for the 1953
American film directed by
Fritz Lang

That rare combination—a
great poster for a great film.
Ballester seems to have been
roused to the heights of his
creativity by Lang's definitive
film noir, even to the point of
including a New York skyline
that powerfully evokes Lang's
1927 film *Metropolis*.

Anselmo Ballester
IL DELITTO DEL SECOLO

WALK EAST ON BEACON

Offset, 6'6¾" × 55⅛"
(200 × 140 cm)
1953 poster for the 1952
American film directed by
Alfred L. Werker

Ballester appears to have
spun this unforgettable noir
image out of pure imagination; nothing in Werker's
rather ordinary thriller about
an FBI agent on the trail of a
Soviet spy comes close to it.

Anselmo Ballester
MI CHIAMO GIULIA ROSS

MY NAME IS JULIA ROSS
Offset, 6'6¾" × 55⅛"
(200 × 140 cm)
1947 poster for the 1945
American film directed by
Joseph H. Lewis

The artist packs a lot of
iconography—a black cat, a
butcher knife, and a roiling
sea—into this atmospheric
poster for the cult classic by
Lewis. The director's name is
rendered here as Joseph
Illewis by an apparently over-
worked Ballester.

Anselmo Ballester
SINDICATO DEL PORTO

RUMBLE ON THE DOCKS
Offset, 27 ½ × 13"
(70 × 33 cm)
Undated poster for the 1956
American film by Fred F. Sears

The studio may have been
pushing James Darren, who
made his debut in this
Columbia Pictures programmer, but Ballester characteris-
tically shifts his attention to a
threatened woman and a
dramatic New York skyline.

Anselmo Ballester
LA STATUA CHE URLA

SCREAMING MIMI
Offset, 27½ × 13"
(70 × 33 cm)
Undated poster for the 1958
American film directed by
Gerd Oswald

Fredric Brown's disturbing
pulp novel became a sharp
little thriller under Oswald's
direction.

Anselmo Ballester
LA STRADA È BLOCCATA

THE LONG HAUL
Offset, 55⅛ x 39⅜"
(140 x 100 cm)
Undated poster for the
1957 British film directed
by Ken Hughes

The story centers around an
infernal struggle for an icy
blonde. Ballester spins the
pneumatic figure of Diana
Dors, Britain's answer to
Marilyn Monroe, into one of
the ultimate "bad-girl" images.

Alfredo Capitani
LA STRADA È BLOCCATA

THE LONG HAUL

Offset, 27½ × 13"
(70 × 33 cm)
Undated poster for the
1957 British film directed
by Ken Hughes

This is one of the rare
occasions when two artists,
Capitani and Anselmo
Ballester, worked on the
same publicity campaign.
Capitani signed this small-
format poster for Hughes's
truckdriving drama. The larger
poster by Ballester (see p.
117) offers a very different
perspective on the action.

Luigi Martinati
L'ALTRA BANDIERA

OPERATION SECRET
Offset, 27½ x 13"
(70 x 33 cm)
Undated poster for the 1952
American film directed by
Lewis Seiler

French resistance fighter
Cornel Wilde copes with a
traitor in his group, while
Martinati creates a tense
image that suggests an Orson
Welles-like deep-focus composition.

119

Gargiulo
SOTTO I PONTI DI NEW YORK
WINTERSET
Lithograph, 6'6¾" × 55⅛"
(200 × 140 cm)
1937 poster for the 1936
American film directed by
Alfred Santell

Not much is known about
Gargiulo (even his first name,
if he had one), but his signature appears on several of
the most striking stone lithograph posters of the 1930s.
Here is a typically bold Deco
design, which manages to
make Santell's sleepy adaptation of the Maxwell Anderson
play *Winterset* looks like a
Warner Brothers crime
thriller.

Luigi Martinati
LA CITTÀ SPENTA

CRIME WAVE
Offset, 6'6¾" × 55⅛"
(200 × 140 cm)
1955 poster for the 1954
American film directed by
Andre de Toth

There are intimations of René
Magritte and Giorgio de
Chirico in Martinati's wonderfully surreal poster, very freely
inspired by de Toth's economic
gangster thriller.

Anselmo Ballester
**CELLA 2455, BRACCIO DELLA
MORTE**

CELL 2455, DEATH ROW
Offset, 55 ⅛ × 39 ⅜"
(140 × 100 cm)
Poster for the 1955 American
film directed by Fred F. Sears

Based on a best-selling book
by Caryl Chessman, who
spent twelve years on San
Quentin's death row before
being executed in 1960, Sears's
film becomes the occasion for
Ballester to deploy some
classic film noir iconography,
including prison bars, haunted
eyes, and clutching hands.

Anselmo Ballester
LA CITTÀ SI DIFENDE

FOUR WAYS OUT
Offset, 27½ × 13"
(70 × 33 cm)
Undated poster for the
1951 Italian film directed
by Pietro Germi

Better known for the social
comedies he made later in his
career (*Divorce Italian Style;
Seduced and Abandoned*),
Germi directed this *film noir a
l'italiana*, with a plotline—
crooks rob a soccer stadi-
um—that anticipates Stanley
Kubrick's *The Killing* (1956).
Among the five credited
screenwriters are Federico
Fellini and Luigi Comencini.
The film was released in the
United States, dubbed, in
1954, as *Four Ways Out*.

Luigi Martinati
UNA PALLOTTOLA PER ROY

HIGH SIERRA
Offset, 55 ⅛ × 39 ⅜"
(140 × 100 cm)
1949 poster for the 1941
American film directed by
Raoul Walsh
Collection Museo Nazionale
del Cinema, Turin

Martinati ingeniously reworks
the American poster art for
High Sierra into a much more
dramatic composition.

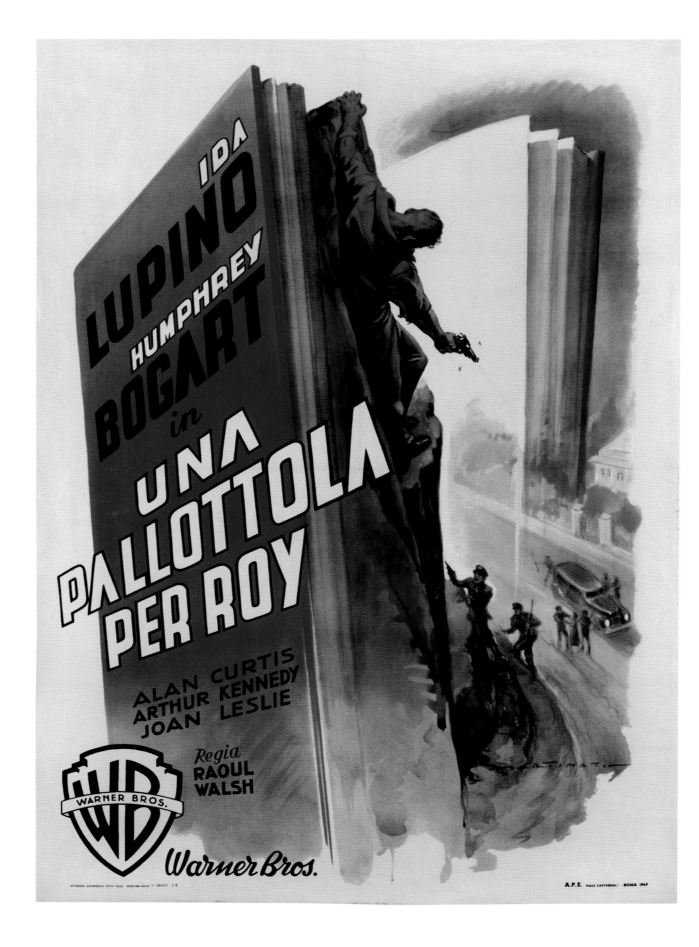

Luigi Martinati
LA PATTUGLIA DEI SENZA PAURA

"G" MEN
Offset, 55 ⅛ × 39 ⅜"
(140 × 100 cm)
1951 poster for the 1935
American film directed by
William Keighley
Collection Museo Nazionale
del Cinema, Turin

In 1935 *"G" Men* was Warner
Brothers' attempt to put their
great gangster star James
Cagney on the right side of
the law (and the right side of
the new production code)
by making him a member of
J. Edgar Hoover's fledgling FBI.
By 1951, when the film was
re-released in Italy, gangsters
were glamorous again, and
Martinati's poster, with Cagney
striking a definitive tragic hero
pose, returns the star to his
Public Enemy persona.

Anselmo Ballester
SEDUZIONE

THE LADY IN QUESTION
Offset, 6'6¾" × 55⅛"
(200 × 140 cm)
1951 poster for the 1940
American film directed by
Charles Vidor
Collection Museo Nazionale
del Cinema, Turin

Of all Ballester's portraits of
Rita Hayworth, this image, created for the postwar release
of a prewar film, is perhaps the
warmest and most sensual.

Anselmo Ballester
LA SIGNORA DI SHANGHAI
THE LADY FROM SHANGHAI
Offset, 6'6¾" × 55⅛"
(200 × 140 cm)
Poster for the 1948 American
film directed by Orson Welles
Collection Museo Nazionale
del Cinema, Turin

Rita Hayworth's gown offers a
new definition of diaphanous
in Ballester's magnificent poster
for Welles's ultra-stylish, and
subtly satirical, film noir.

Luigi Martinati
LA CITTÀ È SALVA

THE ENFORCER
Offset, 6'6¾" × 55⅛"
(200 × 140 cm)
Poster for the 1951 American
film directed by Bretaigne
Windust and Raoul Walsh
Collection Museo Nazionale
del Cinema, Turin

Humphrey Bogart's last great
gangster film finds a worthy
interpreter in Martinati, who
imagines Bogart's crusading
district attorney as a literally
larger-than-life hero striding
across a detailed Manhattan
cityscape.

Luigi Martinati
L'ALTRO UOMO

STRANGERS ON A TRAIN
Offset, 55 ⅛ × 39 ⅜"
(140 × 100 cm)
1952 poster for the
American 1951 film
directed by Alfred Hitchcock
Collection Museo Nazionale
del Cinema, Turin

Martinati's trademark inversion
of foreground and background
produces a roaringly dynamic
image for the Hitchcock classic.

Alfredo Capitani
ASSALTO AL CIELO

CHAIN LIGHTNING
Offset, 6'6¾" × 55⅛"
(200 × 140 cm)
1951 poster for the1950
American film directed by
Stuart Heisler
Collection Museo Nazionale
del Cinema, Turin

Humphrey Bogart plays a test
pilot in this minor postwar
drama, which is transformed
by Capitani's wildly imagina-
tive poster into Bogey's only
science-fiction epic.

Anselmo Ballester
M
Offset, 6'6¾" × 55⅛"
(200 × 140 cm)
Poster for the 1951 American
film directed by Joseph Losey
Collection Museo Nazionale
del Cinema, Turin.

Losey's unfairly overlooked
1951 remake of Fritz Lang's
1931 classic rouses the
Expressionist in Ballester, who
here produces a masterpiece
of shifting perspectives and
leaping colors.

The late 1940s and early 1950s saw the emergence of a new breed of filmmaker in Italy, directors who saw themselves as the complete authors of their films rather than craftsmen executing the designs of others. The first sign of this new movement, evident when Italy was still at war, was Luchino Visconti's 1942 film *Ossessione,* an unauthorized adaptation of James M. Cain's novel *The Postman Always Rings Twice.* Visconti's defiantly de-glamorized film was shot on grim, provincial locations. Roberto Rossellini's *Roma, città aperta (Open City),* filmed in 1945 while German troops were still in the streets of Rome, confirmed the authorial status of this ambitious young director. Combined with Vittorio De Sica's *Ladri di biciclette (Bicycle Thieves;* 1948) and Visconti's *La Terra trema (The Earth Trembles;* 1948), Rossellini's film opened a new aesthetic that critics called neorealism, defined by a preference for location over studio shooting, proletarian characters rather than the carefree aristocrats who had populated many of the Fascist-era films, and a simplified technique that approached the newsreel while turning from the ostentatious "calligraphic" style favored by prewar filmmakers.

A second generation of authors quickly followed after the first. Federico Fellini, one of the writers on *Open City,* introduced broad swaths of fantasy, autobiography, and dreamy stylization in his films, beginning with *Lo Sceicco bianco (The White Sheik)* in 1952. Michelangelo Antonioni moved from melodrama (*Cronaca di un amore [Story of a Love Affair];* 1950) to metaphysics (*L'Avventura;* 1960), developing a crispy modern visual style. The poet Pier Paolo Pasolini discovered a revolutionary blend of politics and eroticism.

Inspired by the Italians—and particularly by Rossellini—a group of young French film critics took to the streets with their cameras, and by the early 1960s had established themselves as "la nouvelle vague"—the New Wave. Of this group, Jean-Luc Godard remained most closely aligned to the discoveries of the Italians, a debt he repaid by making his masterpiece *Le Mepris (Contempt)* at Rome's Cinecittà studios (where one sequence shows the Italian poster of Godard's *Vivre sa vie* in the background; p. 145).

New authors and new films required a new kind of poster, the birth of which can be seen in the anonymous design for Visconti's *Ossessione* (p.135). Here, for one of the first times, was a simple, almost unadorned black-and-white photograph being used to summarize a film, rather than the elaborate artwork provided by Averardo Ciriello for Visconti's *La Terra trema* (p. 134). As the decade wore on, photomontages slowly replaced original artwork; photographs were more in keeping with the modern spirit of the films, and were certainly faster and easier to produce than full-color illustrations. Still, there were some remarkable exceptions to the rule in the 1960s, such as the posters reproduced here for the episode film *RoGoPaG* (1962; p.143) and Giuliano Nistri's chilling poster for Antonioni's *La Notte* (1960; p. 142).

Sandro Simeoni. Detail of **ACCATTONE.** See also p. 144

THE NEW WAVE

Averardo Ciriello
LA TERRA TREMA

THE EARTH TREMBLES

Offset, 55⅛ × 39⅜"
(140 × 100 cm)
Poster for the 1948 Italian film
directed by Luchino Visconti

Primarily a magazine illustrator,
Ciriello created several memorable posters after World
War II, including this dynamic
interpretation of the climactic
sequence from Visconti's neorealist drama about Sicilian fishermen. Though Ciriello worked
in the painterly Ballester-
Martinati tradition, he here
allows some strikingly impressionistic effects of movement.

Anonymous
OSSESSIONE
Offset, 27 × 19"
(68.6 × 48.3 cm)
Undated poster for the 1942
Italian film directed by
Luchino Visconti

An early use of photomontage
defines this unusual image
from *Ossessione*, Visconti's
unauthorized wartime adaptation of James M. Cain's ultra-
noir novel, *The Postman Always
Rings Twice*. This is one of at
least four medium-format
posters issued for this film.
Though long unreleased in
the United States because of
copyright problems, the film is
often credited with crystallizing
the style that, after the war,
became known as neorealism.

Anonymous
UN CONDANNATO A MORTE È FUGGITO

UN CONDAMNÉ À MORT S'EST ECHAPPÉ

A MAN ESCAPED
Offset, 27½ × 13"
(70 × 33 cm)
1958 poster for the 1956
French film directed by
Robert Bresson

This is an anonymous Italian
variation on the famous
French poster designed for
Bresson's masterpiece by Paul
Colin, which showed only the
end of a rope hanging over a
prison wall. The Italian illustration, quite literally, adds the
human touch.

LA **GLOBE FILMS INTERNATIONAL** PRESENTA

UN CONDANNATO A MORTE E' FUGGITO

GRAN PREMIO FESTIVAL DI CANNES 1957
GRAN PREMIO ACADEMIE DU CINEMA 1957
VICTOIRE DU CINEMA 1957 - GRAN PREMIO O.C.I.C. 1957

PER LA MIGLIORE REGIA • PER IL MIGLIORE FILM FRANCESE
PER IL MIGLIORE FILM EUROPEO • PER IL MIGLIORE FILM DEL MONDO

REGIA DI **ROBERT BRESSON**

Vecchioni & Guadagno, Via del Casal de Merode, 8 - Ottobre 1958

Anselmo Ballester
ROMA, CITTÀ APERTA

OPEN CITY
Offset, 39 ⅜ × 27 ½"
(100 × 70 cm)
Poster for the 1945 Italian film
directed by Roberto Rossellini
Collection Museo Nazionale
del Cinema, Turin

Filmed in the streets of Rome
days after the departure of
the Germans, Rossellini's film
established a new standard of
screen realism, an aesthetic
reflected in Ballester's decid-
edly unglamorous image of
Aldo Fabrizi, who played the
film's hero, a priest working
with the anti-Nazi under-
ground.

Ercole Brini
LADRI DI BICICLETTE

BICYCLE THIEVES
Offset, 6'6¾" × 55⅛"
(200 × 140 cm)
Poster for the 1948 Italian film
directed by Vittorio De Sica

Brini, a specialist in depicting
musicals and romantic comedies, seems at first an odd
choice for De Sica's neorealist melodrama—a film soon
to become a worldwide success. But with a touch of
Expressionist lighting—in
the odd background shift
between midnight and
noon—Brini turns his usual
breezy style into something
more somber, suggestive of
the film's social message.

Ercole Brini
LADRI DI BICICLETTE

BICYCLE THIEVES
Offset, 55⅛ × 39⅜"
(140 × 100 cm)
Poster for the 1948 Italian film
directed by Vittorio De Sica
Collection Museo Nazionale
del Cinema, Turin

Brini's two-folio poster for
De Sica's neorealist classic
offers an impressionistic rendering of the film's characters
and settings—reality captured
very much on the fly, as if in
an artist's sketchbook.

Anonymous
ROCCO E I SUOI FRATELLI

ROCCO AND HIS BROTHERS

Offset, 27 ½ × 13"
(70 × 33 cm)
Poster for the 1960 Italian film
directed by Luchino Visconti

This poster is a strong but
unsigned image for Visconti's
epic of social injustice, a late
neorealist masterpiece in
which the realism has begun
to evolve into the operatic, as
the poster suggests.

Carlantonio Longi
L'AVVENTURA
Offset, 55 ⅛ × 39 ⅜"
(140 × 100 cm)
Poster for the 1960 Italian
film directed by
Michelangelo Antonioni
Collection Martin Scorsese

Caught between the old
school of illustration—highly
colored, dramatically charged,
extremely emotional—and
the new school of oblique,
elemental Italian filmmaking
pioneered by Antonioni,
Longi's poster for *L'Avventura*
seems only tangentially related to the film. It is hard to
recognize in these traditional
romantic images the movie
that caused a major scandal at
the Cannes Film Festival for
its enigmatic situations and
unresolved ending.

Giuliano Nistri
LA NOTTE
Offset, 55⅛ × 39⅜"
(140 × 100 cm)
1960 poster for the
Italian film directed by
Michelangelo Antonioni

Antonioni's existential drama
about a night of crisis for a
married couple (Jeanne
Moreau and Marcello
Mastroianni) comes off almost
like a horror movie in Nistri's
eerie rendering. One can
already feel the tension
between the new forms in
filmmaking and the old forms
of advertising in this dramatic
but uneasy image.

Anonymous
ROGOPAG
Offset, 6'6¾" × 55⅛"
(200 × 140 cm)
Poster for the 1962 Italian
film directed by Roberto
Rossellini, Jean-Luc Godard,
Pier Paolo Pasolini, and Ugo
Gregoretti

The omnibus format, popular
in the 1950s and early 1960s,
here unites the elder states-
man of the Italian cinema,
Rossellini, with two of his
most dedicated followers,
Godard and Pasolini. (The
fourth filmmaker, Ugo
Gregoretti, was an aspiring
documentary director.) A
handsome presentation from
Cineriz, distributor of several
of the most important auteur
films of the 1960s.

Sandro Simeoni
ACCATTONE
Lithograph, 27½ × 13"
(70 × 33 cm)
Poster for the 1961 Italian film
directed by Pier Paolo Pasolini

Several posters by well-known
artists were commissioned for
Pasolini's first feature, the story
of a brutal Roman pimp, but
the most memorable is this
sinister composition by veteran commercial artist Simeoni
(who sometimes, as here,
signed his work "Symeoni").

Donelli
QUESTA È LA MIA VITA

VIVRE SA VIE

MY LIFE TO LIVE
Offset, 6'6¾" × 55⅛"
(200 × 140 cm)
Undated poster for the 1962
French film directed by Jean-
Luc Godard

Little is known about the
artist who signed this very
unusual piece, but Godard
was impressed enough with it
to feature it prominently in
the background of *Le Mepris
(Contempt)*, his 1963 film
partly shot at Rome's
Cinecittà studios.

Anonymous
OTTO E MEZZO

8 1/2
Offset 55 ⅛ × 39 ⅜"
(140 × 100 cm)
Poster for the 1963 Italian film
directed by Federico Fellini
Collection Martin Scorsese

A pleasing example of the
photomontage style as it
emerged in the early 1960s.
More modern in appearance
than the painterly designs of
Anselmo Ballester and his
followers, the photomontage
style seems more in tune with
the revolutionary narrative
techniques then being
explored by the leading directors of the burgeoning Italian
art cinema. Here the stark
black-and-white photographs
do much to capture the feeling of this high-contrast black-
and-white film. Marcello
Mastroianni, playing a character based on Fellini himself,
sports the director's trademark felt hat.

Giorgio Olivetti
LA DOLCE VITA
Offset, 55⅛ × 39⅜"
(140 × 100 cm)
Poster for the 1960 Italian film
directed by Federico Fellini
Collection Martin Scorsese

This large format *quattro foglio*
(four-sheet) poster is the best
of many produced for Fellini's
international hit, an indictment
of decadent postwar Roman
society that provided as much
titillation as moral instruction
to the millions who saw it
around the world.

SELECTED BIBLIOGRAPHY

Baroni, Maurizio. *Platea in piedi*. Bologna: Bolelli Editore, 1995. A three-volume history of Italian filmmaking, presented through statistics and a generous selection of posters

Bertetto, Paolo, ed. *Schermi di carta: La collezione di manifesti del Museo Nazionale del Cinema di Torino, Il muto italiano 1905–1927*. Torino: Edizioni d'Arte Fratelli Pozzo, 1995. A handsome collection, with essays by Gillo Pontecorvo, David Robinson, and others, of silent-film posters from the collection of the Turin film museum.

Bolaffi, Alberto, et al. *Catalogo Bolaffi del manifesto italiano: Diszionario degli illustratori*. Torino: Giulio Bolaffi Editore, 1995. An indispensable guide to the artists who created the Italian poster tradition, including, but not limited to, film posters.

Brunetta, Gian Piero. *Il colore dei sogni: Iconografia e memoria nel manifesto cinematografico italiano*. Torino: Testo & Immagine, 2002. A collection of essays on cinema, memory, and film posters.

Campeggi, Silvano. *Come dipinsi il cinema*. Castello: Edimond, 1994. An exhaustive collection of the work, almost all of it for MGM, of the illustrator who signed his posters "Nano," accompanied by an autobiographical preface.

Capitaine, Jean-Louis, and Balthazar Charton. *L'Affiche de cinema: Les plus belles stars d'Hollywood*. Paris: Edition Frédéric Birr, 1983. A fine collection of international posters, including several examples from Italy.

Dell'Anno, Michele, and Matteo Soccio, eds. *Cinema di Carta: 50 anni di manifesti cinematografici*. Foggia: Edizioni Bastogi, 1984. The earliest study of Italian film posters, and still one of the most useful; includes essays on and biographies of many of the leading artists.

Delle Torre, Roberto, and Elena Mosconi. *I manifesti tipografici del cinema*. Milan: Il Castoro, 2001. A history of typographical film posters, drawn from the collection of the Fondazione Cineteca Italiana.

Edwards, Gregory J. *The International Film Poster*. Salem, New Hampshire: Salem House, 1985. A survey of the form that includes several examples from Italy.

Giniès, Michel. *Les plus belles affiches du cinéma italien*. Paris: Dreamland, 2002. A collection of color reproductions, with particular emphasis on the 1960s.

Manzato, Eugenio, et al., eds. *L'Italia al cinema: Manifesti dalla Raccolta Salce 1911–1961*. Venice: Marsilio Editori, 1992. Exhibition catalogue of film posters drawn from the Salce Collection; contains short biographies of many of the principal artists.

Morandini, Laura, et al. *Il Morandini: Dizionario dei film*. Bologna: Zanichelli, 2002. Updated annually, a dictionary-style guide to films from Italy and elsewhere.

Werde, Stuart. *The Modern Poster*. New York: The Museum of Modern Art, 1988. Catalogue of the Museum's ground-breaking 1988 poster exhibition; no Italian film posters but a wealth of information on technology and design.

INDEX

FILM DIRECTORS